DILEMMAS OF DEMOCRACY IN NIGERIA

DILEMMAS OF DEMOCRACY IN NIGERIA

edited by

Paul A. Beckett and Crawford Young

 UNIVERSITY OF ROCHESTER PRESS

Copyright © 1997 Contributors

All Rights Reserved. Except as permitted under current legislation, no part of this work may be photocopied, stored in a retrieval system, published, performed in public, adapted, broadcast, transmitted, recorded or reproduced in any form or by any means, without the prior permission of the copyright owner.

First published 1997

University of Rochester Press
668 Mt. Hope Avenue
Rochester, NY 14620   USA

and at P.O. Box 9
Woodbridge, Suffolk IP12 3DF
United Kingdom

ISBN 1–878822–98–5
ISSN 1092–5228

Library of Congress Cataloging-in-Publication Data

Dilemmas of democracy in Nigeria / edited by Paul A. Beckett and
    Crawford Young.
        p.   cm. — (Rochester studies in African history and the
    diaspora, ISSN 1092–5228 ; v. 2)
      Includes bibliographical references and index.
      ISBN 1–878822–98–5 (alk. paper)
        1. Democracy—Nigeria.   2. Nigeria—Politics and government—1984–
    I. Beckett, Paul.   II. Young, Crawford, 1931–   .   III. Series.
JQ3096.D55   1997
321.8′09669—dc21   97–17411
                                                                      CIP

British Library Cataloguing-in-Publication Data
A catalogue record for this book is
available from the British Library

Designed and typeset by Cornerstone Composition Services
Printed in the United States of America
This publication is printed on acid-free paper

CONTENTS

List of Tables — viii

List of Contributors — ix

Preface — xiii

Introduction:
Beyond the Impasse of "Permanent Transition" in Nigeria — 1
Paul A. Beckett and Crawford Young

HISTORY AND SOCIETY

1 Crises and Transitions in the Political History of Independent Nigeria — 15
Richard L. Sklar

2 Nigeria: A Political Entity and a Society — 45
Funso Afolayan

THEORETICAL PERSPECTIVES

3 Permanent Transition and Changing Conjuncture: Dilemmas of Democracy in Nigeria in Comparative Perspective — 65
Crawford Young

4 The Concept of Second Liberation and the Prospects of Democracy in Africa: A Nigerian Context — 83
Peter P. Ekeh

5 Legitimizing Democracy: The Role of the Highly Educated Elite — 111
Paul A. Beckett

THE FAILURE OF TRANSITION

6 Democratization under Military Rule and Repression in Nigeria — 137
Richard Joseph

7	Obstacles to Democratization in Nigeria *Jibrin Ibrahim*	155
8	Transition Without End: From Hope to Despair—Reflections of a Participant-Observer *Oyeleye Oyediran*	175
9	1993: Crisis and Breakdown of Nigeria's Transition to Democracy *David Emelifeonwu*	193

IDENTITIES AND CONTEXTS

10	Women and the Dilemma of Politics in Nigeria *Pat Ama Tokunbo Williams*	219
11	Nigerian Unity and the Tensions of Democracy: Geo-Cultural Zones and North-South Legacies *John N. Paden*	243
12	Christian Radicalism and Nigerian Politics *Toyin Falola*	265
13	Muslims, State, and the Struggle for Democratic Transition in Nigeria: From Cooperation to Conflict *Sabo Bako*	283
14	Politics and the Economy: A Downward Spiral *Peter Lewis*	303

INSTITUTIONAL FRAMEWORKS

15	Politics and the Search for Accomodation in Nigeria: Will Rotational Consociationalism Suffice? *Chudi Uwazurike*	329
16	Federalism, Ethnicity and Regionalism in Nigeria *Rotimi T. Suberu*	341
17	Party Systems and Civil Society *Adigun Agbaje*	361
18	Local Institutions, Civil Society and Democratization in Nigeria, 1986–1993 *Alex Gboyega*	389

19	Traditional Rulers and the Dilemma of Democratic Transitions in Nigeria *Olufemi Vaughan*	413
Index		435

LIST OF TABLES

Table 11.1	Presidentail elections, 1979	252
Table 11.2	Presidential elections, 1983	253
Table 11.3	Results (by state) of June 12 1993 presidential election	255
Table 16.1	Vertical allocation of the federal account, 1981–1995	348
Table 16.2	Horizontal revenue allocation formulae, 1970–1995	350
Table 16.3	Recent demands for new states in Nigeria	354

LIST OF CONTRIBUTORS

Funso Afolayan took his Ph.D. in history at Obafemi Awolowo University, Ile Ife, in 1991. His main historical research has been on pre-colonial Yorubaland. He has also written on state formation in the Central Sudan. He has taught at Obafemi Awolowo University, Amherst College (as Visiting Copeland Fellow), Washington University in Saint Louis, and presently teaches in History at the University of New Hampshire, Durham. He is co-author of *Yoruba Sacred Kingship: A Power Like That of the Gods* (1996).

Adigun Agbaje took his Ph.D. in political science at the University of Ibadan in 1988. He is Senior Lecturer in the Department of Political Science at Ibadan. He was Visiting Commonwealth Fellow at the University of Oxford in 1991-92. He is author of *The Nigerian Press, Hegemony, and the Social Construction of Legitimacy, 1960-1983* (1992), as well as many articles on democracy, civil society and the media in Nigeria.

Sabo Bako teaches in the Department of Political Science of Ahmadu Bello University in Zaria, Nigeria, where he completed his Ph.D. in 1992. Bako is a leading scholar on religion and politics in Nigeria's northern states. His study of the PRP political party and Class Struggles in Kano, 1979-83, is forthcoming, and he has completed a book-length study of the Maitatsine religious crisis in Kano, 1980-85. During 1994-5 he served as a member of the Constitutional Conference which formulated recommendations for the next democratic constitution of Nigeria.

Paul Beckett took his Ph.D. at the University of Wisconsin in 1970, and taught and carried out research at Ahmadu Bello University in Zaria, Nigeria, from 1969 to 1976. He is co-author of *Education and Power in Nigeria* (1978). His work has always focussed on Nigeria's highly educated elite in its relation to the post-colonial state, but he has also written on Nigerian democracy and political parties, and on aspects of African political theory. He is Assistant Dean of International Studies at the University of Wisconsin-Madison.

Peter Ekeh earned his Ph.D. in sociology at the University of California-Berkeley in 1970. He taught at the University of Ibadan from 1974-89, and since that time has served on the faculty of the State University of New York-Buffalo, where he currently chairs the Department of African American Studies. He was an invited fellow at the Woodrow Wilson International Center for Scholars in 1988-89. He is the author of *Social Exchange Theory: the Two Traditions* (1974) and many other publications. His seminal article, "Colonialism and the Two Publics in Africa," which appeared in *Comparative Studies in Society and History* in 1975, remains one of the most widely cited contributions in Africanist social science. His current research explores the issue of kinship and state in African history.

DAVID EMELIFEONWU is a doctoral candidate at McGill University. His dissertation focusses on the relation between characteristics of authoritarian regimes and the dynamics of political transitions. He has completed exceptionally detailed research on the circumstances of the failed transition to democracy in Nigeria under the Babangida regime (culminating in the June 12 1993 presidential election), and draws on that research for his chapter in this volume.

TOYIN FALOLA is a member of the Department of History at the University of Texas-Austin. Falola has been a prolific contributor to the study of Nigerian politics and society, and is co-author of *History of Nigeria* (three volumes). His recent work on radical Christian organization and religious competition in Nigeria is particularly noteworthy, including his *Religious Militancy and Self Assertion: Islam and Politics in Nigeria* (with M. H. Kukah, 1996).

ALEX GBOYEGA is Professor of Political Science at the University of Ibadan in Nigeria. For many years he has been among Nigeria's leading academic contributors on issues of local government in Nigeria, and on the Nigerian Public Service. He has edited a number of volumes, published many articles, and has served on a number of important study commissions on the local government and the Public Service systems in Nigeria. Gboyega was an influential participant in the design of the system of elected local government and local level mobilization which he analyzes in his chapter in this volume.

JIBRIN IBRAHIM teaches in the Political Science Department of Ahmadu Bello University in Zaria, Nigeria. He took his Ph.D. at the Institut d'Etudes Politiques in Bordeaux in 1991. He has quickly become a leader among younger African political analysts in both the Francophone and English-language intellectual worlds. He has published widely, in English and French, on Nigerian political parties, the Nigerian state, democratization, and religion and politics in Nigeria. He is an editor of the *Review of African Political Economy* and is editor of two forthcoming volumes on democratization in Nigeria and in Africa.

RICHARD JOSEPH is Asa G. Candler Professor of Political Science at Emory University. He lectured at the University of Ibadan, Nigeria, 1976-79. His major publications include *Democracy and Prebendal Politics in Nigeria: The Rise and Fall of the Second Republic* (1987), and *Radical Nationalism in Cameroun: Social Origins of the U.P.C. Rebellion* (1977), as well as many articles and book chapters. From 1988-1994, he worked with the Carter Center, participating actively in a number of its crisis mediation efforts and electoral monitoring for democratizing African states.

PETER LEWIS completed his Ph.D. at Princeton in 1992. Lewis already is recognized among the top American specialists on Nigerian politics and Nigerian economic developments. His work on the 1992-93 failed democratic transition (see "Endgame in Nigeria?", *African Affairs*, 1994), and on the political economy of structural adjustment in Nigeria, have been influential. Lewis teaches comparative politics and international political economy at American University; during 1995-96 he was at the Hoover Institution as a National Fellow.

OYELEYE OYEDIRAN is among the most distinguished of Nigerian social scientists. He has taught at a number of Nigerian and American universities, and presently is a member of the Department of Political Science at the University of Lagos. He is author or editor of a number of books (including *Nigerian Government and Politics under Military Rule*, 1979) and many articles on Nigerian politics and government. Among other honors and service roles, from 1975 to 1979 Oyediran served on the important Constitution Drafting Committee and the subsequent Constituent Assembly to develop the constitutional system of the Nigerian Second Republic.

JOHN PADEN has been regarded as a leading student of Northern Nigerian politics and Islamic culture in Kano for more than 20 years. Noteworthy among many books and articles are *Religion and Political Culture in Kano* (1973) and *Ahmadu Bello: Sardauna of Sokoto* (1986). A former professor and Director of the African Studies Program at Northwestern University, Paden now teaches at George Mason University.

RICHARD SKLAR has followed Nigerian politics over the whole period of Nigerian independence. His *Nigerian Political Parties* (1963) set a standard of scholarship and analysis which has rarely been equaled, and he has continued throughout a long career to contribute some of the most stimulating and influential theoretical perspectives on Nigerian and African politics. Sklar is Professor Emeritus at UCLA.

ROTIMI SUBERU is one of Nigeria's brilliant younger political scientists. He took his Ph.D. in 1990 at the University of Ibadan, and is a member of that university's political science department. His research focuses on Nigerian federalism, especially in relation to problems of instability, ethnic competition, and democratization. His book, *Federalism and Ethnic Conflict in Nigeria*, is in progress.

CHUDI UWAZURIKE is Associate Professor of Sociology at City College, City University of New York. He took his Ph.D. at Harvard University in 1987. A published author of novels, poetry and drama, his scholarly publications focus on Nigerian politics, problems of democracy in Nigeria, and intellectuals and the state in Nigeria and other African countries. Two books--on democracy and development in Nigeria and on rethinking development--are forthcoming. Before going to City College he taught at Harvard, Framingham State College, and Columbia University.

OLUFEMI VAUGHAN studied at St. Johns University, and took his Ph.D. at Oxford in 1989. He is Assistant Professor of Africana Studies and History at the State University of New York at Stony Brook. He is co-editor and contributor to *Legitimacy and the State in Twentieth Century Africa* (London, Macmillan, 1993), and is widely recognized for his work on traditional rulers and grassroots politics in Nigeria.

PAT AMA TOKUNBO WILLIAMS took her Ph.D. in political science at the University of Ibadan in 1989. She has taught at Ogun State University, and served as Principal Research Officer in the Centre for Democratic Studies, Abuja, Nigeria. Presently, she is Visiting Scholar in the Centre for Refugee Studies at York University as well as coordinator of the West African Research Network. She is co-author of *Religious Impact on the Nation State: the Nigerian Predicament* (1995) and has published a large number of articles from Nigerian and comparative perspectives on topics such as women and democratization, religion and violence, women and urban violence, and power, authority and the gender crisis.

CRAWFORD YOUNG is H. Edwin Young and Rupert Emerson Professor of Political Science at the University of Wisconsin-Madison, where he has taught since 1963. He has served as visiting professor in Uganda, Zaire, and Senegal. Two of his major works, *The Politics of Cultural Pluralism* (1976), and *The African Colonial State in Comparative Perspective* (1994), have won awards, the former from the African Studies Association and the American Political Science Association, the latter from the Comparative Politics Section of the APSA. A former President of the African Studies Association, he received the Distinguished Africanist Award from ASA in 1991.

PREFACE

On the afternoon of November 10, 1995, 29 scholars gathered on the campus of the University of Wisconsin-Madison to begin three days of intensive work together on the problem of democracy in Nigeria. Three or four hours before the conference convened came shocking news: the Nigerian author and activist Ken Saro-Wiwa, together with eight Ogoni movement colleagues, had been abruptly executed in Port Harcourt by the military regime headed by General Sani Abacha.

Several of the conference participants were longtime friends of Saro-Wiwa. All felt a profound symbolic impact as the event gave dramatic and tragic expression to the looming questions surrounding Nigeria's failure over more than two decades to establish lasting democracy and to forge an inclusive and lasting solution to the Nigerian "national question" on which Saro-Wiwa's last years had focused.

Under these circumstances, to say that the ensuing dialogue was intense would be an understatement. The perspectives the participants brought to the conference were diverse. Twelve were scholars based at six of Nigeria's universities. A number of others were Nigerian scholars based at American or Canadian universities. Several American long-term students of Nigerian politics and history were present. Different regional perspectives, and different personal positions on recent political events, were represented among the participants. The discussion was informed with a sense that this large and complex country is almost certainly on the verge of momentous change, toward better, or toward worse.

Of the twenty-three scholars who presented papers at the conference, eighteen agreed to revise their papers for publication in this volume. It is clear that the resulting chapters have come to reflect in deep ways the proceedings of the whole conference and the contributions of paper-givers and discussants alike.[1] Subsequently, Dr. Pat Williams of York University kindly agreed to contribute a chapter on the crucial topic of gender. Together, these nineteen essays seem to us to make a significant contribution to understanding the events of the past and the national options that lie before Nigeria. All cluster around a consensual understanding of the ever-increasing centrality of the question of democracy to the future of the Nigerian polity. Included with that understanding is the idea that dissolution of the political unit we call Nigeria has become, once again, as Sklar remarks, a possible consequence of failure.

The "Dilemmas of Democracy in Nigeria" conference was made possible by financial support from the United States Information Agency under the broad theme of "Democracy in Africa," and grew out of our collaborative project on democracy and American Studies with the University of Jos. We appreciate the support of USIA officials both in Washington and Lagos; needless to say, USIA has no responsibility for the content of the conference proceedings, or for the revised contributions published in this volume. We also benefitted from the generous support of Dean David M. Trubek and the Office of International Studies and Programs of the University of Wisconsin-Madison, as well as the African Studies Program of the University of Wisconsin-Madison.

Grateful acknowledgement is due to several University of Wisconsin-Madison graduate students who provided invaluable assistance at various stages of this project: Michael Williams, Bruce Magnusson, and Cathlene Hanaman. Michael Afolayan offered particularly important assistance, and the Nigerian community in Madison provided support and generous hospitality. Our appreciation also extends to our primary collaborator at the University of Jos, former Deputy Vice-Chancellor Shamsudeen Amali, and to his faculty team at the University of Jos.

Note

1. A brief summary of the conference proceedings has been published by the African Studies Program of the University of Wisconsin-Madison (1996): "Summary: Conference on the Dilemmas of Democracy in Nigeria, University of Wisconsin-Madison, November 10–13, 1995," prepared by conference Rapporteur Bruce Magnusson. (Copies of this document, including the names of all papergivers and discussants, may be requested from: The African Studies Program, 205 Ingraham Hall, University of Wisconsin-Madison, Madison WI 53706.)

INTRODUCTION: BEYOND THE IMPASSE OF "PERMANENT TRANSITION" IN NIGERIA

Paul Beckett and Crawford Young

The Scope of the Effort—and of the Failure

Nigeria, home to a quarter of Africa's population, faces a profound and multi-faceted crisis: "the running sore of a continent," in the title of a scathing critique by one of its most talented sons, Nobel Laureate Wole Soyinka (1996). The survival of Nigeria is at issue, with chilling scenarios of what a breakdown—or breakup—might bring in its wake, casting a long shadow over the entire region.

The stakes are great. Nigeria can be seen as a defining case among the African nations that have, in the decade of the 1990s, moved to re-democratize. In no African country has the effort to create democracy been more far-reaching or of longer duration than in Nigeria. While tending to extremes in scale and complexity, however, the Nigerian experience at the same time illustrates underlying circumstances and obstacles common to democratization cases throughout the continent. A number of the obstacles are highlighted in this volume:

- The essential artificiality of the political entity (Afolayan)
- The incongruity of indigenous and imported patterns of political theory and culture (Ekeh)
- Extremes of ethnic diversity, resulting in a political mosaic and "national question" of extraordinary diversity (as one illustration,

see Suberu's remarkable compilation of recent demands for new states in Nigeria)
- Persistence of colonial patterns of regional division (Paden)
- A disastrous and traumatic first experience with democracy in the immediate post-colonial period (Sklar)
- The rise of religious polarization (Bako, Falola)
- Enormous concentration of power, distortion of political culture, and increasingly repressive practices through decades of military rule (Ibrahim)
- Deepening patterns of corruption and declining standards of economic management (Lewis)

If such characteristics and patterns of experience are emblematic of many African post-colonial polities and societies, the experiences of other African countries equally illustrate—at the extremes—the potential costs of continued failure to institutionalize democracy in Nigeria. Zaire is often advanced as negative reference point. Cases of sustained civil strife and even state collapse—Liberia or Sierra Leone—together with such extra-African extremes as ex-Yugoslavia— weigh heavily on Nigerian intellectuals as they consider the future of their country.

In his chapter, Young offers a comparative perspective in an assessment and chronology of the African democratization process that coincided with and to some extent was unleashed by the sudden end of the Cold War in 1989. Certain it is that the significance of the Nigerian effort to create democracy extends far beyond the country's border and, as a case of democracy in a post-colonial, multi-ethnic society, beyond the continent.

The Overlooked Interest of the Nigerian Case

It is common to argue that the Nigerian case is of political importance for Africa and beyond. But our chapters go beyond this everyday observation to demonstrate the cumulative *intellectual* interest from more than twenty years of almost unbroken "transition" to democracy in Nigeria. The ultimate failure, thus far, of the effort to re-democratize that began in August, 1975, has obscured much that is of high comparative interest, including some significant successes. Detailed in the papers in this volume are the remarkably open processes of consultation, reflection and collective self-study that resulted in the constitutions of 1979 and 1989 (the account of Oyediran, a participant, provides a particularly fascinating set of reflections). As Uwazurike remarks, a tendency to political theorizing has been a pronounced characteristic of Nigeria since the 1950s. An ingenious and aggressive strategy of constitutional engineering has been carried forward and developed since 1975, culminating in the remarkable and elaborate "consociational" formulae for power-sharing and rotation included in the proposed 1995 "Abacha constitution" (see Uwazurike, in particular). Democratic "constitutional engineering" in Nigeria—aimed at reducing the blatant and destructive regionalism and ethnic organization of the failed First Republic—has, in fact, produced remarkably innovative institutional experiments (see Paden and Beckett for illustrations). And, almost unnoticed and little analyzed, an enormous volume of electoral experience has accumulated in Nigeria (complete rounds of nationwide elections at local, state and federal level were held in 1978–79, 1983 and 1989–93). Despite frequent mismanagement by governments in power there have been many unsung achievements. Finally, and least noticed of all, a proliferation of local level associations announces a deepening of civil society (Gboyega; see Agbaje on its limits). In the process, Nigeria's critically important traditional rulers have been alternately courted and repulsed in the course of the ebb and flow of military rule and democratic transition (Vaughan).

Yet for all the effort, and the intellectual interest of the effort, each transition has so far failed: the first, from colonial rule to independence, dissolved in January 1966, leading to civil war; the second (December 31 1983) after four years of increasingly prebendal democratic rule; the third (in June 1993) before transition to democracy was quite complete. The 1983 failure was a missed opportunity of major proportions—one to which the country now struggles to return (Oyediran). But to most of these authors the 1993 failure to carry through a transition on the edge of completion represents a national catastrophe. At stake since that event is not simply democracy, but the existence of Nigeria as a political entity.

Democracy and the Legitimacy of Military Rule: The Nigerian Paradox

Looking at the three failed transitions, as well as at events *since* June 1993, we identify a pattern we term "Permanent Transition." What is Permanent Transition?

Permanent Transition turns on that paradoxical situation—visible over many years—in which Nigerian military rule is legitimated by a sense of *progress* toward creating its own alternative: civil democratic government. The postwar colonial state, under growing nationalist challenge, purchased some time and a modicum of legitimacy by a promise of transition to independence. The Gowon regime extended its legitimacy beyond the crisis of the Civil War by promising (in October 1970) to create democracy. Conversely, the regime de-legitimated precipitously when (in October 1974) Gowon reneged on the promise of transition to democracy. The Muhammed/Obasanjo military regime, established in August 1975, was legitimated as the regime (unlike its predecessor) carried through an energetic and systematic program of transition to democracy. The connection was strengthened as the regime in fact handed over power on schedule and returned to the barracks.

By contrast, the Babangida-managed transition—begun in 1985—wore on and on. An increasingly complex transition process continually drew new waves of civilian members of the political, commercial and intellectual elites into participation. Ultimately, in the nationwide partisan elections that occurred between 1989 and 1993 at least 5,000 office holders were elected at local, state and federal levels, including party offices (see Emelifeonwu).

But as the process went on, the rules of the political game were frequently altered by the Babangida regime, usually on very short notice. Thus, parties were invited to apply for registration—and then rejected en masse. Whole categories of politicians were banned—and then unbanned. At one point all the leading presidential candidates were suddenly proscribed from further participation. At another, the parties—initially organized by the government—were declared in receivership and taken under the direction of government-appointed managers. The Babangida regime continually pushed back the dates of stages and extended the timetable for completion of the democratic transition. Meanwhile, speculation increased that Babangida's personal intention was to ensure that the transition was *never* completed. Many suspected that as Babangida presided over a seemingly endless transition, he watched for an opportunity to civilianize and overtly politicize his own rule.[1]

In this perspective, the presidential elections of June 12, 1993 represented an embarrassment. Almost in spite of the regime that managed them, the elections were accounted fair, and the results they produced were remarkably "national" and in keeping with the goals of constitutional engineering. (In his Table 3 Paden presents a state-by-state and regional analysis of the results.) Permanent Transition was thus threatened by unexpected success in achieving transition. The regime's awkward response was to suppress the electoral data (which had already been leaked and published) and to announce the annulment of the election.

Complex events (chronicled and analyzed by Emelifeonwu and Sklar) ensued, leading ultimately to full remilitarization, with General Sani Abacha taking over. Illustrating both the centrality and inescapability of Permanent Transition, Abacha immediately set in motion his own transition process, following the now well-worn paths developed since 1975.

The Anatomy of Permanent Transition

At the most superficial level, Permanent Transition represents a relatively simple stratagem to provide legitimizing cover to military rule. Military rule is justified to the extent that an illusion of progress toward the creation of civil democratic government is maintained. This basis of legitimacy becomes the more important as alternative claims to legitimacy (probity, nationalism and "military virtues") erode. The ideal of Permanent Transition is to somehow freeze in place that idyllic stage where the military plans a distant handover, intellectuals and other elites devise a constitution, and politicians form clubs and (in astonishing numbers) dream personally of the presidency.

But Permanent Transition goes deeper. Permanent Transition has both accompanied and facilitated significant changes in class rule patterns. Permanent Transition makes possible simultaneous military rule *and* the participation of broad sections of the "political class" in the party politics and the elections that are part of the transition program. In effect, Permanent Transition can be seen as a confused and chaotic form of that military-civil *diarchy* which has been considered as a form of government—and, in the main, rejected—by Nigerian intellectuals since the First Republic (see Uwazurike).

Yet for all the furious circulation of elites through political and governmental offices as Permanent Transition has developed, our essays suggest that true participation has narrowed sharply from the level of the "conciliar" military governments of the 1970s (Joseph). While the economic resources distributed through the state remain the central target of both political and economic activity, the public sector administrative elite has become far less central to events than in the first two decades of independence. The broader spectrum of Nigeria's highly-educated elite—those who have not themselves joined the dance and game of Permanent Transition—increasingly are marginalized in the face of a new ruling class composed by overlapping military, political and commercial elites (Beckett).

Permanent Transition is closely associated with significant changes in economic behavior patterns. If Nigeria is a politically blocked country, it also is an economically blocked one. The "nurture capitalism" of the first phase of independence, did not lead to mature capitalism, but rather to "pirate capitalism" as Schatz (1984) termed it. The focus of economic behavior has turned continually back upon the resources (primarily derived from oil) accumulated and distributed by the state, rather than outward toward productive and creative economic activity. The political game has grown to comprise an ever more central part of the economic one.

Permanent Transition, with its rapid circulation of elites (and immense political investment requirements) has given a quality of feeding frenzy to the pursuit of oil-derived and state-distributed resources. Our contributors suggest Nigeria's movement to yet another phase, as "pirate capitalism" has moved through the stage identified by Joseph (1987) as "prebendalism" to reach a new stage of buccaneering accumulation, termed by Lewis predatory or avaricious dictatorship. In comparison with the earlier stages of corrupt practices, contemporary predation, as Lewis and Joseph indicate, has taken somewhat different forms, is more direct, is on quite a different scale, and clearly has had devastating consequences for the polity and society. Predatory accumulation has both accompanied and promoted unprecedented levels of power concentration around the personality of the general in power.

A particularly disconcerting trend identified by some observers is the sharpening distinction, in terms of the global economy, between a "useful Nigeria," essentially composed of the Niger delta and especially the offshore oil production zone, and the rest of the country. New investment flows into the enclave, doubtless secure in the belief that—as in Angola—the oil producing areas can be virtually sealed off from the remainder of the country and thus insulated from its fate. The substantial rents from a growing petroleum production accrue solely to the center and to the military-political apparatus which remains ensconced in Permanent Transition.

With substantial increases in Nigerian oil production and hence revenues in prospect, the managers of Permanent Transition appear likely to dispose of sufficient resources to avert the fate of those African autocratic regimes such as neighboring Benin, driven to cover by the simple incapacity to remunerate the public service or to offer minimal prebendal distributions. Nigeria, by some estimates, is poised to become the third or fourth largest oil producer. The absence of either accountability or transparency in the disposition of these revenues is a fundamental attribute of military rule, as evidenced by the 1994 official report detailing the disappearance of $12.2 billion of windfall oil revenues produced by the last price spike into "dedicated accounts" removed from any scrutiny (Lewis). This in turn intensifies the deep resentments felt in the on-shore producing areas, whose populations believe they pay an exorbitant ransom in the destruction of their environment, and receive the barest pittance in return.

During the course of the Permanent Transition, Nigeria has emerged as a major transit point for the international narcotics traffic (Lewis). The risks of a partial criminalization of the state are high in this development; as Lewis notes, some degree of official forbearance is indispensable to the operation of the narcotics rings. The damage to Nigeria's standing in the international community, reflected in the demeaning scrutiny Nigerian travelers experience at immigration posts, is one of many consequences.

The Impasse of Permanent Transition

In one sense, our contributors provide unwilling testimony to the success of Permanent Transition. Permanent Transition has functioned as intended as a stratagem and political technique of rule to divide and marginalize potential opposition from elite groups and civil society, and to divert and confuse public attention. Certainly, it has been of crucial importance for the military regimes of the 1980s and 1990s whose obvious corruption and dereliction in economic management obviate any other claims to legitimacy.

But at a far more profound level, these chapters chronicle the bankruptcy of Permanent Transition, and point to a looming national impasse. Governance in Nigeria is seen in disarray as corruption, cynicism, tyranny and *personalismo* reach unprecedented levels (Ibrahim, Joseph, Lewis). Nigerian federalism—the lifeline of national existence since independence—

is, in the view of a number of our authors (for example, Suberu, Ibrahim), corrupted both by decades of military centralization, and by the spreading and compounding effects of a *rentier* national lifestyle. Regional relations have become so exacerbated as to recall the worst times of the 1960s (Sklar, Bako). Illustrated and tragically dramatized by the execution of Saro-Wiwa and his colleagues, the relations of Nigeria's many ethnic peoples to each other and to the whole (the "national question") have deteriorated so sharply as to call into question—for many—the Nigerian union itself. Bako and Falola not only show the sharp and disturbing deterioration of the culture of civility which so long prevailed in inter-religious relations, but also are able to trace the deterioration to the characteristics and dynamics of prolonged military rule. Written from the point of view of a primarily northern Islamic intelligentsia, Bako's chapter itself serves to illustrate the dangerously sharp differentiation of perception that presently divides religious and regional groups in Nigeria. Meanwhile, as Abgaje and others show, the years of Permanent Transition have divided and weakened civil society in general as the sphere of operation of pro-democratic forces has shrunken. Gender is another negative entry on the balance sheet; women, argues Williams, have *remained* marginalized under military rule and in the "charade" of Permanent Transition. And with the failure (in 1993) of the transition to a Third Republic, democratization at the local level has been reversed; the vertical articulations of Nigerian federalism linking local government and its functions to the state and national levels are in disarray.

In the repertoire of identities all Nigerians possess, the relative valence of local community, ethnic, religious and national attachments evolves in a complex dialectic. The close association of the national attachment with the performance and legitimacy of the state itself makes Permanent Transition an increasingly risky strategy. As its credibility steadily declines in the 1990s, the disposition of the citizen to perceive security and affective legitimacy in other forms of social attachment (see Ekeh) is likely to increase. At some point the cynical disengagement of the average Nigerian citizen from the state may give way to the conclusion now drawn by Soyinka—that the very notion of a Nigerian nation has become a "farcical illusion." In Soyinka's pungent terms, the illusion of the nation has become "that mangy, flea-infested flag that the sanctimonious nationalist drapes around his torso to cover a repulsive nudity!" (Soyinka 1996, 126).

Symptomatic is the renewed search for revitalized ethnic community by a variety of cultural entrepreneurs. Language authentification and ethnic history are important tools. In some instances, such as the Ogoni in the Niger delta oilfields, intense deprivation is a mobilizing force. For many in southern and Middle Belt areas, the conviction that a Hausa-Fulani clique insists on monopolizing power is a motivating factor.[2]

One clear measure of the drift of identity politics is the differing reactions in various regions to the annulment of the 1993 presidential elections. Reaction was angriest in the Yoruba zones of the southwest; the north remained largely silent, and protest in the east was relatively muted and short-lived. Indeed, some perceive a trend towards a semi-detachment of the southwest; the transfer of government from Lagos to Abuja continues, and animosity towards the Abacha regime remains particularly intense in these areas.

Of profound significance is the increasing religious polarization. As Bako and Falola point out, the Muslim-Christian divide played little role in the early years of the republic. Indeed, in comparative terms, the initial absence of religious mobilization in politics is striking, even extraordinary; few countries with roughly equal Muslim and Christian populations have enjoyed comity. However, since the middle 1970s tension has steadily increased across the confessional divide. The Bako and Falola chapters trace the various ways in which mutual suspicions have deepened; both perceive conspiratorial designs in the actions of the other. Both major religious communities have acquired more aggressive, at times inflammatory spokesmen.

Closely inspected, as these chapters show, neither the Muslim nor the Christian community is a monolithic block. Both are internally divided by sect, doctrine, and organizational structure. But each in the eyes of the other is readily aggregated into a single threatening force.

Mobilized religious solidarity as a political force has some special properties worthy of note. For the faithful, identity carries a divine sanction, and difference is compounded by the error of the other. A charismatic religious leader — found in both communities — enjoys an ascendance over the following whose transcendental underpinnings may provide a more robust mobilizing potential than ethnic politicians can muster, in their more secular quest for a larger serving from the "national cake".

Our chapters indicate the growing sense that after the decades of Permanent Transition the military is simply not capable of curing the ills that it has created, and not capable of creating its own alternative, whether through the complex constitutional formulae announced late in 1995 by the Abacha regime, or otherwise. Yet, with Permanent Transition as its main technique of rule, and with full control over the distribution of oil-derived resources, the military seems to retain the ability and the determination to block any visible alternative. Hence derives the sense of *impasse* which could ultimately call into question the future existence of Nigeria itself.

Indeed, suspicion grows that Sani Abacha contemplates riding Permanent Transition into continued office as an ostensibly elected president, under the provisions of his new constitution. The success of Niger president Ibrahima Bare Mainassara and Gambian president Yahya Jammeh in 1996 in orchestrating a metamorphosis from military putschist to constitutional head of state offers tempting examples. Many believe that Ibrahim Babangida had hidden hopes of such a feat, which proved beyond even his fine Italian hand in political management.

Beyond Permanent Transition

There is agreement among these contributors: Nigeria has arrived at a crossroads. Since 1975—and, indeed, over the whole period of independence—Nigeria has oscillated between military dictatorship and democracy. The pattern has been extravagantly developed, embroidered and ultimately corrupted and ruined in the Permanent Transition of Babangida and Abacha. As Joseph shows so clearly, a "stable" circulation among relatively benevolent regime types of mixed character must give way to more decisive national options. Most of our authors argue, in one way or another, the bankruptcy of the practices and strategems that, together, comprise Permanent Transition.

A number of these essays look beyond the national impasse. Suberu details and critiques the argumentation forming an emergent debate on alternative political options for Nigeria, and finds some degree of personal hope in the concept of a recaptured and reformed Nigerian federalism that could provide the basis for national reconciliation. For Ibrahim also, hope requires deconcentration of the enormous centralization of power that has occurred over all the years of military rule, through the restoration of a genuine federal mechanism. Joseph lays out the alternative routes that effective political transition might take. Sklar derives from analysis of the major political crises of the past and present three empirical propositions that augur favorably for the ultimate construction of an "inclusive national unity." Uwazurike gives careful analysis to, and finds promise in, the consociational aspects of the rotational power-sharing arrangements that emerged from the Constitutional Conference of 1995. Paden likewise shows the deep historical roots of the regionalist schema which is central to the new constitutional propositions.

These and other features of these essays represent the beginning of a vision of Nigeria beyond impasse. But it would be false to the contributors to suggest a euphoric solution. The collection is far from bereft of hope—yet these mainly hard-headed and frequently somber assessments are replete with the caution born of hard experience.

Shared by all, however, is the sense that ultimately democracy represents the only escape from impasse. In his formulation, Oyediran puts it: "hope lies in the realization of the transition [to democracy], despair lies in the triumph of authoritarian and reactionary forces." Few, if any, of the contributors would disagree in terms of the choice. On the basis of comparative analysis, Young argues that the liabilities "and indeed mortal dangers" inherent in further prolongation of military rule in the context of Permanent Transition greatly outweigh the liabilities and perils of democracy. The route is uncertain, but the goal is clear. Democracy represents the only visible exit from the "dismal tunnel" of the present impasse. Oyediran says simply: "We must break this tragic circle."

Notes

1. Significantly, the forthcoming and excellent examination of Nigerian politics and civil society during the period of Ibrahim Babangida's rule edited by Larry Diamond, Anthony Kirk-Greene, and Oyeleye Oyediran is entitled *Transition Without End* (Lynne Reinner, forthcoming, 1997).

2. The fact that only two of the seven military rulers (Murtala Muhammed and Muhammadu Buhari, who together ruled only two of the 27 years of military incumbency) have been of the "Hausa-Fulani" ethnic background in exact terms does not shake this perception. Even in the simplified terms represented by the personal ethnic-regional identity of top leaders, the question of regional "domination" in Nigerian politics is complex. The present military ruler, Sani Abacha (from Kano with a Bornu family background) is a somewhat debatable case (and Paden underscores the significance of regional distinctions *within* "the north"). Interestingly, the two military heads of state of longest tenure each exemplified ambiguity in regional-ethnic terms. The long-time "northern" head of state General Yakubu Gowon is a Christian member of a small Middle Belt minority ethnicity (Angas)

who was raised in a Hausa-Fulani heartland area (Zaria). The "Maradona" of military-political rule, Ibrahim Badamasi Babangida, is Muslim and hails from one of the traditional emirate areas (Nupe). His parents and grandparents were Muslim, and claim connections to Kano and Sokoto. Yet his main ethnic affiliation seems to be Gbagyi (Gwari), and thus he can be considered a Middle Belt minority (Forrest 1993, 127). Finally, based partly on a misunderstanding of his middle name, he was often said to have Yoruba antecedents as well! Among civilian leaders, on the other hand, Ahmadu Bello and Shehu Shagari were indeed Hausa-Fulani; Tafawa Balewa came from the outer fringe of the Hausa-Fulani empire (Bauchi), and a semi-secret was his family's slave background (Whitaker 1970, 339). Southerners (Ironsi, Igbo and Obasanjo, Yoruba) have held the head of state position twice, but for a combined total of less than four years. (There was an element of accident in the accession of each to the head of state position.) The question of regional domination is extremely central in Nigerian political discourse. Yet, as Bako's and other contributions in the volume illustrate, domination is a phenomenon that may be defined in the eye of the beholder.

References

Diamond, Larry, Anthony Kirk-Greene and Oyeleye Oyediran, eds. 1997 (forthcoming). *Transition Without End: Nigerian Politics and Civil Society Under Babangida*. Boulder: Lynne Rienner.
Forrest, Tom. 1993. *Politics and Economic Development in Nigeria*. Boulder: Westview Press.
Joseph, Richard. 1987. *Democracy and Prebendal Politics in Nigeria: The Rise and Fall of the Second Republic*. Cambridge: Cambridge University Press.
Schatz, Sayre. 1984. "Pirate Capitalism and the Inert Economy of Nigeria." *Journal of Modern African Studies*, 22, I: 45–57.
Soyinka, Wole. 1996. *The Running Sore of a Continent: A Personal Narrative of the Nigerian Crisis*. New York: Oxford University Press.
Whitaker, C.S. Jr. 1970. *The Politics of Tradition, Continuity and Change in Northern Nigeria, 1946–1966*. Princeton: Princeton University Press.

PART 1
History and Society

1

CRISES AND TRANSITIONS IN THE POLITICAL HISTORY OF INDEPENDENT NIGERIA

Richard L. Sklar

From the time of its emergence as a sovereign state in 1960, Nigeria has weathered recurrent threats to its corporate existence. More often than not, however, Nigerian political leaders have failed to exploit concurrent opportunities to strengthen their nation by responding creatively to the challenges of crisis management. While there have been many informative studies of particular crises in Nigerian political history, comparative studies of these events are needed for the derivation of general conclusions. This account considers five major political crises, one each in the 1960s, the 1970s, and the 1980s, and two in the 1990s.

It would not be realistic to suppose that the crises chosen for this assessment of responses and their effects are either isolable or self-contained events in recent Nigerian history. Each one represents the culmination of many related circumstances and events that both complicate the quest for causation and produce multiple effects in politics and society. In each case, the starting point has been selected for expository reasons mainly, since historical origins are never determinate. For the sake of narrative continuity, I have adopted the concept of transition, believing that it would be conducive to the identification of other significant events which might be selected for examination in a more thorough survey of political crises. This concept is often used by political scientists to analyze passages from military to civilian rule. Although two such passages in Nigeria have been compared systematically by Koehn (1989), the second of those transitions, still in progress when his account appeared, was eventually aborted by the military rulers (Lewis 1994).

I have taken yet another liberty with the historical record by choosing to identify each crisis with the name of a protagonist who was also the nation's incumbent chief executive officer during a portion, at least, of the crisis in question. This presentational device does tend to personalize and, for that reason, possibly misrepresent the causes and elements of complex situations. In each instance, the person whose name is featured was but one among several principal actors. In any case, the aim of this analysis is to elicit lessons from the crisis behavior of political leaders rather than determine the causes of their predicaments.

Nigeria's history since independence can be represented, graphically and plausibly, as a continuous crisis with occasional peaks, some valleys, and several plateaus. This writer has traversed that metaphorical distance mainly from afar, but also in close proximity to the first crisis examined, having lived in Nigeria for a portion of it and known many of those who experienced it as participants and observers. For the subsequent crises chronicled herein, my reliance on the public record increases in proportion to diminished degrees of personal knowledge. In no case, however, does information acquired by means of personal conversation, direct observation, or examination of documents and published commentaries outweigh the importance of interpretation influenced by reflection on the era in its entirety.

Abubakar Tafawa Balewa's Crisis, 1962–1966

Alhaji Sir Abubakar Tafawa Balewa was appointed Prime Minister of the Federation of Nigeria by the British Governor-General in 1957 on the unanimous recommendation of the leaders of three rival political parties. He was then, and for the remainder of his life, vice president of the predominant party of Nigeria's northern region. With some 54 percent of the national population, the northern region would be entitled to a comparable majority of seats in a reconstituted federal House of Representatives. Following the general election of 1959, itself a decisive stride toward full independence, Sir Abubakar formed a coalition government comprising his own party, the Northern Peoples' Congress (NPC), and one of the two other parties in control of a regional government, namely, the National

Convention of Nigerian Citizens (NCNC), which controlled the eastern region. The Action Group of Nigeria, which controlled the western region, formed the official opposition in the House of Representatives at the time of independence.

Shortly after independence, Chief Obafemi Awolowo, leader of the federal Opposition and president of his party, clashed with Chief Samuel Ladoke Akintola, deputy leader of the Action Group and Awolowo's successor as Premier of the western regional government. Chief Akintola disagreed with Awolowo's political strategy involving the use of western regional resources to challenge the dominant parties of the eastern and northern regions in order to gain control of the federal government. Awolowo particularly wished to divide the north into two or more regions and then to minimize the power of its traditional aristocracy and those modern conservatives with whom the traditionalists were allied. Ever since 1903, when British forces subdued recalcitrant northern rulers, particularly the Sultan of Sokoto, colonial officials had relied upon Muslim traditional rulers to govern most of the northern peoples. The adaptation of those rulers and their retainers to modernity, indeed their ability to incorporate commercial institutions, social services, and various liberal reforms into a theocratic order, accounts for their immense political authority in postcolonial Nigeria (Whitaker 1970). Awolowo's challenge to the northern rulers—collectively, the emirs, their titled officials, and other supporters—was revolutionary in nature, although his personal ideology was closely akin to British Fabian socialism.

Contrary to Awolowo, Akintola advocated respect for the northern principle of regional security, meaning that no party in control of a regional government should employ its resources to support opponents of another regional government (Sklar 1965b). The ideological implications of this political formula were profoundly conservative. Faced with the refusal of authorities in the north to countenance effective cross-regional electoral campaigning, Awolowo and his lieutenants resorted to desperate measures, including rudimentary training of cadres for paramilitary actions. An attempt by Awolowo's supporters in the Western House of Assembly, comprising a majority of members, to remove Akintola as premier provoked disorderly conduct within the chamber and resulted in a decision by the prime minister to propose a parliamentary declaration of public emergency in the western region. That measure, taken in May 1962, authorized the appointment of a federal official to administer the western region. A subsequent investigation disclosed that public funds in large amounts had been diverted to political activities by officials of the regional government who were loyal to Awolowo. Furthermore, Awolowo, himself, was arrested, prosecuted for allegedly conspiring to seize power by means of a coup d'état, convicted of treasonable felony, and sentenced to a ten-year term of imprisonment (Sklar 1966).

Soon thereafter, the NCNC had reason to rue its support of the parliamentary resolution declaring an emergency in the west. When the emergency administration ended, in January 1963, Chief Akintola was reinstated as premier with NCNC support. Ineluctably, the regionalist interests of most Yoruba members of the NCNC outweighed their loyalties to a party identified primarily with the eastern region and its Igbo majority. The decisive breach occurred in February 1964, as a result of the announcement of disputed census results, which preserved the northern region's population edge over the rest of the country. These results were accepted by the northern and western regional governments but rejected by the eastern regional government and its political ally, the government of a newly-created midwestern region, which had been carved out of the west by excising Edo and other non-Yoruba-speaking areas. Most NCNC members in the west abandoned their party and joined a new regionalist party led by Akintola. By September 1964, the proponents and opponents of regional political security had formed rival alliances in preparation for an impending election for the federal House of Representatives. The strict regionalists, including the NPC, Akintola's party in the west, the midwestern opposition, and small parties in the east, formed a Nigerian National Alliance (NNA), while their opponents, including the NCNC (in control of both the eastern and midwestern regional governments), the western Action Group, and the combined (emirate- and non-emirate-area) opposition in the north established a United Progressive Grand Alliance (UPGA).

The ensuing campaign was marred by tribalistic propaganda, sporadic violence, and maladministration, resulting in an UPGA boycott of the election, protesting the decision of electoral commissioners that in nearly 40 percent of the northern regional constituencies NPC candidates would be unopposed due to the failure of their potential rivals to qualify for inclusion on the ballot. President Nnamdi Azikiwe, who had been premier of the eastern region until 1959 and president of NCNC until shortly before independence, tried to persuade the prime minister to postpone the election, but without success. After consulting leaders of the armed forces, who insisted upon their constitutional duty to obey the Prime Minister rather than the President, Azikiwe negotiated an agreement with Sir Abubakar, who then formed a government controlled by the NNA with provision for the inclusion of UPGA members of parliament in the cabinet once supplementary elections had been conducted in the eastern region, where no voting had taken place.

By early 1965, the NPC and its allies had prevailed in several successive political contests: Awolowo's political organization had been humbled, shorn of its resource base, and reduced to dependence on a former rival, the NCNC. The government of the western region was controlled by the NPC's principal ally; the census controversy had been settled, for the time being, to the NPC's satisfaction; and the federal government was firmly under the control of NPC ministers. Yet deep resentment among the Yoruba in western Nigeria, combined with the determination of UPGA leaders in all regions to redress the balance of political power, signified a precarious peace and severe challenge to the government of the federation, one that leaders of the NPC could neglect to address only at their peril. Their capacity to contain the danger would soon be tested by an impending election to the Western House of Assembly. An Action Group victory in the west would place the governments of all three southern regions under the control of UPGA leaders who rejected the NPC doctrine of regional political security. Dr. Michael I. Okpara, Premier of the Eastern Region and president of the NCNC, was reliably reported to have expressed his willingness to accept Chief Awolowo as leader of UPGA should he be released from prison. It was also thought that the Prime Minister would not have been averse to the inclusion of Awolowo in a government of national unity.

How would Alhaji Sir Ahmadu Bello, Premier of the northern region and president of the NPC, regard the prospect of political reconciliation with his arch-rival, Awolowo? Sir Ahmadu, whose title, Sardauna of Sokoto, attested to his great eminence as a traditional authority in the domain of the exalted Sultan of Sokoto, was a staunch ally of Chief Akintola; yet he did state publicly that Awolowo would be released from prison should the Action Group win the western regional election. He was also evidently agnostic on the question of reconciliation among the Yoruba rivals, regarding it as a domestic issue for them to decide. Despite the strength of partisan passions, the logic of national reconciliation was plausible. Neither the NNA conception of a regionalist political system based on strictly regional parties, nor the UPGA conception of a relatively centralized federal system based on truly national parties was an inflexible dogma that would preclude a reasonable compromise. To all intents and purposes, the Action Group had become a western regional party, while the NCNC was an eastern and midwestern party. A timely compromise, based on those realities and involving the reactivization of Awolowo, might have facilitated serious consideration of his social-democratic policies. In January 1965, the present writer suggested the formation of a united national front, consisting of freely-affiliated political parties, in the inaugural issue of *Nigerian Opinion*, published at the University of Ibadan:

> Within the framework of a National Front regional leaders would be able to pursue bold programs of modernization and development free from the fear that political vulnerabilities resulting from such programs might be exploited by outsiders for opportunistic purposes. At the same time, progressive elements, now in opposition to regional governments, would no longer be compelled to exploit ethnic or religious discontents that are extraneous to their basic concerns in order to win votes. Within such a framework, there might be reconciliation without dishonor, and the energies of the nation might be harnessed more efficiently to accomplish the unfulfilled goals of the nationalist movement (Sklar 1965a).

Tragically, the reconciliationist option was foregone in October 1965 when Akintola's regime blatantly rigged the western regional election, thereby provoking insurrections in several parts of the region, outside of Akintola's own (Oyo) section of Yorubaland (Osuntokun 1984, 158–67). Moreover, the premiers of the north and the west learned of plans by dissident army officers to seize control of the federal government. Their resolve to crush opposition to the NNA regime was blocked by the coup d'état of January 15 1966 in which rebellious elements of the armed forces, led by junior officers, assassinated the prime minister, the northern and western premiers, and other high officials, including several senior army officers, mainly northerners and westerners who did not share their political outlook. It is not unreasonable to think that the course not taken—a free election in the western region coupled with national reconciliation based on a feasible compromise—could have averted the ensuing calamities.

Transition: Ironsi, Gowon, the Civil War, and Oil

Twenty-seven of the thirty-two officers who were identified as participants in the audacious coup d'état were Igbos of eastern or midwestern regional origin (Miners 1971, 167–70). Rather than escalate the conflict, they surrendered to Major-General Johnson Aguiyi-Ironsi, an Igbo, who had assumed authority as head of state at the request of a depleted cabinet. General Ironsi's attempt to replace federalism with a unitary form of government, and a centralized system of administration, provoked bitter resistance among regionalists, leading to mob violence against Igbo communities in northern towns. On July 29 1966, mutineers, mainly commissioned and non-commissioned officers of northern origin, killed Ironsi and many other Igbo officers. Their leaders, and the surviving senior officers in Lagos, chose Lt.-Colonel Yakubu Gowon to head the military government. A Christian from the southerly, non-emirate sector of the northern region—the so-called Middle Belt—Lt.-Colonel Gowon shared the predominant political outlook of Middle Belters, who were numerous, if not indeed the largest sectional group, among rank and file soldiers as well as non-commissioned officers. They resented the historical domination of their home areas by rulers of the Muslim majority in the northern region, most, but not all, of whom were emirs of Fulani descent. Like minority peoples in the eastern region, and a large majority of people in the recently-created midwestern region, they had been disadvantaged by political regionalism and were disposed to favor a federal system of government with a strong center. At the same time, they resented the industrious immigrants from other parts of Nigeria, mainly Igbos from the densely-populated eastern region, who settled in their home areas and prospered there in commerce and skilled occupations.

Lt.-Colonel Gowon began his tenure of office as head of state by reaffirming the principles of federal government and releasing the ardent federalist, Chief Awolowo, from prison. Now the main challenge faced by Gowon was to conciliate the eastern leaders and persuade them to help reconstruct the federation on equitable foundations. This aim was thwarted, on the eve of a crucial meeting of regional delegates, by the sudden, evidently planned, massacre of easterners in various parts of the north, resulting in some 30,000 deaths and the flight of more than a million refugees from the northern to the eastern region. Thereafter, the eastern government, headed by Lt.-Colonel Chukwuemeka Odumegwu-Ojukwu, prepared to secede from Nigeria. After several unsuccessful attempts to negotiate a settlement, Gowon countered the eastern threat by dividing the northern region into 6 states, the eastern into 3, and the western into 2; with the midwest, the total number of states would be 12, including 2 non-Igbo states in the east that were expected to oppose secession. Immediately thereafter, on May 30 1967, the east proclaimed its secession as the Republic of Biafra. Simultaneously, Chief Awolowo joined Gowon's government as its leading civilian figure (Deputy Chairman of the Federal Executive Council) and commissioner for finance.

Nigeria's civil war lasted 31 months, culminating in Biafra's surrender on January 12 1970. It resulted in more than a million deaths, including a vast number of children who starved and suffered from malnutrition in the beleaguered, land-locked, Igbo heartland. Yet the end of armed hostilities was followed by a remarkably genuine reconciliation of former adversaries, indicating that the war had been fought, not primarily to give vent to hatreds, but to settle significant issues. While the goal of self-determination for an aggrieved people motivated the Igbos, the threat of political disintegration and chaos that could result from a successful secession strengthened the resolve of other Nigerians to preserve the federation intact. Gradually, hostility toward the Igbos was transformed into an appreciation of them as an integral, and valued, part of Nigeria's multiethnic mosaic of peoples.

In 1970, Nigeria was on the verge of a boom in oil production that would change the nature of the country's economy. At independence, agriculture had accounted for three-fourths of the value of exports; by 1975 that figure would decline to 10 percent, while oil, stimulated by pricing policies of the Organization of Petroleum Exporting Countries (OPEC), would escalate to more than 80 percent, rising to 95 percent by 1980. Nigeria was awash in oil, extracted mainly from the Niger Delta, the southeastern coastal swampland, and adjacent deposits offshore.

In 1974, General Gowon, citing the virulence of ethnic politics, declared that it would not be feasible to restore civilian government in 1976, as had been promised in 1970. Meanwhile, in an apparent attempt to mollify the upwardly-mobile intelligentsia, huge salary increases were given to employees in the public sector. This bounty, reproduced for employees of large private firms, was accompanied by an economic policy known as indigenization, meaning that foreign owned enterprises were required to sell shares, often controlling amounts, to Nigerians at prices that were set beneath market valuation by a governmental agency. In this way, wealth generated by oil production fueled a demand for private share-ownership in existing companies rather than creative entrepreneurship (Joseph 1978). This practice was a basic element of the nationalist economic pathology that Sayre P. Schatz (1984) subsequently characterized pungently as "pirate capitalism."

General Gowon's decision to prolong military rule proved to be exceedingly unpopular. His inability to cope effectively with various administrative and economic problems demoralized the intelligentsia, civilian and military alike. On July 29 1975, nine years to the day after his assumption of power, he was deposed without bloodshed by fellow officers while he was abroad, leading a Nigerian delegation to a summit conference of the Organization of African Unity. His successor as head of state and Commander-in-Chief of the armed forces, Brigadier Murtala Ramat Muhammed, 38 and a prominent northern officer, turned out to be a crusading reformer. He cracked down on corruption and maladministration, retired thousands of public employees, prosecuted the former military governors of ten states for misappropriating public funds (recovering substantial amounts), created 7 new states in response to popular demands, and resolved to restore civilian rule in accordance with a strict timetable.

In October 1975, General Muhammed appointed a Constitutional Drafting Committee of 50 persons, including two members from each state with the remainder chosen on the basis of their knowledge of the disciplines of history, law, economics, and political science. He instructed them to propose a constitution that would establish a "free," "democratic," and "federal" system of government. Furthermore, he directed, the constitution should provide for an executive president and an independent judiciary; it should also guarantee human rights. This declaration, 15 months before President Jimmy Carter made human rights a guiding principle of American foreign policy, boosted the level of respect for the military guardians of the state to unprecedented heights.

Olusegun Obasanjo's Crisis, 1976

On February 13 1976, General Murtala Muhammed, at the height of his popularity, was assassinated by a group of disgruntled officers who plotted to take control of the government. The general was killed when a few conspirators fired into his car, which was caught in heavy Lagos traffic. Within hours, however, the coup attempt collapsed. Its principal organizer, Lt.-Colonel B. S. Dimka, director of the army's physical training corps, his senior collaborator, Major-General I. D. Bissalla, Commissioner of Defense, and more than 30 others were executed following secret trials by a military tribunal.

Two distinct issues surfaced in the wake of this unsettling episode. First, it was painfully evident that the planned demobilization of some 40 percent of Nigeria's bloated army of approximately 250,000 would require sensitive management and caution. Second, ethnic tensions, prevalent in Nigerian society, were not absent from the milieu of the army's high command. These issues merged in the figure of Maj.-General Bissalla, who personalized his opposition to proposals for reorganization of the army and related reductions in force. Specifically, he objected to the appointment of Brigadier Yakubu Danjuma, an officer junior to himself, as Chief of Army Staff, and to the latter's subsequent promotion to the rank of Lieutenant General (Obasanjo 1990, 23). It also appears that Bissalla, Dimka, and most of the other leading conspirators were natives of Plateau State and adjacent districts in Kaduna State, a core sector of the so-called Middle Belt (Campbell 1978, 88). Evidently, they harbored a grudge against those officers who had been instrumental in the overthrow of General Gowon (also a son of Plateau State) and then promoted to positions of high authority.

The conspirators failed in their attempt to assassinate General Muhammed's second-in-command, Lt.-General Olusegun Obasanjo, Chief of Staff, Supreme Headquarters. At first, Lt.-General Obasanjo declined to become head of state, but he was the unanimous choice of the Supreme Military Council and finally agreed to serve in order to fulfill the destiny of Muhammed's reformist regime. At 38, Obasanjo, an engineering specialist, had compiled a distinguished record in peace and war; he was also the first person of Yoruba ethnic descent to become Nigeria's chief executive. Since Lt.-General Danjuma was a Christian of Middle Belt ethnic origin, it was deemed politic, indeed necessary, to elevate a Muslim officer from the emirate sector of the north to the office of Chief of Staff, Supreme Headquarters, that is to say, second-in-command. The officer chosen was Lt.-Colonel Shehu Musa Yar'Adua, who was then promoted to the rank of brigadier, "over and above many who were his superior officers" (Oyediran 1980, 5).

General Obasanjo's memoir of this time draws attention to the climate of mistrust between Christians and Muslims that nearly resulted in outbreaks of sectarian violence. Christian alarmists speculated that Muhammed had been killed to forestall the establishment of an Islamic state, a proposition that had no basis in fact and nothing whatever to do with the motivations of the conspirators. Yet rumors of that sort did elicit dangerous responses from militant Muslims, and could have resulted in panic and chaos had they not been countered effectively by many responsible leaders (Obasanjo 1990, 36–37). It is important to recognize that, in Nigeria, serious political antagonism between Christians and Muslims is almost always associated with ethnic and related cultural tensions. Neither Christians nor Muslims in the southern states or the Middle Belt feel particularly threatened by the political aims of persons within their own ethnic communities who espouse either Christianity or Islam. Their religious beliefs are normally compartmentalized and do not impede the formation of purely secular political associations, which recruit members and supporters from both groups. Invariably, dangerous religious conflicts arise from disputes that range the emirate peoples, whose political traditions are theocratic, against southern and Middle Belt peoples, as for example in the vexatious dispute over the creation of a Shari'a Court of Appeal, a confrontation that nearly disrupted the progress of the 1977 Constituent Assembly (Laitin 1982, 411–30). In that circumstance, General Obasanjo persuaded his colleagues on the Supreme Military Council to set aside their differences and facilitate the voluntary adoption of a pragmatic compromise by the Constituent Assembly (Obasanjo 1990, 61–63; Dudley 1982, 162–64). His earlier, adroit management of the assassination and succession crisis may be said to have borne a fruitful sequel.

Transition: the Second Republic

In September 1976, the Constitution Drafting Committee, chaired by the eminent barrister Chief F. R. A. Williams, submitted its report to the head of state. In addition to a draft constitution, this learned document contained a tightly reasoned argument in support of liberal-democratic government based largely on reports of the deliberations of six sub-committees (Federal Republic of Nigeria 1976). Among the main structural proposals were these: separation of powers with a directly elected executive president; federalism with equal representation of states in the federal Senate; and multiparty competition for elective office, although the formation of parties on an ethnic, religious, or sectional basis was prohibited. After a full year of public commentary and debate, the draft was scrutinized and modified by a Constituent Assembly, comprising mainly persons elected by local government councils, and then approved with slight modification by the Supreme Military Council.

The restrictive provision concerning party organization was less consequential than had been intended by the framers of this constitution. Despite an injunction to the effect that every political party must "reflect the federal character of Nigeria" (defined to mean that it must have established a credible presence in at least two-thirds of the 19 states), the five parties that were authorized to contest elections in 1979 were still identified with particular ethnic and sectional interests. Hence the formidable National Party of Nigeria (NPN), a party of "heavyweights" or "men of timber and caliber," in Nigeria's political idiom, was a broadly-based conservative party, which chose as its presidential candidate Alhaji Shehu Shagari, 54, a councillor of the Sultan of Sokoto, former federal minister, and rising star in the NPC during the first republic. Its vice-presidential candidate was a prominent Igbo architect; its chairman a prominent Yoruba barrister. Reminiscent of the NNA, formed in 1964 to defend the northern principle of regional security, the NPN projected an up-to-date national image to cloak its core, northern establishment.

Awolowo and Azikiwe were also back in the field. At 70, Awolowo led the Unity Party of Nigeria (UPN), based primarily in the Yoruba-speaking west yet seeking to expand through the popular appeal of its social democratic policies. At 75, Azikiwe led the Nigerian People's Party (NPP), based solidly in the Igbo-speaking east. Many Nigerians of socialist persuasion who did not care to support any of these three establishmentarian parties rallied to the People's Redemption Party (PRP), whose presidential candidate, Alhaji Aminu Kano, 59, was widely admired throughout Nigeria for his egalitarian principles and redoubtable opposition to the ruling class of the northern emirates, despite his own patrician standing in that social system. A fifth party, the Great Nigeria People's Party (GNPP), was led by Alhaji Waziri Ibrahim, 53, a northerner of Kanuri descent. This party's emergence was a reminder of the most significant intra-emirate political division—between the Hausa-speaking majority of the emirate sector, with its traditional ruling class of mainly Fulani descent, on the one hand, and the Kanuri-speaking people of northeastern Nigeria, on the other.

In the 1979 presidential balloting, Shagari obtained roughly 34 percent of the vote to Awolowo's 29 percent and Azikiwe's 17 percent, while Aminu Kano and Waziri Ibrahim each polled 10 percent. Despite his plurality, Sharagi's claim to be president was challenged by Awolowo on the ground that he had not obtained at least 25 percent of the vote in two-thirds of the states, as required by the constitution. In a controversial judgement, the Supreme Court ruled that, in a 19-state federation, it was sufficient for Shagari to have obtained at least 25 percent in 12 states and 25 percent of two-thirds of the vote in a thirteenth state. But for that ingenious (many said tortured) decision, a complex and unpredictable electoral college procedure, involving both federal and state legislators, would have been implemented.

As in 1959, the northern-oriented NPN (comparable to the old NPC) formed a governing coalition with the eastern-based NPP (successor to the NCNC), while the western-based UPN (in the tradition of the Action Group) organized the official opposition. It has been suggested that Azikiwe, who did not seek to serve under Shagari, had always been mainly concerned to ensure that a party representing organized Igbo interests would be strongly entrenched in the governing coalition of the Second Republic (Dudley 1982, 217). However, the coalition lasted just 21 months before being dissolved, by mutual agreement, amidst reciprocal recriminations. Although the NPN could no longer rely on party discipline to muster majorities in the bicameral National Assembly, it managed to enact its legislative program with the assistance of free-floating senators and representatives who voted for NPN proposals in their individual capacities without joining that party, since the constitution did not permit members of the Assembly to retain their seats in either house if they changed parties prior to expiration of the term of office for which they had been elected (Diamond 1983, 48).

In addition to its insecure condition as a minority government at the center, the NPN held gubernatorial office in but 8 of the 19 states, including six of the nine northern states. In 1981, the PRP governor of Kaduna State sought to diminish the powers of emirs and their councils in relation to land, local government and taxation, although he did not command a majority in the state legislature, which body then retaliated by impeaching the governor and removing him from office. In adjacent Kano State, where the PRP controlled the legislature in addition to gubernatorial authority, traditionalists and conservatives produced a political stalemate through resort to violence. Once again, as in 1964 and 1965, two opposing political movements were marching toward an electoral showdown; once again there was far too much at stake for either side to accept defeat at the polls as a normal and tolerable outcome.

Shehu Shagari's Crisis, 1983

In the summer of 1983, a series of elections left the NPN firmly in control of the federal government and a majority of the state governments. Shagari was re-elected easily; his party won majorities in the Senate and the House of Representatives; and NPN gubernatorial candidates were successful in a majority of the states. However, these results were tainted by gross malfeasance in the organization and conduct of the various elections. Many informed analysts have suggested that the outcomes of most of these elections, in particular the presidential contest, would have been the same had the registers of voters been properly prepared, fraudulent balloting minimized, the votes tallied accurately, and then reported reliably. In the absence of acceptably fair procedures, a potentially strong popular mandate for Shagari's second term moldered in the haze of duplicity and related spasms of violence (Diamond 1984).

Although the legitimacy of Shagari's government was gravely impaired by massive electoral fraud, the crisis of the Second Republic had even more fundamental causes, involving, at bottom, the role of the state in economic life. Wherever societies have evolved from early to intermediate and advanced stages of industrialization, the state has been relied upon to undertake essential economic and social tasks that are beyond the capacities of private enterprise to accomplish. Except for a few cases of communist industrialization, notably the former Soviet Union and China, modern economic development has been contingent on a salutary balance between private entrepreneurship and state enterprise. If the business community becomes excessively dependent on the state, experience shows that it will not develop a normal capacity to create viable capitalist institutions; instead it will become chronically addicted to governmental favors, patronage, and other parasitical practices. In Nigeria, that degenerative tendency was strengthened by the previously noted policy of indigenization, which drained the wealth derived from oil into acquisitions of already existing foreign-owned assets rather than self-reliant entrepreneurship. Meanwhile the state itself acquired control of the commanding heights of the economy, including financial institutions and the giant oil industry. Optimistic expectations of general economic development fueled by oil revenues were destined to be disappointed.

When the state becomes the major source of private income, the temptation to abuse power is enormous. And when a corrupted state dominates the economy, it becomes the biggest racket going; government is all but reduced to the giving and taking of money. Inexorably, oil revenues accruing to the state became the principal source of private enrichment, including huge "kickbacks," or payments to officials for contracts and licenses. Immense sums of ill-begotten gains were stashed abroad by officials and their partners in crime; public buildings were set aflame by arsonists in order to destroy incriminating evidence. Meanwhile, during the first few years of the 1980s, a superabundant supply of oil, due largely to the impact of production in the North Sea, caused oil revenues to decline precipitously "from a peak of $24 billion in 1980 to $10 billion in 1983" (Diamond 1984, 909).

Suddenly the government could not pay its bills. Teachers and civil servants went on strike after many months without pay; hospitals ran out of medical supplies; cities went without basic utilities; in some parts of the country, schools were shut for over a year. Many Nigerians hoped, desperately, for reform through democratic elections. Their hopes were dashed when, in 1983, the electoral system failed dismally to produce the semblance of an acceptably democratic process. To no small degree, this abysmal outcome was due to the statist economy. When the state becomes the sole major source of revenue, political power appears to be an irreplaceably precious commodity; its potential loss presents a horrifying prospect. Unwilling to entrust their personal and political fortunes to the voters, power holders tampered with the electoral process in many ways. By and large,

Nigerians were free to vote as they pleased, but the results announced were not reliably related to the votes cast.

Following the 1983 elections, President Shagari tried to restore public confidence in the political process by affirming his personal commitment to multiparty electoral democracy and genuine political reform. His new cabinet included a majority of new faces, among them reputable figures from all parts of the country. But this attempt to retrieve legitimacy for the widely despised "rogue government" was too late. On December 31 1983, a coup d'état occurred without public protest, eliciting a vast, collective sigh of relief.

The Second Republic's travail and demise is memorable as a textbook case of debilitating economic statism and the abuse of political power for private ends. Yet the personal probity of President Shagari was not in question; two years after his fall from power, he was formally exonerated by an official inquiry, which found no evidence of personal enrichment during his term of office. Scholarly assessments of chronic misrule in Nigeria have focussed mainly on structural, rather than behavioral, explanations (although these analytical categories are not separable in reality). Among them, Richard Joseph's (1983, 1987) thesis of "prebendel politics," meaning the virtual conversion of public offices into private assets to be manipulated for the extraction of personal wealth, has been especially influential. Other explanations attribute economic decline and predation to excessive state ownership and control of productive property (Diamond 1987); to the pathologies of early capitalism (Schatz 1984); to neocolonialism and peripheral capitalism (Ake 1981; Falola and Ihonvbere 1985; Graf 1988). Still others have noted the destabilizing effects of discontinuity in the moral commitments of Nigerians to their traditional communities, on the one hand, and official governmental institutions, on the other (Ekeh 1974; Whitaker 1984). In their ensemble, these diverse explanations of economic stagnation and political turmoil mirror Nigeria's desperate search for redemption.

Transition: Which Way?

Pledged to reform, the military junta that succeeded the Second Republic installed Major-General Muhammadu Buhari, a northern officer from Daura emirate, as head of state, with Brigadier Tunde Idiagbon, a Yoruba, as Chief of Staff, Supreme Headquarters. Defining the country's basic problem as one of social inefficiency, attributable largely to indolence, disorderly conduct, and the corruption of public officials, the new military rulers proclaimed a "war against indiscipline." Rapidly, it became apparent that these rulers, unlike their military predecessors, were not disposed to plan for the restoration of civilian, constitutional, government. A series of decrees provided for the detention of persons who were alleged to be security risks; for punishment, including imprisonment, of persons who might broadcast or publish "false accusations" against public officials, or expose such officials to "ridicule or disrepute"; and for the establishment of military tribunals, conducted *in camera*, to try persons accused of various offenses. Unable to arrest the country's economic decline and the related growth of urban unrest, due in part to massive retrenchments in the private as well as the public employment sectors, the Buhari regime relied increasingly on repressive measures. Its overthrow, by a palace coup on August 27 1985, elicited no less enthusiasm than had its assumption of power twenty months before. The new regime, headed by Major-General Ibrahim Badamasi Babangida, who had been Chief of Army Staff, ranking third in the previous hierarchy, immediately abrogated the decree that abridged freedom of the press, and pledged to respect the fundamental rights of Nigerians (Diamond 1985/86). The name of the Supreme Military Council was changed to Armed Forces Ruling Council (AFRC). More ominously, Maj.-General Babangida became the first head of a military government in Nigeria to assume the title of President.

Shortly after his assumption of power, President Babangida initiated a "plebiscite by newspaper" on the merits of accepting a $2.4 billion loan, offered by the International Monetary Fund (IMF) on condition of currency devaluation and the elimination of various state subsidies. Taking his cue from public opinion, the president rejected the conditional loan, but adopted a self-directed reform program, including devaluation, that satisfied foreign creditors, including the World Bank. Meanwhile, Babangida weathered an attempt to assassinate him and seize power planned by disgruntled officers, including a sometime rival from his own state, Niger, in the former northern region. He also provoked an acrimonious debate between Christians and Muslims by arranging for Nigeria to become a member of the Organization of the Islamic Conference, an intergovernmental association based on religious affinity. This highly controversial decision appears to have been motivated mainly by economic considerations, involving Nigeria's role in OPEC, but it was taken without having consulted Christian members of the government, which created intense consternation.

At the same time, and in keeping with Babangida's pledge to govern with "the consent of the people," the AFRC appointed a study commission, named the Political Bureau, consisting of 17 members, of whom a majority were university-based scholars. The Bureau was instructed to identify and address the causes of problems that have impeded national progress, to elicit the views of citizens about such matters, and to suggest a "basic philosophy of government" for the future. The Bureau's report of 1987 recommended, inter alia, the restoration of constitutional and representative government based on the principles of federalism, separation of powers, and party competition. However, the Bureau departed from liberal precepts by recommending that the number of political parties be limited to two, and that each party should subscribe to a national philosophy of socialism, differing from one another only on "priorities and strategies of implementation" (Federal Republic of Nigeria 1987a, 50, 126). These recommendations were contrary to an emerging consensus throughout Africa and the world on the desirability of freedom of association to form multiple parties, and the centrality of private enterprise, both domestic and foreign, in economic development. In its response, the pragmatic military government opposed "the imposition of a political ideology on the nation," declaring that "the principle of democracy and social justice" is a suitable expression of the national philosophy (Federal Republic of Nigeria 1987b, 14). Accordingly, the government also rejected the bureau's proposal to halt and reverse the policy of privatizing state enterprises as well as its recommendation to fully nationalize the oil industry (60 percent of which was already owned by the state). However, the two-party recommendation, with each party to be funded substantially by the government, was accepted by the AFRC, which also adopted a timetable for the return to civilian rule by October 1992.

The constitution for a Third Republic was crafted, over a two-year period, mainly in the image of its predecessor by these bodies: an appointed Constitution Review Committee; a subsequent Constituent Assembly, most of whose members were elected by local government councilors in the 450 federal parliamentary constituencies; and the AFRC itself as final arbiter (Koehn 1989). In May 1989, political associations, in gestation among members of the Constituent Assembly, were permitted to organize openly and apply to the National Electoral Commission to be one of the two parties that would be chosen to compete in elections by the AFRC. From a field of thirteen parties claiming to meet the extravagently detailed criteria of national, rather than sectional or sectarian, identity, only six were referred by the NEC to the AFRC for its consideration. Even these were referred with little enthusiasm since all of them appeared to the NEC to be stamped indelibly with the regional and other undesirable characteristics of parties in previous eras. Then, in October 1989, President Babangida exercised his penchant for the element of surprise by abolishing all of the aspirant parties and directing the NEC to *create* two national parties—"one a little to the left and the other a little to the right of center"—named, respectively, the Social Democratic Party and the National Republican Convention. Many Nigerians praised this maneuver for its common sense; others wondered what kind of democracy Nigeria would have if the government permitted only two parties, created both of them, and prescribed the program for each.

Babangida was proving to be a national leader of uncommon acumen. He had manipulated the two-but-only-two-party idea to establish a balance between two parties that would be no more than mildly ideological, thereby thwarting the aims of many intellectuals and political activists who believed that Nigeria should choose decisively between capitalist and socialist conceptions of economic organization. From May until October 1989, citizens were permitted to organize political associations although no more than two such associations would be registered as parties. When Babangida changed the rules, citizens could no longer organize potential parties, but they were free to join either of the two official parties. Informed commentaries on these events reflect the mixture of critical respect and trepidation inspired by this adroit, articulate, yet enigmatic and Machiavellian ruler (Uwazurike 1990; Oyediran and Agbaje 1991).

Ibrahim Babangida's Crisis, 1990

Before Babangida's regime, four of the five previous military rulers had been either assassinated or deposed as a result of conspiracies within the armed forces. Both assassinations—of Aguiyi-Ironsi and of Muhammed—involved serious ethno-sectional tensions. Nearly four months after assuming the presidency, Babangida averted an attempt on his life by a group of conspirators from all three service branches, one of whom was minister for the federal capital territory; two others were former governors. Fifteen officers were convicted by a military tribunal; ten of them were subsequently executed. Although Babangida emerged unscathed and with enhanced public support, this episode limned the deadly threat posed by dissension within Nigeria's highly politicized armed forces.

During the next four years, Babangida wrestled with economic problems while the process of political transition was wending its way toward a resumption of representative government. Having resolved to implement a self-directed (rather than IMF-prescribed) program of market-based economic reform, the regime accepted the consequences of increasing privation at home in return for the restoration of Nigeria's credit as a trading partner and in capital markets abroad. Currency devaluation and import restrictions resulted in severe shortages of supply, hyper-inflation, the erosion of social services, and a sharp decline in the average standard of living. Austerity measures involved retrenchments in the civil service, pay cuts for all employees of the government, including armed service personnel, and wage freezes. These entailed labor unrest as well as unemployment leading to curtailment of the right to strike, escalating protests by the labor movement, and retributive reorganization of the country's central labor organization. While it implemented such painful, yet necessary, economic reforms, the regime deviated sporadically from the path of liberalism, which it continued to profess, into the byways of repressive rule. Its reputation as a trustee of the rights of citizens was badly tarnished by numerous instances of detention without trial, confrontations with students involving the use of deadly force, and the notorious assassination of the principled editor of a newsmagazine (Diamond 1991a). Inevitably, repression breeds corruption: officials who violate the rights of citizens with impunity scarcely hesitate to enrich themselves at public expense. Thus, immense sums were stolen from the national treasury for transference to secret accounts abroad. Furthermore, military leaders of northern emirate origin manipulated the mechanisms of economic reform, such as privatization and credit facilitation, to enrich their civilian patrons in that part of the country as well as themselves (Diamond 1991b; Reno 1993). When insecure rulers resort to plunder as a means of protection, they court the wrath of the people and the enmity of disaffected members of the empowered elites.

On April 22 1990, Babangida's regime was shaken violently by an attempted coup d'état. Fighting, reported to be deadly during a span of several hours, was confined to Lagos, where Babangida himself narrowly escaped injury or death. The mutineers were doomed when they failed to eliminate any of the regime's top leaders. Had they decapitated the regime, as planned, and gained the support of sympathizers in the armed forces, the outcome, given their aims, could have been civil war.

Upon seizing the radio station in Lagos, Major Gideon Oguaza Orka, speaking on behalf of the mutineers, broadcast an extraordinarily divisive message, one that virtually declared political warfare against the emirate areas of the north in the name of the "middle belt and southern parts of the country." Specifically, he proclaimed that the insurgents meant to exclude five northern states, containing the vast majority of emirates, from the Nigerian federation. They could, he said, be readmitted on two conditions: the incumbent Sultan of Sokoto, whose 1988 installation had been supported by President Babangida, must be deposed in favor of a rival, alleged to have a "rightful" claim; the latter must then lead a delegation of northern leaders who would be required to "vouch that the feudalistic and aristocratic quest for domination and oppression will be a thing of the past." Meanwhile, all southerners living in the five northern states and northerners in the south would be required to move to their respective states of origin; and northerners from the affected states would cease to hold either public or private office in the Middle Belt and southern states (Ihonvbere 1991, 617).

Reacting harshly, the regime arrested and interrogated more than 800 people, including journalists, civil rights lawyers, and critics of the government. While the vast majority were released within a few months, sixty-nine officers and enlisted men, including Major Orka, were convicted by military tribunals and executed. As in the attempted coups of 1976 and 1985, officers of minority ethnic identity were prominent among the conspirators of 1990. In 1976, the leading conspirators were identified with the Middle Belt state of Plateau; in 1985, Benue state origin, also in the Middle Belt, was conspicuous. In 1990, Major Orka, a Tiv of Benue state, decried the alleged subjugation of Middle-Belt people by the northern "aristocratic class"; however, most of the executed mutinous officers were persons of minority ethnic identity from the midwestern state of Bendel. As a gesture of good will, Babangida selected Admiral (ret.) Augustus Aikhomu, outgoing Chief of General Staff, whose home state is Bendel, for the office of vice-president. Similarly, Domkat Bali, a highly regarded general officer of Plateau state origin, was promoted to the rank of full general despite the fact that he had previously been compelled to retire following his replacement as Minister of Defence. These measures, and others designed to enhance the "federal character" of the high command, helped to assuage the hard feelings that surfaced in the aftermath of an alarming display of rebellious anger. During the relatively brief watch of a previous head of state, namely General Obasanjo (1976–79), national values eclipsed sectional hostilities more completely than ever before in Nigerian history. Eleven years later, the corrosive forces of corruption in government, military dictatorship, and economic stagnation had resuscitated the hydra-headed specter of ethnosectional conflict.

Transition: Towards a Third Republic, but in Vain

President Babangida had created two official political parties, the National Republican Convention (NRC) and the Social Democratic Party (SDP), to minimize the political effects of ethnosectional particularism, religious sectarianism, and ideological extremism. That maneuver produced the desired result because it compelled activists and voters alike to prioritize their values and cooperate with fellow citizens who held different beliefs on major issues. Inevitably, each of the two parties was identified in public opinion with a set of specific orientations: the NRC with the northern emirate system, Islam, and capitalism; the SDP with the south and Middle Belt, Christianity, and socialism. Thus, the northerner who was inclined to elevate his or her commitment to social justice above other political values would gravitate toward the SDP; conversely, the southerner who valued capitalism, as a political value, ahead of Christianity or regional identification would be attracted to the NRC. Given the innumerable combinations and permutations of choice, over and above local rivalries and personal ambitions, each party became reasonably representative of the nation as a whole. It was also fitting that each party's elected national chairman should be a personality from the "opposite" region: Chief Tom Ikime of the NRC, an Edo-speaking Christian from the southern state of Bendel; Ambassador Baba Gana Kingibe of the SDP, a Kanuri Muslim from the northern emirate state of Borno. However, these selections also reinforced the disconcerting presumption that the eventual presidential candidates would be a northerner for the NRC and a southerner for the SDP. *Plus ça change, plus c'est la même chose.*

In May 1990, the National Electoral Commission (NEC) inaugurated a sequence of intra- and inter-party elections designed to culminate in a presidential election towards the end of 1992. These contests were conducted by means of an "open ballot" system: voters were required to queue in front of photographs of the candidates of their choice and be counted. Devised to counteract electoral fraud, this innovation effectively disenfranchised a large section of the intelligentsia, perhaps a majority, which valued the secret ballot as an elementary freedom. Approximately 22 percent of the eligible electorate voted in the local government elections of December 1990; the SDP emerged with a slight edge in councils controlled. Following the creation of nine additional states, in August 1991, and gubernatorial primaries in the fall, gubernatorial and state assembly elections were held in December with approximately even outcomes: the NRC won 16 governorships, while the SDP gained control of 16 state legislatures. Outside of its northern-emirate heartland, the NRC was notably successful in the southeast, while the SDP won in northeastern and Middle Belt states in addition to its primary electoral base of states in the southwest.

In March 1992, the transition was both boosted and mildly disturbed by the published results of a national census, conducted the previous November. The official count of 88.5 million was some twenty million less than the inflated estimate which had been current for several years. Particularly noticed was the remarkably close approximation of the percentage of the national total accounted for by the sixteen states of the former northern region (53 percent) to that region's percentage of the national total recorded in the census of 1963. A somber reflection was the shadow cast on the register of voters, which then contained approximately 50 million names despite the belief of demographers generally that not less than 60 percent of the population was below the voting age of 18. Having recently purged 20 million fictitious names, including the names of dead persons, from the electoral roll, the NEC endeavored to produce more reliable lists for use in the July elections to the bicameral National Assembly and the subsequent presidential election.

In July 1992, the SDP forged ahead of its rival, winning the Senate by 52 seats to 39, and the House of Representatives, by 314 to 275, including notable victories in the northern-emirate states of Kaduna and Kano. However, the electoral process faltered abruptly in August and September during staggered presidential primaries in various states. Citing massive fraud, voting irregularities, and corrupt practices, the regime announced that the primaries which had been held were invalidated and all twenty-three aspirants for the presidency were summarily disqualified from any further participation.

The regime then required the two parties to nominate their respective candidates for president and vice president by means of successive conventions of delegates elected at ward level and ascending to local government, state, and national levels. At this juncture, the open ballot system, which had failed dismally to reduce the level of electoral corruption, was modified in favor of the use of ballot boxes; voters would no longer be required to queue in front of the photographs of candidates of their choice. In anticipation of military withdrawal, the AFRC appointed a Transitional Council, composed of civilians, to replace the cabinet. This council then elected Chief Ernest A. O. Shonekan, a prominent Yoruba businessman, formerly chairman and managing director of United Africa Company, Nigeria, the country's largest conglomerate enterprise, to serve as chair—in effect, as acting Prime Minister. Simultaneously, in January 1993, the ruling AFRC was renamed the National Defense and Security Council (NDSC).

In late March 1993, the parties chose their respective candidates at conventions, each attended by approximately 5,000 voting delegates. The

NRC selected Alhaji Bashir Tofa, 46, of Kano, a wealthy financier of Kanuri descent; his chosen running-mate was Dr. Sylvester Ugoh, a former minister of science and technology, and an Igbo. The SDP nominated Chief Moshood K. O. Abiola, 56, of Abeokuta (seat of the Egba section of the Yoruba people), chief executive of ITT Nigeria Limited, publisher of a newspaper, and vice-president of the Nigerian Supreme Council of Islamic Affairs. Abiola's vice-presidential choice was Ambassador Baba Gana Kingibe of Borno, the national chairman of the SDP, who had vied for the presidential nomination. Together, these tickets appeared to resemble an all-too-familiar political pattern: the northern emirate sector allied with the southeast versus the southwest and minority sectors in the north.

Two days before the election of June 12, a pro-military group, the Association for a Better Nigeria (ABN), persuaded a justice of the High Court at Abuja, the federal capital, to order the NEC to suspend the election on grounds of alleged malpractice by the SDP candidate at the nominating convention. However, the NEC exercised its legal right to disregard this order and conducted an election for the presidency that was virtually free of violence and fraud. The relatively low turnout—14 million of the registered 39 million, or 36 percent—may have been, in part, a consequence of confusion due to the court order. Three days after the election, the ABN, with NRC support, obtained yet another injunction against the release of final results on the ground of electoral malpractice. However, a justice of the High Court in Lagos ordered the NEC to make the results public. At this point the Lagos-based Campaign for Democracy released reliable, albeit unofficial, reports of the results which gave Abiola 8.1 million (58 percent) to Tofa's 5.9 million (42 percent). Abiola had won in 19 states and the Federal Capital Territory to Tofa's 11; he had also received one-third or more of the vote in 28 states—eight more than the constitutional requirement; he even won in Tofa's home state of Kano. Finally, on June 23 1993, the ruling NDSC, professing its desire to "rescue the judiciary" from "wranglings," (sic) and spare it further ridicule, annulled the election, suspended the NEC, and terminated the transition to civil rule.

Babangida's address to the nation, on June 26, impugned the conduct of both candidates and their parties by alluding to unsubstantiated conflicts of interest and electoral malpractice, but his words did not clarify the momentous decision to abort an historic process in which so much of his, the regime's, and the nation's energies had been invested. He repeated his pledge, and that of the NDSC, to withdraw in favor of a civilian government on August 27 1993, and proposed to organize a new presidential election to that end. Eventually, a tripartite committee, including members of the government and both parties, recommended the installation of an interim government. On the day before the appointed date, Babangida, 52, retired from the army and stepped down as president in favor an interim head of state, Chief Shonekan, 57, Chairman of the Transitional Council and, like Abiola, a son of Abeokuta. Despite his administrative competence, personal probity, and pledge to hold new presidential elections in the near future, Shonekan's position was undermined irretrievably by resolute partisans of the Campaign for Democracy, who insisted on the validity of the June 12th election. Meanwhile, Abiola defended his electoral mandate vigorously, both abroad, where he canvassed support during an eight-week sojourn in Britain and the United States, and upon his return to Nigeria. When the beleaguered interim administration decreed a sevenfold increase in the price of gasoline, to approximate the cost of production, its popular support dwindled to virtually nil. On November 10, a justice of the High Court in Lagos ruled, in favor of petitioners Abiola and Kingibe, that the interim government was illegal. One week later, with an appeal of that decision pending, Chief Shonekan abruptly resigned; his Secretary of Defense, General Sani Abacha, 50, assumed office as head of state. Abacha immediately dissolved the interim government, the national assembly, all state assemblies, executive councils in the states (where governors were replaced by military commanders), local government councils, the NEC and both political parties.

Sani Abacha's Crisis, 1993–

Although Abacha was born and educated in the Hausa-Fulani heartland state of Kano, his descent, like that of both Tofa and Kingibe, is Kanuri (termed Beriberi in Hausaland). He became nationally prominent on December 31 1983 as the brigadier who announced the coup d'état that terminated the Second Republic. Twenty months later, in August 1985, he broadcast the decision of the military rulers, who had deposed Buhari, to elevate Babangida to the highest office. In 1990, as Chief of Army Staff and Chairman of the Joint Chiefs, he was instrumental in quelling Orka's attempted coup and duly appointed Minister of Defense. He was Secretary of Defense in the Transitional Council and its successor, Shonekan's Interim National Government, in which he was clearly the most powerful figure. Upon his assumption of office as head of state and commander-in-chief of the armed forces, Abacha secured the retirement of seventeen officers, including nine generals, who had been identified closely with Babangida.

He also created a Provisional Ruling Council (PRC), empowered to legislate, and he appointed a surprisingly representative federal executive council, including several democratic activists and political associates of Chief Abiola, notably Ambassador Kingibe as foreign minister. Those democrats who accepted Abacha's invitation to join his government, particularly Onu Onagoruwa, a civil liberties lawyer who became Attorney-General, urged him to convene a representative National Conference that would restore democracy in Nigeria on a new and lasting basis. When, in March 1994, Abiola, in the United States, endorsed an American congressional resolution in favor of sanctions against the Nigerian military government, Kingibe responded, in a letter to members of the Congress, that he and Abiola had "actively canvassed" for military intervention to rescue the nation from political paralysis and instability during Shonekan's administration.

In late May 1994, after a six-month absence abroad, during which time he solicited support, mainly in Britain and the United States, Chief Abiola returned to Nigeria to fight for his mandate. Amidst supporters, he was defiantly "sworn in" as President on the eve of the annulled election's first anniversary. Eventually, he was arrested and charged with treason, destined to remain in prison, without bail, for more than two years (at the time of writing). Despite ill health, Abiola has firmly refused to accept bail in return for renunciation of his claim; meanwhile his trial for treason has been adjourned repeatedly. In support of his cause, the powerful petroleum and gas workers union and the industry's senior staff association went on strike for two months before capitulating under pressure, including the dissolution of their executive committees by governmental edict, and in the absence of sufficiently broad labor solidarity. Like defiant labor leaders, some outspoken leaders of the organized democratic movement have been arrested while others have fled the country. An especially portentous development was the arrest, in March 1995, of former head of state (1976–79), General (ret.) Olusegun Obasanjo, and his erstwhile deputy, Major-General (ret.) Shehu Musa Yar'Adua, who had subsequently become a leading politician and presidential aspirant. They were tried and sentenced, by a military tribunal, to a prison term of 25 years in Obasanjo's case, and to death in Yar'Adua's and 13 other cases; the death sentences were subsequently commuted to life imprisonment by the head of state.

Those democrats who, like Onagoruwa, had chosen to give Abacha a chance, and had joined his administration, were destined to experience bitter disappointment: the national Constitutional Conference that eventually convened in late June 1994, consisted of 273 elected and 96 nominated delegates, the former chosen by electoral colleges, the latter by the regime itself. In December, conferees adopted a resolution, promoted by Yar'Adua, then an elected delegate, calling for a transition to civilian government no later than January 1 1996. In late April, however, the conferees, having been rebuked by the PRC, reversed that decision, and advised the regime itself to set a timetable. The final report of the conference, including a draft constitution, was reviewed by several committees and executive bodies following its submission to the head of state in June 1995. In a broadcast to the nation, on October 1 1995, General Abacha disclosed a number of recommendations, including a 3-year timetable for the restoration of civilian rule, which had been approved by the PRC. He also revealed that the PRC had modified the draft constitution without specifying differences between the conference report, subsequent committee recommendations, and the PRC's final decisions. In previous constitution-making processes, neither the voters nor their elected representatives had ever been empowered to ratify the final document. But there has never been as little public disclosure of issues arising during the course of deliberations in a constitutional assembly and succeeding reviews of a draft document as in the process managed by Abacha in 1995 and onward.

As in the crisis the 1962–1966, the current crisis, in its third year at the time of writing, signifies a widening rift in the Nigerian body politic between those who value Nigerian national identity over and above divisive, subnational identities, and those who are more passionately attached to the cultural and political heritage of a traditional community. During the latter 1960s, Nigerian unity was preserved by force of arms. Subsequently, in the crises of 1976, 1990, and 1993 to date, national identity has prevailed against challenges mounted by the partisans of assertive regional, ethnic, and politicized religious identities. The following propositions, derived empirically from this comparative analysis of political crises, bode well for the future of inclusive national unity: (1) to a great extent, potentially divisive ethnic and religious identities are also transregional; (2) to a significant degree, ethnic and regional identities are also inter-religious; (3) virtually all regional and religious identities are also multi-ethnic.

Thus, regional boundaries in Nigeria have always been controversial. Until the former Northern Region was divided into six states, in 1967, people of the so-called Middle Belt bridled against the domination of their sub-region by the emirate sector. However, the emirates themselves have never constituted a consolidated political bloc. There is a pronounced political divide between the Hausa-Fulani emirates of northwestern and north-central Nigeria, established by Shehu Uthman Dan Fodio (during the years from 1804 to 1812) and his descendants, on the one hand, and the northeastern Kanuri emirate of Borno, on the other. In the general elections of 1979 and 1983, northeastern political sentiment crystallized in the Great Nigeria People's Party, led by Waziri Ibrahim. Today, once again, northeastern consciousness appears to be a factor of no small importance in the regime of General Abacha; Kingibe's early and continuing commitment to Abacha has that appearance. More to the point, analysts who track military affairs in Nigeria observed a pronounced shift in the army hierarchy away from Babangida's Sokoto orientation towards the northeast, far in advance of Abacha's decision of April 1996 to depose the Sultan of Sokoto in favor of a successor who was apparently more popular, but far less dangerous to the regime. Nor is the evident shift of power within the northern emirate sector, from west to east, inconsistent with reports to the effect that Abacha's only unconditional supporter among the powerful traditional rulers of the north has been the Fulani Emir of Kano, given the traditional rivalry between the north-central emirate of Kano and its historic suzerain, Sokoto.

Among those who have lost confidence in the viability of a strictly federal system of government in Nigeria, the idea of a six-region confederation has been seriously considered. The proposed regions are these: northeast, northwest, middle belt, southwest, mid-west, and southeast. In any such confederation, Igbo-speaking sections of the midwest would doubtless elect to join the southeast. However the sizeable non-Igbo portion of the southeast, possibly 40 percent of that region's population, has always objected to its inclusion within an Igbo-dominated political entity, as shown by its political tendency during the first republic, the swift capitulation of the Calabar-Ogoja-Rivers area to federal forces in the civil war, and the respectable level of its electoral support for northern-oriented political parties ever since. To cope with this problem within a framework of government that would remain federal but also assuage regional grievances, constitutional planners have recently delimited six zones—three northern, three southern—for the purpose of rotating high federal offices. One such zone, designated "southern minority," combines the midwest with southeastern minorities. This arrangement, which would be anomalous from the geographical standpoint, like other proposed delimitations of large political jurisdictions, would inevitably create new reasons for sectional discontent.

In a six-region confederation based on geographical, rather than specifically ethnic, criteria, only the Yoruba-speaking southwest would be cohesive politically. Furthermore, a confederal form of government would surely release pent-up centrifugal tendencies. One predictable result would be an attempt by Yoruba-speaking sections of the northwest to join the southwest, which effort would be bitterly resisted by the Fulani emir of mostly-Yoruba Ilorin. Should confederation prove to be a step toward the emergence of successor sovereign states, the emirate and middle-belt regions would be landlocked and deprived of access to the revenues derived from Nigeria's oil, in the Niger Delta and offshore, a *casus belli* that could easily become inflamed, given the probable control of that immense resource by the southeastern and, to a far lesser extent, midwestern regional authorities. In brief, separatist political regionalism is likely to entail severe inter-regional conflict to the point of warfare.

Concerning religion as a potential basis for political separatism: from time to time, conflicts over questions that are essentially religious in nature (involving, for instance, education, legal systems, the status of women, or rivalries between doctrinal organizations within a cohesive faith) have resulted in violence between religious groups. However, such conflicts are unlikely to escalate into civil war, secession, or demands for territorial change (Abernethy 1969; Paden 1973; Ibrahim 1991). In all sections of the country, ethnic communities include people of different religious persuasions living in relative harmony (Amucheazi 1986; Laitin 1986; Paden 1986). Episodes of religious violence that threaten Nigerian national unity have always occurred in connection with tensions produced by the basic division between emirate and non-emirate forms of society (Kukah 1993). The essential basis of such conflict is ethnic, not religious; it is but one form of the broader issue of ethnic political identity in Nigeria.

In Africa, as elsewhere, ethnic diversity can be managed to promote inclusive, rather than parochial and exclusive, forms of nationhood. Nigeria's richly textured mosaic of diverse ethnic, linguistic, and religious elements could form the backdrop for a blueprint of inclusive national integration. The educational, cultural, and social blessings of unity are manifest in the multitude of complementary relationships that bind the various peoples and sections of the country to one another. Thus far, the missing ingredient for balanced and sustained national development has been political leadership of a consistently integrative character.

References

Abernethy, David B. 1969. *The Political Dilemma of Popular Education.* Stanford: Stanford University Press.

Ake, Claude, ed. 1985. *Political Economy of Nigeria.* London and Lagos: Longman.

Amucheazi, Elochukwu C. 1986. *Church and Politics in Eastern Nigeria, 1945–1966.* Lagos: Macmillan.

Campbell, Ian. 1978. "Army Reorganization and Military Withdrawal." In Panter-Brick, Keith (ed.), *Soldiers and Oil: The Political Transformation of Nigeria*: 58–95. London: Frank Cass.

Diamond, Larry. 1983. "Social Change and Political Conflict in Nigeria's Second Republic." In *The Political Economy of Nigeria*: 25–84. New York: Praeger.

———. 1984. "Nigeria in Search of Democracy." *Foreign Affairs*, 62, 4 (Spring): 905–27.

———. 1985/86. "Nigeria Update." *Foreign Affairs*, 64, 2 (Winter): 326–36.

———. 1987. "Class Formation in the Swollen African State." *The Journal of Modern African Studies*, 25, 4 (December): 567–96.

———. 1991a. "Nigeria's Search for a New Political Order." *Journal of Democracy*, II, 2 (Spring): 54–69.

———. 1991b. "Nigeria's Perennial Struggle." *Journal of Democracy*, II, 4 (Fall), 73–85.

Dudley, Billy. 1982. *An Introduction to Nigerian Government and Politics*. Bloomington: Indiana University Press.

Ekeh, Peter P. 1974. "Citizenship and Political Conflict." In Okpaku, Joseph (ed.), *Nigeria: Dilemma of Nationhood*: 76–117. New York: The Third Press.

Falola, Toyin and Julius Ihonvbere. 1985. *The Rise and Fall of Nigeria's Second Republic, 1979–84*. London: Zed Books.

Federal Republic of Nigeria. 1976. *Report of the Constitution Drafting Committee, vols. I & II*. Lagos: Federal Ministry of Information.

———. 1987a. *Report of the Political Bureau*. Lagos: Federal Government Printer.

———. 1987b. *Government's Views and Comments on the Findings and Recommendations of the Political Bureau*. Lagos: Federal Government Printer.

Graf, William D. 1988. *The Nigerian State*. London: Currey.

Ibrahim, Jibrin. 1991. "Religion and Political Turbulence in Nigeria." *The Journal of Modern African Studies*, XXIX, 1 (March): 115–36.

Ihonvbere, Julius O. 1991. "A Critical Evaluation of the Failed 1990 Coup in Nigeria." *The Journal of Modern African Studies*, XXIX, 4 (December): 601–26.

Joseph, Richard A. 1978. "Affluence and Underdevelopment: the Nigerian Experience." *The Journal of Modern African Studies*, XVI, 2 (June): 221–39.

———. 1983. "Class, State, and Prebendel Politics in Nigeria." *The Journal of Commonwealth and Comparative Politics*, XXI, 3 (November): 21–38.

———. 1987. *Democracy and Prebendel Politics in Nigeria*. Cambridge University Press.

Koehn, Peter. 1989. Competitive Transition to Civilian Rule: Nigeria's First and Second Experiments." *The Journal of Modern African Studies*, XXVII, 3 (September): 401–30.

Kukah, Matthew Hassan. 1993. *Religion, Politics and Power in Northern Nigeria.* Ibadan: Spectrum.

Laitin, David D. 1982. "The Sharia Debate and the Origins of Nigeria's Second Republic." *The Journal of Modern African Studies*, XX, 3 (September): 411–30.

———. 1986. *Hegemony and Culture: Politics and Religious Change among the Yoruba.* Chicago & London: University of Chicago Press.

Lewis, Peter M. 1994. "Endgame in Nigeria? The Politics of a Failed Democratic Transition." *African Affairs*, 93 (July): 323–40.

Miners, N. J. 1971. *The Nigerian Army, 1956–1966.* London: Methuen.

Obasanjo, Olusegun. 1990. *Not My Will.* Ibadan: University Press.

Osuntokun, Akinjide. 1984. *Chief S. Ladoke Akintola: His Life and Times.* London: Frank Cass.

Oyediran, Oyeleye. 1980. "In Search of a New National Political Charter." In Oyeleye Oyediran (ed.), *Survey of Nigerian Affairs, 1976–1977.* Lagos: Nigerian Institute of International Affairs.

Oyediran, Oyeleye and Adigun Agbaje. 1991. "Two-Partyism and Democratic Transition in Nigeria." *The Journal of Modern African Studies*, XXIX, 2 (June): 213–35.

Paden, John N. 1973. *Religion and Political Culture in Kano.* Berkeley: University of California Press.

———. 1986. *Ahmadu Bello, Sardauna of Sokoto.* London: Hodder and Stoughton.

Reno, William. 1993. "Old Brigades, Money Bags, New Breeds, and the Ironies of Reform in Nigeria." *Canadian Journal of African Studies*, XXVII, 1: 66–87.

Schatz, Sayre P. 1984. "Pirate Capitalism and the Inert Economy of Nigeria." *The Journal of Modern African Studies*, XXII, 1 (March): 45–57.

Sklar, R. L. 1965a. "For National Reconciliation and a United National Front." *Nigerian Opinion*, I, 1 (January): 5–6.

———. 1965b. "Contradictions in the Nigerian Political System." *The Journal of Modern African Studies*, III, 2 (August): 201–13.

———. 1966. "Nigerian Politics: The Ordeal of Chief Awolowo, 1960–65." In Gwndolen M. Carter (ed.), *Politics in Africa: 7 Cases*: 119–65. New York: Harcourt, Brace & World.

Uwazurike, P. Chudi. 1990. "Confronting Potential Breakdown: The Nigerian Democratization Process in Critical Perspective." *The Journal of Modern frican Studies*, XXVIII, 1 (March): 55–77.

Whitaker, C. S., Jr. 1970. *The Politics of Tradition: Continuity and Change in Northern Nigeria, 1946–1966.* Princeton: Princeton University Press.

———. 1984. "The Unfinished State of Nigeria." *Worldview*, 27, 3 (March): 5–8.

(*Note*: The foregoing references include only items cited in the text. The author owes a much wider intellectual debt to a variety of works too numerous for citation here.)

2

NIGERIA: A POLITICAL ENTITY AND A SOCIETY

Funso Afolayan

> Nigeria is not a nation. It is a mere geographical expression.
> —Obafemi Awolowo (1947).

> Nigerian people themselves are historically different in their backgrounds, in their religious beliefs and customs and do not show themselves any sign of willingness to unite . . . Nigerian unity is only a British intention for the country.
> —Tafawa Balewa (1948).

The area of present day Nigeria was referred to by many terms during the nineteenth century. Notable among these terms were "Soudan," "Nigritia," "Houssa" states, Central Sudan, Niger empire, Slave Coast and Niger Sudan, to mention a few. The use of the term "Nigeria" received its first official recognition in a debate in the British House of Common in 1899 (Coleman 1958, 44). Earlier in 1897, the *London Times* had written about the need

> to coin a shorter title for the agglomeration of pagan and Mohammedan states which have been brought . . . within the confines of a British Protectorate, and thus need for the first time in their history to be described as an entity by some general name. . . . The name 'Nigeria' applying to no other portion of Africa, may without offence to any neighbours, be accepted as coextensive with the territories over which the Royal Niger Company has extended British influence (quoted by Coleman 1958, 44).

In this circumstance "Nigeria" became the name of the territorial entity conquered or acquired around the Niger and Benue rivers by the British during the closing years of the nineteenth century. This chapter examines the emergence of Nigeria as a political entity and as a society. It looks at the roles of ethnicity, class and social distance in Nigerian politics. In its analytical framework, it argues that the presence of sociocultural differences in themselves will not explain the Nigerian crisis. Using a primordialist approach, it attempts to explore and elucidate the nature and congruents of Nigeria as a conglomerate society. It sees ethnicity as a dependent, rather than a primordial variable, among other forces at work in the struggle for power and resources in the state. Benefiting from a synthesis of an instrumentalist and a constructivist perspective (Young 1994, 76–81), it maintains that it is the continuous, systematic, and regressive manipulation of these differences by the ruling elite for the furtherance of their narrow, individual and elite-group interests, that has continued to shape and reshape, sharpen and further entrench these differences, while hampering economic and political progress as well as national unity and integration.

Colonial Rule and the Creation of Modern Nigeria

Before the colonial period, the area of Nigeria did not constitute a political entity. It was not a nation; there was no encompassing sense of belonging to a single community. Instead, there were several political entities and groups in the region. These groups spoke different languages, possessed different traditions of origin, had different though sometimes overlapping historical experiences, developed and possessed different cultural traditions, were organized into different political systems and polities as well as different, sometimes competing states and empires. However, these differences and distinctions should not be exaggerated. These societies and groups were not self-contained and exclusive units. Available evidence shows that there were intensive and extensive interactions between the groups as well as considerable overlapping of sociopolitical jurisdiction and interests. In the area of state formation, wars and conquests took place between and among the various groups. Considerable interactions also occurred in trade and commerce, as well as in demographic migrations and intermingling of peoples and groups. Ideas of politics, religion and other forms of cultural innovations also flowed from one group to the other. The advent of the Islamic religion and its consolidation as the official religion of the Hausa and Kanuri states introduced a new and potentially powerful unifying force to the region.

Nevertheless, all these developments notwithstanding, it is still largely correct to contend as many have done, that the emergence of Nigeria as a single political entity was a by-product of British imperialism. In creating Nigeria, the British welded into a single political entity the vastly different groups and cultures existing in the area. To ensure their effective control of the conquered regions, for the efficient running of the administration and the promotion of commerce, the British embarked on large-scale infrastructural developments. The by-product of these developments was to provide the basic physical infrastructures for the further integration of the various groups and peoples who were thus dramatically and suddenly thrust into membership in this single political entity called Nigeria. On the other hand, throughout the colonial period, the British pursued policies that were not meant to unify the country but to maintain the status quo, to preserve and if possible solidify the ethnoregional differences and distinctions in the country. As Coleman (1958) said, "the system of native administration was designed to foster love for and loyalty to tribe" (210). In every case, especially after the war, "every effort was made to encourage 'regional' thinking" (323), which prevented the development of a national identity. The consequences of this divisive colonial policy were counterproductive for the country. It deepened regionalism, intensified and created new north-south differences, fostered ethnic nationalism and reinforced the dichotomy between the north and the south.

The Nigeria that gained independence in 1960 can hardly be regarded as a nation, except as a territorial and geographical term. Rather it was something akin to a patchwork of semi-autonomous units who viewed one another with considerable fear and suspicion. Independent Nigeria could be viewed as an experiment, an attempt to forge a nation out of a conglomeration of states and societies with differing and conflicting interests and conceptions of authority. There is nothing new or unique about the experiment itself. After all, many nations and empires have come into being by a combination of luck and accident. The tragedy of the Nigerian case was that it was a half hearted experiment. It was neither vigorously nor resolutely pursued. The British organized the nationalists to fashion and experiment with a federal constitution with a fairly weak center and with much power delegated to the region. But it was an experiment doomed from its inception. It never worked. In the hands of an elite tutored under British imperialism to think regionally and to glory in ethnic consciousness, the system broke down. The fallout for the nation was nepotism, tribalism, thuggery, corruption, political repression, the breakdown of law and order, a permanent state of tension and civil strife, and civil war and protracted and resurgent military rule.

Independence and the Emergence of Nigeria as a Conglomerate Society

But how do we account for this failure? While the colonial legacy factor cannot be ignored, it must be placed in its proper context. It alone will not explain the Nigerian crisis. The answer appears to be located somewhere in the nature of Nigeria as a political entity and a society. Examining the issue of Nigeria as a political entity and a society reminds us that Nigeria is a nation of diversity. This diversity is evident in the geography of the country: from the Sahel savanna grassland of the Saharan desert fringe in the north with its open and undulating prairies, rolling plains and tall grasses; to the thick forests, rivers and impenetrable mangrove swamps and hilly terrain of the south. Environmental differences became the basis for differing ecological and economic adaptation, from the nomadic pastoral Fulani and sedentary grain producers in the north to the forest root crop cultivators and fishermen of the south. Similarly, ethnic plurality remains a major feature of Nigerian society. Estimates of the country's ethnic groups have ranged from 200 to 400, depending on the criteria of differentiation. Of these number three ethnic groupings have predominated: the Hausa-Fulani in the north, the Yoruba in the southwest and the Igbo in the southeast. Between them these three groups constitute about two thirds of the nation's population. The Middle Belt, and the extreme southeast contained the largest concentration of the smaller or minority ethnic groups. What is most striking is the fact that each ethnic group inhabits a geographically contiguous territory, and has continued to preserve its own distinct historical tradition, to possess its own culture and sociopolitical institutions, and to speak its own language.

No one is quite certain about how many languages are spoken in Nigeria especially since the point of differentiation and categorization between a language and a dialect remains a contentious issue among linguists. Estimates of the number of languages have ranged from 250 to 500 (Allan 1978, 402). The Hausa language is spoken by over half of the northern population and there is considerable incidence of bi- and tri-lingual proficiencies in the border areas, especially among minority groups. Nevertheless, no one indigenous language is spoken by more than a third of the population. The consequence of this is that English, the colonial language, has become the nation's lingua franca. Successive, although often half-hearted, attempts to adopt one or more indigenous languages as the national language or languages have foundered on the rock of ethnolinguistic rivalries and mutual suspicion. The end result has been that the multiplicity of mutually unintelligible languages have continued to hinder intergroup communication and the development of national identification, while reinforcing group differences. On the other hand, the use of the English language as the principal medium of national politics and education has created and sharpened the cleavage between the elites and the majority of the population, whose lack of western education has continued to keep them divided, largely uninformed and vulnerable to intra- and inter-elite manipulations (Graf 1988, 5).

The elite-mass cleavage can be seen in the division of the country into rural and urban areas. Urbanization in the Nigerian area antedated the colonial era, but colonialism accentuated the process of urbanization. By concentrating its development in the urban areas, colonialism created the phenomenon of unequal development. More than two-thirds of the Nigerian population still live in rural areas, made largely of the "masses" who continue to complain of neglect and lack of infrastructural facilities. In the rural areas, communal loyalty, at the level of the village or lineage communities, is primary and paramount. For the mass of the rural population, kinship connections usually command absolute and unquestioned commitment, far above loyalty to region or ethnic group. For all practical purposes, the rural population carries on its subsistence existence, largely independent of the state and oblivious to the power struggle perpetually going on in the political capitals. However, as the state increases its control of the nation's economy, it has become more difficult for the peasant population to be insulated from the negative and destabilizing consequences of intra-elites' perennial competition for power and continuing mismanagement of the economy. National and local elections become the occasion for the peasants' latent sense of political sensibilities to be ignited, activated and mobilized by the largely urban political elites, who have become adept at fanning the ember of ethnicity to gain votes. The political elites also strive to maintain their hold on their local constituencies through patronage, palatial buildings in the home village, developmental projects such as schools, industries, hospitals, and others, and donations at communal launchings of development funds for roads, churches, mosques, palaces and town halls, to mention just a few.

Closely related to the rural-urban cleavage is the dichotomy between the state and the civil society. Made up largely of middle class professionals, lawyers, journalists, teachers, organized market women, labor unions and other nongovernmental and professional associations, the powers and the potential of the civil society have remained largely latent and undeveloped. The state, through its monopolistic control of the repressive and coercive capacities, has always been able to compel obedience and submission to its will. It has continued to do this through corrupting overtures to the undernourished, leaderless and fractious middle class, including cooptation into the privileged class through appointments, contract awards or gifts, and other implicating assistances. And if all these fail then subservience or cooperation can be enforced through material exaction, property confiscation, psychological insecurity, incarceration, constant harassment and intimidation. In the worst case, the government might resort to total liquidation through the use of letter bomb, hired assassins, police brutality or the anti-riot police squad, which Nigerians have labeled "kill and go" or "operation no mercy." While it is true that Nigerians "have a shrewd understanding of their political needs" and are "actively concerned about their political system" (Peil 1976, 3, 6), political experience in the country shows that the low level of literacy, the grueling poverty and the limited political conscientization continue to render the masses of the populace including the civil society vulnerable and susceptible to manipulation, exploitation and oppression by the nation's ruling elites. The relentless and ruthless repression of student and labor unions, pro-democracy nongovernmental and human rights organizations attest to how far the political class will go to cow its enemies and detractors to preserve its elite hegemony.

The diversity of the Nigerian society is also reflected in the multiplicity of religious loyalties. Each ethnic group has its own religious traditions. However, the two universalistic religions of Islam and Christianity have had the most impact on national politics and intergroup relations. Between them, these two command the largest followings in the country. With the exception of the Middle Belt, the north is dominantly Islamic, Christianity predominates in the east, while the west is nearly uniformly divided between the two religions. Generally, Nigerians have been quite tolerant of differing religious beliefs. It is not uncommon to find individual members of the same family adhering to different religions while living amicably together, especially in Yorubaland and the Middle Belt. In recent years, however, the resurgence of religious fundamentalism and intra- and inter-religious competition, as well as the distrust and tension created by the exploitation and manipulation of religious differences by the political elites, have provoked violent clashes and riots, especially in the northern part of the country.

Diversities of geography, language and culture are not in themselves inevitable catalysts of conflict and malintegration. That they have continued to fulfill these functions in Nigeria is a consequence of other intervening variables. The most persistent of these variables has been the negative and destructive use of ethnic nationalism. Generally and derogatorily described as tribalism, ethnonationalism has many facets. The word tribalism is a "catch-all" term. The phenomenon rears its head in almost every sphere.

It is associated with corruption, class formation, nepotism and the sociopolitical malaise bedeviling the nation. The failure of nation building and integration has most often been explained through references to the pernicious evils of tribalism. For many it is the root cause of all the sociopolitical crises in the country.

Ethnic nationalism and tribalism are closely interrelated concepts. It is often quite difficult to differentiate them. Ethnic nationalism can be a positive commitment to the advancement of the interest of one's ethnic group without prejudice to the interest of others. But in its negative and extreme form it can become tribalism. Tribalism can be described as a kind of morbid loyalty and commitment to one's ethnic group to the exclusion, prejudice and often at the expense of other ethnic groups. It is usually inward looking, ethnocentric, and parochial in its exclusiveness. The ultimate objective is the survival, aggrandizement and supremacy of one's ethnic group, usually to the detriment of other groups. In its strategies it entails the appeal to and mobilization of ethnic consciousness and the use of ethnic favors and preferences, as well as nepotism and corruption.

This form of tribalism did not exist in pre-colonial Nigeria. While the various ethnic groups and states fought and competed with each other, tribalism as a decisive force in the ordering of intergroup relations came with British colonialism. By continually fostering a feeling of separate identity and keeping the educated elite divided and fragmented through a policy of "divide and rule," the British attempted to assure their own hegemony while forestalling the emergence of a mass-based, supra-regional and unified anti-colonial movement that could successfully challenge the colonial system itself. Regionalization of politics resulted in the regionalization of ethnicity, as the three regions were carved and constructed during the 1950s to be dominated by the three principal ethnic groups: the Hausa-Fulani in the north, the Yoruba in the west and the Igbo in the east. The minorities in each region were left to develop their own form of ethnonationalism. The periodic exercises at state creation (from twelve in 1967 to thirty-six in 1996) have weakened but not entirely eliminated the perception and use of regional hegemony in national politics.

Primordial Loyalties, Ideologies and the Consolidation of Social Distance

Besides ethnic pluralism, another dominant feature of Nigerian society is the presence and continued resilience of a plurality of sociopolitical cultures and attitudes. This is brought out clearly through an examination of how differences in political perspectives and deference to authority have continued to affect political behavior and social distance among Nigerians. Precolonial Hausa-Fulani society was organized along feudal lines. With the triumph of the Fulani jihad in the early nineteenth century, a theocratic state was established under the supreme rulership of the Sultan of Sokoto, the Commander of the Faithful. His representatives in the provinces were the emirs, who stood at the top of a vertical structure of authority that was hierarchical in nature. Combining in his person secular and religious authority, the emir was able to command the absolute loyalty of his subjects. A Hausa phrase puts it, "*addinimmu addini biyyaya ne*" (our religion is a religion of obedience). Thus power, commands, protection and favors flowed from the top downwards in exchange for obedience, loyalty and submission. Hausa-Fulani society is a highly stratified one in which hereditary legitimacy and personal connections remain central. Elaborate and complex principles of stratification worked together to divide the society into two classes, the ruling (*sarakuna*) and the commoner (*talakawa*) classes. While the number of categories within the two classes varied in time and in place, Whitaker (1970, 314; see also Smith 1955, 83–108), in a study of twelve selected emirates, was able to identify at least 26 major categories into which the two classes were divided. Membership in each class was usually fixed at birth, although available evidence shows that the system was neither completely ascriptive nor entirely restrictive and inflexible.

Similarly, the advent of independence and modernization have brought into prominence a new class of elites whose claim to power and status has not depended primarily on ascription, but on western education and employment in new national and state positions of governmental authority. The new modern elites, by virtue of the strategic position of power they occupy, are in a position to challenge or threaten the traditional dominance of the *sarakuna*. Conflict and confrontation have, however, not generally been the nature of the relations between the two groups for a number of reasons. In the early phase of their emergence, most members of the new political class were drawn from members or kinsmen of the *sarakuna*. The fact that the first premier of Northern Nigeria, Sir Ahmadu Bello, was an heir of the Uthman Dan Fodio ruling dynasty was hardly an accident. Secondly, realizing the strategic positions occupied by members of this new class, the old ruling aristocracy has tried to work with, rather than antagonize, this group, who in any case were usually their sons or kinsmen. Thirdly, for the modern political elites, determined to maintain their privileged position and realizing the enormous hold of the emirs over the *talakawa*, gaining the support of the emirate authority in their attempt to mobilize and consolidate their local or regional position was more than a passing concern. Traditional rulers, in spite of modernization or even because of it, have continued to exercise residual influence in the society, especially because of the prestige and importance attached to their position as enduring symbols of cultural and communal identities. The Nigerian political experience has demonstrated time and again that the overt or covert support of the emir can be decisive in determining the voting direction of his people. This has in turn turned the emirs into "kingmakers" as aspiring politicians have scurried to emirs' palaces to curry favor, competing to outdo each other in promises, fealty and presents. Few politicians have successfully attempted to win the votes of the people against the opposition of their emir. Finally, both the traditional and the modern political elites have realized that it is in their common class interest to ally together to maintain a firm hold over the peasants, preserve their privileged position and stifle every attempt by the *talakawa* to mobilize along class lines to challenge the ruling elites' commanding position in the society. In this they have been largely successful, in spite of the occasional galvanization of *talakawa* discontents into open rebellions. Thus "kingship, marriage, clientage and other ties bind officials together, and provide the bases for their corporate solidarity and action against *talakawa* who dispute their authority and power" (Smith 1960, 275).

Like the Hausa, Yoruba society was hierarchical in structure. At the same time, like the Igbo, it was not authoritarian. Although the Yoruba Oba was perceived as a sacred monarch, he did not exercise absolute power. Hedged about by numerous taboos and usually restricted to the palace, he had to rule by the advice of his chiefs. These chiefs formed the Oba's ruling council. Since most of their offices were hereditary, they could not be removed by the king, who, in spite of the prestige and ritual sanctions of his office, was regarded as a primus inter pares vis-à-vis his chiefs. They were usually responsible for the selection of a new ruler and could organize the deposition of a king who had lost the respect of his chiefs and people. While the Oba's status brought him respect, obedience to him was neither absolute nor unquestioning. Yoruba society can be divided into two groups, the royal and the non-royal lineages. The royal lineages supplied candidates for the throne while the non-royal lineages held the other principal titles. This resulted in a system of checks and balances in the society. The two groups were, however, not rigidly categorized into ranks. Members of the royal family were not usually richer than the non-royal groups, who usually constituted the bulk of the population and held more prominent titles. Like the Igbo, the Yoruba placed a high premium on hard work, personal achievement and occupational excellence. Loyalty and ties to one's lineage (*ebi*), as well as clientage relationships of subservience and obedience to political superiors, were also emphasized. Conflicts, rivalry, competition for power and the playing or balancing of one group against the other appear to have been prominent features of Yoruba history and politics, making the political system somewhat unstable and social mobility quite fluid. The pervasive state of internecine warfare in the nineteenth century created new cleavages that have continued to impact Yoruba politics. These have also continued to hamper intragroup solidarity and unity except when necessary to compete with other groups (Bascom 1969).

The traditional Igbo society exemplifies the sociopolitical organization that was dominant in many southern and middle belt societies. Many of these societies were small-scale in their organizational frameworks, for the most part lacking in centralized kingship institutions, until the colonial period. Among the Igbo, the most prominent feature of the government was the village representative assembly. In a typical village, the assembly consisted of all the adult male members and some notable women in the community. Debate was always open and everyone was free to participate, and decisions were reached by consensus of the general assembly. Above this assembly was the village-group assembly made up of representatives of all the component villages. The process of decision-making followed the pattern already enunciated for the village assembly. Each village however, remained autonomous and could not be compelled to accept decisions of which it was not part. Age grade associations, secret societies, title societies and sanctions of oracles were instrumental in helping to enforce order in their respective villages. There was a strong emphasis on equality and equivalence as well as on rivalry and competition tempered only by reasoned moderation. Attitudes of subservience, dependency and servility were deprecated. Hard work, self-assertiveness, enterprise, individualism and personal achievement were stressed. Helping one's kinsman or brother (*nnam*) was considered the highest moral obligation. In this society, "individual rivaled individual, segment rivaled social segment and gods rivaled gods" (Afigbo 1973, 23).

Pluralism and Intra-Elite Struggle for Power and Dominance

Looking at these differences in traditional values, political attitudes and perspectives on authority, it is tempting to conclude that the groups are irreconciliably predetermined not only to competition but to conflict and crisis. Many have attempted to explain Nigerian troubles as inevitable consequences of primordial loyalties and attachments. This is, however, a simplistic approach. While not underestimating them, it is maintained here that these objective and subjective differences in political systems and social attitudes are not in themselves sufficient prerequisites for intergroup conflict and the emergence of ethnicity. That they have continued, in many ways and at various levels, to remain salient and significant in national politics and intergroup relations, is a direct consequence first of the policies of British imperialism, and then of the divisive activities of the successor ruling elites. To assure their survival as "spokespersons" for their region or state, the emerging elite consciously created and propagated a myth of irreconcilable differences. Following in the traditions of the colonial administration, the emerging elites have continued to reconstruct, invent, manipulate and reinvigorate these ancient hierarchical structures and ethics to create and consolidate new patterns of dominance and inequalities that are legitimated through references to "real or imagined practices of the past" (Fatton 1992, 89). Ethnic and regional disequilibrium and group frustration were explained as the result of control of the state and its commanding heights by "the others." The ethnoregional elites emphasized differences between the ethnic groups to generate ethnic solidarity and "arouse deep fears, anxieties, and insecurities" while triggering "collective aggression inexplicable in terms of simple material pursuits of interest" (Young 1994, 79). Groups who hitherto had not perceived themselves as corporate ethnic units, began to develop active and powerful forms of collective consciousness, vis-à-vis other groups. Ethnicity, became one of the many "instrumentalities of survival" (Young 1982, 85), a mask for the furtherance of "the constitutive interests of emerging social classes" (Sklar 1976, 151) in the keen contest for power and the control of resources characteristic of the modern state. As a flexible and dependent ideology, it was constantly defined and redefined, constructed and reconstructed, by the dominant elites and their followers, depending on the exigencies of the time, to further their group and vested interests. Meanwhile, strenuous steps were taken to mystify and obfuscate the glaring disparity between the elite and the mass of the population, the ever widening gap between the "haves" and the "have-nots." All this was done to prevent the perception by the populace of the class nature of the intra-elite struggle for power, principally by constant appeals to ethnicity. For instance, during the 1983 presidential campaign, one of the presidential candidates told the people of his home state not to vote for his leading opponent who, apart from being an infidel, could not speak to them in their own indigenous language, but only in an alien language through an interpreter.

It is important to note that the results of the 1993 presidential election also demonstrate that ethnicity need not be a divisive force in national politics. The presidential candidate of the SDP, though a southerner, won more votes in the north than the NRC candidate, a northerner who was defeated in his home state of Kano. The cancellation of the election results was initially condemned all over the nation. When the government began immediately to play the ethnic card, the nation's political class soon joined. They trooped to Abuja to negotiate a better deal for themselves in whatever new arrangement the government would allow. Instead of a struggle for the triumph of democracy, the crisis transformed itself into a struggle among ethnic groups for dominance, as old wounds, fears and distrust resurfaced. Far from being managers of conflict, the ruling regional elite, by fragmenting the society into antagonistic units and by routinely and unscrupulously deploying the demagogic weapon of ethnicity, became generators of conflict. As Dudley (1973, 35) aptly puts it, more than any other group in Nigerian society, the Nigerian ruling elites, civilian and military, have remained "the chief proponents and purveyors of parochialism and particularistic values" in the nation's body politic.

Though differentiated into regions, the emergent classes shared objectives, the most important of which was the preservation of their dominant position of power in the state. Since the state controls almost everything, possession of political power meant access to the resources of the state, promotion, security of status, enrichment, influence and power. To secure and entrench its dominant position in its region, while striving to gain national power, each group of the regional elites needed some forms of populist ideology to mobilize the support of its peoples. Usually lacking in charismatic appeal, and uncommitted to and skeptical of appeals to universalistic ideology, the elite resorted to the regressive specter of ethnicity. Thus the masses who had earlier been politicized to achieve colonial liberation, now had to be re-politicized in the service of elite domination.

The emergent ruling class was not an economic one. Its dominance in the society did not result primarily from its relation or control of the instruments of economic production, but by its "relations of power" (Sklar 1979, 537). Before long, ethnicity became a moderating and mediating factor in intra- and inter-group relations. In its manifestations, tribalism operates at various levels and with varying ramifications. Political appointments meant fat salaries, attractive fringe benefits and other official and unofficial perquisites of office, such as "kick backs," "ten per cent," "dash," or to use a recently coined term, "*egunje*" (spoil) by grateful business contractors. Everything, from securing admission to choice schools, or military academies, trading licenses, scholarship awards, appointments and promotions to plum civil service and ambassadorial posts, contracts, public funds and investment loans, access to shares of privatized and indigenized companies, and many other things beside, came to depend, to an extraordinary extent, on one's ethnic affiliation or as Nigerians put it, on "who you know" (Peil 1976, 70–72; Diamond 1988, 32–33). Thus class dominance developed as an ethnic and regional phenomenon.

In the relative isolation and dislocation of the urban centers and the anomie of an industrial economy, migrants to the cities turned to members of their own ethnic or cultural groups for psychological and sociological solidarity and support. For the dominant political elites this was advantageous. They developed and maintained an array of patron-client relationships. In a capitalist economy that has come to be characterized by limited resources and extreme disparities of wealth and privilege, where the mass of the populace continue to live in a state of "the most grinding and dehumanizing poverty" (Osoba 1977, 378), control of political power became the principal means for the elites to secure and consolidate their class dominance. Politics became a struggle for the control of resources, increasingly characterized by zero-sum rules. Elections were fought as mortal combats and apocalyptic undertakings between implacable and irreconcilable enemies, in which victory and the liquidation of the opponents must be secured at all costs and by all means. In this context, acceptance of defeat was out of the question

Creating a More Perfect Union: Challenges and Prospects

The emphasis on sociocultural distinctiveness and diversities runs the risk of overemphasizing differences at the expense of similarities, of conflict at the expense of collaboration. Old and new factors of commonalties have continued to serve as centripetal cements, blunting the differences between regions, states as well as ethnolinguistic groups. Integrating factors include western education, the use of the English language, the spread of the major indigenous languages, the expansion of supra-ethnic religions such as Islam and Christianity, exposure to liberal and democratic ideas from the west, and the daily reality of living and working together. Colonialism itself provided the basic infrastructural framework for the forging of national unity. Important more recently has been the presence of a general commitment on the part of the intelligentsia to articulating, understanding and eventually prescribing solutions to the problems of democracy and national unity. Closely related to this has been the reawakening, resurgence and maturing of civil society, despite relentless pressure to tame, suppress or coopt it by the ruling elite. Similarly, the cause of democracy has continued to be promoted by the activism of a vigilant and indefatigable free press and a resilient, albeit continuously assaulted, labor union movement. Not least in importance has been external support from pro-democracy groups and human rights organizations all over the world.

Thus, the projection of ethnoregional cleavages must not be pushed too far; the picture is often more complex. Indeed, there are many intervening and mediating variables making apparently monolithic ethnoregional compartmentalization more fluid and more flexible than it appears on the surface. None of the principal regions has remained completely monolithic. In virtually all the regional blocks there are different types of centrifugal forces weakening or circumscribing the limits of ethnoregional solidarity. The north, though predominantly Islamic continues to contend with the restiveness of its Christian population, whose territorial incidence also coincides spatially with ethnic minorities' locations. The traditional rivalries between the Kanuri-dominated northeast and the Fulani-dominated northwest, which dates to the nineteenth century jihad wars, remain salient in northern and national politics. The contingencies and the dictates of the mutual interests of the dominant ruling elites in the two areas have always worked to either sharpen or contain these rivalries. In addition, beside having to deal with the particularistic claims of its numerous ethnic minorities the northern political class has also had to confront centripetal tendencies within the majority Hausa-Fulani-Muslim society. The rise of Islamic fundamentalism and the rivalry between the Quadriyya and the Tijanniyya brotherhoods have periodically created tension and turbulence. The career and qualified success of Aminu Kano (himself a Fulani malam) and his use of an Islamic ideology of liberation to mobilize and catalyze into popular revolution the disenchantment of the *talakawa* Hausa peasantry against the oppression and feudalistic domination of the Fulani ruling aristocracy is noteworthy in this regard (Paden 1973; Feinstein 1973, 90–120).

Similarly, the minority groups have continued to serve as levelers in the political process, sometimes weakening, sometimes strengthening regionalism while time and again complicating ethnoreligious conglomerations. Over the years, they have adroitly exploited their strategic positions as balancing forces in the struggle for power and supremacy among the leading ethnolinguistic groups. Ever suspicious of the intentions of the dominant groups, they have often coalesced to demand and defend their interests, while zealously fighting to frustrate every attempt to marginalize them in national politics. They have been vocal and strident in the agitation for local autonomy, most especially as expressed in the creation of new states and local governments. In the west, the resentment of the Edo and other ethnic minorities of Yoruba domination created agitation that provided the background for the creation of the mid-western Region in 1963. In the east, the several ethnic minorities in the Delta and south-eastern sections of the region have remained resentful of Igbo dominance, explaining their reluctance to follow the secessionist cause in 1967. Uncertain of the fate that awaits them as new minorities, in any breakup of the country into two or more nations, the minorities have always voted for the maintenance of the status quo. Juxtaposed between powerful groups, minorities have introduced factors of fluidity and incoherence in national affairs, mediating the quest for hegemony among the regional blocs of ruling elites.

Nearly four decades after independence, Nigeria, as a political entity and as a society, remains. But in the last few years, especially following the abortive election of June 1993, the most serious and most volatile issue in the Nigerian political landscape and discourse is still what it was in 1900, 1914, 1953, 1958 and 1967: whether the nation can, will and should continue as a single political entity or break up into how many and on what and whose terms. Unfortunately no debate on this issue is permitted in the country where critics and opponents are routinely ending up in prison and informed opinion is ruthlessly stifled, suppressed and silenced. Critical issues of national significance, especially where they pose a potential challenge to the dominance of the political class, are routinely swept under the carpet with the hope that they will go away. Repression of the opposition, incapacitation of civil society, the emptying of democratic institutions of their democratic contents and the imposition of democracy by undemocratic means have become the standard procedure in the country. These do not augur well for the establishment of solid foundations for democratic governance. Years of irresponsible and coercive leadership, economic corruption and mismanagement have resulted in impoverishment, and a paralyzing sense of powerlessness and despondency. What we are dealing with here is the story of forty years of a nation in the making. The record speaks for itself: nine years of civilian misrule, close to three decades of one form of military dictatorship or another, the doubling of the nation's population, a collapsed economy, gross indebtedness and corruption, unabated brain drain, political malaise, ethical deterioration and social incoherence.

The civil war and the 1993 election crisis have shown that the unity of Nigeria can no longer be taken for granted. Many believe that the Nigerian "gold," oil, is what is presently keeping the country together. But survival of the entity will depend on whether a new crop of leadership can and will be able to emerge. This new leadership will not only have to be representative of all groups and sections but will have to be conscientious and visionary in its commitment to democracy, development, the rule of law, freedom of expression, open and unfettered discourse and dialogue, justice and equity, national unity, mass mobilization and the political conscientization of the whole society. Overcentralization will have to be progressively eliminated and a new system devised to ensure a dynamic equilibrium between the centripetal and centrifugal forces in the nation and to accommodate differences and diversities without jeopardizing national unity and integration. After this happens, one will be able to speak of Nigeria as a political entity not only in theory but also in practice, a nation with a self existing, self contained, distinct and objective reality. Such a nation can continue to develop as a grouping or conglomeration of peoples and cultures but with emerging common national traditions, ethos, institutions, collective activities and interests. This is not an utopian dream; it is a realistic and attainable goal, if the conditions are consciously and deliberately cultivated and developed. Nigerians may yet be able to look back at the last fifty or more years as a prolonged period of gestation, of trial and error in the arduous task of forging a "more perfect union."

References

Adamu, M. 1973. *The Hausa Factor in West African History*. Zaria: Ahmadu Bello University Press.

Afigbo, A. E. 1973. "The Indigenous Political Systems of the Igbo." *Tarikh*, 4, 2: 13–23.

Allan, Keith. 1978. "Nation, Tribalism and National Language." *Cahiers d'Etudes Africaines*, 18, 3: 397–415.

Bascom, William. 1969. *The Yoruba of Southwestern Nigeria*. Prospect Height: Waveland Press

Chazan, Naomi, Robert Mortimer, John Ravenhill, and Donald Rothchild. 1992. *Politics and Society in Contemporary Africa*, 2nd ed. Boulder, Colorado: Lynne Rienner Publishers.

Coleman, James S. 1958. *Nigeria: Background to Nationalism*. Berkeley: University of California Press.
Diamond, Larry. 1988. *Class, Ethnicity and Democracy in Nigeria: The Failure of the First Republic*. Syracuse: Syracuse University Press.
Dudley, B.J. 1968. *Parties and Politics in Northern Nigeria*. London: FrankCass.
———. 1973. *Instability and Political Order*. Ibadan: Ibadan UniversityPress.
Falola, Toyin and Julius Ihonvbere. 1985. *The Rise and Fall of Nigeria's Second Republic 1979–1984*. London: Zed Books.
Fatton, Robert. 1992. *Predatory Rule, States and Civil Society in Africa*.Boulder & London: Lynne Rienner Publishers.
Feinstein, Alan. 1973. *African Revolutionary: The Life and Times of Nigeria's Aminu Kano*. New York: Quadrangle/The New York Times Book Company.
Graf, William D. 1988. *The Nigerian State: Political Economy, State Class and Political System in the Post-Colonial Era*. London: James Currey.
Joseph, Richard A. 1987. *Democracy and Prebendal Politics in Nigeria: The Rise and Fall of the Second Republic*. Cambridge: Cambridge University Press.
Nnoli, Okwudiba. 1978. *Ethnic Politics in Nigeria*. Enugu: Fourth Dimension Publishing Company.
Olorunsola, Victor A., ed. 1972. *The Politics of Cultural Sub-Nationalism in Africa*. Garden City, New York: Anchor Books Doubleday & Company, Inc.
Osoba, Segun. 1977. "The Nigerian Power Elite, 1952–65." In Peter W. Gutkind and Peter Waterman (eds.), *African Social Studies*. New York: Monthly Review Press.
Paden, John. 1973. *Religion and Political Culture in Kano*. Berkeley: University of California Press.
Peil, Margaret. 1976. *Nigerian Politics: The Peoples View*. London: Cassel Ltd.
Post, K.W. J., and Vickers, M. 1973. *Structure and Politics in Nigeria*. London: Heinemann.
Sklar, Richard L. 1963. *Nigerian Political Parties: Power in an Emergent African Nation*. Princeton: Princeton University Press.
———. 1976. "Ethnicity and Social Class." In Sanda, A. O. (ed.), *Ethnic Relations in Nigeria*: 146–57. Ibadan: Department of Sociology.
Smith, M.G. 1955. *The Economy of Hausa Communities of Zaria*. London: Her Majesty's Stationary Office.
———. 1959. "The Hausa System of Social Status." *Africa*, 29, 3.
———. 1960. *Government in Zazzau, 1800–1950*. London: Oxford University Press.
Whitaker, C.S., (Jr.). 1970 *The Politics of Tradition: Continuity and Change in Northern Nigeria, 1946–66*. Princeton: Princeton University Press.
Young, Crawford. 1982. "Patterns of Social Conflict: State, Class and Ethnicity." *Daedalus*, 3, 2.

———. 1994. "Evolving Modes of Consciousness and Ideology: Nationalism and Ethnicity." In D.E. Apter and C.G. Rosberg (eds.), *Political Development and the New Realism in Sub-Saharan Africa*. Charlottesville: University of Virginia Press.

PART 2
Theoretical Perspectives

3

PERMANENT TRANSITION AND CHANGING CONJUNCTURE: DILEMMAS OF DEMOCRACY IN NIGERIA IN COMPARATIVE PERSPECTIVE

Crawford Young

The military managers of the Nigerian state, after dissolving the First and Second Republics, appear to propose to a disabused citizenry a novel form of governance: the permanent transition. Since General Ibrahim Babangida announced the initiation of a process of return to constitutional democratic rule in early 1986, Nigerians have observed a slowly unfolding, elaborately scripted political spectacle, replete with disqualifications and rehabilitations of key actors; scheduling, postponement, and annulment of electoral events; creation and dissolution of political parties; multiple institutions of democracy monitoring, tutelage, and pedagogy. The appearance of purposive transition direction is carefully nurtured, at first with reasonable credibility. With each new artifice extending the culmination of the transition just over the edge of an ever-receding time horizon, the skepticism of Nigerian and other publics grows. Some might say that Murray Edelman was right after all; the essence of politics is "construction of the political spectacle" (Edelman 1988).

Prolonged transitions are not entirely a novelty in Nigeria. We may take the starting point of the decolonization transition to be 1945, when the end of World War II compelled Britain to begin a process of fulfilling wartime pledges that imperial custody was directed towards preparing the colonies for self-government, still perceived to be decades away for West Africa. Over this final fifteen years of colonial rule, no less than five constitutional dispensations replaced one another (the prewar legal framework as point of departure, the 1946 Richards constitution, the 1951 MacPherson constitution, the 1954 constitution, and finally the 1959 independence constitution). As nationalist pressures increased and the Nigerian voice in shaping these documents enlarged, the timetable of transition foreshortened, from generations to months. Although the dominant trope of this terminal colonial transition was self-rule, its subtext was democratization, assumed by both parties as the end point. But until the end game, the inarticulate major premise of the colonial managers was that time was a crucial prize to be wrested in the negotiations; a protracted transition would permit a more perfectly crafted end product, and meanwhile whatever advantages accrued from proprietary title to the imperial domain would continue to flow. But then, as today, the transition concept was indispensable discourse of legitimation.

For much of the 1966–79 military period, episodic transitional ventures punctuated an epoch when a number of officers made the profitable discovery of the rents available to power holders.[1] After a fruitless search for a constitutional formula to save the unity of the country in 1966, the civil war which began in 1967 provided ample justification for army tutelage until 1970. However, after the triumphant conclusion of the war, transition promises needed to be revived. In October 1970, Gowon announced a six-year preparatory period, during which a reformed constitution would be drafted.

In the early 1970s, leading officers sought to persuade a skeptical Nigerian public that the military was uniquely suited for a long-term vocation of nation-building and developmental management. Public lectures by influential officers were delivered across the country in 1972, to test this message, drawing heavily upon themes of "modernization" theory of the day; the military, ran the argument, was imbued with a national ethos, and possessed the unity, hierarchy, and discipline to serve as efficacious macro-manager of rational development (Bienen 1968; Johnson 1962; Janowitz 1964). Former chief of state Olusegun Obasanjo, subsequently broker of the 1979 transition, gave one of these encomiums to the military institution in 1972:

> [The soldier is] no longer regarded merely as a gun-toting robot. It is his lot to create a world community devoted to stability and socio-economic progress. . . .[Africa should recognize] his role as a nation-builder, his commitment to modernization (Campbell 1978, 318).

A quizzical Nigerian public compared the claimed nation-building prowess and modernization skills with the daily observed realities of the 1973 census fiasco, the cement scandal, and the brazen venality of the twelve military governors.[2] When Gowon announced an indefinite postponement of the return to civilian rule in October 1974, he violated the rules of the permanent transition game, and was overthrown to general acclaim in July 1975 (Diamond 1988).

Public confidence was regained in the politics of transition under the remarkably vigorous but short-lived rule of Brigadier Murtala Muhammed, and General Obasanjo. Although four more years elapsed before restoration of a constitutional democratic regime, the respect of timetable promises, and broad political consensus in support of the new institutional design, combined with the fructifying flow of rapidly expanding oil revenues, produced an era of relative good feeling perhaps comparable to the analogous period of the first transition era. Note may be taken of the emergence of a strategem subsequently deployed with manipulative effect on repeated occasions in the post-1983 transition era: cleansing as a mechanism for relegitimation. Brigadier Murtala, to the delight of the public, instantly sacked and arrested the twelve military governors. There followed a purge of some 10,000 civil servants, for sundry abuses or sloth.

The current transition will be thoroughly covered by other contributors. As an exercise in permanence, it has already outlasted the French Fourth Republic, and will certainly exceed the duration of the second transition; the fifteen year record of the terminal colonial transition is within sight. Before turning to the broader African context within which the Nigerian drama unfolds, one may suggest a few observations about transition life cycles. First and foremost, prolonged transitions are inherently unstable over time. The impossibility of a legitimating argument for indefinite military rule in the Nigerian circumstances, well demonstrated by the 1972 campaign failure, shows that a constantly reconstructed "political spectacle" of movement towards the end point is required: constitutional commissions, preparatory moves (censuses, electoral registration, political party formation, subnational electoral exercises). Only a brief interlude of entry legitimacy is available, as the citizenry celebrates the demise of an *ancien régime* rendered contemptible (the colonial state, the First and Second Republics). Thereafter, some years of time may be purchased through investment in elaborate institutional design exercises. Interim legitimacy is sustained though involving influential members of the civilian political and intellectual elite in this process. Displacement of the existing supreme manager of the transition may also be a mechanism of delay; one may note that both the second and third transitions had (to date) four different superintendants. Ultimately, the permanent transition is impermanent; extended periods without convincing forward momentum produce deepening cynicism, disaffection, and citizen disengagement. In the first and second transitions, credibility was recaptured by reasonably faithful, rule-bound fulfillment of a constitutional compact with civil society, broadly conceived. Whether this will be possible for the current transition remains an open question.

The stakes for Nigeria—and Africa as a whole—are great. Along with South Africa, Nigeria is a defining case for the outcome of the democratization process unleashed in Africa in 1989 simultaneous with (but not simply caused by) the fall of the Berlin wall. An effective transition and above all a consolidated political liberalization would lend powerful impetus to democratization throughout Africa. Conversely, an extended prolongation of military rule gives rise to chilling scenarios of accelerating state decay or even disintegration.

The preceding observation may be reformulated to suggest that transition politics in Nigeria do not occur in a vacuum. The broader conjuncture of African and global events shapes perceptions, creates expectations and pressures for Nigeria to conform to world historical trends, and provides comparative yardsticks for the domestic public and external world to judge Nigerian performance. The contrasts in conjuncture between the initial two prolonged transitions, and the contemporary version, bear reflection. As well, a striking aspect of the present transition is the remarkable change in the broader conjuncture over its life cycle.

The decolonization transition occurred at a moment of soaring hopes for Africa, and general optimism concerning the constitutional structures put in place for power transfer. State revenues rapidly swelled in the 1950s, permitting for the first time a significant public investment in educational and health services, and basic public amenities; as well, contrary to prewar practice, Britain made substantial public capital available. The prolonged primary commodity price boom brought new prosperity to farmers. The terminal colonial decade was the only one during the colonial era of steadily rising real incomes in both the urban and rural sectors. And, in the Nigerian case, substantial oil revenues were in prospect.

In one significant respect, Nigeria swam against the tide of mainstream African nationalist opinion. At the hour of independence, a number of particularly influential African leaders—Sekou Toure, Modibo Keita, Habib Bourguiba, Julius Nyerere, Kwame Nkrumah—developed the doctrine of the democratic mass single party. Rapid African development required united and concentrated authority; thus unitary forms of state were indispensable. On both counts, Nigeria demurred; by the late 1950s, all realized that a single party was not realizable in Nigerian circumstances, and that "federal character" was indispensable to any constitutional formula. Significantly, at a 1959 conference of African intellectuals organized in Ibadan by the Congress of Cultural Freedom, Nigerian participants alone spoke out against the single party system.

Nonetheless the mood within and without Nigeria was of robust optimism. Some senior colonial officials privately expressed apprehension, but their perspectives seemed redolent of an antiquated nostalgia for the guardian role. Most Nigerian elites and the nascent community of Africa specialists elsewhere perceived the transition as a triumphant fulfillment of the promise of history as progress. The tides of the Huntingtonian "second wave" of democratization still flowed, and the liberal constitutional state was a natural concomitant of independence. For the ordinary Nigerian, in metamorphosis from subject to citizen, the promises of the political leaders of a life more abundant were entirely plausible, set against the lived experience of rapid spread of basic amenities which had accompanied responsible government in the three Regions, and the steady increase in real incomes of the 1950s. The potency of the ethnic factor in competitive electoral politics was plainly evident, in reflecting upon the outcomes of the 1954 and 1959 elections, and the vocal concerns expressed by the "minorities." But the powerful though then largely invisible legacy of the autocratic heritage of the colonial state was deeply embedded in the habits, routines, and mentalities of its successor; as Michael Crowder ruefully observed a quarter century later, "if the colonial state provided a model for its inheritors, it was that government rested not on consent but force" (Crowder 1987, 13).

The conjuncture for the second transition was radically altered. For Africa at large, the expectation of democratic politics had all but vanished. The claims advanced for the single party system as a more authentic and locally viable formula for true democratic practice had lost their credibility, in the face of the transparent autocratic realities poorly concealed by the radical populist rhetoric of many ruling parties. More generally, the tides of authoritarianism appeared to flow strongly throughout the third world.

Once set firmly on its path by General Murtala Muhammed in 1975, the Nigerian restoration of democracy stood out against the continental trends. Nigeria, at the time, seemed an economic exception as well, at a moment when Afropessimism was beginning to flower. The vast surge in both price and production of petroleum permitted an extraordinary expansion of state expenditures. Government outlays, a mere 7.4 million pounds as late as 1937, rose to 60.7 million pounds in 1954, but were still only 214 million pounds at the end of the First Republic. During the second transition epoch, from 1971 to 1980, state expenditures ballooned from 997.4 million naira to 17,513.1 million naira (Kilby 1969; Schatz 1984; Baker 1984; Joseph 1984).

There were, to be sure, some other episodes of democratic opening contemporary with the Nigerian second transition. In Ghana, a short-lived democratic restoration occurred in 1979, in conditions of public revulsion at military regime performance amply measured by the public executions of three former army rulers. Senegal opened the door in 1976 to relatively open political debate, and peripheral competition from the margins of the system. Burkina Faso likewise had its democratic moment in the late 1970s; Gambia and Botswana remained throughout moderately democratic without political alternation (Wiseman 1990). But these were exceptional cases, in all instances relatively small polities. The Nigerian experiment, in the size, scale, and importance of the country, far transcended the other examples. Yet at the time it had little resonance in Africa in terms of demonstration effect. Conversely, because Nigerian opinion had always excluded the single party formula, whether of civil or military provenance, the still widely rooted authoritarian practice elsewhere had little influence upon Nigerian constitutional reflection.

The extended political debates surrounding the formulation of the Second Republic institutions stand out as an exercise in constitutional engineering. However ephemeral the actual political framework proved, the originality of the collective reflection which shaped their design deserves emphasis. The broader crisis of the postcolonial African state was not yet apparent, but the reality of cultural pluralism as a fundamental challenge to institutional design clearly was. In its conception, the Second Republic constitution represented at the time, in comparative terms, an innovative venture in political design which explicitly acknowledged cultural diversity as a fundamental and ongoing attribute of civil society, and abandoned illusions that it could be forcibly contained, marginalized by "national integration," or dissipated by "modernization."

The second transition was virtually exempt from external pressures. Neither of the contending parties to the cold war, which reached a virulent level in the later 1970s, exhibited a disposition to query authoritarian formulas in Africa. The Soviet Union was generally pleased during the 1970s with African trends, with seven states declaring themselves of "Afro-Marxist" disposition, and others claiming "socialist orientation." The Western powers were beginning to question socialist and statist development strategies by the end of the 1970s, but not life presidents. The erratically applied "human rights" preoccupations advanced by President Jimmy Carter did not extend to political liberalization more broadly. France, singularly influential within the orbit of *francophonie*, cultivated and protected incumbents who valued the intimacy of the French connection, and quietly encouraged apprehensions of the West African states under its umbrella regarding the possible threat of Nigerian "hegemonism." In short, in contrast to the third conjuncture, there was virtually no international pressure for democratization.

The environment of the present Nigerian transition is dramatically different, and has significantly changed during its prolonged life cycle. By the time that the first promises of a move toward transition were made in 1984, international pressures on Africa had radically escalated. Initially these centered on the economic domain, with intensifying insistence upon economic liberalization; the term "structural adjustment program" entered everyday vocabulary for the first time. The acknowledgement of an impasse on all sides dates from the birth of the Second Republic in 1979, with the nearly simultaneous 1980 Organization of African Unity (OAU) Lagos Plan of Action. Two years later the blistering critique of African development performance in the World Bank "Berg Report" placed African states on the defensive, further constrained by the appearance of a widespread debt crisis. At the same time, the 1981 COMECON rejection of the Mozambique application for membership, and the Soviet rebuff in 1982 to a Ghanaian delegation plea for backing for a radical strategy of response to the economic crisis, made clear that the "camp of socialism" was shifting to a posture of disengagement from Africa. Ronald Reagan and Margaret Thatcher were beginning to change the terms of debate on macro-economic policy in the industrial world, and French President Francois Mitterand veered sharply away from the *socialisante* strategy pledged in his 1981 election campaign within a year. The progressive discrediting of state socialism during the 1980s, well before the fall of the Berlin wall, made economic liberalization the only game in town. Africa, including Nigeria, had little choice but to accept at least the discourse of reform.

By the time that a Third Republic constitution was promulgated in 1989, the global conjuncture further altered, with democratization elevated to become an integral part of the terms of engagement between Africa and Western states. The stunning 1989 collapse of state socialist regimes, and the 1991 death of the Soviet Union, powerfully reinforced these trends. Even within the international financial institutions, influential voices urged political reform as an indispensable concomitant of economic liberalization, antiseptically labelled as "governance." Accountability and transparency, ran the argument, could only be achieved with more open political institutions. Even President Mitterand suggested at the 1990 francophonic summit that the *pré carré* was not exempt; France, he suggested, would become more lukewarm towards countries under its sway which failed to join the democratizing trend.

Dramatic developments within Africa interacted with external pressures. The unending economic crisis had corroded the legitimacy of many states, as had the corruption and dispiriting performance of most regimes. The debt crisis and structural adjustment sharply reduced the resources available for patrimonial autocracy to lubricate the clientelistic networks which had kept such regimes in place (Bayart 1993; Medard 1991).

Powerful internal pressures as well as the altered international conjuncture set in motion the wave of democratizing ventures across the continent. Serious riots in Algeria in 1988 punctured the revolutionary mystique of the ruling *Front de Libération Nationale*, and led to a political opening aborted in 1991, when it appeared that the Islamist *Front Islamique de Salut* would actually win. In 1989, long-time Benin ruler Mathieu Kerekou found himself unable to meet the state payroll or obtain external credits, abandoned by his erstwhile clientele, faced with a crescendo of street protests and a barrage of criticism from "civil society": intellectuals, teachers, functionaries, unions, students. Acceding to their demand for a "national conference" of the "*forces vives*" of the nation seemed the only way out. But when the conference delegates declared themselves sovereign, and proceeded to put in place transitional institutions, Kerekou stood bereft of any possibility of resisting. Within the francophone world, contagion took hold; the Benin national conference, writes one of its admirers, "had the beauty of something unique, incomparable" (Boulaga 1993). National conferences succeeded in displacing incumbents in Mali, Niger, Congo-Brazzaville, and Madagascar; they failed in this respect in Gabon, Zaire and Togo, but nonetheless altered the parameters of politics.

In Zambia, the underpinnings of the Kenneth Kaunda regime suddenly unravelled, and the three-decade monopoly of the United National Independence Party ended. And in South Africa, the unexpected release of Nelson Mandela and legalization of the African National Congress set into motion a process which led ineluctably to the 1994 elections and genuine majority rule. These stunning developments, when placed in tandem with the new international pressures, created almost irresistible momentum for change. By my count, of the 53 independent African states, only Libya, Sudan, and Swaziland have held out entirely against the continental version of the Huntingtonian third wave. In Liberia and Somalia, the disintegration of the state excluded any form of political change.

The last two instances, along with Sierre Leone and Rwanda, illustrate another conjunctural factor which has assumed increasing, even frightening weight: the incubus of the collapsed state. Until the Charles Taylor band triggered a dialectic of disintegration in Liberia in 1989, and the ouster of Siad Barre in 1991 in Somalia brought a chain reaction of armed factional struggle highlighting the complex clan structure of society, the disappearance of state structures was never included in the range of possible scenarios imagined by analysts of African politics. The weaker African states might be, in Jackson's terms, mere "quasi-states," whose supply of sovereignty-sustaining oxygen flowed through the tubing connected to the international state system (Jackson 1990). But the failed state becomes a significant category in the most recent period; to the countries named might be added Zaire, Burundi and Chad, where for different reasons the institutional apparatus of a "normal" state shrivels into near irrelevance in the daily struggles of the citizen.

In the most recent period, the conjuncture evolves in a significant way. Democratizing pressures from the international arena become markedly less intense. Partly this arises from the inevitable hypocrisy in applying such a standard. Neither France nor the United States reacted negatively when the Algerian military aborted the electoral process in 1991; when Islamists are the alternative, the steam behind external democratization pressure swiftly dissipates. Nor is Hosni Mubarak of Egypt the object of public remonstrance at the very circumscribed range of permitted public debate and tightly managed electoral politics; the two billion dollars of annual American support are unchallenged even by congressional enemies of aid to Africa such as Senator Jesse Helms, and the eradication campaign directed towards the armed end of the congeries of Islamist currents evokes no protest. Countries such as Tunisia and Ghana, whose economic management earn high marks in international financial milieux, have a large range of tolerance in political matters. The grizzled veterans of autocratic statecraft, such as Daniel Arap Moi of Kenya or Gnasingbe Eyadema of Togo, have developed agile skills in playing out the reform pressures. Within Africa, some of the democratization experiences have led to debilitating impasses (Niger) or violent ethnic conflict (the youth militia in Congo-Brazzaville who ethnically cleansed various Brazzaville neighborhoods in 1993).

Thus, the third Nigerian transition meanders towards its uncertain conclusion in a far different environment than the second. Simple military restoration still encounters vigorous external response, particularly in small and highly vulnerable states. The Sao Tome and Principe 1995 military coup was reversed within a week, by energetic international pressures and Angolan mediation. The Gambian military intervention in 1994, overthrowing (for the second time) Dawda Jawara, encountered a sharp rebuff from foreign donors; although Jawara had clearly overstayed his welcome, the partial disconnection of the external life support system compelled nominal action toward restoration of civilian rule. In 1996, the military coup in Niger, although apparently welcomed initially by a citizenry weary of the impasse of failed cohabitation, encountered a much less indulgent reaction from the international community. About the same time in Lesotho, energetic South African intervention blocked an imminent military intervention.

What, then, is the balance sheet of African democratization, which provides the broader context within which the current permanent transition of Nigeria plays itself out? The African surge of democratization is now well into its second half-decade, with the decidedly mixed results many analysts anticipated after the initial burst of enthusiasm faded. If one takes full measure of the extraordinary difficulty of the political and economic environment in which it was undertaken, one can even pronounce a cautiously positive verdict. In no other region were the economic difficulties so debilitating, the underlying societal cleavages so exacerbated by the prolonged state decline and corrosion of the effectiveness and legitimacy of the public realm. One moves in many countries beyond the initial phase of transition, to the more complex processes of consolidation and institutionalization. In a number of others, effective transitions were aborted in midpassage, without necessarily being entirely arrested or abandoned.

In only a few cases can one speak of a reasonable degree of consolidation, measured by at least a second fairly conducted set of competitive elections reasonably open to opposition forces (Benin, Botswana, Mauritius, and Namibia might qualify, although only Benin and Mauritius have experienced alternation). In several other cases, initial elections did permit displacement of long-standing incumbents (Cape Verde, Central African Republic, Congo-Brazzaville, Madagascar, Malawi, Sao Tome and Principe, South Africa, and Zambia). The most extensive classification of degrees of democratization is provided by *Africa Demos*. By their categorizations, only three states are irretrievably authoritarian (Libya, Nigeria and Sudan); there are seven other unclassifiable cases, because sovereignty is contested (Algeria, Angola, Burundi, Liberia, Rwanda, Sierra Leone and Somalia). All others fall into some form of partial or substantial democracy. These categories, reproduced below, are open to debate, as are some of the attributions. The same would be said of any other taxonomy; thus for purposes of this discussion let me accept the *Africa Demos* schema. The classifications have been carefully made by Richard Joseph and his colleagues at the Carter Center in various issues of *Africa Demos*:

Democratic—15
(Benin, Botswana, Cape Verde, Central African Republic, Congo-Brazzaville, Madagascar, Mauritius, Malawi, Mali, Namibia, Niger, Sao Tome and Principe, Senegal, South Africa, Zambia);

Directed democracy—6
(Burkina Faso, Cameroon, Egypt, Guinea, Morocco, Togo);

Transition with moderate democratic commitment—16
(Comoros Islands, Eritrea, Gabon, Ghana, Guinea-Bissau, Ivory Coast, Kenya, Lesotho, Mauritania, Mozambique, Seychelles, Tanzania, Tunisia, Uganda, Zimbabwe);

Transition with ambiguous democratic commitment—6
(Chad, Djibouti, Equatorial Guinea, Gambia, Swaziland, Zaire);

Contested sovereignty—7
(Algeria, Angola, Burundi, Liberia, Rwanda, Sierra Leone, Somalia);

Authoritarian—3
(Libya, Nigeria, Sudan).

In a substantial number of cases, incumbent rulers were able to legalize opposition parties and profit from their proliferation and the substantial advantage accruing from control of the administration (and whatever life remained in the former single party, in many cases) to win an electoral mandate. Opposition formations generally contest the legitimacy of the elections, not infrequently boycott the resulting institutions, and partially delegitimate the process. Cases which might fit this pattern would include Burkina Faso, Cameroon, Egypt, Ethiopia, Gabon, Ghana, Guinea, Guinea-Bissau, Ivory Coast, Kenya, Mauritania, Togo, Tunisia and Zimbabwe. Opposition protests were particularly vehement in the Cameroon and Kenya cases; in instances such as Burkina Faso, Ghana, Tunisia and Zimbabwe, claims of the invalidity of the electoral process were more muted. Deeply flawed elections may serve some cosmetic legitimating purposes externally, and may operate to divide and even partly discredit the opposition (Kenya, for example). But they fail in their purpose of rehabilitating a regime in the eyes of its public.

One may speculate, however, that the political learning process within presidential palaces in Africa has refined a survival science applicable to the new rules of democratic politics. With careful orchestration, the more wily rulers discover, "democratization" can be turned to the advantage of the incumbent. The capacity of rulers to find instruction in observed experience should not be under-estimated. In an earlier post-colonial age, after the shock wave of the barrage of military coups in 1965–66, over time autocrats developed an array of protective schemes to coup-proof their regimes (scrambled command lines, ethnic security maps, presidential guards staffed by foreign mercenaries, multiple security forces) (Enloe 1980). Where the upswell of public animosity is too powerful in key regions or sectors (Zambia in 1990), or the ruler loses control over the process (as in the national conference scenarios in Benin, Niger, Congo-Brazzaville, and Madagascar), presidential restoration through an apparent democratic transition becomes impossible. But rulers such as Ben Ali, Felix Houphouet-Boigny (and Henri Bedie), Omar Bongo, and Robert Mugabe are agile enough to retain the initiative.

Two major arguments were advanced by those skeptical of democratization as therapy for African discontents. Firstly, competitive political parties and open elections would inevitably mobilize and politicize ethnic, regional and religious solidarities, and thus intensify disintegrative pressures on already fragile states without notably contributing to either stability or legitimacy. Secondly, the depth of the economic crisis, and the intrinsic difficulty of persuading electorates of the necessity of painful remedial actions, would place economic recovery beyond reach, and guarantee a further downward spiral; such is the gravamen of the Thomas Callaghy warning of a "high historical correlation in the contemporary era between authoritarian rule and the ability to engage in major economic restructuring in the Third World" (Callaghy 1993, 467). An interim appraisal of these two arguments is in order; one may recollect that the 1960 brief for the single party system invoked parallel themes: the imperative of national unity, and the necessity for unified, unchallenged developmental state authority.

There can be little doubt that electoral competition readily flows along lines of cleavage defined by ethnicity, religion, or race, in Africa and elsewhere. Communal consciousness supplies vote banks which are tempting targets for political organizers. The political formations which sprang up in the wake of liberalization often offered little identifiable differentiation on grounds of doctrine or program, beyond systematic opposition to incumbents, and vague slogans of change ("*sopi*," in the Senegal war cry). Only in a few instances (again, Senegal is an example) are alignments largely unaffected by cultural pluralism.

Yet the striking fact is that in only three of the current transitions does one find one find communal conflict escalating to uncontrollable levels: Congo-Brazzaville, Burundi, and Rwanda. Of these three cases, only the first represents an instance where a dialectic of violent conflict attributable to the contending political factions issuing from electoral politics overwhelmed civil order, during several months in 1993. The culprits here were factional leaders in the capital, who organized ethnic youth militias bearing the sinister labels of "Ninjas," "Cobras," and "Zulus" who terrorized Brazzaville. These tragic months, reviving unhappy memories of the serious ethnic violence which tore the capital apart in 1959, wreaked much havoc, and drove ordinary citizens into the relative safety of their own ethnic enclaves. But even here the violence subsided when the leaders who had fomented it reverted to more civil forms of rivalry, and when an OAU mediation mission played a fruitful role. The liberalized regime remains nonetheless precarious, teetering on the edge of bankruptcy; Congo-Brazzaville is a cautionary tale by any interpretation.

In Burundi, after the searing experiences of ethnic massacres in 1965, 1972, and 1988, the Tutsi-dominated military regime of Pierre Buyoya undertook meaningful steps towards national reconciliation, and accepted political opening. Doubtless Buyoya expected that his UPRONA party, despite its association with Tutsi hegemony, would be rewarded with electoral triumph; the 1993 FRODEBU victory was not expected. The hopes were not entirely misplaced; the FRODEBU margin was only 60 percent, well below the 85 percent Hutu percentage of the population. Buyoya gracefully ceded power to his FRODEBU opponents. The fatal flaw was the Tutsi monopoly in the security forces, an extremist fraction of which savagely annihilated hopes for a new dispensation by assassinating newly elected President Melchior Ndadaye and several other FRODEBU leaders in October 1993 (Reyntjens 1993). Consolidation of this dramatic transition was doubtless problematic, but the calamitous military intervention not only unleashed a wave of ethnic killings, but leaves Burundi teetering on the edge of a genocidal precipice.

In the case of the Rwanda holocaust, the evidence is more stark: rather than causing the calamity, only political opening and some power-sharing formula could have averted it. Although the single party autocracy of Juvenal Habyarimana performed with moderate effectiveness by legitimacy and economic measures, if not in ethnic equities, until the later 1980s, its decline was swift thereafter. The 1990 *Front Patriotique Rwandais* invasion precipitated a crisis which was inevitable. The parties which emerged after their 1991 legalization fell far short of overcoming a deepening disaffection of civil society towards state institutions, but they had at least the possibility of brokering the escalating ethnic and regional tensions, and providing the indispensable power-sharing framework. The 1994 assassination of Habyarimana, and genocidal massacres which followed instigated by extremist Hutu elements associated with the former regime, left a devastated state without citizens or resources, and a large fraction of its populace as stateless refugees.

Worthy of particular note in surveying the impact of the ethnic problematic in democratization are the contrasting cases of Ethiopia and Uganda. The dialectic of events in recent political history of Ethiopia created a situation where integral ethnicization of the political institutions was probably unavoidable. The empire building of Menelik, followed by the centralizing state construction of Haile Selassie, intensified in new doctrinal clothing by the Derg from 1974 to 1991, produced a wave of armed insurrection around the periphery. The core of the Ethiopian state became intimately tied to an Amharic cultural personality. Resistance in turn became defined by difference, with the three most important insurgent movements mobilizing Eritrean, Tigrean, and Oromo consciousness. The defeat of the center by the periphery thus translated ideologies of ethnoregional mobilization (or territorial nationalism, in the Eritrean case) into doctrines of state. The new Ethiopian constitution goes farther than any other extant in the world in embedding comprehensive ethnic self-determination, including the right of secession. The first national elections, in 1995, were largely conducted on the basis of ethnoregional formations.

Actual political practice naturally imperfectly reflects constitutional norms. State power remains closely held by the best organized of the liberation movements (excepting the Eritrean Peoples Liberation Front, which chose independence), the Tigrean Peoples Liberation Front, residues of whose erstwhile Leninist perspectives on power exercise subsist. Operating through the umbrella of the Ethiopian Peoples Revolutionary Democratic Front, the regime has stimulated the formation of client ethnic movements in a number of regions. Key opposition formations such as the Oromo Liberation Front boycotted the elections, diluting their legitimacy. And large segments of the former core nationality, the Amhara, remain sullenly disaffected, attached to an older and probably irretrievable vision of the empire as nation-state. Whether the ethnic self-determination state can survive as a democratic polity is at best problematic; it does so to date by the very circumscribed nature of its liberalization.

In the Uganda case, Yoweri Museveni has maneuvered to prolong the period of a party-free democracy. A new constitution, framed in a reasonably democratic spirit and process, postpones the decision on reintroduction of parties for five years, while proceeding in other respects with the construction of a liberal state. The reality of a political monopoly by the National Resistance Movement sits uneasily with important segments of Ugandan civil society. Regime legitimacy is sustained by the tangible progress in restoring Uganda as a viable political economy, after the utter wreckage of the Amin years and the second Obote period. Some time has been purchased by major concessions to the core region of Buganda: restoration of the Kabaka Ronald Mutebi, a formula for semi-federalization. Enthusiasm for a return to political parties is tempered by the likelihood of a return to prominence of the Uganda People's Congress and Democratic parties, whose sectarian practices in the 1960s served the polity poorly. But the permanent viability of NRM rule thinly disguised as no-party politics is doubtful; the clock of inevitably eroding legitimacy for a ruler, however admired in his first years, ticks on.

Thus the evidence to date on contemporary African transitions suggests that cultural diversity constitutes a significant challenge to national comity and state effectiveness in a politically liberalized environment, but not an insuperable obstacle. Careful constitutional design can facilitate (though not guarantee) accommodation of ethnic, religious or racial difference. In such institutional practice, accumulated experience demonstrates that cultural pluralism needs to be acknowledged, through arrangements which ensure inclusionary politics, and create structural incentives for inter-communal cooperation.

The critical question of whether a politically liberalized state can supply the kind of rigorous macro-economic management imperative for African economic recovery remains to date unresolved, in my view. The mediocre developmental performance of the patrimonial autocracies which preceded the present post-transition regimes provides little support for the thesis that authoritarianism assures escape from underdevelopment. The lack of accountability, responsibility, and transparency to such regimes contributed powerfully to their decline and discrediting. But the lodestar of the East Asian model exerts its magnetic pull, reflected in a sometimes hagiographic literature (Amsdem 1989; Haggard 1990; Wade 1990). Probably the most impressive developmental performance in Africa is found in the highly plural polity of Mauritius, resolutely democratic since its independence; whether its experience is replicable is open to question. Scrutiny of World Bank tables or other country-level statistical indicators yields no clear answers as to the overall causal impact of third wave regime type on developmental performance.

By way of conclusion, returning to the politics of permanent transition in Nigeria, despite the doubts and uncertainties of the contemporary African political scene, the certain liabilities and indeed mortal dangers in the further prolongation of a military regime unacceptable to large, even overwhelming, segments of Nigerian society far outweigh, in my judgement, whatever perils may await the Third Republic. Nigerian civil society, in contrast to the mood of the first and second transitions, is deeply skeptical of the political class which would succeed to power. Possibly these low expectations provide some latitude for a successor regime. But the confidence of the citizenry, indispensable for a secure legitimation for the *longue durée*, will require much more than a credible election to restore. In contrast to the soft budgetary constraints which the rapidly rising state revenues of the first and second transitions provided, the debilitating debt burden and inescapable need for painful austerity measures will severely constrain a liberalized political order.

Can a new leadership rise to the historic occasion? The stakes for Nigeria are exceedingly high. A politics of endlessly rotating military and civilian regimes no longer can ensure even minimal survival for a Nigerian polity. And a return to the politics of avarice and predatory rent-seeking under civilian stewardship, which destroyed the First and Second Republics, would threaten not only the longevity of the Third Republic, but the existence of Nigeria itself.

Notes

1. The cement scandal of the early 1970s was paradigmatic. At one point in 1975, 360 ships queued off Lagos harbor, with half of all merchant ships suitable for cement haulage racing to profit from this bonanza. The cement purchased was ten times the amount specified in the third development plan, ordered at prices $15 per ton over the going rate. Lucrative demurrage charges were collectible, with profits shared between the officers and the shippers. For detail, see Williams (1987, 70).

2. I attended in 1972 a sample of this military pegagogy, delivered to a University of Ibadan student audience by Brigadier Rotimi in a packed auditorium. Rotimi offered a very academic lecture on "the role of the military in developing nations," drawing liberally on the aforecited literature. The audience was entertained but not persuaded.

References

Amsden, Alice. 1989. *Asia's Next Giant: South Korea and Late Industrialization*. New York: Oxford University Press.
Baker, Pauline H. 1984. *The Economics of Nigerian Federalism*. Washington: Battelle Memorial Institute.
Bayart, Jean-Francois. 1993. *The State in Africa*. London: Longman.
Bienen, Henry S., ed. 1968. *The Military Intervenes: Case Studies in Political Development*. New York: Russell Sage.
Boulaga, F. Eboussi. 1993. *Les conférences nationales en Afrique Noire: Une affaire à suivre*. Paris: Karthala.
Callaghy, Thomas M. 1993. "Political Passions and Economic Interests: Economic Reform and Political Structure in Africa." In Callaghy and John Ravenhill (eds.), *Hemmed In: Responses to Africa's Economic Decline*: 463–519. New York: Columbia University Press.
Campbell, Ian. 1978. "Military Withdrawal Debate in Nigeria: The Prelude to the 1975 Coup." *West African Journal of Sociology and Political Science*, 1, 3 (January): 316–337.
Crowder, Michael. 1987. "Whose Dream Was It Anyway? Twenty-Five Years of African Independence." *African Affairs*, 86, 342 (January): 7–24.
Diamond, Larry. 1988. "Nigeria: Pluralism, Statism, and the Struggle for Democracy." In Diamond, Juan J. Linz, and Seymour Martin Lipset (eds.), *Democracy in Developing Countries: Africa*: 33–91. Boulder: Lynne Rienner Publishers.
Edelman, Murray. 1988. *Constructing the Political Spectacle*. Chicago: University of Chicago Press.
Enloe, Cynthia. 1980. *Ethnic Soldiers: State Security in Divided Societies*. Athens: University of Georgia Press.
Haggard, Stephan. 1990. *Pathways from the Periphery: The Politics of Growth in Newly Industrializing Countries*. Ithaca: Cornell University Press.
Jackson, Robert H. 1990. *Quasi-States: Sovereignty, International Relations and the Third World*. Cambridge: Cambridge University Press.
Janowitz, Morris. 1964. *The Military in the Political Development of New Nations: An Essay in Comparative Analysis*. Chicago: University of Chicago Press.
Johnson, John J., ed. 1962. *The Role of the Military in Underdeveloped Countries*. Princeton: Princeton University Press.
Joseph, Richard. 1984. "Affluence and Underdevelopment: The Nigerian Experience." *Journal of Modern African Studies*, 16, 2: 221–240.
Kilby, Peter. 1969. *Industrialization in an Open Economy: Nigeria 1945–1966*. Cambridge: Cambridge University Press.
Medard, Jean-Francois, ed. 1991. *Etats d'Afrique Noire: Formation, mécanismes et crises*. Paris: Karthala.

Reyntjens, Filip. 1993. "The June 1993 Elections in Burundi." *Journal of Modern African Studies*, 31, 4 (December): 563–583.
Schatz, Sayre P. 1984. "Pirate Capitalism and the Inert Economy of Nigeria." *Journal of Modern African Studies*, 22, 1 (March): 45–58.
Wade, Robert. 1990. *Governing the Market: Economic Theory and the Role of Government in East Asian Industrialization*. Princeton: Princeton University Press.
Williams, Robert. 1987. *Political Corruption in Africa*. London: Gower.
Wiseman, John A. 1990. *Democracy in Black Africa: Survival and Renewal*. New York: Paragon House Publishers.

4

THE CONCEPT OF SECOND LIBERATION AND THE PROSPECTS OF DEMOCRACY IN AFRICA: A NIGERIAN CONTEXT

Peter P. Ekeh

Since the collapse of functionalism as the dominant paradigm in the social sciences and in African studies, and since the decline in the use of dependency theory to account for Africa's problems of backwardness, there has grown a practice, among Africanists, of inventing metaphors for conveying the meanings of African social structures and processes. Of the slew of metaphors that have been so coined, none is more engaging, nor more mysterious, than "second liberation." It is engaging because it is suggestive of large new prospects for democratic horizons with which the notion of second liberation is freely associated. It is mysterious because little has been said about the contents and problems of the implied unsuccessful "first liberation" which this political frontier of a brave new liberation movement is expected to supplant.

"Second liberation" is a metaphor that currently lacks analytical force. Subjecting it to historical and theoretical explorations may therefore enhance its value for our understanding of the nature of politics and democracy in Africa. At the very least, it suggests the importance of understanding democracy as an aspect of the theory of freedom, which has its own rich history in African social thought. Studying democracy in terms of conceptions of freedom in African history may indeed be one important way of grounding it in African political thought and of avoiding an unprofitable mimicry of Western scholarship in this area.

This paper seeks to shed light on the context, contents, and the ideational attributes of the concept of second liberation along the following lines. First, I shall demonstrate that there is an underlying historical dilemma in the meanings of freedom in Africa's public affairs in its fluctuating uses to refer collectively to the liberties of whole communities (including especially ethnic groups) in contradistinction to the liberal meaning of freedom as an attribute of individuals. This sharp distinction between two meanings of freedom can be grounded in the problems of liberty facing communities and individuals during the prolonged era of the slave trade in African history. I shall therefore first resort to this corner of African history in our quest for unearthing the meaning of democracy and freedom that the evocative notion of second liberation suggests.

Second, I shall characterize the implied premier counterpart of second liberation by examining the democratic implications of the struggle for freedom waged by Africa's freedom fighters during the colonial period. In doing so, we will seek to define its meaning of freedom as a collective possession of whole nations and peoples, which conceptually ignored the freedom needs of unique individuals—compelling a notion of democracy as a people's self-determination. Third, I will contrast second liberation's promise of freedom for individuals with the notion of liberation in the colonial period as collective freedom, emphasizing their implications for differing meanings of democracy in African social thought. To provide a forum for these analyses, I will choose my examples and contexts from Nigerian history and politics.

Two Meanings of Freedom in African History

The prolonged era of the slave trade, spanning several centuries of active endangerment to individuals and whole communities in virtually every corner of Black Africa, has been unfairly neglected for its role in the development of social structures and ideas that have subsequently dominated African societies and politics, even in our own times. To choose one prominent area for illustrating its important social formations, the freedom of individuals was most problematic in societies and politics of the slave trade era. The concept of freedom, along with its opposite forms of oppression and loss of freedom, was well developed in the political thought of most African societies, and should be presumed to be of substantial significance in Africans' intuitive conception of democracy in modern times. Paul Lovejoy (1991, 7) points out, possibly with a touch of exaggeration but not without some merit, that the variety and intensity of servile relationships and methods of oppression that can be equated with slavery were probably more developed in Africa than anywhere else in the world at any period in history. Furthermore, there were certainly more slaves in Africa in the nineteenth century than there were in the Americas at any time.

The French anthropologist Claude Meillassoux (1986) locates the conception of freedom in African social thought in kinship and its practices. Borrowing from Beneviste's (1969, 1: 324) semantic tracing of the concept "free" in Indo-European languages to "membership in an ethnic stock described by a metaphor taken from plant growth," which "confers a privilege which is unknown to the alien and the slave," Meillassoux (1986, 23–24) links the social conception of freedom in African societies to the idea of "congeneration"—which he invests with a meaning from the Madinka saying, "to be born together, to mature together." Congeneration includes, for Meillassoux, kinsmen and those others who have been socially accepted into the kinsfolk by way of marriage or other institutions of social integration. They constitute the free-born, the gentles.[1] On the other hand, those individuals in nineteenth century African societies who were not freeborn, being neither kinsmen nor gentles, were regarded as aliens and were denied the rights and privileges of kinsmen and gentles. Indeed, aliens, lacking the privileges of kinsmen, had the status of slaves:

> the slave's juridical inability to become 'kin' . . . makes slavery the *antithesis of kinship* and is the legal means of subordination of the slave in all forms of enslavement [in precolonial African societies] (Meillassoux: 1986, 35; also compare Bohannan 1963, 180).

Such an anthropological conception of individual freedom located in kinship, and its antithetical phenomenon of slavery, is not really far removed from our history. It can be best illustrated from the history and politics of a region of Africa that suffered enormously from the slave trade. The Igbo in modern Nigeria have usually been credited with traditional practices of democracy, at least dating back to the nineteenth century. In *Ibo Village Affairs*, Margaret Green (1937) provided an early picture of the management of Igbo public affairs on the basis of open discussions involving all adult male members of the community in a democratic forum. Victor Uchendu (1965), the Nigerian social anthropologist, characterized Igbo political system as an "equalitarian" society that recognized individual achievement and fostered "a democratic sociopolitical system." Chinua Achebe's world-famous novel *Things Fall Apart* is so compelling because it demonstrates the dilemmas fomented from challenges posed by the dictatorial ways of European colonial rule to indigenous proto-democratic forms and the habits of thought they engendered from a previous era. Individuals' freedom and their democratic role in the communities' public affairs were cherished commodities in Igbo societies—as much in the past as they are today.

And yet Igbo society of the nineteenth century, and before then, was also the arena for one of the most vicious forms of oppression and individuals' loss of freedom in African history. The intensity of the slave trade in Igbo country led to the development of the institution of *osu*, which deprived kinless persons of any rights and privileges belonging to kinsmen and free-borns. Osu were kinless persons who sought the protection of community gods from severe victimization by free-borns. But as community possessions they and their progeny lost their freedom and were regarded as community slaves. If Igbo society was deemed to be a model of democracy in precolonial Africa, it also provided one of the worst instances of an institution of oppression that totally deprived kinless individuals of their freedom. "All over [Igbo] country," Basden (1938, 245) wrote on its conditions early in the twentieth century, "are men and women who have not the remotest idea where they were born" because they were among the large number of people kidnapped as children:

> A man or woman, labouring under the impression that he or she was in danger, could flee to the [public village deity's] shrine and claim protection. In return for benefits of sanctuary, such an one forfeited liberty and became an *osu*, the property of the deity. . . . If the person demanded safety for life, the choice was irrevocable; such an one could under no circumstances be redeemed (Basden 1938: 247).[2]

Such were the consequences of the slave trade for the social formation of ideas of freedom at its loss, in slave trade Igboland. They probably were replicated in many other societies in Africa of that period, although to a lesser degree, depending on the scope and ravages of the slave trade. The slave trade clearly has a major impact on the conceptions of individual freedom and of proto-democratic practices in most African societies.

The slave trade introduced a second conception of freedom into African history and societies. It is the notion that whole ethnic groups and peoples could be regarded as free or unfree. This notion that whole ethnic groups could lose their freedom is perhaps best discussed from the disputes regarding Islamic theories of enslavement which were intensified following the fall of Songhai at the hands of Moroccan invaders in 1591. Among those carried away to the Maghreb by the invading Moroccans was the theologian and scholar Ahmad Baba (1556–1627) of Timbucktu. On his return from captivity, Baba complained that Muslim Arabs were unfairly treating African Muslims: "The Muslims among [the Blacks], like the people of Kano, Katsina, Bornu, Gobir, and all of Songhai are Muslims, who are not to be owned. Yet some [Muslims] transgress on the others unjustly by invasion as do the Arabs, Bedouins, who transgress on free Muslims and sell them unjustly" (see Hilliard 1985, 162). The Arab response was theologically nuanced: Africans could not be included in rules forbidding the enslavement of Muslims because they were the children of Ham cursed by Noah in the enslavement of his progeny to his brothers' descendants, an interpretation that was bitterly disputed by African Muslim theologians (see Hilliard 1985).[3]

In countering Arab arguments condemning all blacks to enslavement, Ahmad Baba introduced a notion that has proved pernicious in African history. While precluding certain Muslim communities from enslavement, he provided a list of ethnic groups from among which it was proper to practice enslavement on the grounds of their non-belief:

> Those who come to you from the following [sic] clans: the Mossi, the Gurma, the Busa, the Yorko, the Kutukul, the Yoruba, the Tanbugbu, the Bobo are considered non-believers who still adhere to non-belief until now. . . . You are allowed to own all these without questioning. This is the ruling about these clans, and Allah, the Highest, knows and judges (Baba c.1622, 137).

This authoritative statement about enslavable groups in the Sudan[4] became the basis of theories of freedom and enslavement propounded by the most significant political figure in the Western Sudan of the nineteenth century: Uthman dan Fodio. As leader of the successful jihad revolt by immigrant Fulani against the host Hausa, his thoughts and pronouncements carried special weight and determined the meaning of freedom and enslavement imposed by his successors on communities in Hausaland and the surrounding ethnic groups in the nineteenth century. While safeguarding the freedom of Muslims, Dan Fodio refined and enlarged Ahmad Baba's list of enslavable ethnic groups to include Mossi, Gurma, Busa, Kutukuli, Yoruba, Tabangbu, Bobo, Borgu, Daghomba, and Gambia (see Willis 1985, 19).

Uthman dan Fodio further contributed to the theories of collective freedom in his jihad admonitions to his followers. This is especially the case with respect to Fodio's conception of the special status of the ruler as the determinant of his subjects' freedom: "The government of a country is the government of its king without question. If the king is a Muslim, his land is Muslim; if he is an Unbeliever, his land is a land of Unbelievers"

(Fodio c.1811, 53). Or, as he put it in his jihad memorandum, "the status of a town is the status of its ruler: if he be Muslim, the town belongs to Islam; but if he be heathen the town is a town of heathendom" (Fodio c.1803, 240). Fodio quoted with complete approval the warning to the Hausa king of Kano from the Sheikh Abd' Rahman As-Suyuti: "[The King] is the Shade of God . . . on the Earth, for verily if he has done righteously, he has the Reward and grateful remembrance, but if he does evil, the Bondage awaits him and *his people suffer*" (Fodio: c.1811, 57; emphasis added). According to this view, the king's sins shall be visited upon the inhabitants of his realm. They are enslavable if their sovereign lord practices the wrong religion, and will be spared from enslavement if he is a true Believer of Islam.

Although it might appear that his views provided a charter for the conduct of enslavement in the Fulani jihad, it would be unfair to indict Uthman dan Fodio for the untoward consequences that flowed from the misdeeds of his successors in prosecuting the revolution which he led and justified on moral grounds. However, as Lugard and other admirers of the Fulani have admitted, the Fulani jihad set a pattern of state misbehavior which has haunted the prospects of freedom and democracy in its region of impact in modern northern Nigeria and northern Cameroon.[5] As the most significant state formation in nineteenth century West Africa, the Fulani revolution challenged and diminished the prospects of both individual and collective freedom in our region.

Both of these conceptions—of individual freedom and collective freedom—were active in African societies in the nineteenth century and in early parts of this century, before colonial rule took hold in much of Africa. While individual freedom was a subject of great concern to particular societies, in the bigger scheme of West African geopolitics, to select one area of our consideration, many ethnic groups were condemned to harassment and enslavement because of their lack of prescribed faith.

The "First Liberation": Africans' Struggle for Collective Freedom from Colonial Rule

European colonial rule was superimposed on these ideas of freedom in African societies in ways that compounded the meanings of individual freedom and collective freedom in African social thought. Colonialism was in one sense the great equalizer between free-borns and aliens, citizens and slaves. While those who were unfree gained some liberation from oppression, all Africans lost the opportunity of running their own affairs—losing important political freedoms in the management of their own affairs. Such loss of individual freedom was paralleled by a political separation of ethnic groups from one another, which minimized the opportunities to differentiate between those (like the designated slave-raiding areas of Northern Nigeria)[6] who were collectively unfree and those who were deemed to be collectively free (like the Fulani and the Kanuri who were sufficiently protected by their own states). On the other hand, there is a sense in which colonialism represented the collective loss of freedom by all colonized Africans before the colonizers who as a group were now collectively regarded as political masters of the African political situation.

Colonial policy makers were not unmindful of these limits to the political circumstances that Africans were subjected to under colonial rule. Writing in an age in which it was fashionable to be blunt about the true intentions of imperialism, Lady Lugard gave a hint of these restrictions in her treatise on Northern Nigeria:

> The administration of this quarter of the [British] Empire [lying within the tropics] cannot be conducted on the principle of self-government as that phrase is understood by whitemen. It must be more or less in the nature of an autocracy which leaves with rulers full responsibility for the prosperity of the ruled. The administration of India, where this aspect of the question has long been appreciated, is among the successes of which the British people is most justly proud. The work done by England in Egypt is another proof of our capacity for autocratic rule (Lugard 1906, 1).

Colonialism embodied "autocratic rule" that compelled some loss of individual freedom. But it also led to the diminution of Africans' collective freedom. Frederick Lugard, the foremost policy mogul of British imperialism in Africa, saw Africans' lots under colonialism as their historical and inherited legacy that did not have to entail an Englishman's concept of government or freedom: "the true conception of the inter-relation of colour: complete uniformity in ideals . . . [but] in matters social and racial a separate path, each pursuing his own inherited traditions, preserving his own race-purity and race-pride" (Lugard 1922, 87). This was the premise of indirect rule which created numerous "native authorities" to "pursue [their] own inherited traditions." These had very little freedom in their practices. Rather, the doctrine of indirect rule borrowed from the Fulani system its notion of the ownership of the state by its rulers.[7] Just as the Fulani had alienated the landed possessions of the Hausa, so did Lugard and subsequent British governors proclaim ownership of land by the colonial state in Northern Nigeria (see Lovejoy and Hogendorn 1993, 127–58). Above all else, the colonial doctrine of indirect rule led to the antidemocratic principle that the public domain is the sole property of rulers and that it is theirs to control as they please—perhaps the most damning consequence of colonialism and the bane of democracy in modern Nigeria.

It was the loss of freedom under colonialism and its ensuing dictatorship that Pan-African nationalists and freedom fighters highlighted in their intellectual struggle for the liberation of Africans from colonial rule. Already W.E.B. DuBois (1945, 81), the African American intellectual and activist, had accused European colonialism in Africa of becoming the antithesis of democracy and freedom:

> [Democracy's] greatest successful opponent today, [argued DuBois], is not Fascism, whose extravagance has brought its own overthrow, but rather imperial colonialism, where the disenfranchisement of the mass of the people has reduced millions to tyrannical control without any vestige of democracy.

Nationalism in Africa in the nineteen-thirties, forties and fifties gained its intellectual current from a motivation to dethrone colonialism and promote in its place what nationalists regarded as its opposite, that is, democracy. Kwame Nkrumah became African nationalism's standard bearer because he condemned colonialism and preached that Africans deserved to rule themselves. Nkrumah (1945, 25) complained that all colonial systems in Africa made it "impossible to vote the 'government' out of office," adding that they "also deliberately prevent[ed] and curb[ed] any aspirations towards independence on the part of the colonial peoples. . . . In fact, [they] definitely nullif[ied] the ideas of true democracy." Nkrumah (1945, 28) energetically affirmed that "it will not be incorrect to say that democracy, self-determination, independence and self-government are incompatible with the doctrines" of European colonial rule in Africa.

It is noteworthy that neither democracy nor freedom had for Nkrumah and the African nationalists of his age the conventional meanings that these epithets bear in modern political discourse. The nationalists were concerned with gaining collective freedom for all Africans, not for individuals. This point becomes rather clear in the thoughts of another brilliant freedom fighter, the Nigerian Mbonu Ojike. Ojike condemned "British colonialism in Nigeria because . . . it contradicts the principles and practices of democracy. *It makes one people to rule another under the guise of an advisory relationship*" (1946, 271; emphasis added). Ojike thus saw democracy in Wilsonian lights as self-determination by a people, not necessarily in terms of individuals' rights to participate in their communities' public affairs.

Thus, in its earliest appearance in modern African affairs, democracy was an advocacy of freedom-fighting nationalism that sought to rid Africa of foreign domination. Often paired with "freedom," nationalism's democracy bore connotations that were radically different from the meanings of democracy in the West. This is clearly so on two separate counts. First, this early conception of democracy in Africa concerned itself with freedom from foreign rule. Its imprint was carried forward to the Fifth Pan-African Congress at which a statement prepared by Kwame Nkrumah was adopted:

> We believe in the rights of all peoples to govern themselves. We affirm the right of all colonial peoples to control their own destiny. All colonial peoples must be free from foreign imperialist control, whether political or economic. The peoples of the colonies must have the right to elect their own government, a government without restrictions from a foreign power (Fifth Pan-African Congress 1945, 44).

Stretching from its pioneering representations in Nnamdi Azikiwe (e. g., 1937) to those of his younger and more militant colleagues, Kwame Nkrumah and Mbonu Ojike, African nationalism's democracy was concerned with the freedom of peoples and collectivities from *foreign* domination and was silent on the problems of their freedom from *domestic* tyranny. Thus, Africans were ill-prepared from the advocacy of democracy in the nationalist era to tackle the problems of domestic tyrannies. In contrast, democracy developed historically in Western Europe in the context of the struggle for freedom from domestic repression. Although African nationalists had metaphorically copied the association between democracy and freedom from European political history, the contents and contexts of freedom were quite different in these two epochs.

There is a second source of difference between the native conception of democracy in the West and its adoption by African anti-colonial nationalism. In the West, the individual is the unit of operation of democracy. It is the expansion of the individual's legal, political, and social rights (Marshall 1950) and the ordinary individual's enfranchisement that entrenched democracy in Western political culture. In contrast, African nationalism's advocacy of democracy was solely concerned with people's rights. It was largely uninterested in the rights of the unique individual. More likely, the nationalists could not imagine that there was a valid difference between, on the one hand, the collective rights of a people to self-determination and, on the other, individuals' rights to possess their own niche of democratic expression concerning their rights of citizenship and freedom of speech.

These meanings of freedom and democracy contributed substantially to the tyrannies that have arisen in Nigeria and elsewhere in post-colonial

Africa. These extraordinary conceptions of democracy during the nationalist era posed sharp problems for African political life precisely at the point of the triumph of nationalism. Basil Davidson (1992, 14), the Scotsman who has been one of the few Britons to support African nationalism, has been led to ask the frustrating question: "if nationalism has been and can be a liberating force, why then has it so often become the reverse?" Nationalism's democracy ironically sowed the seeds of tyranny that came to wreck the prospects of individual-based democracy in post-colonial Africa. As matters turned out, a people's collective freedom could generate conditions that heighten lack of freedom for the individual. Nowhere is this irony more fulfilled than in the lives of the two most articulate spokesmen for nationalism's democracy in Africa. By sheer force of determination, Kwame Nkrumah broke down Britain's imperial maneuver and won independence for Ghana in 1957. W.E.B. DuBois followed the younger man to Ghana as his principal adviser, apparently to live a fulfilled dream, in this land of freedom where he died in an independent African country in 1963. But Nkrumah soon came to be accused of being a tyrant who denied individuals the right of free speech. Nationalism's freedom from foreign rule may have been realized; but democracy's freedom also requires that the individual be free from domestic tyranny, a problem for which nationalist movements had not been prepared.

The peculiar direction of nationalism's sense of democracy may best be illustrated from its incorporation into the most benign dictatorship in post-colonial Africa. Nyerere, one of the most respected of the post-colonial rulers of Africa, tells of the design of democracy in Tanzania:

> In 1965 Tanzania adopted its own form of democracy—we rejected the Western model and said it was not appropriate for our circumstances despite the fact that all our constitutional development had until then been based on it. We looked at different democratic systems around the world, and studied the work of different thinkers. . . . Then we worked out a system of one-party Government which seemed to us to include the essential elements of democracy at the same time as it provided for unity and strength in Government, and took account of our poverty, our size, our traditions, and our aspirations. The resultant constitution is not perfect; but it suits us better than any system operating elsewhere, *and we believe that it safeguards the people's sovereignty at the same time as it enables the effective and strong Government so essential at this stage of our development* (Nyerere 1968, 19; emphasis added).

Note Nyerere's stress on the people's collective sovereignty and the absence of any reference to individuals and their rights. Elsewhere, the necessity for strong government and state's sovereignty have wreaked havoc on individual liberties—subverting the essence of liberal democracy in Nigeria and scores of other African nations. Despite Nyerere's affirmation, African history of the post-colonial era has shown that the people's sovereignty has fared poorly before the ruthlessness of tyrannical rule by Africa's post-colonial states.

Post-Colonial Nationhood and the Abuses of Collective Freedom

The story of the tyranny of the post-colonial state in Africa and its betrayal of ordinary individuals has been well told in a large number of sources and its Nigerian versions are clearly recited in several chapters in this volume. They range from personal dictatorships to military monopolies of power and one-party state dictatorships. Their severity has ranged from mild political deprivations, as in Nyerere's Tanzania, to cunning if destructive political follies, as in Ibrahim Babangida's Nigeria, and to more terrifying political madness, as in Idi Amin's reign of terror in Uganda. In all these instances, individuals and their liberties have suffered enormously.

While the details of Africa's difficulties with democracy in our post-colonial times are worth documenting, it is also as important that we establish the principles of democracy that have been violated by the multiple forms of dictatorship that have wrecked Africa's public affairs since the attainment of national independence. I will emphasize two such areas in this paper: the absence of individualism and the crisis surrounding the ownership of the state and the public domain.

The Absence of Individualism and the Destiny of Democracy in Africa

Of all the cultural traits that Westerners have introduced into Africa, none has been more disparaged as unworthy of Africans, nor has any other drawn greater wrath from established tradition, than individualism. It has earned such negative epithets as selfishness, greed, materialism, and even wickedness (compare Jahoda 1961, 48–54). The introduction of many of individualism's corollaries—like wills regarding what should be done with their makers' property after death, or such other matters as their burial preferences—has been resisted and often rejected as offensive and a threat to African traditions. The resistance to individualism is understandable in view of the hold of corporate kinship on the lives of Africans. Assertive individualism is a threat to kinship and would be possible only if the individual could rely on the state for his existence. After centuries of being abandoned and even persecuted by the state the individual has ceased to trust the African state. The more the mistrust between individuals and the state, the more they rely on corporate kinship and the less their individualism. It is kinship corporations that have undertaken to care for the welfare of individuals while they are alive and to arrange for their proper burial when they die. The welfare of a deceased person's family has also been the kin group's responsibility. The vast majority of Africans rely on kinship for their social security. The post-colonial state has followed in the footsteps of its predecessor colonial state in pushing any matters relating to the birth of individuals and the arrangements for their burial to the sphere of kinship.

While corporate kinship has thus embraced the individual in much of Africa's troubled history, the state has steadily alienated him from its domain. The onset of the mistrust between the individual and the state must be traced back to the sordid history of the international Arab and European slave trade from Africa. In it, many states in various areas failed to protect the individual from Arab slave raiders, while others served as agents and active participants in many other regions, ruining the lives and families of millions of people in their realms, especially those where the European slave trade was active (see Ekeh 1990, 673–83; also Davidson 1992). While the colonial states that took over the administration of most of Africa in the last quarter of the nineteenth century and the first two decades of the twentieth did not send the individual into enforced migration in slavery, they did nothing to reassure him that he was a worthy object of their attention. The colonial state was satisfied that the colonized feared its capacity to punish those not complying with its decrees. At most, the individual was treated more like the subject in medieval society in Western Europe than a citizen of the modern Western state.[8]

It was a failure of decolonization that there was never a genuine transformation in the status of the individual from that of a *subject* under colonialism to that of a *citizen* in post-colonial Africa. In spite of a bubble of excitement and great expectations in the first few years of independence, the post-colonial state in Africa reverted to the wonted ways of colonial rule in the relationship between the individual and the state. Especially under military and personal dictatorships, the individual was subjected to considerable humiliation by the state. For its operations, the post-colonial state has relied on the fear of its physical implements of violence rather than on the legitimating attitudes of respect from its citizens.

What are the consequences of the troubled relationships between the individual and the state and the contrasting firmer relationships between kinship and the individual for the destiny of democracy in Africa? The individual has a great deal of significance within the perimeter of his kin group. Outside of it, he loses his inherent respect and dignity. This denies the state a common value-definition of the individual that seems vital for a functioning democracy. Human rights and the individual's rights have a function in a democracy only if the individual enjoys a common definition on the national scene.

Must democracy disappear in the face of such absence of individualism in Africa? We may provide some answer to such a question from the Nigerian experience in democratization and constitution making in the effort to create the Second Republic. In 1976 to 1979 the question that confronted Nigerian constitution-makers was this: How will the individual be able to relate meaningfully to the state in the face of the history of close ties between him and his ethnic group and his predilection to rely on his kinsmen to make joint decisions for him on issues of national significance? The realist position that the constitution makers adopted was that the individual should be allowed to exercise dual allegiance to the state and his ethnic group. It is in order to express this point of view that the constitution makers chanced on the famous phrase, *the federal character* of Nigeria, which they defined as

> the distinctive desire of the peoples [read: ethnic groups] of Nigeria to promote national unity, foster national loyalty and give every citizen of Nigeria a sense of belonging to the nation notwithstanding the diversities of ethnic origin, culture, language or religion which may exist and which it is their desire to nourish [and] harness to the enrichment of the Federal Republic of Nigeria (Williams 1976, x).

Put differently, democratization was going to be a learning experience of gradually bringing the state and the individual together in a stable relationship built on trust and loyalty. But until it proves to be a success, until the individual can trust the state, it would be futile to ask him to imitate the formal status and kinship-free appearances of democracy in the West and cast aside his trusted relationship with his kinship networks.[9]

Fragmented Public Spheres and the Problems of Democracy in Africa

Democracy implies standard rules of politics and contest for power that are played out within the fold of a single public realm. The contest for democratic power makes sense because the public realm is premised on a common idiom and grammar of politics. Democracy has thrived in the West and in such other political cultures as Japan's because their nations possess single public realms. Individuals' commitments to the preservation of their public sphere is related to the fact that they assume that they own it in common with the rest of the citizenry. In this sense such constructs as *the common good, the public interest,* and *the national interest* are vital instruments in a functioning democracy.

In contrast to such a model, African politics are remarkable for the fact that their public sphere is fragmented. There is, first, a thin-layered *civic* public realm that is identified with the apparatuses of the state. It is the segment of the public sphere that is held in common by all those who live in any African nations. Its health would seem to be vital for the survival of democracy, and yet it is frail in most African nations. Parallel to the civic public are *primordial* public realms which are the exclusive public contexts of different ethnic groups. A great deal of what is political in Africa is transacted in these primordial publics, outside the purview of the state and the civic public. With such fragmentation of the public sphere, democracy has had great difficulties surviving because its rules are interpreted differently in the various public realms (compare Ekeh 1975).

But the bane of democracy in Africa lies elsewhere, beyond the fragmentation of its public sphere. It is the apathy that derives from lack of commitment to the civic public realm in which democratic politics affecting all persons and ethnic groups in the state take place. Few Africans have risen to defend the civic public realm from attack, whereas they would be ready to sacrifice their lives defending their own exclusive primordial public realm. While they say that the sphere of the primordial public belongs to them, many openly exclude themselves from the ownership of the state, breeding apathy whenever the fortunes of the state are at stake.

Who then owns the state? This is a problem of political thought that has troubled African politics since precolonial times and that has much significance for the democratization of modern African politics. Evidence from the precolonial forest states of West Africa (see Connah 1987, 121–49 for a definition of these state formations) indicate strongly that the common man felt very much a part of the state and that royal privileges were constitutionally circumscribed. Thus, the kings of the powerful states of Benin (see Egharevba 1934; Ekeh 1976) and Oyo (see Johnson 1921; Fadipe 1970; Morton-Williams 1960; Law 1977) were often removed for egregious transgressions and misrule. Clearly, then, in these precolonial traditional societies, the state belonged to ruler and ruled, to all free citizens of the state.

Such political thought as Benin and Oyo exemplified changed with conquest and rule of African states by outsiders. One of the most important of these changes in rulership, with active consequences for modern-day Nigerian politics, came with the Fulani conquest of Hausaland in 1804–10 under the jihad movement led by Uthman dan Fodio. As we have already noted, dan Fodio had clear ideas about the ownership of the state: the state belongs to its ruler. What has not been adequately emphasized in Nigerian political history is how much dan Fodio's legacies have dominated modern Nigerian history. British indirect rule borrowed from this doctrine of government. Increasingly, the themes of indirect rule are being fulfilled in subsequent Nigerian history. To cite from one important development extending Fulani notions of government, one of the most important failures in Lugard's attempt to carry his principle of indirect rule to the south in 1914 and thereafter concerned the public ownership of lands. Flushed with oil wealth and optimism that government could do everything it wanted, the military dictatorship of Murtala Muhammed and Olusegun Obasanjo changed all that in 1978, extending the government's control of lands to southern Nigeria (see Federal Republic of Nigeria 1978). In another critical area, colonial practice has been continued and extended with the doctrine that the airwaves belong to the state exclusively and not to any other segments of the public domain and its citizens, leading to the state's monopolization of the radio and television industry and its networks.[10]

This widespread element of political thought weakens the democratic pulse in African politics. Rulers have been able to do as they please, almost as a matter of routine course, because ordinary individuals see themselves as subjects of the state's rulers, and not as citizens and therefore part-owners of the state.[11] Any thoroughgoing program of democratization should include some effort to override Africa's history in this respect. If the ordinary individual can be as bold in respect of the civic public and the state as he is in asserting his ownership of his ethnic primordial public, democracy may have a good chance of surviving in Nigeria and Africa.

The Second Liberation: The Search for Individuals' Freedom from Domestic Tyranny

The term second liberation was coined in the 1980s to identify efforts aimed at restraining the post-colonial African state from its dictatorial ways and of finding alternative ways of enhancing the individual's democratic worth and liberties in the face of oppression.[12] As distinct from "first liberation" concerns with struggle from foreign rule, the second liberation movement is about gaining democratic rights from post-colonial domestic tyrants whose arrogance had been fattened by the machinations of the Cold War. As a matter of fact, the second liberation movement is a post-Cold War phenomenon. The end of the Cold War exposed the emptiness of dictatorship in many of these post-colonial states, offering fresh opportunities for revamping African politics in a manner that would maximize democratic prospects.

As in the struggle for freedom from colonial rule, the fight for second liberation has been multi-faceted. Enabled by the defrosting effects of the Cold War, Western institutions concerned with human rights have generously assisted, even led the way, in the campaign for restructuring African politics in the direction of democratic privileges. Thus, the African program of the Carter Center of Emory University and its *Africa Demos* magazine has highlighted successes and failures in African nations' approaches to this new-era politics. Inside Africa, there have arisen fresh calls for democracy and some courageous opposition to domestic tyranny by human rights campaigners. Importantly, Peter Anyang Nyong'o (1987), the Kenyan political scientist and now politician, and his fellow African coauthors saw popular struggles against domestic tyranny as the cure for the absence of democracy in Africa.

As the Carter Center's *Africa Demos* has been the first to publicize, the second liberation movement has scored some important victories in many African countries (including, for good examples, Benin, Malawi, and Zambia). But the problems of tyranny remain entrenched in such potentially key African nations as Kenya, Zaire, and Nigeria. While Kenya and Zaire may justifiably be regarded as holdovers from the Cold War—probably involving some payback to African dictators who supported the West during the Cold War—Nigeria's military dictatorship challenges the prospects of the second liberation in a special manner. An examination of the nagging defiance to democracy posed by Nigeria's military dictatorship will enable us to formulate the problems that face the campaign for second liberation, to identify its central issues and principles, and to discuss the strategies and solutions for tackling the crisis of tyranny that the Nigerian situation exemplifies.

Problems Confronting the Struggle for Second Liberation

The struggle for second liberation is in response to an incrustation of tyranny subsisting from the eras of the slave trade, European colonial rule, and the dictatorship of the post-colonial state. Going by its Nigerian instance, this struggle is mired in palpable confusion between a desire for ethnic group rights and the international campaign for individual and human rights, between the wish for collective freedom and the advocacy of individual freedom. While much of the international involvement in this struggle tends to be phrased in abstractions of individual and human rights, local internal struggles for liberation from tyranny have largely been organized in terms of collective rights.

Definitions of the *national interest* and the *common good* have been exiguous in the Nigerian struggle against military tyranny. When Tam David-West, one-time Oil Minister, was imprisoned without trial, his Rivers people were expected to fight for his freedom—with little input from anywhere else. He was in fact released to his people by dictator Ibrahim Babangida. Now a free man, he has had no reservation justifying the arbitrary imprisonment, by the new dictator Sani Abacha, of several eminent Nigerians from outside his ethnic base in the Rivers. Ken Saro-Wiwa's ordeals arising from his bouts of confrontation with tyranny have been visited upon his Ogoni ethnic group, with other ethnic groups showing less concern than the international community.[13] The bizarre imprisonment of Moshood Abiola, widely assumed to have won the presidential elections of 1993, and Olusegun Obasanjo, who headed a previous military regime, have been chiefly mourned by their fellow ethnic Yoruba. Indeed, it sometimes appears that Igbo leaders, the erstwhile rivals of the Yoruba, now mock the predicament of Yoruba leadership—a payback time for the dissensions of the Nigerian Civil War. In all these instances, there is clear inability to transcend particular ethnic interests to search for a larger national common denominator of the national weal. There is a failure to see a reflection of ourselves and our liberties in everyone's freedom, and to imagine a potential threat to our common freedom in the arbitrary loss of others' liberties. In the Nigerian struggle for a second liberation, few have seen a common threat to everyone's liberties—including the liberties of the most privileged Fulani aristocracy, as Shehu Yar'Adua's imprisonment demonstrates.

Such fractured responses to tyranny in Nigeria is an attestation to the fragmentation of its public realm. It also propels Nigeria's public affairs backwards to Dan Fodio's notion of the state and British colonial practice of statehood: the state is the ruler's to rule and possess as he pleases. The public domain is solely occupied by the state and any agencies it licenses. Hence, the airwaves and the public media—including newspapers, radio, and television—are wholly ruled by the state.

An adjunct development flowing from these attitudes is a severe attack on the precept of public accountability, an essential component of democracy (see Sklar 1987). Administrative and law-enforcement immunity now seem fully entrenched as central canons of military dictatorship in Nigeria. Perhaps the greatest threat to liberty in Nigeria is total involvement of the Nigeria Police Force in lawless acts in their interactions with individuals, sometimes killing defenseless persons, in the worsening crisis in Nigeria. All this is surrounded by a growing political culture of impunity in the conduct of public officials (see Usman 1982; Lawyers Committee for Human Rights 1992).

Issues and Principles of the Second Liberation Movement

It is important to step back from the maddening details of military dictatorship in Nigeria in order to spell out the principles and issues of the second liberation movement. First and foremost, it involves an age-old problem of relating individuals to their state's public affairs. The issue of the alienation of the individual from the state stalks African history, from the evil era of the slave trade unto our times. Overcoming this problem should be the supreme goal of the second liberation movement. It should pursue the goal of bringing the individual closer to the state, involving the state in the personal security of ordinary Africans. Ultimately, this is a matter of trust. It is only the individual's trust in the state that will win him over from his allegiances to his primordial public.

The severity of the African political situation may ironically provide an important opportunity for the state to win over the individual. Recent political tragedies in Rwanda and Somalia strongly indicate that the burden of providing adequate personal security for individuals is well beyond the capacity of ethnic groups. An imaginative political leadership may be able to win over the individual's allegiance in a sustained attempt to engage ordinary persons and the African state. Such an opportunity is not beyond possibility in future Nigerian political reforms.

There is a second important principle in the second liberation movement: the uses and management of the public domain. Bad academic habits of imitating Western assumptions of politics have obscured the important point that colonial and post-colonial African states have consistently monopolized the uses and management of the public domain. An important task of the struggle for second liberation should be to eliminate the state's monopoly of the public domain. Sharing the public space with other organizations would be a major departure for the history of the state in Africa, but training the state to do so is essential for the success of democracy in Africa.

Strategies and Solutions for Achieving the Goals of Second Liberation Movement

Although we can nowadays look back at the previous struggle for freedom from colonial rule in the luxury of armchair analysis, the problems of the second liberation are urgent and imminent and cry for winning strategies and solutions. If there is justification for praxis, for engaging in "theory-informed political activity" (see Kilminster 1993) in African affairs, it deserves a place in the second liberation movement. However, as the demise of problem-solving and theory-wielding communism in Eastern Europe should remind us all, praxis has its own pitfalls. False solutions may hinder, rather than advance, the prospects of democracy in Africa.

One false trail for the second liberation movement is the advocacy of civil society as an *alternative* to the state, apparently enabling individuals to do without the state. Properly structured, civil society will enable individuals and groups to engage the state in the public arena. Unfortunately, a peculiar meaning of civil society in African studies sees it as a congeries of institutions that are alternative to the state's existence in Africa. A shade of this view of civil society is apparent in Michael Bratton's (1989) influential statement on this subject:

> The African state is weak by any conventional measure of institutional capacity; yet it remains the most prominent landmark on the African institutional landscape. . . . In Africa the state projects upwards from its surroundings like a veritable Kilimanjaro, in large part because the open plains of domestic society appear to be thinly populated with *alternative institutions* (emphasis added).

This conception of civil society imagines it, falsely in my view, as operating "in the political space beyond the state's purview." In my view, far from being estranged from the state, civil society presumes a degree of political pluralism that allows autonomous institutions and organizations to function in the same public domain as the state.[14]

Indeed, the best strategy available to the second liberation movement is to develop a sharp focus on the behavior of the state, especially in its uses of the public domain and in its interaction with the institutions of civil society. It is the reform of the African state—in a manner that allows autonomous organizations of civil society to exist outside the dictation of the state—that should preoccupy the minds of political activists, for instance. In this matter, an issue of great strategic value stands out: the conception of sovereignty has been appropriated and monopolized by the state while the notion of the people's sovereignty has fallen into disuse.

Rethinking the Sovereignty of African Nations

In modern African political thought, it was assumed that gaining national independence from colonial rule endowed the post-colonial state with sovereignty. The conception of sovereignty was phrased in terms of the freedom of the state from intrusive behavior from the former colonial powers. In this sense sovereignty has come to mean exclusively the state's power to be free from foreign control. The state gained its sovereignty negatively from its capacity to be independent from outside control, not positively from its affirmative relationship with the people. Despite the initial Bonapartist character of military regimes, invoking the needs of the people in such African nations as Ghana and Nigeria, African dictatorships have cared little about the concept of the people's sovereignty. On the contrary, the need for national sovereignty from foreign domination has been the excuse invoked for tyrannical excesses in the state's behavior in dealing with the people.

In objective terms, African states' autonomy has rarely been violated by outside forces — the Congo crisis of the 1960s provided one glaring, if rare, instance of an external attack on an African state's sovereignty. The greater assault has been on the people's sovereignty by state functionaries who have in many instances warded off international queries on their conduct by insisting on the state's sovereignty within its borders. Although the more thoughtful African leaders acknowledged the province of the people's sovereignty, they have tended to subordinate it to the exigencies of a strong state. Thus, both Nkrumah (see 1945, 43) and Nyerere (1968, 19) clearly treated the concept of the people's sovereignty as no more than the need for a strong government. Nigeria provides ample evidence on the violation of the people's sovereignty. Military regimes have consistently claimed to have the last word and authority on the constitutions formulated by Nigerians. For instance, moves to make military coups d'état illegal in Nigerian constitutions have been disallowed by the military.

Clearly, there is need to balance these two views of sovereignty. If

Nigerians are not able to have their will entrenched in their own constitutions, can they not ask for foreign assistance to help them achieve such a goal? If Nigerians wish to ban military rule, as I believe they currently want to, can they not ask international bodies to restrain the military from externally representing Nigeria in international forums? The expression of such views would probably be disallowed in modern Nigeria. But silencing them is the clear indication of the violation of the people's sovereignty. It is entirely possible that Nigerians may be unable to regain their civilian voice and sovereignty without help from the international community. Here then, we have a clash between an inherited notion of sovereignty from colonial rule and the older and well established concept of a people's sovereignty. In an increasingly internationalized world, there is no reason why the sovereignty that came with national independence should override the people's desire to rid themselves of dictatorship—which, if there is freedom, it is their sovereign privilege to seek. Tyranny in the post-colonial African state is a misuse of hard-won national sovereignty. More importantly, it is an assault on the people's sovereignty.

Notes

1. Meillassoux (1986, 339) defines a *gentle* as an "individual who, born and brought up in a *free-born* social milieu, is acknowledged to be free of all *servitude*."

2. Basden (1938, 249) adds the following: "It has been suggested that this Osu System is an institution going back not more than three or four generations and that, at its initiation, the 'osu' held an honorable position until the slave trade brought it into degradation, and caused it to degenerate to its present unhappy condition" (also see Isichei 1976, 47–48). The closest parallel in Western European history to the Igbo *osu* system is that of the "broken men" of medieval Ireland. This is how Maine (1888, 172–75) analyzed it: "The territory of every Irish tribe appears to have had settled on it . . . certain classes of persons whose condition was much nearer to slavery than that of [impoverished] free tribesman. . . . It consisted of *Fuidhirs*, the strangers or fugitives from other territories, men, in fact, who had broken from the original tribal bond which gave them a place in the community, and who had to obtain another as best they might in a new tribe or a new place. . . . Now, the Fuidhir tenant was exclusively a dependant of the Chief, and was through him alone connected with the Tribe. The responsibility for crime, which in the natural sense of Irish society attached to the Family or Tribe, attached in the case of the Fuidhirs, to the Chief, who in fact became to this class of

tenants that which their original tribesmen or kindred had been. Moreover, the land which they cultivated in their place of refuge was not theirs but his."

3. See Ephraim Isaac (1985) for the reduction of the original story of Noah's curse on Ham to an ideological campaign against Africans. On the Christian side of this issue, see Pontifical Commission "Iustitia et Pax" (1988, 13): "In places where missionaries were more closely dependent on political powers, it was more difficult for them to curb the colonists' attempt to dominate. At times, they even gave it encouragement on the basis of false interpretations of the Bible. For example, the interpretation that some fundamentalists gave to the curse made by Noah on his son Shem, condemned, in his grandson Canaan, to be his brothers' slave is well known (Genesis 9:24–27). They misunderstood the meaning and scope of the sacred text which referred to a certain historical situation: the difficult relations between the Canaanites and the people of Israel. They wanted to see in Shem or Canaan the ancestor of the African peoples whom they had subjugated and, consequently, they considered marked by God with an indelible inferiority which destined them to serve whites for ever."

4. I use this term in the sense in which historians have come to use it. Thus, see Rodney (1972, 56): "To the Arabs, the whole of Africa south of the Sahara was the *Bilad as Sudan*—the Land of the Blacks. The name survives today only in the Republic of the Sudan on the Nile, but references to Western Sudan in early times concern the zone presently occupied by Senegal, Mali, Upper Volta, and Niger, plus parts of Mauritania, Guinea, and Nigeria."

5. See, for example, Lugard (1912–1919, 56): "The population of North [Nigeria]—described some 60 years ago [in the 1850s] by Barth as the densest in all of Africa—had by 1900 dwindled to some 9 million, owing to intertribal war, and, above all, to the slave raids by the Fulani. . . . A rapid deterioration had . . . followed the decay of the religious zeal which had prompted the Fulani *jihad* . . . in 1900 the Fulani Emirates formed a series of separate despotisms, marked by the worst forms of wholesale slave-raiding, spoilation of the peasantry, inhuman cruelty and debased justice."

6. Abubakar Tafawa Balewa, Nigeria's first Prime Minister, has provided an ethnohistory of the slave trade which gave accounts of the internal working of slave raids in the designated slave-raiding Gwari country. The insecurities and indignities that ordinary individuals endured, and the duplicity of state officials who ruled the slave trade, were well indicated in Balewa's (1967) pseudo-novel, *Shaibu Umar*. Thus consider the following fragment from Balewa's story: "the Chief [a Fulani state official] had all his courtiers summoned. When they had assembled he said to them, 'The reason I have summoned you is this. I want you to make ready, and set out on a raid to Gwari country'. . . . When the courtiers heard what the chief had to say, they all went mad with joy . . . The reason for their delight was because . . . on a raid they would gain many cattle, and slaves as well. And then when they

returned, the Chief would give them a part of everything which they had won. Thus if a man were to capture three slaves, the Chief would take two of them, and he would be allowed to keep one" (Balewa 1967, 21–22).

7. The British colonial doctrine of indirect rule emerged in its first historical instance from negotiations on power-sharing between Frederick Lugard, representing the British, the new conquerors of Hausaland, and the Fulani aristocracy, its old conquerors. The outcome was that the Fulani remained the direct rulers of Hausaland while the British emerged as its indirect rulers. What was at issue here was not the straight-forward adoption and respect for local traditions. In Northern Nigeria the British were operating on the basis of dual conquest. The British conquest of Northern Nigeria did not terminate the Fulani conquest of these areas a century earlier. Rather, in its pristine Northern Nigerian format, indirect rule was a theory of dual conquest in which the newest conquerors recognized the rights, albeit now circumscribed, of the previous conquerors and rulers of these lands. It involved power-sharing between the old and new conquerors in an arrangement that recognized the system of government devised by the old conquerors as a proper basis for their mutual administration of the conquered lands (see M.G. Smith 1960, 203; also Perham 1963, xl).

8. The transformation of the individual in the course of Western history from a lowly status of a *subject* in the medieval world to his empowerment as a *citizen* in modern democracies has been well captured by Walter Ullmann (1966): "the historical recognition of the vital difference between the individual as a mere subject and the individual as a citizen is long overdue. The two conceptions, subject and citizen, reflect and epitomize . . . the basic standing of the individual in the public sphere. . . . In a rough sense one may well say that for the larger part of the Middle Ages it was the individual as a subject that dominated the scene, while in the later Middle Ages and in the modern period the subject was gradually supplanted by the citizen."

9. Horowitz (1991) has suggested that Nigeria's innovation and flirtation with the concept of *federal character*, which compels contestants for power to look beyond their ethnic base (see Ekeh and Osaghae 1989), may be helpful in the construction of a constitution for South Africa.

10. See Mamdani (1992, 314): "Whereas state-controlled broadcast media coexisted with state supervised print media in the colonial period, both came under state control under the new [postcolonial] regime" in many African nations.

11. Richard Joseph's (1987) idea of "prebendal politics" may well be related to this notion of ownership of the state. Certainly, Nigerian military rulers have behaved along the ways that Joseph discussed. Even more alarming is the wholesale commercialization of the bureaucracy, with most civil servants no longer relying on salaries but on bribery and other gains from their impoverished offices.

12. As far as I am aware, the term "second liberation" was first used, with respect to the democratization of African politics, by a conference on "The State and the Crisis in Africa: In Search of a Second Liberation" organized by the Dag Hammarskjold Foundation and attended by participants from many African countries and Sweden (see Dag Hammarskjold Foundation 1992). This conference followed a seminar (with the same title) which was directed by Goran Hyden and Walter Bgoya and convened by the Dag Hammarskjold Foundation in 1986 in Uppsala, Sweden, to mark the 25th anniversary of the death, in September 1961, of the Secretary General of the United Nations while on a peace mission to Central Africa. The term has since been widely used in the literature on democratization (see e.g., Diamond 1992).

13. Ken Saro-Wiwa's struggles for autonomy for his Ogoni people and his death at the hands of the Nigerian Government should recall the memories of an earlier hero of struggles in the same region against the might of an arrogant state apparatus. Isaac Buro, a "maverick" Ijo student leader, led a futile movement to secede from Eastern Nigeria in the 1950s, declaring the independence of the Ijos, neighbors of Saro-Wiwa's people, the Ogoni, on the grounds that his people were oppressed and cheated of their oil revenues. He too was killed by government forces.

14. Bayart (1986) does offer a definition of civil society that places the state and civil society's institutions in the same political space, allowing society thereby to restrain the state's totalitarian tendencies: Borrowing from Fossaert (1981), Bayart (1986) defines civil society as "'society in its relations with the state' or, more precisely, as the process by which society seeks to 'breach' and counteract the simultaneous 'totalisation' unleashed by the state" (Bayart 1986, 111). He adds, "Civil society exists only in so far as there is self-consciousness of its existence and of its opposition to the state" (Bayart 1986, 117; see also Ekeh 1994).

References

Achebe, Chinua. 1959. *Things Fall Apart*. London: Heinemann.
Azikiwe, Nnamdi. 1937[1968]. *Renascent Africa*. London: Frank Cass.
Baba, Ahmad. c. 1622. "The Mi'raj: a Legal Treatise on Slavery by Ahmad Baba." Translated and edited by Bernard Barbour and Michelle Jacobs. In John Ralph Willis (ed.), *Slaves and Slavery in Muslim Africa*. Volume I: Islam and the Ideology of Enslavement: 125–38. London: Frank Cass.
Balewa, Abubakar Tafawa. 1967. *Shaibu Umar*. English Translation by M. Hiskett. London: Longmans.

Basden, G. T. 1938[1966]. *Niger Ibos.* London: Frank Cass.
Bayart, Jean-Francois. 1986. "Civil Society in Africa." In Patrick Chabal (ed.), *Political Domination in Africa*: 106–25. Cambridge, England: Cambridge University Press.
Beneviste, E. 1969. *Le Vocabulaire des Institutions Indo-Europeennes,* Ed. de Minuit, 2 vols.
Bohannan, P. 1963. *Social Anthropology.* New York: Holt, Rhinehart & Winston.
Bradbury, R. E. 1973. *Benin Studies,* Peter Morton-Williams, ed. London: Oxford University Press.
Bratton, Michael. 1989. "Beyond the State: Civil Society and Associational Life in Africa." *World Politics,* 41, 3: 407–29.
Connah, Graham. 1987. *African Civilizations: Precolonial Cities and States in Tropical Africa: an Archaeological Perspective.* New York: Cambridge University Press.
Dag Hammarskjold Foundation. 1992. *The State and the Crisis in Africa: In Search of a Second Liberation.* Report of the Mweya Conference in Uganda, May 12–17, 1990. Uppsala [Sweden]: Dag Hammarskjold Foundation.
Davidson, Basil. 1992. *The Black Man's Burden. Africa and the Curse of the Nation-State.* New York: Times Books.
Diamond, Larry. 1992. "The Second Liberation (Transformation from Autocracy to Democracy)." *Africa Report,* 37 (November-December): 38–41.
DuBois, W. E. B. 1945[1975]. *Color and Democracy: Colonies and Peace.* Millwood, N.Y.: Kraus-Thomson.
Egharevba, Jacob. 1934[1968]. *A Short History of Benin.* Ibadan: Ibadan University Press.
Ekeh, Peter P. 1975. "Colonialism and the Two Publics in Africa: A Theoretical Statement." *Comparative Studies in Society and History,* 17(1 January): 91–112.
———. 1976. "Benin and Thebes: Elementary Forms of Civilization." In Werner Muensterberger, Aaron H. Esman, and L. Bryce Boyer, (eds.), *The Psychoanalytic Study of Society,* Volume 7: 65–93. New Haven and London: Yale University Press.
———. 1990. "Social Anthropology and Two Contrasting Uses of Tribalism in Africa." *Comparative Studies in Society and History,* 32: 660–700.
———. 1994. "Historical and Cross-Cultural Contexts of Civil Society in Africa." In USAID, *Civil Society, Democracy, and Development in Africa: Proceedings of a Workshop for Development Practitioners*: A21–A45. Washington, D.C.: USAID.
Ekeh, Peter P. and Eghosa E. Osaghae, eds. 1989. *Federal Character and Federalism in Nigeria.* Ibadan: Heinemann Educational Books.
Fadipe, N. A. 1970. *The Sociology of the Yoruba.* Edited with an Introduction by Francis Olu Okediji and Oladejo O. Okediji. Ibadan: Ibadan University Press.

Federal Republic of Nigeria. 1978. *Land Use Decree*. Lagos: Federal Ministry of Information, Printing Division.

Fifth Pan-African Congress. 1945. "Declaration to the Colonial Peoples of the World." [Written by Kwame Nkrumah. Approved and adopted by the Pan African Congress held in Manchester, England, October 15th–21st, 1945.] Reprinted in pages 44–45 in Nkrumah, Kwame. 1945[1962]. *Towards Colonial Freedom. Africa in the Struggle against World Imperialism*. London: Panaf.

Fodio, Uthman dan. c.1803. [2] "The Wathiqat ahl al-Sudan: A Manifesto of the Fulani Jihad." Translated and edited by A. D. H. Bivar, *Journal of African History*, 2, 2 (1961): 235–43.

———. c.1811. "Tanbihu'l Ikhwan." Translated and edited by H. R. Palmer, *Journal of the African Society*, 13 (1913–14): 411–14; 14 (1914–15): 53–9, 185–92.

Fossaert, Robert. 1981. *La Société. Le Etats*. Paris: Seuil.

Green, M. M. 1937 [1964]. *Ibo Village Affairs*. New York: Praeger.

Hilliard, Constance. 1985. "Zuhur al-Basatin and Ta'rikh al- Turubbe: Some Legal and Ethical Aspects of Slavery In the Sudan as Seen in the Works of Shaykh Musa Kamara." In John Ralph Willis (ed.), *Slaves and Slavery in Muslim Africa. Volume I: Islam and the Ideology of Enslavement*: 160–81. London: Frank Cass.

Horowitz, Donald L. 1991. *A Democratic South Africa? Constitutional Engineering in a Divided Society*. Berkeley: University of California Press.

Isaac, Ephraim. 1985. "Genesis, Judaism, and the Sons of Ham." In John Ralph Willis (ed.), *Slaves and Slavery in Muslim Africa. Volume I: Islam and the Ideology of Enslavement*: 75–91. London: Frank Cass.

Isichei, Elizabeth. 1976. *A History of the Igbo People*. New York: St. Martins Press.

Jahoda, Gustav. 1961. *White Man. A Study of the Attitudes of Africans to Europeans in Ghana before Independence*. London: Oxford University Press.

Johnson, S. 1921[1966]. *The History of the Yorubas: from the Earliest Times to the Beginning of the British Protectorate*. London: Routledge & K. Paul.

Joseph, Richard. 1987. *Democracy and Prebendal Politics in Nigeria*. Cambridge: Cambridge University Press. Routledge and K. Paul.

Kilminster, Richard. 1993. "Praxis." In William Outhwaite and Tom Bottomore (eds.), *The Blackwell Dictionary of Twentieth-Century Social Thought*: 507–09. Oxford: Blackwell Publications.

Law, Robin. 1977. *The Oyo Empire, c1·600–1836: A West African Imperialism in the Era of the Atlantic Slave Trade*. Oxford: Clarendon Press.

Lawyers Committee for Human Rights. 1992. *The Nigerian Police Force: A Culture of Impunity*. Washington, D.C.: Lawyers Committee for Human Rights.

Lovejoy, Paul E. 1991. "Foreword." In Claude Meillassoux, *The Anthropology of Slavery, The Womb of Iron and Gold*: 7–8. Chicago: The University of Chicago Press.

Lovejoy, Paul E. and Jan S. Hogendorn. 1993. *Slow Death for Slavery. The Course of Abolition in Northern Nigeria, 1897–1936*. Cambridge: Cambridge University Press.

Lugard, Flora L. (Lady). 1906 [1964]. *A Tropical Dependency. An Outline of the Ancient History of the Western Sudan with an Account of the Modern Settlement of Northern Nigeria*. London: Frank Cass & Co.

Lugard, Sir F. D. 1912–1919. *Lugard and the Amalgamation of Nigeria. A Documentary Record*. Compiled and Introduced by A. H. M. Kirk-Greene. London: Frank Cass, 1968.

———. 1922[1964]. *The Dual Mandate in British Tropical Africa*. London: Frank Cass & Co.

Maine, Sumner Henry. 1888. *Lectures on the Early History of Institutions*. New York: Henry Holt & Company.

Mamdani, Mahmood. 1992. "Africa: Democratic Theory and Democratic Struggles: Clash between Ideas and Realities?" *Dissent*, 39 (Summer): 312–18.

Marshall, T. H. 1950. *Citizenship and Social Class and Other Essays*. Cambridge [England]: Cambridge University Press.

Meillassoux, Claude. 1986 [1991]. *The Anthropology of Slavery, The Womb of Iron and Gold*. Chicago: The University of Chicago Press.

Morton-Williams, Peter. 1960. "The Yoruba Ogboni Cult in Oyo." *Africa*, 30:362–74.

Nkrumah, Kwame. 1945 [1962]. *Towards Colonial Freedom. Africa in the Struggle against World Imperialism*. London: Panaf.

Nyong'o, Anyang Peter, ed. 1987. *Popular Struggles for Democracy in Africa*. Atlantic Highlands, N.J.: Zed Books.

Nyerere, Julius K. 1968. *Freedom and Socialism. Uhuru na ujamaa. A Selection from Writings and Speeches*. 1965–1967. New York: Oxford University Press.

Ojike, Mbonu. 1946. *My Africa*. New York: The John Day Company.

Perham, Margery. 1965. "Introduction to the Fifth Edition." In Lord Lugard, 1922. *The Dual Mandate in British Tropical Africa*: xxvii-xlix. Mamden: Archon Books.

Pontifical Commission "Iustitia et Pax". 1988. *The Church and Racism*. Rome: Vatican City.

Rodney, Walter. 1972. *How Europe Underdeveloped Africa*. Washington, D.C.: Howard University Press.

Sklar, Richard L. 1987. "Developmental Democracy." *Comparative Studies in Society and History*, 29(4, October): 686–714.

Smith, M. G. 1960. *Government in Zazzau 1800–1950*. London: Oxford University Press.

Uchendu, Victor Chikezie. 1965. *The Igbo of Southeast Nigeria*. New York: Holt, Rhinehart & Winston.
Ullmann, Walter. 1966. *The Relevance of Medieval Ecclesiastical History: An Inaugural Lecture*. Cambridge: Cambridge University Press.
Usman, Yusufu Bala, ed. 1982. *Political Repression in Nigeria*. Zaria: Gaskiya Corporation.
Williams, F. R. A. 1976. *Report of the Constitution Drafting Committee Containing the Draft Constitution Volume I*. Lagos: Federal Ministry of Information, Printing Division.
Willis, John Ralph. 1985. "Jihad and the Ideology of Enslavement." In John Ralph Willis (ed.), *Slaves and Slavery in Muslim Africa. Volume I: Islam and the Ideology of Enslavement*: 16–26. London: Frank Cass.

5

LEGITIMIZING DEMOCRACY: THE ROLE OF THE HIGHLY EDUCATED ELITE

Paul A. Beckett

Two things are striking in the puzzle of Nigeria's conflicted relationship with the goal of democracy. One is the persistence and the strength of the impulse toward democracy. But the other is the weakness of support for democracy, once created and in place. It is these two phenomena together that result in the pendulum pattern of alternation between military and democratic regimes that is so characteristic of Nigerian political history.

Of these contrary impulses, the one toward democracy is far more easily documented. The effort to reconstruct constitutional government and democracy began in the very ruins of the First Republic (Elaigwu 1986, 76–88). Less than ten months after the end of the Civil War, on October 1 1970, General Gowon announced his regime's commitment to create democratic government by 1976. In more than 25 years since that commitment, a democratic government has been in place only four years. But conversely, fewer than four of those more than 25 years have not been characterized by a formal commitment to create and install democratic government. In no other African country—and few anywhere—has so much collective effort and money been expended to create democracy.[1] Meanwhile, over all the years, military rule itself has never been fully institutionalized, and has never claimed any but transitional legitimacy. And paradoxically, progress toward the creation of democracy, and handover to it, has become a principal legitimating criterion of military government.

More difficult to pin down is the second side of this central Nigerian paradox: the abrupt abandonment of democracy. The issue is confused, since the barrel of the gun is the instrument. Yet it seems true, as Nigerian military leaders or their representatives have often asserted (e.g., Kazaure 1993; Garba 1989), that Nigeria's successful military coups (both antidemocratic and intra-military), with the partial and debatable exception of 1993, have been in line with consensus public opinion. In understanding Nigerian military coups the important analytic problem is less the military actions than the background of public opinion that surrounds and underlies them.

This side of the Nigerian paradox of democracy is indeed puzzling. Why did informed public opinion begin to abandon (and un-legitimate) the Second Republic—after prodigious effort to create it—well before the flawed 1983 elections (Diamond 1995, 438)? Why was "the public" so willing to have the baby of the Second Republic structures and constitution thrown out with the dirty bathwater of the 1983 elections, even though remedial actions could have been devised (e.g., Oyediran 1989, 180–81)? And why, a decade later, was the public reaction to the Babangida regime's annulment of the presidential elections of June 12 1993 sufficiently mixed as to permit a divided and politically weakened military to cling successfully to power, and to co-opt a number of respected civilian members of the Nigerian elite and intelligentsia (Diamond 1995, 462)? Why was there so little protest as all the rest of the democratic office holders of the Third Republic (some 5,000 of them, their own democratic legitimation in no way based on the annulled June 12 election) were dismissed with the final Abacha takeover in November 1993?

These events bring to the fore questions of legitimacy. On the one hand, military government clearly has not established a more than custodial basis of legitimacy: one which is conditional and of limited duration (Diamond 1995, 418). On the other hand, even a superficial reading of events, as above, suggests both weakness and conditionality in the legitimacy which surrounds democratic constitutions and institutions.

These are the problems I will address. My underlying hypothesis is the assumption that Nigeria's highly educated elite has played (and continues to play) a critical role in shaping and expressing the "public opinion" that is so often cited in discussion of political events in Nigeria. The essay is difficult in that the shaping impacts of Nigeria's intelligentsia and bureaucratic and professional elites on the events since independence have been generally and sadly neglected in the literature, both because successive scholarly approaches have directed attention elsewhere but also—and ironically—because accepted history has been determined by and large by this same elite. The central hypothesis of the essay is that Nigeria's highly educated, public sector-oriented elite, or "intelligentsia," has played a central historical role in promoting and designing democracy—but also in precipitate flight from democracy and reversion to military rule. To provide a basis for this hypothesis, and a backdrop to a consequent interpretation of the failure of the Second and Third Republics, it will be useful to present a brief social history of this elite.[2]

The Highly Educated Elite in Post-Independence Nigeria

The relatively brief history of Nigeria's highly educated, public-sector oriented elite is inseparable from that of the Nigerian post-colonial state. While the origins of Nigeria's highly educated elite may be traced deep into the colonial period itself (Coleman 1958; Ayandele 1974), this summary will take up the story in the colonial twilight of the 1950s. As British colonialism carried out a rapid withdrawal, leaving the colonial administrative state as its principal heritage to independent Nigeria, two putative ruling elite groups emerged. A historically shallow democratic overlay over the deeper reality of the colonial administrative state was rapidly elaborated through several constitutional stages and a "political class" as it has been called ever since quickly came forward. The new political leaders were the official representatives of the independent-Nigeria-to-be, forming a highly visible and officially designated successor elite to the British "colonial masters."

Somewhat less visible was the second elite group, the "senior service" elite which took over the colonial administrative state through the 1950s and the first years after independence. This elite—the focus of this essay—may be designated the administrative, or bureaucratic, or "structural" (Post and Vickers 1973) elite.

In their historical (and social) origins, these two elite groups were closely bound together (Coleman 1958; Post and Vickers 1973, 43; Paden 1986, 230–45). By the early 1960s, however, a sharper separation was apparent between the political elite and the administrative elite (Post and Vickers 1973, 44ff.).

At the time, political analysts—no doubt correctly—perceived the "political elite" as "rooted more deeply in Nigerian society, and . . . much larger in total numbers" than the administrative elite (Post and Vickers 1973, 48). This changed, however, as the great majority of graduates and professionals emerging from the new institutions of higher education chose administrative roles within the public sector institutions where opportunity, income, status and security all were excellent in an era of both Nigerianization and rapid growth and diversification of the state apparatus. Recruitment of this administrative or "structural" elite was based heavily on high educational qualifications. The rapid development and expansion of universities from 1962 meant that, by the later 1960s, university education (or equivalent professional training) provided the essential definition of the elite.

The highly educated elite was socialized, starting with secondary and higher education, into values of "impartiality, honesty and efficiency, the observance of proper procedures and the maintenance of a hierarchy of responsibility" (Post and Vickers 1973, 44–45). Van den Berghe, writing from research done at the University of Ibadan in 1968–69 (van den Berghe 1973, 59–60) likened the Nigerian preparation of its new bureaucratic elite to a mandarinate:

> The University is in fact training a bureaucratic elite that resembles the mandarin class of imperial China.... The University, as the main source for the country's bureaucratic mandarinate, molds not only the minds of its students, but also their entire life style. The University sets the pace for the emergent class culture of the elite; ... The important fact about this elite ... is that they are not a land-owning aristocracy or a capital-owning bourgeoisie, but controllers of the bureaucratic machinery.

Meanwhile, the ugly political warfare of the 1950s and early 1960s had led to the rapid development, in elite culture, of a stereotypical view of politicians along the lines of Achebe's Chief Nanga (*Man of the People*, Achebe 1966): likely to be a renegade elite in terms of personal background; crude, selfish, corrupt; manipulating violence and ethnicity to personal and partisan benefit. In the same book the highly educated elite is represented, in an enduring elite self-image, by Odili: an honest, moral being, amazed and disgusted by the discovered reality of Chief Nanga's corruption and moral baseness, and semi-helpless in the face of Nanga's control and manipulation of political power.

The political overlay over the older administrative state was removed by the coup of January 15 1966, as the politicians were sent home and all of the representative institutions were dissolved. The political class was eliminated as the active ruling elite, and replaced by a thin veneer of politically inexperienced military officers playing roles in the "military" government, essentially in alliance with the broad base of higher civil servants. Forrest (1993, 47) remarks:

> With military cover and protection, [the senior civil servants] assumed political as well as administrative control of the civil service.... After the civil

war, the military, who had no plans of their own, relied heavily on civil servants to formulate and execute policy. Bureaucratic power was popularly referred to as the rule of the super-permanent secretaries.

Adamolekun (1985, 166) makes a similar point:

> Under military rule, the key feature was the emergence of political technocrats whose role in the policy making process was much more significant than that of senior career administrators under British-style parliamentary government.

It is important to note that this situation of military/bureaucratic rule, so often described as anomaly or aberration, was really not at all anomalous in the longer history of Nigeria (Beckett 1987, 111). To the contrary, the situation of military rule bore a very considerable resemblance to the relatively benign and selectively consultative authoritarianism of post-World War II British colonialism. In this sense, the pattern of military-civil rule without politicians and without formal structures of political input was literally neo-colonialist, representing a resumption of the longer and deeper history of the colonial administrative state.

The era between the coups of 1966 and the resumption of democracy in 1979 marked the apogee of the role of the highly educated public sector elite. The same era was the apogee of the Nigerian public sector with which the elite is so closely associated. It was this elite group, specifically higher civil servants, that played the major role in saving and reshaping the Nigerian federation in the difficult days of 1966–1967 (Elaigwu 1986, 90 and passim). The creation of the 12-state federal structure in May 1967 inaugurated a major expansion of public sector structures and of public service personnel. With the end of the civil war in 1970, oil began to flow, and with the oil pricing revolution of 1974 Nigeria became (temporarily) a rich poor country. (See Richard Joseph (1978) on the results!)

The period from the end of the civil war and the Second Republic saw a vast expansion of the public sector (public sector employment tripled between 1973 and 1981: Forrest 1993, 147), and of ambitions for Nigerian development (as expressed, for instance, by the *Third National Development Plan 1975–80*; see Schatz 1977, 39–46; Elaigwu 1986, 162–63). The power of the Nigerian state and the revenues it could distribute and apply were meant to be the driving force. Each state (12 states, and after February 1976, 19) took on the accoutrements of Regionhood, while a broad range of infrastructural investments, together with direct economic activities through parastatals, were undertaken at both state and federal levels. Meanwhile, through indigenization and "nationalist nurture-capitalism" the historically underdeveloped private capitalist sector was to be developed (as well as controlled) by the state (Schatz 1977).

In education, in 1974 General Gowon committed the country to the goal of Universal Primary Education (UPE). Meanwhile, a huge expansion of higher education, in particular university education, had occurred already and now accelerated, producing a flood of manpower for the "mandarinate." For instance, enrollments in the Arts and in the Social Sciences grew some 800 percent between 1962–63 (in five universities) and 1978–79 (in 13 universities; National Universities Commission 1992.)

In terms of status and economic rewards the public sector elite prospered during the period. The distribution of oil wealth through the huge "Udoji" public sector salary awards in 1974 particularly benefitted senior staff (Schatz 1977, 46; Forrest 1993, 143–44). For a period (which was to prove brief!) the Nigerian bureaucratic and professional elite enjoyed incomes and a standard of living nearly commensurate with the middle class standard of western countries. But within Nigeria, this "middle class" clearly formed part of the Nigerian post-independence upper class.

Politicians and politics, be it noted, were officially absent from the scene during the whole period of military rule from 1966 until the creation of the Second Republic neared. But was the administrative state and its burgeoning public sector of parastatals, utilities, and educational institutions, without politics, and without representation of Nigeria's complex social mosaic? Inevitably, the "authoritarian" administrative state that was the heritage of colonialism had been subtly adapted. The traumas of the First Republic and its tragic aftermath had created exquisite sensitivities to the importance of ethnic-regional balance in what nominally would have been administrative, technical or professional appointments made solely on the basis of merit. Effectively, members of the public sector elite operated, and were viewed by an alert public, as representatives—of home communities, ethnic groups, religious groups, and states (Graf 1988, 204; Beckett 1987, 95). The "federal character" that was to appear in the 1979 constitution (Ekeh and Osaghae 1989; Oyovbaire 1984, 243–44) was less a new idea than a codification of practices developed since independence and especially since the establishment of military rule.

The new federalism of 12 states created on May 27 1967 had saved Nigeria as a political unit. In the 1970s, under military/bureaucratic rule, there was a steady political centralization from the base of the originally decentralized federalism designed in the 1950s (Oyovbaire 1984; Elaigwu 1986, 159–65, 1988, 187; Graf 1988, 47–49). But, at the same time, the evolving revenue allocation system funnelled petronaira on a guaranteed-formula basis to the 12 and then 19 states. By 1975–76, 9 of the 12 states received more than 85 percent of total state revenues from federal sources, mainly through the statutory revenue allocation system (Elaigwu 1986, 164). Viewed from the standpoint of the federal center, the increasing dependence of states on federally distributed shares of the country's oil revenues was a major element of federal centralization (see Suberu, Tables 1 and 2, this volume). But, viewed from the standpoint of the states, one can see in retrospect that the oil wealth distributed through the system of statutory allocation, taken together with the principles of informal representation that were to be codified as "federal character," provided a significant degree of informal *consociationalism* to the working of Nigerian federalism, providing a guarantee of relative equality, autonomy and security to each of the states (Jinadu 1985; see also Onyeoziri 1989).

Thus, during the years of military/bureaucratic rule, the administrative state that had been inherited from British colonialism not only was enormously expanded—it was also changed. With Nigerianization and the development of "federal character" balancing, the administrative state was subtly completed and connected to the states and localities, and was given its own pseudo-political representative dimension. The highly educated elite was at the center of the process. Members were amply coopted by the uniform wearers: as representatives, as expert professionals, and as Platonic wise men. The elite participated widely in the evaluation and development of policy (Onido 1989). The oil wealth that came in after 1973–74 provided the basis for a sense of nearly unlimited possibility and, while it was never expressed as a single coherent vision, the ambitions marked out in economic and infrastructural development, in education and health, and in the improvement of individual lives—all driven, or at least led, by the public sector—amounted to a Nigerian vision of "integral state" (Young 1994).

This quietly momentous period was the context of the redesign of democracy which occurred between 1975 and 1979. Political democracy was to be the culmination and completion of the process of recovery from the nadir of First Republic chaos and Civil War and—at the deepest level—from the humiliation and repression of the colonial experience. As I will note later, the intelligentsia essentially designed and wrote the new (1979) constitution and it was approved and promulgated in "elite consensus" (Dudley 1982, 161).

But to what extent was the constitution and the coming democracy truly rooted in the political culture of the highly-educated elite? In general, solid data on elite opinion are sadly lacking. However, insights of interest are provided by data on Nigeria university student opinion collected in the early 1970s, as the developments summarized above were gathering steam. (Data from a recent partial replication of the work from the 1970s are summarized in the final section, below.)

The Political Culture of an Elite-in-Training: Ambivalent Democrats

James O'Connell and I carried out a major study of Nigerian university student opinion between 1970 and 1973 (Beckett and O'Connell 1977). This generation of students was among the first large wave of university graduates produced by Nigeria's new universities. The largest proportion of the generation of students that we surveyed took up public sector positions following graduation, and have moved into senior ranks in the 1980s and 1990s (Zartman 1983, 7).

Our research identified basic values completely consistent with the characterizations of the bureaucratic public sector elite cited above (Post and Vickers 1973; van den Berghe 1973). Education is highly valued, and technical and administrative skills are seen as those that have made the greatest contribution to Nigeria. Careers in the public sector—not the private—were the ambition of the great majority of the students. Students valued nationalism extremely highly, while acknowledging fully the strength of subnational loyalties within their own personal identities (1977, 69).

Deeper political values are also consistent with van den Berghe's characterization of "mandarin" elite members. The state itself is highly valued, and students in general do not fear government, feeling that weak government is a much greater danger than strong government. Order and unity are the supreme positive values, while disorder and disunity (read, ethnicity) lead as negatives (Beckett and O'Connell 1977, Chapter 5). The great majority of the university students seemed essentially Hobbesian, fearing above all an absence of unity and order, and looking to government to provide order and unity.

Some social characteristics that emerged from our research are important for the arguments made in this essay. Students' sense of connection to families and to home communities is very strongly expressed. Most came from small rural communities and farming families (Beckett and O'Connell 1975). Strikingly, despite their objective personal separation from home communities (both cultural and physical) the majority of students felt as much members of home communities as peers who had not had education and who lived there permanently (1977, 65). A majority feel that in the make-up of their personal identity home community is even more important than Nigeria (1977, 69). Respect for family and local leaders, in the local context, is pronounced, and the students consistently felt strong sympathy for the economic problems of the rural communities and their members (1977, 131–32).

Were these elites-in-training elitist? In what was probably the single most important finding with specific relevance for democracy, we found that in strong majority (about 75 percent or more) the university students agreed that "the masses in African countries are not yet capable of making rational choices in elections for national political office" (1977, 154). In interpreting these findings, my colleague and I noted the attitudes of respect and affection for relatives and elders of rural communities, and suggested that the students feel that outside the local community, the "masses" are removed from their proper sphere. We suggested (1977, 155) that for the students, "the business of pan-Nigeria is the business of 'elites,'" i.e., the highly educated.

Responses to direct questions on democracy produced patterns of ambivalence and greater diversity of opinion than on most other problems we examined. In the abstract, and as an aspiration for Nigeria, the university students were generally strong democrats. Our surveys were done after General Gowon's October 1 1970 announcement that the country would return to "normal constitutional government," and before his announcement on October 1 1974, that "the target date of 1976 is unrealistic." Already, the military (in power since January 1966) was unpopular and democratic government was the only practicable alternative. After the Gowon regime reneged on its promise, university students and lecturers, together with journalists who themselves were generally recent university graduates, were among the groups most vocal and effective in generating opposition to continued military rule and in demanding democracy (Falola and Ihonvbere 1985, 21).

However, when our survey instruments put democracy in competition with other values the picture became complex (see 1977, Chapter 6). On the one hand, support for democracy was substantial. Around half of respondents considered a democratic form of government more important than economic development (if one had to choose). Remarkably, a strongly democratic minority (one-third or more) ranked democracy as a value ahead of political stability. Students split about evenly on the question of whether a "governing elite elected in free and fair elections" is more important than a "competent governing elite"—and we knew the latter to be highly valued by these "mandarins" in training.

However, the strongly-democratic minority became small indeed when democracy was put in competition with "national unity" (1977, 158–59). Furthermore, the personnel of democracy—the politicians—were persistently ranked as the lowest of the low in terms of the contribution they had made to Nigeria, and were strongly associated with the evils of ethnicity, disunity and corruption.

An important insight into the meaning of democracy for the students was provided as students were asked which among a number of criteria was most important in defining what is "democratic" (1977, 156). Interestingly, "honest government in the interests of the people" was ranked first of five alternatives by a majority of students. Meanwhile, "competing politicians and political parties" received last place rankings from the largest number of students. Thus, the majority of students seemed inclined to define democracy by its results (good government) rather than its processes (competitive elections).

Support for democracy, therefore, was conditioned by a number of negative associations (above all, with politicians, and through them to disunity, ethnicity and corruption). Only a small minority valued democracy above the central order/unity constellation of political values. Students seemed by nature oriented far more positively toward the administrative dimension of the post-colonial state. The vast majority entertained strong doubts as to the ability of "the masses" to understand the national issues on which national electoral campaigns are supposed to turn.

Yet it is important not to understate the "residual" (as we called it, 162), support for democracy among a majority of students, and the strength of stronger and less conditioned support by a significant minority of more resolute democrats. In a final test, my colleague and I asked the students to assume the premise (which we knew that most accepted)—that the masses are not able to choose rationally in national elections—and then to choose one of three alternatives: full democracy with all its risks; indirect election; and benign technocratic rule (1977, 160). We were surprised to find that about as many students chose full democracy (with all its risks) as chose the indirect alternative, while only a small proportion chose benign technocratic rule (1977, 160).

Overall, our work on democracy resulted in a picture of ambivalence. In a summation that seems to describe later events we stated (1977, 163):

> There is considerable support among university students for a return to electoral democracy, but we think it is likely that the structure of ambivalence that underlines this . . . means that that position is prey to circumstances. At

the moment democracy benefits from its own absence, and from the general unpopularity of the military regime. These factors undoubtedly help shift the "balance of ambivalence" toward support. But one must keep in mind the negative value patterns, in particular, the strong association of democracy with ethnic division and with corrupt and ignorant politicians. If circumstances should render these associations more relevant, then the "balance of ambivalence" could shift massively in the other direction, with probably only a very small hard-core minority of true democrats remaining to support democracy.

A Cycle of Ambivalence: 1975–1983

The 1979 constitution expressed and codified a vision of a maximal Nigerian "integral state": a powerful and pervasive state based on popular sovereignty and dedicated to democracy and social justice and to the security and welfare of the people. The constitution presents a picture of a state deeply engaged in both economic and social development within a diverse but unified Nigerian society (Federal Republic of Nigeria 1979, Chapter II and passim).

The 1979 Constitution was designed in elite consensus as it was put by a leading member of the 49-member Constitution Drafting Committee or CDC) that wrote it (Dudley 1982, 161; Adamolekun 1985, 20ff; for the limits of "elite consensus" in the process see Falola and Ihonvbere 1985, 35–44). Together with the subsequent work of the Constituent Assembly (dominated according to Dudley (1982, 161) by the business-commercial elite, as the CDC was by the intelligentsia), and a remarkable "great debate" via symposia and newspaper media (Ofonagoro 1977), the process of constitutional formulation and approval seemed to involve at one level or another a large proportion of Nigeria's educated populace.

This extraordinary period of collective reflection, and debate (so suggestive of the summer of 1787 in Philadelphia), produced an ingenious plan of constitutional engineering designed to prevent the ethnic/regional sectionalism that was such a prominent and disastrous feature of the First Republic. If the central goal of the U.S. constitutional fathers was a "non-tyrannical republic" (Dahl 1956, 10), then the Nigerian "wise men" of the CDC aimed above all at the creation of a non-tribalist republic, breaking free from the "bitter shadow" (Achebe's phrase; cited by Kirk-Greene 1971, 6) of the First Republic experience. The central strategy of constitutional engineering aimed at providing rewards for national political behavior, and punishments for sectional (ethnic, regional, religious) political behavior.

The constitution's main thrusts are very much in line with the values and concerns we identified among our university student respondents. The students regarded ethnic antagonism, disunity, and disorder as the supreme ills that could befall African societies. We saw that students also held profoundly negative views of "politicians." The 1979 constitution was replete with attempts to mandate via constitutional provisions good politicians, and integrative national political parties. Central to the strategy was the powerful Federal Electoral Commission or FEDECO, meant to operate as a politically neutral policeman and arbiter of the process of competitive politics (Constitution Chapters V and VI; Schedule Three; Graf 1988, 64). Clearly FEDECO was expected to be the elite's enforcer of politicians' good behavior.

Between 1975 and 1979, therefore, the highly-educated elite played a historic role of leadership to design a new, putatively permanent, democracy for Nigeria. The democracy reflected values and concerns shared widely within the elite, and the constitution as it emerged from the process was the expression of "elite consensus." Undoubtedly, to most, democracy seemed to represent a completion of the Nigerian state in its most ambitious conception. It is noteworthy that the democracy was to be full, complete, and unconditional (with allowance made for the watchdog provisions referred to above), with competitive election of all significant power holders from top to bottom (1,911 offices in all were elective).

It seems clear that there was broad and solid support for the Second Republic system of democracy among the Nigerian highly educated elite at the time of the constitution's promulgation in 1979.

Yet less than four years later "elite consensus" in support of the democratic system was in ruins. Sharp erosion of this support was clear even *before* the 1983 elections that were the official explanation for suspension of democracy (Diamond 1995, 438).

The problem of this essay is to account for this apparent massive and swift shift in opinion. Can it adequately be accounted for by a general failure of the strategy of constitutional engineering that had been devised by the CDC and the Constituent Assembly? I do not believe so. The constitutional engineering of 1979 proved a qualified success. The central strategy of providing political incentives to nation-wide alliance building, and disincentives to First Republic-style ethnic/regional appeal or mobilization, resulted in significant cross-region patterns of competition in the 1979 elections (Beckett 1987, 101–106; Diamond 1995, 468–69; Ollawa 1989, 145; Bienen 1987, 229–42). The 1983 elections were marred by a very significant increase in rigging and violence over 1979 levels (Diamond 1995,

436–37; Falola and Ihonvbere 1985, 210–11). Undoubtedly these had the effect of distorting electoral effects, especially increasing old-style regional ethnic/regional electoral domination in some areas (e.g., 91 percent in Sokoto for NPN and 95 percent in Ogun for UPN in the Presidential election: Falola and Ihonvbere 1985, 220). Recognizing their flaws, the 1983 elections should also be viewed as having extended the 1979 "progress" in terms of inter-regional, inter-ethnic alliance and crossover and thus the "national" quality of party competition (Beckett 1987, 103–104).

But such "successes" (and such a disengaged level of analysis) held little relevance for public opinion. To the contrary, the actual experience of democracy in action from 1978 through 1983 had had the effect of invoking the deepest negative values we identified in our study of university student opinion and culture. In this perspective, the new politicians of the Second Republic seemed to the observant public sector elite and its intelligentsia every bit as bad as the old ones of the First Republic. While at the national level of aggregation Second Republic electoral politics might be said to have turned less exclusively on ethnic/regional considerations than in the First Republic, the building blocks of politics on the ground were far less changed, and little reformed. Individual corruption, which had grown alarmingly in scale and character during the final years of the Gowon regime, now achieved hitherto unimagined levels during the Second Republic (Falola and Ihonvbere 1985, 107–14; Diamond 1995, 437; Joseph 1987). Political violence had grown to rival the levels of the First Republic, calling forth not only the negative of political corruption, but of disorder and instability. Politics once again seemed divisive, characterized by hostility, suspicion, and bitterness, raising the specter of disunity based on ethnicity, regionalism and religion. In terms of policy outputs, terrible levels of wastage of public resources were obvious. (Falola and Ihonvbere 1985, Chapters 5–6.) To the major sector of the highly educated elite—themselves largely disengaged from political rule and politics—the country undoubtedly seemed to be in the hands of rulers that were selfish, sectionalist, corrupt, and incompetent.

Meanwhile, the quality of the Nigerian public sector and the services it was supposed to provide (e.g., in health and education) was regressing under political rule from the levels achieved by the mid-1970s. The ambitions of what I have described as the vision of the Nigerian "integral state" (e.g., "adequate medical and health facilities for all person(s)"; "equal and adequate educational opportunities at all levels": 1979 Constitution, Chap. II) began to seem a perverse joke. The initiation of the Second Republic had approximately coincided with a major downturn in Nigeria's economic fortunes that commenced with the world recession of 1980–81 but has continued on indefinitely. The negative effects of world economic trends and forces interacted with and were exacerbated by the corrupt and incompetent management of Second Republic leaders.

To borrow words from our opinion survey instruments, the democracy of the Second Republic was not good government; it was not "honest government in the interests of the people." For the great majority of thoughtful people, "competing politicians and political parties" did not make the Second Republic a proper democracy—and would not have done, even had the 1983 elections themselves been free and fair. As it was, the rigging and violence associated with the elections of 1983, far from legitimating the regime and the system removed the last shreds of legitimacy.

Thus far, we have looked at events in relation to values and culture to explain the rapid de-legitimation of the Second Republic. Now, let us speculate as to the extent that the class interests of the highly-educated, public-sector-oriented elite reduced support for democracy.

We noted earlier that through the years of "military" government members of the public sector elite functioned as connecting links between the administrative state and their own home communities, providing an element of representation at state and national levels. Now, politicians—equipped with a claimed legitimacy derived from elections—became the intermediaries and the representatives. The tacit alliance of the administrative elite with a relatively limited number of military officers in administrative/political roles was replaced, in the democracy, by service under a numerous, energetic (and rapacious) "political class."

Meanwhile, the 1970s had seen a huge expansion of the commercial/business elite driven by forced "indigenization" and by the flood of oil money. This new economic elite was well-prepared for alliance with a political elite in need of money to fuel political machines, and in need of private sector connections to complete the transactions of "contractocracy," i.e., to liberate and transfer public sector resources into private hands.

Second Republic democracy was thus associated with a complex pattern of supplantation of the public sector elite in favor of political and commercial elites. This was in part the direct result of democratic rule per se, and in part the reflection more general historical and economic patterns. By the end of 1983, four years into the democratic experiment, the balance of ambivalence had shifted its whole extreme to the anti-democratic side. Once again, that ultimate oxymoron, a "democratic coup" (Garba 1989) against democracy (on December 31 1983) seemed to come as a response to popular will. Public opinion seemed quite ready to accept the military regime's diagnosis: the Second Republic democracy was not sick; it was dead.

A Second Cycle of Ambivalence: 1985–1993

The cycle of the abortive Third Republic bears a close resemblance to that of the Second Republic. Only a brief summary of major points can be presented here.

Following the Babangida coup of August 27 1985, a new transition to democracy was set in motion (Koehn 1989). Once again, members of the intelligentsia were called upon as "wise men" as a seventeen-member Political Bureau was set up to carry out a broad review of the 1979 constitution and the country's political aspirations. Of the seventeen members of the Political Bureau at least twelve could be described as academics (Report of the Political Bureau 1987, 6–7). A broad range of the educated elite was involved as members of the Political Bureau visited all local government areas in the country and elicited contributions and commentary according to two elaborate and detailed questionnaires, one for the "national political debate" and one for interviews with "grassroots population" (Report, Appendix III, C and D).

The resulting 1989 constitution mainly carried on the constitutional engineering of the 1979 constitution. It is noteworthy that the 1979 strategies to control the quality of politics and politicians were strengthened and extended. A stronger National Electoral Commission (NEC) was meant to provide a stronger quality control than the Second Republic FEDECO had done. Interesting, the quality of voters at the base was now to be improved with the Directorate of Social Mobilization or MAMSER to create the political culture of democracy among the rural masses. With the beginning of the transition, controls over the quality of parties and politicians were extended as the "old breed" politicians of First and Second Republics were banned from participation, and as a two-party system was imposed, with the two parties eventually designed and organized by the military government. An open ballot system was designed to guard against traditional methods of electoral rigging.

Despite the government's frequent abrupt and authoritarian changes in the schedule, procedures and personnel of the electoral competition, reasonably credible elections were carried out at local, state and national levels producing local government councils, state legislatures and governors, and the federal two-house National Assembly. The oft-delayed Presidential elections to complete the process, finally held on June 12 1993, were widely attested as acceptably free and fair (Lewis 1994)—and also unprecedentedly "national" in character, with southerner M.K.O. Abiola of the SDP carrying 58 percent of the vote nationwide and 19 of 30 states including, remarkably, Bashir Tofa's home state of Kano.

As is well-known a slow-developing coup halted the creation of the Third Republic at this point, with the June 12 election results suppressed, the NEC suspended and, by November 1993 as General Sani Abacha seized full power, the elected bodies and executives at all levels dissolved and sent home.

Many, throughout the country, reacted with shock and dismay to the suppression of the June 12 election and the gradual reimposition of full military rule. Yet the reaction was weak enough, nationwide, and sufficiently mixed, to permit a military clique—itself divided and on the point of collapse—to prevail. Politicians divided in their pursuit of short-term and selfish interests, and both politicians and intellectuals permitted themselves to be coopted into Abacha's cabinet (Diamond 1995, 462; Lewis 1994, 329). Reaction from a broader public was strong in the southwest and in the oil-producing areas of the southeast—but generally muted in the north. It was possible within months for the military regime, with some credibility, to characterize opposition to suspension of the June 12 election (and the Third Republic) as partisan, sectional, and ethnic in character, and hence invalid.

With the cancellation of the transition to democracy, the 1985–93 cycle was incomplete. Nevertheless, the main features of the "cycle of ambivalence" are clear. The public, led by members of the intelligentsia, participated widely in the design of a new democracy. The main strategies of the 1979 Constitution were confirmed, while new elite safeguards against the disappointments of the First and Second Republics were devised. The cycle began in relative optimism (but, undoubtedly, much less faith in the process than had existed in 1979). The electoral process itself functioned relatively well, and the aggregate patterns of competition and alliance across the old lines of region and ethnicity continued on from the trend of the Second Republic experience to diverge positively from the "bitter shadow" of First Republic regionalism.

Yet reports of corruption and some political violence accumulated as the process continued (Diamond, 1993). Wholesale changes by government fiat in political leadership (banning of "old breeds," unbanning of "old breeds," cancellation of primaries and disqualification of Presidential candidates, etc.) undoubtedly weakened the public's faith and sense of involvement in the process of choosing national leadership. The long delay in completing the elections at the presidential level meant that legislators at local, state and federal levels were frozen in an incomplete transition, and often seen in the worst possible light as they inhabited luxury hotels in Abuja and competed for perquisites. To most thoughtful observers, the enormous effort to create political "new breeds" must have seemed to have failed.

By the time of the presidential elections on June 12 the cycle of ambivalence had already shifted a long distance from the extreme of pro-democracy toward the extreme of disillusionment with democracy. Thus the mixed and and often muted reactions from Nigeria's large and influential highly educated elite in the face of cancellation of elections and, finally, of the transition to democracy itself.

Cycles of Elite Ambivalence and Permanent Transition

The failure of the Nigerian highly educated elite collectively to defend democracy (the Second Republic, the nearly-complete Third Republic) has been a critical factor in the failure of Nigeria—thus far—to institutionalize democratic government. I have extrapolated from data on university student political culture collected at the beginning of the 20-year effort to construct democracy to suggest more general patterns of elite opinion surrounding democracy. I have combined that view with an analytical historical one, reviewing the special role of the highly educated elite as the Nigerian state has evolved and changed over the years of independence. We have seen elite ambivalence regarding democracy playing itself out historically in cycles of ambivalence that correspond with Nigeria's pendulum swings from full military rule toward democracy and back again.

In this pattern of ambivalence elite support for, and belief in, democracy—while genuine and strong as an ultimate aspiration for Nigeria—is conditioned in four important ways.

First, support for democracy is conditioned by deeper and completely unconditional adherence to central political values of order and unity. Support for democracy in the abstract is reduced to the extent that democracy-in-practice seems to threaten order and unity. Support for democracy also is conditioned, and potentially reduced, as democracy-in-action produces conflicts with "mandarin" values of honesty, dignity, nationalism, and service.

Secondly, support for democracy is conditioned by an understanding of democracy as *good* government—and not simply as *elected* government. Thus, support for democracy in the abstract is quickly eroded by the reality of seemingly *worse* government as inexperienced politicians, anxious to recoup the costs of their election, take over the reins of the public sector, the quality and effectiveness of which is particularly crucial to the public sector-oriented highly educated elite.

Thirdly, in a more complex argument I suggested that support for democracy is conditioned by the subtle but far-reaching evolution and adaptation of the Nigerian state over more than 35 years of independence, of which more than 25 years have been without a formal democratic dimension. I suggested that informal practices have adapted the heritage of the colonial administrative state to make it more complete, more participatory, and more representative. Closely connected to home communities, as our survey data indicated, the members of the highly educated public sector elite are central in these adaptations. In the situation of military rule, the elite has participated in quasi-political roles both in terms of policy determination, and in terms of providing connecting links as pseudo-representatives between the state and the society made up of home communities. Undoubtedly, the evolution of the administrative state has made the creation of formal democratic institutions of input seem less necessary to many of the participants in military-civil rule in its more benevolent phases.

Along the same lines, I suggested that the new federalism of 30 states, and with the development of "federal character" and a statutory revenue allocation system that distributes guaranteed shares of petronaira both to states and local governments, provides a consociational element to the Nigerian polity which increases group security and system stability, and consequently makes the achievement of democracy seem less urgent and less necessary.

Fourthly, and deriving from the third conditionality, democracy in fact tends to run counter to the "class interests" of the highly educated public sector elite. In this view we see the politicians, claiming a legitimacy based on election superior to the educational/experiential legitimacy of the elite, shouldering the elite aside, both in determining public policy and in representing communities.

These four conditionalities produce the cycle of ambivalence pattern. Support for democracy is highest under military rule as a process of transition is set in motion. Members of the intelligentsia lead in planning and shaping the democracy. The plan is replete with constitutional provisions and mechanisms to make sure that the next democracy will produce a good democratic process, good leadership, and good government. But once the democracy begins, the values associated with democracy tend to come into conflict with the more deeply held values of order and unity. Disappointment sets in with the quality of political leadership and with the quality of government that result from democracy. At the other extreme of the cycle, disillusionment with the democracy is extreme. The legitimacy of both the democratic regime and the constitutional system that produced it erodes sharply. I postulated that elite opinion has a broad shaping influence on public opinion as it relates to national political events. Thus, the opinion climate favorable to new military intervention is created. With a new military government—its own legitimacy of limited duration and conditional on performing cleanup functions and organizing a new transition—the cycle is complete.

The stratagem of "Permanent Transition" which seems to be behind the machinations of "Presidents" Babangida and Abacha capitalizes on the cycle, attempting to freeze it at the happy point where members of the intelligentsia design a revised constitution while politicians form clubs and parties, make alliances and dream of the presidency. For all, positive expectations are at their height.

But "Permanent Transition" is a political strategy that contains its own seeds of bankruptcy. To work, and to provide the presiding military regime a cover of legitimacy, there must be *belief* in transition. Yet belief is precisely what "Permanent Transition" erodes and ultimately destroys. This is the heritage of the Babangida/Abacha transitions.

The Present and the Future

Is the future for democracy hopeless? A recent (1995) partial replication of the earlier university student survey research on which this analysis is largely based provides interesting insights into the role the highly educated elite may play.[3] Overall, the stability of university student opinion over more than two decades is remarkable. Yet the impact of events is evident in several areas relevant to the future of democracy. Overall there is a decline in optimism. Students perceive less nationalism among Nigerians (even among their own numbers), and ethnicity is seen as a yet more completely dominating force in politics and society. Today's students are less optimistic about Nigeria's economic development and about the quality of Nigerian politics in the future. A significant shift toward private sector orientations is clear. Unsurprisingly after all the years of military rule (and broken promises) respect for the military has declined sharply from the middling rankings the officers were given in the early 1970s. Meanwhile, the contribution of businessmen to the society is ranked somewhat higher.

But little change in core political values (unity, order, strong government) is apparent. Significantly, however, more of the 1995 respondents are positively oriented toward democracy. Democracy is generally ranked higher in relation to other values (although large majorities still rank democracy behind the central order/unity political values). A much larger proportion of students consider constitutional structures a crucial component of "democratic" government, no doubt reflecting the national focus on constitutional design since 1975. (However, the proportion thinking of democracy in terms of competing parties and politicians is even smaller than it was 20 years before!) Significantly, the proportion agreeing with the proposition that "the masses" are not capable of making rational choices in national elections is smaller (but still comprises slightly more than 50 percent of respondents).

If taken as broadly indicative of elite opinion, these university student opinions may suggest some shift in the "balance of ambivalence" toward the democracy side.

There are, as well, historical reasons to expect change. Over the first decades of independence, the public sector-oriented, highly educated elite that played such a crucial role in state and society over the first two decades of independence has undergone "class demotion" (Beckett 1987, 109–10). The real value of legitimate remuneration (salaries and legal perquisites) of public service employees has fallen radically from the post-Udoji highs of the middle 1970s. Moreover, as the author Kole Omotoso perceptively remarked (Omotoso 1983), the coincident decline in quality of the Nigerian state and its services has affected the public sector elite with particular severity, since, in general, members of this elite are more completely dependent on infrastructural, health, education, and other services from the public sector than are the new commercial and political elites. A numerous commercial elite has developed with an economic base derived from but outside of the public sector. A "political class" of politicians and military power holders (active or retired) is closely intertwined with the commercial elite (Diamond 1993, 223; Reno 1993). Thus the public sector elite now finds itself a true middle—not upper—class. It seems unlikely that higher civil servants, professionals, academics, and writers and artists will ever again enjoy the position of high influence and status which they enjoyed after the first coup and through the process of designing the Second Republic.

In the short run, these profound changes have probably weakened support for the two democratic experiments represented by the Second and Third Republics. But in the longer run loss of status, influence, and access to power may well further strengthen the pro-democracy side of the structure of elite ambivalence. The group's participation in power and public policy determination will never again be so central and so automatic as in the 1960s and 1970s. Consequently, the future class interests of the highly educated public sector elite and intelligentsia will require institutionalized access and input through constitutional electoral democracy. The highly-educated middle class may become truer democrats, and may provide the social base of legitimacy for democratic institutions that has so strikingly been absent heretofore. Ambivalence would thus be resolved in favor of democracy, as the process of democracy comes to be seen as a superior value to be fought for, above and beyond the quality of its particular outcomes moment to moment, and as faith is put in the long-term adjustive and self-regulative capacities of an electoral democracy.

Notes

1. During just part (1987–91) of the failed transition to the Third Republic budgetary and extra-budgetary allocations to the National Electoral Commission, the political parties, and other levels of government to support the electoral process totalled 2.6 billion naira. At least as much was spent on other parts of the strategy to restore democracy such as the Directorate of Food, Roads and Rural Infrastructure, and the Directorate for Social Mobilization (Olagunju et al., 1993, Addenda A, C, D, E).

2. My conception of the post-independence, highly educated, public sector-oriented elite is made clear in the historical summary section that follows. As a shorthand I shall follow common Nigerian practice (Ayandele 1974) in referring to the intellectual, bureaucratic and professional elites and their members collectively as "the elite." As is recognized in my historical summary and elsewhere, there is much de facto overlap between this "elite" and the other principal higher elite groups viz., the political elite referred to in Nigeria as the "political class," the business/commercial elite, and the military elite. Distinctions are contextual, and in terms of individuals slippery, yet essential, in my interpretation, to an understanding of the otherwise puzzling history of democracy in Nigeria.

3. In the first half of 1995 my colleague Dr. W. O. Alli of the Political Science Department of the University of Jos carried out an administration of a questionnaire which we formulated comprised of the more politically-focussed questions from the questionnaires employed in the Beckett-O'Connell study of the early 1970s. In the non-random sample, 338 questionnaires were completed by University of Jos students. The summary presented here is based on preliminary analysis; a more complete report on the data produced by the replication is forthcoming.

References

Achebe, Chinua. 1966. *A Man of the People*. John Day Company.
Adamolekun, Ladipo. 1985. *The Fall of the Second Republic*. Ibadan: Spectrum Books, Ltd.
———. 1986. *Politics and Administration in Nigeria*. Ibadan: Spectrum Books.
Ayandele, E.A. 1974. *The Educated Elite in the Nigerian Society*. Ibadan: Ibadan University Press.
Beckett, Paul and James O'Connell. 1975. "Social Characteristics of an Elite-in-Formation: Nigerian University Students." *British Journal of Sociology*, September.
———. 1977. *Education and Power in Nigeria: A Study of University Students*. London: Hodder and Stoughton.
Beckett, Paul A. 1987. "Elections and Democracy in Nigeria." In Fred M. Hayward (ed.), *Elections in Independent Africa*: 87–119. Boulder and London: Westview Press.
Bienen, Henry. 1987. "Nigeria." In Weiner, Myron and Ergun Ozbudun (eds.), *Comparative Elections in Developing Countries*: 201–47. Duke University Press.
Coleman, James S. 1958. *Nigeria: Background to Nationalism*. University of California Press.
Dahl, Robert A. 1956. *A Preface to Democratic Theory*. Chicago and London, University of Chicago Press.
Diamond, Larry and Marc F. Plattner, eds. 1993. *The Global Resurgence of Democracy*. Baltimore and London: Johns Hopkins University Press.
Diamond, Larry. 1995. "Nigeria: The Uncivic Society and the Descent into Praetorianism." In Larry Diamond, Juan J. Linz, and Seymour Martin Lipset, eds. (1995), *Politics in Developing Countries: Comparing Experiences with Democracy*: 417–91. Boulder and London: Lynn Rienner Publishers.
Dudley, Billy. 1982. *An Introduction to Nigerian Government and Politics*. Bloomington, Indiana, Indiana University Press.
Ekeh, Peter P. and E.E. Osaghae, eds. 1989a. *Federal Character and Federalism in Nigeria*. Ibadan: Heinemann Educational Books.
Ekeh, Peter P., Patrick Dele-Cole, and Gabriel O. Olusanya, eds. 1989b. *Politics and Constitutions: Vol. V of, Nigeria Since Independence: The First 25 Years*. Ibadan: Heinemann Educational Books.
Elaigwu, J. Isawa. 1986. *Gowon: The Biography of a Soldier-Statesman*. Ibadan: West Books Publisher, Ltd.
———. 1988. "Nigerian Federalism Under Civilian and Military Regimes." *Publius*, 18 (Winter): 173–88.
Falola, Toyin and Julius Ihonvbere. 1985. *The Rise and Fall of Nigeria's Second Republic: 1979–84*. London: Zed Books.

Federal Republic of Nigeria. 1976. *Report of the Constitution Drafting Committee*. Lagos: Federal Ministry of Education.

———. 1979. *Constitution of the Federal Republic of Nigeria 1979*. Enugu, Fourth Dimension Publishing Company. (Intro by Turi Muhammadu.)

———. 1987. *Report of the Political Bureau*. Lagos: Federal Government Printer.

———. 1989. *The Constitution of the Federal Republic of Nigeria [1989] (Promulgation) Decree 1989*. Lagos, Daily Times of Nigeria, Ltd., 1990.

Forrest, Tom. 1993. *Politics and Economic Development in Nigeria*. Boulder, San Francisco and Oxford: Westview Press.

Garba, Joseph. 1989. *New York Times International* (interview), Sept. 30, A3.

Graf, William D. 1988. *The Nigerian State: Political Economy, State Class and Political System in the Post-Colonial Era*. Portsmouth, N.H.: Heinemann Educational Books, Inc.

Ibrahim, Jibrin. 1991. "Religion and Political Turbulence in Nigeria." *Journal of Modern African Studies*, XXIX, 1 (March): 115–36.

Jinadu, L. A. 1985. "Federalism, the Consociational State and Ethnic Conflict in Nigeria." *Publius*, 15, ii.

Joseph, Richard A. 1978. "Affluence and Underdevelopment: The Nigerian Experience." *Journal of Modern African Studies*, 16, 2 (June): 221–39.

———. 1987. *Democracy and Prebendal Politics in Nigeria: The Rise and Fall of the Second Republic*. Cambridge University Press.

Kazaure, Zubair Mahmud. 1993. "Nigerians Prefer Military Rule to Chaos." *New York Times*, Letter to the Editor, December 18, 1993.

Kirk-Greene, A.H.M. 1971. *Crisis and Conflict in Nigeria: A Documentary Sourcebook, 1966–70*, vols. I, II. London, Oxford University Press.

Koehn, Peter. 1989. "Competitive Transition to Civilian Rule: Nigeria's First and Second Experiments." *Journal of Modern African Studies*, 27, 3 (September): 401–30.

Lewis, Peter M. 1994. "Endgame in Nigeria: The Politics of a Failed Democratic Transition." *African Affairs*, 93 (July): 323–40.

———. 1995. "Nigeria: Domestic Crisis Challenges International Intervention." *SAIS Review*, XV, 2 (Summer-Fall): 17–38.

National Universities Commission. 1992. *NUC at 30*. Abuja: National Universities Commission.

Ofonagoro, Walter Ibekwe and Olatunde B. Ojo, eds. 1977. *The Great Debate: Nigerian Viewpoints on the Draft Constitution 1976/1977*. Lagos, Daily Times Publication.

Olagunju, Tunji, Adele Jinadu and Sam Oyovbaire. 1993. *Transition to Democracy in Nigeria (1985–1993)*. Ibadan, Spectrum Books.

Ollawa, Patrick E. 1989. "The 1979 Elections." In Peter P. Ekeh et al. (eds.), *Nigeria Since Independence: The First 25 Years: Vol. V: Politics and Constitutions*. Ibadan, Heinemann Educational Books.

Omotoso, Kole. 1983. "A Writer's Diary: 25: 'Power to the People.'" *West Africa*, 3441, 25 July: 1719–20.
Onido, Anujobe Ademoh. 1989. "Elitist Public Policymaking: Reflections on the Structure, Behavior and Impact of the Nigerian Policy Making Elite." *Development Studies Review*. (University of Jos), III, 1&2.
Onyeoziri, Fred. 1989. "Consociationalism and the Nigerian Political Practice." In Ekeh, Peter P. and E.E. Osaghae (eds.), *Federal Character and Federalism in Nigeria*. Ibadan: Heinemann Educational Books.
Oyediran, Oyeleye, ed. 1979. *Nigerian Government and Politics under Military Rule, 1966–79*. New York: St. Martin's Press.
———. 1989. "The 1983 Elections." In Peter P. Ekeh, Patrick Dele-Cole, and Gabriel O. Olusanya, (eds.), *Politics and Constitutions: Vol. V of Nigeria Since Independence: The First 25 Years*: 165–82. Ibadan: Heinemann Educational Books.
Oyediran, Oyeleye and Adigun Agbaje. 1991. "Two-Partyism and Democratic Transition in Nigeria." *Journal of Modern African Studies*, 29, 2 (June): 213–35.
Oyovbaire, S. Egite. 1984. *Federalism in Nigeria*. New York, St. Martin's Press.
———. (ed.). 1987. *Democratic Experiment in Nigeria, Interpretive Essays*. Benin City, Omega Publishers.
Paden, John N. 1986. *Ahmadu Bello, Sardauna of Sokoto: Values and Leadership in Nigeria*. Zaria: Hudahuda Publishing Company.
Post, Kenneth and Michael Vickers. 1973. *Structure and Conflict in Nigeria 1960–66*. Madison: University of Wisconsin Press.
Reno, William. 1993. "Old Brigades, Money Bags, New Breeds, and the Ironies of Reform in Nigeria," *Canadian Journal of African Studies*, 27, 1: 66–87.
Schatz, Sayre P. 1977. *Nigerian Capitalism*. Berkeley, Los Angeles, London: University of California Press.
———. 1984. "Pirate Capitalism and the Inert Economy of Nigeria." *Journal of Modern African Studies*, 22, 1: 45–57.
Sklar, Richard L. 1963. *Nigerian Political Parties: Power in an Emergent African Nation*. Princeton University Press.
Uwazurike, P. Chudi. 1990. "Confronting Potential Breakdown: The Nigerian Democratization Process in Critical Perspective." *Journal of Modern African Studies*, XXVIII, 1 (March): 55–77.
van den Berghe, Pierre L. 1973. *Power and Privilege at an African University*. London: Routledge and Kegan Paul.
Young, Crawford. 1994. "Zaire: the Shattered Illusion of the Integral State." *Journal of Modern African Studies*, 32, 2: 247–63.
Zartman, I. William, ed. 1983. *The Political Economy of Nigeria*. New York: Praeger.

PART 3
The Failure of Transition

6

DEMOCRATIZATION UNDER MILITARY RULE AND REPRESSION IN NIGERIA

Richard Joseph

Despite its restrained language, the March 1996 Human Rights Report of the United States State Department conveys a chilling picture of Nigeria under the regime of General Sani Abacha which it ranked with Burma in the perpetration of human rights abuses. Arbitrary arrests and detentions, extrajudicial killings, endemic corruption, excessive use of force, torture of detainees, life-threatening prison conditions, imprisonment without charge or trial, harassment of journalists and democratic activists, corruption of the judiciary, arson attacks on media houses, seizure of passports—in virtually every sphere, Nigeria has become one of the world's most oppressed nations. Decree 12 of 1994 declares that "no act of the federal military government may be questioned henceforth in a court of law" and it divests the courts of "jurisdiction in all matters concerning the authority of the federal government." When the courts were also forbidden under Decree 14 to order the government to produce prisoners in court, what was thereby shredded was perhaps the most fundamental of civil liberties, the right of habeas corpus. It is no wonder that the Abacha government stands accused of flaunting "the most basic international norms and universal standards of human rights."[1]

Nevertheless, at every turn, the Abacha regime proclaims its commitment "to establish the foundations of a durable democracy," and it has launched another multiphase process of transition to civilian rule to be completed in October 1998. As one set of analysts report, the regime's technique is to "weaken, divide and confuse opponents by simultaneously combining reform (or the illusion of reform) with repression" (Butts and Metz 1996, 14–15). These authors also contend that "the military is incapable of self-reform and cannot lead to successful democratization" (17), an assessment which confirms a prediction made two decades earlier. After the first four years of military rule concluded with the signing of the armistice that ended the Biafran war in January 1970, one of Nigeria's leading politicians, Obafemi Awolowo, resigned from the government of General Yakubu Gowon on the grounds that the military had no legitimate basis to continue ruling Nigeria with peace restored. Five years later, when Gowon's regime was overthrown, Awolowo restated his position and added a warning of the risks posed by prolonged military governance. Their exceptional rule should serve, he argued, as "an essentially corrective regime, and not a reconstructing Administration with ready and lasting answers to all our political and economic ills . . . It would be too much of a task for it to attempt the massive and never-ending task of rebuilding or reconstructing the body politic" (Awolowo 1975).

Awolowo could be suspected of having his own self-interested motives in seeking to get the armed forces to limit their political agenda. However, in this and other matters, his comments went to the heart of the Nigerian dilemma. Nigeria first entered what Awolowo labeled "the dismal tunnel" on January 15 1966 when the military overthrew all the institutions of a democratically-elected government. Recently, that date echoed in the decision of the Constitutional Conference, established by General Sani Abacha after he seized power on November 17 1993, to set January 1996 as the date on which his regime would transfer power to elected civilians. It took considerable effort and persistence to obtain such a declaration from a Conference packed with Abacha appointees and subject to all forms of inducements, cooptation and coercion. In April 1995 the democratic hopes of the Nigerian people suffered another grave setback: the Conference reversed itself and left the termination date open. On October 1 1995 Abacha demonstrated his dominance over all internal political forces, and his disregard for international opinion, by declaring that he would remain in power until 1998. One month later, despite urgent appeals from numerous world leaders, nine civilian activists of the Movement for the Survival of the Ogoni People including its leader, Ken Saro-Wiwa, were hanged. Their execution followed months of brutal treatment in prison and a trial that was universally judged to be a travesty. As Nelson Mandela led the international chorus of condemnation, it seemed as if the former apartheid state of South Africa, with its dehumanizing institutions and instruments, had switched places with Nigeria, once the great hope for a constitutional democracy on the continent.

How did this state of affairs come to pass? Why did Nigeria, which has conducted perhaps the most extensive attempts of any developing nation to construct a constitutional democracy fail so abysmally? The Nigerian military governed the country during much of the post-civil war decade (including even the early years of the regime of Ibrahim Babangida) in a manner that allowed for a high level of openness and autonomy in civil society. How did this country end up being one of the few today still ruled by a military dictatorship? Why did a country which had a deserved reputation as a principled leader of the continent on international matters, especially the struggle against racist regimes in Rhodesia and South Africa and against the conduct of Cold War proxy wars on the continent, such as in Angola, come to be described by a British foreign minister as a place of "growing cruelty" (Hurd 1995)? And finally, is there any hope that Nigeria can emerge in the foreseeable future from the dismal tunnel of rule by a rapacious military establishment and their civilian consorts?

The Consolidation of a Prebendal Republic

General Danjuma, Chief of Army Staff under Obasanjo, stated with some exasperation in the late 1970s: "It is now fashionable in Nigeria to talk about a military regime being an aberration, and that a return to civilian rule means a return to democracy. This is a fallacy because we never had a democracy in Nigeria" (Jemibewon 1978, x). After having closely studied the transition to civilian rule after Gowon's downfall in 1975, and before a vote was cast for the Second Republic, I wrote that there was a deep flaw that could undermine the new political system. That flaw was the relationship between the administering of public offices and the acquisition and distribution of material benefits which had also become central to the processes of party-building and the making of political alliances. The party that won power in the elections was successful for a number of reasons among which was its willingness to capitalize on this logic. Moreover, I argued that these well-established practices in Nigerian sociopolitical life would yield short-term gains but contribute inexorably to the sapping of the authority, legitimacy, capacity and finances of the state (Joseph 1979).

According to the theory of prebendalism, offices of state are regarded as prebends which can be appropriated by office-holders and used to generate material benefits for themselves and their constituents or reference groups.

The statutory purposes of these offices, meanwhile, become matters of secondary concern. (Joseph 1984b, 31–32). With the National Party of Nigeria (NPN) leading the way in entrenching these practices at the federal level, and all other parties doing likewise in the state and local governments they controlled, Nigeria between 1979 and 1983 evolved into a full-fledged "prebendal republic." The state was a "national cake" to be divided and sub-divided among office-holders. Politics consequently degenerated, as Claude Ake pointed out, into an unrelenting war to acquire, defend or gain access to its offices (Ake 1981, 1162–63).

Although the civilians had fashioned this system while Nigeria was still under colonial rule, the Nigerian military proved equally adept at its execution. There was little difference between the final years of the Gowon administration (1973–75) and that of the Second Republic in this regard. State military governors, as reported by a senior officer, "carried corruption to an unparalleled degree in the history of Nigeria." A visiting scholar concurred: "Government seemed to have lapsed into the private business ventures of its officials" (Joseph 1987a, 72–73). In fact, every Nigerian government, from the regional administrations under colonial rule in the 1950s to the Abacha regime four decades later, has carried corruption to an unparalleled degree. Justice Akinola Aguda stated it quite simply in the late 1970s: the one achievement of every Nigerian government is that it has created more millionaires than its predecessor. Today, in view of the emergence of what I have called "pharaonic" corruption in place of the milder "prebendal" corruption, that comment should be amended to "multimillionaires."

Babangida's Bogus Transition

Despite these failings, Nigeria usually remained a place of hope. It was and still is, the greatest agglomeration of African peoples within the boundaries of a single nation-state, and it still possesses considerable natural resources. Nevertheless, there came a moment when I recognized that the country was once again lost in the "dismal tunnel." That moment came in 1989. Ibrahim Babangida had already postponed the promised date for the handover of power to civilians from 1990 to 1992. In 1989, the political associations being formed were allowed to seek registration as political parties. The requirements for registration were grossly unreasonable. They included the number of offices each would-be party had to open and operate, and lists of their supporters—with photographs! All this had to be amassed and submitted in just three months. The regime set the rules and it could impose any criteria it wished. After the mountains of materials were delivered to the Electoral Commission in Lagos, the verdict soon followed: none of the associations had met the test and the government was going to create its own political parties, name them, write their manifestos, and oversee their development. The military was now going beyond what Awolowo and others had long cautioned against as "the massive and never-ending task of rebuilding or reconstructing the body politic." The regime was assuming full responsibility for establishing the instruments by which civil society in Nigeria would be allowed to manifest its political wishes and act to achieve them. No wonder many Nigerian critics dismissed the parties created by the federal military government as state-enterprises or "parastatals."

As was revealed by an individual at the center of these transactions, the two-party system imposed by the Babangida regime after it dismissed all political associations in 1989 was a preconceived plan.[2] All the political aspirants and entrepreneurs who took part in these exercises were dupes to one extent or another. The regime had no intention of ceding power. The transition to democracy had become a game in which the rules were changed as soon as the civilian politicians felt they had mastered them. In the hope of inheriting power, or some parcel of it, many Nigerians—soldiers, trade unionists, established politicians, traditional rulers, intellectuals, business persons—had been led further down the dismal tunnel by Babangida. In the election of June 12 1993, he finally allowed two affluent businessmen who considered themselves his cronies to contest the presidency. They were just the last of the many individuals who had been led to believe that Babangida supported their candidacy only to find themselves dismissed as they reached for the brass ring. On the very eve of the June 23rd annulment of the presidential elections, some of Babangida's advisers went away from a meeting with him reassured that he was going to do the very opposite and announce the winner and next president of the nation.[3]

After 1989, there seemed to be little new to be said about Nigerian politics.[4] The prebendal character of the state and of political life generally had been repeatedly confirmed by Nigerian scholars and other commentators (Diamond 1995, 473). The major developments under the Babangida regime—the considerable expansion of the powers of the presidency, the colossal sums being privately appropriated by senior members of the regime, the inexorable growth of drug smuggling and fraudulent financial schemes, the minute stage-managing of an elusive transition process—only deepened the contradictions identified by many analysts. The critical challenge faced by concerned Nigerians and their overseas colleagues was to arouse international awareness of the abyss into which Babangida was leading Nigeria. In a byzantine series of developments, Babangida was finally induced to leave office, clearing the way for Sani Abacha to brush aside Ernest Shonekan's "Interim Civilian Government" of August-November 1993. Abacha, whom Obasanjo has described as Babangida's "eminent disciple, faithful supporter and beneficiary," proceeded to take the nation deeper into the dismal tunnel (Obasanjo 1994). Like Zaire, it is now difficult to imagine how Nigeria will ever re-emerge as one coherent nation.

Military-Civilian Alternation in Power

Although military rule has often been referred to as "an aberration" in Nigeria, it is also the case that civilian rule has not left a commendable record. The violence and mayhem, especially in western Nigeria at the time of the 1983 elections, were reminiscent of the carnage and confusion during the final year of the First Republic. The corrupt behavior of public officials and the gross mismanagement and increasing repressiveness of the federal and state governments during the Shagari era raised fears that Nigeria would experience a severe crisis, perhaps occasioning the loss of much human life. When the armed forces intervened on December 31 1983, "the ease of their takeover reflected the extent to which the civilian government had lost legitimacy in the eyes of the demoralized and anxious population" (Joseph 1984c). Even the embryonic Third Republic, as legislatures and elected governments were established at the local, state and federal levels before the transition was complete, showed signs of continuing this pattern: "in very few states were cases of corruption and obscene malpractice and abuse of office not the order of the day. At the national level, the scale of corruption was monumental" (Obasanjo 1994, 7).

It should be recognized, however, that Nigeria has also known significant peace, some economic progress and a sense of hopefulness during certain periods of military rule. This was the case for the first years following the civil war, for the duration of the Murtala-Obasanjo regime (1975–79), and for the first few years of the Babangida administration (1985–88). During each of these episodes, a distinctive Nigerian military system of governance was in evidence. I described this system as one which, beginning with Gowon, was refined by each subsequent military administration: "In both federal and state governments, a relatively small group of military officers are assisted by civilian appointees who include well-known politicians as well as more private citizens from the professions and the business world . . . the effective sharing of power takes place between the higher military and civil bureaucracies" (Joseph 1984a, 6). This system, when in place, allowed considerable freedom and autonomy within civil society. Indeed, Nigeria had a freer press during these episodes and a more active, autonomous and often effective array of interest and professional groups than most other African countries. Moreover, the balancing of representation of Nigeria's major ethnic groups in the government and in the major public institutions was also handled reasonably well by this system (6).

Each of these governments, however, was subject to decay because the military was an unaccountable body which could not restrain the inevitable abuses of office and, except for the Obasanjo regime, was unable to arrange a smooth succession. It thereby increasingly invited counter-coups. When Sani Abacha seized power in November 1993, even he temporarily aroused hopes that this known system of governance would be re-installed. Although he dismissed all the elective political institutions, he managed to draw into his government an impressive array of known national politicians including the long-time human rights lawyer Olu Onagoruwa as his Minister of Justice. By this time, however, such gestures no longer had any substantive meaning: they were merely decorative and diversionary, rituals to obtain compliance with continued military rule.

In 1982, I drew the following diagram to try and capture the cyclical pattern of Nigerian politics, especially the alternation between military and civilian systems, and to identify the possible options if the military intervened again. It is worth revisiting (see Figure 1).

The unbroken arrows in the Figure 1 diagram show the main cycle of regime change in Nigeria since 1960. If the military intervened again, as seemed increasingly likely (by 1982) as the Second Republic became a full-fledged prebendal republic, there appeared to be four possible outcomes: the return to a corrective/conciliar republic, an attempt to establish a socialist democracy, some process leading to a stable liberal democracy, or a new corporatist/authoritarian system. The options of a socialist or stable liberal democracy were considered less probable and hence the smaller arrows. More likely was the return to the starting point of a corrective/conciliar regime similar to that of Murtala/Obansanjo (1975–79), or a new form of military government that Nigeria had never known and whose characteristics would likely be authoritarian and corporatist.

When the harsh military government led by Buhari and Idiagbon was overthrown by Babangida in August 1985, it seemed that Nigeria was being returned to the familiar conciliar system of governance. As Babangida stated in criticizing his predecessor: "a diverse polity like Nigeria required recognition and the appreciation of differences in both cultural and indi-

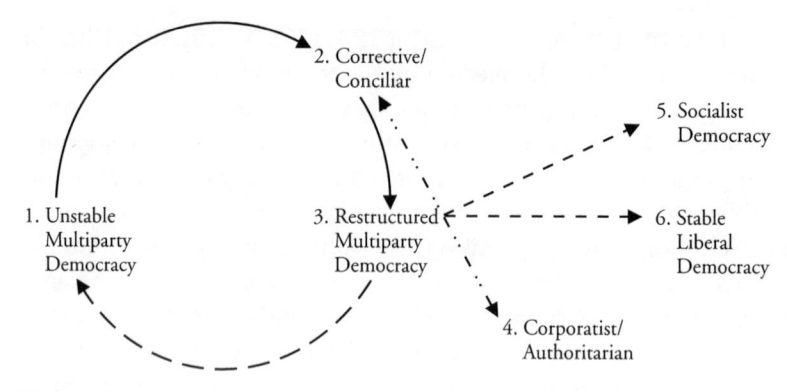

Figure 1.

1. Unstable Multiparty Democracy
2. Corrective/Conciliar
3. Restructured Multiparty Democracy
4. Corporatist/Authoritarian
5. Socialist Democracy
6. Stable Liberal Democracy

vidual perceptions" (Babangida 1986). In fact, the first year of Babangida's rule with its wide degree of consultation and his open style, especially in contrast with the practices of his immediate predecessors, kept at bay criticisms of his self-described "military democracy." By the end of his eight years in power, however, what the country had experienced, in the words of one its erstwhile agents, was "organized confusion."[5] The regime eventually adopted, at one time or another, elements of all four options which will be indicated below by the numbers in the diagram. It claimed to be laying the basis for a "stable liberal democracy" and pushed through reforms in the early years that seemed to create the foundation for a more market-oriented economy (6). The Political Bureau appointed by Babangida shortly after he came to power recommended the construction of a socialist republic, a goal the regime rejected while accepting the need for extensive social and ethical mobilization of the population and the creation of a costly bureaucracy to conduct it (5). It initially adopted the conciliar mode of interest accommodation (2) but gradually supplanted it with a corporatist propensity to charter new institutions and make formerly autonomous bodies dependent on presidential largesse (4). From a regime that began by touting a vigorous human rights policy (2), it ended up harassing and imprisoning the country's leading human rights lawyers and democratic activists and detaining journalists and banning publications (4).

Alternatives to Another Superficial Transition

A "restructured multiparty democracy" created under military auspices, according to the 1982 diagram, was likely to deteriorate once again into an unstable system and prompt another military intervention. In 1991, as the final stage of the supposed transition was being prepared, it was evident that it was going to be still-born. There could be no winners in the political games that Babangida had forced Nigerian politicians to play and whose rules he changed at whim. I therefore made the following suggestion: "Nigerians should go along with the government's transition plan. Once power had been transferred to civilians, the political leaders should convene a national conference to discuss what should be salvaged, and what should be jettisoned, from the system that had been rammed down their throats. They should then proceed to establish a Government of National Unity for a fixed number of years which would lay the basis for genuine multiparty elections." I referred to this proposal as a "transition within the transition" or the creation of the Third and a half Republic.[6]

By the end of the 1980s, the Campaign for Democracy led by Dr. Beko Ransome Kuti and its affiliates were calling for a National Conference to lay the basis for a genuine transition in place of Babangida's manipulations. In neighboring francophone countries, this approach had brought an end to military regimes in Benin, Congo and Niger but was stoutly resisted or derailed in others such as Cameroon and Zaire. Nigeria needed a new basis for civilian politics that would emerge from an "ingathering" of all political and social forces rather than a renewed top-down crafting by a military regime. Obasanjo (1994, 7) has also added his voice to that of the radical democratic movement, with which he is normally at odds, by calling for a National Conference to "deal comprehensively with the fundamental issues of Nigerian existence."

In addition to the need for a transitional process that would mobilize the broad forces (*forces vives*) of Nigerian society, there was also the issue to be tackled of these transitions being largely phases in the circulation of powerful elites. Since civilians have occupied governmental positions under military as well as civilian regimes, they have also tended to become involved in promoting changes within military systems, or even military coups (as those of 1983 and 1993), to further their own material interests. The idea of a period of non-partisan civilian government as a probationary exercise has regularly surfaced in Nigerian political discourse. One flaw of the transition to the Second Republic was the absence of such an experience at the national level. Three years of the Mohammed-Obasanjo regime's four years in power, 1975–79, were devoted to the making of the constitution and only one year to legalized party-building, campaigning and elections (Joseph 1981). The diverse polity of Nigeria required a bridge between the system of governance established by the military and the re-establishment of an open system of competitive party politics, perhaps similar to the transition that took place in Brazil from the mid-1970s. Such a bridge was also advocated in 1975 by Awolowo who suggested that Nigeria should not move directly to a winners-take-all system. He revived a recommendation put forward earlier by Aminu Kano that a "political probationary period" should last five years in which a sharing of all governmental positions would be proportional to the votes won by parties in the elections (Awolowo 1975), a proposal that is remarkably similar to the transitional arrangements put into effect in South Africa two decades later.

The Nigerian military has always preferred to oversee the building of each new civilian system rather than allow civilian politicians to experiment with their own transitional arrangements. The Abacha regime unveiled in 1995 a new draft constitution whose most striking feature is the introduction of a rotational presidency in which the position of head of state will revolve among the country's major ethnolinguistic groups. A new multiphase transition program, involving sequential elections at local, state and federal levels, similar to that of the Babangida regime, has started with nonparty local government elections in March 1996. Nigerian political aspirants have wasted no time, despite the continued detention of many of their colleagues and the flight into exile of others, in creating new political associations to compete for the new electoral offices. As long as the Abacha regime maintains effective control of the security forces, it can dictate any "transition" program it wants in the knowledge that politically ambitious Nigerians will dance to the new tune. Despite the country's economic shambles, oil production continues and there will always be major fortunes to be made via state offices.

What are some of Nigeria's options as it undergoes yet another exercise in "democratization under military tutelage" (Joseph 1981)? There is the formal plan now laid before the nation to re-elect civilian governments at all levels and to introduce "for thirty years" a system of rotation and power sharing among senior executive and legislative officials. Even if this plan is enacted as drafted, the likelihood is that it would return Nigeria to the starting points of 1979, namely the installing of an unstable, highly prebendalized, civilian republic that another group of military adventurers could easily topple. A second option is a replay of the Babangida scenario: a supposedly democratizing regime that uses its leverage to revise constantly the "transition program" thereby prolonging its stay in power until it is forced out. A third option is a different transition program based on a national conference/power-sharing framework suggested above. This option would depend on the termination of the rule of Sani Abacha by a military regime more committed to a genuine transition. A fourth option is one that has always been rumored within the country but never executed: a radical military coup comparable to the second seizure of power by Jerry Rawlings in Ghana in 1981 with the intention of establishing a revolutionary government and sidelining the established military and civilian political class.

Although junior officers have played a significant role in the making of coups in Nigeria, once successful they have often ceded place to more senior officers. Periodic purges of junior officers, including their liquidation, have often been rumored in Nigeria. And the threat they allegedly posed has frequently been used to justify a pre-emptive move by their more conservative superiors. As will be seen from all the suggested options, a military establishment that has become a highly politicized and corrupted entity will continue to determine the structure and composition of future Nigerian governments. Butts and Metz (1996, 17) contend that "the only way democracy can be built and sustained" in Nigeria "is through a radical transformation of the military to include the wholesale replacement of the officer corps." They do not see, however, how this can be done, "without provoking national fragmentation, revolution, civil war, and a human disaster of vast proportions."

The Missed Opportunity of June 12 1993

Pini Jason, a Nigerian journalist, contended that "General Babangida annulled Nigeria's best chance to enter the 21st century as a modern democracy" when he blocked the publication of the results of the June 1993 elections and the declaration of Moshood Abiola as the first democratically elected southerner of the country (Jason 1995). Something unusual took place in Nigeria on June 12 1993, and the report by Peter Lewis, who was present for the occasion, is instructive. The party-building process leading up to the presidential elections replicated the misconduct normally associated with civilian politics in Nigeria: "aspiring political factions employed fraud, financial inducement and violence in the bid for advantage" (Lewis 1994, 324). Hardly a week passed, it seemed, that one party official or another was not suspending a colleague or jumping ship to the opposition. In 1992 the regime had cancelled the presidential primaries on the basis of alleged irregularities and substituted an even more complicated system. When the day of the presidential elections in 1993 arrived, however, Nigerians performed a collective and national act that rendered these elections one of the most peaceful to take place in Africa during the current wave of democratic transitions.

The report by Lewis echoes another issued by the Nigerian Centre for Democratic Studies which had organized its own election monitoring exercise: "the election campaign was conducted with unprecedented decorum;" [it] "reflected little of the political violence or electoral manipulation characteristic of politics under the First and Second Republics;" "there was little evidence of systematic fraud or vote-rigging;" "polling was generally conducted in a peaceful and orderly manner;" "the NEC [National Electoral Commission] promptly collated the results. . . ." Any observer of previous Nigerian elections is likely to blink upon reading these words. Something very unique had happened in Nigeria. The unannounced results of the election, which would have shown a 58 percent majority for Moshood Abiola, was also noteworthy in the size of his plurality and the fact that he drew significant support from all areas of the country. Larry Diamond reports that the suppressed results would have shown that Abiola, a Yoruba and Muslim, had won 48 percent of the vote in the predominantly Igbo and Christian states in the east, although his opponent had an Igbo running-mate. Abiola also won a majority (9 of 16) of the northern states, a result that stunned the Babangida regime and the northern establishment (Diamond 1995, 458).

The deliberately contrived judicial pronouncements cancelling the 1993 elections, then blocking the announcement of the returns, and the tragic-comic exertions of Arthur Nzeribe's Association for Better Nigeria, reflect the panic within government circles and among some of its constituencies that, despite all the road-blocks and "organized confusion," the Nigerian people were going to elect a President who could not be relied upon, once in office, to do the bidding of the outgoing military regime. Moshood Abiola is no paragon of democratic accountability. He has become fabulously wealthy through mastering the avenues for acquiring power and wealth in Nigerian society, whatever the regime in power. However, only someone who can play the game as well as he can would have reached the endpoint in Babangida's "transition." The Nigerian electorate was voting for much more than a man. After all the delays, they had been granted one final chance to get the military out of power and restart the Nigerian political calendar. As Lewis (1994) points out, "the combined influences of apathy, apprehension and confusion kept many away from the polls." The resulting 35 percent turnout (some 14 million voters) was subsequently used by the regime's supporters in its campaign to weaken Abiola's claims. In fact, in view of all that Nigerians had been through since the "transition" started eight years earlier, it is remarkable that so many were still prepared to go to the polls.

June 12 1993 should not be seen in isolation. The argument can be made that it represents one of several elements of a citizens republic, the expressed will of a demos in its most profound sense, whose emergence has been stymied by the misconduct of civilian politicians as well as the deliberate interference of a politicized military. During the First Republic, the country was gradually evolving into a political system with two broad political groupings. A similar process, as Larry Diamond (1988, 1995) has reported, was in evidence during the Second Republic. Both trends were halted by the irresponsible behavior of the political class and the arrogation by the military of the absolute right to rule.

When Babangida rounded up several politicians in 1991 and detained them for violating the ban on political activities, another remarkable thing happened that presaged what took place on June 12 1993. Although these politicians came from different parts of the country and belonged to different political formations, they discovered that they shared much common ground. When they were released, they put forward a set of common positions on the political process much to the chagrin of the Babangida administration. This is an indication of the kind of experience that a national conference, or its equivalent, could force Nigeria's senior politicians to undergo, similar to the transition proceedings after 1991 in South Africa. It could also lead to the fashioning of a minimum common political program together with a commitment to try and overcome the country's sectional divisions—regional, ethnic, religious—and make possible the national concord that could sustain an extended period of civilian rule. Although such a scenario can be imagined, and readily justified, it is still far from apparent how it will ever come to pass as long as Nigeria's military regimes closely supervise each transition and deliberately blunt the emergence of a stable civilian system that can transcend the divisions of region, religion and ethnicity.

Beyond Military Overrule

For decades, the Nigerian state, even under military regimes, allowed some scope to the judiciary and the exercise of the rule of law. Nigeria also sought to carve for itself a position of leadership within the African continent and in the world community at large and Nigerians served with distinction in many U.N. peacekeeping operations beginning in 1960 in the Congo (Zaire from 1971 to 1997). There were occasional indications that this "benign giant" could turn into its opposite. In early 1983, for example, several hundred thousand West Africans were summarily expelled from the country, even though "freedom of movement" was one of the hallowed goals of the Economic Community of West African States (ECOWAS) of which Nigeria was the acknowledged leader. However, it was the Buhari/Idiagbon Administration of 1984–85 that gave Nigeria a foretaste of a government that would be willing, as a regular mode of governance, to ride roughshod over its fundamental legal obligations, national as well as international, and be dismissive of all protests whatever their provenance.

Shortly after coming to power, General Buhari declared that those individuals who used their offices to rob the nation would not be allowed to escape by resorting to the "nonsenses of litigation." The regime then introduced a number of exceptional decrees. Nigerians, who had clamored for relief from the misrule of the Second Republic, "awakened to find a militarized Leviathan which bolstered its command of organized violence by what it regarded as a popular mandate to serve the nation in an exceptional manner" (Joseph 1987b, 82). The Buhari regime, as that of Sani Abacha after 1993, did not consider itself bound by any of the nation's laws or by any act of the civilian courts. Moreover, the security services were increasingly used by both the Buhari and Babangida regimes as instruments of repression. When in October 1986 the dynamic journalist and publisher, Dele Giwa, was blown apart by a parcel bomb as he investigated the connections between criminal and military networks, a signal was sent of what was potentially in store for other Nigerians who threatened the consolidation of a mafia style of governance. With the military's growing belief in its right to rule Nigeria free of legal and constitutional encumbrances, the risk of an unbridled tyranny grew closer. Moreover, this tyranny extended to the manipulation of language itself in ways that recall George Orwell's *Animal Farm* and *1984*. In his October 1995 national address, Abacha, who had been a major player in three successful coups in Nigeria, proclaimed his determination to end "the cycle of coups and counter-coups that have perennially dogged" the nation's evolution. And although he has systematically manipulated the courts to keep Abiola from being released, he explained his reluctance to release him by claiming that "the matter is still sub-judice." Finally, Abacha, who had ordered the arrest of an elected Abiola on a charge of treason for declaring himself president in June 1994 was the same military officer who, in December 1983, had publicly announced the overthrow of an elected government and the dismantling of a constitutional republic.

The legal and moral inversion evident in Abacha's actions and pronouncements is the culmination of a long train of sophistic argumentation by Nigeria's military rulers. Less than a year after he had returned power to civilians in 1979, General Obasanjo took part in a debate with a law lecturer on the campus of the University of Ibadan. That confrontation can now be seen to have taken place across the philosophical faultline in the construction of the Nigerian polity. Rejecting the argument that the Nigerian military undermined the rule of law, Obasanjo contended that the military invoked an alternate, and equally authoritative, legal system whenever it dismissed civilians and suspended the constitution. As a consequence, he argued, the "ability, competence and authority" of the Nigerian military "to make law that is valid and binding on all citizens should not be in doubt or questioned once they are effectively in political power" (Shyllon and Obasanjo 1980, 24). Obasanjo also extended this authority to include the right to disregard not just constitutional procedures but such fundamental principles as the inadmissibility of retroactive laws: "when occasions do call for such laws to save the nation from political or economic destruction, the governing majority must be able to act in defence of the nation" (25).

Fifteen years later, Obasanjo has been arrested, tried and imprisoned on the basis of the very alternate legal system he once defended. A spokesperson for the Abacha regime dismissed criticisms of the 1995 secret trials by arguing that "this is not the first time we have had this type of trial" in Nigeria. He wondered why "past secret coup trials in Nigeria did not attract this kind of attention" (Chijuka 1995). In the Kafkaesque world that Nigeria has become since the Babangida era, Emeka Ojukwu, who led an armed struggle against the Nigerian nation from 1967 to 1970, can today rebuke an Olusegun Obasanjo, who defended the nation in that civil war, in the following dismissive words: "if there is any punishment that comes, should he be found guilty of whatever it is, it will be prescribed by no other person than himself" (Ojukwu 1995).

Conclusion

For the first time since the Biafran war, the Nigerian nation-state is itself a contested entity. Calls for a national conference to reconsider the fundamental composition of the country rose steadily during the later years of the Babangida regime. As has been effectively demonstrated in analyses of the Ogoni dispute, the campaign against environmental degradation in the oil-producing areas broadened to include a determined challenge of the very nature of the Nigerian state and its dominance by northern civilian and military elites (Osaghae 1995; Naanen 1995). The annulment of the election of Moshood Abiola deeply alienated southern intellectuals, many of whom now regard the federal state as being firmly in the grip of a northern military and civilian ruling group, feudal in its attitudes, which they refer to as "the Caliphate." While there will be no shortage of political aspirants of all regions who are prepared to follow the narrow paths permitted by the Abacha regime to gain access to the corridors of power, more Nigerians than at any time since independence are likely to adopt direct forms of struggle perhaps including organized violence.

It is unlikely that the Nigerian people will be permitted by the Abacha regime to experience the open competition for political power via the electoral process that has taken place since 1989 in such African countries as Benin, Malawi and Zambia. The Abacha regime has shown no willingness to allow the restoration of the rule of law and the observance of fundamental civil liberties, two basic prerequisites of a democratic process. In this regard, Abacha's policies resemble those of contemporary regimes in Cameroon, Guinea and Mobutu's Zaire with the important difference that the Nigerian ruler has denied any wish to stay in power beyond his self-appointed five-year term. There are several countries that have made a gradual transition from highly authoritarian systems to semi-democratic states and from there to liberal polities in recent decades, as the cases of South Korea, Taiwan, Chile and Brazil exemplify. From this perspective, it cannot be asserted that Nigeria will remain indefinitely confined within the dismal tunnel of military authoritarianism. However, the fact that the tentacles of this tyrannical system are daily infiltrating every nook of this once civic polity, and are being used to snuff out all sources of dissent and autonomy, suggest that the democratic polity being erected under Abacha will require the skills of a Nigerian Orwell or Kafka to be adequately depicted.

Notes

1. This quote is from a statement issued by the U.S. government following the execution of the Ogoni dissidents on November 10 1995. Similar condemnations were made by other governments, the European Union, and the Commonwealth.

2. Eme Awa, former head of the National Electoral Commission, speaking at the Conference on Democratic Transition and Structural Adjustment in Nigeria, Hoover Institute, Stanford, 1990.

3. Personal communication.

4. At a conference in 1990 in Lagos attended by American and British longtime students of Nigeria, Nigerian scholars who had been recruited into the Babangida administration and served as spokespersons for its democratic commitments, expressed their surprise that their overseas colleagues seemed convinced that the transition process was now largely a ruse. In addition to Lewis (1994), for further information on the various twists in this process, see Peter Koehn (1989), Uwazurike (1990), and Larry Diamond (1991). For a comprehensive account of Nigeria's economic, political, and social evolution, see Joseph, Taylor, and Agbaje (1996).

5. Abimbola Davis of the Association for Better Nigeria in his press statement on the methods used to deceive and confuse the Nigerian public, given before fleeing the country in July 1993.

6. These points were publicly stated at the time of the second phase of the Conference on Democratic Transition and Structural Adjustment, held in Lagos, Nigeria, in January 1991. Since an extensive interview with the *Sunday Times* in which they would have appeared was never published, I am citing here my Congressional testimony of August 1993 in which these views were summarized.

References

Ake, Claude. 1981. "Off to a Good Start but Dangers Await. . . ." Presidential Address to the Nigerian Political Science Association in Kano. *West Africa* (25 May): 1162–63.

Awolowo, Obafemi. 1975. "Advice to New Federal Government." *Daily Sketch* (Ibadan) 21 August.

Babangida, Ibrahim B. 1986. *Newswatch*, 3, 3: 50.

Butts, Kent Hughes and Steven Metz. 1996. "Armies and Democracy in the New Africa: Lessons from Nigeria and South Africa." Strategic Studies Institute.

Chijuka, Brigadier Fred. 1995. *Reuters*. 8 July.

Diamond, Larry. 1988. "Introduction: Roots of Failure, Seeds of Hope." In Larry Diamond, Juan J. Linz, and Seymour Martin Lipset (eds.), *Democracy in Developing Countries: Africa*: 1–32. Boulder: Lynne Rienner Publishers.

———. 1991. "Nigeria's Search for a New Political Order." *Journal of Democracy* 2, 2.

———. 1995. "Nigeria: The Uncivic Society and the Descent into Praetorianism." In Larry Diamond, Juan J. Linz, and Seymour Martin Lipset (eds.), *Politics in Developing Countries: Comparing Experiences with Democracy*: 417–92. Boulder: Lynne Rienner Publishers.

Hurd, Douglas. 1995. *Times* 5 July.
Jason, Pini. 1995. *New African* June.
Jemibewon, David B. 1978. *A Combatant in Government*. Ibadan: Heinemann Educational Books.
Joseph, Richard A. 1979. "Political Parties and Ideology in Nigeria." *Review of African Political Economy* 13: 83–84.
———. 1981. "Democratization under Military Tutelage: Crisis and Consensus in the Nigerian 1979 Elections." *Comparative Politics*, 14, 1.
———. 1984a. "Alternation between Military and Civilian Rule in Nigeria: Can the Cycle be Stopped" (typescript).
———. 1984b. "Class, State and Prebendal Politics in Nigeria." In Kasfir, N. (ed.), *State and Class in Africa*. London: Frank Cass.
———. 1984c. "The Overthrow of Nigeria's Second Republic." *Current History*, 83, 491.
———. 1987a. *Democracy and Prebendal Politics in Nigeria: The Rise and Fall of the Second Republic*. Cambridge: Cambridge University Press.
———. 1987b. "Principles and Practices of Nigerian Military Government." J.W. Harbeson (ed.), *The Military in African Politics*: 67–92. New York: Praeger.
———. 1993. "Nigeria: The Way Forward." Testimony before the Sub-Committee on Africa, The House Committee on Foreign Affairs, Washington D.C. 4 August.
Joseph, Richard A., Scott Taylor and Adigun Agbaje. 1996. "Nigeria." In K. Kesselman, M. J. Krieger and W. Joseph (eds.), *Comparative Politics at the Crossroads*: 616–89. Lexington: D.C. Heath.
Koehn, Peter. 1989. "Competitive Transitions to Civilian Rule: Nigeria's First and Second Experiments." *Journal of Modern African Studies* 27, 3: 401–30.
Lewis, Peter M. 1994. "Endgame in Nigeria: The Politics of a Failed Democratic Transition." *African Affairs* 93: 323–40.
Naanen, Ben. 1995. "Oil-Producing Minorities and the Restructuring of Nigerian Federalism: The Case of the Ogoni People." *Journal of Commonwealth & Comparative Politics*, 33, 1: 46–78.
Obasanjo, Olusegun. 1994. "State of the Nation: Which Way Forward" (typescript).
Ojukwu, Emeka. 1995. Quoted: Internet. Newsgroup: soc. culture, Nigeria Article: 4090 14 July.
Osaghae, Eghosa. 1995. "The Ogoni Uprising: Oil Politics, Minority Agitation and the Future of the Nigerian State." *African Affairs*, 94, 376: 325–44.
Shyllon, Folarin and Olusegun Obasanjo. 1980. *The Demise of the Rule of Law in Nigerian under the Military: Two Points of View*. Ibadan: Institute of African Studies.
Uwazurike, Chudi P. 1990. "Confronting Potential Breakdown: The Nigerian Redemocratization Process in Critical Perspective." *Journal of Modern African Studies*, 28, 1.

7

OBSTACLES TO DEMOCRATIZATION NIGERIA

Jibrin Ibrahim

Until recently Nigeria enjoyed a relatively advanced democratic culture, at least within the context of Africa. The development of this democratic culture was rooted in two historical aspects of the evolution of the country. First, there has been the differentiation in space and time of the development of the country's political structures and institutions. The political elites coming from different regions and backgrounds were so culturally and politically different that the evolution of a unified hegemonic bloc was impossible. That development hindered the emergence of a tyrannical system of the sultanic or oligarchic type that was the norm in many other African countries. In addition, Nigerian civil society has a well established tradition of fighting for democracy. The press, the trade unions, and the judicial system in particular are regularly involved in the struggle for democracy, supported by a highly politicized population.

Democracy is never a static situation; it is a dynamic process in which there is movement between the expansive and repressive ends of the continuum depending on the relative strength of the forces at play. Simply put, these forces are, on the one hand, actors from the civil society who want to increase democratic spaces and, on the other hand, the strata who control the state apparatus and who want to reduce the democratic spaces. Not surprisingly, the democratic drive rooted in the civil society in Nigeria often confronts the authoritarianism of the regimes in power which resort to repression to safeguard their power. The result is a contradictory situation:

on the one hand, we have democratic assets and, on the other, we have authoritarian forces who try to destroy the said assets. The major obstacles to democratization in Nigeria have been the patrimonial and rentier nature of the state, the militarization of society and the determination of the officer corps to remain in power.

The Obstacles Posed by the Patrimonial and Rentier State

The Nigerian state is a patrimonial and rentier one in which those who are in control of state power and strategic bureaucratic offices use their positions for private appropriation. Patrimonial and rentier states create structural constraints that erode the impersonal state based on rule of law that is necessary for democratic practice. In his analysis of state domination, Max Weber posits that there are three bases for legitimacy—traditional, charismatic and legal-rational—which justify different forms of authority. Traditional authority is derived from the notion of "eternal yesterday," of "customs which have been sanctified by their immemorial validity and by the habit that is rooted in man to respect them." Traditional domination relies on the authority of one person, the patriarch. Patriarchal domination is usually based on kinship and exercised by the oldest male. As Medard has argued (1991), patrimonial power appears when political authority differentiates from domestic authority as a result of being exercised beyond kinship boundaries and of no longer relying only on relatives but on faithful followers, clients, and patrimonial servants who constitute a veritable administrative staff. Personal power which characterizes patrimonialism does not exclude the growth of a differentiated administration. According to Weber, patrimonial administration is different from bureaucratic administration because of the amalgamation of the private and public domains that one finds in the former:

> The patrimonial office lacks above all the bureaucratic separation of the 'private' and the 'official' sphere. For the political administration too is treated as a purely personal affair of the ruler, and political power is considered part of his personal property, which can be exploited by means of contributions and fees (1978, 1023–24).

Political reform and democracy are therefore seen as privileges that could be granted or refused as a personal decision by the ruler, as was illustrated by Babangida's annulment of the June 12 1993 elections. The patrimonial state does not feel the need to promote the common good and its logic is essentially limited to the distribution of prebendal offices and to the reduction of the access of the people to power wielders as Weber (1951) shows in his analysis of patrimonialism in China.

Nigeria is not only a patrimonial state but also a rentier one. The major characteristic of the rentier state is that its main relationship with the society is mediated through its expenditures on the military and state security, development projects, consumption subsidies, and construction (Skocpol 1982, 269). Rent, it should be recalled, is not merely an income earned by landlords but is in general a reward for ownership of all natural resources. A rentier economy is one that relies on substantial external rent. The creation of wealth is centered around a small fraction of the society, the rest of the society being engaged only in the distribution and utilization of the wealth so created. In a rentier state, the government is the main recipient of external rent and one of its major features is that production efficiency is relegated to the background and in fact,

> There is at best a tenuous link between individual income and activity. Getting access to the rent circuit is a greater preoccupation than attaining production efficiency (Beblawi and Luciani 1987, 13).

There is thus a glaring contradiction between rentier and production ethics.

The rentier state is oriented away from the conventional role of providing public goods that have been extracted from the people through taxation; it is a provider of private favors. It becomes what Luciani (1987, 70) has called an allocation (as distinct from a production) state. Luciani argues that the fact that rentier states do not have to wrest taxes from their citizens has serious implications for political reform or, rather, the lack of it:

> Whenever the State essentially relies on taxation the question of democracy becomes an unavoidable issue, and a strong current in favour of democracy inevitably arises. This is the result of the fact that people will naturally be induced to coalesce according to their economic interest, and those groups that find no way to influence the decision-making process in their favour claim appropriate institutional choice. The State for its part must give credibility to the notion that it represents the common good (1987, 73).

While it is logical that the necessity for sustained taxation demands the construction of legitimacy in production states, it does not follow that the marginality of taxation in rentier states reduces the importance of legitimacy and democratic reforms.

Rentier states are capable of generating a certain level of legitimacy when they succeed in guaranteeing access to resources to a relatively large cross section of society. When they are no longer able to do that, due to a shortfall in rent or to the fact that the rent is monopolized by a small oligarchy, or both, they lose their legitimacy and are often able to remain in power only through extreme coercion. They tend to face regime crisis when they experience drastic shortfall in rent and are thus unable to allocate resources at a level they have accustomed their populations to. The tendency is for ruling elites to exclude more and more people from access to state resources, thereby creating the basis for widening political crisis. This has been the situation in Nigeria.

Nigeria has a rentier economy similar to the Arab rentier economies described by Beblawi and Luciani (1987) which revolve around petroleum revenues. Petroleum exports which accounted for only 10 percent of export earnings in 1962 rose to account for 82.7 percent of total export earnings in 1973 and for a period peaked at 90–93 percent. The price of crude oil jumped from US$11 per barrel to US$40 per barrel in 1980 with output reaching 2.05 million barrels a day in the same year (Olukoshi 1991, 29). The country was turned overnight into an allocation state and there was a dramatic rise in public expenditure. Government spending rose from naira 1.1 billion in 1970 to naira 6.5 billion in 1975, thus raising state expenditure as a percentage of GDP from 15.5 percent to 30.5 percent (Olashore 1989, 156). The then Head of State, General Yakubu Gowon, declared that "finance was not a problem to Nigeria" (Ayagi 1990, 73) and a spending spree on cement imports, festivals of arts, sports jamborees, universal primary education, and all sorts of public works commenced. The boom did not last long. Indeed, by 1978, an economic crisis was set in motion, due to a decline in oil exports and revenues. Income from petroleum dropped from naira 7 billion in 1977 to naira 5.9 billion in 1978 while production plummeted from 2.1 million barrels in 1977 to 1.57 million barrels in 1978 (Olukoshi 1991, 29). Oil revenues rose briefly to a record naira 10.1 billion in 1979 but collapsed to naira 5.161 billion in 1982. By 1985, oil prices had fallen to US$28 a barrel and by 1986, a barrel of oil was selling at only US$10 (Olukoshi 1991, 30). The economic crisis was by now in full steam.

Meanwhile, the rentier state in Nigeria had lost much of the production capacity of its economy. Agricultural production which was the mainstay of the economy in the colonial period and during the First Republic had gone into decline. Its contribution to the GDP declined from 61 percent in 1964 to 18 percent in 1982 as the state lost interest in the extraction of peasant agricultural surpluses. Manufacturing and employment also declined significantly and between 1980 and 1983 over one million workers were retrenched (Olukoshi 1991, 28–33). As a way of getting out of the economic crisis, the state, under the impulsion of the IMF, adopted a structural adjustment program (SAP) in 1986, aimed at reducing the staggering external debt that had built up, the chronic balance of payments crisis, hyperinflation and rising unemployment. The positive effects of SAP are yet to be seen, however. The employment scene has been devastated by mass retrenchment, galloping unemployment and underemployment as well as underutilization of installed capacity. The workforce of the UAC, one of Nigeria's biggest conglomerates, has been compressed from 23,850 workers in 1985 to 9,000 in 1988 (Fadahunsi 1993, 93). Capacity utilization since the introduction of SAP in 1986 has remained low, between 30 and 37 percent, and income per capita has collapsed from US$778 in 1985 to US$108 in 1989 (Fadahunsi 1993, 91–101). while the decline in income per capita in dollars undoubtedly is exaggerated by changes in exchange rates, it remains true that all indices of economic production and efficiency are on the decline, the standard of living has fallen to a historic low point, and the rentier state seems to have given up on the economy. The various sections of the power elite have focused their attention on struggles of access to the declining rent produced by the state.

In patrimonial and rentier states, the most important resource for accumulation is access to those who run the state. Indeed for Ken Post (1989, 4), access is one of the fundamental elements in the analysis of the state itself:

> The state is not an entity which does things, as it time and again appears in discussions. Only people can do things. Obviously, therefore, the people who can gain access to, and a monopoly over, the institutions within which the authoritative policy-making process occurs, or who already staff them, and who thus control the state-as-resources, using them and state policies to favour groups either directly or indirectly.

According to him, therefore, access determines what social classes or other social groups are able to find a direct voice in the policy process.

Access constitutes acts of navigation by actors, (i.e. the political entrepreneurs) in waters where the conditions and rules of admission cannot be clear, open or equal. In economies where the market is more or less open, the most important problem is that of the income at the disposal of consumers, access being easy if income is available. Nobody in such a situation is forced to resort to particular forms of influence and the market becomes a sort of "democratic" distribution mechanism. According to Bernard Shaffer and Huang Wen-Hsien (1976, 15), access becomes a problem from the moment distribution is done outside the open market. When that happens, there is the need to assert particular linkages to gain access. The problem which at the beginning was economic thus becomes a political one since the person who is looking for access has to use his voice to justify why he and not somebody else should have access to the resource in question.

The neopatrimonial state promotes booty capitalism and in so doing, it makes the state more fragile. The neopatrimonial bourgeoisie is parasitic and predatory. It goes without saying then, that this class has no particular interest in transparency, in accountability, in the existence of political opposition or in the culture of public debate that democracy breeds. The interest of individuals, factions, or cliques within the neopatrimonial bourgeoisie is to secure, maintain and expand their access to state resources while trying to exclude the access of others. This ruthless struggle for access fuels the increasing instability of the state. Since the bourgeoisie does not have a true autonomous base for accumulation, the struggles do not take place at the level of the economy. Primary sociological categories of an absolute nature such as sect, religion, tribe, ethnic group, or language are the most effective instruments. In other words, there is a contradiction between the modernist ideology of a neutral state which plays the role of arbiter and the reality of the Nigerian state which is the patrimony of the agents who run it. The state they have molded has become a major obstacle to the democratic aspirations of the people.

The Military Obstacle

The military has ruled Nigeria for all but 9 of the more than 35 years in which the country has existed as an independent entity. Military rule has strongly impacted the country's culture and institutions. Our argument is that military rule ultimately impacts negatively on society by generalizing its authoritarian values which are in essence anti-social and destructive of politics. Politics in this sense is understood as the art of negotiating conflicts related to the exercise of power. Military regimes have succeeded in permeating civil society with their values—both the formal military values of centralization and authoritarianism and the informal lumpen values associated with "barrack culture" and brutality that were derived from the colonial army. The contemporary Nigerian elite has been acquiring a lot of "barrack culture" over the past few years; for example, many of them starch and press their clothing in a military style. The army barracks have become a major social center for sports, discotheques, consumption of alcoholic beverages, gambling, prostitution, and mammy markets. At a more significant level, there is a decline in civility and a rise in violence in social interaction. In terms of governance, the most devastating impact of the military has been to spread the myth that they play a useful political role as an institution that can use its "monopoly" of force to prevent chaos. It will be recalled that since the Gowon era, the military regimes have used the "impending chaos" argument to postpone promised democratization. The specific legacy from the military is therefore neither corruption nor authoritarianism, much as they took both to new heights. The military legacy is the fabrication of a political culture oriented towards the imposition of a command and control structure on the political process, which has the effect of destroying the residual democratic values that have survived in the Nigerian society.

The Nigerian military is today the major segment of the power elite. They are the most wealthy people in the country and occupy the summit of most powerful organizations in the country's polity and economy. We include the large crop of retired army officers in this category. The military power elite in Nigeria has always claimed that they were playing a role similar to the one played by Cincinnatus (Oyovbaire 1987, 178). In Roman mythology, Cincinnatus was the model par excellence of human selfless service and civic consciousness. He had been invited by the representatives of the people in a period of national decay to carry out a fundamental civic responsibility—to repair and reconstruct the decomposing institutions, structures, and norms of the society. Having brilliantly carried out his civic duty, he scorned the glory of power and the appeals for him to remain as ruler and left the scene.

In contrast to the mythical Roman hero, the soldiers in power in Nigeria have found it increasingly difficult to relinquish power. The erosion of a culture of limited military intervention was gradual, over two decades. In January 1966 General Aguiyi Ironsi, who had become Head of State after the coup d'état organized by the "Five Majors," declared that he was a temporary impartial arbiter accepting the responsibility of power only for the short time that was necessary to reorganize the world of civilian politics which would then take back the power that belongs to it. For that reason he was advised not to take a political title like President or Prime Minister but to restrict himself to being a temporary Head of State. The three other military regimes that succeeded his regime more or less remained faithful to this idea. A discernible pattern of political culture evolved in Nigeria in the 1960s and 1970s—one that delegitimated military rule, except as short "corrective" regimes intervening at moments of political crisis. Consistently, when military regimes were settling down as "natural rulers," Nigerian civil society has arisen, fought for the departure of the military to their barracks, and insisted on a return to democracy. A certain form of professional political ethical code was thus imposed on the Nigerian military by civil society. This culture provided for military interventions for the resolution of acute political crisis, the reorganization of structures and institutions and the organization of elections, but specified that the military should not try to perpetuate their rule.

Within the military institution itself, a resistance to this culture of limitation developed gradually. The Gowon regime sought to perpetuate its rule but the Murtala coup of July 1975 led to the acceptance of the agenda of civil society and eventually to the Second Republic. The Buhari regime that ended the Second Republic sought to impose on Nigerians a clearly military value system—based on the idea that discipline and force, applied in a military manner, could resolve the numerous problems confronting Nigeria. The Buhari regime represented a frank attempt to militarize Nigeria, and Nigerians abhorred it. That created the conditions for the emergence of the Babangida regime which consciously and deliberately broke with the tradition of the military as "impartial arbiter." General Ibrahim Babangida was the first of Nigeria's military rulers to take the title of "President," and he embarked on a trajectory of personal, as opposed to the tradition of collegial, military rule. For example, he dissolved and reconstituted the ruling military council at will and informed his military colleagues of his decisions rather than consult with the official decision making bodies.

Cumulatively, the Nigerian military has transformed the country's body politic in a significant manner. In the first place, the military has entrenched the culture of public corruption. It is a major change in the country's political culture. In the past, corruption was corruption—unethical or illegal advantages procured through official positions. Under the Babangida and Abacha administrations, what used to be known as corruption has become the art of government itself. There is a complete prebendalization of state power, and virtually all acts by public officials involving public expenditure or public goods of any kind leads to the appropriation of state finances or property by officials. The routine operations of government are being subjected to prebendal rules. It is widely known for example that officials of state governments and parastatals have to pay, as they put it, 'up front,' a percentage of their statutory allocations to the Presidency, the Ministry of Finance, and Central Bank officials before their allocations are released. They in turn simply take their own personal shares, "up front," from government coffers. Contractors who used to bribe officials for government contracts have been completely sidelined. Numerous press reports indicate that the president, military governors, and ministers now simply allocate contracts to their own front companies, and they do not even have to pretend they are doing the job because few can dare pose questions. The country's major resource, petroleum, is now allocated to individuals who then sell their allocations to petroleum companies. Custom officers have been reported to have refused to release equipment imported by government because they had not been paid their percentage "up front." The military has succeeded in transforming corruption from a deviant activity by public officials into the raison d'être of the Nigerian state.

Secondly, the military has succeeded in destroying Nigerian federalism, sacrificing it on the alter of overcentralization. The military are structurally incapable of running a federal system because their unified command structure is incapable of accepting that a state government, which they consider to be hierarchically subordinate to the federal government, could have domains over which the state is sovereign, which, as is generally recognized, is the essence of federalism.

Nigeria's geopolitical realities have been completely modified. The old tripartite structure, which had become quatripartite with the creation of the Mid West in 1963, has changed drastically as a result of the multiplication of states whose number now stands at 36. The multiplication of states has produced a Jacobin effect that strengthens the center by eroding the autonomy of the regions. Nigeria thus finds itself now with a so-called Federation that is for all practical purposes a unitary state with some limited devolution of power to the states. This tendency was reinforced with the decision by Babangida on October 1 1988, to scrap Ministries of Local Governments and establish a Directorate in the Presidency to directly finance and control local governments. The Abacha administration which took over from Babangida in 1993 has gone a step further. It insisted not only on determining the criteria for the appointment of state commissioners and local government caretaker chairpersons, but has also insisted on a right of veto over those chosen. It is clearly anomalous for the president of a theoretically federal country to seek to control appointments in 589 local governments in the country.

The heritage of centralization established by the military is so strong that it has permeated the civilian political establishment. In 1976 the Nigerian political class seems to have accepted that the First Republic failed because the Westminister system, applied to Nigeria, produces a weak prime minister and that the solution is a strong executive president who could act in a decisive and unhindered manner (Ibrahim 1986). This resulted in the allocation of enormous powers, hitherto held by the regions or the cabinet, to the president or the state governors in the 1979, 1989 and 1995 Constitutions. The military succeeded in making the civilian politicians accept the principles of military government as a basis for Nigeria's "democratization." The political class forgot that Nigerians had accepted federalism as a guarantee that would help reduce the fears of ethnoregional domination and that these fears could only be allayed if the federating units had real powers that could guarantee people some autonomy in their local operations.

Nigeria's heritage of a federal and parliamentary tradition, both of which tend to encourage the dispersal of power, was replaced by an excessively centralized executive system that concentrated power in one person, thus opening the gates not for an American-style system, but for the worst form of Jacobin dictatorship. Nigeria has certainly not developed its own military Cincinnatus; instead, it has created the conditions for the rise of absolute dictators whose totalitarian ambitions are very difficult to contain.

The centralizing features that the military has imposed on Nigeria have resulted in the extensive use of public law as an instrument for the control of the political process. The single most ominous impact of the military legacy on Nigeria's political process is the imposition of a state command and control system on political parties and party politics. The military seems to believe that good politics is non-party politics, and indeed the 1976, 1987 and 1996 non-party local government elections were presented as strategies to initiate wholesome politics before parties messed them up. Both the Gowon and Murtala regimes tried to steer the country towards a zero party or one party system with the clear intention of establishing more effective state control over the political process. When these attempts were rejected by civil society, the military used the national unity argument to popularize the idea of the necessity of imposing conditions for the registration of parties. The immediate result of this was that the definition of a political party was changed from what it was in the First Republic, an organization formed by a number of people to propagate certain ideas and contest for power, to an organization that is recognized by the state to contest elections. Sections 201 of the 1979 Constitution and 219 of the 1989 Constitution specifically limit the definition of a political party to an organization recognized by the state to canvass for votes. The law forbids any organization, not so recognized, to canvass. More importantly, both on the juridical and political levels, parties were no longer considered as popular organizations that aggregate and articulate interests and opinions but as corporate entities that are registered with the state. This meant that the political significance of parties was no longer determined by popular support, as is the case in open democracies, but by administrative fiat.

Thus in the run-up to the Second Republic, 150 parties were announced and about 50 of them were fully constituted as parties. However, only 18 were able to feel that they had any chance of meeting the conditions imposed by the government, and submitted their applications. The state recognized 5 of them. The Constitution also banned independent candidates from contesting elections. In the naive thought that seemed to underlie these decisions, it was hoped that if regional, ethnic, religious, or extremist parties were disallowed, then the forces that they represented would somehow disappear. It is the same argument that was used in many African countries to justify the establishment of one party regimes; but the tragedy is that as more "national" parties have been imposed in the various countries, ethnic and regional tensions have increased as more and more people and groups have felt they were being excluded from the political process. The 1979 Constitutional provisions eliminated the right of minorities who believed they had specific local problems to form parties to articulate these problems. The concerns that had led to the popularity of parties such as the Bornu Youth Movement, United Middle Belt Congress and the Niger Delta Congress during the First Republic were thus disregarded. In addition, the constitutional provisions for the establishment of party offices nationwide meant parties must necessarily be big and rich because a large financial outlay was necessary for establishing the party infrastructure. Parties with non-mainstream ideological positions were also excluded by the system. The democratic ideal that a small poor party representing popular interests could develop into a major party was thus foreclosed.

The 1979 constitutional provisions also created the basis for the elimination of internal party democracy. The fact that parties were parties only because they were recognized by the state meant that party leaders were party leaders not because they were popular with their grassroots members, but only because they were so recognized by the state. During the Second Republic, politicians ceased trying to persuade their rivals: they simply expelled rivals for anti-party activities by using money, thugs and sometimes the police. The role of party officials became more important than that of party members because they decided nominations for electoral posts. Factions developed in all the parties and the state became the arbiter to decide which faction was the "genuine" representative of the party. The state however, through the courts and FEDECO, was less than neutral. In the GNPP and PRP factional crisis, for example, the factions that represented the majority of party members and the elected legislators of the parties were declared illegal and the minority factions were recognized. The frustrated and alienated members were reduced to negotiating with other parties to work out deals for electoral purposes. Many popular politicians were thus denied the right to contest in elections. The logic of democratic politics is that parties try to get popular candidates to improve their electoral chances. The logic of the Second Republic was that powerful and rich political entrepreneurs sought to exclude popular candidates from their parties so that they could get a nomination.

General Ibrahim Babangida fabricated the most antidemocratic program of return to "democratic" rule in the history of Nigeria. His program covered a long transition period during which, a group of political scientists drew up a program of "political crafting" that was supposed to create a new democratic political culture (Olagunju, Jinadu, and Oyoubaire 1993). There were two aspects to the plan. The first involved the resolution of the country's economic and sociopolitical problems through institutions such as the Directorate for Social Mobilization, the Center for Democratic Studies, and the Structural Adjustment Program that would turn Nigeria into a genuine democracy operated by honest people with a sound economy. The second aspect was the political transition program itself which had a series of elections that would eventually culminate in a handover to an elected civilian administration. The handover date, however, proved to be a mirage which was postponed from October 1990, to October 1992, to January 1993 and finally to August 1993. At that point, Babangida's military colleagues eased him out of power, only to set the stage for reimposition of full military rule in November.

The military closely supervised the design and implementation of the transition program to ensure that it conformed with their worldview. They used university intellectuals to produce the drafts and brought in military officers to fine tune the program. After the Political Bureau drew up the program for example, it was handed over by the government to a nine man committee chaired by and with a majority of military officers for the drafting of the government's position. The committee charged with drawing up a white paper on democratic transition was said to have worked in close consultation with critical elements of the armed forces and the military administration (see Olagunju, Jinadu, and Oyoubaire 1993, 165).

The first concern of the soldiers and their intellectual friends was to destabilize the country's political class. The military was conscious that previous military attempts to control the political process had been derailed by politicians. In 1986, the military junta announced a ten year ban on some old politicians. In September 1987 the ban was extended to the totality of those who had held political office in all preceding civilian and military regimes. In 1989 the ban was further extended to all those who had been heads of the various transition agencies. A new breed of "grassroots politicians," "untainted" by multiparty politics, was to be created. The idea was that persons elected from the "grassroots" in the 1987 non-party local government elections were suitable material for the formation of the new breed parties. When, however, these local government councilors started consulting nationally in an attempt to form a nationwide grassroots party, the effort was destabilized by the government which summarily dissolved all local government councils eighteen months before the end of their terms.

For the Third Republic, the military leaders and their friends rejected a multiparty framework and proposed a two party system with both parties requiring state registration. To determine the two political parties to be registered, the National Electoral Commission (NEC) and the government imposed very expensive and virtually impossible preconditions that only the upper section of the bourgeoisie or old politicians with established networks could have afforded or met. In three months, the parties were to establish well-equipped offices with at least three paid staff in all the (then) 435 local government areas in the country. In addition, they were to supply 25 membership lists of their parties comprising the names, photographs and personal details of at least 200 members from each local government area in the country (making at least 87,000 individual membership files per party) to the NEC. For good measure, prospective parties were to submit their applications with a registration fee of 50,000 naira. In spite of these draconian measures, 13 parties were able to submit their files before the deadline. It was a Catch 22 scenario. In a broadcast to the nation on October 6 1989, the Head of State announced that *all* the parties had:

> failed to comply with key conditions in the guidelines such as documentation on members, declaration of assets and liabilities of individual members of the national executive committees [. . .] most of them (parties) had operated underground prior to the lifting of the ban on politics on 3rd May 1989 [. . .] (and) had deep roots in the party politics of the First and Second

Republics. There were very strong indications of the wealthy individuals in the executive committees of the associations that confirm fears that they were being hijacked by money bags.

The idea that a mass party should know all its members and have files on each of them is a military one. To control the political process, the military was ready to deny the reality of democratic parties, such as differential levels of commitment including sympathizers who might not bother to register but might vote for the party. In addition, the whole idea of democratic elections is that candidates attempt to transfer loyalty of voters from one party to another, so adherence to parties is never a rigid bureaucratic issue. No democratic party in the world can give exact and detailed information on all its members at any point in time, so when the military and their intellectuals insisted on these conditions, one cannot but be suspicious of their motives. Their insistence that the politicians of the Third Republic must have no contacts or connections with old politicians was unconnected with reality. Similarly, the rule that wealthy people must not play a major role in the parties or use their money to win votes, at a time when their economic policies were creating a tiny minority of excessively wealthy people in a sea of mass poverty, was nothing short of pure fantasy.

In the end, the government decided to dissolve all the 13 would-be parties. Essentially, the military wanted full control. The next step they took was to create two new parties, allegedly for the "ordinary people"—the Social Democratic Party and the National Republican Convention, with the former leaning "a little to the left of center" and the latter leaning "a little to the right of center." The task of overseeing and coordinating the institutionalization of the two parties was given to a transition committee under the chairmanship of another military man and former Chief of Air Staff, Ibrahim Alfa (Olagunju, Jinadu, and Oyoubaire 1993, 215). Under his military direction, the government drew up the manifestoes and constitutions of the two parties, and decided to fund and staff them, before calling on individuals (as opposed to organized groups) to sign up. What was clear from the transition program was that the military government had decided to define and apply each "democratic" step on behalf of the people. They were determined to, and had the capacity to, stamp their world view on the so called democratization process.

Apart from imposing manifestoes and constitutions on the two parties, excessive powers were given to government-appointed administrative secretaries to organize the parties' take-off and to exclude from them radicals, socialists, anti-Structural Adjustment Program agitators, as well as alleged ideological and religious extremists. In addition, Decree 48 of 1991 gave the National Electoral Commission (NEC), established by the Military Government, wide ranging powers to disqualify any political aspirant whose action was "likely to disrupt the process of grassroots democracy." This was amended with Decree 6 of 1992 which widened these powers by absolving NEC of the duty of explaining or giving reasons for disqualification. Under this law the NEC disqualified thirty-two aspirants who had already won their party's nominations for the Senatorial and House of Assembly elections in July 1992. In October 1992 the government sacked elected party leaders and appointed caretaker committees to run their affairs. In the spirit of the times, one of the appointed chairpersons, Air Vice Marshall Shekari, was a retired military officer. As *Tell* reported, January 18 1993, the caretaker committees were directed by NEC to re-register party members with the provision that they should not accept more than 2,000 members in each ward. An extraordinary level of arbitrariness was displayed by NEC.

The politically acute Nigerian press discerned after two to three years that General Babangida had a hidden agenda which involved using the supposed program of transition to civilian rule as a ploy to cling to power as long as possible. While launching the Political Bureau in January 1986, General Babangida had announced that power would be handed over to a democratically elected civilian regime in 1990 and the Report of the Political Bureau confirmed this date. However he clung to power till August 1993, when he was finally pushed out by his equally ambitious military colleagues. At every twist and turn of the convoluted transition program, General Babangida's government tried to create conditions that would make the process collapse. The National Electoral Commission was established in 1987 to manage the political parties and the elections under the leadership of a respected retired professor, Eme Awa. When the Government realized he was not amenable to manipulation, he was removed in 1989 and replaced by a more pliable professor, Humphry Nwosu.

The most dramatic aspect of the transition was, however, the commercialization of the nomination and electoral process through the use, or rather abuse, of the open ballot or queuing system in which the secret ballot was disallowed and voters queued up in public behind the party symbol of their "choice." The most serious problem with the open ballot system was its fundamentally anti-democratic character. When it was proposed, the Sultan of Sokoto, Ibrahim Dasuki, complained about its anti-democratic character, citing possible problems such as that of virtually denying wives and peasants the possibility of benefitting from the secret ballot to vote against the candidates of their more powerful husbands and patrons

(*Citizen* October 15 1990). He was later proven right, but in the meantime he had, for whatever reasons, recanted and claimed that he was misquoted. Most informed opinions in Nigeria were against the open ballot but the government went ahead to implement it in 1990. The direct effect of the system was that candidates paid people to vote for them and party aides could directly observe and ensure that people who had been "bought" joined the queue of the aspirant who had paid for their vote. The NEC Chair, Humphry Nwosu, once complained that Nigerian voters were corrupt because they would take money from one candidate and vote for another. What a tragedy that Nigerian citizens were denied even this meager right to frustrate their wealthy enemies.

Not surprisingly, the state governors who were elected in 1991 were known to be some of the most corrupt and notorious elements in the society. They included a well known cocaine dealer and someone who had been found guilty by a Judicial Tribunal of bankrupting a state-owned National Supply Company by stealing its resources. They were political entrepreneurs who had decided to invest in the political game to make more money. It has been estimated that no serious presidential candidate spent less than 50 million naira for his campaigns (see *African Concord* September 21 1992).

Starting from the primaries for the 1990 local government elections, the political parties revealed their paramilitary character. They became embroiled in serious squabbles over who is defined as a genuine party member, that being the qualification necessary to participate in rigging. The general principle was that the faction that succeeded in capturing the party executive issued party cards to its clients and made sure possible supporters of its rivals were not officially registered as party members. The issue of party cards became a do-or-die issue because it was used to rig nominations of party candidates. In a manner reminiscent of communist parties and in direct contradiction to the tradition of democratic parties, belonging to the faction became a central pre-condition for belonging to the party.

In addition, after successfully running the gauntlet of intraparty competition, nominees had to have security clearance from the state to be recognized as genuine nominees. It was the worst travesty of democracy in Nigerian history. The level of manipulation was so high that all prospective presidential candidates had to see General Babangida personally and seek his blessing, as it were, to contest. He encouraged many of them to go ahead and it is generally believed that he gave a lot of them money to contest so that he could later accuse them of unethically using money to influence voters.

Most of the elections were characterized by what former governor Bola Ige called "free style rigging that made the occurrences of the Second Republic appear sluggish and amateurish" (*Guardian* December 12 1992). The first set of leading Presidential candidates for the two parties were disqualified by the NEC for using money and rigging the primaries. The adoption of Option A4 method was purportedly designed to resolve the problem of undue influence from rich patrons, or "moneybags." The idea was to organize primaries through a series of elections from the ward level, through the local governments and states, to the national level. However, by multiplying the number and levels of elections, the costs of transporting and feeding supporters skyrocketed, thus making the nomination open to the highest bidder. Not surprisingly, the 1992 presidential primaries were characterized by massive rigging and falsification of figures.

In a last ditch attempt to get General Babangida to hand over power, the two parties both nominated close personal friends and business associates of Babangida as their presidential candidates—M. K. O. Abiola for the SDP and Bashir Tofa for the NRC. Presidential elections were finally held on June 12 1993. The candidate of the SDP won decisively in an election that, surprisingly, was generally considered free and fair. The elections were above all a referendum in which Nigerians voted *out* Babangida, but he would not take no for an answer. He cancelled the elections and tried to initiate yet another round of "political crafting," but there was so much protest against the cancellation that he had to leave power in haste and hand over to an incompetent and powerless civilian without any mandate, creating the basis for yet another coup in November 1993 by his former second in command, General Abacha.

The "new" Abacha administration seems to be determined to keep to the Babangida policy of perpetuating military rule using the ruse of an interminable transition program to keep the democrats and politicians occupied. A Constitutional Conference was convened in the second half of 1994 and finished its deliberations in mid-1995. Since the Constitutional Conference proposed in December 1994 that the military junta should hand over power to a democratically elected government in January 1996, the regime became very hostile towards it and the conference was even prevented from sitting for some months, until the members got the message that they would not be allowed to challenge the longevity of the Abacha regime. The new junta finally announced a political transition program that would lead to a hand over of power in October 1998, thus giving themselves an initial life span of five years, exactly as Babangida had done.

The signs of more of the same are very clear. In the March 1996 non-party local government elections for example, all those perceived as potential anti-Abacha forces such as National Democratic Coalition (NADECO) activists, human rights organizations members, or Ogoni struggle sympathizers were disqualified from contesting by the National Electoral Commission. Already, Nigerians are concerned about postponement of the handover date, and strategies for pushing the junta out of power are being devised.

Conclusion

A patrimonial and rentier state has emerged in Nigeria and has created difficult structural conditions for a transition to democratic rule. In addition, the long period of military rule has set in motion the militarization of society and the entrenchment of a military oligarchy that is opposed to democratic rule. The erosion by military dictators of the multiple poles of political power that earlier existed in Nigeria has exacerbated the specter of the fear of domination in the country. The Nigerian state is no longer seen as a neutral arbiter. Conflict resolution mechanisms are breaking down and political actors are taking maximalist positions and treating compromise with disdain. Saving the Nigerian nation will require not only a return to civilian rule but also a deconcentration of the central government powers through a restoration of genuine federalism. More power centers have to be created in the country. It is also necessary to give up the idea of "garrison" political parties crafted by a few gurus and allow all groups to form parties. As the struggle of Nigerians for a democratic Republic continues, the expansion of democratic space is the most effective method of overcoming the fear of the dictator which the masses often transform into the fear of the "other."

References

Abbese, P. O. 1968. "Defence Expenditure and Private Capital Accumulation in Nigeria." *Journal of African and Asian Studies*, 23.

Aniagolu, A. N. 1993. *The Making of the 1989 Constitution of Nigeria*. Ibadan: Spectrum Books.

Awa, E. 1985. "The Nigerian Political System : A Critical Assessment of Twenty-five Years of Independence from Colonial Rule." *Studies in Politics and Society*, 4 (October).

Ayagi, Ibrahim. 1990. *The Trapped Economy*. Ibadan: Heinemann.
Bangura, Y. "Structural Adjustment and the Political Question." *Review of African Political Economy*, 37.
Beblawi, Hazem and Luciani, Giacomo, eds. 1987. *The Rentier State*. London: Croom Helm.
Beckman, B. 1987. "The Post-Colonial State: Crisis and Reconstruction." *IDS Bulletin*, 19, 4.
Civil Liberties Organization. 1993. *Human Rights in Retreat*. Lagos.
Fadahunsi, Akin. 1993. "Devaluation: Implications for Employment, Inflation, Growth and Development." In Adebayo Olukoshi (ed.), *The Politics of Structural Adjustment*. London: James Currey.
Ibrahim Jibrin. 1988. "La Société Contre le Bipartisme." *Politique Africaine*, 32.
———. 1986. "The Political Debate and the Struggle for Democracy in Nigeria." *The Review of African Political Economy*, 37.
———. 1992. "The State, Accumulation and Democratic Forces in Nigeria." In Lars Rudebeck (ed.), *When Democracy Makes Sense: Studies in the Democratic Potential of Third World Popular Movements*. Uppsala: AKUT.
———. 1993. "The Transition to Civil Rule: Sapping Democracy in Nigeria." In Olukoshi, Adebayo (ed.), *The Politics of Structural Adjustment in Nigeria*. London: James Currey.
———, ed. forthcoming: 1996. *The Expansion of Nigerian Democratic Space*. Dakar: CODESRIA.
Luciani, G., 1987. "Allocation vs Production States: A Theoretical Statement." In Hazem Beblawi and Giacomo Luciani (eds.), *The Rentier State*. London: Croom Helm.
Medard, Jean-Francois. 1991. "L'Etat neo-patrimonial en Afrique." In Jean-Francois Medard (ed.), *Les Etats d'Afrique Noire: Formation, Mecanismes, et Crises*. Paris: Karthala.
———. 1982. "The Underdeveloped State in Tropical Africa: Political Clientelism or Neo-Patrimonialism." In C. Clapham (ed.), *Private Patronage and Public Power*. London: Pinter.
Olagunju, Tunji, Jinadu, Adele, & Oyoubaire, Sam. 1993. *Transition to Democracy in Nigeria: 1985–93*. Ibadan: Safari Books.
Olashore, Oladele. 1989. *Challenges of Nigeria's Economic Reform*. Ibadan: Fountain Publication.
Olukoshi, Adebayo O., ed. 1991. *Crisis and Adjustment in the Nigerian Economy*. Lagos: Jad Publishers.
———, ed. 1993. *The Politics of Structural Adjustment in Nigeria*. London: James Currey.
Oyovbaire, S. E., ed. 1987. *Democratic Experiment in Nigeria, Interpretive Essays*. Benin City: Omega Publishers.
Post, Kenneth. 1989. "The State, Civil Society and Democracy in Africa:

Some Theoretical Issues" ROAPE Conference on Taking Democracy Seriously, England.

Schaffer, Bernard & Wen-Hsien, H. 1976. "Distribution and the Theory of Access." *Development and Change*, 6, 2.

Skocpol, Theda, 1982. "Rentier State and Shi'a Islam in the Iranian Revolution." *Theory and Society*, 11, 3.

Suberu, Rotimi. T. 1993. "The Challenge of Ethnic Conflict: The Travails of Federalism in Nigeria." *Journal of Democracy*, 4, 4: 39–53.

Theobald, Robin. 1982 "Patrimonialism." *World Politics*, 34.

Ukwu I. U. (ed.) 1987. *Federal Character and National Integration*. Kuru: National Institute.

Weber, Max. 1978. "Economy and Society II." In Roth and Wittich (eds.), *Economy and Society: An Outline of Interpretative Sociology*. Berkeley: University of California Press.

———. 1951. *The Religion of China*. Glencoe: The Free Press.

8

TRANSITION WITHOUT END: FROM HOPE TO DESPAIR—REFLECTIONS OF A PARTICIPANT-OBSERVER

Oyeleye Oyediran

> The most populous black nation, Nigeria, is now in a state of decay if not despair . . .
> —Ibrahim Agboola Gambari
> Nigerian Permanent Representative to the
> United Nations (May 1994)

> Four years ago, *Africa Demos*, listed Nigeria among countries with a strong commitment to democracy, while South Africa's commitment was described as ambiguous. Today, it would be most charitable to describe as ambiguous the commitment to democracy of the ruling military regime in Nigeria headed by General Sani Abacha.
> —Adigun Agbaje (1994)

Nigeria has commenced yet another journey, another transition to civil democratic rule. August 27 1993 marked another beginning, the fourth program of transition since independence. Yet we cannot ignore the fact that independence itself was a project of transition—the watershed of transitions in Nigeria. While that "Mother of Transitions" was midwifed by departing colonialists, the others have been presided over by military rulers—the traditional custodians of national defense and equity. Yet each transition, it seems, has taken us further from the "promised democratic paradise," and deeper into the authoritarian purgatory, where militarism and the most cynical forms of political opportunism hold sway.

Reflecting on the subject of "transitions without end," one is not inviting the world to join the chorus of despair. Despair in this context is not synonymous with the loss of hope, it is a projective meditation on the cost of hope. Despair only comes when we know that the cost of hope now escalates by the second, and as the minutes tick away, one must weigh the options that confront Nigeria today by way of a collective catharsis. Is it too late to have another peaceful transition? Have we passed the last gate?

While putting these thoughts together, the Sisyphus image came to mind repeatedly. It would seem that Nigeria, as in the story of Sisyphus, succeeds in rolling up the rock of democracy to the top of the hill, only to let it roll back into the valley, over and over again. Is there some inevitability to the crisis of transitions in Nigeria? Who are the greatest culprits in the crisis of political succession in Nigeria, and what portents do the most recent developments hold for Nigeria? Can one find a basis for hope in the despair of the current conjuncture?

In setting about the analysis, we shall take transitions in turn and examine their ramifications for the current descent to despair. Of particular interest would be the identification of the forces obstructing and advancing the transitions and the objective interests embedded in their position. In dealing with the current phase of the "transitions without end," one examines the very nature of the ongoing struggles, and the economic and social contexts and the serious peril that some outcomes portend in the wake of re-charged authoritarian resistance to peaceful change and a truly democratic outcome. In the last and concluding part of the discourse, we link the theme of our reflections which encapsulate the aspirations of Nigerians—currently on the verge of despair—with a new hope for democratic redress, shorn of despair, tears and blood.

The First and Second Transitions

It would seem that the intractability of the present process of regime change and political succession has its seeds in the fruit of independence. A lot has been written of Nigeria's colonial experience. Whichever way one looks at it, pre-colonial societies in Nigeria gave way to the Nigerian colonial state, a state "created" by Britain to cater for largely economic interests—access to cheap and steady supply of raw materials, and the creation of a market for goods manufactured in Britain, or sold by companies with British interests. Through access to western education and the lower rungs of colonial commerce, a Nigerian elite emerged, an elite which was to be politically fractured along regional lines at the formative stages of the nationalist struggles (Ayandele 1974; Coleman 1958). As it turned out, these cleavages were not only caused by the struggles for political power at the various defined levels, but by the drive to acquire the economic power of the colonial class, or at least a share of it. In the bid to inherit the colonial state, the nationalist elite papered over the more fundamental cracks in their coalition, while fashioning exclusive territories or political spaces defined as regions, ethnic enclaves or a combination of both. These were to be "defended" at all cost and to be closed to "outsiders," usually members of a competing party, by any means necessary, while rewarding loyalty over and above merit or efficiency (Sklar 1963).

By the time of the first military coup in January 1966, the cracks in the power elite had deepened into bitter irreconcilable factions. The manipulation of rules and institutions, the high premium on political power, and the view of politics as war not only tore apart the post-independence power elite, it sounded the death knell of the First Republic. Thus, the first transition was not a clean break from the past; neither did it lead to any transformation. The seeds of mistrust, avarice and division sown in the decades before independence found good soil and thrived from 1960 onwards. Perhaps the greatest tragedy to befall politics in Nigeria was the failure of the power elite or political class in these most critical formative years to imbibe the values of accepting the will of the people and the spirit of give and take.

The second transition (1975–79), unlike the first, was about civilian succession to a disengaging military regime. Being a "new" type of transition, the process of the transfer of power had to contend with the issues of modus operandi and modus vivendi. It also raised issues on the ethical limits of military involvement in selecting its own successors out of the motley crowd of political office seekers and "king-makers," without losing its legitimacy as a neutral umpire, and its ability to act as ever-ready government-in-waiting, should the squabbles of the civilian governing elite threaten the stability of the state.

This second transition, the first for transferring power from the military to civilians, was predicated on two grounds: the belief that military incursion into national politics and governance is an aberration; and that the process of military disengagement was ultimately a purely military act of political benevolence to a civilian political class that had learnt its lesson. The second chance therefore was an opportunity for the civilian class to democratically resolve its differences and compete for public office without threatening the stability of the political system. For the military, it was a chance to demonstrate its integrity and legitimacy. As Obasanjo, who presided over the final stages of that transition remarked:

> For those of us who count on institutional integrity and credibility for the military as the last bastion of hope and defence for the unity and integrity of Nigeria, our words on behalf of that institution must be matched by our actions (Obasanjo 1987).

As it would turn out, not all factions of the "politicized generals" shared this view, but their opposition did not become obvious till the third and fourth transitions.

The Third Transition: From Transition to Transition

When General Babangida seized power in 1985 from the Buhari-Idiagbon junta which had terminated the crisis-ridden Second Republic, one of his first actions directed at winning support and legitimacy for his administration was the promise of a program for the return to civil-democratic governance. His strategy was based on populism and in the early months of 1986, he opened the question of the country's political future to public debate. To facilitate and document the debate, the Political Bureau, made up of seventeen members under the chairmanship of Dr. S. J. Cookey, was set up by the Babangida administration. The Political Bureau was asked to travel the whole country, getting the views of Nigerians, analyzing, synthesizing and documenting their views. In addition, the Bureau was given the task of proposing a blueprint of a new political model for consideration by the Babangida regime. Fired by patriotic zeal and the determination to build a grassroots democratic order which would be free from the possible political forays of the militarized state, the Bureau widened its assignment. The members travelled the length and breadth of Nigeria to animate the debate and collated their different views before painstakingly synthesizing the huge pile of documentation into a report submitted to the government. In setting about the task, the Political Bureau did so in the settled knowledge that their report would provide a basis for a better and more enduring process of transition, based on the lessons from the aborted Second Republic and bearing in mind the widest possible consultations that had taken place and were reflected in its report.

Elsewhere we have analyzed the composition, debate, division and uncertainties in the Political Bureau (Oyediran in Diamond, Kirk-Greene and Oyediran, forthcoming; Oyediran and Badejo, forthcoming). Three of the closest political advisers of General Babangida in the first six years of his administration have in their own way looked at the role of the assignment given to the Political Bureau (Olagunju, Jinadu and Oyovbaire 1993). Though there is a very critical difference in these two analyses (understandable in the light of the role played by each) both agreed that "the objective of the Political Bureau was to shift the debate on the content and direction of the transition (political) programme away from in-house discussions and exchange of memoranda to a publicly-organized and populist based discussion which would, in a systematic and scientific manner, elicit, sift and analyze the views of the common man on the programme" (Olagunju, Jinadu and Oyovbaire 1993, 109).

In *Transition to Democracy in Nigeria, 1985–1993* Olagunju, Jinadu and Oyovbaire devoted five of the ten chapters in the book to the Political Bureau. If nothing else, this shows how important they considered the assignment given to the Bureau. The present author, a member of the group, can confirm that on a personal basis it was a pleasure to have been privileged to serve Nigeria as a member of the Political Bureau. It gave one a unique opportunity to be more familiar with the problems facing different parts and groups of Nigeria. It was that assignment that turned one into a great defender of the case which people from the oil-producing areas make on the sharing of revenue derived from petroleum. The plight of the Ogoni people and others in the oil-producing areas, and the plight of the men and women who live in the desert areas of Nigeria, were brought home to those who wished to notice, however completely different the plights might be. These were the realities that influenced the Report of the Political Bureau and the recommendations made to the government.

As expected, members of the Political Bureau did not agree on all issues. Probably the most controversial issue, which if not for the role played by the chairman would have led to a break-up of the Bureau before submitting its report, was that of state creation. The Bureau was split into two equal groups—those in favor of recommending the creation of more states (who split again as to the number and what they should be), and those of us who argued that more states will not solve the critical problems facing Nigeria and believed that, on the contrary more states will compound Nigeria's problems. Closely following this issue was the transition schedule. Should it end in 1990 as General Babangida announced when inaugurating the Bureau, or in 1992 as a minority argued?

Members were able to maintain the solidarity of the group only to a limited extent. There were seventeen members at the inauguration of the Bureau; only fifteen ended the fifteen-month assignment. One left in frustration because other members did not agree with his style; the other was eased out because he refused to obey the simple rule of keeping the happenings in the Bureau within the group rather than use the newspaper he worked for to publicize the division within the Bureau. Despite such internal frictions, the Political Bureau Report remains the most sought-after document that has comprehensively looked at the past and suggested the way to the political, economic and social future of Nigeria.

But as it turned out, the report was manipulated and twisted out of context in order to subvert the process of transfer of power to elected civilians. This process of delay was justified by the Babangida regime's ideologues as a process of political experimentation/engineering. To give an example, the Political Bureau Report included the following analysis of the transition process that led to the creation of the Second Republic in 1979:

> With the precision and speed with which all these activities were completed were commendable in retrospect, it would seem that the modalities and strategies for effective disengagement were not carefully worked out. The assumption that the old politicians had learnt their lessons during the thirteen years of non-partisan political activities was soon proved wrong. No new leadership had emerged to chart new course for the country, the old combative attitudes were to surface again during the Second Republic. It soon become clear that it would have been more responsible for the military to withdraw in stages to ensure proper supervision and monitoring of the new system that came into force in 1979 (Political Bureau Report 1987).

This single point was deployed to tinker with the duration or lifespan of the Babangida-led transition and to justify under the rubric of political experimentation the twists and turns of the increasingly convoluted transition process. All were explained away as shifts necessitated by "the learning process." Thus, the terminal date of the transition moved from 1990 to 1992 to 1993. In 1993, the date was shifted twice, and it was only when the pro-democratic forces in Nigerian civil society coincided with contradictions in the ranks of the politicized generals that Babangida "stepped aside," after hastily handing over power to an unelected and illegal handpicked Interim Government on August 26 1993.

There is no doubt that the events that took place between 1985 and 1993 are linked to the personality and highly manipulative style of the Babangida leadership, the greed of the politicized generals and power elite, the unprecedented level of official corruption, and the deep-seated economic crisis which further raised the stakes of political contest and exacerbated the politics of anxiety. As it turned out, the seeds of 1960 which had borne fruit in the Second Republic had multiplied a thousandfold. The banning of the so-called "old-breed" politicians and the funding and imposition of a two-party structure on the political arena manifested the desire of the government not only to be a supervisor of the political process, but to define and control it. As Fred Onyeoziri put it (*The Guardian* January 29 1988), the transition became a gift to, not the right of, citizens. To this end, the presidency embarked on a profuse creation of institutions: the Constituent Assembly, the Constitution Review Committee, the National Electoral Commission, the Centre for Democratic Studies, the Directorate for Social Mobilization, the National Council for Inter-Governmental Relations, and the Movement for Mass Mobilization for Self-Reliance and Economic Recovery among others. Amounting in part to an essay in class formation, the process of institution creation acted through cooptation and patron-client linkages to bring in new elite participants, the majority of whom were highly educated or were university professors. Apart from forming the ideological prop of Babangida's personal rule, and benefiting from his patronage and generosity to loyalists, they were involved in personal projects linked to either political career hopes, or to the perpetuation of the Babangida-led neopatrimonialism. To this group could be added the motley crowd of political jobbers, contractors, individuals seeking to settle political scores, ambitious bureaucrats and a new generation of politicized Colonels. In all, Babangida sought to capture the transition process, while he was captive to the contending factions and tendencies in both wings of the Nigerian power elite—military and civil—whom he played against each other and sought to compensate at the same time in his ingenious scheme of clinging to power. Hailed by his ideologues, and condemned by his critics, Babangida's annulment of the June 12 1993 Presidential elections, as a final act in a series of manipulations of "his" transition, turned out to be the final straw of his rule and his transition to nowhere. As we noted elsewhere:

> Within the context of what happened in the latter years of Babangida's administration—cancellation of the process for the formation of political parties, creation of new government named, sponsored, funded and directed political parties; banning and unbanning of groups and individuals from political participation; execution (assassination?) of opponents; regular postponement of return to civil rule, institutionalization of corruption and flamboyant living; indiscriminate dissolution of executive committees of politi-

cal parties; nullification of court decisions; unleashing of organized confusion and annulment of the widely acclaimed, freest and fairest and most peaceful election ever held in Nigeria - the misuse of the Report of the Political Bureau was simply the beginning of the unfolding of "the hidden agenda" of an authoritarian military who refused to surrender political power until he was disgraced from office on August 26, 1993 (Oyediran forthcoming).

How then can the Babangida phenomenon be explained in the context of the politics of transition in Nigeria? There is no doubt that the wily dictator took full advantage of the competing selfish interests that ranged free in the ranks of the politicized Generals; the desperation, avarice, immodesty and longing for power at any cost which fractured the civilian power elite; the atomization, anomie, and low level of organization for democratic governance in Nigerian civil society (most of the groups were elite-led urban creations); and the tacit support of the Western powers for an African leader "courageous" enough to impose structural adjustment on his people and to openly declare support for free enterprise and liberal democracy. The politicized Generals had an internal crisis in the post-Second Republic years. Many ambitious and relatively young Generals were retired and forced to leave the "house of power" when General Olusegun Obasanjo handed power to Alhaji Shehu Shagari. Now "civilianized," many of them sought to return to power via the ballot box, putting to use their old and existing connections, their immense economic resources and their newly won credentials as convert-democrats. Relatively new to the turf of civil politics, they manifested a dual character reflective of their military antecedents and their new ambition to be civilian democrats. Among the political class they generated an ambiguous response. While some civilian politicians pandered to their side, others distrusted them as pretenders and opportunists in pursuit of power which they had enjoyed for a long period. Either way, some of the retired Generals found their way into the two parties while others abstained from partisan politics but commented on political issues from time to time. Many distrusted the ruling General and his cohorts, whom they suspected of having a "hidden agenda."

In such a treacherous terrain, everything remained in a state of flux, and the ruling coalition constituted and reconstituted itself with Babangida remaining as the unchangeable constant and head. Meanwhile the civilian power elite, many of them freed from incarceration, rehabilitated and having participated in the Constituent Assembly, were ready for the race to the "House of Power." This obsession for power turned out to be their greatest undoing. They were successfully played against one another, tired by the long and cumbersome nature of the transition, bought out, humiliated, rehabilitated and tossed around. At the center of it all, Babangida remained the unchangeable constant.

Based on their experience with the Buhari-Idiagbon junta which resisted structural adjustment and refused to discuss a transition program, the Western powers saw in the Babangida regime a renewed commitment to economic structural adjustment, liberal democracy and laissez-faireism. They were prepared to tolerate his "political engineering" in the hope that the immense resources he had sunk into his transition would yield a more enduring, stable and sustainable democracy that would protect long-term Western economic and political interests. Their hopes came to grief on June 23 1993 when the June 12 presidential election globally recognized as free and fair was annulled by the author of the third transition—a most tragic assault on democracy in Nigeria.

Any doubt as to the motive of the annulment was soon removed by several developments. The role of the antidemocratic group, the Association for a Better Nigeria (ABN) in a Babangida-Must-Stay Campaign and the annulment of the Presidential elections was exposed in the confessions of Chief Abimbola Davies, one of the ABN henchmen. Likewise, the resignation of the editor of the *New Nigerian* newspapers in protest against inflammatory editorials being forced on him, and the controversial rulings of the Abuja courts were indicative (Suberu, forthcoming).

What legacy was left by the 1985–93 failed transition? Chief Tony Enahoro answered that question succinctly:

a. deification of suddenly-acquired wealth with no obvious source;
b. a free wheeling society where no questions are asked so long as the end and the means coincide;
c. economic policies which proved disastrous to the Naira and the common people of Nigeria;
d. closure of factories all over and mounting numbers of beggars in the streets;
e. decline in educational and moral standards;
f. corruption which General Danjuma observed had become "so abrasive, so flagrant and pervasive that it is frightening" (*Tell* July 19 1993, 25–27).

Having successfully derailed the transition with the annulment of the June 12 1993 presidential election, the next step was to conjure a political crisis in which the only option would be to let Babangida remain in power. The ethnicization of the post-June 12 crisis tore the political parties, and even the entire citizenship, and brought the nation to the brink of collapse. New elections were scheduled and then cancelled. The executives of both parties were divided over how to respond to the annulment, and later over whom to nominate into an Interim National Government. Meanwhile, the democratic forces in Nigerian civil society rendered the country ungovernable. At this point Babangida gave up power, and it was left to Shonekan, his unelected civilian hand-picked successor, as head of the Interim National Government (ING) to ride the storm. He could not. Lacking popular legitimacy and unacceptable either to the "politicized Generals" or to the power elite who saw him as a usurper and traitor, Shonekan's rule received a major jolt when the government he presided over was declared illegal by a Lagos Court in early November 1993. On November 17 General Abacha struck and dealt the final death blows to the ING and the third transition. In one fell stroke, all the elected national and state assemblies were dissolved and state executive councils were sacked. The elected local governments were not spared, neither were the political parties. Politics was banned.

In his maiden speech as Head of State in November 1993 General Abacha promised to enthrone a lasting and true democracy. In the warped logic of the politics of transition, the Babangida transition had been replaced by the Abacha transition. The cornerstone of this "new" Abacha transition was to be the Constitutional Conference in which representatives of the Nigerian people would fashion a firm, just and equitable basis for peaceful co-existence and national development. Like its precursor, its historicism denied any links to the transition process just aborted and presented itself as free from the "encumbrances" of the annulled June 12 Presidential elections. Thus it was argued the regime would need time for another phased program of disengagement, another transition. In embarking on his own transition, Abacha unwittingly compounded the political crisis with the forceful imposition of a teleological-political approach which seeks to structure the democratic choice so clearly and validly delivered by the Nigerian electorate June 12 1993.

The Fourth Transition: From Crisis to Despair

The constitution of the fourth transition as an obstruction to the actualization of the third is at the root of the current political crisis. Yet both transitions converge in terms of a pathological antidemocratic ethos, the constriction of democratic space in a highly militarized terrain. In this personalized form of rule, access, entry and participation are solely at the pleasure of His (military) Excellency, and opposition to his will is seen as an attack or disloyalty, to be met with stiff punishments in the interest of "national peace and security." In the current dispensation, the stakes of hanging onto power have escalated in a context where the economy has continued to decline and the avenues for accumulation have become fewer and more competitive. Within the power-elite, the factional cleavages have become sharper and the conflicts deeper. Anxiety at the possibility of the opposition capturing power or destabilizing the state has made the present rulers dig into their trenches, lashing out in paranoia in all directions. The regime seeks to crush all opposition and to guarantee that it is the only gladiator, unchallenged in the Nigerian political space to pursue a self-defined, self-timed and authoritarian program of transition.

If the current hegemonic faction of the politicized generals and their civilian power-elite allies have been so ready to crush all opposition at any cost and by all means at their disposal, how has the opposition fared in facing up to the new Leviathan? What does the current struggle for democracy portend for Nigeria? Is this a mere struggle for political office or is it a quest for a true democracy? How far will each of the opposing forces go in pursuit of its interest? Can Nigeria survive the violent onslaught of the trapped state?

In our reflections, we have come to the conclusion that what Nigeria is going through are the final rites of passage to democracy. At this conjucture, Nigerians are confronted as a people by a state trapped between a hostile international community, a bitter and frustrated civil society bent on seeing the immediate end to military rule, a devastated economy, and a badly fractured, unprincipled, opportunistic and corrupt ruling class. Unwilling to retreat, as retreat would spell surrender and the risk of being overrun by a vengeful civil society and the sidelined victors of the June 12 1993 cause, the state has plodded. The cost has been high, including draconian decrees, the jailing of all opposition, the banning of all unofficial politics, open hostility to well-meaning friends of Nigeria seeking a speedy return to democracy in Nigeria, and immense suffering borne by ordinary Nigerians. The concern of this paper lies at the heart of this insensitivity to the voice of democracy.

How has the opposition fared against the trapped state? Its fortunes have been mixed. The opposition has fared badly and well, but on balance it has succeeded in making matters worse for the trapped state, at a heavy cost to itself. Due to the linkages between the third and fourth transitions, the opposition has undergone some changes and shifting membership. In its ranks were new entrants after the June 12 1993 crisis, namely the civilian faction of the powers that felt cheated by the annulment of the presidential election. Yet its ranks had simultaneously been depleted by those who jumped ship into the ING, and then into the Abacha Administration. Among the politicized Generals (and Colonels), while most vocal ones preferred a broad-based National Government to be constituted, others felt democracy should be given a chance. As it turned out the democrats in this group were drowned out by those who favored annulment and hoped to benefit from it. But when it became clear that some of them could not benefit from the events that followed, they switched camps and joined the opposition.

At the level of the power elite—civil and military—the opposition took the form of the National Democratic Coalition (NADECO), a broad union of political associations, human rights groups, nationalists, minority rights groups and even political fortune seekers. Their effort was complemented by the activities of the Campaign for Democracy—a coalition of human rights groups, student organizations and labor unions. Their demands ranged from the reinstatement of all dissolved democratic institutions and the proclamation of Chief M.K.O. Abiola as President-elect, to the formation of a National Government with Abiola as the Head to convene a sovereign National Conference to resolve the nation's problems. But all were agreed on the need for an immediate end to military rule. Through legal actions, strikes and demonstrations they rendered the country ungovernable and attempted to block Abacha's new transition. As attempts to influence events were outlawed by new decrees, and as the entry into political dialogue was shut, some members of the opposition resorted to counter-violence.

The opposition in Nigeria gained strength from the support given to the cause of democracy by the international community. In particular the United States and the European Union, and Canada as well as the Mandela-led government of South Africa have shown concern about the grave political situation in Nigeria. In order to express displeasure at the annulment and the scuttling of democracy in Nigeria, the world's leading democracies imposed limited sanctions on the Nigerian military and their civilian cohorts in the hope that this would push the Nigerian state out of the trap into which its unbridled authoritarianism and sit-tight posture has put it. Today, the patience of the international community with the trapped state is fast wearing thin. Appeals are giving way to threats in the face of rising domestic pressures in Europe and the U.S. for their governments to act decisively in the defense of democracy in Nigeria.

Smarting from their losses, the "democratic" faction of the politicized Generals (and Colonels) and others who lost in the changing of guards of August 26 and November 17 1993, decided it was time to hit back, either by blocking Abacha's transition and forcing the acceptance of the June 12 election results, or by entering Abacha's transition to take it over from within for their own purposes. In one of his critiques of the Abacha political ethos, a former Head of State (now in detention) noted, inter alia:

> . . . responsive governments and societies can be better chastised and sanitized through speech debate, discussion and dialogue no matter how unpleasant, than through violence (Obasanjo 1994).

This course was a frontal attack on Abacha's refusal to discuss the resolution of the June 12 question outside the parameters of his transition—a discussion which he feared could render his transition irrelevant and his claim to power destroyed. Being linked himself to the failed third transition and knowing what fate had befallen Babangida, he wanted to avoid the "mistake" Babangida made when he withdrew on August 26 1993. As the ex-head of state cited above further noted:

> General Babangida is the main architect of the state in which the nation finds itself today and General Sani Abacha was his eminent disciple, faithful supporter and beneficiary (Obasanjo 1994, 1).

What is obvious from the above is the strong link of continuity that connects the third and fourth transitions as political projects of the hegemonic antidemocratic forces in Nigeria: insecure and desperate to remain in control of state power. To ask them to give up state power is akin to asking them to drink hemlock. Under their power democracy cannot but be cast in a tightly controlled authoritarian image. It is a mask of convenience to be worn when the occasion demands and to be cast aside when threatened by democratic forces.

From the trend of events that have followed the recently concluded constitutional conference, it is all too clear to the discerning mind that the outcome of this government-sponsored conference will be heavily "doctored" by the government. In a recent public forum, the Secretary to the Chief of General Staff, Lt. General Ladipo Diya, said that the constitution will not be promulgated until 1998 when the transition is to end. As an editorial in the *National Concord* (February 9 1996) reminded the regime, "The military regime on its own volition imposed on the nation a 36 month program of 'transition to democracy' in October last year. A prominent item on the first quarter (October to December 1995) of the schedule was the promulgation of the 1995 constitution." The setting up of a Constitutional Review Committee, along with the pronouncement of many government functionaries underscore that the work of the constitutional conference is regarded as a mere proposal subject to vetting by the Provisional Ruling Council, over which the "eminent beneficiary" of the third transition, General Abacha, holds unchallenged sway.

From every angle, it would appear that things are not going well with the regime. General Abacha lost his eldest son in a plane crash when the presidential jet in which Abacha's son was traveling with thirteen of his friends crashed at Kano Airport in January 1996. Several bombs have exploded in Kano, Kaduna and Lagos.

At the same time, the opposition has suffered heavy losses. Many of its leading members are in exile, in detention, have been convicted for treason, are on the run, or are living in daily fear of any of the aforementioned happening to them. Others have been penetrated and bought out. Meanwhile the populace has become weary from long periods of crisis in 1993 and 1994 and sinks into despair. The labor movement has been penetrated, discredited and weakened as a potent source of opposition, while the new political associations, lacking a united democratic goal, study the unfolding scenario to see where their political fortunes may lie. The weakening of the opposition internally has fed into the strength of the opposition in exile which has waged an effective campaign for the restoration of democracy in Nigeria. What remains to be seen are the links between external and internal opposition. More will be learnt in the months and years to come.

The greatest casualty of the current crisis has been the state. National institutions have been left in shambles, and with the obsession with politics and material gain at the expense of everything else, people have lost confidence in institutions, in structures, in due process, and, of course, in leaders of all kind. The problem of the blockage of democratic transition by the forces of authoritarianism—military and civilian—poses the greatest danger confronting Nigeria, and indeed Africa, today. It transcends Babangida and Abacha who, at the end of the day, may well have been victims of stronger now hidden hegemonic forces. And time is running out.

How do Nigerians look beyond the immediate climate of doom to the future? Unfortunately for many, there appears to be no future. Many Nigerians have come to accept that the minimum number of years to return to what the Nigerian political scene was at the end of 1983 is ten. Sam Nwanze, writing in the *National Concord* of February 16 1996, speaks for this group when he said, "My view . . . is that the nation is completely ruined. There is just nowhere to hide." He goes on:

> Look at the educational sector. . . . Today education from primary to university level is on the verge of total collapse.
> Students in both secondary and tertiary institutions face the threat of total breakdown of the educational sector.
> The health sector is not different; we have moved from "consulting clinics" to "mortuaries" in our hospitals. No drugs, no infrastructure, no equipment, nothing, except beds. The private and teaching hospitals are out of the reach of the common man.
> Look at the transport sector. Road, rail, air, sea, all are in shambles. Vehicles, ferries, wagons and coaches have simply disappeared. Aeroplanes are "flying coffins" according to the minister in charge . . .
> Now, the housing sector. A bag of cement is over N500. You do not talk of roofing sheets. Landlords and tenants keep on getting at each other's throat everyday over rents on the few available houses in the cities.
> And then food. How many Nigerians can afford a comfortable two square meals these days? Garri which used to be the "arbiter" as people soaked it in water with groundnuts is no longer there . . .

Nwanze ends with hope. "But I know we will rise again if we come together with sincerity of purpose to discuss how to begin all over again . . . Nigeria will not go under. We will rise."

Conclusion

One searches for a solid basis of hope in despair. But the obstacles are great. One notes the deep fractionalization of the Nigerian political class, the "over-politicization" of the military, and the mercenary character of the civilian power elite. Likewise one must note the cynicism of the Nigerian populace, the castration of the judiciary, and the complication of the unresolved but blocked third transition. It is possible the politics of brinkmanship may backfire, with disastrous consequences for Nigeria.

The other side of the coin is that Nigerians now know who the enemies of democracy are. They know how not to go about a transition to democratic governance. They know that the resolution of the National Question—the relations of Nigeria's constituent groups—has to be done through dialogue, negotiation, consensus and democracy. Increasing numbers also believe in consonance with the global trend that military rule has outlived its usefulness and must be replaced immediately with democracy.

But with the "democrats" of yesterday now functioning as supporters of military rule as a necessary step towards democracy, while some generals of yore become converts to democracy asking the military to leave at once, the confusing scenario is a recipe for more bitter contestations over power.

The reliance on state terror to deal with the opposition, shutting the door to dialogue except on the terms of the "trapped state" in the midst of an economy crippled by inflation, corruption, factory shut-downs and a weakened oil sector, is a recipe for more social convulsions and greater violence. Frustrated and bitter, the democratic opposition is bound to overcome its present temporary reversals and engage the state headlong. With all avenues for peaceful dialogue blocked, and the confidence and trust needed to solve problems eroded by past experiences of betrayal, deceit and treachery, the signs of a possible violent resolution begin to take the form of an inevitability. The cost of such would be too grievous to imagine. Are there any trade-offs that can convince the contending forces to step back from the precipice? Will the current efforts by well-intentioned individuals, groups in Nigeria, and governments in Africa, Europe, Asia and America succeed in reversing our rapid descent into fratricidal crisis and conflict? Or might an unknown factor—a third force—emerge in Nigeria to clear the mess created by the squabbling factions of the ruling class through a violent process of social and political re-birth? The Nigerian situation includes all these possibilities and shows that Nigeria is on the verge of a momentous political event.

The action of the military government of General Abacha in hanging Ken Saro-Wiwa and eight of his colleagues in the Movement for the Survival of Ogoni People (MOSOP) on Friday, November 10 1995, for asking for a fair and ethical treatment of their people in the distribution of the rent that the nation collects from petroleum which comes from their backyard, turned Nigeria into a pariah state worldwide. That incident becomes part of the despair in which Nigerians and all those who love Nigeria find themselves today. The hope is that whenever civilian political leaders, as bad as most of them are, do not get it right in the future when they take over political power (as they must), it will not be the military that Nigerians will look to for salvation.

Any Nigerian who experiences the type of encounter which Professor Niyi Osundare had with two other Africans at a conference soon after the hanging of Ken Saro-Wiwa and his compatriots cannot but weep for the low esteem in which his country is now held. According to Osundare (1996), by far the most moving encounter he had during the month of the hanging in November 1995 was with a Zambian, who held to my arm and asked with agonizing concern . . . Tell me, my brother, why is your country Nigeria doing this to us? Why have you brought all this shame on Africa? Look, they called me murderer at my place of work yesterday. All of them, white folk so appalled by those terrible hangings in your country. Why has Nigeria done this to Africa? His grip tightened on my arm, even as tears rolled down his middle-aged face.

But that was not all for Osundare. Another African met him on the same spot—this time a South African. This is what he said:

What has come upon Nigeria? Tell me, what? First a fouled-up election, now these murders. What gods has Nigeria offended? See, when Nigeria spoke in the seventies and eighties, the world listened. The rest of Africa lined up behind her. Speak for us, they said. See, I am a South African. I know what I am talking about. I have the memory of Sharpeville. I nearly perished in Soweto. You see, Nigeria was part of the South African struggle for freedom. Spatial distance notwithstanding, she was regarded as a front-line state. Nigeria took part in the Liberation of my country. A very big shame, Nigeria now needs to be liberated from its own black Boers!

The question of "the military as the last bastion of hope and defence for the unity and integrity of Nigeria" (Obasanjo 1987) has been forcefully answered in the negative. Hope lies in the democratic realization of the transition, despair lies in the triumph of authoritarian and reactionary forces.

As Larry Diamond noted as far back as 1991 while reflecting on the importance of a democratic Nigeria, "if democracy is to take hold in the Africa of the 1990s, it must succeed in Nigeria" (Diamond 1991). Nigeria is the key. We must break this tragic circle.

References

Agbaje, Adigun. 1994. "Beyond the Generals: Twilight of Democracy in Nigeria." *Africa Demos*, 3, 3 (September): 4–5.
Ayandele, E.A. 1974. *The Educated Elite in the Nigerian Society*. Ibadan: University of Ibadan Press.
Babangida, Ibrahim. 1987. Address to Senior Armed Forces Officers. Abuja, October 17 (mimeograph).
Coleman, James S. 1958. *Nigeria: Background to Nationalism*. Berkeley: University of California Press.
Diamond, Larry. 1991. "Nigeria's Search for a New Political Order." *Journal of Democracy*, 2, 2 (Spring): 54–69.

Falola, Toyin and Julius Ihonvbere. 1985. *The Rise and Fall of Nigeria's Second Republic, 1979–1984*. London: Zed Press.

Joseph, Richard. 1987. *Democracy and Prebendal Politics in Nigeria: The Rise and Fall of the Second Republic*. Cambridge: Cambridge University Press.

Obasanjo, Olusegun. 1994. [Key Note] Address at the Conference "State of the Nation: Which Way Forward?" February 2 (mimeograph).

———. 1987. Address at the launching of the book, *Diplomatic Soldiering* by Major-General Joe Garba.

Olagunju, Tunji, Adele Jinadu, and Sam Oyovbaire. 1993. *Transition and Democracy in Nigeria 1985–1993*. Ibadan: Safari Books.

Osundare, Niyi. 1996. "Not an Internal Affair." *Newswatch*, (February 19): 6.

Oyediran, Oyeleye. 1988/89. "The Gospel of the Second Chance: A Comparison of Obasanjo and Babangida Military Disengagement in Nigeria." *Quarterly Journal of Administration*, 23, 1 & 2.

———. forthcoming. "The Political Bureau." In Larry Diamond, Anthony Kirk-Greene and Oyeleye Oyediran, eds., *Transition Without End in Nigeria, Politics, Governance and Civil Society 1985–1993*.

Oyediran, Oyeleye and Babafemi Badejo. forthcoming. "The Political Bureau Report and Government Reaction to it." In M. Oluyemi-Kusa (ed.), *Governance and Political Economy in Nigeria under Babangida Administration*.

Sklar, Richard L. 1963. *Nigerian Political Parties: Power in an Emergent African Nation*. Princeton: Princeton University Press.

Suberu, Rotimi. forthcoming. "Crisis and Collapse: June-November 1993." In Larry Diamond, Anthony Kirk-Greene and Oyeleye Oyediran (eds.), *Transition Without End in Nigeria, Politics, Governance and Civil Society 1985–1993*.

9

1993: CRISIS AND BREAKDOWN OF NIGERIA'S TRANSITION TO DEMOCRACY

David Emelifeonwu

Widespread public protests greeted President Babangida's decision to annul the June 12 1993 presidential elections. In major cities throughout the southwest region, people took to the streets to vent their anger not only at the news of the annulment but also at the arbitrary way the administration had managed the political transition process (Adeosun 1993, 10). In the face of these protests, the administration searched for a solution which, among other things, could reassure the public while maintaining a strong, organized front. To this end, on June 26, President Babangida addressed the nation to offer explanations as to why the June 12 elections were annulled and to reveal the administration's immediate plans to put the transition program back on track.

On July 31, this speech opened a rather confused period including many rounds of acrimonious negotiations as the military regime attempted to define what had become a full-blown political crisis. The three protagonists—the administration and the chairpersons of the two political parties—settled on the idea of an interim national government as a way to resolve the political crisis. On August 26 1993 President Babangida stepped down as head of state and Chief Ernest Shonekan was sworn in as the head of the Interim National Government (ING).

The foregoing summary of events raises a number of questions: for example, what events precipitated the annulment of the June 12 presidential elections? What was the response of the two political parties to the President's announcement? How and why did the three protagonists in this drama—the two parties and the military government—settle for the interim government solution? This chapter will consider these questions.

This essay is divided into two sections. In the first section, I will examine the crises which preceded the administration's decision to annul the June 12 presidential elections as well as the explanations proffered by President Babangida for so doing. In the second section, I will discuss the negotiations between the government and the two political parties. In a concluding section, I will view these events in the larger context of the patrimonial state.

Behind the Annulment

The first crisis of the June 12 presidential elections began five days before the election. On June 7 1993, Mr. Abimbola Davies, National Director of a previously unknown political organization—the Association for Better Nigeria (ABN)[1]—sought a court injunction restraining the National Electoral Commission (NEC) from proceeding with the planned presidential elections. At the time, no one, not even NEC or the two political parties, took the lawsuit seriously (Agbroko 1994, 12). The political parties and officials of NEC were confident that the lawsuit would be thrown out and the ABN's legal antics brought to an end. Officials of NEC reasoned, and at the time correctly, that under the Presidential Election Decree 13 of 1993 they could not be taken to court.

To the surprise of NEC officials, on June 10 1993, Judge (Mrs.) Bassey Ikpeme of the Abuja high court granted the ABN the court injunction it sought. In her ruling, Judge Ikpeme said:

> I have the jurisdiction to hear this matter. NEC is not to determine a stable stage for democracy but only to conduct [elections]. [Decree 13] does not preclude me but encourages NEC to disregard any ruling. . . . NEC is hereby restrained from conducting the presidential election pending the determination of the substantive suit before the court (Opara 1993, 12).

On June 11, two residents of Lagos, Sunbo Onitiri and Richard Adejumo, filed a lawsuit compelling NEC to go ahead with the election. On the same day, Judge Moshood Olugbami of the Lagos high court also ruled that NEC must proceed with the election. In his ruling, Olugbami said:

> The court is aware that the effect of not having an election may be a breakdown of law, order and a disaster. It is obliged under the law to uphold and enforce obedience to [the] law (Agbo 1993a, 9).

NEC chairman Humphrey Nwosu had decided in any case to proceed with the scheduled presidential elections. Nwosu reasoned that Decree 13 gave him the legal backing to ignore any court order restraining NEC from performing its legally assigned duties. On June 12 the presidential election was held and from all accounts the polling was mainly free and fair. Thus ended the first crisis of the presidential elections.

The second crisis of the June 12 presidential elections started the following week. Unbeknownst to members of the public, to the two political parties, and to NEC, the now infamous ABN had filed another court injunction against NEC. The ABN now wanted the courts to restrain NEC from releasing further results of the presidential elections. On June 15 1993 the ABN obtained a court order to this effect from the Chief Judge of Abuja, Dahiru Saleh. In his ruling, Saleh observed that: "it was illegal for NEC to have conducted the [June 12] election in the first instance, because it was held 'contrary to a court order prohibiting the same'" (Agbo 1993a, 12).

In the face of the latest court ruling, on June 16 1993, Humphrey Nwosu announced to a bewildered nation that NEC would comply with the latest court ruling. As Nwosu explained the court ruling:

> [NEC had gone to court] to challenge the right of the Abuja high court to enter contempt proceedings against the commission or any of its officers. [He added that NEC would] file an appeal to the court of appeal, together with a motion for accelerated hearing, challenging the jurisdiction of the said court to entertain the suit and the motion restraining the commission from conducting the said election. [Lastly Nwosu said that] in the light of the current development, the commission has in deference to the court's injunction and other actions pending in court, decided to stay action on all matters pertaining to the presidential election until further notice (Agbo 1993a, 13–14).

It did not help matters for the NEC chairman that earlier that same week, NEC had released provisional results from 14 states of the federation showing SDP flagbearer—Moshood Abiola—with a commanding lead over his NRC opponent, Bashir Tofa.

The public was stunned by the news that NEC had suspended further release of the results from the presidential elections. The general public could not understand why Nwosu had bowed to the court order. They reasoned that if Nwosu had ignored the previous court order, he should also ignore the present one. What the public did not know at the time was that more powerful social forces had pressured Nwosu to suspend further release of the presidential results.[2] Following Nwosu's announcement, the NRC chairman, Dr. Hammed Kusamotu, issued a statement to the effect that the NRC did not approve of the decision. The NRC chairman said:

> This is another unfortunate action against the development of democracy in Nigeria. This frequent arbitrariness of NEC in the handling of sensitive national issues is a recipe for confusion and chaos which all right thinking Nigerians who love genuine democracy must reject (Agbo 1993a, 15).[3]

For his part, SDP chairman, Chief Tony Anenih, observed that NEC's action was "inciting, undemocratic and unfortunate...." (Agbo 1993a, 15).

Thereafter, the leadership of the two political parties converged on Abuja on June 17 to establish a joint response to the NEC chairman's decision (Agbo 1993a, 15). At the close of their meeting, the leadership of both political parties resolved to unite their forces against the ABN and in a show of support, the leadership of the NRC pledged to assist the SDP in its struggle to reinstate the June 12 results. However, the NRC's apparent show of support belied the conditionality of its pledge. In fact the NRC's pledge was contingent upon the SDP's willingness to share with it government portfolios. According to *Newswatch* magazine:

> At the meeting, the NRC pledged its support if the SDP will as well pledge to form a government of national unity, zone six ministerial positions to the party and ensure reasonable spread of other governmental positions, such as chairmanship and membership of boards of government parastatals (Agbo 1993a, 15).

For its part, the government delayed issuing a statement on the NEC chairman's decision. Overall, the attitude of the government was to feign ignorance about the political crisis. When the government managed to issue a statement, it was to the effect that it had not yet received a report of the election from NEC (Agbo 1993a, 9). Moreover, it did not help the administration's image that newspapers and magazines had earlier reported that senior military officers and key government officials were operating behind the scenes to scuttle the June 12 elections. According to *Newswatch*:

> Senior military officers feared that the first duty of an Abiola government was to retire some of them. [Such action the officers feared] would dislocate

seniority within the armed forces and allow the emergence of military chiefs who ordinarily may never have attained that position. [For their part, key government officials feared that] Abiola may use the opportunity of his being in government to reverse all the policies of Babangida, and disgrace his tenure. [In addition] they [saw] Abiola as excitable and populist, a man who, once in power, would dance to the peoples' tune at the expense of Babangida's name (Agbo 1993a, 10).

It is significant that for almost two weeks the President had not issued a detailed statement on the suspended election results. His continued silence fueled widespread public suspicion that his administration had aided and abetted the ABN. Official word came, at last, on June 26 1993, when President Babangida addressed the nation on the events of the past week and a half.[4]

Aside from explaining to the nation why the results of the June 12 elections were suspended, President Babangida's broadcast was instructive in other respects as well: first, it revealed to the nation what the administration planned for the remainder of the transition program. Second, it showed that the administration was very much opposed to an Abiola presidency. Lastly, it demonstrated the arbitrariness of the administration.

Concerning the administration's plans for the remainder of the transition program, President Babangida announced that the National Electoral Commission (NEC) would be reconstituted and a new chairperson appointed. In addition, the President indicated that the newly reconstituted NEC would organize a fresh presidential election for the end of July 1993.

But the president tabled a new set of criteria for contesting the next round of presidential elections: first, each presidential candidate must not be less than 50 years old. Second, each must have been a registered member of one of the two political parties for at least one year. Third, their business interests must not conflict with the interests of the nation.[5] Lastly Babangida mentioned that the administration had undertaken to unban politicians who had previously been banned from contesting the presidential elections.[6]

Setting aside the allegations of bribery and corruption,[7] it is more instructive to focus attention on the issue of conflict of interest as described in President Babangida's broadcast. The compelling reason for focusing attention on this issue is that it illuminates the patronage relationship between members of Nigeria's political class and officials of the state. Furthermore, it reflects upon the imperiled nature of transitions under conditions of neopatrimonialism.

Conflict of interest, per se, had less to do with the two presidential candidates than it had to do with the relationship of the political class to the state. Moreover, the issue had more to do with power and control than it had to do, at least at the time, with the capacity of both presidential candidates to govern the nation effectively.

The majority of Nigeria's political class are beholden to the state because of the enormous opportunities to acquire wealth (Nwabueze 1994, 86–88; Ibrahim 1992, 121–24; Joseph 1991, 55–59; Graf 1988, 218–41). They struggle to gain access to the state or to capture the state outright for the purposes of wealth accumulation. As a result, the struggle among members of the political class for such access is not only intense but is often characterized by intolerance and violence. In this struggle, both winners and losers risk everything; thus the much repeated observation that politics and the electoral game in Nigeria and throughout much of sub-Saharan Africa is a zero-sum competition.

There are two basic implications with respect to political transitions which flow from the foregoing relationship. First, due to the dependent relationship of the political class on the state, the former lacks the autonomy and scope of action it needs to challenge regime officials, especially when they act in an arbitrary fashion during the transition process. The political class is also exposed to threats of blackmail by the regime. Take for example, Babangida's charge of conflict of interest against Moshood Abiola. Second, through the linkages of the political class to the rest of society, the dependent relationship is spread to the grassroots with the consequence that the masses have limited scope for action against the political class and the authoritarian regime. The dysfunctional relationships between the state and the political class and consequently the political class and the masses work to thoroughly impede the development of civil society.

Could the issue of conflict of interest have been avoided? At the present time, it is doubtful. For the most part, members of the political class are not engaged in any meaningful productive economic activity. Their livelihoods depend, as it were, on the economic rents they farm from the state. To do otherwise would be tantamount to committing class suicide because outside the orbit of the state few opportunities are available for wealth accumulation. Therefore, breaking the ties of the political class to the Nigerian state would require, at a minimum, that members of the class first cease collectively to farm economic rents from the state; and second, that the way in which the state manages the economy and conducts its affairs is changed. Associated with the first requirement, however, is the difficult problem of policing and enforcing collective behavior among rational egoists. With regards to the second requirement, the difficulty lies in creating alternative avenues for private capital accumulation as well as improving the transparency in state budgetary allocations.

Thus the significance of President Babangida's last minute allegations of conflict of interest against the two presidential candidates is that insofar as members of the political class themselves do not ascribe to rational-legal norms, they should not expect the administration belatedly to adhere to strict democratic rules. President Babangida was emboldened to raise the issue of conflict of interest because he was aware of the business activities of many members of the political class, not the least of which were the two presidential candidates. Of course, this is not to say that while in office the President did not enrich himself, quite the contrary. However, by rationalizing the annulment of the elections on the grounds of conflict of interest, Babangida was challenging the democratic credentials of the political class.

A measure of the administration's exercise of power and control can be seen through its successive rounds of banning and unbanning members of the political class from participating in the presidential elections. The effects of such activities are twofold: first, by exercising the power to include and exclude presidential candidates at will, the administration was able to divide members of the political class and thus prevent them from acting against it; second, by being able to determine who can and cannot compete in the elections, the administration was able to shape and influence the quality and substance of the presidential contest.

Beginning with the first effect, it is often members of the political class who pressure state officials to ban one or more of their members from the presidential race. The motive behind this action is to pave the way for their own candidacy and to make the competition less demanding.[8] With regard to the second effect, by exercising the power to pick and choose players, the administration can vary the caliber of candidates as well as the substantive issues debated during the electoral campaigns, thereby ensuring that the status quo is maintained.

President Babangida and members of his administration were aware that by unbanning previously banned politicians they would sow the seeds of discord among members of the political class, as well as gain the upper hand in the upcoming negotiations with leaders of the political parties. In addition, by opening the door to more presidential candidates the administration was, in effect, challenging members of the political class to reveal their true behavior, namely their perennial infighting and recourse to regionalism, ethnicism, and political thuggery.

What emerges from the foregoing discussions is the dependency of

Nigeria's political class on the state as well as the arbitrary nature of rule under Babangida's administration. As can be seen from the ensuing negotiations, this dependency cost the political class the resolve to challenge the administration's annulment.

After the Annulment

In the face of negative public response to its decision, the administration initiated a campaign of damage control by consulting with all manner of politicians and leaders of thought in the country (Akintunde 1993, 15). For their part, leaders of both political parties met separately to analyze the contents and implications of the President's broadcast. In the NRC, party leaders resolved to submit to another round of presidential elections. In the SDP, party chieftains resolved to oppose any new elections and to stand by June 12. The latter's position, however, belied the fact that not all the SDP members were opposed to another round of presidential elections.

The SDP's public opposition to a fresh presidential election at first would imply that the government had no room for maneuver; not so. The government did not have to look very far for a safe berth as infighting among members of the SDP gave it the opening it sought. In the June 26 broadcast the president had unbanned previously banned politicians; this decision served to rekindle the presidential ambitions of those politicians. However, before those candidates could realize their ambitions they had to first persuade their respective parties to forget the annulment and accede to a new round of presidential elections. As the jockeying for power and position intensified inside both political parties, more so inside the SDP, cracks began to appear within their ranks. The administration took full advantage of the divisions to sell its vision for the remainder of the transition program to the political parties.

Before discussing the cracks inside the SDP and the government's strategy for the remainder of the transition, it is useful to briefly discuss the meaning of elections under conditions of prebendalism.

Because capturing political power is the main avenue for self enrichment, elections are generally not about selling competing policies or ideas about governance to the electorate or, most importantly, about the electorate exercising their franchise. Rather, elections are formalities (stepping stones) on the road to capturing power. Elections provide an opportunity for politicians to rouse sectarian interests, rather than an occasion for aggregating and representing broad public interests. Because of the stakes involved, it is unsurprising that elections are conducted as a "war of all against all." With reference to the June 12 crisis, the NRC welcomed another opportunity to face its political rival, the SDP, because it had never accepted the verdict of the first election. Had the tables been turned, the SDP surely would have behaved likewise.

For their part, formerly banned politicians welcomed the opportunity to compete again because it drew them closer to their ultimate goal of capturing state power. Like leaders of the NRC and some elements within the SDP, it was of no particular consequence to them that the administration had exercised a veto on the electoral proceedings. From their perspective, the most recent victims of the administration's veto deserved what they got; after all they—the formerly banned politicians—had been victimized by a similar veto following the 1992 presidential primary. Foremost on their minds was the opportunity to compete again; thus they tacitly supported the administration's plans to schedule another round of presidential elections.

After due consideration of the president's June 26 announcement, the parties reached the following decisions: for the NRC, to submit to a fresh presidential election; and for the SDP, to stand by June 12. Before delving into the specifics of the ensuing negotiations, it is useful to consider three important questions: first, what were some of the expectations of the three participants? Second, why did the SDP enter into negotiations with the administration and the NRC? Third, over what exactly were they negotiating?

The three protagonists—the administration, the SDP, and the NRC—had different expectations and goals as they approached the negotiations. The government's expectations were based on two possible outcomes: first, both parties would refuse the government's offer following which there would be a breakdown of law and order giving the administration the excuse to perpetuate itself in power; second, both parties, including the SDP, would ultimately submit to another round of elections. The NRC had one specific goal in mind, namely to demand a fresh presidential election and hope to win the second time around. Due to internal divisions, the SDP's expectations were divided.

The SDP entered into negotiations with the administration and the NRC on the assumption that if the party stood its ground and public pressure were sufficient, the administration might experience a change of heart and rescind the annulment. However, the steps taken by Babangida after his June 26 broadcast left no doubt that he did not desire to have Moshood Abiola succeed him in office. Moreover, for Babangida to have rescinded his decision of June 26, as the SDP would have had him do, would have meant further loss of credibility not only for him but also for the military, and the real possibility of a coup. Ultimately, the growing fissures inside the ranks of the SDP were what forced the party into negotiations with the administration and the NRC. A significant fraction of the SDP was negotiating because it wanted its point man—Shehu Yar'Adua—to have a shot at becoming the next president in new elections. They were interested in negotiations if it would undo the government's verdict of June 26 to annul the elections.

Heading into the negotiations, the administration took two important steps to signal that it would not rescind its decision to annul the June 12 elections. First, as promised, the administration appointed a new chairperson, Professor Okon Uya, to head NEC. Second, the administration announced the new dates for the next round of presidential elections.[9] Lacking a common strategy because of internal divisions, the leaders of the SDP (much to the chagrin of Moshood Abiola) agreed to participate in the negotiations with the administration and the NRC. The administration interpreted the SDP's willingness to participate as a signal that the party was amenable to reaching a compromise solution.

At the opening round of the negotiations, the administration tabled two options: (1) repeat the process of presidential primaries as a prelude to choosing candidates for the new round of presidential elections or (2) skip having another presidential election and instead allow each political party to submit a candidate to an electoral college. The administration preferred the second option because it would "make the two political parties work together for a more enduring foundation for the Third Republic" (Agbo 1993b, 10). As *Newswatch* put it:

> [The second option was] the military option. . . . In this case, all local government chairmen and members of the state national assemblies would constitute an electoral college to elect the president. Whoever wins in the election becomes the president while the loser becomes the vice president. They will now form a national government for an interim period of two years (Agbo 1993b, 8 and 10).

With respect to the first option, the administration also considered allowing a third party candidate or an independent candidate to contest the next round of elections. According to *Newswatch*:

> There was a strong lobby for the president to approve the formation of one or more [additional] political parties. The argument was that many people

in the existing political parties were only there because they had no other choice. The presidency, however, rejected the proposal because of the cost involved and the short time left in the transition programme. A middle-of-the-road decision was therefore adopted, that is to tinker with the constitution to allow for independent candidates (Agbo 1993b, 10).[10]

Thus, confronted with the administration's twin options—accede to a fresh presidential election or submit two candidates to an electoral college, the NRC chose the first option. NRC party executives reasoned correctly that they would lose in an electoral college arrangement because the SDP had a majority in both houses of the National Assembly. For its part, the SDP rejected both options citing time and money. Moreover, party leaders had not come to terms with the annulment of the June 12 elections. As party chairman Chief Tony Anenih explained: "[the SDP had] not changed [its] mind. We are not ready for fresh election because the one held on June 12 is still valid" (Ukim 1993, 10). In response to the SDP, the administration insisted that a fresh election would be held with or without the party's cooperation.

Over the weekend of July 3–4 both parties met separately to discuss with their members the administration's latest insistence on a new round of presidential elections. The SDP met in Benin while the NRC met in Port Harcourt (Anyanwu 1993, 8; Agbo 1993d, 13). At the close of the meeting, SDP leaders resolved "to stick to the June 12 election from [their] heads and not [their] hearts" (Ohakwe and Olaniyonu 1993, 9). Conversely, NRC leaders resolved to participate in the new round of presidential elections. Party chairman, Dr. Hammed Kusamotu, rationalized the decision thusly: "what is paramount now is that the NRC believes that nothing should be done to derail the transition programme. To us all hands should be on deck to make August 27 realistic" ("SDP, NRC Shape Up" 1993, A2).

As previously scheduled, the administration met with leaders of the two parties on July 5 to learn whether or not they had agreed to participate in another round of elections. The meeting did not start well because of the resolution adopted by the SDP over the weekend, to the effect that the SDP would "not sponsor any candidate for a fresh poll, nor should its supporters participate in any new election" ("Political Crisis: Anxiety" 1993, A10). With this resolution, the SDP had determined its position. In response, at the close of the July 5 meeting, the administration issued an ultimatum to leaders of both political parties "to decide within 72 hours whether to accede to a new election or form an interim national government which would necessitate the demolition of all democratic structures existing since 1990" ("Political Crisis: Anxiety" 1993, A10; Ogunleye and

Efeni 1993, 9).[11] By this threat, the administration succeeded finally in breaking the already fragile resolve of the SDP.

The administration's threat to dissolve all existing democratic structures was a stroke of genius. The threat had the intended effect of exacerbating the divisions within the SDP. In addition, it frightened elected office holders of both parties into pressuring their party executives to reach a compromise with the administration. The implication of the threat, according to one published account, was:

> [It would have meant] the sacking of, at least, 5,000 political office holders made up of 30 governors, 91 senators, 589 members of the House of Representatives, 1,178 members of state assemblies, 589 local government chairmen, more than 2,000 councillors and, at least, 1,000 party officials at the ward, local government, state and national levels (Ukim 1993, 12).

The panic of elected office holders in reaction to the government's threat gives us an additional insight into Nigeria's political class. In the context of neopatrimonialism, running for elected office is an investment to be recouped by the successful candidates at a later date. In other words, public offices are treated as personal domains through which elected officers can acquire wealth. Thus, by threatening to abolish all democratic structures, the administration had knowingly threatened the dividends that would have accrued to elected office holders. As one source put it:

> [Lawmakers] have invested money in their elections and their investments are still to yield financial dividends as there have been no opportunities created by their circumscribed legislative activity. Even before the latest development, many were already agitated by the bleak financial prospects (Anyanwu 1993, 9).

Therefore, notwithstanding pleas from party leaders for personal sacrifice and perseverance, elected office holders on their own initiatives pleaded with the administration not to make good with its threat. Aside from the pleas by elected office holders, sectional leaders within the SDP were no less interested in cutting a deal with the administration. As one member reasoned:

> Abiola needs to be punished for acting as Babangida's ambassador plenipotentiary last year when they were banned. He [Abiola] was said to have gone around the country to canvass support for the cancellation (Ukim 1993, 12).

For his part, Abiola issued a statement:

> [asking all] political office holders to ignore the threat as Babangida would be acting 'beyond his authority'. . . .This latest blackmail is another example of the General's total disregard for the ordinary Nigerian people at every level and there is therefore no basis whatsoever for any Nigerian to continue to give regard to such a person. To accept this dictation is to admit that this man is indeed superior to all Nigerian people put together (Ogunleye and Efeni 1993, 9).

The behavior of elected office holders as well as that of sectional leaders within the SDP showed the administration that its strategy of divide and rule was working. At the close of the meeting with the administration, SDP executives met in Abuja and agreed on an interim national government ("Political Crisis: Anxiety" 1993, 9).

On July 7, the executives of both parties announced that they had agreed to form an interim national government with some conditions (Agbo 1993d, 13; Ifijeh 1993, 6–7; Anyanwu 1993, 10). Reactions to the announcement were mixed. For their part, members of the NRC reacted positively to the announcement. In the words of the NRC party chairman, Dr. Hammed Kusamotu: "This is the best option for the nation now" (Anyanwu 1993, 10). On the SDP side, news of the agreement served to exacerbate the tensions within the party. Abiola's supporters feared that by this agreement the party executive may have sold out their man ("Political Crisis: Anxiety" 1993, A10). The rest of the party, however, was elated by the agreement reached with the NRC. One newspaper report quoted a source from the SDP:

> We have reached a gridlock. We either take a hard position and go the way of Bosnia or do otherwise. [The report went on to add that] some senior members of the SDP in the North and East [took offense to] Abiola's inflammatory remarks. But they cannot come into the open to say so ("Political Crisis: Anxiety" 1993, A10).

For its part, the administration welcomed the agreement by leaders of both parties but withheld final approval until the National Defence and Security Council (NDSC) had reviewed the agreement.[12]

On July 9, the NDSC met and tentatively accepted the agreement reached by leaders of both political parties pending another review by senior military and police officers. Describing the July 9 meeting of the NDSC, *Newswatch* magazine observed that: "there was a sharp division between those who were opposed to the formation of an interim government and the acceptance of the June 12 election" (Ukim 1993, 11).

Another meeting of senior military and police officers occurred on July 12. At the conclusion of this meeting they moved to reject the interim government agreement reached by both parties and called instead for another presidential election. A number of factors gave the officers cause to reject the interim government agreement (Oduwole 1993, 1–2; Ukim 1993, 11–12; Zubar 1993, 1 and 12). One factor which stood out, apparently, was that leaders of the SDP seemed to be hoping to use the offer of an interim national government to install Abiola as president through the back door. According to *Newswatch*:

> The plan, which even Abiola was not aware of, favoured the formation of a national interim government as a way of getting the military to relinquish power. Thereafter, the interim government will be voted out of power and replaced by the winner of the June 12 election (Ukim 1993, 12).

All sides were negotiating in bad faith or, at least, misinterpreted what the other meant by interim national government. From the point of view of the two parties, especially the SDP, the idea of forming an interim national government meant creating a consensus national government. Both parties would share government portfolios among themselves, with Moshood Abiola as the head of the interim national government. The administration, however, considered an interim government as a holdover administration that would complete the task of conducting a fresh presidential election at a later date.

As could be expected, the rejection of the agreement by senior military and police officers, and their insistence on holding another presidential election, was not well received by the two political parties. As Chief Tony Anenih put it:

> This is another one of those rash and insensitive decisions which this government is always taking. After all the sacrifice we went through last week (during the joint proposal for an interim national government) and the names people have been calling us, this is the result (Oduwole 1993, 2).

For their part, the NRC publicity secretary, Mr. Okey Uzoho, observed that: "as far as [the party] is concerned August 27 [when the military was to leave power] is irrevocable but if the SDP declines to participate in the election, the government should go ahead [and] conduct another election" (Ogunleye 1993a, 9; 1993b, 9).

In view of the decision by senior military and police officers, the SDP withdrew its participation from future negotiations with the administration and the NRC. Thus, it was left to the NRC and the administration to find a way out of the political impasse. With time running out and barring a last minute change of heart by the administration, the only recourse left was to consider holding another election with just one political party. At the time, there was a real possibility that the administration might do just that. According to section 131 of the 1989 constitution,

> a candidate for the office of president shall be deemed to have been duly elected to such office where, being the only candidate nominated for the election he: has a majority of 'yes' votes over the 'no' votes cast at the election; has not less than one third of the votes cast at the election in each of at least two-thirds of all states of the federation. But where the only candidate fails to be elected in accordance with this section then there shall be fresh nominations (Ogunleye 1993b, 9).

For his part, Moshood Abiola met with the SDP negotiating team and cautioned them against reaching any hasty agreement with the administration. Responding to the prospect that the administration might hold another election with the participation of the NRC only, Moshood Abiola said:

> That the army now supports fresh [elections] means the army and the NRC are together. The fact that the army and NRC are now together is a cause for concern for those who believe in democracy (Ogunleye 1993a, 9).

And with regard to whether the SDP should participate in another presidential election, Abiola observed that NEC was not duly constituted to conduct such elections. As he put it:

> There is no way we can have another election. Quite apart from anything else, the NEC that is composed at the moment is either [the] Association for Better Nigeria (ABN) or [the] National Republican Convention. . . . The new secretary of NEC is a card-carrying member of the NRC, a polling agent for the NRC who was also at the Port Harcourt convention. The new director of research is a cousin of Arthur Nzeribe. What type of election do we expect from people like that (Ogunleye 1993b, 9)?

Meanwhile, Abiola continued to rally his supporters within the SDP as well as in the general public for the reinstatement of the June 12 election results (Ogunleye 1993a, 9; 1993c, 11).

At the arrangement of Chief Ernest Shonekan, Chairman of the Transitional Council, Moshood Abiola met with President Babangida on July 13 and 16, to try to find an amicable solution to the political crisis (Ukim 1993, 13; Omonijo 1993, 22). Abiola came away with nothing from both meetings. President Babangida even met with Abiola's son, Kola, to discuss a suitable political role for his father. The meeting with Abiola's son is significant in that the president repeated his offer of a prime ministership position for Abiola (Ukim 1993, 13). Abiola refused this offer. In the end, none of these meetings were successful in resolving the political crisis.

With time running out for another election, the administration went on the offensive to try and rejuvenate the negotiations broken off by the SDP (Omonijo 1993, 21). There were rumors to the effect that due to the uncooperative stance of the SDP, the government might postpone the handover date from August 27 to October 1 1993, so as to enable the government to have more time to work out a solution to the political crisis (Ukim 1993, 9; Ogunleye 1993b, 9; Omonijo 1993, 21).

On July 23 1993, after much acrimony, the SDP returned to the negotiating table (Ogunleye 1993b, 9; 1993c, 11). At first little progress was made because the three sides stuck firmly to their positions. They resolved, however, to meet again the following week (Ogunleye 1993b, 9). When they met on July 26 and 27 there was still no breakthrough. Finally, on July 28 both political parties announced that they had agreed to an interim national government plan ("SDP, NRC Shift" 1993, 1 and 14; Ohakwe and Olaniyonu 1993, 10). The announcement read as follows:

> Following our continuing resolve to find an acceptable political solution to the present political impasse and the need to avoid further violence and bloodshed, the end of which may be unpredictable and unmanageable, we, the two political parties have resolved to revisit the option of [an] interim national government as a way out of the present crisis in the greater national interest (Ogunleye 1993c, 11).

After receiving news of the agreement on July 31, the President inaugurated the Augustus Aikhomu Tripartite Committee "to study and make recommendations on the modalities of [implementing the agreement]" (Agbroko 1993b, 14). On August 3, the Committee submitted its recommendations to the President for approval by the NDSC. On August 12, the NDSC met and endorsed the recommendations of the Aikhomu Committee report. On August 26 1993 without pomp and circumstance, Ernest Shonekan was formally sworn in as head of the interim national government by Chief Justice Mohammed Bello in Abuja. The ceremony marked the end of the Babangida administration, though not the end of the 12 June debacle.

Conclusion

The crisis which precipitated the annulment of the June 12 elections and the events thereafter serve to illuminate two aspects of Nigeria's political structure. First, due to the structure of the political economy, the class which ought to be the engine of change, namely the political class, is incapable of acting against the neopatrimonial state because it is tied to it through business links. The political economy of Nigeria is premised on export-import trade more than manufacturing. At the center of the economy and the export-import trade is the state. By necessity, then, members of the political-economic class must depend on the state for the award of economic contracts as well as economic opportunities. Consequently, the struggle among members of the political class for access to the state for the purposes of obtaining business contracts is intense and open to corrupt practices. With respect to members of Nigeria's political class then, they do not function as an economic class in the true sense of the word, or better still, they do not behave as a class for itself. The upshot of this economic arrangement is that members of the political class do not openly question the arbitrary nature of state administration, let alone consistently advocate a transparent political and economic system.

In the context of the June 12 elections, it is highly possible that some members of the political class were instrumental in the decision taken by the administration to annul the results. The events of June 12 are not unprecedented in the annals of Nigeria's political history. We can remember the 1979 electoral crisis between Shehu Shagari (then the NPN party flagbearer) and the Obasanjo administration on one hand, and the late Obafemi Awolowo (the UPN flagbearer) on the other hand. That crisis was over the mathematical interpretation of two-thirds of 19 states. Like June 12 1993 that crisis also created divisions within the body politic and almost brought about the annulment of the 1979 presidential election results. A telling point from both crises was the failure of the political class to unite in defense of the electoral process.

On another level, the dependent relationship between the state and members of the political class is carried over into the wider society, most especially in the relations of the political class to civil society groups. The emergence of civil society associations with an expressly democratic agenda is a recent development in Nigeria. Insofar as they exist, such associations are urban-based with poor links to the rest of society. In addition, due to the extremely limited resource base of many civic organizations and the underlying pluralism of the Nigerian society, there are few avenues for cross-fertilization of ideas and concerns among associations and between civic groups and members of the political class. Until moments of grave political crisis, members of the political class are aloof from civil society organizations. The disconnected nature and poor organization of the relationship between social formations weakened the struggle against authoritarianism.

The second point touches upon the arbitrariness of the Babangida administration, evident in the way it handled the entire transition program as well as the crisis of June 12. The entire transition program was stage-managed by the administration with very little input from members of the political class, let alone civil society groups. A key aspect of neopatrimonial authority is the low tolerance for other rival centers of authority outside the orbit of the state as well as for the emergence of other key players or groups not sanctioned by the state. Understandably: for the neopatrimonial authority to allow otherwise is to undercut its authority and power base.

In the context of the June 12 elections, Moshood Abiola may have posed such a threat to the prevailing neopatrimonial authority structure as well as to members of his own class. The principles of neopatrimonial authority demand that such an individual not be allowed to assume power for fear that he may take advantage of his new-found position to change the rules of the game. Although the possibility of Abiola effecting such a change might be remote (in the past Abiola himself had benefitted enormously from the neopatrimonial political economy) there may well have been the perception of possibility that, once in power, he might have elected to change the existing rules of the game. This possibility must have been a factor influencing the administration to nullify the June 12 election results.

Notes

1. On July 16 1993, at the height of the June 12 crisis, this same Mr. Davies confessed that President Babangida was behind the court injunction filed by the ABN (see Nwabueze 1994, 88–89). Very little is known about the origins of the ABN or even when it was founded. We do know that it was headed by Chief Francis Arthur Nzeribe, a maverick businessman and Second Republic senator, who was among the group of 23 presidential aspirants

banned by the administration in October 1992 from competing in the then scheduled presidential election of December 1992.

2. *Newswatch* magazine reported that: "a senior military officer [had] prevailed on Dahiru Saleh, . . . to compel NEC to respond to the court order after that notice was served on him restraining him from announcing the result of the election." The report went on to say: "It was learnt that Nwosu received a directive from the presidency to await the order of the Abuja high court." While this was going on, some senior military officers were also making frantic efforts to have Nwosu sign a statement suspending announcement of the results of the election and accepting instead to make representations in the case brought against NEC. Lastly, the report said: "the NEC chairman signed the letter suspending further processing of the election results under duress" (Agbo 1993b, 10).

3. The party's publicity secretary, Mr. Okey Uzoho was, however, elated by Nwosu's decision. As he put it: "We commend the Federal Government for coming to the aid of the majority of disenfranchised Nigerians who could not vote due to the discriminate action of the NEC on the election. We urge the government to go ahead and accede to our demand that fresh elections be held" (Ogunleye 1993a, 9).

4. For an official report of the president's address and the explanations he gave for cancelling the results of the election, see *The Transition Programme and the June 12, 1993 Presidential Election*.

5. Not surprisingly, most of the administration's allegations were directed at Moshood Abiola. It is instructive to detail some of these charges because they give us some insight into past business alliances of Moshood Abiola with the Nigerian state. The specific conflict of interest issue which the president may have had in mind during his broadcast concerned the debts owed by the government to International Telephone and Telegraph (ITT). Between 1969 and 1970 Abiola was the comptroller of ITT Nigeria Limited. According to *Newswatch* magazine: Abiola's companies won government contracts in the amount of $844,979,751.75. Out of this sum, $648,046,638.41 [had] been paid leaving a debt of $196,933,113.34. Part of this money [was] said to be loan repayment by the federal government to International Telephone and Telegraph, ITT, for a telecommunication equipment supply and installation contract entered into in 1975 (Akintunde 1993, 9; For a brief discussion of Abiola's tenure with ITT see Eka-Enang 1992, 5). The other body of evidence was contained in a report put together by the Central Bank of Nigeria. According to the report, between 1985 and 1990 alone the federal government awarded 10 contracts to companies which were either owned by or related to Abiola. For these contracts and loan repayment made to ITT within that period, the federal government paid out $196,933,113.34. The contracts listed included four for the supply of equipment and spare parts to NITEL which were said to have been awarded to ITT, Harris International

Telecommunications and Alcatel S.A. The total cost of the project was $4,506,338.66. Radio Communications of Nigeria (RCN), one of Abiola's companies in conjunction with HFR Intertel also received contracts for the supply of signals equipment to troops of the Economic Community of West Africa Monitoring Group (ECOMOG) in Liberia, while Abiola Farms was contracted to supply fertilizer worth $44.5 million to the Federal Ministry of Agriculture (Agbo 1993c, 10). In response to those allegations, Abiola dismissed them as false and unfounded. In an interview with *Newswatch*, Abiola said: "That the federal government is owing ITT or owing me . . . that there's an ITT debt of an unverified nature which I will pay myself immediately I get power? That is a lie. There is no truth at all about it. Any debt owed to ITT will be paid on the loan which ITT was given, which is based on an agreement. There is nothing like unverified debts. . . . No company will get into an unverifiable open account of that magnitude, no company. . . . Are they saying that those who are in business with the government and are owed money must not hold office?" (Akin-Aina and Ette 1993, 14).

6. When he imposed the ban on the previous set of presidential candidates, in October 1992, President Babangida observed that: "It should be noted that the former aspirants imbibed the worst culture of the Nigerian political class that feels and sees any election as the last election which must be contested, fought and won at all costs. The explanation can be sought in the heavy financial investment committed to politics and hence the view of political contests as a do-or-die battle" (Akintunde 1993, 20 and 23).

7. My reasons for not exploring the allegations of bribery and corruption are twofold: first, in the context of neopatrimonialism, illegal use of money can never be ruled out because of the high premium placed on capturing power; second, in most instances there are few people who are willing to corroborate such allegations. Moreover, since neither of the two candidates had accused the other of undue use of money, it is difficult to understand why the administration was making an issue of the alleged indiscretions of both presidential candidates.

8. In this connection, it is significant to keep in mind the administration's ban of 23 presidential aspirants in October 1992. Ironically, the leader of the Association for Better Nigeria (ABN)—Arthur Nzeribe—was one of those banned by the administration in October 1992. Furthermore, in the context of June 12, it did not help Abiola's cause that within the SDP were other members of the political class who suffered a similar fate as Nzeribe's in October 1992. One such member is Shehu Yar'Adua. The NRC also had its share of failed presidential aspirants, people such as Adamu Ciroma and Umaru Shinkafi. These names figured prominently in the crises and drama surrounding the cancellation of the June 12 elections and thereafter.

9. On July 2 1993, Babangida tabled the schedule for holding the next round of presidential elections. Nomination of candidates was set for July 1–

10. The campaign was slated for July 10–30. On July 31 the election would take place. Between August 1–4 election results would be announced. Between August 4–10, election petitions would be heard. Handing over ceremonies would commence from August 11–25. Lastly, the administration would quit power on August 27. According to *Newswatch*, retired head of state General Olusegun Obasanjo along with Adamu Ciroma (former NRC presidential candidate and victim of the administration's ban in October 1992), Shehu Yar'Adua (former SDP presidential candidate and also a victim of the October 1992 ban), Patrick Dele Cole (former SDP presidential candidate), and Olu Falae (former SDP presidential candidate) had collaborated in putting together the new timetable (Ukim 1993, 10; Esajere and Oduwole 1993, 1; Esajer 1993, A5).

10. The strong lobby for a third party or an independent candidate illustrates how the political class collectively undercuts itself. Note the administration's strategy: The decision to unban previously banned politicians not only increased the number of presidential aspirants but also meant that room would have to be created within the existing two-party structure to accommodate those aspirations. Such a tactical move by the administration played on the underlying distrust among members of the political class. To understand, then, why there was a strong lobby for a third party or for independent candidates, one has to understand the administration's tactical decision as well as the internal makeup of both political parties. Each party operated like a political machine and reflected the unequal relations prevailing in the larger society. Within each party there were several bosses; however, some bosses were more powerful than others. The value of each boss lies in his/her capacity to mobilize and to deliver the votes at election time. The euphemism for this arrangement in Nigerian politics is called "zoning." Upon closer reflection, zoning is a poor attempt by the political class to cope with the pluralistic nature of the society. The characteristic problem with zoning is that it tends to reinforce regionalism, ethnicism, and "religionism." In the context of the annulled elections, this problem was especially acute. Starting with the SDP, there were two main factions inside the party: one faction belonged to Shehu Musa Yar'Adua and the other to Moshood Abiola. It is noteworthy that Shehu Musa Yar'Adua was a former SDP presidential candidate. His presidential aspirations, however, were terminated by the October 1992 ban by Babangida. Having had his presidential wings clipped by the administration, Yar'Adua moved inside the SDP as one of the kingmakers. If he could not run himself, he could influence the party's choice of candidate. At the SDP convention in Jos in March 1993, Yar'Adua campaigned vigorously for one of his clients, Abubakar Atiku, to stand as the party flagbearer. Atiku's bid was unsuccessful. Be that as it may, Yar'Adua was not about to bow out of the political scene. Because of his prominence as leader of the far north within the SDP, Yar'Adua was responsible for delivering the Hausa-

Fulani votes. Under the terms of Babangida's broadcast, Yar'Adua would be free to contest again the next round of presidential elections. However, standing in his way was Moshood Abiola. Yar'Adua would have welcomed the formation of a third party should his bid to unseat Abiola prove to be difficult or if the opportunity arose to run as an independent candidate. The NRC also had its factional leaders and leading individuals who would have welcomed either the opportunity to compete as independent candidates or the creation of a third party. However, unlike the SDP, the major factions inside the NRC were led by northerners. Two prominent factional leaders in the NRC were Alhaji Adamu Ciroma and Alhaji Umaru Shinkafi, both from the far north. Like Yar'Adua in the SDP, both men played the role of kingmakers on the NRC side.

11. Meanwhile, on July 5 1993, "a serving General of the security establishment visited [General Olusegun Obasanjo] a former head of state in Ogun State. [Obasanjo] was offered the headship of an interim government on the ground that the country needed him at this crucial period and that he was deemed to be acceptable to both the military and the civil population." "[The same day Obasanjo visited Abiola], [b]ut it [was] not clear if he fully apprised Abiola of the requests on him to help resolve the lingering crisis" ("Political Crisis: Anxiety" 1993, A10).

12. Speaking on behalf of the President, the Information and Culture Secretary, Comrade Uche Chukwumerije said: "I express the appreciation of the President and the Federal Government to the leaders of the two political parties for the statesmanlike maturity with which you have approached the impasse facing the nation today" (Makinde 1993, 7). The following day, on July 8, "a day after the parties' joint meeting, [Obasanjo] was revisited in Ogun State with the earlier proposal to help rescue the situation by coming on the 'interim board.' Sources said [Obasanjo] did not firmly reject the offer" ("Political Crisis: Anxiety" 1993, A10).

References

Adedoyin, Ademola. 1993. "Nwosu Appears and Bows Out . . . Uya Takes Over." *TSM: The Sunday Magazine*, (18 July): 16.
Adeosun, Dele, Nwabuko, Chukwudi, Akhigbe, Bayo, and Cosmas Attayi-Elaigu. 1993. "Transition: Decoding New 'Rules and Regulations.'" *Sunday Champion*, (4 July): 10–11.
Agbo, Nats. 1993a. "Cloud of Uncertainty." *Newswatch*, (28 June): 8–15.
———. 1993b. "New Game Plan." *Newswatch*, (5 July): 7–18.
———. 1993c. "Why Abiola Was Blocked." *Newswatch*, (12 July):10–13.
———. 1993d. "Shonekan Takes Over." *Newswatch*, (6 September): 10–14.
———. 1994. "June 12." *Newswatch*, (10 January): 10–13.
Agbroko, Godwin. 1993b. "Judicial Babel." *Newswatch*, (12 July): 16–17.

———. 1993b. "Fear of War." *Newswatch*, (23 August): 11–15.

———. 1994. "Four Steps Back." *Newswatch*, (3 January): 11–12.

Ake, Claude. 1981. "Off to a Good Start but Dangers Await . . ." *West Africa*, (25 May): 1162–63.

Akin-Aina, Wale. 1994. "Hero of Tragedy." *Newswatch*, (10 January): 14–15.

Akin-Aina, Wale, and Mercy Ette. 1993. "I Leave Things to Allah." *Newswatch*, (12 July): 14–15.

Akintunde, Muyiwa. 1993. "How the Military Flaunts Its Might." *Newswatch*, (12 July): 9–23.

Akpan, Mike. 1993. "Finding Mr Clean." *Newswatch*, (12 July): 18–19.

Anyanwu, Chris. 1993. "Uncertainty Unlimited." *TSM: The Sunday Magazine*, (18 July): 8–10.

Bienen, Henry. 1987. "Nigeria." In Myron Weiner, and Ergun Ozbudun (eds.), *Competitive Elections in Developing Countries*: 201–47. Durham, NC: Duke University.

Dare, Olatunji. 1994. "The Year of the Debacle." *The African Guardian*, (3 January): 11.

Diamond, Larry. 1988. "Nigeria: Pluralism, Statism and the Struggle for Democracy." In Larry Diamond, Juan J. Linz, and Seymour Martin Lipset (eds.), *Democracy in Developing Countries: Africa*: 33–91. Boulder: Lynne Rienner Publishers.

Eka-Enang, Anthony. 1992. "Profile of the Big-Four." *Sunday Punch*, (21 November): 5.

Esajere, Akpo. 1993a. "Babangida Unfolds New Agenda." *The Guardian on Sunday*, (27 June): 1.

———. 1993b. "The Last Laugh." *The Guardian on Sunday*, (4 July): A5.

Esajer, Akpo and Yinka Oduwole. 1993. "Government Proposes Election for July 31." *The Guardian*, (3 July): 1.

Federal Ministry of Information and Culture. n.d. *The Transition Programme and the June 12, 1993 Presidential Election*. Lagos: Federal Ministry of Information and Culture.

Graf, William. 1988. *The Nigerian State: Political Economy, State, Class and Political System in the Post-Colonial Era*. London: James Currey.

Hart, Christopher. 1993. "The Nigerian Elections of 1983." *Africa*, 63, 3: 397–429.

Ibrahim, Jibrin. 1992. "The State Accumulation and Democratic Forces in Nigeria." In Lars Rudebeck (ed.), *When Democracy Makes Sense: Studies in the Democratic Potential of Third World Movements*. AKUT Stockholm: Uppsala University.

Ifijeh, Victor. 1993. "Interim Government: Recipe for Chaos." *Sunday Concord*, (11 July): 6–7.

Joseph, Richard. 1991. *Democracy and Prebendal Politics in Nigeria: The Rise and Fall of the Second Republic*. Ibadan: Spectrum Books.

Koehn, Peter. 1989. "Competitive Transition to Civilian Rule: Nigeria's First and Second Experiments." *The Journal of Modern African Studies* 28, 3: 401–30.

Makinde, Kunle. 1993. "August 27: The Day of Destiny." *Daily Sunray*, (6 August): 7.

Maku, Labaran. 1993a. "Presidential Election at Last Tofa or MKO." *Daily Champion*, (12 June): 1.

———. 1993b. "Transition Suspended." *Daily Champion*, (24 July): 1.

Nwabueze, B.O. 1994. *Nigeria 93: The Political Crisis and Solutions*. Ibadan: Spectrum Books Limited.

Obi, Comfort. 1993. "New Government Before August 27." *TSM: The Sunday Magazine*, (15 August): 17–19.

Ochiama, Christina. 1993. "No Superior Partner in Interim Government." *Sunday Champion*, (11 July): 1 and 3.

Oduwole, Yinka. 1993. "Government Insists on New Elections." *The Guardian*, (13 July): 1–2.

Ogunleye Gbemiga. 1993a. "Dark Clouds Over Fresh Poll." *The Guardian*, (19 July): 9.

———. 1993b. "Still Striving to Stave off a National Crisis." *The Guardian*, (26 July): 9.

———. 1993c. "Transition Hiccup: Looking for a Safe Berth." *The Guardian*, (2 August): 11.

———. 1993d. "Again It's Back to the Drawing Board." *The Guardian*, (9 August): 9.

Ogunleye, Gbemiga and Emmanuel Efeni. 1993. "Transition Quagmire: In Search of a Safe Passage." *The Guardian*, (12 July): 9.

Ohakwe, Steve, and Yusuph Olaniyonu. 1993. "Interim Chaos." *TSM: The Sunday Magazine*, (15 August): 8–14.

Ojigbo, Okion. 1982. *Shehu Shagari*. Ljubljana, Yugoslavia: Mladinska Knjiga.

Opara Reginald. 1993. "Conflicting Signals." *African Concord*, (21 June): 12–18.

Omonijo, Mobolade. 1993. "Will It Be?" *The Nigerian Economist*, (26 July): 20–25.

"Political Crisis: Anxiety Beclouds SDP, NRC Deal." 1993. *The Guardian on Sunday*, (11 July): 1 and A10.

Rahman, Tunde. 1993. "Court Stops the Election." *Daily Times*, (11 June): 1.

Sanyaolu, Kunle. 1993. "Why June 12 Election was Cancelled, by Babangida." *The Guardian on Sunday*, (27 June): 1.

"SDP, NRC Shape Up New Gameplan." 1993. *The Guardian on Sunday*, (4 July): A1–A2.

"SDP, NRC Shift Ground on Crisis." 1993. *Vanguard*, (28 July): 1. "Tension, Criticisms Mount Over Withheld Result." 1993. *The Guardian*, (19 June): 1.

Ukim, Utibe. 1993. "Fresh Elections: Mission Impossible." *Newswatch*, (26 July): 9–13.

Zubar, Aliu. 1993. "FG Orders Fresh Poll." *Daily Times*, (13 July): 1 and 12.

PART 4
Identities and Contexts

10

WOMEN AND THE DILEMMA OF POLITICS IN NIGERIA

Pat Ama Tokunbo Williams

The extant literature on Nigerian politics, particularly the early scholarship, pays little attention to women (see Coleman 1958; Burns 1972; Hodgkin 1975; Olagunju et al. 1993; and Diamond 1995). For the most part, the literature on the Nigerian political situation has pursued the subject mainly from male-centered perspectives. For instance, Coleman in his epochal book has only one paragraph on women's activities and two obscure lines on women's groups in Lagos (1958, 42, 212). Sklar on the other hand, gave relatively more space and time to women's activities and their organizations (1963, 23, 84, passim). The reason for this overwhelming gender bias in favor of men is not difficult to fathom. Men were, and are, the main actors in partisan politics, and therefore, their activities on the political terrain claimed center stage in the various investigations and writings on Nigerian politics. (The omission by Olagunju et al. (1993) is particularly grievous since their book focuses on an administration which claimed to be supportive of women.) Because of this oversight in the scholarship, women and their activities have remained invisible in Nigerian political discourse and (mis)governance. To rectify this dearth of literature on women, some female scholars have written on the past glories of women and touched on the possible positive roles of women in the contemporary period (e.g., Mba 1982; Afonja 1986; Awe 1992).

This essay attempts to further highlight some of the activities of Nigerian women since the advent of partisan politics in Nigeria. This is not to claim that the political situation would have been better if women had more say in governance from the start, or if their activities had been better featured in writings. Rather, it is the submission of this essay that given women's performances in the context of the few opportunities some women have had in government, and given the conservative and patriarchal structure of the society generally, not much could have been achieved by women. Nonetheless, the very absence of women from the political arena ought to be documented for posterity. Because of the dearth of literature on women's activities, it is difficult to retrace their public life. Therefore, their contributions must be gleaned from the limited available literature during the period of review. Using historical analysis, this essay examines the contributions of women since the advent of partisan politics in Nigeria and submits that generally, women have often failed to be critical of events or to make critical statements when they were most needed and would be most effective.

The paper begins with the examination of the position of women in the unfolding socio-political events in Nigeria. It outlines some past developments in order to provide historical perspective with respect to women's role in the contemporary situation.

Background to Women and Nigerian politics

Significantly, Nigerian women are not an homogenous social class. They are diverse with varied social persuasions. Certainly any study of Nigerian women must include cultural, social, economic and political dimensions. The focus in this essay however, is on the political aspect. Nonetheless, through this medium, glimpses of other activities can be seen. Nigerian women's positions and political roles have been a mixed bag since the turn of this century. Men began their upward climb in society through their early exposure to western education. On the other hand, women were not given that opportunity early enough. When women were exposed to western education, they were segregated by sex and the subject matter was sexist in content, and limited to southern Nigeria (see Phillipson 1948 and Coleman 1958, 113–66 on western education and western elite). Thus, there was an educational imbalance. Some women had an advantage over their contemporaries in other parts of the country through their early exposure to western influence and education. The better educated women obtained better jobs than did women in other parts of the country. Yet these elite women were not able to compete successfully with men in the political sphere. This means that there were problems other than financial status and literacy.

Ironically, about the time women were unable to make any impact on partisan politics, two "women's wars" were fought and won. The "women's wars" took place in 1929 and 1948 when women rejected the colonial and patriarchal tax imposed on them (see Mba 1982, chapters 4 and 7). But, apart from the immediate achievements of getting a respite from taxation and limited representation in local politics, women remained on the political sidelines during the 1950s and the 1960s.

The fact therefore remains that the position of women has not dramatically improved either since independence in 1960 or since 1976 when Nigerian women were granted universal suffrage, and certainly not in 1987 when the Babangida government began to pay lip service and attention to women. In contemporary times, the situation of women seems to have worsened. They appear to have lost the few gains they had made over the years, through heightened male chauvinism and patriarchy, the perpetuation of military rule and their restructuring and deregulation programs since 1986, and the fact that some women have jumped on the political bandwagon. It becomes the case of: if you can't beat them, then join them!

Certainly there cannot be applause for the roles played by a small group of privileged women. Over the years, they have contributed to the political charade which has resulted in the present political situation. Thus, it is necessary to demystify the claim that women might be the solution to the present Nigerian political quagmire. The capitalist system which Nigeria is aping has inevitably created and entrenched a class structure which is not explicitly gendered. Hence there are bourgeois women, and proletarian/peasant women; there are upper class, middle class and lower class women. All these different classes of women perceive the problem of Nigeria through different lenses and proffer different solutions to the problem.

Scholarship on Nigerian women has ranged from conservatism, feminist conservatism, feminist radicalism to socialist feminism perspectives (Itayavyar and Obiajunwa 1992, 13–32). The role of women can also be examined from Patricia Stamp's feminist political economy (1989) framework. It focuses on the manner in which Nigerian women cared for themselves and those they look after materially, physically and emotionally. But the ability to put a meal on the table does not necessarily create the capability to move into the decision making realm. While these categories of women are neither time nor culture bound, it is significant to observe also that the categories often overlapped with each other.

The conservative strand offers biological explanations for the continued subjugation of women in Nigerian society and submits that women are inferior to men and therefore cannot be expected to occupy roles naturally designated for men. Modern feminist conservatism similarly recognizes the biological superiority of males but adds the modernization of the subordinate position of women in society through the introduction and acquisition of modern household gadgets in order to lessen the burden of household chores. It adds that women's education must be geared towards the perfection of their natural feminine roles as mothers, wives and daughters. For instance, Stamm and Ruff (1982, 191–93) have argued that women wield personal power which can be far reaching and complex. But this is still begging the issue. The fact remains that personal power is not the positional power (political power) which men wield.

Feminist Marxism/radicalism focuses on the eradication of inequality in society, but this struggle for equality in society does not envisage the inclusion of women by their elevation from lowly status. Feminist socialism recognizes this limitation within Marxism and thus pursues the elevation of this radicalism to include the lifting of women from their drudgery and places women on par with men in the struggle for the eradication of injustices at all levels in society. Stamp discusses the relationship between political and economic policies from a feminist perspective and their influence on social institutions. Thus, the notion that African women are totally dependant on men is an erroneous conclusion of western feminist scholarship. Stamp submits that through economic activities and empowerment, women can venture into the public sphere from which patriarchy has excluded them (see Stamp 1989, 20, 23, 74).

Nigerian women contribute to the economic development of the society generally. Fairly well established in the informal sector, Nigerian women can be independent of men economically. From their limited proceeds in the informal sector, women, as producers and reproducers, have been able to care for their family and the education of their children, particularly male children. However, women's contribution has not been adequately recognized and rewarded in society. The general notion is that both men and women have their role to play in the economy, but, while men are cash crop farmers, women mainly produce food crops. This further underlines the subordination of women in society (see Itayavyar and Obiajunwa 1992).

When it comes to who occupies decision-making positions in politics, the mere ability to survive is not enough. Money made at the subsistence level by women is not enough to catapult them into decision-making roles. Proceeds from the informal sector are quite insufficient to meet the demands of contemporary politics where huge amounts of money are required for future political gains. These socio-economic points were not taken into consideration when women occasionally ventured into Nigerian politics.

Nigerian Women in the colonial period

Generally, politics has been a male affair in Nigeria. Those who made the first incursions into politics were men in such professions and businesses as newspaper proprietorships, entrepreneurship, engineering, law, medicine and journalism. Through the newspapers, men were able to criticize the colonial government and its policies. Men also founded the early political associations. Thus by the turn of the 20th century, there was a flurry of political activity first in Lagos and later in other parts of Nigeria. When the colonial government decided to open up the public terrain to partisan politics in 1922, Herbert Samuel Heelas Macaulay founded the main political party, the Nigerian National Democratic Party (NNDP) on June 24 1923. What is not often acknowledged is the financial support of the Lagos Market Women's Guild. Their financial support enabled the NNDP to win elections between 1923 and 1938 until it was defeated by the Nigerian Youth Movement (NYM) in 1938. Ironically, the NYM did not have the overall backing of the rank and file of women as did the NNDP. The NYM held sway over Lagos politics until the early 1940s when it too fizzled out of existence, giving way to other new political parties (see Sklar 1963, 42, 23, 55–64). Political exigencies led to the formation of the National Council of Nigeria and Cameroons (NCNC), an amalgamation of 87 organizations. Again, the Lagos Market Women's Guild gave it its blessing. In the ranks of the NCNC was the fiery Mrs. Ransome-Kuti and her Nigerian Women's Union. Mrs. Ransome-Kuti was part of the NCNC team that went to Britain to protest the 1946 constitution. The team achieved very little and after their return the NCNC became moribund. It was later revived in 1948 as the National Council of Nigerian Citizens (NCNC).

Significantly, despite these activities and exposure, women accepted their subordinate role within the various political parties which emerged in the final struggle for independence. They failed to attain the decision-making positions, nor did they demand them. Their socialization prevented them from indulging in "brazen acts" such as vying for public positions alongside men. Neither could many of the women understand why other women should put themselves forward for elective posts. Hence, their lack of sympathy for women who dared to form their own political parties or who were vocal in their opinions. Consequently, they did not support political parties founded by women such as the Women's Party of Lady Oyinkan Abayomi founded in 1944 and Mrs. Ransome-Kuti's Nigerian Women's Union founded in the late 1940s. Women maintained this stand even when women were officially enfranchised in southern Nigeria in 1950. They voted for men rather than for women. Conservative southern women opined that it was enough to influence things from "behind the scenes" and voting for men was just the right thing to do. The women's wing in the Action Group (AG), a party founded in the West in 1950, and the NCNC, ensured this. At Independence in 1960, however, men magnanimously rewarded this loyalty by appointing a few women into ceremonial posts.

Nigerian Women in the Post-Colonial Period Under Democratic Regimes

This section highlights 1960–1966 and 1979–1983, when democratic administrations were in office. These dates coincided with the period of the two republics. Two types of systems were practiced during these periods. From 1960 to 1963, the British Queen was the Head of State. Between 1963 and 1966, Nigeria severed allegiance to the British Crown but remained a member of the Commonwealth. A system of government was modelled on the Westminsterial bi-cameral legislature. Thus, during this period, at various times there were the Queen/Governor-General/President, a Prime Minister and his cabinet, and the Parliament comprising the houses of Senate and Representatives. During the Second Republic (1979–1983), an Executive Presidential system was practiced. It was also bi-cameral with the President and his cabinet, and a National Assembly comprised of the Senate and House of Representatives.

There was no dramatic difference in the position women occupied in Nigerian politics during the two republics. Between 1960 and 1966, two women were appointed to the Senate at the federal level. In 1961, three women were elected to the Eastern House of Assembly. But there were no female ministers in the regional governments. The AG and the NCNC had allowed women's wings in their parties, but no woman occupied the top echelon of the parties where decisions were made. Also, few women were elected into the local government councils in the south.

Incidentally, the formation of the National Council of Women's Societies (NCWS) coincided with the first federal elections in 1959, and one would have thought that its existence would bring women some political dividends. With branches all over Nigeria, the NCWS was meant to promote the education of women, the welfare, and the status of women. While its executive was heavily elitist, the organization was made up of both elites and non-elites, professionals and non-professionals. Though it claimed to be non-partisan and national in posture, it failed to mobilize women politically and educate them on their rights. This failure of women's organizations was repeated in later years.

In the Second Republic, women occupied less than five percent of the total political positions occupied by men in the federation. Yet, in the period under review, many more women became better educated and occupied professions similar to their male counterparts. With the advantage of hindsight, women's poor representation in politics could not have been due to the want of suitable women. In the Shehu Shagari administration, three women were appointed federal ministers between 1979 and 1983. Later, in the second short-lived segment of that Republic following general elections in 1983, more women won elections into the National Assembly and more women were appointed ministers. It was also customary to have at least one woman each in cabinets at the state level. On the surface, judging by the numbers, one might agree with Nina Mba's assessment that: "In terms of the numbers of women holding formal political office and participating in the political system, the Second Republic measured greater success than the First Republic or the military regimes." But in terms of improvements in the quality of life, the implementation of rights and liberties, proper management of human and natural resources of the country and the people, "the Second Republic measured greater failure than the first . . . [it] betrayed the trust of the citizens in an elected representative government" (Mba 1988, 14). Under the Shagari administration, Islamic and customary laws were employed to discriminate against women, in spite of the existing statutory laws. Similarly, the presence of women in the Shagari government made no difference to its chauvinistic style.

In 1981, in response to the demands of the NCWS and other women's organizations for the establishment of a women's commission/bureau, the Shagari regime established the National Committee on Women and Development, which was a grandiose term for a women's unit in the child and family welfare section of the Directorate of Social Development in the Ministry of Social Development, Youths and Sports! It was merely an advisory committee. This unit was replicated at the state level. The government thereafter remained impervious to all appeals to upgrade the committee to a technical department with executive functions as advised by various international organizations namely: the Lagos Plan of Action in 1980, the

Organization of African Unity and the United Nations. Yet more women were involved in this government than any hitherto. Is participation in any government advantageous, then, to women? Incidentally, during the Second Republic, the few women in government not only did not live up to expectations, several female politicians were also among those accused of abuse of office by the various tribunals set up by the Buhari administration (see Osoba 1996, 371–86; Diamond 1995, 470–71; *Report of the Political Bureau* 1987, 215; Forrest 1995). While no woman was convicted, female politicians became guilty by their association and membership of the discredited political class in the Second Republic.

Nigerian Women in the First and Second Military Regimes

In 1966, the first military regime began. Under Yakubu Gowon's administration (1966–1975), it became fashionable for state governors to appoint at least one woman as commissioner in the cabinet. It was left to individual governors to appoint more than one. Yet, some state governors could not find one female suitable enough for their cabinet and so women were left out. During the Murtala/Obasanjo administration (1975–1979), while the transition program was under way, Nigerian women were granted universal suffrage so that they could participate in the local government elections of 1976. Northern Nigerian women voted for the first time in that election. In the subsequent December 12 1976 elections, few women were elected and they constituted a minority in the 299 local government councils. The councils were to serve as electoral colleges for elections into the Constituent Assembly (CA). The elections were hotly contested and there were abuses. Among those elected were former politicians, commissioners, retired members of the military personnel and police force, professionals and academics. Only one woman, the late Mrs. Janet Akinrinade, a large-scale tobacco leaf farmer and contractor, won election to the CA. Nigerian women were not often able to hold their own in male elite-dominated competition given their lack of education, wealth and the entrenched patriarchal culture. To appease women, four other women representing the three main language groups and the Kalabari were appointed by the military government into the CA (Mba 1988, 10). Thus in a body of 250, there were 5 women, making women only 2 percent of the CA membership. These token appointments to the CA were made in order to quiet critics after the selection to the 50-member Constitution Drafting Committee (CDC) in 1975 which did not have a single female member. It is also important to note that at the final stage in the Obasanjo/Yar'Adua transition program, when state Administrators were withdrawn, Mrs. Womiloju Idowu was appointed to head the Ogun State Administration and thus became the only female Deputy Chairperson in the federation.

In the compilation of voters registered for the 1979 elections by the Federal Electoral Commission (FEDECO), there were 47,710,680 voters of whom 24,465,683 or 51.3 percent were women, thus setting the stage for women to vote for their kind. However, in the subsequent lifting of the ban on certain political activities, 52 associations were formed of which five were led by women. None of these five associations was registered as a political party. The NCWS, under the leadership of Mrs. Kofo Pratt who was a one-time Lagos State commissioner, formed the League of Women Voters. The objectives of the League were to educate women on how to exercise their civil rights and thereby identify persons and parties likely to do their best for women and to create a strong forum to raise the status of women and also involve them in policy making (Mba 1988, 11). The League and NCWS stressed the non-partisan nature of their activities and therefore forbade their executives to hold political posts. As political campaigns gathered momentum, the NCWS lost some very active members to politics. Nonetheless, FEDECO viewed the League as a political association and asked it to register. Even though it was not eligible for registration being an all female organization, the League did not resist the request of FEDECO to register. Eventually, it was disbanded, scuttling its enlightenment drive.

Women, during the transition to the Second Republic, reverted to the practice of participating in the women's wing within the five registered political parties. Even though these wings were represented in the national executives of the parties concerned, these representatives were not part of the policy making caucuses. Thus, women were left to occupy token and ceremonial positions. Usually, women were one of several vice-chairpersons of political parties. Finally, it was customary for the various political parties to nominate fewer women than men as candidates for election and to unviable, or unsafe constituencies. In the end, no woman stood for election as a presidential candidate. There were no female gubernatorial candidates, although there were several female running-mates. None of the four women who contested elections for the Senate won. For the Federal House of Representatives, 10 women ran for election out of 2,000 candidates, and three won. At the level of state Houses of Assembly, 42 women ran for election out of 5,000 candidates and five won (see Mba 1988, 13).

With the military's return on the last day of 1983, women's token representation was intensified by the administration of General Muhammadu Buhari. It was Muhammadu Buhari who first insisted on including women in all state cabinets in spite of his fundamentalist and chauvinist bent. But this tokenism was not extended to the local governments which would have been easier to penetrate. This shows that the system of patriarchy is more firmly entrenched at the grassroots level and the military was not in hurry to upset this situation.

Women and the Babangida Administration

Nigeria's first military (self-declared) president, Ibrahim Badamasi Babangida, continued with the token representation of women at the state level. This token representation of women was extended to all levels in the socio-economic sectors. Significantly, during the eight years of military dictatorship of Babangida (1985–1993), no women held posts in the federal cabinet or the Armed Forces Ruling Council (AFRC). The AFRC remained exclusive to men. The reason for this was not obscure: there were no women occupying senior combatant positions in the Army or the equivalent in the other branches of the armed forces. But Babangida also announced the inclusion of one woman for every four nominated local government councillors and a woman on every government board or parastatal. Also during his tenure, two women became Vice-Chancellors (at the University of Benin and Lagos State University). Thus Babangida could claim: "we have started what appears to be a silent revolution to higher institutions" (*The Guardian* May 8 1986). According to *The Guardian*, the emancipation of women was part of a government crusade to guarantee equal opportunities to all.

Quite early in the life of his administration, Babangida began to woo women with the inclusion of two women in the Political Bureau in 1986. These were the President of NCWS, Mrs. Hilda Adefarasin, and an academic, Mrs. Rahmatu Abdullahi. Thus Babangida demonstrated his superiority to the shortsighted military administration of Murtala/Obasanjo in 1975. Many women's associations made presentations to the Political Bureau demanding political power for women and for 30 to 40 percent of seats in the legislature and cabinet. They also called for the revival of the League of Women Voters (Mba 1988, 15–16). The NCWS particularly demanded the removal of all administrative and legal barriers to women's equality. However, the "progressive" stand of the NCWS was often countered by other women's groups, either from a religious perspective or from some other ideological standpoint. For instance, the Muslim Sisters of Nigeria, later known as the Federation of Muslim Women Association of Nigeria (FOMWAN), considered NCWS a "Christian and Zionist" organization. This is not surprising given the fact Nigerians had just gone through a trying period over Nigeria's surreptitious entry into the Organization of Islamic Conference (OIC). The OIC issue had divided Nigeria into Islamic and Christian groups and often public actions were viewed in religious terms (see Williams 1991 and 1996). Similarly, the radical women's group, Women In Nigeria (WIN), seemed to believe that the fight for the empowerment of women should not solely be spearheaded by bourgeois women's groups such as the NCWS, but that the fight against women's oppression must be carried out in alliance with other groups and forces which are struggling against all forms of discrimination in society (*Women in Nigeria Today* 1985, 7).

The *Report of the Political Bureau* considered women's demands and recommended that:

> ... full involvement of women in politics is one method of defending and promoting women's interest in society. They can participate fully if they are members of the legislature and executive arms of government. For this reason, we recommend the allocation of 5 per cent of the legislative seats to women in all the three tiers of government. This 5 percent of seats allocated to women is to be filled by nominations through the political parties (1987, 159).

However, the good intentions of the Political Bureau were undone by the Omu Panel (to which no woman was appointed) which reviewed the Report and made recommendations to the government. It was on the Omu panel's recommendations that the final white paper of the government was based (see Olagunju et al. 1993, 163; 243). The five percent reservation of positions at all levels for women was rejected by the government though it noted the reason for the Bureau's recommendation on representation of women:

> ... But Government does not accept the implication of reverse discrimination embedded in that recommendation. Government believes in equality of sexes, individuals and groups. Given equal opportunities in the political parties and other institutions, Government believes that these groups can effectively stand on their own without special constitutional provisions (*Government Views* 1987, 32).

Subsequently, 6 women were appointed to a 46 member Constitution Review Committee (CRC) on September 7 1987 and in March 1988, fourteen women (of which five were elected and nine appointed) were members of a 567 Constituent Assembly (CA). In these two fora, some women understudied their male counterparts and perfected the political art, the Nigerian way.

The government further appealed to women as the wife of the president formed an ad hoc committee of professional women to advise her on how to improve the life of rural women. This later metamorphosized into the Better Life for Rural Women (BLP) Program in 1987. The irony of the situation was that the benefits from BLP went to a few urban women! Meanwhile, in 1986, the government had embarked on a Structural Adjustment Program (SAP), endorsed by the International Monetary Fund (IMF) and the World Bank. This had the effect of impoverishing everyone, especially women who were dependent on the informal sector. Similarly, the various people-oriented programs such as the Directorate of Food, Roads and Rural Infrastructure (DRRFI) were not alleviating the problems. The BLP was then the magical instrument to alleviate the problems of women both in the rural and urban areas.

The government at all levels pumped money into the BLP and it became a household word. By 1991, Mrs. Maryam Babangida won the African Prize for Leadership, a prize she shared with another African, Professor Wangarri Maathai, the Kenyan environmentalist. The BLP could catalogue a long list of so-called achievements namely: 6,635 cooperatives, 997 cottage industries, 1,751 new farms and gardens, 487 new shops and markets, 419 women's centers and 163 social welfare programs (*African Women* 1991, 26). In addition, women were empowered to improve their lives through adult education programs, primary health programs and agricultural, trade, crafts and food processing. According to the report, "women were not only becoming self-sufficient but in some areas, they were in the vanguard of agricultural production in their various districts and ensured increased food production while minimising post harvest waste" (*African Women* 1991 in Williams 1994, 24). The BLP had also ensured women's easy access to credit facilities through cooperatives such as the People's Bank and Community Bank. The BLP had also discouraged child marriage by encouraging girls to stay longer in school thereby reducing the incidence of vesico vaginal fistula (*African Notes* 1990). Finally, BLP assisted in mobilizing women politically so that more women than men registered for and voted at the various elections for the two government created parties: National Republican Convention (NCR) and the Social Democratic Party (SDP). It is difficult to accept the above assessment given the fact that it was when this rosy picture was being painted that the structural adjustment program was further impoverishing people due to the government's restructuring and down-sizing programs. Parents could no longer keep their children, especially the female children in school, hospitals became consulting clinics, and the incidence of vesico vaginal fistula rose as more young girls were married off for economic reasons.

President Babangida, in response to pressure from women's organizations, but also in compliance with a UN recommendation, established the National Commission for Women by decree No. 30 in 1989. The Commission constituted the political teeth that Nigerian women needed to really make an impact on the political sphere. The board of the Commission, appointed by the President, was made up of a Chairperson and 10 members, all of whom worked part-time. The Commission chairperson was the renowned professor of history, Bolanle Awe. An executive secretary headed the Commission's secretariat and was responsible for the implementation of the decisions, policies and recommendations of the board. Appointed by the president and situated in the presidency, it was expected that the Commission would have the ear of the president. The BLP was one of three departments within the Commission. However, Mrs. Babangida was reluctant to relinquish her leadership role in the BLP to the National Commission for Women. Inevitably, competition, rivalry and suspicion marred the effectiveness of the Commission. Just before Babangida left office, roles were changed. The First Lady became the Chairperson of the Advisory Board of the Commission thereby becoming the effective head of both the Commission and the BLP. Subsequently, the main programs of the Commission suffered while only the BLP activities undertaken to attract publicity were pursued at various levels of government. BLP failed to reach the grassroots. It remained the toy of privileged women.

With the intervention at the federal level of some female Director Generals such as Mrs. Francesca Emmanuel, some of the discrimination policies against women ended through government decrees, such as those providing for equality in pay for both genders in government positions, the eradication of discriminatory taxes, and tax relief for women with children. However, in the political sphere women were not overly favored. The National Electoral Commission (NEC) did not permit women's wings in the two political parties. They were abolished and declared illegal under Decree No. 27 in 1989. Similarly, the Women's League was not revived even though the National Commission for Women and the NCWS made a great show of insisting that the two presidential candidates in the 1993 elections discuss their party's programs for women in the new Third Republic. The men did not take this demand by women seriously and only made noncommittal statements with respect to women's concerns. Between 1989 and 1993 various elections took place, yet there were no major successes by women at the various levels of government or in terms of decision-making positions within the two parties. Women constituted more than half of the 8 million members of both parties, yet once again women had to be content with token recognition. Government's rejection of the Political Bureau's recommendation that 5 percent of positions be reserved for women should be seen for what it was—a lack of support for the empowerment of women. Mrs. Babangida did not support it because it could be detrimental to her wish to remain in the limelight. Later, her wish to entrench the First Lady position in the 1989 constitution was thwarted by the short-lived National Assembly in 1993. Towards the end of the Babangida administration, more women came to the fore such as Alhaja Latifat Okunnu, who headed the SDP after the dissolution of the parties' executives in 1992. More women were appointed to the Transitional Council and later to the interim government.

Women were finally galvanized into action during the period of acute crisis after the annulment of June 12 1993 elections by Babangida. With the annulment it suddenly dawned on Nigerians that their hopes for civilian rule after almost a decade of military rule were dashed. There were pockets of protests among the old women in Ijebu Ode, Ogun State who marched in the streets half-naked with the effigy of Babangida. Later, they conducted a mock burial and "outing" ceremonies and ended with the frying and distribution of *akara* (fried bean cakes). The action of these women was symbolic: it meant the rejection of Babangida by the people, and it threatened to hasten his death.

Two women's groups joined the throng at Aso Rock, the seat of government in Abuja, either to persuade Babangida to leave or to stay in power. One group was led by Mrs. H.I.D. Awolowo, the wife of the respected politician, Chief Obafemi Awolowo. She was accompanied by traditional and market women leaders from all over Yorubaland. In their plea, they asked that "Government should reconsider its stand on the June 12 elections because following the annulment, an uneasy calm had enveloped the country which has been giving us grave concern." Stressing that their paramount concern "is the continued existence of the country as one indivisible entity," they warned that the country "should not disintegrate because our late elder statesman, Chief Obafemi Awolowo fought relentlessly for the unity of the country" (*The Guardian* 12 August 1993, 1).

On the heels of this group came another women's group led by Professor Grace Alele-Williams, the first female Vice-Chancellor, and in the entourage were female politicians, academics, administrators and businesswomen from all over Nigeria. They urged Babangida not to hand over power which would result in chaos. It was widely believed that this visit was staged-managed by the government. WIN dissociated itself from the call made by the Alele-Williams group. It said, inter alia, "Nigeria's toiling and patriotic women who have come under assault on account of this contrived stalemate preferred to associate themselves with the wish of Nigerians expressed freely on June 12, 1993" (*The Guardian* August 2 1993, 5). It is interesting how the word *peace* was used by both parties. The Awolowo group stressed "justice and fair play" in order to achieve "peace" while the Alele-Williams party was more concerned with "peace" without thinking how it could be attained. Babangida left office ignominiously, a day before he completed eight years in office. He handed power over to Chief Ernest Shonekan who had headed the government during the period of the Transitional Council (see Olagunju et al. 1993, 246). General Abacha seized power on November 17 1993.

Women and the Abacha Administration

Since Abacha came into office, some women have been active either in support of his government or in opposition to it. Some women have willingly served in his government and have enjoyed favors from the government. A case in point was the election of the national executive of the NCWS which necessitated the subtle intervention of the new First Lady for the emergence of the present team. The former Laila Dogonyaro team, similarly, was not above putting pressure on women in the bid to retain office. On the opposition side, some women's groups teamed up with the National Democratic Coalition (NADECO). A case in point was WIN. Yet women have also been actively involved in the organizations canvassing for Abacha's continued stay in office.

Abacha's overtures to women closely followed the pattern established by the Babangida administration. The regime created a Ministry for Women and this has been hailed in some quarters as a progressive move. (These supporters did not wait to see it in operation and ascertain whether or not it would become moribund like the BLP and the National Commission for Women). True to type, the present First Lady, Mrs. Maryam Abacha, has set up her own pet project: the Family Support Program which, judging by its objectives, is retrogressive. Women were no longer the focus in government activities but simply "added-on." The Family Support Program relegated the articulated needs of women to the background once again in an attempt to embrace family projects with the hope that the present ills of society would be alleviated.

Abacha embarked on another transition program which began with elections to the local government councils which later constituted the electoral college for the Constitutional Conference. Many pro-June 12 groups and individuals boycotted this election and that allowed the government the opportunity to pack the Constitutional Conference with people sympathetic to its policies. The constitution which emerged in 1995 from this exercise was mainly a tinkering of the 1989 constitution. For instance, four rights which were formerly in Section Two of the 1979 and 1989 constitutions were added to the Fundamental Rights section. They are: the right to eradicate corrupt practices (35); the right to medical consultation (43); the right to primary education (45: 1–2); and the right to immovable property anywhere in the Federation (46). Clearly, these are mere sentiments which the government is not willing to implement (see Williams 1996, 15). It is certainly true that women are primary victims of rights abuses. It is women who are denied access to education, good health care, who are the victims of corrupt practices, and who do not always have the right to immovable properties. Yet, who applies to the Constitutional Court (49), a provision in the 1995 constitution, against the infringement of rights? Inevitably, it is the educated, rich male.

It is alleged that Abacha has personally reviewed the 1995 constitution and has inserted some provisions which will pave the way for him to remain in power à la Rawlings of Ghana; Mainassara of Niger; and Jammeh of Gambia (see *Africa Confidential* 18 October 1996, 3). On October 1 1996, the ban on partisan politics was lifted and five political parties have been registered out of 15 political associations, effectively excluding the "dominant clique of northern conservatives" from contesting. The parties are: United Nigeria Congress Party (UNCP), the Committee for National Consensus (CNC), National Center Party (NCP), Democratic Party (DP), and Grassroots Democratic Movement (GDM). "All the parties are seen as close to government" (*Africa Confidential* 18 October 1996, 3).

Since the demise of the Better Life for Rural Women Program and the inactivity of the National Council for Women, two elections have been conducted (for the local government councils and to the Constitutional Conference). Even though these elections were on a non-party basis, the performance of women in the elections was not impressive. Several reasons account for this relatively poor performance: political fatigue, indifference, and male chauvinism. There were women who stood their ground on the June 12 issue and had subsequently become alienated, a-politicized or victimized. There are also women who are political opportunists and who are busy canvassing actively for Abacha and his government to be given a chance, and there are those who want him elected President in 1998. Some women turn to religion, asking for prayers to be said for the government or advocating prayers and fasting so that God may intervene. Some women employ ethno-religious devices to explain the present quagmire, for instance, "the pollution of the *Ummah*" (see Nuhu n.d.). One clear conclusion from all this is that there are women from all states of the federation who are scrambling for political positions just like their male counterparts. So far, no military administrator has failed to fill the token positions reserved for women. As long as women continue to serve in dictatorships, it cannot be suggested that women are not part of the problem or that they did not contribute to its making.

Meanwhile, to satisfy personal ambition and opportunism, grandiose terms such as the "empowerment of women" have been employed by some women's organizations. The President of the NCWS, Amina Sambo, claimed that her organization had been involved in the mobilization of women for political and economic empowerment and further claimed that 80 women were elected as councillors and 9 women as heads of local governments. As well, the NCWS planned to raise funds for women politicians. Similarly, since the next local government elections will be on a party basis, some Ogun state women launched a $250,000 appeal fund to assist women in their campaigns. Titi Ajanaku, the Ogun State coordinator, observed that the launch was one of a series of awareness and education programs for women. She indicated that although in past elections no woman contested the chairmanship position in Ogun state, this will not be the situation for the next election. Already, it is claimed that the new CNC party has women chairpersons in Lagos, Oyo and Ekiti states. Its Lagos chairperson, Dayo Perera-Nwachukwu, was optimistic that more women would run for posts as local government chairpersons and councillors (Olori 1996).

Some western powers and NGOs are participants. Under the auspices of the British Council, the United States Agency for International Development, the Center for Development and Population Activities, and Gender and Development Action (GADA), women's groups were mobilized, ostensibly to improve the socio-economic and political lot of women. There was the "One Day Post-Beijing Women's Political Summit" held on March 2 1996 in Lagos, with "about 124 women representing politicians, NGOs and activists from all states of Nigeria." The summit deliberated on issues of women, democracy and governance. It made 11 observations among which were:

1. that the electoral process and the existing legal and structural framework do not effectively address women's rights, consensus and participation;
2. that whereas women constitute 60 percent of voters they are grossly underrepresented in all organs of the transition program;
3. that continued undemocratic rules do not provide a conducive atmosphere for the realization of women's potential;
4. that, as a result of prolonged military government and the negative atmosphere, women have remained apathetic to the political process and development;
5. that the abuse of human rights and essential freedoms has deterred women from participation in politics and hampered the realization of democratic ideals;
6. that the realization of women's rights through political participation is subverted by such tokenism as women's wings of political parties;
7. that the monetization of the political process by both government and politicians further deters women from political participation; and
8. that many women and women associations lack sufficient sensitivity and commitment to issues of politics and human rights.

The participants agreed on the following resolutions:

1. the political horizon should be broadened to encourage women's participation and the "open ballot" system should be scrapped and replaced with a modified open ballot system;
2. provisions should be made for independent candidates and financial conditions for candidates should not be excessive;
3. women's legal and professional groups should embark on advocacy to ensure that at least 30 percent of all legislative seats are reserved for women to ensure proportional representation;
4. national policy should be formulated and implemented immediately;
5. a Women's Coalition should be established to ensure greater cohesion and it should monitor all activities for gender sensitization and political participation;
6. gender sensitive women should be elected into leadership positions and an enforceable code of conduct should be established; and

7. a women's political trust fund should be established to support female candidates (Communiqué 2 March 1996).

A similar meeting was held in Enugu on April 20 1996 for women in the eastern states who were unable to attend the March meeting. Ninety women including politicians and activists discussed the "active role of women in the transition process." These women noted that money played a major role in the earlier election; that cultural constraints continue to impede women's ability to succeed in their political aims; that women went unprepared to the political arena given the absence of adequate information; and that religion could help to sensitize women. Therefore, they resolved inter alia, to establish a non-partisan trust fund for women politicians; that cultural constraints over women's participation could be removed through the raising and sustenance of public opinion and interest; that 40 percent of the hierarchy of political parties and government transition bodies should be occupied by women; and that women should develop their capacity, and build upon existing political skills, so as to effectively represent women (Communiqué 20 April 1996).

Not to be outdone, on the heels of the Post-Beijing Women's Political Summit, a heavily publicized one-day meeting of the Forum of Nigerian Women in Politics took place in Abuja. Similar meetings were held at the state level. Yet government failed to implement the suggestions made at any of these meetings. The election for local government councils, held soon after the Lagos Summit in March 1996, was the first test of Abacha's transition program and its commitment to democratization. Some women ran for election or worked towards the success of women candidates, but it was obvious that things had not changed much. Women still occupy marginal positions.

Since the murder of Ken Saro Wiwa and eight Ogoni colleagues in November 1995, the Abacha government's human rights ratings have plummeted and the standard of living of Nigerians has deteriorated. More non-governmental organizations have taken on the tasks of alleviating the sufferings of the masses. These NGOs not only have concentrated on bringing relief to people, they also have embarked on providing economic assistance through training people, particularly youths who are at loose ends given the total collapse of the economy. Also, some NGOs have worked to build democratic culture and encourage the empowerment of women. Some of the NGOs are: the International Reproductive Rights Research Action Group, the Girls' Power Initiative and the Inter Church Fund for International Development. In various ways, they have been helpful in working to build up civil society without incurring the wrath of government. But the effect of all these efforts is yet to be seen in positions women subsequently occupy.

As if steered by the efforts of the NGOs, the Abacha government has now established a program known as Vision 2010, with 173 members of which there are only 10 women (among whom is the 85-year-old Lagos market women leader, Alhaja Abibat Mogaji). Alhaja Mogaji is expected to speak to her members on how to support government programs (*The News* December 16 1996, 16). The membership of the Vision 2010 committee shows clearly that it is a body which is designed to woo the west as well as announce to the undiscerning world Abacha's date of departure from office. To get into the good books of the IMF and other financial bodies, the government is privatizing several parastatals including the National Electric Power Authority (NEPA), the Nigerian Telecommunication agency (Nitel) and the oil and gas sector. Many western countries want to "have a bit of the action" particularly in the oil sector which is worth up to $50 billion. Thus, the West is "soft-peddling" on sanctions against Nigeria (see *Africa Confidential* 18 October 1996, 2–3; *Nigerian Now* Sept./Oct. 1996, 2, 4–7; *Socialist Congress* December 1996, 1–2). Similarly, the Abacha government woos women with the proposed flooding of markets with "essential commodities" which are presently priced beyond the reach of ordinary people.

Conclusion

In this essay, I have attempted to use historical analysis to review the position of women in Nigerian politics beginning with colonial times and moving up to the present. I examine women's political activities and find that they have lacked planning and continuity. Women's responses to women in politics and the political situation have occurred on an ad hoc basis. It seems as if women have had to be pushed to the wall before they react to situations—and once the problem has been solved, they have reverted to complacency. This attitude is due to cultural traits, socialization and patriarchy. The attitude is embedded in society.

Colonial hegemony does not help matters. Its background is patriarchal "where women were tucked away in Victorian families" (Williams 1995, 11). Helen Callaway underlines the Victorian mentality of colonial men when she observes, " . . . in men's memoirs of the colonial period European women appear, if at all, as nameless figures in the background . . . the successive reconstructions of the colonial record have either left women out altogether or presented them in negative . . . roles" (1987, 3). Religion has not helped women shrug off subordination either. African traditional religion, Christianity and Islam helped to justify the superiority of males and the subordination of females. Christianity, and later, colonialism, helped enlighten women but not to the extent that they could emerge freely from the constraints of society. Islam was used for many years to disenfranchise northern Nigerian women, while it was used to keep western Nigerian women from achieving prominent roles in politics.

Thus, Stamp's feminist political economy only helps to identify the partial dependence of most Nigerian women on men. It was neither sufficient to shake women out of their lethargy nor does it elevate them to be on par with men in the political struggle. With the entrenched cultural constraints and economic limitations, some women stood out as enemies of progress. The few women who attempted to equal men, by virtue of their wealth or education or both, were not supported by women. For instance, Lagos market women were indifferent to the political situation and Babangida's transition program. They were more concerned about their business than politics. They were jolted from their stupor by Maryam Babangida who demonstrated what it meant to be able to call the shots. For instance, loans from the People's Banks and, later, Community Banks were easily available to women who were in the Better Life cooperatives. The Family Support Program of Mrs. Abacha is similarly employing the same strategy to win women's support. Thus, presently for most Nigerian women, it is still business as usual in spite of the poor economy, government's draconian laws and its poor human rights record. Token representation of women will continue for as long as there are not enough vocal, enlightened, educated/professional and wealthy women ready to make their impact felt in the sociopolitical spheres.

Though patriarchy will persist, its influence can be greatly diminished when a society's population is highly literate, wealthy and healthy. A Women's Ministry and the Family Support Program could disappear, but good education and health should not. Women's education is a priority, because to educate a woman is to educate a nation. Good health is another necessity. A healthy literate woman will participate fully in the development of the nation. The continued good heath of women is dependent on their economic wellbeing. All three are now rare among the people of Nigeria, particularly females. For the progress of Nigeria, there is a need to work for the common good. This entails that women and their organizations must achieve cohesion not only among themselves but also be in league with progressive men's groups in the struggle. The ambition to acquire political power should not blind women to certain decent behavior. The present apathy among some Nigerian women, particularly Yoruba women, may well be a demonstration that women have not lost all sense of decency after all, as is popularly believed. Finally, Nigerian women have not always spoken in unison. Thus their near silence has been interpreted as acquiescence to the present situation.

References

Afonja, Simi. 1986. "Women, Power and Authority in Traditional Society." In Leela Dube, Eleanor Leacock and Shirley Ardener (eds.), *Visibility and Power: Essays on Women in Society and Development*. Delhi: Oxford Univeristy Press.
Africa Confidential. 1996. 37, 21, October 18.
African Notes. 1990. Ibadan, WORDOC.
African Women. 1991. Autumn.
Awe, Bolanle. 1992. "Saviours of their Societies." In B. Awe (ed), *Nigerian Women in Historical Perspective*. Lagos: Sankore Publishers.
Burns, Allan. 1972. *History of Nigeria*. London: George Allen & Unwin.
Callaway, Helen. 1987. *Gender, Culture and Empire: European Women in Colonial Nigeria*. Chicago: University of Illinois Press.
Coleman, J. S. 1958. *Nigeria: Background to Nationalism*. Berkeley: University of California Press.
Coles, C. and B. Mack. 1991. *Hausa Women in the Twentieth Century*. Madison: University of Wisconsin Press.
Communiqué. 1996. Post-Beijing Women's Political Summit in Lagos. March 2.
———. 1996. Women's Political Awareness Meeting, Enugu. April 20.
Constitution of the Federal Republic. 1979, 1989, 1995. Abuja.
Diamond, Larry. 1995. "Nigeria: The Uncivic Society and Descent to Praetorianism." In Larry Diamond, Juan J. Linz and Seymour Martin Lipset (eds.), *Political Developing Countries: Comparing Experiences with Democracy*. Boulder: Lynne Rienner Publishers.
Forrest, Tom. 1995. *Politics and Economic Development in Nigeria*. Boulder: Westview Press.
Government's Views and Comments on the Findings and Recommendations of the Political Bureau. 1987. Abuja.
Hodgkin, Thomas. 1975. *Nigerian Perspectives: An Historical Anthology*. London: Oxford University Press.
Ityavyar, Dennis A. & Stella N. Obiajunwa. 1992. *The State and Women in Nigeria*. Jos: Jos University Press.

Mba, Nina. 1982. *Nigerian Women Mobilized: Women's Political Activity in Southern Nigeria 190–1965*. Berkeley: Institute of International Affairs, University of California.

———. 1992a. "Heroines of the Women's War." In B. Awe (ed.) *Op. Cit.*

———. 1992b. "Olufunmilayo Ransome-Kuti." In B. Awe (ed.) *Ibid.*

———. 1988. "Kaba and Khaki: Women and the Militarized State in Nigeria." Working Paper. Michigan State University.

Nigerian Now. (London).

Nuhu, H. Not Dated. *Religious Crises in Northern Nigeria: An Appraisal.* Unknown Publisher.

Olagunju, Tunji, Adele Jinadu and Sam Oyovbaire. 1993. *Transition to Democracy in Nigeria (1985–1993)*. Ibadan: Safari and Spectrum Books.

Olori, Toye. 1996. "Nigeria-Politics: Come and Vote, But Be Voted For Too." Inter Press Service.

Osoba, S. O. 1996. "Corruption in Nigeria: Historical Perspectives." In *Review of African Political Economy*, 69, 23 (September): 371–86.

Phillipson, S. 1948. *Grants-in-Aid of Education in Nigeria*. Lagos: Government Printer.

Report of the Political Bureau. 1987. Abuja.

Socialist Congress: Organ of the Socialist Congress of Nigeria.

Sklar, R. L. 1963. *Nigerian Political Parties: Power in an Emergent African Nation*. Princeton: Princeton University Press.

Stamm, Liesa and Carol D. Ruff, ed. 1982. *Social Power and Influence of Women*. Boulder: Westview.

Stamp, Patricia. 1989. *Technology, Gender and Power in Africa*. Ottawa: IDRC.

Williams, Pat. 1991. International Organization and National Interest: The O.I.C. Question in Nigeria. Unpublished Paper.

———. 1994. Power, Authority and Gender. An Unpublished Paper.

———. 1995. Nigerian Women in Conflict Resolution. Unpublished Paper.

———. 1996a. Women, Religion and Politics in Nigeria. Unpublished Paper.

———. 1996b. Constitutional Rights are not Women's Rights: An Examination of Nigerian Women as Full Citizens. Unpublished Paper.

———. forthcoming. "Religion, Violence and Displacement in Nigeria." *Journal of Asian and African Studies*.

Women in Nigeria Today. 1985. London: Zed Press.

Yusuf, Bilkisu. "Hausa-Fulani Women: The State of the Struggle." In C. Coles and B. Mack, *Hausa Women in the Twentieth Century*. Madison: University of Wisconsin Press.

11

NIGERIAN UNITY AND THE TENSIONS OF DEMOCRACY: GEO-CULTURAL ZONES AND NORTH-SOUTH LEGACIES

John N. Paden

Introduction

Despite the general air of pessimism about issues of unity and democracy in Nigeria, the Federal Republic of Nigeria is one of the few "federations" to have emerged from British colonial rule which has not fractured into its component parts. The nature of the "component parts" in Nigeria has undergone several transformations over the years, from regions, to provinces, to states, to the idea of six geo-cultural zones.

Although Nigeria is persistently analyzed in north-south terms, the more enduring reality is a six zone division, which can be traced to earliest British perceptions and has surfaced more recently in the constitutional proposals of General Abacha in October 1995. The persistence of a north-south set of perceptions and the realities of a sixfold set of dyadic relations will be explored in this essay.

During periods of civilian regimes (First and Second Republics), and military regimes (1st set, 1966–79; 2nd set, 1983–present) many of the political tensions in Nigeria have involved relations between the six "component parts." Yet, there is a tendency to regard Nigeria as consisting of two main political blocks: north and south (see Ake 1993; Metz 1992; Forrest 1993).

This essay will explore the implications of "north-south" legacies, as they impact issues of national unity and issues of transition to democratic rule in the independence period. It is important to distinguish between some of the structural experiments in federalism—(e.g. three tier levels, federal character, distribution of resources, division of powers, and federal capital territory)—and the politics of networks, coalitions, and symbolisms. Clearly, such structural and political aspects persist during both civilian and military regimes.

According to General Abacha's announcement on October 1995, the idea of rotation and a six zone structure was designated in the new constitution announced in 1995 as follows: "The PRC has also endorsed a modified Presidential system in which six (6) key executive and legislative offices will be zoned and rotated between six identifiable geographical groups. In the implementation of this provision, the country has been divided into six zones: North-East, North-West, Middle Belt, South-West, East Central and Southern Minority."

In historical perspective, these six zones may be translated into (1) emirate states; (2) Borno and environs; (3) middle belt minorities; (4) Yoruba areas; (5) Igbo areas; (6) southern minorities. It is far from clear how such zonal power sharing will be implemented, and the exact demarcation of zonal boundaries remains vague. Yet, the constitutional endorsement of what appears to be a "four tier federalism"—national, zonal, state, local—reflects the complexity of the "components" issue.

Indeed, there is perhaps a fifth level as well, at the neighborhood, or ward level. Also, there may be variations on the zonal clustering of states, depending on circumstances. Thus, at the time of the local government elections of March 16 1996, the thirty states were clustered into seven electoral zones, which roughly equate with the geo-cultural zones: (1) Borno, Yobe, Adamawa and Taraba; (2) Kano, Jigawa, Katsina, Sokoto and Kebbi; (3) Kwara, Kogi, Benue and Niger; (4) Lagos, Oyo, Ogun, Osun and Ondo; (5) Enugu, Abia, Imo and Anambra; (6) Edo, Delta, Rivers, Cross River and Akwa Ibom; (7) Plateau, Bauchi, Kaduna, and FCT, Abuja. The thirty states were divided into a total of 589 local government areas (LGAs) and a total of 6,927 electoral wards.

Zonal interactions are a persistent theme through much of Nigerian history. Yet, the persistence of a simpler "north-south" dichotomy likewise has both real and symbolic significance. How has this pattern evolved?

Background on North-South Relations

Between 1880 and 1905, most of Nigeria was conquered by the British, first in the south along the coast, and later in the interior north. In 1900,

Frederick Lugard declared Northern Nigeria to be under British rule and set up headquarters in Lokoja. Between 1907 and 1914, the British set up "Native Authorities" throughout Northern Nigeria, and introduced the policy of "indirect rule," utilizing pre-existing political units for administrative purposes.

In 1912, Lugard was appointed Governor of the Protectorate of Northern Nigeria, as well as Governor of the Colony and Protectorate of Southern Nigeria. The amalgamation of north and south was accomplished in 1914, although it was not until 1946 that Nigerians from these two regions had much administrative or political contact with each other. During this period, a lieutenant-governor in Kaduna (the new northern capital) administered the north, a lieutenant-governor in Enugu administered the south, and the governor general was located in Lagos. Later, indirect rule also became the policy in the south.

Within Northern Nigeria, the British envisioned three distinct political/cultural components: (1) the Sokoto "Empire" (sometimes referred to as the "Fulani empire"); (2) the Borno "Empire" (or "Kanuri empire"); (3) the "minorities" in the "Middle Belt." Within Southern Nigeria, the British also envisioned three distinct political/cultural components: (1) the Igbo speaking areas of the east; (2) the Yoruba states of the west; (3) the various "minorities" in the mid-west and east.

During the period of decolonization (1946–60), a series of constitutional discussions occurred, involving British officials, plus representatives from the northern region and the southern regions (the eastern and western provinces). The national conference in Ibadan in 1950 involved delegates from northern and southern regions, and it was agreed that regional assemblies would have legislative powers. Regional assemblies would select from their members to participate in a central House of Representatives in Lagos. The north insisted on equal representation with the south and a formula for sharing ministerial positions. Elections were held in 1951 and 1952 with political parties forming in each of the three regions.

A London conference in 1953 agreed on a federal formula for Nigeria, with residual powers remaining in the regions. At the Constitutional Conference of 1957, it was agreed that the east and west would become self-governing as soon as possible, and the north would set its own date for self-government (1959). Federal elections were held in 1959 to determine the composition of the independence government. With independence on October 1 1960, the major northern party won a plurality (143) of the 312 seats in the federal parliament and went into a governing coalition with the dominant party from the east, leaving the dominant party from the west as the opposition.

During the First Republic (1960–66), the dominant coalition continued to be major elements from the north and east. The lack of involvement of major elements from the west contributed to the breakdown of the First Republic.

During the Second Republic (1979–83), the dominant coalition again was major elements from the north and east. Again, tensions in the west led to the military takeover on December 31 1983.

In the presidential elections in June 1993, a west-based coalition with significant northern linkages appeared to be successful against a more traditional north-east coalition. This apparent "upset" of the coalition alignment of the two preceding republics caused alarm (and, apparently, threats of secession) in several parts of Nigeria, and the military annulled the election prior to the announcement of official results.

Thus, the question as to the relationship between the "regions" of Nigeria has a long structural and political history. As we noted earlier, on October 1 1995 General Abacha announced that a rotating power sharing formula had been approved and that six zones would be designated as the basis for the next transition to civilian rule.

The Idea of Six Geo-Cultural Zones

A six zone model of political culture in Nigeria includes the following components: (1) emirate states; (2) Borno and environs; (3) middle belt minorities; (4) Yoruba states; (5) Igbo states; (6) southern minorities. (The first three are "northern;" the second three are "southern.") To some extent, this follows the original assessment of the British colonial period, which became reified in part because of the indirect rule policy. These component zones have certain cultural and/or historical characteristics which have profoundly affected Nigerian efforts at unity and democratic rule.

The emirate states share the legacy of having been part of the Sokoto caliphal experience in the nineteenth century. Within the "northern region" of the twentieth century they stretch from Sokoto in the west to Adamawa in the east, and Ilorin and Niger in the south. They are, by definition, predominantly Muslim in their traditional political structure. In the twentieth century, they have evolved into distinctive "emirates" (i.e., with an emir, or equivalent, as symbolic head of the unit). While Hausa language tends to predominate as a lingua franca, the emirate states are a multilingual cluster, including Fulfulde, Yoruba, Nupe, and several minority languages. Often there are traditional rivalries among these states (e.g. Kano and Sokoto, which split into civil war in the 1890s). There are many occasions where the cluster does not act as a unified block. Yet, within this zone, the Sultan of Sokoto has special salience in spiritual matters.

Borno (and environs), in the northeastern corner of Nigeria, is the oldest continuous Islamic community in sub-Saharan Africa (dating from the eleventh century) and has the same sort of recognizable Muslim authority structures as Sokoto. In the nineteenth century, when Sokoto tried to conquer Borno, there was a standoff, and Borno "resistance to Sokoto" became part of the historical legacy. Within the "far north" the delicate balance between Sokoto and Borno was an important feature of colonial rule, and an important challenge in the post-independence political coalition process. The dominant language group in Borno is Kanuri, although, like Sokoto, Borno is a multi-lingual cluster, (increasingly with Hausa as a lingua franca).

The middle belt minorities within the "north" are a residual cluster consisting of a large number of smaller ethnolinguistic groups, many of whom have historically resisted the large scale Muslim political powers (e.g. Sokoto and Borno) of the savanna/horse culture zones. Some of these minorities have structured political systems, with leaders such as the Aku Uku of Wukari (Jukun), the Och'Idoma (Idoma), the Atta of Igala, and the Atta of Igbirra. Others, such as the Tiv, the Gwari, the Dass area peoples, the Ningi, and the Bachama are segmental societies without hierarchical structures (although in some cases, e.g. the Tor Tiv, the British policy of indirect rule "created" central authorities). In the nineteenth century, these minorities were traditional in their religious beliefs. In the twentieth century, there have been increasing inroads by both Christianity and Islam. Hausa has come to be a language of wider communication in the middle belt minority group.

In the southwest, the fifty or so traditional Yoruba states share a common linguistic heritage, and a political culture in which the city states have "chiefs" (obas), which tend to be symbolic in their powers with decision-making powers often vested in a council of representatives from the various lineages. A common myth of origin traces back to Ile Ife, and much of the cosmology is similar. In the eighteenth century, many Yoruba city states (except the Ijebu) were loosely united under Old Oyo. They were later split into four states (Oyo, Egba, Ketu, and Jebu). By 1850, after the Sokoto conquest of Ilorin, four new states emerged (Ibadan, Ilesha, Ife, and Ekiti Parapo). With British conquest, more fragmentation occurred. A certain amount of pan-Yoruba sentiment exists which has been heightened in the independence period by the "outsider" role of the dominant political factions. By the 1990s, it is generally acknowledged that the Yoruba states are about half Muslim and half Christian, with strong traditional elements permeating both faiths. (Moreover, there have been close intrafamily ties between Christian and Muslim adherents.) Notably, the "emirate state" of Ilorin (in the "north") is predominantly Yoruba, and hence is an important overlap in zones. In the June 1993 presidential elections, the focus was on the city-state of Abeokuta, home of Chief Abiola, the apparent winner.

In the southeast, the Igbo states share a common linguistic identity, and a political culture based on decentralized/village structures (including age grade and gender grade associations). There are numerous locational identities, but the important descriptors are extended families and clan groupings. In the twentieth century, there is an important distinction between Onitsha Igbos and others. During the independence era, many of the Igbo political factions have associated themselves with dominant groups in the north, and hence have been part of governing coalitions. The Biafra secession movement/Nigerian civil war (1967–70) has underscored the ambiguity of Igbo participation in Nigerian political life.

The southern minorities cluster, as a residual zone, includes large ethnolinguistic groups such as the Edo of Benin, with its powerful history along the Guinea coast, as well as a large number of other midwest and eastern groups, such as the Ibibio, Efik, Ijaw, Ogoni, and others. Politically, such groups have often been suspicious of their larger southern neighbors (Yoruba and Igbo), and often find themselves in coalition with northern political partners. Much of the oil producing area is located within this minorities cluster.

Dyadic Relations of Geo-Cultural Zones in "North" and "South"

There is a tendency outside of the northern zones of Nigeria to lump the three northern clusters together as part of a politically homogeneous whole. Under certain circumstances this may be appropriate, but often it tends to obscure the dynamic balances between these zones. The three dyadic relationships are as follows: (1) emirate states and Borno; (2) emirate states and middle belt minorities; (3) middle belt minorities and Borno. Often, the symbolism of power sharing, or political representation, is more important in coalition building than the actual political realities. This has been true in both civilian and military regime periods.

The historic tensions between Borno and Sokoto have been mentioned. During the colonial period, the British moved cautiously through the educational system to integrate the sons of notables from these two zones into a common, Islamic-sensitive educational structure. This allowed for a younger generation to take the mantle of leadership in the early independence era and try to find a balance of interests between these two zones. Perhaps emblematic of this coalition were the careers of Ahmadu Bello (Sokoto) and Kashim Ibrahim (Borno) during the First Republic (see Paden 1986).

During the Second Republic, with presidential leadership coming from Sokoto (Shagari), there was no predominant political figure from Borno. In the countdown to the aborted Third Republic it remained for the dominant Social Democratic Party (SDP) to select a vice presidential running mate from Borno (Kingibe). Yet this time, it was not in coalition with the emirate states, but with a candidate from the Yoruba states (Abiola).

The sensitivity of representation from Borno, as distinct from Sokoto, is illustrated in the leadership structure of the Nigerian Supreme Council for Islamic Affairs. The Sultan of Sokoto is chair of the council. The Shehu of Borno is the vice-chair, and a representative from the Yoruba states is secretary (see Paden 1995a).

During military regime periods, while most of the heads of state have been "northern," there are important zonal differences: Gowon (middle belt), Mohammad (emirate), Buhari (emirate), Babangida (middle belt), Abacha (Borno). The fact that the current head of state, although born and raised in Kano is regarded as originally from Borno, has had a distinct impact on Nigerian military regime politics. The Abacha regime has built a national coalition of commercial elites, educated elites and traditional elites who see the alternative as chaos. The center of this coalition is Kano-Borno which plays on their historic rivalry with Sokoto to create a counterbalance in the north which may be welcomed in other parts of the country.

Emirate relations with the middle belt minorities has partly centered on issues of religious identity. Many of the prominent military leaders from the middle belt tend to be identified as either Christian or Muslim. Thus, Yakubu Gowon, of Angas ethno-linguistic heritage, is clearly seen as Christian, while Ibrahim Babangida, of Gwari ethno-linguistic heritage, is Muslim.

During the 1st republic, the dominant northern party (Northern Peoples' Congress/NPC) made every effort to find allies among middle belt factions. This was complicated by the open challenge to Muslim political leaders, especially in the Tiv areas, and in large missionary-influenced cities such as Jos.

During the Second Republic, the fact that the dominant Tiv politican (Tarka) went into coalition with "the north," helped account for the Shagari presidential success. Yet, areas of Benue and Plateau have problematic relations with emirate states.

Borno-middle belt relations have sometimes been facilitated by a shared sense of grievance against the emirate states. Opposition groups in both zones joined forces during the First Republic. Generally, there have been better relations between Borno and the middle belt, because, unlike the emirate legacy, there has been much less tendency for Borno to proselytize in the religio-political realm.

Having noted some examples of dyadic relations among northern zones, one should mention that both during the First Republic, and under the Abacha military regime, there have been elite efforts to reinforce an overarching sense of "northerness." The creation of a northern identity ("yan arewa") which transcended religion, geography and history was clearly a major objective of the NPC during 1960–66 (see Paden 1986).

More recently, the stresses of political role reversal, especially in the emirate states, have revived efforts to reinforce a sense of "northern" identity. (See, for example, the report of the establishment in London of the Arewa Association, a forum for Northern Nigerians resident in Britain in *West Africa*, September 4–10 1995.)

Patterns of dyadic relationships are apparent within the southern group of zones as well. Within the "south," the complexities of Yoruba-Igbo relations are beyond the scope of this essay. A cover story of *Newswatch* (February 13 1995, "The Forces Against Igbo/Yoruba Unity") argues that "History, politics, old animosities, make a new alliance between the Yoruba and the Igbo an uphill task" (12). On January 28 1995, a meeting of eminent persons met in Ibadan under the auspices of the National Unity Organization (NUO), led by Olusegun Obasanjo (Abeokuta) aimed at "promoting understanding, unity, harmony and solidarity between the east and the west." The final communique suggested that much work remained to be done. Tensions between Igbo and Yoruba go back to the First Republic and to the civil war.

With regard to southern minorities, the article continues, " . . . eastern minorities have always preferred to deal with non-Igbo. An example was in the 1979 elections when the votes from Cross River and Rivers secured for Shehu Shagari and the NPN victory at the polls. Rivers State gave 72.65 percent of the total votes to former President Shagari, while Cross River gave 64.40 percent. This was more than the votes cast in core northern states of Sokoto (66.58 percent), Shagari's home state, and Bauchi (62.48 percent). The feeling of the minorities, *Newswatch* gathered, is that any agreement between the Igbo and the Yoruba would not be binding on them" (17). In short, southern minorities seem to distrust both Yoruba and Igbo clusters, and prefer coalitions with northern zones.

The 1979 and 1983 presidential elections

In the multi-party elections of 1979 and 1983, the final coalitions occurred after the elections rather than before (as in a two party system). In the 1979 presidential elections, the parties which won 50 percent or more of the votes are shown in Table 11.1, by state, arranged by geo-cultural zones. (The party abbreviations are as follows: National Party of Nigeria, NPN; Great Nigeria People's Party, GNPP; People's Redemption Party, PRP; Nigerian People's Party, NPP; Unity Party of Nigeria, UPN.)

The three northern based parties (NPN, PRP, GNPP) won majorities in all of the three northern zones: emirate states (NPN), plus Kano (PRP) and Borno (GNPP); (i.e., the dominant party, NPN, lost in Kano and Borno).

The two southern based parties (UPN, NPP) won in their respective zones: Yoruba areas (UPN) and Igbo areas (NPP). The UPN was able to win only one state outside its zone, i.e., the neighboring state of Bendel. The NPP split the vote in Plateau (with a near win of 49 percent) but did not capture any state outside the Igbo zone.

The only party with a significant showing outside its zonal base was the NPN, which won in the middle belt (Benue) and among southern minorities (Rivers and Cross River). To some extent this represented a coalition of emirate states, middle belt and southern minorities, i.e., a northwest to southeast axis.

After the election (perhaps because the presidential/vice-presidential team represented an emirate/Igbo alliance) and with the close cooperation of the GNPP (Borno), the only "outsider zone" not participating in government was the Yoruba area. (Note: the splits in the PRP in Kano into a hard line faction and accommodating faction made it possible for certain Kano elements to cooperate with the NPN.)

In the 1983 presidential elections the northern based party (NPN) again won majorities or pluralities in six of the seven emirate states. In Kano, the race tightened between the NPN and PRP, with the latter winning only a slight plurality. Yet neither of the two northern smaller parties (PRP/Kano, GNPP/Borno) won a majority in any state. (Note that the death of Aminu Kano in April 1983 prior to the election, and the succession of Hassan Yusuf to leadership of the PRP, clearly affected the election results in Kano.) As in 1979, the NPN won majorities in minority states of Benue, Rivers and Cross River, and after the election, worked in coalition with Igbo and Borno elements. The NPP won the Igbo areas, and the UPN won the Yoruba areas, plus Bendel, with a strong showing in Kwara.

Table 11.1. Presidential Elections, 1979: parties with 50 percent of votes cast per state (note: "X" indicates majority vote)

	NPN	PRP	GNPP	NPP	UPN
A. Emirate states					
1. Sokoto	x				
2. Bauchi	x				
3. Kwara	x				
4. Niger	x				
5. Kaduna	x				
6. Gongola	(34%)		(34%)		
7. Kano		x			
B. Borno area					
8. Borno			x		
C. Middle belt					
9. Plateau	(35%)			(49%)	
10. Benue	x				
D. Yoruba areas					
11. Oyo					x
12. Ogun					x
13. Lagos					x
14. Ondo					x
E. Igbo areas					
15. Anambra				x	
16. Imo				x	
F. Southern minorities					
17. Bendel					x
18. Rivers	x				
19. Cross River	x				
Totals:	8.7	1	1.3	2.5	5

(Key: X=party won state)

Table 11.2. Presidential Elections, 1983: parties with 50 percent of votes cast per state

	NPN	PRP	GNPP	NPP	UPN
A. Emirate states					
1. Sokoto	x				
2. Bauchi	x				
3. Kwara	(49%)				(45%)
4. Niger	x				
5. Kaduna	x				
6. Gongola	(44%)				
7. Kano	(32%)	(37%)			
B. Borno area					
8. Borno	(49%)			(25%)	
C. Middle belt					
9. Plateau	(45%)			(43%)	
10. Benue	x				
D. Yoruba areas					
11. Oyo	(38%)				x
12. Ogun					x
13. Lagos					x
14. Ondo					x
E. Igbo areas					
15. Anambra	(33%)			x	
16. Imo	(25%)			x	
F. Southern minorities					
17. Bendel	(41%)				x
18. Rivers	x				
19. Cross River	x				
Totals:	7(+)	0	0	2	5

(Key: X=party won state)

The 1993 Presidential Elections

The prelude to the June 1993 elections was clearly the series of presidential primary elections within the two parties which were cancelled in November 1992 by the military government. Yet, by October 1992 the primaries had resulted in strong leads for Shehu Musa Yar'Adua (from Katsina) of the Social Democratic Party (SDP), and Adamu Ciroma (from Borno) of the National Republican Convention (NRC). President Ibrahim Babangida (originally from the Federal Capital Territory/FCT area), pointed to instances of voting irregularities, but there was also a clear concern that both leading candidates were from the far northern part of the country, and the issue of locational balance was not far from the surface.

The two parties were asked to nominate new candidates through a process of bottom up nominations for presidential candidates by means of a series of primary elections within each party. Presidential candidates, once nominated, then selected vice presidential candidates. This process culminated in national elections on June 12 1993 between the SDP team of M.K.O. Abiola (presidential candidate from Ogun) plus Baba Gana Kingibe (vice presidential candidate from Borno) and the NRC team of Bashir Tofa (presidential candidate from Kano) plus Sylvester Ugoh (vice presidential candidate from the former eastern region). All four team members were carefully vetted prior to the election to ensure their eligibility.

The results of the June 1993 presidential election were never announced officially, but the unofficial results gave the SDP 58.5 percent of the votes to the NRC's 41.5 percent. The SDP appeared to have won the election in 19 states, and the NRC in ll states.

A central question is whether the distribution of these votes reflect patterns which are clearly different from previous Nigerian federal elections (1959, 1964, 1979, 1983). These patterns are ascertainable from an assessment of the strength of the SDP and NRC in each of the six major geo-cultural zones within Nigeria, as indicated in Table 11.3. (Note: regardless of the number of new states, the continuity of geo-cultural zones seems fairly well established in Nigeria.)

The voting patterns cross cut the two major religious zones (Muslims, mainly in the north, and Christians, mainly in the south). Yet, are religious identity patterns reflected in the results? Since both presidential candidates were Muslim there was not a clear pattern of demarcation. As usual, the cross-currents within the Muslim community were significant. Of the four major ethno-cultural groups within the Nigerian Muslim community—former Sokoto caliphal states (i.e., the "emirate states"), Borno, Yoruba communities, and middle belt "minorities"—

Table 11.3. Results (by state) of June 12 1993 Presidential election (arranged by socio-cultural zones)

	SDP	NRC
A. northern emirate states		
1. Kebbi		x
2. Sokoto		x
3. Niger		x
4. Katsina		x
5. Bauchi		x
6. Adamawa		x
7. Kano	x	
8. Jigawa	x	
9. Kaduna	x	
10. Kwara	x	
B. Borno area		
11. Borno	x	
12. Yobe	x	
C. Middle belt minorities		
13. Plateau	x	
14. Taraba	x	
15. Benue	x	
16. Kogi		x
D. Yoruba speaking areas		
17. Oyo	x	
18. Ogun	x	
19. Lagos	x	
20. Osun	x	
21. Ondo	x	
E. Igbo speaking areas		
22. Abia		x
23. Enugu		x
24. Imo		x
25. Anambra	x	
F. Southern minorities		
26. Edo	x	
27. Delta	x	
28. Akwa Ibom	x	
29. Cross River	x	
30. Rivers		x
Totals:	19	11

(Key: X=party won state)

the SDP won in the latter three zones, and made clear inroads into the emirate states.

In short, the NRC won the *emirate states* (except Kano, Jigawa, Kaduna, Kwara) and the *Igbo speaking areas* (except Anambra). The SDP won the *Yoruba speaking areas*, the *Borno area*, the *middle belt* (except Kogi), and the *southern minority areas* (except Rivers).

Geo-Cultural Identities and Coalition Building (1993)

How have geo-cultural identities affected coalition building, and what are the effects of such coalitions on the prospects for a workable democratic system in the future?

In the 1993 elections, it would have been in the clear interests of the NRC to have been able to keep the northern emirate block of states (10) intact, to have kept the Igbo speaking states (4), and to have held the middle belt minority states (4). They might have hoped to keep at least two of the southern minority states, which would have given them two-thirds of the total number of states.

By contrast, the SDP needed to hold the Yoruba speaking states (5 plus Kwara = 6), hold the Borno area (2), take most of the middle belt states (4), and make inroads into the northern emirate states (especially Kano, Jigawa and Kaduna, i.e., 3). Then, with a few southern minority states (e.g., Edo, Delta) the SDP would have held the balance of voting power.

Both the SDP and the NRC strategies required north-south coalitions and alliances, as distinct from north versus south block voting. The results show that for the first time in Nigerian presidential elections a north/middle/east coalition did not prevail. Instead, a northeast (Borno)/ middle/ west coalition held together to form the winning team.

To what extent did the geo-cultural identities of the presidential teams affect coalition building? The selection of two relatively unknown candidates by the NRC (Tofa and Ugoh), was perhaps meant to be an echo of the successful team in 1979 and 1983 of Shehu Shagari (Sokoto), and Dr. Alex Ekwueme (Anambra). Such regional balance also provided religious balance (Muslim/Christian). In addition, as part of the transition to the Third Republic, the governorship of Kano had been won by an NRC candidate (due to splits within the Kano SDP). There was a sense that another Sokoto based presidency might not seem fair in terms of regional balance, but that a Kano-based presidency might appeal to a broader constituency.

Kano itself was crucial, as the largest single state in the federation. (As it turned out, the NRC lost Kano by about 52 percent to 48 percent.)

The selection of two well known personalities by the SDP (Abiola and Kingibe) was somewhat of a risk, and a coalition of Yoruba speaking areas with the Borno area had never held in the past. Also, both Abiola and Kingibe were Muslim, and there was a question as to whether Christian groups would defect. (As it turned out, the Christian Association of Nigeria/CAN endorsed the SDP ticket, and the SDP held most of the "Christian" geo-cultural zones.)

The fact that the SDP ticket won four of the emirate states (Kano, Jigawa, Kaduna, Kwara) plus the Borno states (Borno, Yobe) meant that there was not a north-south, or Christian-Muslim split. The fact that Abiola was identified as a "Yoruba Muslim" meant that he could appeal both to predominantly Yoruba groups, and to predominantly northern Muslim groups. Since Abiola was regarded as a "renewal" (*tajdid*) Muslim by some of the younger northern Muslims, he was also a challenge to the widespread northern Muslim view that "Yoruba Muslims" were not as religiously committed as "far northern Muslims" (Birai 1993).

The annulment (on June 23 1993) of the June 12th elections resulted in the military appointment in August of a Christian Yoruba (Chief Ernest Shonekan) as head of an "interim council" to oversee fresh elections. In November 1993 the military restored military rule under Sani Abacha. A Constitutional Conference was convened to draft a new constitution, which was unveiled in late spring 1995. This, inter alia, recommended rotating the presidency between six zones.

On October 1 1995 General Abacha endorsed a variation of this recommendation: "The national political offices which will be filled by candidates in a rotational basis are: the President, the Vice President, Prime Minister, Deputy Prime Minister, Senate President and Speaker of the House of Representatives. This power sharing arrangement which shall be entrenched in the Constitution shall be at Federal level and applicable for an experimental period of 30 (thirty) years."

Implications of the 1993 Experience

The events of 1993 pose the question whether any leadership team can govern Nigeria without the active participation of all six of the geo-cultural zones. In particular, many in the Igbo speaking areas seem to be washing their hands of the national power struggle—which some see as being between "the Yoruba and the Hausa." There was some evidence of people returning to their village areas after June 12 due to the growing tensions. Having been the major participants in a secessionist effort between 1967 and 1970, some in Igbo areas felt that what they needed now would be a real autonomy within a loose federation.

In the northern emirate state areas, including Kano and Kaduna—(where the margins of victory for the SDP were very close)—there was strong feeling that regardless of party, if there were fresh elections some of the candidates who were northern front-runners in the 1992 primaries might compete again and be successful nationally. There was also, no doubt, a good deal of shock at having a "southern" elected president for the first time in Nigerian history.

Given the sub-national/regional basis of national coalition building in Nigerian presidential elections, and the intensity of geo-cultural identities, some "healing processes" will be needed along with mechanisms for inclusion of all areas of the country in any future attempt at democratic rule. Whatever the status of the 1993 presidential elections, the experience presents clear patterns of "continuity and change" within the socio-political arena. Understanding such patterns may suggest answers about "north-south" legacies, and focus on underlying dynamics of Nigerian unity and the tensions of democracy.

The Idea of Zonal Power Sharing and Rotation

The Constitutional Conference established under Sani Abacha in 1994 debated issues of power sharing, and a rotational presidency. The recommendations in 1995 included the idea of a rotational presidency and multiple vice presidents. According to *West Africa*, "While the South is enthusiastic about rotational Presidency, many politicians and people of the North do not seem to be happy with it. The Northern Elders Forum said, however, that it was not completely against rotational presidency as long as it was not permanent. The Presidency, said the forum, should rotate between the North and South for 10 years, and should begin with the North. . . . Compare this with the views of the South-West Obas who not only support rotational Presidency but say that the Southern part of the country should be allowed to produce the next President. For the Igbos, in the eastern part of the country, the best thing they got out of the Constitutional Conference is the issue of rotation" (September 25–October 8 1995, 1515). Yet, rotation would require attention to zones, and not just north-south regionalism (see Figure 1).

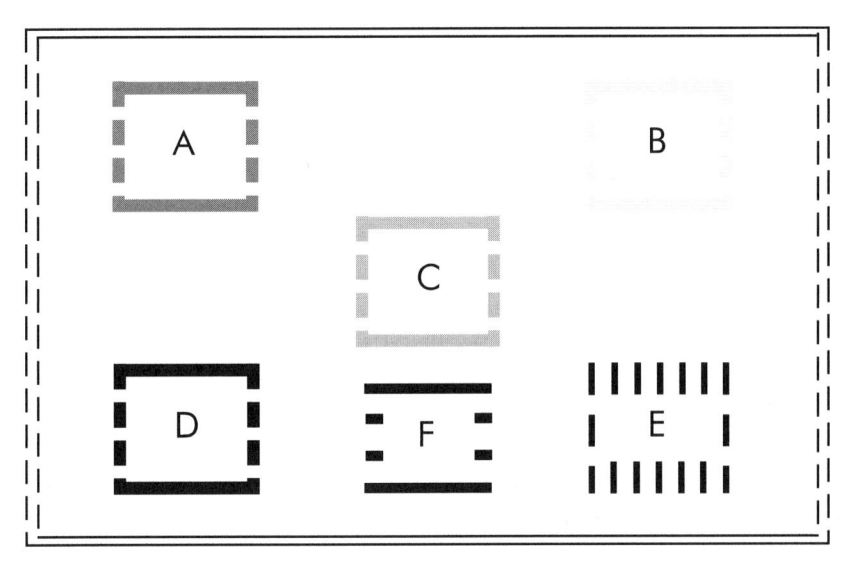

1. previous federal winning coalitions: ABCEF
2. June, 1993, federal "winning" coalition: DBCF
3. June, 1993, federal "losing" coalition: AE

Key: A = northern emirate states
   B = Borno area
   C = middle belt minorities
   D = Yoruba speaking area
   E = Igbo speaking area
   F = southern minorities

Figure 2. Diagram of Coalitions.

As mentioned above, the October 1 1995 speech of the head of state confirmed the idea of rotational powers, plus a multi-party system (to be phased in over a three year period). *The Economist* summarized as follows:

> The proposal is that, for the first time, power will be rotated between the six regions. This is in answer to the criticism that Nigeria is nearly always governed by northerners. The president, vice-president, prime minister, deputy prime minister, senate president and speaker of the House of Representatives could all be from different parties and different ethnic groups. This could make for gridlock—or total chaos. The programme provides for the creation of more states, although there are already too many, and multiple parties which must be 'federal' in character. The choice of which region will

get the first turn at the presidency is a potential flash-point. Moreover, the boundaries of the regions will be hard to define since Nigeria's 90m people come from over 200 ethnic groups (October 7 1995, 47).

Within Nigeria, many of the concerns about Abiola's release, and residual hopes for his ascendence to the presidency, are located within the Yoruba-speaking zone. The original coalition which produced the apparent victory for the SDP team in 1993 has splintered into a variety of emerging coalitions, often with inter-zonal links. Strikingly, the SDP vice-presidential candidate, Kingibe, along with other Abiola supporters, joined the military government in November 1993.

The details of a rotational presidency and/or other forms of zonal power sharing remain to be seen. Indeed, even the exact nature of the "six regions" is in a state of flux. The resurgence of "north" and "south" designators in the debates has added to the complexity of finding a workable political formula to accommodate regional diversity and still provide a sense of national cohesion.

Geo-Cultural Zones and "North-South" Federalism Issues

The central question in Nigerian political life continues to be national unity. Tensions in the aftermath of the June 12th election have reinforced the historic sense in the Yoruba areas of being excluded from political power. Beneath the surface calm of military rule, there are numerous examples of pan-Yoruba conferences which articulate these grievances. Clearly, the detention of Abiola, and later Obasanjo, plus the flight of Wole Soyinka—all three from the Egba-Yoruba town of Abeokuta in Ogun state—have served as symbolic focal points for discontent in the southwestern/Yoruba zone.

The discontent, in turn, has sparked speculation, or conspiracy theories, about potential secessionist behavior in the Yoruba areas. This speculation in turn has prompted other areas of Nigeria to face, once again, the issue of national unity and the potential impact of a partition movement. While such partition is sometimes articulated in "north-south" terms, it is unlikely that the south would be unified on such a matter. The role of Kwara state, which straddles the emirate zone (in the "north") and the Yoruba zone (in the "south"), would be especially complex. Indeed, the mere speculation about partition strengthens the hand of military nationalists who have, more than once, been called on to "save the federation."

This blurring of "north-south" demarcations is nowhere more apparent than in the relocation of the federal capital from Lagos to Abuja. A decision of the Mohammad-Obasanjo regime in the mid-1970s, the site selection of Abuja was intended to remove the federal capital from any particular zone and to create a new territory on the borderline between north and south.

The creation of a Federal Capital Territory (FTC) in the center of the country, with equal access from all zones, has been popular in all zones except the Yoruba areas. The Shagari-Ekwueme civilian regime in particular encouraged Igbo contractors to participate in the building of the new city. The middle belt minorities, in whose area the capital territory was created, have felt a special sense of access to Abuja. Other minorities in the south and north have welcomed the fact that Abuja was not in any one of the "big three" zones (Hausa, Yoruba, Igbo).

Yet, the move from Lagos to Abuja has been slow and fraught with politics. The fact that many Yoruba civil servants in Lagos did not choose to relocate to Abuja, plus the slow pace of building physical facilities, created a "dual capital" phenomenon, with "parallel" ministries, until quite recently. Indeed, there were many in Nigeria, during the 1993 election, who may have felt that only a Yoruba president could effectuate the relocation to a truly "federal" capital.

Most Nigerians seem to recognize that of the three national options—centralization, partition, federalism—the costs of centralization and partition are very high. Centralization, particularly in an oil producing economy, tends toward corruption and abuse of power. It tends to follow military chain of command precedents, from top down, even when the formal level structures are more differentiated in terms of autonomy.

The partition option has been tried, with the attempted secession of the Eastern Region, and a bloody civil war resulted (1967–70). Most observers agree that any future partition in Nigeria would not be an amicable divorce, but probably tend toward domestic violence. Indeed, the mere threat of partition is likely to prolong military rule.

Thus, the option of federalism has remained the consistent choice of most Nigerians over the years since independence. Yet, the questions as to the nature of Nigerian federalism remain in a state of constant transformation and debate. It is beyond the scope of this essay to summarize all of the issues and permutations of these debates.

Suffice it to note that the idea of "federal character" has been a consistent theme since the period of the First Republic. Thus, cabinets and top political leadership are expected to be balanced by state-of-origin, in some approximate way. All political parties, since efforts to restore democracy began in 1975, have been required to have a national base of support rather than a regional base. (Indeed, in the contemporary political culture of Nigeria, many argue that there should be some rough parity of Muslims and Christians in senior leadership positions.) This federal character principle has been applied in both military and civilian periods.

This "horizontal federalism" among the various states and regions of Nigeria has been part of the impetus for the creation of new states. It has also been the theoretical basis for the idea of a rotational presidency and power sharing among regions.

Although experience in other countries varies, from Yugoslavia to Switzerland, the challenge seems to be to avoid gridlock, and be able to provide national coherence and effective decision-making. The need for some alternatives to winner-take-all systems (whether parliamentary or presidential) within a regionally based federal system is part of the experimental evolution of Nigerian horizontal federalism.

By contrast, vertical federalism in Nigeria seems clearly set on a three tier model, with federal, state and local levels constitutionally demarcated. The question as to the nature of the "states" is central, and the Nigerian legacy is not to use ethnicity as the sole criteria. The reemergence of zones in the constitutional package announced in 1995 may add another tier.

It is clear that "military federalism" is a contradiction in terms. Thus, a transition to democratic rule is a precondition for effective federalism, both horizontal and vertical.

Whether "north and south" will continue to play a major role in Nigerian federal experiments remains to be seen. There are clear indications that six zone models have already transcended the colonial regionalism of north and south. Yet political dynamics during times of stress may resuscitate any number of in-group/out-group designations.

Also, north/south regional identities may be surrogates for other factors, such as religion, even though religious identities now are mixed in most parts of the federation.

The danger of "north-south" designations in a functioning federal system is that the political use of regional symbolism is often a symptom of out-group anger and frustration. Political talk of "northern political domination" or "southern economic domination" is hardly conducive to the health of a national system. When such regional symbols are used in a threatening or pejorative manner, the specter of partition hangs overhead.

Conclusions

Conclusions about unity and the tensions of democracy, with special reference to "north-south" legacies, are difficult because of the transitional nature of Nigerian political life. It has been argued in this essay that the historic distinctions between "north" and "south" remain only one of several ways of cultural clustering in Nigeria. Within the political realm, the concept of six geo-cultural zones with cross-cutting linkages is far more useful than a simple north-south dichotomy.[1]

Yet, the question remains: how can "federal character" and national unity be achieved through the symbolism and structure of the presidency? The idea of balanced tickets—(i.e., one from the north and one from the south)—was put to the test in 1993, when the apparent winners were not from the emirate zone of the north, or the Igbo zone of the south. With a winner-take-all system, at best only two of the six zones can be represented at any one time by such a team balance. A central lesson in Nigerian political history is that the perceived exclusion of major segments of the country leads to instability and regime collapse.

The search for alternatives within the federalist paradigm will continue in Nigeria. Indeed, this is part of the tension of democratic process. The danger is that the culture of military rule will be so ingrained over time, that the whole concept of democratic federalism will be reduced to formalities, rather than an integral part of a vibrant civic culture.

Notes

1. It seems significant that as six new states were created (in October 1996), one fell into each of the six zones discussed in this essay.

References

Ake, Claude. 1993. "Nigeria." In Joel Krieger (ed.), *The Oxford Companion to Politics of the World*. New York: Oxford University Press.
Birai, Umar. 1993. "Islamic Tajdid and the Political Process in Nigeria." In Martin Marty and Scott Appleby (eds.), *Fundamentalisms and the State*. Chicago: University of Chicago.

Forrest, Tom. 1993. *Politics and Economic Development in Nigeria*. Boulder: Westview Press.
Kastfelt, Niels. 1994. *Religion and Politics in Nigeria: A Study in Middle Belt Christianity*. New York: British Academic Press.
Metz, Helen, ed. 1992. *Nigeria: A Country Study*. Washington DC: Federal Research Division, Library of Congress.
Paden, John. 1986. *Ahmadu Bello, Sardauna of Sokoto: Values and Leadership in Nigeria*. London: Hodder & Stoughton.
———. 1995a. "Nigeria." In John Esposito (ed.), *The Oxford Encyclopedia of the Modern Islamic World, Volume 3*. New York: Oxford University Press.
———. 1995b. "Sokoto Caliphate." In John Esposito (ed.), *The Oxford Encyclopedia of the Modern Islamic World, Volume 4*. New York: Oxford University Press.

12

CHRISTIAN RADICALISM AND NIGERIAN POLITICS

Toyin Falola

Since the late 1970s, religion has become a major factor to consider in the analysis of Nigerian politics and issues relating to the democratic process. While analysts tend to underplay its role before then, this can no longer be so because of the use to which religion is put in political campaigns, the violence that is associated with it, and the debates surrounding the *shari'a* and the character of the state itself.

The linkage between religion and the democratic process in Nigeria takes a variety of forms, a few of which can be mentioned in brief. Religion has generated one of the most controversial issues in drafting the constitutions for the country since 1975, specifically in relation to how to define the basis of democracy in legal terms. The continuous search for alternatives to, or adaptations of, western political models has led to the examination of what religion can contribute. For instance, a number of *Ulama* (Islamic teachers/preachers) have insisted that answers to the country's political and democratic problems lie in the Qur'an and Hadith and the collective Islamic experiences rather than borrowed models from the west, thereby offering an alternative ideology. The difficulty of institutionalizing military or democratic regimes provides religious leaders with a high-profile platform that is political in nature. Religious leaders and organizations have become part of a broad-based "civil society" that continues to challenge the state and to demand democracy. As an avenue to express opinions, places of worship have been used to make far-reaching political statements, condemn corruption, and even to demand political reforms and democracy. A reaction to the country's deep problems has been religious violence. Religious tension led to encroachments on individual liberty. There is a perception by the Christians that northern Muslims dominate politics for their own good and to further the interests of their religion. There is equally the perception by the Muslims that Christians benefited the most from British rule and have used this opportunity to entrench many "Christian practices" into both the private and public lives of Nigerians. Finally, there has been a need to factor religion into the distribution of political and bureaucratic offices in order to attain not only a "federal character" but also a "religious character" to reflect the country's pluralism.

As one of two contributions on the subject, this chapter examines the role of the Christian Association of Nigeria (CAN) in contemporary politics. While not representing the entire Christian community, CAN is recognized both by the state and public as speaking for the Christians. More importantly, it is recognized by such powerful Islamic organizations as the *Jama'atu Nasril Islam* (JNI) and the Supreme Council of Islamic Affairs (SCIA) as a "rival" or an "enemy." These organizations view CAN's leadership as cantankerous. In the period under review CAN has in fact responded to all issues pertinent to the understanding of democracy in Nigeria, has pushed its own concerns, and has offered a major challenge to Islam in the struggle for hegemony.

To understand why CAN is able to dominate the political scene, it is important to underscore two related issues. The first is to restate the relevance of religion in politics in a Third World country like Nigeria, and the second is to explain why a religious organization such as CAN has become so visible, even labelled by a Muslim cleric as an "alternative political party"[1] that represents millions of people.

The Religious Factor

Applying the paradigms of modernization in the 1960s, most analysts underplayed the religious factor in such countries as Nigeria. The claim was that as the society abandoned its "traditional" elements and moved towards westernization, religion would play a lesser role in intergroup relations and the management of the state (Haynes 1994). Historical events disproved the modernization thesis. Rather than weaken, religious forces became stronger. In the case of Nigeria, not only were new areas converted to one of the two universal religions of Islam and Christianity, but values and ideas continued to be drawn from religion. Both are competitive religions; not only did they try to displace indigenous religions, but each has always attempted to impose its domination on the other as well. Historical circumstances have provided a great imbalance in the spread of religion: Islam is prominent in the north, Christianity in the east, and both have established their presence in the west. Each tries to consolidate and win new converts (Olupona and Falola 1991).

In Nigerian intellectual circles, Marxism emerged as a counter to the modernization thesis in the 1970s. Both in its writings and politics, Marxists devalued religion in their discourse, focusing instead on class and economic analysis. This attitude is founded in an intellectual tradition which regards religion as the "opiate of the masses," to cite the well-known cliché. In the application of Marxist approaches to Nigeria, there is either an attempt to minimize the role of religion or to see it primarily as a tool of manipulation (Usman 1987).

Since the 1970s, political events in such diverse places as Poland, Iran, Libya, and Sudan have shown clearly that religion is a powerful force in politics and is relevant to the understanding of both democratic and revolutionary changes. This awareness has influenced a number of new studies, both theoretical and empirical (Ahanotu 1992; Hunwick 1992; Williams and Falola 1995).

With reference to Nigeria, religion has always been a factor of identity and political mobilization. Islam and the jihad of the 19th century contributed to the emergence of a Hausa-Fulani power elite that has been prominent for almost two hundred years (Usman 1979; Dudley 1968; Paden 1973, 1986; Whitaker 1970; Sulaiman 1987). This elite has profited from Islam to define itself, make claims to power, exclude others and challenge its rivals. Several studies have shown how Islam became an effective tool in building the Northern Peoples' Congress (NPC) and providing a source of unity in the north since the 1950s. Profiting politically from Islam has remained a major strategy since the country's independence, to the extent that Christians have expressed the fear of domination. Since the 1970s, this fear has been compounded by a feeling of persecution and a sense of impending Islamization of the country. This perception has instigated a more militant Christianity and has influenced the nature of political competition and the democratic process.

Contrary to the current image presented by a Christian elite, Christianity, too, has been connected with politics since the 19th century. Combined with western education, Christianity was responsible for the creation of the first "modern elite"—educated, mobile, and ambitious. This elite, based mainly in the southern part of the country, began to participate actively in all the modernizing sectors of society. After 1945, it expected the British to transfer power to it, and many of its members regarded Islam and the north as conservative forces. This elite has drawn many of its ideas and values from the west. Post-colonial politics have seen this elite struggling to retain its influence, and at the moment facing a serious crisis of marginalization. To the Christian elite, Islam presents challenges and competition that are highly political and difficult to handle. The politics of CAN is in part a reflection of the challenges faced by a Christian elite in post-colonial Nigeria and contestations over the values to predominate in managing the country and moving it forward.

The creation of CAN can be located in the context of the relevance of religion in society. In its present form, CAN was established in 1976, originally as an ecumenical group to address Christian issues, especially in dealing with the government. Most of its functions were originally designed to facilitate interactions among Christian organizations and with the government in an amicable manner. As CAN itself would admit, its formation was owed to the government that wanted to have a unified Christian body with which to negotiate.

A few years after its formation, CAN became involved in politics. By the 1980s and 1990s, it had turned militant to the extent of being called "an opposition group," a "political party in the making" and "the thorn in the flesh of government." Its membership now comprises over a dozen denominations: the Catholics, the Protestants, and a large number of "Others" such as the Pentecostal Fellowship of Nigeria or the ECWA Fellowship and Charismatic Movements. Membership is by churches rather than individuals. It is a voluntary association, always ready to open its door to new churches, except the Jehovah's Witnesses and those who do not believe in the idea of the Trinity, that is the belief in "one God in the Trinity of the Father, Son, and Holy Spirit" (CAN 1988; Makozi and Ojo 1982). It has a National Executive Committee, headed by a President who speaks for the association, an Assembly comprised of all the representatives of the members that meets annually, and state Standing Committees that liaise with the executive. Funding sources include membership contributions, dues, and gifts (Enwerem 1995; Tanko 1991). Using the media, places of worship, and state branches, CAN is able to reach its members rather quickly.

CAN's prominence and political visibility since the 1980s owe much to a combination of two factors: the role of the state and the fear of Islam. Both factors are political in nature and have shaped the orientation of CAN since the 1980s. First, the military-dominated state, when it prevented the emergence of active political associations, created a vacuum for religious organizations to fill. Student societies, trade unions and others struggle to be visible and to constitute "opposition parties" to the military. Religious organizations are very successful partly because of the high number of worshippers, and partly because the state finds it more difficult to cripple them than is the case with student and labor unions. Nigeria's honeymoon with the military was short-lived. Originally regarded as less prone to corruption, by the 1970s, the weaknesses of the military had become exposed. Nevertheless, the military has continued to entrench itself, thereby generating more alienation and contempt. It has never been difficult for CAN to get Christians to listen to criticisms of the military and the state.

To compound the problem, CAN regarded the state as oppressive and as discriminatory towards Christians, a belief which further promoted radicalism. CAN has repeatedly alleged that the government is pro-Islam, citing many instances. According to CAN, while the government took over the Christian schools, it allowed Muslims to establish new ones; while it curtailed the number of its foreign missionaries, it allowed Muslims to enjoy access; while some states in the north made it difficult to obtain land to build new churches, more mosques were allowed; the government subsidized the pilgrimages of Muslims while ignoring similar Christian demands (CAN 1989). To get those things it wanted, CAN believed it must fight for them, thus moving to the arena of protest politics.

The Islamic factor seems more important than that of the military. For CAN the greatest fear is of Islamic domination. This fear is both perception and reality. It is perception because motives of domination are read into everything that Islamic leaders do. It is real in that Islam has been used for political ends, mainly in the north (Kukah and Falola 1996). Since the 1970s, Islam has exhibited a resurgence expressed in increasing militancy, violence, and attacks on the state. A number of prominent Islamic leaders and preachers have called for an end to the influence of Christianity in the country in such areas as the law, the calendar, and the days set aside for holidays. Furthermore, they have called for a society that will be based on Islamic values and a state that will make religion its center. Alhaji Abubakar Gumi, the influential Islamic scholar who died in 1992, was at the forefront of making a case for Islam for almost three decades. Many of the actions of Islamic leaders have been interpreted by Christians as deliberate designs to impose Islam on the country, either by diplomacy or force (Enwerem 1995). Examples of the success of Islam in such places as Libya, Iran, Pakistan and Bangladesh were used by many Christian leaders and writers to support their argument that Islamization was possible and that their religion was in severe danger.

This fear drove CAN into radicalism, to the extent that relations degenerated into violence and into anticipation that the country might disintegrate into smaller units. While the country is yet to disintegrate, it is far from being united and is definitely unable to manage effectively its plurality and attain political stability in a democratic political context. There is still no consensus on such important questions as: who should govern the country and what his/her religion should be; what should be the legal basis; and what kind of state it should be.

In what follows, I analyze the nature of CAN's involvement in politics and conclude with the implications for the democratic process. It is rather early to make definitive statements as to the long-term impact of CAN on the country's politics. However, its political objectives (CAN 1991), all of which impact governance and the democratic process, are clear. In order of priority, they are to ensure that:[2]

i. Nigeria remains a secular state;
ii. Islam does not assert itself beyond a limit that is tolerable to Christians;
iii. federal resources are distributed rationally and justly to both religious groups and their regions;
iv. Christians are adequately represented in power at the federal level, partly in order to demonstrate that the country is not Islamic, and to have people who can represent the interest of Christianity; and finally,
v. political sensitivity is extended to all matters relating to the welfare of Christians, such as education and health.

These objectives became clearer in the 1980s, and the methods to achieve them more militant as well. The person that epitomizes the politics of CAN has been Archbishop Olubunmi Okogie who became its president in 1987 (Tomori 1991). His predecessor, Cardinal Ekandem, believed in private dialogue with government and a diplomatic, nonconfrontational strategy. Quite early in his presidency, Okogie rejected this approach, saying that it never worked. He has used the media, protest and the courts to make his points.

Confrontation with Islam

CAN defines Islam as an enemy, not just for religious reasons, but also for political ones. The issues involved are primarily the character of the state, the law to govern it, and the distribution of power. While most issues have involved domestic politics, they have spilled over into the conduct of foreign policy, as in the case of the controversy over membership in the Organization of the Islamic Conference (OIC).[3]

Should the Nigerian state be secular or religious? "The government of the federation or of the state," declared the Constitution of the Second Republic, "shall not adopt any religion as the state religion" (Constitution of the Federal Republic of Nigeria, Section 10, 96). Since the mid-1970s when a new constitution was to be drafted, how to interpret this provision, or even whether to retain it in the constitution, have generated political heat. A number of Muslims have objected to the clause. The JNI, a leading Islamic organization established in 1961, defined secular to mean opposition to religion and also as approval of the "worldly or material."[4] To endorse a secular state, argued the Muslims, was to reject God, accept disorder and ridicule the religion of Islam.[5] From the point of view of CAN, the state should be separated from religion. Religion should be treated as a private affair. The state should treat everyone the same way, irrespective of religion. In December 1987, *Monthly Time* quoted Archbishop Okogie as going so far to say he did not care "a hoot about anybody's religion" to emphasize the need for this separation (9). In making its case for separation, CAN never said that religion was not important, as some Muslims have alleged, but that the state should have little to do with religious matters. The state can relate with religion when it is necessary to do so, and without any element of power but of cooperation (Makozi and Ojo 1982, 24).

To the Muslim leaders, especially the *Ulama*, the idea of a secular state has no place in Islam, which recognizes no separation between the temporal and the spiritual. Allah owns the individual and the state and recognizes no such thing as religion as the private affair of an individual. Many of the anti-secular statements connect well with the early history of Islam and with the successful establishment of theocratic states where the Caliph was both a religious and political leader. To the *Ulama*, the ideal state for modern Nigeria was a theocracy, similar to the one founded by Uthman Dan Fodio in the 19th century (Sulaiman 1987). The state must never be neutral in religion (and its choice should be Islam).

This debate has never been resolved and continues to impose a severe burden on the political process, allowing the military to tinker with the constitution and the politicians to obtain the support of religious leaders. The debate reveals doctrinal differences and serves to widen the gulf between the two religions.

Related to the problem of defining the state is that of law, specifically the extent to which the *shari'a* should be employed in the country. The *shari'a* is Islamic law, and was used in many parts of the north following the jihad. During British rule, it was gradually modified, as the western legal system spread and took root. The *Ulama* complained against the marginalization of the *shari'a*, but the issue did not assume significant dimension until 1978 when it became part of the debate in the Constituent Assembly (CA) over the ratification of the draft Constitution for the Second Republic. A second controversy occurred in similar circumstances in 1989 (Kukah 1993; Federal Republic 1976, 1978; Kumo 1972; Aniagolu 1993).

The confrontations over the *shari'a* and the secular state were exacerbated by yet a third crisis: the country's membership in the OIC. In January 1986 the regime of Babangida clandestinely obtained membership in the OIC. Before then, the country had only enjoyed an observer status, which did not become an issue.

When the news of the membership leaked, Christians were enraged, and for the first time spoke loudly about an impending religious war. To those who had been talking of an Islamization agenda, the OIC confirmed their nightmare that Nigeria was soon to be declared an Islamic state. Within a few days, millions of Christians were mobilized to attack the decision. A war was conducted in the media and churches, so strongly that the country was thrown into confusion. The first casualty was Commodore Ebitu Ukiwe, a deputy to President Babangida and a Christian, who publicly stated that the federal government had never deliberated on the issue. He lost his job, taken by CAN as more evidence that a Muslim-controlled government was about to unleash its religious agenda (CAN 1989, 27).

The *Ulama*, Muslim politicians and others fought back, dismissing Christians as selfish, unrealistic, and mean. They warned the government not to withdraw from the OIC unless it wanted the Muslims to request the state to withdraw all Christian aspects that were affecting the Muslims, such as the use of Sunday as a nonworking day (*New Nigerian*, March 17 1986, 18). The JNI called for the country's withdrawal from diplomatic relations with the Vatican in view of the opposition by the Christians to the OIC membership (*New Nigerian*, March 3 1986). Babangida profited from the crisis, as many Muslims endorsed his actions and regime.

Given the extent of anger on the part of Christians and the bitterness in response by the Muslims, the government resorted to damage control. It formed a committee on February 3 1986 to advise how to handle the uproar. About six weeks later the committee submitted its report, but its members continued to hold different public positions. The Christian members dissociated themselves from the report which alleged that an amicable solution had been found to the crisis. Their Muslim counterparts described them as dishonest and warned them against opposing membership in the OIC (*The Reporter*, June 15 1990, 14).

These three issues—secularism of the state, *shari'a*, and membership in the OIC—show clearly that Nigerians differ as to what type of state they want and how they should be governed. While Christians would appear to draw ideas from the west, many Muslims look to Iran, Libya and others for ideas, eulogizing such leaders as Gadaffi and Khomeini.

Distribution of Power

CAN has also demanded greater representation for Christians in the government at the national level, again interpreting the appointments of Muslims to key cabinet positions as evidence of domination. This reflects the long-held view of many Christians that the country is governed by the Muslims and in ways to satisfy the Islamic constituencies.

When Babangida changed his cabinet in December 1989, CAN alleged that it was dominated by Muslims: 27 of the 35 ministers were Muslims, and only five were Christians, with inconsequential ministries over which to preside. Not only did CAN condemn the new government, it embarked on its first antigovernment public demonstration early in 1990. The protest was a huge success, especially in Kaduna where thousands of Christians participated.

CAN decided to attack what it perceived as injustice by publishing what has become one of the most important published documents in contemporary politics. Titled *Leadership in Nigeria*, the book points to the Islamic domination of power since 1960 and argues that Islam has deliberately been used to keep Christians out of power (CAN 1989). According to this book, unless the Muslims want the country to split along religious lines, they should be worried about their greed for power. Christians were requested to mobilize to fight for their legitimate rights as citizens of Nigeria. *Leadership in Nigeria* will pass as perhaps the most politically charged document to emanate from CAN, for its documentation and for its prescription. To Muslims, it seemed a document to incite Christians to warfare.

The arguments of *Leadership in Nigeria* were to put CAN in serious trouble in April 1990 when the instigators of an unsuccessful coup mentioned some of the points that had been made by CAN. Not only were the leading members of CAN suspected of instigating the coup, almost 60 Christians were arrested. They were later released for want of evidence after

53 days in unlawful detention. The government seemed to move quickly away from characterizing the attempted coup as religiously motivated, probably because of the grave consequences for peace.

Muslims were unhappy with the arguments and activities of CAN. "From the assessment of the situation," argued the Nigerian Council of Ulama in a public statement in 1986 and repeated many times thereafter, "the Muslims believe that the blame must squarely rest on the shoulders of the church leaders who couldn't believe that the days of the British Colonialists who collaborated with church missionaries in running the affairs of Nigeria and giving it a favorable Christian character and culture were gone with Nigeria attaining independence in 1960" (*New Nigerian*, March 17 1986, 18). After the coup attempt of April 1990, many Muslims warned the government to proscribe CAN. The military faced a dangerous opponent in CAN, concluded a Muslim commentator, "Dangerous not because it cannot subdue, or does not have the wherewithal to quash, the opponent but because it has grown too magnanimous in dealing with 'provocative demonstration' such as Okogie's and which is now known to be brewing for an ultimate onslaught on a maligned and scorned Hausa-Fulani for the simple reason that they are Muslims" (*The Triumph*, May 29 1990, 3—essay by Musa Tijani).

The confrontations summarized above over the distribution of power and political offices raise a number of issues. To start with, merit is subordinated to other considerations. Second, political actors are able to use religion to attain power. Cases abound in which ambitious aspirants justify their claims on the basis of religion. Third, in order to balance religious and other considerations, more political positions have had to be created, thus increasing the cost of administration and adding to existing interpersonal rivalry.

The Politics of Interest

CAN has acted as an interest group in other ways when it thinks the interests of Christians are at stake. Notable areas include the control of schools, demands for government subsidies for Christian pilgrims to Jerusalem, acquisition of land to build churches, and compensation for victims of religious violence. Many of these issues have been explored elsewhere; thus a few examples should suffice.

The role of the state in the organization of religious pilgrimage has been criticized by CAN as favoring Muslims from public funds. CAN demanded subsidies to assist those Christians traveling to Jerusalem as well.

Muslims, meanwhile, have been offended by the comparison of pilgrimages, on the grounds that their pilgrimage has more justification in Islamic beliefs, while those of the Christians verge on tourism.

Regarding Israel as a holy land, CAN criticized the break in diplomatic relations with Israel in 1973 as unwise. Until diplomatic relations were renewed in 1992, CAN criticized the government for the policy considering that it was maintained to please Muslims, in spite of the fact that Israel had much to offer Nigeria.

The role of CAN as an advocacy group has received severe criticism from the Muslim intelligentsia. To the Muslims, CAN has transformed itself into a political organization manipulating Christianity to obtain power for its leadership. Many times in the 1980s, JNI's prominent members called on the federal government to proscribe CAN and to regard it as an agent of instability. In 1990, JNI issued its most powerful statement on CAN, describing it as the nation's third political party:

> When a religious person or body takes issue on such matters as civil service appointments, ministerial selection, armed forces deployments, and pardon for assassins, and when, moreover, use is made of a platform or a reference group not validated but in fact outlawed by the constitution of the country, then we are in the zone of incitement, sedition, attempts to cause disorder, and disturbance of the peace, if not out-and-out subversion (*The Triumph*, May 29 1990, 13).

Okogie was accused of working for South Africa and a victim of "the Jewish-propaganda-laden Christian organization."

Perhaps the most effective strategy that the Islamic intelligentsia has used against CAN has been to present Muslims as helpless victims in a country controlled by greedy, ambitious, power-hungry Christians. If CAN had carefully projected itself as a victim, attacks on it took the same form. The Muslim intelligentsia accused CAN of wanting to perpetuate the Christian domination of the country and the colonial structure of Christian elitism. Both the JNI, and a pro-north newspaper, the *Hotline*, complained in public that CAN wanted to deny the Muslims of their share of the "national cake"—the euphemism for wealth and power.[6]

Implications for Democracy

CAN has shown both the strength and limitations of a religious organization acting as pressure group. Its activities and the reactions that they provoke demonstrate the connection between spirituality and politics and also the relations between religion and secular government. While the impact of the resurgence of Islamic fundamentalism is not captured in this chapter, it is important to note that Islam imposes its own pressure on culture and on government and has inevitably provoked aggressive responses from CAN.

CAN has succeeded in some ways in defending Christian or/and southern interests. It has alerted the country to the dangers of religious domination. It has turned Christianity into a "force" that can challenge the state and Islam. It has raised the level of political consciousness among millions of Christians, especially in the north where Christianity is rapidly developing into a strong political ideology. It is partly responsible for the creation of the Pilgrim Board to assist Christians traveling to Jerusalem, the restoration of diplomatic relations with Israel, and greater caution in the government's handling of political appointments, to mention a few examples.

CAN has effectively brought the issues of politics and democracy to churches and alerted Christians about their role. In northern Nigeria, especially among Christian groups that regard themselves as oppressed minorities, CAN has succeeded in defining the "political responsibility" of a Christian. To cite a major document, this responsibility includes the following:

i. Pray for those in authority and those seeking to be in authority.
ii. Participate responsibly in Local, State and National elections, in the fear of Christ and love one's neighbour.
iii. Make a serious and sustained attempt to keep fully and reliably informed on political issues.
iv. Be prepared to criticise the Government, its policies and its agents, in the light of the Gospel and Law of God.
v. Be prepared to endeavour to support just and humane policies and to oppose those policies and particular decisions which are unjust or inhumane, by helping to build an enlightened public opinion and in the various other ways (besides voting in elections) which are constitutionally open to one (*Leadership in Nigeria*, 70–71).

Thus Christians were alerted to their political duties, encouraged to run for election, and also to vote for like-minded people. They were prepared for possible confrontation with the government.

The role of CAN explains some of the complications of Nigeria's search for political stability and the transition to democracy. CAN's competition with Islam affects the distribution of power, the perception of one group by another, and the general conduct of politics. The intensity of the competition turns both Islam and Christianity into "political ideologies" perpetually seeking strategies to dominate political space and impose narrow values. The leaders of both religions, and the political actors manipulating the religions, continue to regard their task as unaccomplished. To the Muslims, political power is yet to lead to the emergence of an Islamic state; to the Christians, their education and culture are yet to translate into power. In working to achieve their final goals, religion is equally as important as politics.

The contest for hegemony has combined with socioeconomic factors to generate violence since the 1980s, starting with the Maitatsine outbreak, and many other subsequent ones, as recently as this year in Kano (Falola forthcoming). As I have argued elsewhere, it is also misleading to interpret periods without violence as ones of peace, primarily because a war of words has become permanent, conducted in sermons, in audiocassettes, and in the media. Hate literature is widely circulated, thus sharpening the divisions among the adherents of both religions. Both religions are very aggressive in their conversion campaigns. While there are no hard figures to go by, the growth of mosques and churches has been impressive in recent times. This growth has exhibited intense spirituality and encouraged the critique of the state.

The state has failed to mediate inter-religious conflicts in such a way to prevent future ones or to bring about better understanding between the two rival religions. In 1987, the government established the Advisory Council for Religious Affairs (ACCRA) to promote dialogue and seek the means to use religion to promote national development.[7] The Council could not agree on its Chair, and its members never relented in making allegations directed at one another to gain attention and sympathy. The state has wisely reckoned that it cannot proscribe such powerful religious organizations as CAN or JNI. Thus, it has resorted to the strategy of playing one against the other and finding the means to reward their leadership with money and positions in order to silence them. The state has also profited from CAN and similar bodies as agencies to manipulate to reach the public. The military has always sought arbiters to manage crises. Traditional chiefs and religious leaders have served in this capacity, intervening in the politics of transition to civil rule, and in student protests. As radical as CAN might appear, one regime after another has also used it for its own propaganda purposes.

The criticisms of the activities of CAN by other groups and by the state do reveal serious tensions. On the one hand, the state is critical of those activities it regards as challenges to its legitimacy and authority. As far as the state is concerned, CAN should make suggestions in private and assist the government in propaganda work. Those in power have often accused CAN of intolerance, a way of stigmatizing its politics as dangerous.

On the other hand Muslims reject the demand made by CAN for a secular state and for a greater role for Christians in politics. CAN is depicted as irreligious and its leadership as infidels. When Okogie went public to demand a secular state, he was quickly dismissed as a "satan" and "demon in disguise" (*The Triumph* May 29 1990, 13). The JNI affirmed categorically that Okogie is not a man of God, but an anarchist bent on destroying the country (*The Reporter* June 15 1990, 19).

The attack on Okogie is usually to an extreme, partly because he is seen as politically ambitious and as standing in the way of Islam. He has been described as a sadist, and a power-hungry cleric. Okogie and a number of prominent leaders of CAN have been accused of exploiting religion for a variety of motives: to seek public attention, gain power, win converts, and create trouble. These criticisms turn CAN into part of the country's problems rather than a body seeking solutions and working for a better future.

A number of Christians, too, would like CAN to stay out of politics or to avoid "militant politics" altogether. Some raise an issue of strategy: instead of always combating the government, why not befriend it in order to negotiate in private? CAN's actions do not promote religious tolerance in a plural society, some of these Christians have argued.

Politicians manipulate religion to the extent that it enables them to consolidate positions, reach their followers and find the means to discredit or destroy their rivals. The ramifications of this manipulation have become established. Politicians play upon a north-south divide, and on the tension between Islam and Christianity. Campaigns for votes since the 1970s have revealed how open this manipulation can be. Voters in Islamic areas have been told in many campaigns not to vote for Christians, while Christian politicians have deployed the same strategy. Threatening remarks have been made to the effect that Muslims would not accept a Christian to lead the country.[8]

Beyond the issues of manipulation are others relating to suggestions that religion should drive political agendas and perhaps form the basis of political parties. A tiny minority among Christians advocate the use of an organization such as CAN as a real political platform that will launch a full-scale attack on Islam and will be strong enough to influence politics. Some have become more radical, suggesting that Christianity should take politics more seriously. Liberation theology, or variants resembling it, has provided ideas to a young generation of preachers who believe that theology must address issues of democracy and poverty (Ilesanmi 1995).

A very different, and a more pan-Nigerian suggestion, is that "progressive-minded" peoples in both religions should organize a different "ecumenism" that would capture power. They would be united by the need to transform Nigeria in a radical way, drawing on lessons from their religions, but disregarding those aspects that promote competition (Enwerem 1995). There is little indication that religious-based political parties will emerge, or if they do that they will have answers to the country's problems. The challenge of the military remains strong, based so far on profiting from the control of violence rather than ideas. In addition, while religious leaders continue to talk about the relevance of religion, there are as yet no full-blown manifestoes on how religion can transform the country and form the basis of its democracy.

Finally, in many ways, CAN has equally revealed the limitations of religious organizations in the democratic process. To start, CAN represents the interests mainly of Christians, thus exposing its partisan nature. Even then, not all Christians identify with it, especially those members in the small, loosely organized charismatic movements. The way CAN represents itself is somewhat ambivalent. On the one hand, it wants to build a solid ecumenism, and speak as if to distance itself from politics, to satisfy the "moderate" elements. At other times, it makes radical statements, to satisfy those who want it to check the excesses of the government. Both positions create a problem of identity, one that generates mistrust from time to time in different quarters.

While its criticisms of the military and Islam tend to portray CAN in a radical light, many of its ideas, as expressed by its leadership, are conservative and perhaps insensitive to democracy or to large segments of the population. It is opposed to anything that resembles a revolution. The focus is on the struggles with Islam.

However, the struggles in the Nigerian political arena also involve class and ethnic dimensions. CAN has been unable to deal with the contradictions of class and ethnicity, either within its own organization or in relation to the country itself. To start with ethnicity, many people still identify with their groups, towns and communities in a way that may prevent them from uniting as Christians. Within the established churches, religious leaders call on ethnicity to compete for power. Individuals make claims to leadership in dioceses because they are born in those areas. In the church hierarchy, positions are distributed on the basis of ethnicity.

If the leadership engages in power struggles along ethnic lines, the followers do too. CAN, or Christianity, does not resolve the tensions between say, Igbo and Yoruba politicians. The regional branches of CAN occasionally fight in ways that resemble ethnic competition among the politicians. For instance, the North-CAN sometimes stands alone in its viewpoints on such issues as the solutions to the problems of religious violence. When the North-CAN is criticized for being too aggressive, it responds by saying that its members face daily struggles with Muslims in ways that southerners cannot comprehend. A few have even complained that southern Christians have more power and wealth than their northern counterparts. Ethnicity adds to the politics of denominationalism in CAN,[9] with the effect of preventing it from becoming a stronger agency of change.

With respect to class, CAN is not established to build alliances with progressive forces who speak for the poor. Neither is it in a position to mobilize the masses. It creates the impression that it is satisfied with a few Christians in positions of authority, even if these are incompetent.

The inability to resolve such contradictions has opened CAN to criticisms along ethnic and class lines. Some northerners have accused it of serving the interests of southern politicians. More radical Christians have criticized it for not being progressive enough. Its leaders in different parts of the country sometimes say different things. Its attitude toward women reflects an unwillingness to empower and involve them in politics. Notable CAN leaders have spoken against giving power to women in the church and are vehemently opposed to suggestions to establish "Women Wings" of CAN (*The African Guardian* September 5 1988). In addition, CAN is dominated by male officers who espouse views that are more consistent with patriarchy than democracy.

To conclude this essay, the activities of CAN have shown the role of religion in politics, one that continues to grow in importance. At the same time, CAN's activities have equally revealed its inability to resolve issues relating to ethnicity and class, gender, and the perception of the future. These limitations show clearly how complicated Nigeria's problems are and how the insights of a religious organization such as CAN are inadequate to address them.

Acknowledgments:

I would like to thank the Guggenheim Foundation for supporting my project on religious violence in Nigeria. Also, I have benefitted from profound discussions and arguments with four foremost scholars of religion in contemporary Nigeria: Drs. Hassan Kukah, Pat Williams, Segun Ilesanmi and Iheanyi Enwerem.

Notes

1. Field Notes, Malam I. Idris, Kaduna, 1991.
2. These are not derived from the Constitution of CAN but from its activities. Even the revised Constitution of CAN of 1991 did not specify political functions.
3. The OIC was established in 1971 by Islamic countries to promote, among others, the cause of Islam, fight racism and colonialism and assist member nations with resources. See also Sabo Bako's chapter in this volume.
4. See for instance, the statement by its Secretary in *New Nigerian*, April 18 1987.
5. See for instance, the interview with the influential Islamic leader and scholar, Sheikh Abubakar Gumi, in *This Week*, April 1987, 20.
6. See for instance the various editions of *Hotline* from 1986 onward.
7. See inaugural address by the President in *New Nigerian*, June 30 1987.
8. See for instance, the famous statement by Alhaji Gumi that if a Christian emerged as president, the country had to be divided because "a good Muslim cannot choose a non-Muslim as his leader," *Quality*, October 1987, 35.
9. The Catholics have been accused of dominating CAN.

References

Ahanotu, Austin, M., ed. 1992. *Religion, State and Society in Contemporary Africa*. New York: Peter Lang.
Aniagolu, Anthony Nnaemezie. 1993. *The Making of the 1989 Constitution of Nigeria*. Ibadan: Spectrum Books Ltd.
CAN. 1991. *Constitution of Christian Association of Nigeria*. Lagos.
———. 1989. *Leadership in Nigeria (to date): An Analysis*. Kaduna: CAN Publicity, Northern Zone.
———. 1988. *The Constitution of the Christian Association of Nigeria*. Lagos.
Dudley, B. J. 1968. *Parties and Politics in Northern Nigeria*. London: Frank Cass.
Enwerem, Ihenayi, M. 1995. *A Dangerous Awakening. The Politicization of Religion in Nigeria*. Ibadan: IFRA.
Falola, Toyin. forthcoming. *Religion and Violence in Nigeria*.
Federal Republic of Nigeria. 1976. *Report of the Constitution Drafting Com-*

mittee Containing the Draft Constitution. Vol. 1. Lagos: Federal Ministry of Information.

———. 1978. *Proceedings of the Constituent Assembly. Offical Report.* Vol. 1. Lagos: Federal Ministry of Information.

Haynes, Jeff. 1994. *Religion in Third World Politics.* Boulder: Colorado.

Hunwick, John, O., ed. 1992. *Religion and National Integration in Africa. Islam, Christianity and Politics in the Sudan and Nigeria.* Illinois: Northwestern University Press.

Ilesanmi, Simeon, O. 1995. "Inculturation and Liberation: Christian Social Ethics and the African Theology Project." *The Annal of the Society of Christian Ethics*: 49–73.

Kukah, Matthew, H. 1993. *Religion, Politics and Power in Northern Nigeria.* Ibadan: Spectrum.

Kukah, Matthew and Toyin Falola. 1996. *Religious Militancy and Self-Assertion: Islam and Politics in Nigeria.* Aldershot: Avebury.

Kumo, Suleiman. 1972. "The Organization and Procedure of Sharia Courts in Northern Nigeria." Ph.D. thesis, S.O.A.S., London.

Makozi, J. O. and G. J. A. Ojo., eds. 1982. *The History of the Catholic Church in Nigeria.* Lagos: Macmillan.

Olupona, J. and Toyin Falola, eds. 1991. *Religion and Society in Nigeria: Historical and Sociological Perspectives.* Ibadan: Spectrum.

Paden, John N. 1973. *Religion and Political Culture in Kano.* Berkeley: University of California Press.

———. 1986. *Ahmadu Bello, Sardauna of Sokoto: Values and Leadership in Nigeria.* Zaria: Hudahuda Publishing Company.

Sulaiman, Abraham. 1987. *The Islamic State and the Challenge of History: Ideals, Policies and Operation of the Sokoto Caliphate.* London: Mansell Publishing Ltd.

Tanko, B. P. 1991. *The Christian Association of Nigeria and the Challenge of the Ecumenical Imperative.* Rome: Pontifical University of St. Thomas Acquinas.

Tomori, Rev. Fr. Pascal. 1991. *Anthony Olubunmi Okogie: The People's Bishop.* Lagos: self-published.

Usman, Yusufu Bala. ed. 1979. *Studies in the History of the Sokoto Caliphate.* Zaria: Ahmadu Bello University.

———, ed. 1987. *The Manipulation of Religion in Nigeria, 1977–1987.* Kaduna: Vanguard Printers and Publishers.

Whitaker, C. Sylvester. (Jr.). 1970. *The Politics of Tradition: Continuity and Change in Northern Nigeria, 1946–66.* Princeton: Princeton University Press.

Williams, Pat and Toyin Falola. 1995. *Religious Impact on the Nation State: The Nigerian Predicament.* Aldershot: Avebury.

13

MUSLIMS, STATE, AND THE STRUGGLE FOR DEMOCRATIC TRANSITION IN NIGERIA: FROM COOPERATION TO CONFLICT

Sabo Bako

Introduction

It has been argued elsewhere that the limited programs of democratization and economic prosperity during the colonial period and the First Republic created conditions for relative religious harmony, cooperation, and development between Muslims, the state, and civil society (Bako 1994b; Magbogunje 1992, 169–77). During this period religion was never a serious political issue. Religious conflicts, even where they occurred, were very rare, isolated, rural-based and politically inconsequential (Osuntokun 1974; Bako 1992). This was so primarily because of democratic structures: parliamentarism, political parties, and associational groups; constitutional procedures and principles embodied in the bill of fundamental human rights and civil liberties; and properly constituted federal political structures in place for managing and regulating these conflicts. There was little recourse to large scale violence sponsored by the state or religious movements, which could inflict serious damage on the political and communal relations in the country (Ejimofor 1987; Bako 1994b).

However, the military intervention in the political process which resulted in the overthrow of constitutional and democratic government from January 1966, and its replacement with autocratic and authoritarian rule, has radically altered the situation. In fact, there is a very strong correlation between the militarization of the state, politics and civil society and the increased salience of religion in these structures and relations. These phenomena have grown over the past three decades in the same proportion and intensity. Religion has been transformed from a non-political issue into a leading volatile political phenomenon, substantially engulfing and truncating even the military-organized transitions to civil and constitutional rule between 1975 and 1995.

Militarism and Religiosity

The question is: what are the factors and conditions under military rule that have led to religious resurgence and fundamentalism in Nigeria? A number of factors can be cited:

The first factor is the very manner the military imposes itself on the state and how it utilizes power. The political crises that engulfed the First Republic, particularly in the 1960s, all assumed regional, ethnic, communal, or class characters and dimensions (Post and Vickers 1973; Williams 1976). It was only from the series of events beginning in January 1966 that religious meaning and antagonism began to be read into them. It began with the violent overthrow of the first civilian and democratic government, particularly the perceived religiously-selective pattern of killings of political leaders and military officers in the January 15 1966 coup d'état. The riots that followed the coup, the second coup of July 1966, and the subsequent riots and the civil war hurled religiosity into the political arena of the country (Crampton 1976, 19).

The subsequent intra-military struggles for power expressed through coups and counter-coups further intensified the religious divisions and antagonisms. This came out clearly after the overthrow in 1975 of General Yakubu Gowon, a Christian Middle Belter, by General Murtala Muhammad, a Hausa-Fulani Muslim from Kano. This was later countered by another Christian Middle Belter (Dimka) with the assassination of General Murtala Muhammad in a failed coup in 1976. In spite of his progressive radicalism and extreme nationalism, the Christian Association of Nigeria (CAN), largely sponsored and sustained by the Christian Middle Belters, accused General Muhammad of harboring a secret agenda to Islamize the country (CAN 1989, 12).

Intra-military religious politics reached its crescendo during the eight years of General Ibrahim Babangida. A Muslim minority from Niger State, Babangida came to power in 1985 with support from Christian minority soldiers, overthrowing a member of the Hausa-Fulani power elite (often called the Kaduna mafia), namely, General Muhammadu Buhari. But General Buhari's own accession to power, at the end of 1983, also had religious overtones. Buhari's coup was interpreted as that of the Izala Islamic sect[1] against the Tariqa[2] associated with President Shagari, whose fraction of the National Party of Nigeria (NPN) was rooted in the northern feudal oligarchy and business class (Yusuf 1985). Nevertheless, during Ibrahim Babangida's eight years of rule, Nigeria experienced its highest spate of religious conflicts. Most strikingly, it was in his regime that the attempted coup by Christian minority soldiers from the Middle Belt and the former Mid-West, on April 22 1990, announced the excision of all the far northern (primarily) Muslim states from Nigeria (Orka's speech in *Newswatch*, 7th May, 1990).

The second factor developing from the first one, which has institutionalized religiosity in the body politic, has been the military's dissolution and suppression of democratic structures, principles, and procedures. As argued earlier, it is democratic structures and procedures that sustain religious peace and cooperation and resolve religious conflicts. Democratic structures and principles have been demolished by the decrees which the military promulgated and enforced in 1966, 1983, and 1993 (Adigwe 1985, 269). In short, the abuse of fundamental human rights and civil liberties and the suspension of the rule of law under the military contributed significantly to the rise of religious resurgence and violence, particularly by Muslims (Shyllon 1980; Okoye et al. 1992; and Ubani 1990).

Thirdly, the fundamental restructuring of the Nigerian polity by the military through the systematic abrogation of the federal structure and imposition of a unitary type of government has led to the loss of religious rights and freedom for divergent religious groups. This restructuring started with Decree No. 34, otherwise known as the Unification Decree, issued by the short-lived Ironsi government in 1966. It abrogated the federal structure of governance and replaced it with a centralized military command structure. Even though the Gowon regime in theory and law repealed this decree, in reality, it continued to vigorously implement it. This unification has continued as the military increasingly becomes dictatorial.

Unification under the military has resulted not only in centralizing powers and resources at the center at the expense of other federating units, but it has arbitrarily imposed uniform national political, cultural, juridical, social and educational policies and programs, irrespective of religious differences and peculiarities.

In the same vein, the over-centralization of resources and powers at the center through military centralism, and the continuous arbitrary fragmentation of the federating units with the creation of new states and local governments, have sharpened and opened fresh theaters of religious contradiction and struggles, both at the center and the federating units. The military's remolding of federal governance and policy has enhanced and regularized religious conflicts in the country (Kayode et al. 1994).

The fourth factor that has heightened religiosity lies in the specific relations and interactions the military has maintained with religion. The military relies on religious and traditional institutions in the governance of the state and civil society. This assertion is predicated on the idea that traditional and religious institutions are strategically located to serve military dictatorship by virtue of their closeness with the people at the grassroots, and the influence they have exercised for ages. For example, religious traditional institutions serve as an organ of political communication between the military and the people. In other words, these institutions are utilized for articulation and aggregation of interests from the people, and also work as agents of mass mobilization and to implement military programs and policies.

Furthermore, civil control beyond the instruments and structures of coercion is ideologically sustained by religious and traditional institutions. They assist in the maintenance of law and order within their jurisdiction. And in the event of communal clashes, demonstrations, strikes or protests against the military and its policies and programs (such as the spate of strikes and resistance that have greeted the imposition and effects of the Structural Adjustment Program), religious and traditional rulers act as the Fire-Brigade to quell, appeal and beg for calm, peace, cooperation and understanding with the military. The Babangida administration, because of the series of crises and revolts it faced, incorporated the highest number of ulama, priests, and traditional rulers to its service.

Finally, being an unelected, self-imposed dictatorial regime, the military faced a serious crisis of legitimacy. This point was highlighted by Ukpabi when he said,

> there was also the issue of legitimacy. The military, by intruding into the uncongenial realm of politics would be departing from the traditional roles for which it was well suited into that for which it was ill-prepared either through training or experience. Many politicians therefore thought that unless the civilian population or the politicians conferred such legitimacy on

soldiers, the latter would be venturing into politics of a moral disadvantage which in turn would foreshadow the failure of military rule (Ukpabi 1986, 117–18).

The traditional and religious institutions thus become the military regime's main sources of legitimation and acceptance by the public. This explains why whenever a military coup succeeds in overthrowing a democratic government, the traditional and religious authorities are in the forefront in paying highly publicized courtesy visits and declaring their loyalty and that of their followers.

It can be argued that military regimes that stay longer in power (such as the Gowon and Babangida governments) were the ones that worked with the bureaucrats, university intellectuals, traditional rulers and the clergy. In comparison, those which lasted only two years, or six months, such as the Murtala and Buhari governments, did not solicit the support of these forces.

The military regimes have also used traditional and religious institutions for recruitment of political leadership and partners in the governance of the state. The bulk of the political appointees that serve military regimes in Nigeria are nominees of traditional and religious authorities. Thus, in narrow and somewhat perverted ways, religious and traditional institutions have served the functions in military regimes of political parties in a liberal democratic political system—namely the functions of political legitimization and socialization, and recruitment of civilian leadership into the military regimes.

Consequently, during military rule the religious sector has blossomed and become politically vibrant. The religious sector vis-à-vis the civil society has been empowered and politicized by the military. Old and moribund movements of the colonial periods like the tariqa movements of Qadiriyya and Tijaniyya as well as those of the First Republic such as the Muslim Students Society (MSS), Jama'atu Nasril Islam (JNI), the Council of Ulama, the Supreme Council for Islamic Affairs, the Izala Movement and even the Christian movements such as the Northern Christian Association, have suddenly become alive and dynamic (Bako 1993).

In addition, several dozens of highly militant movements such as the Maitatsine, the Izala movement, the Christian Association of Nigeria (CAN), the Muslim Brothers Group, and the At-Tajdid group were formally organized and invigorated under the military, arising from its essentially dictatorial policies (Bako 1992). It has been correctly argued that the amount of religiosity that has flourished during the last twenty-five years of military dictatorship far surpassed the levels during the colonial period and First

Republic. Thus, the number of mosques, prophets, churches, fundamentalist and born-again movements that emerged during this period far outstripped those of the past century (Bako 1989b).

During this period, religion also became highly commercialized, and a lucrative source of primitive accumulation and class formation due primarily to the political alliance between religiosity and militarism in the country. More than in any previous period the military has empowered, institutionalized and politicized religion in Nigeria, paving the way for the emergence and operation of highly militant movements. This has elevated the religious movements from their previous status of simple legitimizers of power and wealth to that of principal contenders and actors in the political economy of the country.

In the course of this development, religion has emerged to subsume and subordinate ethnic, intra-ethnic, class, intra-class, communal and regional contradictions and struggles. The struggles between the rich and poor, oppressor and oppressed, militarist and democratic forces, have taken on religious coloration.

The Religious Context and Patterns of Democratic Transitions

The struggles for democracy by Muslims should be situated, therefore, in the context of the religiously-charged atmosphere created by the military. In the following pages the major sequences and events in military-led transition to democracy will be briefly reviewed. Our aim is to show the relation of political events with the progressive exacerbation of the relations between the religions which is argued above. The focus of the examination is above all to elucidate the perspective of Muslims, who constitute Nigeria's largest religious community. We will see how it is that many Muslims, including intellectual leaders, see the Muslim side as having been disadvantaged at many points in the constitutional outcomes that set the institutional patterns of the Second and Third Republic (and those that are now prescribed for the next democratic system). Likewise, the major events of political transition as designed and managed by military regimes are seen from the Muslim perspective as working against Muslim interests and even as biased against Muslims. This perception by members of one of the two major religious communities is of great significance (and has been insufficiently appreciated) in understanding the failure of transition to democracy, all the more in its contrast with the commonly received notion of

Muslim (and northern) near monopoly of power throughout so much of Nigeria's independent history (e.g., Nwabueze 1994, 133).

In this review of events we shall see that the crisis of religiosity the military promotes and utilizes inevitably filters into its democratic transitions, creating dilemmas for the democratization process in Nigeria. During military rule—especially in episodes of democratic transition—the secular status of the Nigeria state is hotly debated and questioned. Particularly debated are the ways the state defines its law, its paraphernalia, how it funds and handles religious activities, and how it handles its external relations with religious foreign countries and bodies. Issues include the creation of Muslim courts in southern Nigeria; the status of *shari'a* law; the creation of a federal *shari'a* court of appeal; the issue of religious holidays and state insignia bearing religious symbols; the handling of the Muslim annual pilgrimage to Saudi Arabia; the creation of state religious councils; Nigeria's membership in the Organization of Islamic Conference (OIC); diplomatic relations with the Vatican; and renewing ties with the state of Israel.

It is noteworthy that all the constitutions adopted between 1923 and 1963 in Nigeria were not only silent on the secular status of Nigeria, they were careful not to violate the basic and fundamental rights and freedom of Muslims to live and operate as a distinct component of the Nigerian federation. However, the military not only suspended and dissolved the 1963 constitution but has also been restructuring the Nigerian state and society along unitary lines. As new constitutions emerged from the military-managed transition processes, the question of the secular state has been brought forcefully to the center of political debate, becoming a bitterly divisive issue with Muslims and Christians separating sharply.

During the first military-organized transition to civil rule (1975–1979), the military set up the Constitution Drafting Committee (CDC) to draft a new constitution for the Second Republic. A draft was ready in August 1976, which was thrown open for public debates and comments around the country. A series of seminars organized predominantly by the members of the Council of Ulama were held in Zaria, Minna, and Kano to come up with the position of Muslims on the draft constitution (Kukah 1993, 118–21).

Thus, the National Seminar on Islam was organized by the Islamic Foundation in Kano between July 29–31 1977. The most significant paper was one presented by Alhaji Bappa Mahmoud on the topic: "The Place of Religion in the Draft Constitution." Mahmoud was one of Grandkhadis appointed by the military in Northern Nigeria. Mahmoud drew attention to the Chapter 11 section of the Constitution, which reads: "The state shall not adopt any religion as the state religion." Mahmoud opined that this statement "is something completely new and in fact quite strange to what is contained in the previous constitution we had" (Mahmoud 1977, 2).

After the general public debate, the government set up a Constituent Assembly to deliberate and accept the draft constitution. In the Constituent Assembly the provision which generated the greatest bitterness and division between Muslims and Christians was the one concerning *shari'a* law courts. The Shari'a Court of Appeal had been provided at the regional level in the 1963 constitution for Northern Nigeria. Now, with the demolition of the regional structure and the creation of states, Muslims felt it was essential that such a court be provided above the level of the states as Muslims were now scattered all over the federation. The debate over the Shari'a Court of Appeal caused the first major national religious fracas between Muslims and Christians in the country. Even though it was the political class that carried on this *shari'a* debate, it should be noted that the military created the political and social environment within which it took place.

Religion in Second Republic Politics

After the 1979 national elections, the National Party of Nigeria (NPN) won the Federal election. It should be noted, that in most views, it was the NPN that was groomed to inherit power from the military in 1979. The NPN was never a Muslim political party by its composition, ideology and program as argued by writers such as Kukah (1993, 146–47). It was essentially a national party of the dominant faction of the Nigerian bourgeoisie nurtured and consolidated by military rule. The NPN was a coalition of these dominant groups and individuals that came together to form a national party by subordinating their narrow ethnic and religious outlook and interests to the national class interests. This was the reason why the party declared formally in its manifesto that it stood for the rejection of religious extremism, fanaticism, bigotry and confrontation of any kind or description.

The national successes of its Muslim presidential candidate, Alhaji Shehu Shagari, in 1979 and 1983 general elections against the other parties, led by both Muslims and Christians, was because of the narrower ethnic, religious and ideological appeals of the other parties. They were also characterized by intense internal petty-bourgeois fractionalized leadership struggles. Although the 1983 election was tarnished by substantial fraud, as least arguably the NPN still had a broader appeal than its competitors.

The internal divisions and struggles between the Muslim components of the NPN which began to be apparent in the early 1980s led to the collapse of the party and the Second Republic and the emergence of the Buhari regime. The limited explanations usually offered for the Buhari coup (December 31 1983) are that it was organized and executed by the Hausa-Fulani Muslim power group known as the "Kaduna mafia," composed of the technocratic-bureaucratic military elite against the commercial-cum-feudal based sections of the Muslim bourgeoisie (Takaya and Tyoden 1987; Yusuf 1985).

However, the intra-Muslim sectarian basis of the conflict has not been brought out. While the Kaduna mafia could be associated with the Kaduna-based Izala movement, the other section of the NPN was more with the tariqa coalition of the Jundillahi and Jama'atu Nasril Islam. The first political move by the Kaduna mafia was to start criticizing and attacking the other group through its committee of concerned citizens, which earlier had entered a kind of alliance with the UPN's leader Awolowo for the 1983 general election. The only concession the Kaduna mafia could get from the UPN was a program for the teaching of Islamic and moral education, a lift on the ceiling imposed on the pilgrimage, and the introduction of Islamic banking (Kukah 1993, 169). When the Kaduna mafia failed to influence the result of the 1983 election, it colluded with its military colleagues to overthrow President Shagari in December, three months later.

The resulting military government led by Muhammadu Buhari administration could not last more than two years because—apart from its high-handedness and lack of democratic agenda—it was accused by the Christian Association of Nigeria, as well as Christians generally, of favoring Muslims. The Buhari government was said to be dominated by Muslims as the Head of State, his Deputy, the members of the Supreme Council and the state governors were mostly Muslims. There was a persistent call, especially by the Southern Christians, for a confederal form of government during this period.

Less noted, however, is the amount of repression of some key Muslim figures, especially those belonging to the Shagari faction, that also took place during the Buhari period. This led to protests by Alhaji Abubakar Gumi, who intervened on behalf of his Muslim rival groups and supporters that felt repressed by the Buhari administration. Meanwhile, the number of Muslims attending annual pilgrimage had been drastically reduced by the regime.

Babangida and New Transition

The palace coup led by General Babangida in August 1985 was said to be that of northern Christian minority elements against the Muslim power-elite, the Kaduna mafia. Thus, Ismaila Mohammed popularized this position, when he said the coup was:

> ... the first successful move to put Northern minority elements effectively at the helm of national politics. Significantly, too the northern minorities (i.e., the non-Hausa ethnic, non-Muslim people of the Niger, Ilorin, Kabba, Southern Adamawa, Bauchi, and Zaria) have, by their ascendancy to power, inevitably exposed the myth about the political indivisibility of the North and the invincibility of the Kaduna Mafia (*Sunday Concord* October 20 1985).

Never before in the history of the Nigerian state was it so enmeshed in religious conflicts and so divided between Muslims and Christians as during the Babangida period of military rule. Religious tensions and religious resurgence became prominent during the long transition to civil rule organized by the regime between 1986 and 1993. General Babangida not only used the transition program to perpetuate his power by tinkering with the terminal date and cancelling elections, but also played Christians against Muslims in order to prolong and to divert public attention from his administration.

During this period religious and traditional movements and individuals became politically strong as almost all the popular civil and democratic structures and organizations were either dissolved or incorporated with the state structures. This was done in order for the military to have a fully guarded and controlled transition to civil rule.

From the onset, the objective of Babangida's military rule was perceived by Muslim groups as the displacement of the Hausa-Fulani Muslim groups from state power and their replacement with the northern and southern Christian counterparts. Muslims perceived General Babangida as filling his ruling councils with Christians as members and ministers. As Christian governors were posted to predominantly Muslim states, Muslims perceived an aim to destabilize and displace Muslims from governance.

Muslim religious organizations such as the Izala group, the Muslim Students Society, and the Council of Ulama came out and protested. For example in a paid advertisement published in the *New Nigerian* of June 18 1987, one year after the inception of Babangida's transition program, the Council of Ulama noted:

> There have been long-standing attitude of government to ignore the fact that Muslims constitute the majority of the people in Nigeria; as a result the Muslims presence has often not been reflected in the composition, structure, and policies of the Government. The composition of the Armed Forces Rul-

ing Council presents a false and unjust picture of Nigeria: there is certainly no justifiable reason for the preponderance of Christians in the highest ruling body of a country with a Muslim majority. Similarly, the preponderance of Christian governors, and the imposition of Christian governors over Muslims, as in Bauchi, Lagos, Oyo, and several other states is certainly not the best way to win the confidence of Muslims or have an effective and acceptable administration. It can only be seen as part of a strategy to destablise the Ummah and destroy its cohesion.

In order to assuage the tension rising among the Muslims—as well as to promote the investment interest of the Muslim military-cum-traditional rulers in the Arab world—the Babangida government surreptitiously smuggled Nigeria into membership in the Organization of Islamic Conference (OIC) in 1986.

By 1987 the atmosphere was highly charged. A series of major outbreaks of communal violence pitted Muslim and Christian communities against each other in 1987 and again in 1992, centered first in the Muslim/Christian meeting point of southern Zaria in Kaduna state, and later in the Middle Belt states of Taraba, Adamawa, Bauchi, Plateau and Benue (see Bako 1995b, White Paper on Kaduna Disturbance 1987, Isyaku 1991).

Meanwhile, General Babangida had inaugurated the Political Bureau to organize national debate on the political future of the country, to form the basis and foundation of his transition program to civil rule and democracy in the country. The Political Bureau Report was used in the making of the constitution and restructuring of the Nigerian polity for the Third Republic.

One theoretical issue that emerged during the Political Bureau debate, in the making of 1989 Constitution and in the formation of transition structures and elections, was the volatile relationship between the state and religion (Bako 1990). In the writing of the Political Bureau report, the members were divided on the relations between state and religion. Issues included state membership in religious organizations, ownership of religious schools, and funding of pilgrimages. The Political Bureau was divided into a Christian majority and a Muslim minority over their different approaches to these matters (Political Bureau 1987, 191–181).

The government in its published views and comments on the findings and recommendations of the Political Bureau, took sides with the Christian majority by accepting all their recommendations. Those of the Muslim minority were simply noted, seen by Muslims as a polite way of ignoring and rejecting their views (Government's views and comments on the findings of the Political Bureau 1987, 88).

The government then published the timetable for its political program. Many aspects of the implementation of the program seemed to Muslims to betray a systematic bias against Muslims and Muslim interests. For example, appointments to the top posts in the Directorate of Social Mobilization (MAMSER) and the National Electoral Commission (NEC) were seen as dominated by well-known partisan CAN leaders (such as MAMSER Director Professor Jerry Gana). Recruitment of their assistants was seen as following suit. Thus, MAMSER was seen as being packed with Middle Belt Christian hard-liners (Bako 1988). The NEC was seen as dominated by members regarded in Muslim circles as "fanatical Christians." This latter was of particular importance since the NEC was assigned to conduct all the elections leading to democracy in the country. All of these perceptions were to contribute greatly to the eventual failure of the Third Republic initiative (Bako 1990).

As earlier indicated, neither the 1979 Constitution nor the Political Bureau Report of 1987 resolved the *shari'a* issue. The issue again re-emerged in the deliberation of the 1988 Constituent Assembly. The discussion and debate on the *shari'a* dichotomized and later paralyzed the Assembly. It required the intervention of the military to remove the *shari'a* issue from the jurisdiction of the Constituent Assembly. But this was not the end of the *shari'a* controversy, as even at the submission of the draft constitution in April 1989, the Constituent Assembly was divided as two reports—one for and one against *shari'a*—were submitted. However, the federal government flatly refused to recognize the pro-*shari'a* report (Olagunju, Jinadu, and Oyovbaire 1993, 186).

The processes of party formation and elections between 1987 and 1992 also involved many events perceived by Muslims as pro-Christian and having the effect of discrimination against the Muslim candidates. First, through draconian decrees, the political class was banned, proscribed, and disqualified from participation in politics, election or holding any public or political party office during the transition by (Prohibition) Decree 1987, otherwise known as Decree No. 25 of 1987. The intention was to sanitize the political process by removing corrupt politicians from the political scene. And in fact even those who "held high political offices in the first and second Republics, even though they have not been found guilty of any offence or misconduct were disqualified by virtue of their having held specified public offices at any time during the period from January 15 1966 to the end of (Babangida's) transition" (Olagunju, Jinadu, and Oyovbaire 1993, 201–203). Allegedly, the decrees were intended to give birth to a "New Breed" of politicians, who could play the Babangida regime's kind of politics of democratic transition. But Muslims—especially those of Hausa-Fulani extraction—were heavily represented among this class, accounting for a large number of the most experienced and tested former leaders.

The next major event perceived both as an attack against democracy and against Muslims was at the level of party formation, which could be traced from the 1987 local government elections to the 1988 Constituent Assembly election. Party formation came into the open after lifting the ban on partisan politics in 1989. The National Electoral Commission (NEC) then proceeded to issue nearly impossible guidelines on party-formation, and later the Armed Forces Ruling Council (AFRC) took over the power to register them. No fewer than fifty political associations appeared, but only 13 eventually filed applications for recognition and registration under the NEC's guidelines. In the NEC's verification exercise, the strongest political parties among the 13 emerged from Muslim areas. The highest verification scores given by the NEC were as follows: People's Solidarity Party (44.9 percent); Nigerian National Congress (42.62 percent); People's Front Party (41.20 percent); Liberal Convention (34.08 percent); Nigerian Labour Party (17.10 percent). However, the AFRC rejected all the parties and ordered NEC to form only two parties. Their names, offices, programs and manifestoes would be imposed; civil servants would be in charge of organizing the parties.

The resulting government-designed parties were named the National Republican Convention (NRC) and the Social Democratic Party (SDP). By default or design, since the administration rejected the Political Bureau's recommendation to form ideological parties, it would inevitably be the Muslim/Christian, north/south divide on which working politics would turn. When the SDP elected its officials, Sule Lamaido became the only Muslim member of the party's National Executive Council; the rest were Christians. The NRC, on the other hand, was tilted towards Muslims, with a Yoruba Muslim as its National Chairman.

In most states of the Federation, the elections which were conducted on the platforms of these two imposed parties, from local government to gubernatorial elections, took religious lines. Yau Haruna, who observed the elections in Kaduna State, one of the most religiously divided states, said:

> Shortly after the announcement of the transition programme by this administration, the attempt to manipulate religion for political ends began to assume a frightening and unprecedented dimension that culminated in the 1987 crisis in Kaduna State. Following that crisis, there was no doubt that the dominant religions of Islam and Christianity that became so polarised

and hostile to another that it affected the December 1990 Local Government elections in the state. Although the two political parties were already institutionalized; voting definitely took place along religious lines with Christian candidates contesting under the platform of the S.D.P. and Muslim candidates under the N.R.C. The campaigns were more in the churches and mosques by pastors and mallams rather by the contestants. In an open ballot system, the identity of who voted for which candidates could not be of any doubt, and the line up in Zaria and Kaduna which I personally observed reflected precisely the influence of religion in the voting behaviour (Haruna 1994, 72).

The elections of governors and state and national legislatures followed almost the same pattern. In most of the Middle Belt States such as Benue and Taraba, Christian pastors were elected. Meanwhile, because of its nation-wide structure and appeal to urban and rural petty bourgeois radicals, the Izala group more than other Muslim movements contested and won several gubernatorial and legislative positions in the Muslim northern states, running ahead of the Tariqa movements (Yandaki 1995).

The next governmental actions resented by Muslims came in the wake of the annulment of the presidential primaries which took place in 1992. Muslim candidates from the north had emerged as winners in the primaries of each of the two parties. Citing massive fraud and corruption in the staged primaries, the government not only annulled the primary results, but also disqualified the 23 candidates who contested the primaries from participating in future presidential elections. Several major Muslim candidates were thus taken out of the competition for the Presidency.

The cancellation of these primaries paved the way for the emergence of Chief Abiola (SDP) and Bashir Tofa (NRC), the first a Yoruba Muslim from south-west, and second a Hausa-Fulani Muslim from Kano. It was instructive to note that the subsequent rejection of Bashir Tofa by Muslims in Kano, Jigawa, Bauchi and several other Muslims states was a form of ideological protest: class politics against the ruling clique. It also reflected Abiola's generous previous contributions to Islamic development, unsurpassed by any member of the northern Muslim elite.

Abiola and his running mate were a Muslim-Muslim ticket for the SDP. Yet the bulk of the Christians from Middle Belt and the southern states, as correctly asserted by Nwabueze (apart from Yorubas who voted on ethnic solidarity) voted for Abiola in order to break "the monopoly of the presidency by the Muslim ethnic groups in the North," which the latter regarded, as if it was their exclusive birthright. Outside the Yoruba areas, most people in the south who voted for Chief Abiola did so, not so much because he was their man for the job or on account of loyalty to the SDP his (party) or out of personal identification with its aims and objectives. They did so simply to end the North's monopoly of the Presidency. The annulment of the election is, rightly or wrongly, seen by many in the south as nothing but a plan in aid of the perpetuators of that monopoly. . . . (Nwabueze 1994, 133).

The annulment of the June 12 1993 presidential election has caused a lot of misgivings and open clashes between the Hausa-Fulani Muslims and their Yoruba counterparts. The Yoruba Muslim movements and Chief Abiola himself have accused then-Sultan Dasuki or the nebulous "Sokoto Caliphate," for being party to the annulment at best; or at worst, refusing to do something positive to restore and actualize Abiola's mandate (Sani Kunle Sani, "Dasuki and Muslim Unity in Nigeria," *Nigerian Tribune* 21st June, 1995:2).

The Abacha Period

The political crisis arising from the annulment of the June 12 election brought General Abacha to power. His regime summoned a national Constitutional Conference. However, the Conference ended being what it was tagged: just another another constitution-making exercise. The only additional innovations were a few amendments made on the devolution of federal power to the states. A new power sharing arrangement based on zoning and rotation of the six key federal executive and legislative posts has been accepted for a period of 30 years.

Muslims, many of whom felt they had been on the receiving end since the annulment of the June 12 election, were constrained by the parameters set by the Abacha government from renewed debate on the *shari'a* question. The 1979 and 1988 provisions, which Muslims earlier had rejected, were retained at the Constitutional Conference.

Furthermore, the Constitutional Conference Committee on National Values and Lingua Franca, which was dominated by Muslim and Christian traditional rulers and clergy, traded the creation of a Federal Council of Traditional Rulers for the complete secularization of the state. The Committee decreed that the state should not now belong to any international religious body (i.e., the OIC), or be involved in organizing religious pilgrimages.

Northern Muslims, who were accused of monopolizing the presidency since independence and of the annulment of June 12 election, now conceded to have the presidency rotated and zoned to Christian constituencies as long as the state security agencies and the educational, bureaucratic, financial, and economic federal resources and positions where Christian incumbents traditionally had predominated, should also be rotated and shared, based on the principle of proportional representation.

Meanwhile, Muslims' demand for equitable representation and socioeconomic empowerment has led them to ask for the formation of a Federal Character Commission, which is supposed to be constituted and implemented as part of General Abacha's three-year transition program between October 1995 and October 1998.

Conclusion

Muslims have now found, in spite of their supposed control of the power over most of the period of independence, that they happen to be the least educated and represented in the federal bureaucracy and the most impoverished and dislocated by environmental degradation and uncontrolled urbanization, which have made them more prone to incessant uprisings and revolts against the state, economy and civil society than other religious groups (Bako 1989; 1992; 1991; 1994).

The religious question has been central to Muslims' struggle for democratization, which the militarist state, by virtue of its authoritarian disposition and secularist ideology, has tended to undermine.

Furthermore, the heritage of religious pluralism, federalism, and liberal democracy which colonialism and the First Republic politicians developed to sustain some modicum of religious harmony, dialogue, and development, has been shattered by the military dictatorship.

From all indications, it appears the military as presently constituted, with its structural links to the political economy and religiosity in Nigeria, is incapable of institutionalizing sustainable democratic governance, in the context of which the religious question, which has emerged as a serious political dilemma, could be resolved.

Notes

1. The Izala is the shortened name derived from Izalatul bid'at waikamatul sunnah (Community for eradication of innovation and restoration of tradi-

tions of the prophet Muhammad i.e., Sunnah). A militant and highly organized wahabiyya-oriented post-independence movement, it emerged from the anti-tariqah religious activities organized by Alhaji Abubakar Gumi the first Grandkhadi of Northern Nigeria. From Kaduna it spread. The movement has, though not exclusively, been associated with the northern Muslim active and retired civil servants, intellectuals, military officers, and technocrats who as a power political group are collectively referred to as the Kaduna mafia.

2. The Tariqa refers to Sufi order movements, namely the Qadiriyya and the Tijaniyya which are very prominent in Nigeria. The Qadiriyya has been associated with the northern feudal aristocracy since the foundation of the Sokoto Caliphate, while the Tijaniyya, which evolved significantly during the colonial period, has become popular among the businessmen in the cities and towns of northern Nigeria. Both Qadiriyya and Tijaniyya merged together under the name Jundililahi (holy war in the name of Allah) in the 1970s in order to fight and restrict the activities of the Izala movement in Nigeria.

References

Adigwe, F. 1985. *Essentials of Government in West Africa*. Ibadan University Press.

Bako, Sabo. 1988. "MAMSER and Social Reform." Paper presented at the Conference of Mass Mobilization by the Department of Political Science, University of Jos, May 1987.

———. 1989a. "Religions and the Third Republic." Paper presented at the Conference on Transition to Third Republic by the Political Science Department Association, University of Jos May 16–29 1989.

———. 1989b. "Reception and the Growth of Religious Intolerance in Nigeria." In J.P. Olupno (ed.), *Religious and Peace in Multi-Faith Nigeria*. Ife: Obafemi Awolowo University Press.

———. 1991. "Ecological Crisis and Social Conflicts in Nigeria's Drybelt." In K.O. Ologe (ed.), *Sustainable Development in Nigeria's Drybelt: Problems and Prospects*. Ibadan, Nigerian Environmental Studies Action Team, (NEST).

———. 1992a. "Traditional, Institutions and Religious Conflicts in Northern Nigeria." In A. Kani et al., (eds.), *Traditional System of Administration in Nigeria: Continuity and Change*. Zaria: Ahmadu Bello University Press, Forthcoming.

———. 1992b. "The Maitatisine Revolts: A Socio- Political Explanation of the Islamic Instruction in Northern Nigeria 1980–85," Ph.D. Thesis, Department of Political Science, Ahmadu Bello University, Zaria.

———. 1994a. "Urbanisation and Religious Conflicts in Nigeria." In Herault

G. et al. (eds.), *Urban Management and Urban Violence in Africa*, Volume 2. Ibadan: IFRA.
———. 1994b. *Muslims, Colonialism and Democracy in Nigeria*. Mimeo, Zaria, Nigeria.
———. 1995a. "Muslims and Western Education in Nigeria." Paper prepared for International Conference on Islamic Renaissance. Shefford Lane, Louisville.
———. 1995b. *Religions and the National Question in Nigeria*. Mimeo, Zaria.
CAN. 1989. *Leadership in Nigeria (to date): An Analysis*. Kaduna: CAN Publicity, Northern Zone.
Crampton, Edmund Patrick Thurman. 1976. *Christianity in Northern Nigeria*. London: Geoffrey Chapman.
Ejimofor, Cornelius Ogu. 1987. *British Colonial Objectives and Policies in Nigeria: The Roots of Conflict*. Onitsha: Africa FEP Publishers.
Hansen Holger Bernt and Michael Twaddle, eds. 1988. *Religion and Politics in East Africa: The Period since Independence*. London: James Curry.
Haruna, Y. 1994. "Class, Ethnicity, and Religion in the Politics of Transition to the Nigeria's Third Republic." In O. Omoruyi (ed.), *Democratization in Africa: Nigeria Perspectives Volume 2*. Abuja: Center for Democratic Studies.
Isyaku, B. 1991. *The Kafanchan Carnage*. Zaria: ITN.
Kayode, F. et al. 1994. *Governance and Polity in Nigeria: Some Leading Issues*. Ibadan: University of Ibadan Press.
Kukah, Matthew H. 1993. *Religion, Politics and Power in Northern Nigeria*. Ibadan: Spectrum Books.
Mabogunje, A. and O. Obasanjo, ed. 1992. *Elements of Democracy*. Ibadan: ALF Publication.
Mahmoud, B. 1977. "The Place of Religion in the Draft Constitution." In *Proceedings of the National Seminar on Islam in the Draft Constitution*, Islamic Foundation. Kano, 29–31 May 1977.
Ngoyi, J.P. and Edigheji. 1992. *The Church and Human Rights in Nigeria*. Ijebu-Ode: Catholic Diocese.
Nwabueze, Benjamin Obi 1994. *Nigeria's 93: The Political Crises and Solutions*. Ibadan: Spectrum Books.
Okadigbo, Chuba. 1987. *Power and Leadership in Nigeria*. Enugu: Fourth Dimension Publishing Company.
Okoye, F. et al. 1992. *Justice Denied: The Courts System in Northern States of Nigeria*. Ibadan: Civil Liberties Organisation, CLO, Kraft Books.
Olagunju Tunji, Adele Jinadu, and Sam Oyovbaire. 1993. *Transition to Democracy in Nigeria, 1985–1993*. Ibadan: Safari Books.
Osuntokun, J. 1974. "The Response of the British Colonial Government in Nigeria to the Islamic Insurgency in the French Sudan and the Sahara during the First World War." *Journal of West African Studies*, 10 (July).

Post, Kenneth and Michael Vickers. 1973. *Structure and Conflict in Nigeria 1960–1965*. London: Heinemann.

Shyllon, Folarin and Olusegun Obasanjo. 1980. *The Demise of the Rule of Law in Nigeria under the Military: Two Points of View*. Ibadan: Institute of African Studies, University of Ibadan.

Suleiman, M.O. 1995. "Islamic Fundamentalism: the Shiite in Katsina." In Tsiga, I. A. et al. (eds.), *Islam and History of Learning in Katsina*. Zaria: Ahmadu Bello University Press, Forthcoming.

Takaya B.J. 1992. "Religion, Politics and Peace: Resolving the Nigerian Dilemma." In J.K. Olupona (ed.), *Religion and Peace in Multi-Faith Nigeria*. Ile-Ife :Obafemi Awolowo University Press.

Takaya, B.J. and S.G. Tyoden, eds. 1987. *The Kaduna Mafia*. Jos: Jos University Press.

Ubani, C. 1990. *Annual Report on Human Rights in Nigeria*. Lagos: CLO.

Ukpabi, S.C. 1986. *Strands in Nigeria Military History*. Zaria: Gaskiya Corporation.

———. 1987. *The Origins of the Nigerian Army*. Zaria: Gaskiya Corporation.

Uthman, S. 1984. "Classes, Crises and Coup: The Demise of Shagari's Regime." *African Affairs*, 83.

Williams, G., ed. 1976. *Nigeria: Economy and Society*. London: Rex Collins.

Yandaki, A.M. 1995. "The Izala Movement and Islamic Intellectual Discourse in Northern Nigeria: A Case Study of Katsina." In I. Tsiga et al. (eds.), *Islam and History of Learning in Katsina*. Zaria: Ahmadu Bello University Press.

Yusuf, M.M. 1985. "Class Conflict and Political Change in Nigeria, 1979–85." M.Sc. Thesis, Department of Political Science, Bayero University, Kano.

14

POLITICS AND THE ECONOMY: A DOWNWARD SPIRAL

Peter Lewis

The past decade has witnessed a tortuous course of change in Nigeria's political economy. When General Ibrahim Babangida took power in August 1985, he promised an assertive path of economic and political transformation for Nigeria. In tandem with a scheduled transition to democratic rule, the new President outlined an extensive scheme of economic reform, intended to remedy major distortions in the economy, improve relations with external creditors, and reduce a mounting debt burden. Within a year, the government launched a wide-ranging Structural Adjustment Program (SAP), incorporating key policies advocated by the World Bank and the IMF. The SAP yielded significant early results in stabilizing the economy and resuming growth.

Yet the reform initiative entailed political costs which were increasingly untenable for senior leaders. Within two years of the SAP's introduction, the government wavered on core elements of economic oversight, and by the end of 1990, the adjustment package was in jeopardy. Economic management deteriorated during Babangida's final years, worsening sharply in the period surrounding the mid-1993 political transition crisis. After ousting civilian caretakers in November of 1993, General Sani Abacha turned economic policy over to populist elements in his cabinet, who quickly dismantled the remnants of the adjustment program, prompting further decline. The Abacha regime soon returned to a more pragmatic course in economic policy, though performance remained sluggish. Macroeconomic instability was accompanied by growing corruption, widening social inequality, institutional and infrastructural deterioration, volatile market instability, domestic lawlessness and international isolation.

The Nigerian economy since 1985 has traced a cyclical path from crisis to revival, back to stagnation and decline. While less dramatic than the failed political transition, Nigeria's economic malaise has certainly been more consequential for popular welfare, and injurious to the nation's social and political fabric. The inconsistency and ultimate collapse of economic reform under Babangida mirrored the unsteady path of political transition. Democratic transition and structural adjustment manifested growing tensions as political change gave rise to greater pressures on economic policy and unstable economic management aggravated the discord of political contention (Lewis 1994b, 336). At the core of these contradictions, the military regime increasingly veered from a reformist course. Babangida and his successors eventually presided over a hasty and chaotic disintegration of the reform project.

The economic problems fostered by the Babangida regime draw attention to a fundamental political change during this period, the movement from decentralized patrimonial rule toward the consolidation of predatory dictatorship. The personalization and concentration of power, beginning under Babangida, reflected a new tendency in Nigeria's political economy, which may be regarded as a "Zaireanization" of the military oligarchy. Economic oversight by state elites shifted from a system of dispersed clientalism under relatively stable—if ineffectual—public institutions, to more arbitrary and debilitating control by a single ruler. Military elites took steps to strengthen their hold on state power, employing a mixture of coercion and material inducement. This transformation was significantly consolidated under General Sani Abacha. The deterioration of central institutions, along with alterations in state patronage, created the foundations for an enduring change in the politics of economic management.

This chapter describes the course of economic policy in Nigeria from 1985 through 1996, with special attention to the politics of attempted reform. In addition, I will summarize the central trends and structural changes in Nigeria's political economy during this period. Finally, I offer an account of the changing nature of political domination, with an analysis of implications for the economy.

Background to Reform: Crisis and Stabilization

In the course of the 1970s, Nigeria rode the currents of a heady petroleum boom. Economic growth was driven by prodigious government spending, as oil revenues fueled an ambitious program of state-led development (Williams and Turner 1978; Rimmer 1981). In addition to direct public investment, an array of nominal subsidies were directed toward producers and consumers. Export proceeds were leveraged by foreign borrowing, as successive governments sought to finance ambitious capital projects, and to compensate for fluctuations in oil revenues (Schatz 1984; Bienen 1985). Along with fiscal centralization and growing indebtedness, the economy reflected other symptoms of the "Dutch disease" syndrome common to commodity exporters. Appreciation of the exchange rate subsidized imports, while discouraging non-oil exports (Gelb 1986). The rapid influx of oil rents also fostered a dramatic increase in corruption, alongside deteriorating fiscal management. The bonanza contained the seeds of impending downfall.

Changes in international petroleum markets fostered a precipitous economic decline. The economy was highly sensitive to fluctuations in oil earnings, which furnished more than 95 percent of foreign exchange and 80 percent of government revenues. Oil proceeds peaked in 1980, and then dipped sharply as international prices declined. As export income and national output fell, debts incurred during the boom era came due, compounded by emergency short-term borrowing. The accumulation of external obligations aggravated balance of payments deficits and arrears on debt service, leading to a withdrawal of international lending.

Diminished revenues and rising debt pressures were aggravated by mismanagement during the Second Republic (1979–1983). The civilian administration of President Shehu Shagari was ill-equipped to deal with the unfolding crisis. Political exigencies and widespread corruption created a budgetary fiasco (Dudley 1982; Forrest 1995). Fiscal deficits and foreign indebtedness rose precipitously throughout 1982–83, while the GDP and productive sectors registered declines. The government's improvised austerity measures heightened popular resentment while failing to alleviate major imbalances. In early 1983, the administration initiated talks with the IMF, but the dialogue soon broke down over the key conditions specified by the fund: devaluation of the naira, liberalization of the trade regime, and removal of subsidies on fuel an other commodities.

The Second Republic was ousted by the military at the end of 1983. The new military government under Major-General Muhammadu Buhari improvised a stabilization program, reducing public expenditures, cutting the government payroll and extending administrative controls on trade and foreign exchange (Olukoshi and Abdulraheem 1985). Austerity measures improved the budgetary position and the balance of payments, though outstanding debt service continued to mount and the impasse in discussions with the IMF prevented essential rescheduling. The government attempted to circumvent the Fund by approaching the Paris Club directly, and by initiating countertrade arrangements with Brazil and a few European countries. These initiatives were unsuccessful, and the economy continued to decline.

Babangida and the SAP

Buhari's authoritarian style, set against chronic economic stagnation, quickly depleted the regime's legitimacy. Major-General Ibrahim Babangida deposed Buhari on August 27, 1985. Babangida immediately resolved to arrest the economy's downward slide and to implement fundamental political reform. Within weeks, he opened a nationwide "IMF debate" as a popular outlet for discussing the nation's economic future (Biersteker 1990). The program, conducted in the press, electronic media and other public forums, revealed broad antipathy for IMF and World Bank conditionality. Babangida then performed a deft policy turnabout. Invoking popular opinion, the President publicly repudiated the IMF and announced that Nigeria would not accept conditional finance. Less than a month later, he unveiled an economic package including fiscal restraint, movement toward a more realistic exchange rate, trade liberalization, the reduction of key subsidies, higher agricultural prices, financial liberalization and partial privatization.

Babangida essentially introduced an orthodox reform program under a nationalist guise. Although touted as a "home-grown" package, the program was negotiated with World Bank officials and premised upon supplementary finance from the Bank (Mosley 1992, 230). Some form of accomodation with the IMF was necessary for Nigeria to reschedule its debt with the Paris and London Clubs, and the introduction in July of a formal Structural Adjustment Program (SAP) provided a further step toward such agreement. In November, the IMF approved Nigeria's eligibility for a standby facility. Although Nigeria refused to draw upon the available credits, the Fund's endorsement facilitated debt negotiations and opened the door to lending from the Bank and bilateral donors. While rejecting the "IMF loan", Nigeria acceeded to basic donor conditions with their monitoring and performance requirements (Callaghy 1990).

For about eighteen months after the establishment of the SAP, the regime sustained a fairly consistent course of stabilization. By the end of

1986, these policy shifts significantly changed the character of economic strategy in Nigeria. The import licensing system was abolished and tariffs were substantially reduced, although selective import bans remained. The government instituted a dual exchange rate regime in which most non-government transactions were processed through the Second Tier Foreign Exchange Market (SFEM), an auction-based exchange window. Within a few months the auctions, managed by the Central Bank, created a two-thirds devaluation of the naira (World Bank 1994, 10).[1] Agricultural prices were decontrolled and government commodity boards were dissolved, leading to significant increases in export activity. In addition, preliminary measures were taken to privatize state corporations in agriculture and wholesale distribution. Staff reductions were implemented in several public firms and agencies. Fuel prices nearly doubled at the beginning of 1986, although considerable subsidies remained on both petroleum products and fertilizer (Mosley 1992).

The conclusion of an IMF agreement enabled negotiations with commercial and bilateral creditors over some $19 billion in external debt. The ratio of debt service to exports, which had grown from less than 5 percent in 1981 to more than 33 percent four years later, was reduced significantly after an initial round of rescheduling in 1987 (Central Bank of Nigeria 1993, 19). The balance of payments turned slightly positive, while the fiscal deficit was significantly diminished. These achievements were notable in light of a steep decline in international oil prices in 1986. Despite the general recession, rising agricultural prices and newly-available foreign exchange had beneficial effects on productive sectors of the economy. Traditional export crops such as cocoa, palm produce and cotton registered significant increases in output, while the manufacturing sector witnessed a dramatic (if transient) revival from several years of decline (Lubeck 1992).

However, the SAP also produced considerable hardship as cutbacks and declining real wages cut across a broad band of society. In mid-1987, as the regime was framing its democratic transition program, a series of anti-SAP protests were launched by students, traders and organized labor. The demonstrations, which sometimes turned violent, prompted an expedient retreat from the stabilization program. In January of 1988 the President announced a "reflationary" budget, with a number of compensatory measures including increases in wages and public spending, an interest rate cap and a commitment to sustain the petroleum subsidy (Bevan, Collier and Gunning 1992, 33). The multilateral financial institutions responded by withholding endorsement of Nigeria's economic performance, and the IMF refused to approve a new standby facility when the existing agreement lapsed in early 1988.

The Unsteady Path of Reform

The 1988 budget signaled a period of greater inconsistency in economic policy. While the regime maintained core elements of the adjustment program, there was selective evasion of central policies and a relaxation of macroeconomic discipline (Biersteker 1990). Liberalization of the foreign exchange regime continued with the formal unification of the currency market, and the approval of retail dealers. Despite Central Bank manipulations, the naira continued to depreciate against major currencies. In trade policy, the government implemented tariff revisions and specified new export incentives, while at the same time extending import bans. Continuing discontent over petroleum price increases caused the the regime to hold off further subsidy reductions.[2]

Despite slippage on some targets, other elements of reform attained greater momentum. The privatization program moved forward vigorously, as a 1988 decree allowed the creation of a central agency to supervise public sector divestiture. The sale of state enterprises was accompanied by further retrenchments, involving several thousand workers, in leading public firms. Financial liberalization also advanced incrementally. Entry requirements for the financial services industry were relaxed at the end of 1986, and restrictions on interest rates were lifted several months later. These measures, in tandem with the opening of the foreign exchange market, encouraged a profusion of new banks and finance companies (Lewis 1994a). Entrepreneurs took advantage of lucrative currency deals and the growing demand for credit. Despite some wavering on interest rate policy, a general course of liberalization was sustained through 1990.

By 1989, the multilateral institutions were encouraged by the course of economic performance and policy change. The formal SAP ended in mid-1988, though the government vowed to continue its central policies. A new IMF facility was extended, again without any drawdown by the government. The Fund's endorsement renewed access to supplementary finance from other donors and permitted additional rescheduling of the external debt, which now exceeded $30 billion. Negotiations with the creditor cartels were supplemented by a debt-equity program, inviting greater foreign entry into the domestic market. While key economic indicators remained troublesome, there was a marked improvement in growth. From

1988 through 1990, GDP expansion exceeded 7 percent, while agriculture and manufacturing attained positive per capita increases for the first time in several years (World Bank 1994).

Other elements were less favorable. The debt service ratio remained above 26 percent, unemployment rose sharply and inflation moved into double digits. Demand management policies relaxed significantly after 1988, as the government permitted accelerating monetary growth. Consequently, the full inflationary potential of devaluation was realized. Public restiveness over these conditions erupted again in mid-1989, when the "SAP riots" engulfed universities and commercial districts in several of Nigeria's major cities. The government reported 22 fatalities from the protests, but press estimates were at least twice as high (Ibrahim 1993, 133). Shaken by the outburst, the government quickly announced a compensatory package of job creation, health and transport subsidies, and enhanced food production.

The Political Management of Adjustment

The government's general strategy of reform came to fruition after the 1989 disturbances. Nigeria's adjustment program was inaugurated and maintained by a small group of state elites, largely in the absence of a supportive constituency. The regime tried different tactics to encourage a pro-adjustment coalition, including consultative measures such as the IMF debate, and nominal grassroots participation through local government reform (Biersteker 1990; Forrest 1995). However, popular response to the reform program was oppositional. The diverse groups perceiving losses from austerity bitterly opposed the program, while few potential beneficiaries emerged to support liberalization. Without a popular underpinning for its strategy, the military regime attempted to dictate the pace and content of the process. The adjustment program, driven mainly by Babangida and a small group of advisors, was prone to deviation or reversal.

Comparative experience has shown that some authoritarian leaders, faced with the contending demands of external creditors and domestic constituents, have turned to political liberalization as a means of assuaging the stresses of economic reform (Nelson 1990). Babangida clearly preferred this strategy early in his rule, but he soon shifted to more coercive measures for managing popular demands. At the same time, the regime offered compensation to important constituencies. The government sought relief from external resource constraints, while attempting to deflect the internal political costs of austerity.

Domestically, Babangida relied upon political manipulation, populist gestures, elite patronage, an expanding parallel economy, and overt repression. He soon earned the sobriquet "Maradona" (after the famous Argentine soccer star), to denote his considerable alacrity in selling programs, balancing different interests, and disarming potential opponents. He used a number of diversionary tactics to sustain popular anticipation, including frequent alterations in the schedule and institutions of the transition program, and administrative changes such as the creation of new states. By offsetting the vagaries of political reform with shifts in economic policy, military leaders secured leeway to pursue their agenda.

The regime sought to reduce popular opposition to adjustment through the selective use of compensatory policies for popular groups. In addition to reflationary measures and social subsidies, the government created institutions such as the Directorate for Food, Roads and Rural Infrastructure (DFRRI) to provide special assistance to the rural areas, a network of People's Banks and Community Banks to extend credit to small-scale and local borrowers, and the Better Life Program sponsored by the First Lady, which supported women's microenterprises. These initiatives were underfunded, often short-lived and suffused with corruption, and their impact on popular welfare was limited (Ihonvbere 1993, 146). The regime slowly allowed modest wage increases, while dawdling on the removal of the fuel subsidy.

Compensatory policies were linked to repressive measures, directed especially at labor, students and intellectual critics of the SAP (Jega 1993; Bangura and Beckman 1993). The government took advantage of problems within the peak labor confederation, the Nigeria Labour Congress (NLC), and supervised the election of a more tractable leadership. Independent campus and professional organizations were suppressed, as police quelled student protests, suspended the academic staff union, and cautioned professional groups against protest actions (Jega 1993). The regime banned public discussions of alternatives to the SAP, as decrees established broad powers of detention and supervision of the press.

While the stratagem of carrot and stick was adopted toward popular sectors, elites were mainly accorded dispensation and sidepayments. Structural adjustment entailed an unavoidable contraction of traditional outlets for state patronage, including a sharp reduction in government contracts and the withdrawal of rents from import licenses and subsidized commodity distribution. However, economic restructuring also furnished state officials with a measure of control over emerging markets, providing new sources of political rents and offering a safety valve for hard-pressed economic elites

(Lewis 1994a). The liberalization of agricultural exports provided an early windfall, as cocoa offered a medium for foreign exchange which could be held locally or spirited abroad (Mustapha 1993, 121–22). The privatization program also created a wide circle of beneficiaries as well-connected insiders could take advantage of both equity sales and the divestiture of assets from liquidated companies.

By far the largest arena of burgeoning rents was in the realm of financial services. With the opening of bank licenses at the end of 1986 the industry experienced a spate of new entrants. The number of banks tripled within four years, to 120 institutions (Ojo 1993, 10). In addition, several hundred unlicensed finance and mortgage companies emerged, often connected to the banks. Entrepreneurs were originally attracted by the margins to be garnered from the foreign exchange markets, and later by the arbitrage opportunities in deregulated money markets. Licensing and regulatory procedures were heavily politicised and access to foreign exchange was controlled by the Central Bank. Consequently, financial services offered recompense for groups deprived of rent-seeking outlets in the trading sector and the regime steered opportunities to their cronies (*Financial Times* March 16 1992).

The visible rents which arose in the course of liberalization were augmented by a growing array of parallel markets and illegal activities. These were concentrated in three areas: petroleum smuggling, drug trafficking and commercial fraud. In addition, devaluation of the naira cheapened Nigerian manufactures relative to the surrounding Francophone countries, where the CFA remained overvalued. This discrepancy gave rise to a large unrecorded export trade from Nigeria to the sub-region.

Petroleum smuggling was largely the province of senior military officers and a few civilian associates. Hundreds of millions of dollars in revenue were foregone in this way. In addition, the continued domestic subsidy on refined fuels, along with currency differentials, created an enormous gap in fuel prices with the CFA states. A lively illicit trade in Nigerian fuels, accounting for at least 10 percent of domestic consumption, flowed to regional neighbors (World Bank 1994, 57).

Beginning in the late 1980s, Nigeria became a major transshipment point for South Asian heroin, and cocaine from Latin America. Nigerian syndicates gradually moved their operations to third countries. Many of the proceeds from the trade were laundered through the domestic banking system. Narcotics trafficking enjoyed the forbearance, and possibly the active participation, of senior officials.

An extensive web of international commercial fraud also emanated from Nigeria in the late 1980s. Maintained by dozens of small groups and independent operators, these "419" schemes, named for the local criminal code on fraud, took a variety of guises. Several hundred million dollars were realized from these activities.[3] Again, the "419" operations flourished under government tolerance.

In sum, the Babangida regime managed the adjustment program through a mixture of domestic political orchestration, compensatory measures and coercion. For elites, the state provided special access to emergent markets and illegal activities, and manipulated key policies to provide opportune rents. The regime initially employed these tactics to sustain the implementation of adjustment policies, but senior leaders soon abandoned the commitment to economic recovery. Faced with growing political contention, looming personal insecurity and a fortuitous appearance of new revenues, Babangida engaged in increasingly reckless economic management. This involved a massive diversion of public resources, abdication of basic fiscal and monetary controls, and expansion of the illicit economy.

These strategies created recurrent tensions with foreign creditors and the multilateral institutions, although the government proved capable of periodically salvaging negotiations. External economic relations veered between sufficient compliance with donor conditions and estrangement from international actors. Seeking to alleviate fiscal pressures, senior technocrats persisted with efforts to secure debt relief and new external resources. At the same time, the regime's domestic policies increasingly undermined successful adjustment. The arrangement of IMF facilities in 1987, 1989 and 1991 provided intermittent breathing room, though reform measures faltered and eventually broke down.

Uncertainty and Weakening Reform, 1990–92

The year 1990 was a turning point in the course of economic and political reform. Two pivotal events fostered changes in the calculus of leaders, yielding more personalized, coercive and predatory rule. In April, the regime narrowly averted a coup d'état, led by a group of junior officers from the southeastern portion of the country. The abortive revolt was an ominous manifestation of ethnic and populist resentments, highlighting dangerous internal factionalism within the military (Ihonvbere 1991). During the months that followed, several hundred military personnel were arrested and interrogated, and 69 alleged conspirators were executed. The incident evidently weakened Babangida's intention to transfer power and encouraged the accumulation of illicit revenues as a hedge against further instability (Ihonvbere 1991; Forrest 1995).

Beginning in August, when world petroleum markets were disrupted by the Persian Gulf crisis, oil prices rose sharply. Although prices subsided within a few months, the shock conferred a revenue windfall to Nigeria of perhaps $5 billion. Treating the "mini-boom" as a reprieve from resource constraints, the government embarked on a path of extrabudgetary spending, fiscal and monetary expansion. A large proportion of revenues were diverted to so-called "dedicated" accounts earmarked for special projects. An official report issued during the early months of the Abacha regime estimated that some $12.2 billion was sidelined to off-budget accounts from 1988 through 1993, equivalent to about 20 percent of total petroleum revenues for the period (*Business Times* October 17 1994). Within two years, extrabudgetary spending equalled 17 percent of GDP, or nearly two-thirds of total expenditures (Forrest 1995, 247). The monies were designated for diverse commitments including the new capital at Abuja, the steel and aluminum projects, and the joint peace-keeping mission in Liberia. Once diverted, the funds were entirely unmonitored.

The mini-boom rekindled the pathologies of the Dutch disease, as the growth in public spending surpassed the transient increase in revenues. Government deficits rose from less than 6.7 percent of GDP in 1989, to 8.3 percent in 1990, and 11.3 percent the following year (Central Bank of Nigeria 1993). Rising government deficits were financed by advances from the Central Bank of Nigeria (CBN), and the resultant monetary expansion fueled inflation and depreciation of the naira. The official inflation rate (which probably underestimates the real level of price increases) registered an increase from 7.4 percent in 1990, to 57.2 percent within three years (Central Bank of Nigeria 1995, 1). As prices on fuel, fertilizer and power failed to keep pace with inflation, significant subsidies were restored, which of course aggravated the deficit. Cross-border trade in petroleum products accelerated, creating serious shortages within Nigeria. The fuel crisis led to increased transport fares and a deterioration of public services, especially electricity and waste disposal.

Demand for foreign exchange further weakened the naira. Government management of the auction system had propped up the rate of the naira, and by early 1992, the parallel market showed a 50 percent differential with the formal market price. In March, the government further liberalized the foreign exchange regime by unifying all rates and removing controls on bidding. The CBN attempted to bolster the national currency by injecting additional foreign exchange into the market, but this was unsustainable and could not prevent a rapid 55 percent depreciation of the naira (Ntekop 1992, 30). By the end of the year, however, the government had resolved to halt further erosion, and the prevailing rate of N22=$1 was targeted as a benchmark regardless of movements in the parallel market. This rate was officially fixed in Sani Abacha's 1994 budget.

Macroeconomic instability pushed the turbulent financial system toward insolvency. The rapid growth of banking and financial services, feebly regulated by the state, led to systemic weaknesses which now began to buckle. Many firms were highly leveraged, inadequately capitalized, and heavily exposed in volatile interbank money markets. Following the failure of a prominent state-owned bank and evidence of distress in several private firms, plummeting confidence instigated a torrent of defaults and insolvency throughout the industry. Problems in the financial sector widened steadily over next few years, and by the end of Babangida's tenure, a third of the nation's licensed banks were recognized to be in distress.

Pervasive mismanagement and economic deterioration were fully manifest in 1992, although the multilateral institutions sustained a working relationship almost through the end of Babangida's rule. In February 1991, the government signed its third standby agreement with the IMF and negotiated a substantial package of debt reduction, including a London Club deal allowing a discounted buyback of $3.4 billion in commercial debt along with additional refinancing (Economic Intelligence Unit 1992). The Paris Club also rescheduled $3.2 billion in bilateral debt. Nigeria's total debt stock temporarily declined, from $33.7 billion in 1991 to $27.5 billion a year later. Accumulating arrears soon increased the outstanding debt to earlier levels.

Transition Crisis and the Collapse of Adjustment, 1993-94

Babangida's last year in power was marked by a rapid deterioration in international economic relations and domestic performance. In the course of 1993, Nigeria experienced its gravest political and economic upheaval since the 1960s. An abortive political transition gave rise to two abrupt regime changes, accompanied by growing popular restiveness, ethno-regional tension and stagnation in domestic markets. The growing cost and contention of the political transition undermined economic oversight while senior military officials anticipating a withdrawal from power were increasingly preoccupied with bolstering their own assets and securing perks for the middle ranks. The pretence of macroeconomic management was largely abandoned as policy levers shifted among venal officers and ineffectual civilians.

In November, 1992, the regime announced its third postponement of the transition deadline until the following August. As a consolation to critics who doubted the military's intention to relinquish power, Babangida appointed a civilian Transitional Council, led by Chief Ernest Shonekan, a prominent corporate executive. Without a legal basis to override military prerogatives, the council failed to establish control over economic policy. While some elements of Shonekan's team favored a return to orthodox adjustment, others were committed to nationalist policies, and the council was largely eclipsed by decisions taken within the military and the bureaucracy (Economist Intelligence Unit 1993).

After the third IMF standby arrangement ended in April, 1992, an extended chill was apparent in relations with the multilateral institutions. Poor economic performance and delinquent debt service precluded a new IMF facility, which forestalled further rescheduling with the creditor groups. The budget deficit exceeded 12 percent at the end of 1992, while monetary growth fostered rising inflation. Moreover, the government ceased servicing much of its foreign debt. By early 1993, the country was at least $4 billion in arrears on external obligations, mostly to the Paris Club.[4] Internal mismanagement, a revenue slump, and a dearth of other resources created a significant economic slowdown. The GDP expanded by about 3 percent in 1992, less than half the growth rate two years earlier, and negative in per capita terms (Central Bank of Nigeria 1995, 70).

The regime stalled on key policy changes and reversed earlier reforms. An auction system for foreign exchange was restored by the CBN in early 1993, creating a widening gap between nominal and market rates. Although there was sentiment in Shonekan's council for a reduction in the domestic petroleum subsidy, the military declared that fuel prices would not change until after the transition. This announcement squelched prospects for renewed agreement with the IMF. The privatization program, which had lost momentum during the previous year, was largely suspended save for the divestiture of shares in a dozen major banks.

Beginning in June, a transition crisis plunged the country into political uncertainty and economic paralysis (Lewis 1994b; Diamond 1995). Presidential elections conducted on June 12 1993 apparently yielded a decisive victory for Chief M.K.O. Abiola, a prominent Yoruba Muslim business magnate. However, a few days after the election, Babangida declared the poll invalid, citing purported irregularities. Under intense pressure to cede power, the President stepped down by the August 27 1993 deadline, relegating authority to a caretaker Interim National Government headed by Chief Shonekan. The hasty transfer failed to quell popular indignation over the election annulment, and the absence of a clear transitional framework undermined the government's direction and legitimacy.

The abrogation of the June election incited sporadic civil violence, a resurgence of ethnic tension, and consternation about possible political breakdown (Diamond 1995). For several weeks, the economy was in a state of virtual paralysis as workers demonstrated, fearful depositors staged a run on the banks, financial markets were stalled with trepidation, manufacturers and traders could not gain access to capital, and the business community awaited the outcome of the political impasse. Shonekan attempted to restore public confidence by announcing a date for new elections and releasing a number of political detainees. The government also resumed talks with the multilateral institutions in September, and prepared the way for a removal of domestic petroleum subsidies.

The subsidy issue proved fatal for the interim government. Convinced that this was the decisive sticking point in relations with the IMF, in mid-November the administration announced a 700 percent fuel price hike. The Nigerian Labour Congress (NLC) responded immediately with a general strike. Within three days, Major-General Sani Abacha, whom Babangida had appointed as defence minister in the interim government, forced Shonekan's resignation and siezed control. Having sidelined most Babangida loyalists from the military and the security forces, Abacha proceeded to consolidate his personal power (Lewis 1994b). He abruptly ended speculation about the political transition by revoking the democratization program and dissolving the tiers of elected civilian government. Abacha named a predominantly civilian cabinet, including a number of veteran politicians and Dr. Kalu I. Kalu, a previous finance minister who was a vocal advocate of liberalization.

A segment of Abacha's cabinet including the Secretary to Government and several former politicians advocated a return to populist economic policies. Protectionist measures were also heavily promoted by local manufacturers, while an array of popular groups urged price controls and revaluation of the naira. Dr. Kalu, whose appointment as finance minister was intended to reassure the international community, was quickly sidelined. The January 1994 budget effectively dismantled the SAP in favor of a statist and nationalist agenda. Economic policy returned to a regime of administrative controls on finance, trade and foreign exchange. The exchange rate was fixed at 22 naira to the dollar (in contrast to a prevailing market rate of about 50), and all foreign exchange was allocated directly by the CBN. The parallel foreign exchange market was ostensibly prohibited. Interest rates were also fixed, tariffs were increased and import bans extended.

The reinstatement of currency controls gave rise to a new wave of rent-seeking and corruption. While state officials profited from privileged access to foreign exchange, productive activities were starved of hard currency, and export incentives were eliminated. Capacity utilization in the manufacturing sector reached a nadir of 28 percent, while non-oil exports plummeted to $244 million, little more than half their value two years earlier. The gross domestic product grew by only 1.3 percent (Central Bank of Nigeria 1995, 70). Budgetary profligacy, monetary growth, and artificial scarcities in foreign exchange virtually sabotaged the naira, driving the national currency as low as N120=$1 toward the end of the year, before it settled at about N82=$1.

The government retreated from its populist course in 1995, reopening a market-based foreign exchange window and attempting to stabilize the economy. Seeking a restoration of international credibility, the leadership nominally improved its budgetary performance and attempted a rapprochement with the multilateral institutions. Monetary growth was sharply curtailed, fiscal deficits reduced and off-budget accounts apparently ended. An independent Petroleum Trust Fund was created as a public outlet for channeling "special" revenues derived mainly from improved oil earnings, increases in domestic fuel prices, and a value-added tax. Regulations on capital flows and portfolio investment were liberalized, in a bid to join the international ranks of "emerging markets." These initiatives produced meager results, as Nigeria's international reputation continued to suffer from concerns over corruption, human rights abuses, and policy instability. As the government continued to accumulate $3 billion annually in arrears on debt service, there was little to redeem relations with external creditors. Nagging delinquency in government payments to joint venture partners in the oil industry also created considerable ambivalence among investors.

Building on existing interests in the petroleum sector (including progress on a major Liquefied Natural Gas project), the regime sought to regain international confidence through a dramatic gesture of reform. In October, 1996, the government announced an extensive new phase of privatization, encompassing public utilities and the petroleum industry. Officials declared a willingness to consider a sale of interests in upstream oil producing ventures, as well as downstream refining and distribution. The assets potentially on offer totalled more than $30 billion, promising a new fiscal windfall for government, and a significant increase in foreign capital flowing to the energy sector. The policy pronouncement certainly caught the attention, if not the commitment, of international donors and investors.

Parallel moves in the political arena raised the possibility of a new strategic direction for regularizing Abacha's regime. As the economic initiatives were proposed, authorities also moved forward with its transition schedule, registering five new political parties. Domestic political opponents were not represented in any of the approved parties, reinforcing general expectations that Abacha's transition program would be as constricted as Babangida's. On the heels of successful elections of former military incumbents in Niger and Gambia, many observers interpreted signals from Abuja as an indication of Abacha's intention to enter the presidential contest, in 1998 or beyond. A civilianization of the military regime, linked with a path of limited reform in the economic sphere, would reflect greater likeness to ruling strategies in Ghana—or even Chile—than Zaire. Thus, General Abacha seemed poised between the roads to Kinshasa, or to Accra, as he played out an agenda known mainly to himself.

The Changing Contours of the Political Economy

The Babangida years witnessed a reconfiguration of Nigeria's political economy. As suggested earlier, patterns of distributive politics altered considerably. Economic crisis and ensuing reform curtailed traditional avenues of public patronage. Government contracts, subsidies, grants and employment were substantially diminished, affecting the dispersal of resources among elites and popular sectors. In consequence, the distribution of rents changed substantially. Direct disbursals and administrative favors were increasingly supplanted by politically-influenced arbitrage in a variety of domestic markets.

State officials fomented growing corruption and sanctioned an expanding realm of illegality. The scale of malfeasance increased dramatically in the final years of Babangida's rule. The diversion of revenues depleted investible resources, aggravated the debt burden and worsened relations with external creditors. In addition, overtly illegal activities became a major portion of Nigeria's shadow economy. More than a billion dollars annually—equalling as much as 15 percent of recorded government revenues—flowed to smuggling networks and confidence teams, many of whom operated with the connivance of top elites.

These changes were consequential for inequality and class formation. Income differentials widened dramatically in the decade after 1985 (Ihonvbere 1993). A circle of military leaders and civilian allies made extravagant gains throughout the period, and the rentier economy conferred benefits to a small set of nouveau riche in financial services, real estate, and trade. In contrast, most wage-earners, in both public and private sectors, experienced plummeting real incomes. The middle classes were devastated by inflation, unemployment and deteriorating public services, while low-income urban-dwellers were driven to subsistence levels. The rural economy was not as seriously afflicted, yet the decade brought little more than the perpetuation of an indigent status quo for most agrarian producers.

In the early years of the SAP, economic stabilization, trade liberalization and export incentives had positive effects on productive activities. Manufacturers benefited from renewed access to foreign exchange, agricultural exporters responded to price changes, and investment was encouraged by the removal of bureaucratic obstacles. By 1990, however, domestic markets and public policies had moved in a more adverse direction. A declining naira and rising interest rates impeded access to needed hard currency, while escalating inflation and capricious trade policy created further uncertainties for producers. Agricultural exporters were buffeted by volatile incomes, as speculators created wide swings in commodity prices. Lured by the gains from financial arbitrage, the banking industry largely shunned commercial borrowers, creating severe capital shortages for manufacturers, agrarian producers, transporters and others in the service sector. As the adjustment program proceeded, the inconsistency of government policy created substantial risks for long term investment and the persistence of rent seeking activities undermined incentives for production.

Nigeria's position in the international economy also deteriorated substantially. Nigeria was increasingly marginalized in global trade and capital markets. Despite temporary accomodation with the multilateral financial institutions, the country's increasingly erratic economic policies alienated creditors and investors. By 1992, defaults on external payments and worsening political uncertainty produced widespread economic isolation. Nigeria continued to reflect significant inflows of direct foreign investment, but there was virtually no engagement outside the petroleum sector. Foreign export insurance was rescinded, concessional lending was suspended and commercial capital fled. Added to a steady current of capital flight, the national economy was increasingly deprived of external resources and linkages.

The Emergence of Predatory Rule

The collapse of reform in Nigeria reflected a deeper shift in the political foundations of economic management. This transformation, arising during the latter years of Babangida's rule, can be characterized as the emergence of predatory dictatorship. As a special form of political and economic domination, this should be distinguished from the "prebendal" relations traditionally prevalent in Nigeria, in which patron-client links have been more diffuse and individual authority comparatively limited. This embodied a reconfiguration of neopatrimonial rule, toward more despotic and rapacious control.

Neopatrimonial rule, a syndrome common to many developing countries, embodies the appearance of Weberian "legal-rational" administration, and the essence of patrimonialism. Beneath the trappings of formal bureaucracy, procedural rules and law, these regimes are based upon networks of personal loyalty and patron-client ties (Clapham 1986). Power is typically concentrated in a single ruler or a narrow oligarchy, who occupy the apex of a clientalist pyramid (Jackson and Rosberg 1982). Public and private resources are merged, as state assets come under the discretionary control of political elites, and public office serves as a conduit for private accumulation.

Neopatrimonial administration gives rise to a characteristic pattern of economic management, including arbitrary policy change, deficit financing, capital flight, and the chronic, unrecorded leakage of funds (Sandbrook 1985; van de Walle 1994). The premium on transitory rent-seeking in such economies reinforces an orientation toward political rather than market allocation (Boone 1990; Colander 1984). Moreover, pervasive instability in policy, public finance and the institutional realm give rise to strong disincentives for investment and capital formation. Rational economic actors seek to avoid long-term investment, to diversify their activities, and to keep their assets out of domestic currency and the banking system. Consequently, the private sector gravitates toward short-term, speculative activities and capital export (Sandbrook 1985; Kennedy 1988).

For more than a decade, numerous observers have characterized post-independent Nigeria as a "prebendal" order. Richard Joseph's incisive formulation portrayed three crucial aspects of this system (Joseph 1987). First, there was a widespread appropriation of nominally "public" resources for personal or parochial gain. Second, such allocations were patterned by ethnically-delineated patron-client networks. Third, the distributive arena was largely decentralized, and clientalist relations were diffuse. Prebendalism was sustained by a narrow civil-military elite, and necessarily embodied deep social inequalities. However, in contrast to many other neopatrimonial systems, the Nigerian state was not controlled by an exclusive oligarchy, and there were countervailing influences on the concentration of personal power. Civilian institutions and military affinities hindered the tendency toward personal rule or ethnic monopoly.

These features changed fundamentally after 1990. President Babangida concentrated political authority and economic discretion to an unprecedented degree, fostering the emergence of predatory rule. Max Weber discussed a variety of special forms of patrimonial domination, including extreme personalization and coercive control (Weber 1978, 231–32). More recently Juan Linz, in his important taxonomy of authoritarian systems, offered a pertinent view:

> We encounter a few regimes based on personal rulership with loyalty to the ruler based not on tradition, or on him embodying an ideology, or on a unique personal mission, or on charismatic qualities, but on a mixture of fear and rewards to collaborators. The ruler exercises his power without restraint at his own discretion and above all unencumbered by rules or by any commitment to an ideology or value system (Linz 1975, 259).

This depiction evokes the forms of rule during Babangida's later administration, a pattern deepened under General Abacha.

This emergent order has embodied three essential features. Most important is the concentration of personal power under coercive auspices. Babangida successfully consolidated his authority through a variety of institutional and informal means. Following the abortive 1990 coup, a widespread purge led to the execution or marginalization of dozens of military officers, considerably allaying potential challenges to his tenure. An array of state security forces acquired growing latitude, encouraging increased surveillance and repression against dissidents or putative rivals. Organizations of civil society, notably labor unions, university associations, human rights groups and professional associations, were persecuted and subverted. In addition, the restrictive party system left few openings for autonomous political activity (Diamond 1995). In consequence, Babangida removed potential restraints on presidential power, whether in the military, the political elite or the broader society. Sani Abacha fully availed himself of these instruments of control, extending political repression, enervating the political class, and conducting preemptive indictments (and executions) against perceived opponents.

Second, in both regimes repression has been augmented by material inducement, requiring close discretion over public resources as well as a ready pool of available funds. Compelling evidence has documented massive corruption under the two leaders. The $12 billion in petroleum revenues sidelined to off-budget accounts constitutes an enormous diversion of public resources for discretionary use. The involvement of military leaders in large-scale petroleum smuggling, and imputations of narcotics trafficking, point to further illicit gains. This largesse, supplemented by rents from finance and real estate, has been shared among an elite stratum of loyalist officers, civilian cronies, and acquiescent politicians. Blandishments offered to the military rank and file and the political class were strategically allocated to facilitate personal rule.

A third aspect has been the conscious erosion of central public institutions, and the corresponding hegemony of a close circle of ethnic and personal loyalists. The military has been largely denuded of dissenting voices following the retirement or exile of several prominent advocates of professionalism and civilian rule. Babangida and Abacha have predicated their control on continual reshuffling of division commanders, intensified internal intelligence, selective inducements, and the use of foreign advisors for palace security. The fallout from a series of coups and counter-coups has fragmented and demoralized the military organization (*Newswatch* October 2 1995). In addition, the dissolution of political parties and legislative bodies, and the intrusive manipulation of the judiciary throughout the transition crisis, have depleted other institutional pillars of the state, thereby widening the realm of personal control.

Conclusion

The breakdown of Nigerian economic reform reflects a familiar pattern in the country's economic administration. A legacy of weak central government, fractious ethnic competition, and centralized revenues has sharply politicized economic management (Rimmer 1981; Joseph 1987; Forrest 1995). The interests of Nigeria's political elites have long been entwined with pervasive distributive pressures on the state. Military and civilian regimes have used extensive government control over the economy to bolster their legitimacy and to funnel resources toward favored clients and ethnic constituencies. Nigeria's formidable domestic business class has developed in the shadow of government protection and rent-seeking opportunities.

During the early years of his rule, Babangida was able to manage economic and political reform on discrete, parallel tracks. However, economic and political trajectories grew increasingly contradictory. The record of economic management after 1986 suggests that the regime's reform proclivities were pragmatic and transient. Babangida was motivated chiefly by the desire to obtain a reprieve from debt pressures and capital scarcity. There was little sentiment, either within government or the private sector, for a genuine withdrawal of state economic tutelage, the expansion of competitive markets, or a revival of productive economic activity.

Political impulses dominated the implementation of adjustment and the manipulation of benefits and liabilities. The reform program did not reduce the levers of state distribution. New outlets in such areas as foreign exchange markets, financial arbitrage and privatization sales, offered copious sidepayments to strategic groups. In addition, the military leadership and a small circle of civilian cronies circumvented the formal economy through unprecedented corruption, including large diversions of oil stock and revenues, systematic commercial fraud and intensified drug trafficking. These parallel activities offered refuge from a declining economy to a narrow, predatory elite.

Ultimately, a combination of personal calculation and clientalist pressure induced Babangida to impose more personalistic control of the state. Nigeria's political economy increasingly embodied the characteristics of such autocratic regimes as Mobutu's Zaire, Haiti under Cedras or Somoza's Nicaragua. A transition was soon apparent: from decentralized clientalist rule, to a more purely avaricious dictatorship. Several aspects of this process offered a basis for the consolidation of personal dominance. The decline of state institutions, the fragmentation of private sector elites, and the availability of selective exit from the system encouraged a perpetuation of personal rule. However, there were also historical and structural features of Nigeria's political economy which offered the possibility of reversal. The fragility of personal power, the legacy of institutional development and the persistence of domestic and external opposition to predatory dictatorship, created a potential for retreat from a steep secular decline.

Notes

1. Prior to devaluation, the naira had dropped incrementally, from about $1.50=N1 in the early 1980s, to a value roughly par with the dollar on the eve of the SFEM.

2. In 1989, a two-tiered pricing structure was introduced as a means of easing in a price increase on fuels.

3. Personal interview, western diplomat, Lagos, June, 1993.

4. Interestingly, the government serviced its debt to the World Bank and its obligations to holders of par bonds. An implicit distinction was made between the "lenders of last resort" and creditors regarded as dispensable.

References

Bangura, Yusuf and Bjorn Beckman. 1993. "African Workers and Structural Adjustment: A Nigerian Case Study." In Adebayo Olukoshi (ed.), *The Politics of Structural Adjustment in Nigeria.* London: James Currey.

Bevan, David, Paul Collier, and Jan Willem Gunning. 1992. "Nigerian Economic Policy and Performance: 1981–92," manuscript, Center for the Study of African Economies, Oxford University, May.

Bienen, Henry, 1985. *Political Conflict and Economic Change in Nigeria.* London: Frank Cass.

Biersteker, Thomas J. 1990. "Structural Adjustment and the Political Transition in Nigeria." Paper presented at the Conference on Democratic Transition and Structural Adjustment in Nigeria, Stanford University, August.

Boone, Catherine, 1990. "The Making of a Rentier Class: Wealth Accumulation and Political Control in Senegal." *The Journal of Development Studies*, 26, 3, (April): 425–49.

Callaghy, Thomas. 1990. "Lost Between State and Market: The Politics of Economic Adjustment in Ghana, Zambia and Nigeria." In Joan Nelson, (Ed.), *Economic Crisis and Policy Choice.* Princeton: Princeton University Press.

Central Bank of Nigeria. 1993. *Economic Policy Reforms in Nigeria: A Study Report.* Lagos: CBN Research Department.

Central Bank of Nigeria. 1995. *Annual Report and Statement of Accounts, 1994.* Lagos: Central Bank of Nigeria.

Clapham, Christopher. 1986. *Third World Politics.* Madison: University of Wisconsin Press.

Colander, David C., ed., 1984. *Neoclassical Political Economy: The Analysis of Rent-Seeking and DUP Activities.* Cambridge: Ballinger Publishing Co.

Diamond, Larry. 1995. "Nigeria: The Uncivic Society and the Descent into Praetorianism." In Larry Diamond, J. Linz and S.M. Lipset (eds.), *Politics in Developing Countries: Camparing Experiences With Democracy* (2nd Edition). Boulder: Lynne Rienner Publishers.

Dudley, Billy. 1982. *An Introduction to Nigerian Government and Politics.* Bloomington: Indiana University Press.

Economist Intelligence Unit. 1993. *Nigeria Country Report.* London: EIU.

Federal Republic of Nigeria. 1986. *Structural Adjustment Program July 1986–June 1988.* Lagos: Federal Ministry of Information, November.

Forrest, Tom. 1995. *Politics and Economic Development in Nigeria* (Revised Edition). Boulder: Westview.

Gelb, Alan. 1986. "Adjustment to Windfall Gains: A Comparative Analysis of Oil Exporting Countries." In J.P. Neary and S. van Wijnbergen (eds.), *Natural Resources and the Macroeconomy*. Oxford: Basil Blackwell.

Ibrahim, Jibrin. 1993. "The Transition to Civilian Rule: Sapping Democracy." In Adebayo Olukoshi (ed.), *The Politics of Structural Adjustment in Nigeria*. London: James Currey.

Ihonvbere, Julius O. 1991. "A Critical Evaluation of the 1990 Failed Coup in Nigeria." *The Journal of Modern African Studies*, 29 (4): 601–26.

———. 1993. "Economic Crisis, Structural Adjustment and Social Crisis in Nigeria." *World Development*, 21, 1: 141–53.

Jackson, Robert H., and Carl G. Rosberg. 1982. *Personal Rule in Black Africa*. Berkeley: University of California Press.

Jega, Attahiru. 1993. "Professional Associations and Structural Adjustment." In Adebayo Olukoshi (ed.), *The Politics of Structural Adjustment in Nigeria*. London: James Currey.

Joseph, Richard A. 1987. *Democracy and Prebendal Politics in Nigeria: The Rise and Fall of the Second Republic*. Cambridge: Cambridge University Press.

Kennedy, Paul. 1988. *African Capitalism: The Struggle for Ascendancy*. Cambridge: Cambridge University Press.

Lewis, Peter M. 1994a. "Economic Statism, Private Capital, and the Dilemmas of Accumulation in Nigeria." *World Development*, 22, 3 (March): 437–51.

———. 1994b. "Endgame in Nigeria? The Politics of a Failed Democratic Transition." *African Affairs*, 93 (July).

Linz, Juan J. 1975. "Totalitarian and Authoritarian Regimes." In Fred Greenstein and Nelson Polsby (eds.), *Handbook of Political Science: Macropolitical Theory* (Vol. 3). Menlo Park: Addison-Wesley.

Lubeck, Paul. 1992. "Restructuring Nigeria's Urban-Industrial Sector Within the West African Region: The Interplay of Crisis, Linkages and Popular Resistance." *International Journal of Urban and Regional Research*, 16, 1: 6–23.

Mosley, Paul. 1992. "Policy-Making Without Facts: A Note on the Assessment of Structural Adjustment Policies in Nigeria, 1985–1990." *African Affairs*, 91: 227–40.

Mustapha, Abdul Raufu. 1993. "Structural Adjustment and Agrarian Change in Nigeria." In Adebayo Olukoshi (ed.), *The Politics of Structural Adjustment in Nigeria*. London: James Currey.

Nelson, Joan, ed. 1990. *Economic Crisis and Policy Choice: The Politics of Adjustment in the Third World*. Princeton: Princeton University Press.

———, ed. 1989. *Fragile Coalitions: The Politics of Economic Adjustment*. New Brunswick: Transaction Books.

Ntekop, T.J. 1992. "The Foreign Exchange Market in Nigeria." *Bullion*, 16, 3, (July/September).
Ojo, M.O. 1993. "A Review and Appraisal of Nigeria's Experience with Financial Sector Reform." Central Bank of Nigeria, Research Department Occasional Paper No. 8.
Olukoshi, Adebayo, ed. 1993. *The Politics of Structural Adjustment in Nigeria*. London: James Currey.
Olukoshi, Adebayo and Tajudeen Abdulraheem. 1985. "Nigeria: Crisis Management Under the Buhari Regime." *Review of African Political Economy*, 34, (December): 96–97.
Rimmer, Douglas. 1981. "Development in Nigeria: an Overview." In Henry Bienen and V.P. Diejomaoh (eds.), *The Political Economy of Income Distribution in Nigeria*. New York: Holmes and Meier.
Sandbrook, Richard. 1985. *The Politics of Africa's Economic Stagnation*. Cambridge: Cambridge University Press.
Schatz, Sayre. 1984. "Pirate Capitalism and the Inert Economy of Nigeria." *Journal of Modern African Studies*, 22, I: 45–57.
Van de Walle, Nicolas. 1994. "Neopatrimonialism and Democracy in Africa, with an Illustration from Cameroon." In Jennifer A. Widner (ed.), *Economic Change and Political Liberalization in Sub-Saharan Africa*. Baltimore: Johns Hopkins University Press.
Weber, Max. 1978. *Economy and Society* (2 Vols.). Berkeley: University of California Press.
Williams, Gavin, and Terisa Turner. 1978. "Nigeria." In John Dunn (ed.), *West African States: Failure and Promise*. Cambridge: Cambridge University Press.
World Bank. 1994. *Nigeria's Structural Adjustment Program: Policies, Implementation, and Impact*. Washington, DC: The World Bank.

PART 5
Institutional Frameworks

15

POLITICS AND THE SEARCH FOR ACCOMMODATION IN NIGERIA: WILL ROTATIONAL CONSOCIATIONALISM SUFFICE?

Chudi Uwazurike

> The chances for the survival of democracy in Nigeria might have been better if a consociational pattern had been adopted (in the First Republic).
> —Arend Lijphart (1977).

> I have told people all along that we are not ripe for a system in which there is a fully-fledged Opposition.
> —Prime Minister Abubakar Balewa (*West Africa* 14 January 1966).

> The surest way to kill the idea of democracy in a plural society, is to adopt the Anglo-American electoral system of first-past-the-post.
> —Sir Arthur Lewis (*Politics in West Africa* 1965).

Skepticism naturally greets the latest military promises of a transition to democracy under new constitutional auspices. Yet, one might wager that with the conclusion of the 1994–95 National Constitutional Conference and the proclamation of its core recommendations for a rotational presidential system, something new might well be afoot. The new constitution, on face value, appears to be a long-sought antidote to the fractious politics of one of the most unstable federations in the developing world.

The point must be forcefully made at the outset that, on the face of it, there appears to have been no overarching need for a new constitution following the Abacha coup of 1993. The issue was never the workability of the 1989 Babangida constitution; neither was it the issue for the 1979 Second Republic. With some degree of faith and political commitment to democracy by the impatient military, the systems might have worked out their shortcomings just as the novel 1995 version, if it ever comes to be implemented without further constraints by the presiding regime, would be obliged to do in its turn. The creation of a Constitutional Conference was a side-tracking of the more popular demand for a National Conference where the entire nationhood project itself would be up for dissection. Yet the "down the ladder" rotational principle that was the primary innovation was undeniably popular.

Without prejudice to the well-deserved merits of the June 12 victors, and despite the dubious origins of the Abacha Constitutional Conference, the 1995 constitution may well, in insisting on the principle of power rotationality as an extension of the now-basic principle of "Federal Character," have finally found the knob of the Gordian Knot of Nigerian politics: the issue of geoethnic power imbalance. This is irrespective of the reality that ethnicity is but one of a range of economic, class and cultural issues confronting the dependent state.

Strategies of the 1995 Constitution

Four features in the 1995 document ought to be of interest to students of stable democratization as opposed to nominal democracy. First is the division of the country into six geopolitical zones, more or less the same as most Nigerian observers have been aware of for years: northeast, northwest, middle belt, southwest, east central, and southern minority. It is from these zonal combinations that a winning party ought to come to power with the following offices distributed nationally: President, Vice President, Prime Minister, and Deputy Prime Minister, Senate President and Speaker of the House. The Prime Minister, nominated by the President, is to be an elected legislator who shall work with his colleagues in running the administrative affairs of state. Second is the requirement that this principle be enshrined in the political practices of the secondary tiers of government—state and local government, and by implication, other arenas. Third is the requirement of a multiparty system based on proportional representation, important in a multiethnic polity to ensure the plural expression of group interest. A final proviso is even more critical: the requirement that the system, once in place after the unnecessarily long transition in October 1998, is to last three decades. Nigerians, despite their natural skepticism, seemed to accord the program some interest. The rotationality principle across the board of all three tiers of a federal multiparty system in particular attracted attention, though not unanimous praise. Though the problems of implementation are obvious, the underlying consociational logic may offer Nigeria a chance for stability and the steady economic prosperity that has long eluded her despite the large doubts concerning the sincerity of purpose of the armed forces under Sani Abacha.

A key issue is germane here: Is there a cultural basis for power-sharing by recognized social formations in Nigeria?[1] Contrasted with the logic of open-ended contestational, adversarial democracy, would this modified, even circumscribed pattern, meet the need for development-oriented leadership? An assumption in this chapter is that democratic institutionalization requires time for habituation. Constant learning—and the political will to accommodate—will be central to the process. Any moratorium on purely adversarial politics, capable of offering a breathing space for this to occur, is certainly worth experimentation, as Arthur Lewis (1965) suggested three decades ago. The more central thesis here holds that, in multiethnic plural societies, a measure of consociational accommodation and a system which stresses social, as opposed to merely political, democracy stands a far better chance of surviving. To develop this argument, I first review the main strands in Nigerian debates about democracy then turn to consociation as a possible remedy for the repeated breakdowns of constitutional governance.

Nigerian Political Thought: Five Dominant Tendencies

Despite the venality of Nigerian politics, a systematic effort at political theorizing has been a pronounced characteristic since the 1950s. Five major themes may be identified in this unfolding national dialogue. Of all the voluminous writings by Nigerians on their country's political future, the two state-orchestrated debates, separated by ten years, stand out. The first came with the making of the Second Republic (1975–1978), culminating in the 1979 general election. The second great debate (1986–89) surrounded the proposed Third Republic Constitution, first scheduled for implementation in 1990, then shifted to 1992, and yet again, to 1993.

A dominant conclusion in the most recent efforts was a certain disillusionment with the parliamentary and the presidential systems of government that informed the establishment of the First and the Second Republics respectively. A strong desire emerged for a system at once indigenous, democratic and market-oriented, accommodating of all significant interest groups, yet enduring enough to last the century and beyond. These predispositions among the political literati were sharply focused in the 1989 Cookey Political Bureau recommendations. Some of the same issues would dominate the discussion in the 1994–95 debates, showing their continuing salience.

The Anglo-American Fixation

One predominant pattern in Nigerian politics could be described as a progressive adaptation of some Western model of which the most important have been the British parliamentary or the American presidential systems. This orientation has tended to see the Anglo-American experience as the very essence of democracy. This contestational, *adversarial* system involves a diverse, interests-based inter-party contestation in which fairly simple majorities govern through a two-chamber state structure, with the military expected to remain neutral, and the "loyal" political opposition patiently awaiting a future electoral mandate to attain office. This system was based upon a single-member district plurality electoral practice.

This liberal model, dominant in its parliamentary form in the 1950s, was accepted rather than generally desired, in deference to the colonial British authorities to speed a painless independence. The key political organizations of the political class were largely ethnically defined. The older, larger and more congress-like National Council of Nigerian Citizens (NCNC) was dominant among the Igbo, the ultimately successful Northern Peoples' Congress (NPC) mostly held sway among the Hausa-Fulani Muslims, and the opposition Action Group (AG), was ascendant among the Yoruba. The main intellectual debates in this perspective, especially in the 1950s, were between Nnamdi Azikiwe and Obafemi Awolowo at one level (Dudley 1973), and between southern progressives and northern spokesmen (a mix of progressives, regional nationalists and religious conservatives). These same groups or their ideological legatees, would again attain power along similar geo-ethnic lines at the start of the more presidential Second Republic. Interestingly, halfway through the life of both the First and Second Republics, on each occasion, as ideological leanings and interest-articulation become clearer, class crystallization moves increasingly to the fore alongside the more familiar demon of ethnicity.

Neo-Corporatist Ethno-Regionalism

Yet a pronounced tendency in Nigerian politics has been the urge to create a self-contained regional utopia within which a dominant ethnic coalition—there are no pure ethnic groups really—in a paternalistic fashion, serves as the constellation around which revolve the lesser formations. Then, the regional power brokers could enter into relations with the rest of the federal structure, but on the basis of this understanding. It was partly in response to this that the first wave of new states were created. Yet the additional states did not dim either the sense of a northern "Arewa" region, an Eastern CARIA—(Cross River, Abia, Rivers, Imo and Anambra)—network, or a Western "Oduduwa" tendency.

At the national level, this neo-corporatist model involved all the diverse elements of the Nigerian system, centering on the "traditional" and the modern business and professional elite in conjunction with the organized trade unions and the military. This however, is not all of a kind; two almost radically opposed strands of thinking here run the gamut from the conservative to the radical. This would include, on the "progressive" side, the early nationalists centered around the Nigerian Youth Movement and the pre-1950 NCNC leadership, including the radical "Zikist" tendency (Coleman 1958). For these nationalists, the issue was an attempt to build a mass party akin to the Indian Congress of Gandhi and Nehru. Awolowo exemplified this position following his radical conversion at the Jos Convention of his AG (Sklar 1963).

Ahmadu Bello and the conservative regionalist theoreticians of the NPC would most likely have agreed with the confederal implications of the notion that Nigeria was a "mere geographical expression" cobbled together by empire-building foreigners; unity, if it must be, should function under a corporatist framework if even this were feasible.[2] In general, the neo-corporatist, regionalist elite tendency was not really a cohesive force. These diverse thinkers owed a similarity in the comprehensiveness and similarity of their attempted incorporation of all the diverse elements in the system, perhaps with a score to be settled with recalcitrant "outliers" such as the Marxist far left.

Military-Bureaucratic Developmentalism

Following the demise of the First Republic in 1966 and the ensuing thirteen-year military interregnum, theorists of a bureaucratic authoritarian stripe began to make a case for a system in which the military could rule in conjunction with the bureaucracy to the exclusion of the political class and organized political parties (Dudley 1982, 86). Though a minority tendency up to the present, it was a pattern first articulated during Gowon's lengthy nine-year tenure by the "super permanent secretaries." This orientation drew upon a certain Western literature extolling the military as modernizers, and the example of the bureaucratic-authoritarian state in vogue in Latin America during the 1970s (O'Donnell 1979).

The Dyarchy Realpolitik Option

Since Azikiwe first articulated its modalities in his Mariere Lecture at the University of Lagos in 1972,[3] the volume and intensity with which the dyarchy proposal was debated suggested its vitality. Essentially, it sought to incorporate the three earlier positions, in a bid to forge a degree of ideological consensus of a centrist nature. The proposals taken together reflect five concerns: (i) the overriding need for political stability after a quarter century of intermittent upheaval; (ii) the imperative of rendering the military part and parcel of the state structure in an organic sense, rather than as some alienated watchdog awaiting the moment to "bite"; (iii) the need to institutionalize regional and ethnic social equity in such a manner that no section would feel disaffected on account of being ignored in high-level decision making; (iv) the wish for the same sense of justice to be carried forth to the economic realm, with the prevailing spatial distribution pattern of balanced regional "development" actually institutionalized beyond mere rhetoric; and (v) far more crucially, if the equity balance was to be achieved, for the central political post, the presidency, to be rotational, on a geoethnic basis.

Rotational Exercise of Power

A fifth tendency, it could be argued, is the one that led to the rotational provisions in the 1995 constitution. There is a strong anthropological basis for representation through conscious geo-political inclusiveness. This inheres in a deep-seated African sense of justice and fair play that remains dubious of the logic of majoritarian zero-sum power divisions. Each group, being more or less a semi-autonomous nationality, needs a seat at the table. In Africa where politics and ethnic collectivity, including a "homeland," tend to coincide at the early stages of development, zero-sum politics has the effect of permanently marginalizing those outside the power loop. Opposition thus assumes the character of revolt.

The cultural basis of politics has often been acknowledged in African precolonial polities; the sentiment is strong that African societies need to get back to a theory of "tribal" decision-making, with its realistic attributes of modern "coalitions." Historically, no monarch or body of elders made decisions except through procedural consensus building. And among the autonomous communities, notions of numerical supremacy had no bearing: each group, no matter how small, possessed an embedded sovereignty that did not acknowledge the sort of marginalization that might imperil its corporate existence.

This viewpoint comes across in the words of former Second Republic Vice-President Alex Ekwueme, an original proponent of regional zones on a confederal basis and rotational presidency, in his report of "the last National Constitutional Conference" where "we decided to tackle the problem head-on."

> The Igbo-speaking peoples . . . (desired to be) constituted into one region . . . This arrangement would have given each region the opportunity, as before, to develop at its own pace and within the limits of its resources under the great Nigerian umbrella. This would have resulted in an accelerated development of the whole country. It is true that we did not get a region. But . . . we got a zone. We can start from there.[4]

A survey of most comments at the conference, even the most far-fetched new-wave proponents with sophisticated models, demonstrates that without actually realizing it, most were in effect arguing for some measure of consociational democracy in the sense used by Lijphart (1977). For, despite the bitter disappointment with the shortcomings of the political class in the First and the Second Republics—and their pandering and disarray in the Third—very few are on record as arguing against democracy per se, even after the excesses of the Shagari era. Nor is there very much of an appetite for prolonged military rule.

For some intellectuals, the dream of a socialist alternative still exists, a sixth tendency led at one point by radicals and Marxists like the historian Bala Usman, the social anthropologist Ikenna Nzimiro, the economist Ola Oni, the labor leader Tunji Otegbeye, the mathematician Eddie Madunagu and the political scientist Okwudiba Nnoli. Though hardly a viable alternative, and today on the defensive in Nigeria and elsewhere, radical socialism may not be a completely spent force in highly stratified Nigeria. There is evidence that even the military, in the wake of the political and economic failures of the past three decades, may have become radicalized at the middle and junior ranks.

The 1995 Constitution: Towards a Consociational Future?

The 1995 constitution makers sounded triumphant in the victory of the rotational proviso redolent of a consociational ethos; there is no question that it may have bought the embattled regime a breather. They observe in the summary of the resolutions that the constitutional convention was "mindful of the need to avoid concentration of power in the hands of a few, or a sectional group, and the need to allay the fears in certain quarters that the position of the number one citizen of Nigeria is reserved for a particular area of the country." Therefore, "the Conference in its wisdom, and by consensus, agreed that the Presidency shall rotate between the North and the South . . . and that this principle of rotation shall go down the ladder" (Report of the Constitutional Conference 1995: II, 68).

Given its long history of inter-ethnic conflict, consociationalism of some sort arguably conforms to the incipient culturally-nuanced notion of the political "good society" in the Nigerian psyche. The consociational theories of Lijphart (1977) define the issue in terms of the "segmental cleavages" of plural societies and the imperative of "elite cooperation," drawn from the various segments. It "emphasizes the importance of a high degree of autonomy for each of the separate segments"; federalism or provincial devolution as well as the principle of proportionality in legislative, administrative and executive appointments being crucial ingredients for stability (Lijphart 1977, 146). Taking the cases of Belgium, Holland, Switzerland, and Austria as paradigmatic, Lijphart argues that the European consociational experience is of great normative interest for the Third World, because these countries attained their stability, "not because their societies are only mildly plural, but in spite of the deep segmental cleavages in other societies" (1977, 18).

The experience of the consociational states stands in sharp contrast to the troubled political histories of such countries as India, Nigeria, and Sri Lanka. Specifically addressing the Nigerian case, Lijphart (1977, 164) notes of the First Republic that the "chances for the survival of democracy in Nigeria might have been better if a consociational pattern had been adopted. The multiple ethnic balance of power and the geographic concentration of the ethnic segments were favorable factors."

The promise, as well as the mechanisms, for the instauration of consociational democracy are fairly clear in the Lijphart (1977, 228) conception:

> (I)t can be more plausibly argued that democracy, especially in its consociational form, is a better nation-builder than nondemocratic regimes. Although, in

the short run, consociational democracy tends to strengthen the plural character of a plural society, an extended period of successful consociational government may be able to resolve some of the major disagreements among the segments and thus to depoliticize segmental divergences, *and it may also create mutual trust at both elite and mass levels to render itself superfluous* (emphasis added).

The last portion is noteworthy, since in Lijphart's contention, a successful consociational democracy ultimately outgrows its consociational origins as the system of "mutual security" works into the social fabric.

The consociational option, however is anything but a ready-made panacea, as Jackson and Rosberg caution (1984, 421–42). Apart from the sheer reality that the give-and-take of democratic politics is relatively rare in the African experience, the consociational thesis assumes "conditions of institutional governance that have been largely, sometimes even entirely, absent from political life in most African countries." In fact the essence of their politics has been personalistic and discretionary, and not institutional and procedural. It may also exacerbate cultural insularity at the expense of national cohesion—not to speak of its capacity to foster a degree of mediocre leadership. As Powell (1982, 214) notes, the requirement in classic consociational systems of "mutual vetoes" could lead to the blockage of new policies by recalcitrant groups, "to the great advantage of the supporters of the status quo and the disadvantage of the have-nots." There is also the question of to what degree party leaders could control or retain the confidence of their followers.

A number of Nigerian commentators exhibit an informed awareness of the shortcomings of the consociational option. Others, such as the political scientist and politician C. Anieze Chinwuba, offer a sophisticated defence, worth citing at length to show the high faith placed in the new order by its proponents:

> For the first time in Nigeria's history, the principles of federal character and proportionality will be extensively applied, with a Federal Character Commission (FCC) (overseeing) the implementation of the federal character principle. The federation has been divided into six geopolitical zones (that) will share power and rotate the six to political offices . . . That way the peoples will develop mutual trust faster and the issue of marginalization will be gone. The extra factor that will be needed will be that of consociational leadership. It is clear that unless such leadership emerges, all will not be well. Such leaders must have the virtues of tolerance and accommodation and must show at all times that they are aware of the dangers inherent in their polity and are determined to keep the polity united . . . Nigeria's 1995 Constitution

comes closest to the consociational model of democracy (which) will go a long way to making the Federal Republic of Nigeria democratically governable.[5]

Rotational presidential democracy, then, has much to commend it. Important questions, however, remain. First is the moratorium on open-ended competition for a thirty-year stretch. This, presumably, ought to enable the Nigerian nation attain the stability it badly needs. Secondly, the new system should force the parties to practice a measure of geoethnic zonal representation, as is done out of force of habit in most mature political systems across the world, the wiser after decades, even centuries, of internecine conflict. In these systems, attempts are repeatedly made to ensure that leadership is never cornered by any segment of society for too long, for the nation then becomes obliged to benefit from a narrower base of real input and ultimate legitimacy.

As quickly came to the fore at the Constitutional Conference, the accidental dominance of the military/political organs of power in Nigeria by those from the former northern region could hardly be in the long-term interest of the nation as a whole, if only for the deep anxiety this has continued to evoke in the "south." The indication is strong that Nigerians would accord any leader a chance if only to see if he (or she) could deliver, but would then become sharply critical of the leadership's most blatant failings. This tendency has been repeatedly and powerfully expressed in the course of the nation's tortured history. Abiola's 1993 electoral lead, despite its improbable Muslim-Muslim ticket, was a clear indicator that while ethnicity and religion may have been a trap, they were far from being a lock. The problem was not with the people but with the jockeying power elite—especially the politically ambitious generals who nevertheless dread the prospects of submitting themselves to the electoral will of the people.

A Consociational Fourth Republic: Will It Work?

What is the likelihood that the rotational presidency will actually come to be implemented? Beside the determined opposition of a range of groupings—among them the exiled National Democratic Front inspired by the Nobel prize winner Wole Soyinka—there are as many doubts as there are ex post facto amendments to the new constitution. Already, the various signals have been mixed, with one being a suspected desire to hand-pick a number of associates nationwide as local government electors, but beholden to the center.

The grounds for optimism, in the wake of the precedent of Babangida's treacherous betrayal of faith, must always remain thin. Yet the preeminent challenge of seeking an enduring formula dictates an open mind toward the 1995 Constitution. But there is, in my view, a near-consensus in Nigeria as to the desirability of some form of power rotation among the various groupings. Even a cursory examination of the "Great Debates" that preceded the 1977 Constituent Assembly, or those ten years later that resulted in the Report of the Political Bureau, make clear that the old pattern of regional dominance can only be continued at increasing political and social costs.

Designing regimes requires, therefore, that power circulate rather than coagulate, that regional and individual equitable measures be vigorously pursued, and that the challenge of a viable economy be seen as the very first priority. There is nothing sacrosanct about Nigeria's latest political rearrangement of the checkerboard. Indeed, without attention to the residual problems of annulment of the 1993 election and the prolonged detention of several highly visible public figures, the transition may suffer from a negative perception of insincerity marked by a "hidden agenda" along Babangida's lines. Yet one could wager that of all the various constitutions, this has come closest to presenting a model of a viable system in conformity with the cultural ethos of inter-group equity. The question is open as to whether the rotational presidency option will succeed in fractious Nigeria—though the post-Babangida paralysis ensures that the political elite of a future "grand coalition" will understand that the alternative could be worse. Of course, the survival of any political arrangement will depend on more than consociational mechanisms. For the Nigerian citizenry the degree of social justice will be the ultimate measure.

Notes

1. Most theories of Nigerian political development—by Nigerian as well as foreign scholars—regardless of ideological leaning have been preoccupied, since the late colonial phase, with the question of ethnicity and its pervasive influence and implication. Electoral outcomes since the first general election in 1951/52 seem to confirm what Joseph (1987) has labelled "the ethnic trap." The notion of a "trap"—coined as a result of the outcome of the 1979 general election, the fourth for Nigeria—effectively describes an apparent reality that has recurred, regardless of a political leader's ideological stance or nationalist inclinations. Yet the contrary evidence has existed of the response by Nigerians to differentially-based patterns of interest articulation, even along strictly ideological lines. Regimes, however, have never lasted long enough for these tendencies to crystallize.

2. According to Paden, Ahmadu Bello "thought of himself as a politician, not as Emir of the North (*Sarkin Arewa*) . . . The Sardauna believed that if his own generation had been educated, the north would not be superseded . . . His main concern was the *north*, and northernization was the cornerstone of his belief. i.e., how the people of the north could resist domination by the southerners at the federal and state levels. Yet the Sardauna was a nationalist as well as a regionalist. His tendency was to *unite* people . . . He felt that if the main tribes, Hausa, Yoruba and Igbos, understood each other, there would be less trouble" (Paden 1986, 173).

3. This lecture at the University of Lagos is far better-known than his more sober theoretical work, *Ideology For Nigeria* (1979).

4. This quotation is drawn from his keynote address at the Second Annual Conference of the World Igbo Congress, Los Angeles, 7–9 October 1995.

5. Speech delivered to the Organization of Nigerian Professionals Annual Convention, Kansas City, Missouri, November 1995.

References

Coleman, James S. 1958. *Nigeria: Background to Nationalism*. Berkeley: University of California Press.
Dudley, Billy J. 1973. *Instability and Political Order*. Ibadan: Ibadan University Press.
———. 1982. *An Introduction To Nigerian Government and Politics*. Bloomington: Indiana University Press.
Jackson, Robert H. and Carl G. Rosberg. 1984. "Personal Rule: Theory and Practice in Africa." *Comparative Politics*, (July): 421–42.
Joseph, Richard A. 1987. *Democracy and Prebendal Politics in Nigeria*. Cambridge: Cambridge University Press.
Lewis, W. Arthur. 1965. *Politics in West Africa*. New York: Oxford University Press.
Lijphart, Arend. 1977. *Democracy in Plural Societies: A Comparative Exploration*. New Haven: Yale University Press.
O'Donnell, Guilliermo. 1979. "Tensions in the Bureaucratic Authoritarian State and the Transition to Democracy." In David Collier (ed.), *The New Authoritarianism in Latin America*. Princeton: Princeton University Press.
Paden, John N. 1986. *Ahmadu Bello, Sardauna of Sokoto: Values and Leadership in Nigeria*. London: Hodder and Stoughton.
Powell, G. Bingham. 1982. *Contemporary Democracies: Participation, Stability and Violence*. Cambridge: Harvard University Press.
Report of the Constitutional Conference Containing the Resolutions and Recommendation. 1995. Abuja.
Sklar, Richard L. 1963. *Nigerian Political Parties*. Princeton: Princeton University Press.

16

FEDERALISM, ETHNICITY AND REGIONALISM IN NIGERIA

Rotimi T. Suberu

Nigeria's deep ethnic, regional and religious divisions have made the goal of institutionalizing an enduring system of democratic governance paradoxically both structurally compelling and profoundly problematic. The country's cultural pluralism, it has been observed, "defies successful management through any but democratic and rigorously federalist principles" (Diamond 1991, 55). The presence of "competitive regional and ethnic blocs of the population" not only makes a full-fledged authoritarian system of government unworkable and unthinkable, but also yields a relentless concern with the development of rules, institutions and norms for the accommodation and mediation of diverse group interests (Joseph 1991, 4). For this reason, Nigeria, in spite of its cyclical institutional crises and internecine political conflicts, retains enormous promise as an important African experiment in the creative management of diversity through more or less accommodative or consensual policies and practices.

At the same time, Nigeria's turbulent constitutional odyssey in the post-independence era partly illustrates the tensions that exist between the country's cultural divisions and its federal democratic aspirations. As poignantly demonstrated by developments in the First Nigerian Republic (1960–66), the competitive manipulation and political polarization of ethnic and regional identities have sometimes become so intensive and disintegrative as to endanger the integrity and continuity of the democratic process (Diamond 1988). What is more, the existence of deep-rooted sectional attachments may inhibit the development of the broad societal consensus necessary to support and sustain democratic institutions. Indeed, Nigerian ethnicity severely constrains democratic discourse and procedures, often subordinating the universal democratic values of egalitarian participation and political accountability to particularistic debates and strategies over relative communal access to powers, positions and resources (cf. Szetfel 1994). The tendency to reduce democracy to sectional political competition for positions and resources not only erodes the authenticity of the democratic system, but may also come to endanger the legitimacy and viability of the multi-ethnic state itself (Whitaker 1991, 269).

Such tensions and contradictions, to reiterate, partly account for the structural fragility of democracy and the political visibility of the military in Nigeria. In more than 35 years of independence, Nigeria has been governed by military elites for over 25 years, and by civilian politicians only during brief interregnums in the First Republic and the Second Republic (1979–83). But the military have probably proved to be worse managers of Nigeria's cultural diversity than the civilian politicians. Indeed, according to Matthew Hassan Kukah (1991, 13) "democratic political activities, no matter how limited their ideals have been, have offered a better scope for intercommunal and interreligious integration as politicians seek adherents right across the ethnic or religious divide." The military, on the other hand, have often been driven by the authoritarian, unitarian and often arbitrary or whimsical character of their rule to undermine the delicate basis of Nigeria's federal unity. As former civilian president Shehu Shagari recently lamented, the Nigerian "federal system . . . has been badly battered by the military command system" (*Newswatch* 4 April 1994, 13).

Apart from the tragic Nigerian-Biafran civil war (1967–1970), probably no other event in Nigeria's post-independence political history has better illustrated the precarious and contentious nature of Nigeria's unity, and the contribution of the military to this divisiveness, than the crisis precipitated by the annulment of the results of the presidential election of June 12 1993 by Nigeria's former military president, General Ibrahim Babangida. Succinctly, the brazen abrogation of the imminent electoral victory of a southern presidential candidate, after what many have described as almost three decades of virtually uninterrupted northern monopoly on federal executive power, has spawned a vexatious debate about the manifold inequities and inconsistencies of Nigerian federalism. As reflected in discussions within and outside the Constitutional Conference convened in 1994 by the military administration of General Sani Abacha to fashion a constitution for a future democratic Nigerian Republic, this debate has involved at least four specific issues, namely, the character of ethnic power-sharing in the federation; the politics of resource distribution or revenue allocation; the internal territorial configuration of the federation; and the issue of alternative political structures and futures for multi-ethnic Nigeria.

Power-Sharing and the Federal Character Principle

Since the introduction of an American-style executive presidential system under the 1979 Constitution for the Second Republic, the control of federal executive power in general, and the presidency in particular, has generated deep ethnoregional contention. The 1979 Constitution had tried to contain this acrimony by the requirement that the election of the president, and the composition of his cabinet, should reflect the "federal character" or cultural diversity of the country. Consequently, the President was required to obtain a quarter of the votes in each of at least two-thirds of all the states in order to be elected directly, and to appoint one member from each state of the federation into his cabinet. Under the mandatory, two-party system of the 1989 Constitution for the abrogated, still-born Third Republic, the threshold requirement for the direct election of the president was raised to one-third of the votes in two-thirds of the states, plus a majority, rather than the old requirement for a simple plurality of the votes cast (Suberu 1993, 48). But these provisions have failed to contain fears and allegations of ethnoregional domination of the presidency. To illustrate, several radical proposals for a more ethnically equitable system of executive power-sharing came forward in the process of consideration by the 1994–95 Constitutional Conference. The more prominent of these proposals were:

1. The constitutionalization or formalization of an arrangement for rotating the presidency of the Federal Republic among some recognized geo-ethnic zones of the country. Known as "rotation" or "zoning," this proposal was an implicit stratagem of the ruling party of the Second Republic, the National Party of Nigeria (NPN), and the two official parties of the abortive Third Republic, the National Republican Convention (NRC) and the Social Democratic Party (SDP). Reflecting growing southern paranoia about northern political domination, however, pressures have recently developed for the transformation of "zoning" from an implicit convention of the parties into an explicit and entrenched constitutional provision of the Nigerian State (Ekwueme 1995).

2. The prohibition of consecutive presidential terms or the restriction of each elected president to a single, nonrenewable five-year term. This proposal is often canvassed as an important institutional adjunct to the idea of rotation. In the words of Second Republic Vice-President, Alex Ekwueme (1995), "with the introduction of rotation between zones . . . a single term at a time for each chief executive will ensure a faster rate of rotation." It should be noted, however, that the idea of single terms for political chief executives has the distinct additional potential value of preventing the violence and violations that invariably accompany the reelection bids of political incumbents in Nigeria (Suberu 1993, 50).
3. A multiple vice-presidential system, in which three or more vice-presidents, nominated from different regions of the country, will be elected along with the President. The proposal is intended to allow for the simultaneous representation of the three majority ethnicities and the minorities at the summit of federal executive power. According to its proponents, the multiple vice-presidential arrangement, like the rotatory presidency, would give every region of the federation "a feeling of belonging and sense of participation" in the governance of the country, thereby reducing the fears of sectional domination or marginalization (Ekwueme 1992, 9).
4. A French-style presidential-parliamentary system in which the offices of President and Prime Minister shall be constituted and defined in such a way as to vary, broaden and balance the regional base of federal power. Underlying this proposal is the belief that the undiluted application of American-style presidentialism is unsuited to Nigerian federalism. In the words of one former NRC leader:

> The presidential system, by virtue of the fact that it concentrates total executive powers and functions in the hands of one man, cannot be suitable to Nigeria without very substantial modification. The (president's) near-absolute power to control and distribute resources is the propelling force creating the present heightened geopolitical power confrontation which . . . may rupture the very fabric of our society (Okupe 1992, 8).

5. A full-fledged reversion to the First Republic's Westminster parliamentary system, which is considered to be more institutionally conducive to ethnic power-sharing than the presidential system (Lijphart 1977, 33). In the words of the eminent Nigerian nationalist, Chief Anthony Enahoro, "The parliamentary system recom-

mends itself because of its institutional safeguards, paramount among which is collective responsibility. The cabinet collectively, not the prime-minister alone, as in a presidency, is the executive" (*Sunday Concord* 14 March 1993, 6).
6. The establishment of a Swiss-type federal collegiate council in which (i) federal executive powers shall be collectively exercised by representatives of the country's principal geoethnic zones and (ii) the chairmanship or presidency of the council shall be rotated annually among these representatives (*Vanguard* 17 October 1994, 1).
7. A national coalition or "unity" government in which all major parties shall be adequately and equitably represented in the executive. Specifically, the Constitutional Conference proposed that any party winning not less than 10 percent of seats in the legislature shall be entitled to representation in the cabinet in proportion to the seats won.

In October 1995, the Abacha Government gave partial satisfaction to the agitations for power-sharing by endorsing a presidential-parliamentary system for the proposed Fourth Republic. Under this system, the six key offices of President, Vice-President, Prime Minister, Deputy Prime Minister, Senate President and Speaker of the House of Representatives will be rotated for an experimental 30-year period among six broad geoethnic zones of the country, namely, the north-west, north-east, middle-belt, south-west, south-east and southern minority. A non-renewable five-year tenure for all executive and legislative incumbents is to ensure the rotation of the designated key offices among all six zones by the end of the 30-year period. In addition to this power-sharing arrangement, the Abacha Government approved and implemented the recommendation of the Constitutional Conference that a Federal Character Commission be set up to ensure the equitable distribution of all cadres of public offices and positions among the component units and segments of the Federation.

Yet, much of the contemporary advocacy of power-sharing in Nigeria has been criticized on several grounds. First, these power-sharing proposals often detract from the putative roles of Nigeria's federalism and presidentialism as integrative institutional mechanisms, rather than simply as instruments for reproducing or reinforcing the country's inherent ethnic divisiveness and competitiveness. It was for this reason that the Political Bureau in 1986 dismissed suggestions "for a constitutional provision for rotation" as "an acceptance of our inability to grow beyond ethnic or state loyalty" (Federal Republic of Nigeria 1987, 74). Second, most of these proposals have the potential impact of reinforcing the destructive patrimonialism of Nigerian politics in which political offices are reduced to an object of institutionalized appropriation by sectional elites and their constituents (Joseph 1991). Third, by actually paying relatively little attention to mass-based ethnic concerns, and giving such overriding consideration to the distribution of political offices among sectional elites, these proposals may do little to promote genuine interethnic unity and equity. Rather, they may amount to no more than "a cynical and manipulative mechanism for bourgeois domination," to use Edwin Madunagu's words (Madunagu 1993, 13). Fourth, even among their proponents, many of these proposals have remained profoundly nebulous and contentious. For instance, there has been little or no consensus among advocates of rotational presidency on such basic issues as the demarcation or configuration of the geoethnic zones in the rotatory scheme, the precise ethnic sequencing of the rotatory process, and the overall time frame for implementing such a potentially complex and problematic scheme. Fifth, some of the proposals are antidemocratic since they often detract from the democratic autonomy and responsibility of parties and electorates freely to select or elect key political representatives. Sixth, as already indicated, most of the proposals actually stem from southern paranoia about northern political domination. Meanwhile, elements from the Hausa-Fulani north have portrayed these proposals for power-sharing as "a grand design to exclude them from the scheme of things in a spirit of grand revenge" (*Tell* 29 May 1995, 20). Moreover, they have pointed to the reality and enormity of continuing southern, especially Yoruba, educational, economic and, possibly, bureaucratic domination: an imbalance that has not been rectified by various policies that enforce the "federal character" and/or state equality quotas in education, the bureaucracy, and government-owned enterprises.

Finally, perhaps the most compelling argument that can be made against most of these proposals is that they merely seek to palliate, rather than effectively address, the fundamental problem of Nigerian federalism, namely, the overconcentration of powers and resources in the national government, and the destructive and divisive struggles for control of the center that this centralization invariably engenders (Ekpu 1994, 6). In essence, in the words of ex-Governor Bola Ige (1995b, 2), the key challenge for constitutional design in Nigeria is not the "sharing of positions" but the elaboration of strategies for decentralizing or redistributing powers *and* resources. Although the devolution of federal powers to the states and localities emerged as an important theme in Abacha's transition program, little official attention has been given to the related, but even more critical, issue of the reform of the revenue sharing system.

The Politics of Revenue Sharing

Put succinctly, Nigeria's current revenue sharing principles and practices are a recipe for interethnic tension and intergovernmental contention. Reflecting the country's overwhelming dependence on centralized petroleum export revenues and the simplistic and largely self-serving formulae that have been invoked by the military in allocating these revenues, Nigeria's revenue sharing debates have revolved basically around three issues, namely, (i) the relative proportions of federally collected revenues in the "Federation Account" that should be assigned to the center, the states, the localities and the so-called "Special Funds" (vertical revenue sharing); (ii) the appropriate formulae for the distribution of centrally devolved revenues among the states and among the localities (horizontal revenue sharing) and; (iii) the percentage of federally-collected mineral revenues that should be returned to the oil-producing states and communities on account of the principles of derivation and as compensation for the ecological risks of oil production.

It is possible to speak of a broad, national consensus in Nigeria on the need to prune or streamline the financial resources available to the federal government vis-à-vis the other levels of government. This consensus has emerged as an inevitable riposte to the destabilizing consequences of the continuing financial hegemony of the center in Nigerian federalism.

In the post-war era of "military federalism" from 1970 to 1979, the federal government consistently appropriated about 75 percent of the financial resources of the federation. But the succeeding civilian constitutional government of Shehu Shagari committed itself to "trimming the federal government's resources to the bare bones in the interest of fiscal federalism" (*West Africa* 24 December 1980, 2470). Although that government subsequently reduced the center's share of the federation account to 55 percent, it continued to face intensive pressures for greater financial devolutions to the lower tiers of government. (See Table 16.1.)

These decentralist pressures were ostensibly given satisfaction by the administration of General Babangida, which reduced the allocation to the center to 48.5 percent of the Federation Account, and increased the share of the localities to 20 percent (Danjuma 1994). But Babangida's decentralist rhetoric was heavily contradicted by the sharp reduction in the allocation to the states from 30.5 to 24 percent of the Federation Account, by the transfer of many central responsibilities to the localities, by the Federal Government's continued discretionary control of up to eight percent of the Federation Account designated as special funds and, most importantly, by

348   *Dilemmas of Democracy in Nigeria*

Table 16.1. Vertical Allocation of the Federation Account, 1981–1995

ITEMS	Initial 1981 Act (Nullified by Supreme Court in October 1981)	Revised 1981 Act	1990	January 1992	June 1992 to Date	NRMAFC[a] Proposals	Proposals of the NCC Committee on Revenue Allocation
Federal Government	55	55	50	50	48.5	47	33
State Government	26.5	30.5	30	25	24	30	32.5
Local Governments	10	10	15	20	20	15	20
Special Funds:							
a. Derivation (Oil-producting States)	2	2	1	1	1	2	—
b. Dev. of Mineral Producting Aras	3	1.5	1.5	1.5	3	2	6.5
c. Initial Dev. of FCT, Abuja[b]	2.5	—	1	1	1	1	2
d. General Ecological Problems	1	1	1	1	2	0.5	2.5
e. Stabilization	—	—	—	—	—	2	—
f. Savings	—	—	—	—	—	—	3.0
g. Other Special Projects	—	—	.5	.5	.5	.5	1
Subtotal of Special Funds	8.5	4.5	5	5	7.5	8	14.5
Total 100	100	100	100	100	100	100	100

Sources: Adapted from *New Nigerian* 26 February 1981; Danjuma (1994, 57); and National Constitutional conference (1994, 13 and 30).
Notes: (a) The National Revenue Mobilization Allocation and Fiscal Commission, inaugurated by General Babangida in September 1988. (b) Abuja, the Federal Capital Territory, enjoys the statutory status of a state for revenue sharing purposes and, therefore, may partake in the states' shares of federal revenues.

the Administration's systematic unilateral and extra-legal deductions from the Federation Account. The Abacha government has continued the practice of deliberately manipulating and understating the amount of revenues available for devolution to the states and localities under the Federation Account (*The Guardian* 26 February 1996, 10).

In essence, recent and ongoing attempts officially to decentralize resources to the subfederal authorities in Nigeria still fall short of the expectations of concerned segments of the population. The Political Bureau, for instance, reported a nationwide consensus around a 40:40:20 division of the Federation Account between the center, the states and the localities, while the Revenue Allocation Committee of the Constitutional Conference proposed a 33:32.5:20 sharing formula with the remaining 14.5 percent of the Federation Account going to "special funds" (National Constitutional Conference 1994, 30). These decentralist pressures and related proposals will have to be conceded in the interest of balanced federal governance, or resisted at the price of continued instability and imbalance.

The issue of the appropriate criteria for sharing central revenues among the subfederal units, especially the regions or states, has traditionally been the most divisive distributive issue in Nigeria. Following the civil war, the Gowon administration sought to contain this divisiveness by resorting to two simplistic criteria of horizontal allocation, namely, relative population and equality.

The subsequent periodic modifications of these allocative criteria (Table 2) have achieved three things. First, they have effectively legitimized the criteria of demography and equality as the preeminent principles of horizontal revenue sharing in Nigeria. Currently, for instance, both principles carry a combined weight of 70 percent (i.e., 40 percent to equality and 30 percent to population) in the horizontal revenue sharing scheme. Yet, the role of these principles in fuelling the disruptive ethnic pressures for the creation of new constituent units, and the falsification and politicization of population counts, is broadly recognized and widely lamented. But both principles have remained popular officially because of their ostensibly "neutral," noncontroversial and equitable character.

Second, the periodic changes in the horizontal revenue sharing system have largely compounded the scheme's intensely political and divisive nature. For instance, in 1990, the Babangida Administration re-introduced, and then assigned a weight of 10 percent to, the discredited principle of land mass. Ethnoregional opposition to this apparent bias in favor of the North (which, with only about half of the nation's population, encompasses some three quarters of the national territory) led some southern

Table 16.2. Horizontal Revenue Allocation Formulae, 1970–1995

	Percentage Weight Assigned					
Principles	1970–80	Initial 1981 Act	Revised 1981 Act	1990 to Date	Proposals of NRMAFC	Proposals of NCC Committee on Revenue Allocation
Equality of States (Minimum Responsibility of Government)	50	50	40	40	40	30
Population	50	40	40	30	30	40
Social Development Factor	—	—	15	10	10	—
Internal Revenue Generational Effort	—	—	5	10	20	10
Land Mass and/or Terrain	—	10	—	10	—	10
Population Density	—	—	—	—	—	10
Total	100	100	100	100	100	100

Source: *New Nigerian*, 26 February 1981; and National Constitutional Conference/NCC (1994, 14 and 30).

members of the NCC to propose the inclusion of the countervailing "political" principle of "population density" in the horizontal revenue sharing scheme. The primary effect of such regional political maneuvers is to deprive the nation of the development of a coherent revenue sharing scheme that balances "efficiency" and "equity" principles of allocation in a politically healthy and economically productive manner.

Finally, Nigeria's horizontal revenue sharing policies and reforms over the years give insufficient recognition to such largely nonpolitical principles of allocation as the social development factor and internal revenue generation effort, while blatantly ignoring such other technical principles as budgetary obligation, absorptive capacity, fiscal efficiency and fiscal equalization.

The intergovernmental and ethnoregional tensions and suspicions associated with vertical and horizontal revenue sharing in Nigeria are underscored by ongoing controversies over the sharing of the proceeds of the centrally administered Value Added Tax (VAT). Introduced in January 1994 to replace the unsuccessful state-based sales tax, VAT yielded impressive total revenues of 8.6 and 21 billion naira in 1994 and 1995 respectively (*The Guardian* 16 February 1996, 18). The VAT proceeds were originally and statutorily designed to be shared in the order of 80 percent to the states and 20 percent to the federal government to offset the administrative costs of VAT (*Business Times* 12 December 1994, 16). In January 1995, however, the federal government increased its share of VAT proceeds to 50 percent, reduced that of the states to 25 percent, and assigned the balance to the localities (*Daily Times* 17 January 1995, 1). Trenchant criticisms of this brazen assault on fiscal federalism led General Abacha to announce the following sharing formula for VAT in February 1996: 40 percent to the states and the Federal Capital Territory, Abuja; 35 percent to the federal government; and 25 percent to the localities (*The Guardian* 16 February, 18). Yet, an even more perverse feature of the VAT regime is the federal government's distortion, politicization and centralization of the interstate sharing arrangements, with the consequence that the returns to the biggest contributors to VAT (mainly Lagos and other southern states) are "almost inversely proportional to their contributions" (*Daily Times* 14 January 1995, 1; *Nigerian Tribune* 9 October 1995, 1; Bauchi 1995, F1).

In essence, Nigeria's vertical and horizontal revenue sharing formulae give little consideration to the need to decentralize resources, depoliticize and rationalize the resource allocation process, and encourage Nigeria's financially anaemic states and localities to become more competitive, and less dependent on central revenues. Yet, as the Revenue Allocation Committee of the Constitutional Conference was constrained to acknowledge, "A revenue allocation formula that tends more towards revenue sharing than to generation is a serious depressant to economic development for it generates ethnic rivalry and rancor, and makes government less productive" (National Constitutional Conference 1994, 7–8).

Perhaps the most acrimonious distributional issue in Nigeria today involves the increasingly strident campaign for economic restitution and ecological rehabilitation by the country's oil-producing ethnic minority communities around the Delta region in the south. Since the dramatic expansion in petroleum export revenues in the seventies, Nigeria's revenue sharing policies have explicitly downgraded, and sometimes eliminated, the principle of derivation as a criterion of entitlement. At the same time, relatively little official attention has been given to the need to compensate the oil-bearing areas for the ecological problems of mineral exploration, which difficulties have been compounded by the naturally difficult (usually swampy and creeky) terrain of these areas. Consequently, there has been an upsurge of economic nationalism in the oil rich areas. This has involved vigorous demands for wide-ranging institutional and distributional reforms, including: the amendment of the Nigerian constitution to make mining and minerals a joint federal-state, rather than exclusively federal, responsibility; the vesting of mineral land rents, and perhaps oil royalties, in the communities or states of derivation, rather than in the federal government; the payment of a significant proportion of federally-collected petroleum profits tax to the oil-producing regions in consonance with the principle of derivation; the establishment of appropriate institutional and financial arrangements by which the oil-producing communities may be compensated for, or protected against, the ecological problems and risks of oil exploration and exploitation; the establishment of appropriate legislation to compel the state-backed multinational oil companies to protect the environmental rights, and identify with the developmental aspirations, of their host (oil-producing) communities; and the recasting of Nigeria's defective federal system along genuinely federal, or even ethnoconfederal, lines in order to afford greater autonomy and security to ethnic minority communities (Saro-Wiwa 1992, 1994).

Since the publication and circulation of the *Ogoni Bill of Rights* in 1990, the estimated half million Ogoni people of Rivers State have emerged as the most articulate and militant protagonists for the politico-economic rights of Nigeria's embittered oil-producing minority communities.

Government's response to the agitation by the Ogoni and other oil-producing communities has included the proscription of ethnic minority (and related) associations, the announcement of a treasonable offences law for ethnic minority activists, the military invasion and repression of restive oil-producing communities, and the harassment, detention and arbitrary prosecution of crusading ethnic minority elites, including the noted Ogoni leader and writer Ken Saro-Wiwa. Following a quasi-judicial trial that was denounced as "wrong, illogical, perverse (and) downright dishonest," Ken Saro-Wiwa and eight other Ogoni activists were executed on 10 November 1995 for their alleged roles in the gruesome murders of four pro-government Ogoni elders on May 21 1994 (Birnbaum 1996, 12).

On a more positive note, the federal government in June 1992 announced the establishment of an Oil Mineral Producing Areas Development Commission (OMPADEC). The Commission was assigned three percent of mineral revenues under the "special funds" of the Federation Account. It was charged with undertaking a massive program of ecological rehabilitation and economic development in the oil-rich areas. In addition, in October 1995, the federal government formally endorsed (but did not implement) the recommendation of a plenary session of the Constitutional Conference that 13 percent of revenues from natural and mineral resources be allocated on the basis of derivation as a way of compensating "communities which suffer ecological degradation as a result of the exploitation in their areas" (*Vanguard* 3 October 1995, 10). While these concessions to the oil-producing communities have been undermined by the increasingly murky administrative politics of OMPADEC, and denounced by a few rabid chauvinists from outside the oil-rich areas, it is broadly recognized that the long-term survival of the Nigerian state requires that the southern minorities be compensated for years of neglect and expropriation.

How Many States and Localities?

The role of revenue sharing practices in inducing inexhaustible pressures for the creation of new states and localities has been noted. In 36 years of independence, Nigeria has been fragmented from its original three federal regions into 36 constituent states, with ongoing pressures for creation of some 40 or more new states! Analogous pressures beset the local government system, which has expanded from 301 localities in 1976 to 589 in 1995, with agitations for the establishment of an additional one thousand units of local government!

TABLE 16.3: RECENT DEMANDS FOR NEW STATES IN NIGERIA

Present State	Proposed State	Proposed Capital	Predominant Ethnic Composition
Abia	Aba	Aba	Igbo
Adamawa	Sarduana	Mubi	Hausa-Fulani/NM
Akwa Ibom	Atlantic	Oron	SM
	Itai	Ikot-Ekpene	SM
Anambra	Ezu	Awka	Igbo
Bauchi	Gombe	Gombe	Hausa-Fulani
	Katagum	Azare	Hausa-Fulani
Benue	Apa	Otukpo	NM
	Katsina Ala	Zaki-Ibiam	NM
Cross River	Ogoja	Ikom	SM
Delta	Anioma	Asaba	Igbo
	New Delta	Warri	SM
	Ndokwa	Utagba-Ogbe	Igbo
	Toru-Ebe	Patani	SM
Edo	Afemesan	Auchi	SM
Enugu/Abia	Ebonyi	Abakaliki or Afikpo	Igbo
Imo	Njaba	Okigwe	Igbo
Jigawa	Bayajida	Daura, Kazaure or Gumel	Hausa-Fulani
	Hadejia	Hadejia	Hausa-Fulani
	Lautai	Hadejia	Hausa-Fulani
Kaduna	Gurara	Zonkwa or Kafanchan	NM
Kano	Gari	Dambatta	Hausa-Fulani
	Tiga	—	Hausa-Fulani
	Tigari	Gwarzo	Hausa-Fulani
Katsina	Karaduwa	—	Hausa-Fulani
Kogi	Okura	Idah	NM
	Okun	Kabba	Yoruba
Kwara	Yoruba	Ilorin	Yoruba
Kwara/Kogi	Oyi	Kabba	Yoruba
Niger	Kainji	Kontagara	NM
	Ndaduma	Bida	NM
Ogun	Ijebu-Remo	Ijebu-Ode	Yoruba
Ondo	Ekiti	Ado-Ekiti	Yoruba
Osun	Oduduwa	Ile-Ife or Ilesa	Yoruba
Oyo	New Oyo	Ogbomoso or Oyo	Yoruba
	Oke-Ogun	Saki or Iseyin	Yoruba
Plateau	Nasarawa	Akwanga or Lafia	NM
Rivers	New Rivers	Port-Harcourt South	SM
	Nun-River or Oloibiri	Ogbia or Nembe	SM
	Ogoni	Bori	SM
	Orashi	Ahoada	SM
	Port-Harcourt	Port-Harcourt	SM
Rivers/Delta	Bayelsa	Sagbama	SM
Sokoto	Sakkwato	Sokoto	Hausa-Fulani
	Zamfara	Gusau	Hausa-Fulani/NM
Taraba	Kwararafa	Wukari	NM
	Mambilla	—	NM

Source: Adapted from Report of the Committee on State-Creation, National Constitutional Conference, Abuja, 1995. Key: NM = Northern Minorities SM = Southern Minorities

There can be little doubt that these atomistic pressures constitute a major source of structural instability, regional anxiety and intercommunal envy and enmity in the Nigerian federation today. In the first place, it is now widely recognized that the successive changes in the internal territorial configuration of the federation have served more to satisfy the distributive ambitions of the three ethnic majority formations of Hausa-Fulani, Yoruba and Igbo, than to assuage the fears of politically vulnerable ethnic minority communities. For instance, while *each* of the three majority groups has been divided into no less than four states, the over two hundred ethnic minority communities have been squeezed into a little over ten states. Thus, the prominent minority Ijaw community has trenchantly denounced the current 36-state structure as "fraudulent," and a "clear embodiment of the moral bankruptcy" of the Nigerian system of federalism (*The Guardian* 13 March 1994, A14).

Second, territorial changes in Nigeria have often spawned profound disagreements over the choice, ethnoterritorial composition and location of the administrative headquarters of the new states or localities, and over the disposition of the assets and personnel of the old units from which the new ones had been excised. These disagreements are often compounded, if not generated in the first place, by the arbitrariness arising from the creation of virtually all the Nigerian states and localities by military fiat, rather than by popular ratification and/or constitutional legislation and proclamation. What is more, the creation of new states and local governments immediately fuels pressures for discrimination against new classes of so-called non-indigenes, that is, Nigerians resident in states or local governments other than their own. All of this makes the creation of new states and localities in Nigeria an extremely divisive and disruptive exercise.

Third, Nigeria's internal territorial reforms have remained pathetically inconclusive, as each successive exercise in state and local reorganizations has spawned new minorities, antipathies and agitations for still other new states and localities. The cyclical character of territorial changes in Nigeria contrasts sharply with experiences in most other federations, where initial reforms of state and/or local boundaries have been followed by periods of fairly stable consensus on the internal territorial configuration or morphology of the federal system (McHenry 1986).

Fourth, as Nigeria continues to totter under the impact of its worst economic crisis since independence, the negative economic or financial implications of establishing new state and local administrations are becoming increasingly obvious. Beyond the expansion of bureaucratic and physical infrastructures in the newly established administrative headquarters, the developmental (as distinct from distributive) value of new state and local administrations has become profoundly dubious. Whatever financial devolutions accrue to the new constituent units from the revenue sharing system are immediately consumed by administrative overheads and new patronage positions, which leave little resources for real development.

Fifth, there is the general realization in Nigeria that, far from reflecting a genuine desire officially to resolve some continuing anomalies or inequities in the federal territorial structure, the creation of new states and localities is being promoted and manipulated by the military as a way of prolonging and legitimizing its stay in power and, therefore, circumventing or undermining the redemocratization project. Not surprisingly, the creation of new states and localities has featured prominently in the contentious and circuitous political transition programs of both Generals Babangida and Abacha.

Finally, and most importantly, at a time of deep dissatisfaction and intensive frustration with the overcentralization of the federal system, the repeated creation or proliferation of new constituent units can only compound the imbalance in the intergovernmental system. This is because, in Larry Diamond's words, "the greater the number of states, the weaker and less viable individual states will become, with the direct consequence that the center would actually gather more powers and initiative" (Diamond 1987, 211). Moreover, the direct role of the federal government in reorganizing the boundaries and redefining the structure of the localities is a blatant centrist assault on the received federal doctrine regarding the rights of state administrations and local populations to determine the nature of local authorities. According to Bola Ige, "Today, Nigeria is the only country in the world which says it is federal, but where local government affairs are directed from the federal capital" (Ige 1995a, 34).

Alternative Political Options for Nigeria

The continuing dissatisfaction with, and apprehension about, Nigeria's federal practices and unity has provoked a rigorous debate on alternative political structures and futures for the country. As in Canada, a federation that has also recently been "in question," three broad perspectives have dominated this debate (Watts 1991, 189).

The first perspective proposes a wide range of measures for reforming, improving, and generally decentralizing Nigeria's federal system. The most widely supported reform proposals within this perspective include:

the redistribution of constitutional powers and functions away from the center and in favor of the states and localities; the revision of the revenue-sharing system in order to promote greater financial autonomy and viability at the subfederal level; the modification of the intergovernmental structure to include grassroots, community-level associations or councils as the fourth tier of federal governance; the introduction of effective power-sharing mechanisms and other accommodative arrangements, especially at the federal level; the implementation of special measures to secure the rights of ethnic and religious minorities, including the oil-producing areas; and, most crucially, the rapid democratization of the political system in order to put an end to the current defective system of "military federalism" (Suberu 1993; Olowu 1994). Despite its considerable appeal, the value of this broad political perspective is limited by the absence of any consensus among its proponents regarding the appropriate mix or choice of reform measures, by the continuing hegemony and contumacy of centralizing military elites, and by the severe distortions inherent in the country's mono-mineral political economy.

The second tendency in the debate about Nigeria's political future proposes the restructuring of the Nigerian state along ethnoconfederal lines. But there also has been very little consensus or clarity regarding the composition of the ethnic federations that would make up the proposed Nigerian confederation. However, the Movement for National Reformation/MNR (1993) has published a position paper advocating the recasting of Nigeria into a Union of the following eight federations: Western Federation (comprising the present Lagos, Ogun, Ondo, Osun and Oyo states); South-Central Federation (Edo and Delta States); East-Central Federation (Abia, Anambra, Enugu and Imo); South-Eastern Federation (Akwa Ibom, Cross River and Rivers); Central Federation (Bauchi, Benue, Kaduna and Plateau); North-Eastern Federation (Adamawa, Borno, Taraba and Yobe); Northern Federation (Jigawa, Kano, Katsina, Kebbi and Sokoto); West-Central Federation (Niger, Kogi and Kwara).

Despite the MNR's elaborate proposals, the feasibility or viability of a Nigerian confederation is very dubious indeed. To quote Chuba Okadigbo (1986, 12):

> ... a Nigerian confederation, though perhaps desirable, will be very difficult to negotiate and even harder to create ... Who will implement a confederal plan - the soldiers from Northern Nigeria with cards placed face down, or those from the Middle Belt States ... who may become very vulnerable to domination by their brethren of the far Northern sector? Or do the advocates of confederation think that Nigerians will gladly gather round

a table and gleefully dispense of the federation and its resources by sheer appeal to simple and often fraudulent geographical stratifications?

Moreover, given the volatility and complexity of Nigeria's cultural divisions, it should be obvious that the country's ethnic problems would hardly disappear in a looser confederation (Diamond 1987, 211). But the most compelling argument against confederation is that it is actually "a polite strategy for the dissolution of Nigeria" (Okadigbo 1986, 12). As *West Africa* (5 August 1985, 1579) succinctly opined, "A debate about confederation can hardly be described as a discussion about Nigeria's political future: it is more about how to end the existence of Nigeria as one entity in the future."

A final perspective on Nigeria's political future, while it does not explicitly advocate the dissolution of Nigeria, nevertheless sees the country's disintegration as a real possibility. The respected jurist, Akinola Aguda, for instance, laments that he is no longer "sure that Nigeria will continue to exist . . . (as) we are today faced with the imminent danger of disintegration" (*Nigerian Tribune* 5 April 1995, 5). This view is echoed by S.G. Ikoku who speaks of "a real threat to the corporate existence of Nigeria" (*Newswatch* 1 May 1995, 8). In October 1992, Professor Bolaji Akinyemi warned against the convening of a sovereign National Conference in the country. This was because, in his words, such a convention would "vote for the dissolution of the Nigerian entity" (*Newswatch* 26 October 1992, 14). Adebayo Williams (1994, 16) bluntly contends that the "question is no longer whether Nigeria will break up but when," while Tanko Yakassai (1992, 25) has proposed the organization of a referendum that would enable "Nigerians to decide, once and for all, whether they want the country to continue as a single political entity or not."

Suggestions or prognoses regarding Nigeria's possible dismemberment reflect deep concern, frustration and alarm at the tragic failures and flaws of Nigerian federalism. Yet, as historian J.F. Ade-Ajayi (1992, 29) has insightfully argued, "just as there are problems in keeping Nigeria together, there will be many problems in trying to unscramble it, and the problems of putting it asunder" may, in fact, be more onerous than the challenges of nurturing and sustaining Nigeria's "national integration."

Conclusion

Nigeria is in the throes of a profound, palpable and almost pathetic crisis in its federalism. The Nigerian federation, deeply vulnerable even at the best of times, has been enfeebled and endangered by the exacerbation of ethnoregional struggles for the control of the federal presidency, by the upsurge of economic nationalism in the oil-producing areas, by the seemingly ineluctable but tragically divisive and destructive pressures towards the overcentralization of powers and resources, and by growing cynicism and scepticism regarding the political legitimacy and structural viability of the very idea of a single Nigerian federal state.

Yet, the ruinous implications and contradictions contained in proposals for the confederalization or dissolution of Nigeria seem to underscore the wisdom of maintaining the country as a united federal entity. Moreover, as the deluge of exciting and potentially rewarding ideas for reforming Nigerian federalism indicate, the current political problems of the country are not insurmountable. Indeed, a crucial feature of federalism, as a structural-political device, is the enormous opportunity it provides for the "politics of innovation," or the creative elaboration and adaptation of institutional solutions to societal problems. The challenge for the contemporary Nigerian political leadership and intelligentsia is to muster or foster the moral discipline, historical sensitivity, intellectual imagination and political consensus that will be necessary for the elaboration and consummation of a comprehensive program of federal reforms.

References

Ade-Ajayi, J.F. 1992. "The National Question in Historical Perspective." *The Guardian*, 6 November: 29.
Bauchi, I.A. 1995. "He Who Pays the Piper . . . " *Nigerian Tribune*, 21 November: F1
Birnbaum, M. 1996. "A Travesty of Law and Justice." *AM News*, 5 February: 12
Danjuma, T.Y. 1994. "Revenue Sharing and the Political Economy of Nigerian Federalism." *The Nigerian Journal of Federalism*, 1, 1 (June): 43–68.
Diamond, Larry. 1987. "Issues In The Constitutional Design of a Third Nigerian Republic." *African Affairs*, 86, 343 (April): 209–26.
———. 1988. *Class, Ethnicity, and Democracy in Nigeria; The Failure of the First Republic*. London: Macmillan Press.
———. 1991. "Nigeria's Search for a New Political Order." *Journal of Democracy*, 2, 2 (Spring): 54–69.
Ekpu, R. 1994. "Rotational Palliative." *Newswatch 7*, November: 6.
Ekwueme, A. 1992. "More Than A Government of National Consensus." *The Guardian*, 21 March: 9.

———. 1995. "The Question of Rotation." *AM News*, 7–10 August 1995.
Federal Republic of Nigeria. 1987. *Report of The Political Bureau*. Lagos: Federal Government Printer.
Ige, B. 1995a. "Of Abacha's Constitution and Native Colonialism." *Tell*, (8 May): 34.
———. 1995b. "Share Powers, Not Positions." *Sunday Tribune*, 3 September: 2.
Joseph, Richard. 1991. *Democracy and Prebendal Politics in Nigeria: The Rise and Fall of the Second Republic*. Ibadan: Spectrum Books.
Kukah, Matthew H. 1991. "On Gumi's Conception of the Advocate." *New Nigerian*, 27 January: 13.
Lijphart, A. 1977. *Democracy in Plural Societies: A Comparative Exploration*. New Haven and London: Yale University Press.
Madunagu, E. 1993. "Problems and Prospects." *The Guardian*, 22 April: 13.
McHenry, D. 1986. "Stability of the Federal System in Nigeria: Elite Attitudes at the Constituent Assembly Toward the Creation of New States." *Publius: The Journal of Federalism* 16 (Spring): 91–111.
Movement For National Reformation. 1993. "Position Paper." *The Guardian*, 28–29 January.
National Constitutional Conference. 1994. *Report of the Committee on Revenue Allocation*. (September) Abuja.
Ogoni Bill of Rights. 1990.
Okadigbo, C. 1986. "The People Know Best." *African Concord*, 7 August: 11–12.
Okupe, D. 1992. "Towards Stability of the Third Republic." *The Guardian*, 20 February: 8.
Olowu, D. 1994. "The Future of the Federal System." *The Guardian*, 4 March: 29.
Saro-Wiwa, Ken. 1992. "Federalism and the Minority." *The Guardian*, 30 November: 37.
———. 1994. "Oil and the Issues at Stake." *The Guardian*, 1 April: 17.
Suberu, Rotimi T. 1993. "The Travails of Federalism in Nigeria." *Journal of Democracy* 4, 4 (October): 39–53.
Szetfel, M. 1994. "Ethnicity and Democratization in South Africa." *Review of African Political Economy* 60: 185–99.
Watts, R. 1991. "Canadian Federalism in the 1990s: Once More in Question." *Publius: The Journal of Federalism* 21 (Summer): 169–90.
Whitaker, C. Sylvester. 1991. "The Unfinished State of Nigeria." In R.L. Sklar and C.S. Whitaker (eds.), *African Politics and Problems in Development*: 265–73. Boulder: Lynne Rienner Publishers.
Williams, A. 1994. "An Arewa Liaison." *The News*, (Lagos) 21 February: 16.
Yakassai, T. S.A. 1992. "Hold a National Referendum . . . " *New Nigerian*, 6 July: 25.

17

PARTY SYSTEMS AND CIVIL SOCIETY

Adigun Agbaje

> ... [W]e tend to keep parties separate from other aspects of our lives ... Our social, business, working, and cultural lives ... are almost entirely nonpartisan.
> —James Q. Wilson (1992, 141) on the American experience.

> The crux of the problem of Nigeria today is the overpoliticization of social life. We are intoxicated with politics. The premium on political power is so high that we are prone to take the most extreme measures to win and to maintain political power....
> —Claude Ake (1981a, 1162–63) on the Nigerian experience.

> Our uncertainty about other aspects of the transition process can be diminished ... [when] ... we ... pay much more attention to value change—to how and why leaders in the opposition and in the authoritarian state alter their ideas about what is preferable and what is feasible ... [and when we] ... move much more toward the intensive study of political parties.... [P]olitical parties may be used to perpetuate military as well as civilian rule. The critical political question is when this rule will lead toward democracy and when it will simply contribute to the maintenance of an authoritarian order.
> —Nancy Bermeo (1990, 369, 370) on comparative experiences in the context of political transitions.

In the best of times, the hallmark of the Nigerian polity is its uncertain and unfinished nature (Joseph, Taylor, and Agbaje 1996; Whitaker 1984). It is, therefore, not surprising that this slippery landscape has had lasting and significant impact on the evolution and interface of the country's party systems and civil society. As the prefatory notes above outline, Nigerian economy and society have tended to display the pathologies of suffocating overpoliticization, in sharp contrast to the case of more settled communities which have had time to work out and institutionalize the limits of politics, economy and society in their interconnectedness.

Why does Nigeria remain in an uncertain and unfinished state, several decades after attaining independence? One answer is experiential, since the country has literally been in permanent political transition, suspended between departure and several possible destinations at all points in its history since the colonial amalgamation of 1914 that created Nigeria in its present geographic form (Joseph, Taylor, and Agbaje 1996). All of this transition has taken place under one form of undemocratic rule or the other (colonial, civil-authoritarian, military-autocratic); about 37 years into its history as an independent country, Nigeria has yet to witness three unbroken, uncontested, settled years of democratic rule.

Periods of transition under forms of autocratic rule are by definition moments of uncertainty, and not the best of times for negotiating and renegotiating the construction and revalorization of widely accepted, legitimate organizations, processes, values and rules of conduct that are known, knowable, strong, predictable and efficacious enough to serve as ramparts for democratic rule. This is probably better achieved during periods of democratic consolidation. But these are yet to be fully experienced in Nigeria.

The central argument of this chapter, therefore, is that the manner of constitution and the environment and rhythm of evolution and interaction of Nigeria's party systems and civil society have tended to deepen institutional, processual and value systems supportive of autocratic rather than democratic rule. The rest of the chapter is devoted to the pursuit of this line of argument. But first, in the following section, I will clarify the use of concepts deployed above and below.

Concepts as Key

In the last couple of years, the concepts of party systems and civil society have occupied center stage in the study of political transitions. In the specific case of the African experience, much of the debate has included ringing accusations of ethnocentric theorizing directed mainly at Western academic and policy circles as well as pleas for African exceptionalism emanating mainly from African sources (Bangura and Gibbon 1992, 18–24; Post 1991; Beckman 1993; Mamdani 1990a, b; Osaghae 1995).

Details of this exchange cannot be examined here, but obviously the charge of ethnocentrism can be sustained only in few, including non-Western, instances, while pleas for African exceptionalism cannot by any account be attributed to only African sources. For the purpose of this chapter, it is enough to note that ethnocentrism and exceptionalism are but two sides of the same coin, limiting as it were our ability to conceptually make sense of the African experience in a grounded manner in the context of local and global trends.

On the concept of civil society, for instance, the problem is that in its journey from the classics, it has attracted unto itself Western specificities (Harbeson, Rothchild, and Chazan 1994; Post 1991; Beckman 1993; Lewis 1995; Bangura and Gibbon 1992). Shorn of these specificities, however, what comes out is a conceptualization subscribed to in this chapter utilizing two elements: namely, space and function (Finer 1977; Harbeson 1994, 1–29; Young 1994, 33–50, Bratton 1994, 51–81). Essentially, civil society is then identified with that section of society that engages the state for the purpose of constructing, defining and institutionalizing values, norms, rules and principles by which society is governed as well as the terms of such governance. The relative strength and nature of the organizations and rules of conduct that undergird the political order, as well as the formation of the required basic political values for state and society, are influenced by the nature of this engagement between state and civil society.

The Harbeson, Rothchild, and Chazan volume (1994) makes a seminal contribution to the literature. This contribution is traceable in part to the welcome emphasis it lays on civil society as: helping to define the purposes and rules of society, of the political game, and of government; helping to express the terms of interdependence between state and society; and overseeing the process by which the organizing principles of the state are harmonized with those of society at large.

What then, is the state? To emphasize continuity rather than discontinuity (Agbaje 1991; Manor 1990; Samudavanija 1990; Post 1991; Mbembe 1992; Chazan 1992; Azarya 1988), I follow Azarya(1988, 10) to define the state as an "organization *within* society where it coexists and interacts with other formal and informal organizations;" but which is distinguished from these other organizations "in seeking predominance over them and in aiming to institute binding rules regarding the other organizations' activities, or at least to authorize (i.e. to delegate power to) the other organizations to make such rules for themselves."

In the same vein, a political party "is a group that seeks to elect candidates to public office by supplying them with a label—a 'party identification'—by which they are known to the electorate" (Wilson 1992, 138). A party system is then taken to refer to the pattern of relationships within and among political parties in any given polity. It is possible as is done in this chapter to analytically separate the sphere of social action occupied by parties and party systems from civil society, as others (Diamond 1994, 7; Bratton 1989, 407–29; 1994, 55–56; Lewis 1995) have done. For Diamond (1994, 7) the party system constitutes political society "in essence," while Bratton (1994, 56–57) identifies constituents of political society as including institutions of "political parties, elections and legislatures," distinguished from those of civil society in their concentration on "partisan contestation over state power" in order "to gain and exercise control over state power."

What flows from the foregoing is the point that the nature of a given society as reflected in its dominant structures, practices and processes is contingent on the nature and manner of production of values, norms, ideas, rules and principles of conduct. In turn, the production and reproduction of these intangibles is engaged upon in the context of a complex interaction of state, governing regime, society, civil society and political society in which the roles and provinces of state, governing regime, political society and the rest of society is influenced by civil society and vice versa, and in which the potency of civil society is circumscribed by the nature of the state, governing regime, political society and the rest of society. Within these two alternatives are several possible lines of influence (as, for instance, when the nature of governing regime impacts on political society and the rest of society and vice versa, or when the rest of society pushes for the reformation of political society and vice versa).

A final point at this stage is to note the situational texture of this interaction especially in the context of the length of transition. Literature suggests that the longer a political transition takes, the more civil society is likely to abandon its own traditional role and take on those of political society (i.e. the party system), with attendant risks to itself and the overall search for democracy. The situational picture, as painted by Bratton (1994, 64), is to the effect that

> civil society gives way to political society and is itself transformed during the process of political transition. In the early stages, . . . civil society performs as the refuge of last resort for partisan oppositional groupings. The announcement of 'founding elections', however, brings about a rebirth of political

society and a concomitant transformation in the role of civic institutions. ... Once political parties are available to promote partisan politics, civic organizations can adopt or regain roles that are truly civic.

Even in a properly functioning system, however, civil society retains a political role which is what sets it apart from the society at large. It continues to be central to efforts to invent, validate and reinvent the state and society by performing "distinctive political functions" (Harbeson 1994, 14) that "have both 'horizontal' and 'vertical' aspects":

> horizontal functions . . . characterizing the relationships of actors within society to each other, are . . . as important as vertical ones, those between society and government.

The peculiarities of the Nigerian case, including its characterization as a country literally in permanent transition, the relative salience of the state and governing regimes, as well as long periods of authoritarian rule, and the rough coincidence and deepening of religious, ethnic and regional cleavages in society, raise questions that are addressed in the next section.

Party Systems and Civil Society in Nigeria

An overview of civil society and party systems in Nigeria's political history cannot but bring out the defining forces and moments in their construction, evolution and composition. One such force, which has remained prominent from the founding stage to the moment, is the role and nature of the state and the governing regime.

Unlike much of Western experience, in which civil society preceded and played a decisive role in the construction of the modern state system (Keane 1988), the reverse has been the case in Nigeria as in many African countries, with the state preceding and influencing the constitution not only of contemporary civil society but of political society (party systems) as well (Chabal 1992, 73, 74; Bayart 1986, 109–25; Young 1988, 25–66). Civil society emerged and was powered by core democratic aspirations in the context of society's reaction to the colonial state, perceived essentially as an alien, exploitative force, an excrescence imposed from outside via the agency of colonial rule for the purpose of pacification and plunder rather than as an entity evolving organically from colonial society (Young 1988, 37; 1994, 37; Bayart 1986, 109–25; Chabal 1992, 73–74; Ake 1981b, 76–77).

In Nigeria, in this first stage of development sections of colonized society, composed (especially in the southern port city of Lagos and environs) of an ever-expanding group of Nigerians educated abroad and those educated at home in missionary-sponsored schools, returning freed slaves of Nigerian and other African extractions, and members of the traditional power structure, began to cautiously engage the colonial state. This stage was quickly followed, by the first decade of the twentieth century, by the formation in certain urban centers of associations and groups focusing mainly on local issues of mutual aid for housing and education, and on highlighting evidence of maladministration in the colonial regime or instances of colonial insensitivities in the areas of local customs and tax, land and other legislations, among others (Sklar 1963, 41–45). At this stage, therefore, the nascent civil and political society was first developed and most pronounced in that part of Nigeria exposed most to European influences.

The second stage in the development of civil and political society in Nigeria under British colonial rule started where the first ended with the introduction of the Clifford Constitution in 1922 which for the first time introduced a highly restricted form of the franchise to parts of the colony. Under this principle, residents of Lagos and Calabar, including Nigerians and other members of the British Commonwealth with requisite property qualifications, could vote and be voted for after 1923 to fill three seats (for Lagos) and one seat (for Calabar) in the largely advisory colonial legislative council made up otherwise of unelected colonial officials.

The party system that subsequently developed around elections to the Legislative Council up to 1947 when the Council system ended was essentially Lagos-based and dominated until 1938 by a single party, the Nigerian National Democratic Party (NNDP) organized around the engineer-agitator, Herbert Macauley, and his associates who had been active in the associations of the earlier period. Reflecting its elitist flavor, geographical scope as well as the interests of the highly restricted electorate, the NNDP aimed for "the attainment of municipal status and local self-government for Lagos, the provision of facilities for higher education in Nigeria, the introduction of compulsory education at the primary school level, the encouragement of non-discriminatory, private economic enterprise, and the Africanization of the civil service" (Sklar 1963, 46). In effect, the party, while it remained influential, "was virtually confined to the Lagos political arena and mainly concerned with local matters." This was not surprising, since its primary link with civil society was mainly with Lagos Yoruba elements of chiefs, imams, market women leaders, wealthy merchants, Christian leaders and Nigerian and non-Nigerian professionals (Sklar 1963, 47).

By 1938, however, the NNDP's domination of the party system was brought to an end following the success of the Nigerian Youth Movement (NYM) at the polls; the NYM won control of the Lagos City Council and the three Lagos seats in the Legislative Council. The NYM dated back to 1934 when a Lagos Youth Movement (renamed Nigerian Youth Movement in 1936) was founded by former students of King's College, Lagos, Nigeria's premier institution, led by three professionals (one in government service as an economist and former President of the West African Students Union in the UK) and a trade unionist, to protest and project alternative views to colonial policy on education (which laid emphasis on local vocational training rather than the preferred option of government scholarships to finance education of as many deserving applicants as possible in the UK).

As Sklar (1963, 52) has pointed out, however, the triumph of the NYM from 1938, rather than being "taken as a reflection of popular opinion," should be perceived more as an indication of the triumph and "political leaning of the upper strata of the Westernized elite" in civil and political society. More than the NNDP, the NYM was elitist, drawing membership from the professions and seeking from the start pan-Nigerian membership. The NYM triumph marked, therefore, the highpoint of the reassertion of elite dominance of society-party linkages.

By the early 1940s, business and personal rivalries had led to defections from the NYM and generated tensions wrongly but definitely interpreted along ethnic lines (Sklar 1963, 52–55). One of those who left the NYM at this time was Nnamdi Azikiwe, who had joined in 1937. By 1944 he was able to bring together a coalition of "the growing community of non-Yoruba—mainly Ibo—settlers in Lagos," the rising class of westernized, predominantly Christian, cosmopolitan Yoruba from the provinces, and the largely detribalized Lagos working class to form a new party, the National Council of Nigeria and the Cameroons (NCNC), and to take on the increasingly traditional, predominantly Muslim Lagos indigenes of the NNDP (Sklar 1963, 54–55).

Up to this stage, the colonial state had been propped up by subjugation of colonized civil society, complemented by justification and rationalization to metropolitan (English) civil society (Young 1988, 37). In addition, the world view of the pillars of the emerging colonial civil society, educated as they were in western (especially British) ways of life and values, was basically supportive of the colonial regime, even as it criticized the regime from time to time and pushed for enhanced participation of the local elite in the commanding heights of colonial administration, economy, politics and society. As late as 1947, when the last election into the legislative council was held under the restricted franchise system, the NNDP's motto remained a pledge of "unswerving loyalty to the throne" while its supposedly more irreverent opponent, the NYM, declared "allegiance to His Majesty the King" (Tamuno 1966, 56).

Electoral regulations further ensured that the party system lacked the incentive to cultivate strong links with women and non-elite interests in civil society, and subsequently ensured that the party system was largely denied the benefit of fully reflecting these views without distortions. Between 1923 and 1947, the electorate for Calabar never exceeded 572, and there were instances when it consisted of only three voters. For Lagos, by 1923 the figure was about 3,000 males, including non-Nigerian citizens of the Commonwealth (Tamuno 1966, 57; Sklar 1963, 46). The 1923 regulations that governed the first election to the council, for instance, described the voter as male, twenty-one years or above, a British subject or a native of the protectorate resident for twelve months before registration, with a gross annual income of not less than 100 pounds in the twelve months preceding elections. The origin of a party system conceived as little more than "vote gathering associations" (Graf n.d., 20) of the privileged classes, for the privileged classes by the privileged classes, therefore, can be said to date back to this period.

Another distinctive feature of this period germane to the emerging party system and civil society is the point that up till 1948, when some Africans in the legislative council demanded salaries to 600 pounds per annum for themselves, elective positions in Nigeria held very little promise if any of political power or material reward. Africans did not exercise executive authority or control over government departments; neither were they present in the council in a number large enough to extract concessions from the colonial government.

In effect, the expropriatory powers of government lay outside the control of elected Africans, ensuring that there was little to gain materially from seeking political office. Moreover, those that could seek office or elect people into office also constituted the most privileged among the colonized—privileged as they were by birth, by western education, by firsthand exposure to Euro-American ways of life as former slaves, by wealth, or by a combination of these.

Obviously, therefore, a significant proportion of these groups of politicians, the electorate, and civil society at large, derived much of its income from sources autonomous of the colonial state. This was thanks in part to "the monopoly tendency of the colonial social formation" which was manifested also in the economic sphere by seeking to discourage local incursion into the mainstream of production and distribution (Ake 1981b, 76–77).

In the third phase of the evolution of civil society and party systems (1948–1966), much of this was to change, with fatal consequences in the period leading to independence and thereafter. This phase marked the beginning of a party system that embraced the entire country, rather than being a Lagos affair. But the circumstances robbed specific parties of the opportunities for and inclinations toward genuinely national structures, platforms and reach, as well as of the chance to develop strong links with the mass of the people in a manner that did not ignite, accentuate and feed on communal cleavages in a divisive manner.

Again, as in the previous periods, the defining impetus was provided by colonial policy. Informed by the prevailing climate at home and abroad (including in the colony) in the post-World War II era, the colonial regime began to first examine ways of identifying "potential political and administrative elites who could gradually be trained to assume the enlarged responsibilities of the colonial state" (Young 1988, 53), and shortly afterwards began to prepare to wind up the colonial enterprise. In other words, the colonial state after the war first attempted to become more inclusive by being more welfarist and, shrugging aside its earlier preference for the traditional elite and rural elements (Sklar 1963, 87), it now embraced the urban, western educated elite. The latter had persisted in calling for more local participation in the colonial enterprise and by war's end, were now beginning to call for independence.

This change of view in colonial civil society was complemented by an even stronger and ever-growing denunciation of the colonial enterprise in metropolitan civil society, no longer convinced as to the continued justification for colonial rule. Thus, in Nigeria as in England, civil society began to call for an end to colonial rule. Its initial project of pacification and revenue extraction had been effected and it was becoming difficult to hinge continued colonial rule on the imperative for development, good government or notions of trusteeship. Moreover, within the colonial enterprise was a basic contradiction for, in the words of Young (1988, 37), "the very success of its hegemonic project constituted a civil society which over time was bound to reject its legitimacy." To cope with the increasingly adversarial form of engagement with elite interests in colonial civil society, colonial state policy by the late 1940s began to favor gradualists, ensuring their triumph over revolutionaries as independence dawned.

Thus, while the imposition and prosecution of colonial rule up to the late 1940s marked the triumph of the imperial idea and the colonial state, the unravelling of the enterprise that subsequently unfolded in the form of decolonization highlighted not only the retreat of the imperial state but also the triumph of the norms, values, and preferences of civil society in colony and metropole. This triumph, however, was to have implications for the reconstitution not only of the colonial state and its governing regime but also for the party system and civil society as well.

The early stage of this third phase, in the words of Post (1963, 26), marked "the seminal period for the birth of new political parties in Nigeria." Only the NCNC survived into this third phase from the second as a major party, but even then events of the period from 1948 to 1951 increasingly turned the party into an Igbo-dominated platform closely associated with the Igbo State Union formed in December 1948 (Post 1963, 28–31).

The NCNC, along with the Action Group (AG) and the Northern People's Congress (NPC) were to dominate the political scene until the first military coup of January 1966. The influence of the three parties has outlived their corporate existence, however, for although they were banned after the 1966 coup, dominant perceptions of the Nigerian political scene have to the present portrayed contemporary parties and party systems as lineal descendants and reincarnations of these three parties.

The AG and the NPC were formed just in time for the 1951 election meant to implement the new Macpherson Constitution, the first to incorporate the result of several months of consultation with interest groups all over the colony. The rounds of consultation were done in the context of a "period when the latent antipathies" of ethnic and regional differences "came to the fore, expressed and manipulated by the nationalist leaders . . . as they became rivals for office" (Post 1963, 25).

By 1954 colonial policy had endorsed in principle a federal system for Nigeria with three regions of North, East and West (coterminous respectively with the spheres of influence of the three dominant ethnic groups—namely the Hausa-Fulani, the Igbo and the Yoruba). Moreover, public office for the local elite now held promise of the actual exercise of power and privileges in the context of the promise and execution of decolonization.

It was not surprising that since regionalization was carried out along the three lines of mega-ethnic divides, Yoruba and Hausa-Fulani interests would seek to found their "own" parties in readiness for the 1951 election. Thus, the AG, which held its inaugural congress only in April 1951, grew from a Pan-Yoruba cultural organization, the *Egbe Omo Oduduwa*, while the NPC, formed just in time to participate in the last rounds of the 1951 election, equally grew from the *Jam'iyyar Mutanen Arewa*. The NPC represented the response of conservative northerners to the good electoral performance of the more radical Northern Elements Progressive Union (NEPU) organized around northern *talakawa* (commoners) by Malam Aminu Kano and associates during the early stages of the voting.

The AG, whose name did not reflect its regional and ethnically circumscribed constituency, described itself as the party of the Western Region and drew its strength mainly from traditional chiefs, professionals and wealthy cocoa farmers. The NPC, much more than the AG and the NCNC, embodied in its area of operation the triumph of conservatism and traditional power structures of the mainly Muslim caliphate and its emirate system. This had been in place before colonial rule and was incorporated into local administration via the Indirect Rule system under colonial rule. As Post (1963, 52) bluntly stated, "the party was founded in order to defend the ruling groups" in northern Nigeria "from an apparent threat to their interests." It was unabashedly northern in composition and purpose, utilizing the precolonial network of political fiefdoms built around Islam and dominated by Fulanis (Dudley 1968).

Along with these dominant parties was a constellation of minor parties representing minority ethnic and/or oppositional interests in each of the emerging regions. In the North, the NEPU was soon joined by the United Middle Belt Congress (UMBC) representing minority ethnic groups and Christian elements in the North's middle belt. In the West, the NCNC, increasingly identified with the Igbo, performed the role of the major if weaker opposition party while in the East the United National Independence Party, originally a splinter group from the NCNC, had by 1959 emerged as representative of minority ethnic interests in the East (Post 1963, 67–110; Dudley 1973).

Essentially, the party system remained elitist, although by this time the fragmentation of the elite along ethnic and geopolitical lines had been effected with the attendant lowering of vision from nationalist to parochial aspirations (as happened to the NCNC). The system discouraged and even "punished" parties that sought to expand their horizon from the parochial to the national (as happened to the AG between 1961 and 1962) (Sklar 1963; Post and Vickers 1973; Mackenzie and Robinson 1960, 18–167; Coleman 1958, 271–408).

At independence, the party system at the level of each of the three federating states (then called Regions) was essentially of the one-party variant, in which was "established a close identity between region, party and ethnicity" (Diamond 1988b, 38). The Hausa-Fulani dominated NPC controlled the government of the Hausa-Fulani dominated Northern Region, the Igbo-dominated NCNC did the same in the Igbo-dominated East, and the Yoruba AG dominated the government of the Yoruba West. The highly decentralized nature of the federal system was reflected in political and civil society as well, with the regions being perceived as the ultimate power centers, the control of which was a requirement for control of the federal center.

Under the Westminster parliamentary system, a multiparty system dominated by the NPC, NCNC and AG operated at the center, with the NPC and NCNC forming a coalition government for much of the First Republic (1960–1966). As others have shown, the demise of that republic in the 1966 coup was largely made possible by inter- and intra-party rivalries which spilled over into ethnic and regional clashes. Strong personalities had emerged by the 1950s combining party leadership with leadership of ethnic, religious, regional and media empires and accentuated the spilling over into civil society of issues and crises in political society and vice versa.

This situation was toxic to the democratic order in Nigeria in two senses, as expressed ably by Joseph (1987, 25, 30–31), building on Seymour Lipset and Robert Dahl. First, the composition of party members did not allow for broadbased, cross-cleavaged party structures and, second, the party system in place could pursue the democratic project of expressing and asserting group interests only at the risk of encouraging and deepening channels that were too narrow to support democracy. Thus, the Nigerian situation in this period contrasts unfavorably with democratic expectations and mores. As the argument goes,

> A stable democracy requires a situation in which the major political parties include supporters from many segments of the population. A system in which the support of different parties corresponds too closely to basic social divisions cannot continue to operate on a democratic basis, for it reflects a state of conflict so intense and clear-cut as to rule out compromise (Joseph 1987, 25).

In the second sense, it has been noted that Nigeria at independence did not inherit an authoritarian hegemonic party system, the result being a deepening of polarizations since the only path to democracy has been to "allow considerable room for self expression and the assertion of group interests . . . confined to channels that are more narrowly defined and structured than would be acceptable in most Western liberal societies" (Joseph 1987, 30–31).

The evolving structure of ethnic relations, which falls into the category described by Horowitz (1985, 39) as centralized, in which a few groups "are so large that their interactions are a constant theme of politics at the center," have also had a role to play in making authoritarian rule difficult to sustain, as Diamond (1988b, 35, 68) has vividly indicated, by at least making the kind of consensus conducive to the long-term consolidation of authoritarianism difficult to achieve.

Essentially, however, ethnicity has from the First Republic become "part of the mechanism through which the political elite maintains itself in power and exercises its influence," with the educated elite becoming "the chief proponents and purveyors of parochialism and particularistic values" (Dudley 1973, 41, 51). Ironically, this period had witnessed increased participation of various groups of civil society, including women, students, organized labor, associations of professionals, the mass media, and the urban youth, artisans and the unemployed, in political society. But their participation was largely and unfortunately under the influence and on terms determined by political parties and their barons.

Again, part of the problem is traceable to the nature of electoral regulations which, beginning from 1951 and for much of the 1950s, restricted popular participation and, thereby, did not give the nascent parties the incentive "to make direct contact with the mass of the people" (Post 1963, 27). It was not until the 1959 elections that the principle of universal adult suffrage was widely accepted in southern Nigeria, and it was much later (in 1979), when women were given the right to vote in the North, that the principle gained nationwide usage.

In addition, a tendency toward personalized patrimonial rule emerged during this period, compounding the authoritarian legacies of colonial rule (Diamond 1995, 420; Young 1988, 56; Dudley 1973, 50; Sklar 1963; Schatz 1977; Post 1963; Joseph 1987).

In essence, Nigerian experience with civil and political society up to the demise of the First Republic in 1966 underscores several other points. One is the extent to which civil society and the party system became a variegated machine for electoral competition, often of an extra-legal manner, the endproduct being the satisfaction of the craving for office of notable ethnoregional personalities. Parties were linked with civil society in a manner that ensured the swamping of the latter with partisan and sectional mores and interests. In effect, civil and political society became indistinguishable, with both lacking in effective institutionalization, autonomy, and development of procedures for effective performance.

In addition, the fact that the regions were more powerful than the federal center was reflected in civil and political society not only in terms of electoral regulations but also in terms of the salience of regional interests in national politics. As a result, the party system worked to undermine the potentials for the emergence of strong commitment to the nation-state in civil society, encouraging instead a social pluralism that turned healthy competition into lasting enmity (Whitaker 1981, 1–13); ethnoregional resources and values served as the bulwark and main instrument for political competition at the national level. In this context, it was not surprising that at all levels of government, little distinction was made between public and private resources and aspirations, with public resources being used to lavishly fund party interests and with parties not content with just contesting elections but also seeking to subordinate elected governments and members to party and private dictates. In addition, the evolving political system encapsulated in the federal arrangement was unbalanced, with the North placed in a preeminent position vis-à-vis other regions. Civil and political society was also becoming unbalanced, with power and influence being distributed therein unevenly. All this violated a basic democratic principle that no group be so powerful as to assume with certainty that it can capture the state whenever it wants.

By the 1960s, the electorate had begun to seek pre-electoral gratification, disillusioned by the increasingly self-seeking and arrogant disposition of politicians. Politics and party loyalties were now regarded literally as business ventures. Toward the end of the First Republic (and, later, at the end of the Second), two opposing grand alliances were formed by existing parties for the sole purpose of acquiring or retaining power at the risk of deepening the polarization of civil society into north and south. The electoral system was traduced, and feelings of electoral efficacy among the voters were threatened by elite behavior that not only used government resources to reward loyalists and punish opposition but showed disdain for the voting power of civil society, warning oppositional elements therein that "whether you vote for us or not, we will remain in power" (Mackintosh 1966, 42). Thus did the colonial heritage inform postcolonial practice. That heritage was one of "harsh authoritarian domination that instilled the idea that there were two sets of rules: one for political leaders and another for the citizenry . . . [O]n one hand was the legacy of formally democratic institutions; on the other, an authoritarian political culture" (Joseph, Taylor, and Agbaje 1996, 616–17). Civil society and the party system had come full circle, but the consequences of this transformation were to become fully manifest only much later in the country's political history.

So much space has been devoted to the period up to 1966 because, as indicated earlier, recent and contemporary forms of party systems and civil society owe much of their characters to, and in any event tend to be perceived as lineal descendants of, this early period.

Not even the fact that since the first coup in January 1966, Nigeria has been under military rule for all but four years (1979–1983, when elected civilians governed in the Second Republic) fundamentally detracts from this general point. In fact, the earlier period of colonial rule was itself "a form of military rule" that already had the effect of "socializing the local population to be passive subjects rather than responsive participants" (Joseph, Taylor, and Agbaje 1996, 627).

However, there are elements of the experience of party systems and civil society under military rule (1966–1979, 1983–date) in the post-independence period that departed in form and or in intensity from the experience under colonial rule.

All military coups since the first in January 1966 have had as their first casualty the existing party system and civil society. The first acts of military takeovers invariably include statements removing elected politicians from office, disbanding and placing an official ban on parties and party political activities, suspending those parts of the subsisting constitution crucial to the nurturing of civil society, and putting in place an alternative set of decrees aimed at facilitating governance for the military dictatorship. The long period of military rule since 1966, broken only by four years of civil democratic experimentation, has ensured that civil and political society have not been given enough time and space to negotiate and strike the right balance between and within party systems and civil society and to engage in the routinization and institutionalization required of a democratic order.

However, official bans placed on party political activities under military rule did not in fact put such activities on hold. The bans only drove them underground, ensuring the perpetuation of longstanding patterns of political networking, rather than its disruption, and guaranteeing that, whenever the bans were lifted in the context of democratization, whatever political parties that subsequently emerged would be new only in name, being essentially a reincarnation of the banned (cf., Diamond 1988b, 34–91; 1995, 417–91; 1988a; Joseph 1987; Joseph, Taylor, and Agbaje 1996; Forrest 1995, 73–80, 234–35; Oyediran and Agbaje 1991).

Predictably, the two attempts at transition from military to civil democratic rule (one successfully led to the Second Republic, and the other was initially aborted and is yet to be completed), led to party systems in which constituent parties were perceived as reincarnations of those of a previous era. Of the five parties that dominated the Second Republic, for instance, the National Party of Nigeria (NPN) was perceived as a reincarnation of the NPC; the Nigerian Peoples Party (NPP) as the new face of the NCNC; the Unity Party of Nigeria (UPN) as a reincarnation of the AG; and the People's Redemption Party (PRP) as the new face of NEPU. Even the Great Nigeria People's Party (GNPP), which could not be linked to a party of the First Republic, was founded by an NPC federal minister in that earlier republic. Party organization after 1985 took a similar pattern. Despite the fact that it was the transiting military government that not only decreed a mandatory two-party system (Diamond 1995, 452; Oyediran and Agbaje 1991) but also founded and organized the two parties in the system, the parties that were so created in the late 1980s in the aborted march to the Third Republic were associated in the popular mind not only with parties of the Second Republic but even with those of the First (Oyediran 1981; Agbaje 1990; Agbaje and Oyediran 1990–1991; Oyediran and Agbaje 1991; Adeniran 1991; Suberu 1992; Okoroji 1993).

Thus, the National Republican Convention (NRC), designed by the military regime to have an ideological orientation a little right of center, was associated with interests that dominated the NPC of the First Republic and the NPN of the Second; while the Social Democratic Party (SDP), designed to be a little left of center, was identified with interests that had earlier formed around the UPN, NPP, PRP as well as the AG, NCNC and NEPU, among others.

These basic interests were ultimately of an ethnoregional nature, and the apparent continuity in party stereotyping owed a lot to the persistence of key personalities and issues (Diamond 1988) in the politics and society of the First and Second Republics and the aborted transition to the Third.

As others, especially Diamond (1995, 432–33; 452–58), have pointed out, however, there was a sense in which each of the parties of the Second and aborted Third Republics was in fact "broader than its supposed antecedents" (433, 452–54), suggesting that perhaps the party systems could have evolved into truly crossethnic and crossregional, if not transethnic and transregional, entities if they had been allowed more time to renegotiate and reconstruct terms of interaction among themselves and with civil society and the state.

Apart from its disruptive nature, prolonged military rule has also led to a highly centralized federal state which is now described as an essentially unitary system in federal disguise. Likewise it has encouraged centralizing tendencies in party systems and civil society, in which there is an overconcentration of activity and power and other resources in the higher levels of bureaucracies and in a few urban centers. For the federal government, this tendency, and the advantage it bestows vis-à-vis other levels of government and civil and political society, has been prosecuted mainly from federally collected rents accruing from oil sales which has emerged from the post-civil war period as the main source of national wealth.

In effect, the period after 1966 has witnessed the deepening of the neopatrimonial regime with dire consequences for autonomous and oppositional elements in civil and political society, who have increasingly come to depend on the state for resources and in terms of regulations guiding their conduct.

Changes in the nature of the various military regimes have also had their own impact. While the Murtala/Obasanjo (1975–1979) regime was sincere, and executed its transition timetable faithfully, those since 1983 have either not committed themselves to democratization (as happened to the Buhari regime, overthrown by General Babangida in 1985) or appear to have been insincere in such commitment.

In addition, the military regimes since 1983 have become more repressive and less effective in governance, to the extent that it is now widely agreed that Nigeria "has collapsed into praetorianism" (Diamond 1995, 417), following upon "the increasingly predatory and self-interested character of military rule, a proclivity which has intensified social discord and internal military disaffection" (Lewis 1994, 323).

Up through 1983, the military were considered an alternative in the popular mind to the corrupt and inept rule of elected civilians of the First and Second Republics. From the late 1980s, however, a new consensus has gradually emerged to the effect that "the armed forces have compounded Nigeria's political and economic problems," leading in turn to concerted attempts by groups in civil society to achieve the military's withdrawal from public life (Joseph, Taylor, and Agbaje 1996, 658).

Civil society in this period was strengthened by expansion in education, networking of professional associations, an increasingly vibrant oppositional press, sections of organized labor, market women associations, students, occupational groups, and from 1987 an increasingly vigorous network of human rights organizations. However, a source of weakness remained its elitist nature and its concentration in urban centers and in the Yoruba speaking west. Also the environment in which it operated led it to assume agitational and oppositional roles which traditionally belong to political society, thereby attracting unto itself reprisal from the governing regime. It was also not difficult for the regime to coopt and compromise oppositional groups within civil society: to coerce, intimidate and ban those not amenable to corrupt inducement; and to create or encourage pro-government organizations or movements within this space of civil society. Rents accruing to government from oil sales were deployed generously in this attempt to deepen existing patrimonial tendencies, to strengthen personal rule, and to remold civil society to serve the interests of the increasingly predatory military generals-rulers.

As indicated earlier, civil and political society came under siege under Babangida and Abacha partly because the two initiated and perfected a two-headed project of de-democratization. This involved the use of the promises, imagery and appearances of democratization to de-institutionalize, weaken and cripple democratic processes and structures, while at the same time institutionalizing and invigorating a thoroughgoing system of cooptive rule (Bratton and van de Walle 1994; Joseph 1993b; Suberu 1994; Forrest 1995, 233–56; Agbaje 1994) in the service primarily of the ramparts of neopatrimonial rule.

It was not surprising that Babangida was able to manipulate regime-sponsored groups in civil society as well as the party system to help subvert democratization and to endorse the annulment of the June 12 1993 presidential election. That the party system itself lacked democratic linkages with the people and an effective mass base also explains the ease with which Abacha in November 1993 sacked both the NRC and SDP with hardly a whimper from the people.

Conclusion

Since the amalgamation of 1914, Nigeria's party systems and civil society have been invented by, and in the interests of, the state and its governing regime which, unfortunately, have reflected elements more autocratic than democratic, more uncivic than civic, more unstable than stable, more corrupt and self-seeking than transparent and patriotic, and more predatory than developmental. The recent call by Young (1994, 48) for a redemptive quest in Africa "for a civil society that can reinvent the state," therefore, opens up a vista of opportunities to address in a fundamental manner the inability of civil and political society, as well as the state, to install and consolidate democracy in a country whose peoples have widely been noted for persistently holding on to democratic aspirations in the face of a relentless onslaught of authoritarianism (Joseph, Taylor, and Agbaje 1996; Lewis 1994, 323; Diamond 1995, 417).

In Nigeria, however, the search for a civil (and political) society that can reinvent the state and substitute democratic impulses for its authoritarian mien is hampered by the historical fact that Nigeria has since 1914 been in a more or less permanent transition that has made virtually impossible the emergence of the kind of enduring party systems and civic civil society required for democratic rebirth. The long, broken and uncertain transition, in which most of the time party systems have been officially banned and political society either nonexistent, suppressed or tightly controlled, has caused civil society to have as its primary function the task usually performed by party systems, namely, that of "refuge of last resort for partisan oppositional groupings" (Bratton 1994, 64). A corollary of this development is that, like party systems, civil society has also been robbed of the opportunity to develop its capacities and appetite for its traditional role of deepening civic activities "in more neutral terms." Civil society has been turned into a divided platform for partisan and sectional contestation while political society has been underdeveloped, warped and underinstitutionalized.

All this suggests that the quest for renewal must look far and beyond civil and political society. For Nigerian experience since 1914 emphasizes the extent to which the contemporary problem at hand is multidimensional. The modern Nigerian state began with a tradition of oppressive, arbitrary, exploitative and self-seeking leadership under colonial rule which fostered an authoritarian political culture of leadership and a largely apathetic and passive mass political culture.

Other negative tendencies that surfaced under the later phases of colonial rule included electoral and political systems that increasingly exaggerated the divisive logic of electoral contestation and posed a stumbling block to the emergence of mechanisms for the effective expression and democratic management of cultural diversity in a highly plural context. In addition, the state emerged toward the end of colonial rule as the major source of resources for political and civil society, with major political actors converting access to the state to material advantage to themselves—and to the disadvantage of perceived opposition.

In the postcolonial period, these tendencies have been deepened and new ones entrenched. The political culture of leadership in political and civil society has ensured the persistence and dominance of norms, attitudes, practices and procedures conducive to behavioral and institutional tendencies more exploitative, self-seeking and rent-seeking than was witnessed under colonial rule. In turn, this has further encouraged not only the entrenchment of the logic of patrimonial distribution but that of divisive electoral politics as well. Civil society and party systems (when allowed to operate openly) have deepened exclusionary visions of an inter- and intraregional, ethnic and religious nature under the long periods of authoritarian rule, and equally so under the uncertain and controlled atmosphere of political transitions. The effect is that even after independence, Nigeria has yet to overcome, at the level of rules of conduct and actual behavior, those barriers to effective mediation of Nigeria's multicultural diversity in civil and political society.

Given the near absence of widely recognized and legitimized norms, it is not surprising that both party systems and civil society have not been informed by the requisite level and type of consciousness. In other words, constituencies in these terrains have yet to become fully transformed, to use Marxian language, from passive, objective and atomized elements-in-themselves to active, subjective elements-for-themselves, aware of their corporate existence and interests, and strong enough to defend and pursue such interests. Rather, they have allowed military and civilian autocrats to reconstruct their terrains in a manner conducive more to the needs of autocracy than those of democracy.

The centralization and concentration of party systems and civil society since 1966, arising from the centralization and concentration of the federation, the rise of a strong federal center, and the relative overdevelopment of the executive branch, has further weakened non-state actors at the same time that the powers, prestige and attraction of governmental office have been boosted.

From the outlines of what so far is known of General Abacha's transition program, what is envisaged for the future is a multiparty arrangement under a French-type system of government, since Abacha had on coming to power in 1993 abolished the mandatory two-party arrangement of the NRC and SDP. However, doubts remain about the genuineness of Abacha's commitment to democratic rule. Moreover, the conduct of the March 1996 local government election nationwide on a no-party basis conveyed not only the military's traditional disdain for political parties but, more importantly, underlined the possibility that Abacha's transition could be even more arbitrary, tightly controlled and undemocratic than Babangida's.

An ominous development ever since 1985 has been the institutionalization of military rule in a manner that seeks to compel civil and political society literally to operate under terms handed down by military oligarchs; the purpose being to transplant onto the political and civil terrain the age-old military strategy of surprise, subterfuge, divide, coopt and rule. Given the relative strength, material resources and experience in statecraft available to the military regimes and the relative weakness, poverty and inexperience of political and civil society, especially for oppositional elements therein, the surprising thing, thanks in part to the potency of foreign, especially American, support for democratic forces, is that civil society continues to retain pockets of opposition to military rule. In this regard, the point recently made by Guyer (1994, 215–29), on the pivotal role of citizens abroad, resident foreigners and foreign supporters and powers in the reconfiguration of civil (and perhaps political) society, and in helping to reshape the balance of power between and within non-state and state actors to boost democratic possibilities, is an important one. It sensitizes us to the extent to which civil (and political?) society actors are not necessarily confined to citizens living within the boundaries of a given country.

This is more so since parties and civil society have failed to outgrow their image of being "extremely shallow, fragile and weak," lacking in the "coherence, complexity, autonomy, and adaptability that are the hallmark of institutionalization" (Diamond 1988b, 71–72; 1995, 473–81; Lewis 1994, 323–24; Joseph, Taylor, and Agbaje 1996, 670–75; Lucas 1994, 21–38). Parties and civil society have therefore been unable to establish strong mobilizational links outside of those established by the state and those who govern. In this kind of situation, the nature of the transiting regime becomes crucial to the search for democracy. When such a regime is more interested in perpetuating itself or in stalling, democratic transition becomes only a hope.

This is not to downplay the pro-democratic role of civil society; rather, it is to emphasize that within civil society have equally been found elements vigorously supportive of neopatrimonial military rule and subversive of a rational and stable party system. In fact, given that the sphere of operation of forces supportive of democracy has in fact been shrinking in the face of unrelenting regime pressure, the fear now is that such pro-democracy groups could themselves be increasingly adopting strategies that are toxic to the dream of a stable democratic polity. For now, society appears to be slouching toward autocracy under generals intent on entrenching authoritarian rule by stealth (Dresser 1994, 68).

What is required at the moment is a reinstitutionalization and reinvigoration of civil society and party systems to enhance democratic capacities for managing competition and conflict in a manner that mediates and fully expresses Nigeria's cultural diversity and promotes inclusionary rather than exclusionary politics. Moreover, it is not yet fully clear to the power elite that any attempt to extinguish civil society or distort its constituents is self defeating. Such an attempt imperils civil society's function of defining the basis of legitimacy, thereby raising what has been described as the paradox of elusive power (Harbeson 1994, 11; Migdal 1988).

For the future, a basic step toward resolving the dilemmas of democracy in Nigeria must involve a search for political leadership (civilian and military) committed to democratic regeneration and the lofty ideals of national service. Military rulers and the civilian political elite, ever willing to be coopted into neopatrimonial schemes that thrive on the instrumental misuse of sectional symbols, have jointly imperilled the search for a functional and stable party system and the work of constructing and deepening civil society to serve as a strong prop for such a party system. One hopes that experience would sooner or later teach Nigerian politicians to see military generals who pose as messiahs and generous dispensers of public wealth for what they are—adversaries to be confronted, subjugated, and controlled.

However, this cannot be achieved through fatalistic assumptions regarding voluntaristic and "natural" developments in civil society. Human agency is required, and urgently too. As Azarya (1994, 96) cautions, "civil society does not just exist as a natural component of any society. It has to be constructed, tended to, protected, transmitted from generation to generation; otherwise, it may wither and disappear."

For instance, in the area of party formation and nurturing of the party system, the role of the state needs to be greatly diminished. As indicated elsewhere (Agbaje 1995, 17), perhaps there is much to be said for a system of party formation that emphasizes, as it were, the role of the political market expressed through electoral performance in determining initial public funding, if found necessary, and subsequent survival of parties. In such a system, parties would also be encouraged, again largely through the instrumentality of the political market, to operate within the territorial scope in which their outlook, reach and resources would be most fruitfully utilized. This arrangement would create a situation in which all parties do not have to operate at the national level to satisfy electoral regulations but, rather find their level on the political playing field and limit themselves as appropriate to ward, local, state, group of states, or the entire country.

It would be nice to end on an optimistic note and point to the "potentials for good" in the coming years within party systems and civil society in regard to democratic transition and consolidation. One can quote the popular Rousseau line on the efficacy of "the constitution graven ... in the hearts of the citizens" (Levine 1976, 168). However, experience also highlights the "potentials for evil" within party systems and civil society, and shows that even the constitution graven in the hearts of citizens could literally be reenacted and/or portrayed as serving nondemocratic ends. One is therefore left with long-term optimism laced with medium-term pessimism, anticipating a future in which Nigerians would have overwhelmingly concluded that their country has no future in the comity of nations except a democratic future, and that this future is worth struggling for, and dying for, if necessary.

On a final note, although current literature tends to consider the nation-state as the "proper unit for the democratic process" (Hoffman 1991, 347), it overlooks the point that "the national state is a moment in history" (Dahl 1989, 194), and that as late as the eighteenth century, "democracy was identified only with the city state" (Hoffman 1991, 347). Nigeria is, properly speaking, a multinational state. The issue of mutability, as to whether the national state "in the year 2100 will ... still ... be the natural site and limit of the democratic process," becomes a poignant and suggestive one for Nigeria. If a democratic order with supportive party systems and civil society is unachievable within the borders of the existing contraption, can pressure for its attainment lead to a redrawing of maps, and how are we, as students, friends and citizens of Nigeria, preparing for this possibility?

References

Adeniran, T. 1991. "The Two-Party System and the Federal Political Process." *Publius: The Journal of Federalism*, 2: 31–44.

Agbaje, A. 1990. "Party Formation and the Transition to the Third Nigerian Republic." *Research Projects on Contemporary Development Issues in Nigeria: Final Report.* Ibadan: Social Science Council of Nigeria and Ford Foundation.

———. 1991. "A Quarantine for the African State?" *Journal of Modern African Studies*, 29: 723–27.

———. 1994. "Beyond the Generals: Twilight of Democracy in Nigeria." *Africa Demos*, 3: 4–5.

———. 1995. "The Political Parties, Corruption and Democratization." Presented at *Conference on Corruption and Democratization in Nigeria, 1982–1993*, sponsored by the Lagos Office of Friedrich Ebert Foundation and co-ordinated by Professor Alex Gboyega, Conference Center, University of Ibadan, 19–20 September.

Agbaje, A. and O. Oyediran. 1990–1991. "Party Nominations Under Soft State Conditions—Theoretical and Empirical Notes from a Nigerian Experience." *Administrative Change*, 18: 34–51.

Ake, C. 1981a. "Off to a Good Start but Dangers Await ... " Presidential Address to the Nigerian Political Science Association in Kano. *West Africa* (25 May): 1162–63.

———. 1981b. *A Political Economy of Africa*. London: Longman.

Azarya, V. 1988. "Reordering State-Society relations: Incorporation and Disengagement." In D. Rothchild and N. Chazan (eds.), *The Precarious Balance: State and Society in Africa*: 3–21. Boulder: Westview Press.

———. 1994. In J.W. Harbeson, D. Rothchild, and N. Chazan (eds.), *Civil Society and the State in Africa*. Boulder: Lynne Rienner Publishers.

Bangura, Y. and P. Gibbon. 1992. "Adjustment, Authoritarianism and Democracy: An Introduction to Some Conceptual and Empirical Issues." In P. Gibbon, Y. Bangura, and A. Ofstad (eds.), *Authoritarianism, Democracy and Adjustment: The Politics of Economic Reform in Africa*: 7–38. Uppsala: The Scandinavian Institute of African Studies.

Bayart, J.F. 1986. "Civil Society in Africa." In P. Chabal (ed.), *Political Domination in Africa: Reflections on the Limits of Power*: 109–29. Cambridge: Cambridge University Press.

Beckman, B. 1993. "The Liberation of Civil Society: Neo-Liberal Ideology and Political Theory." *Review of African Political Economy*, 58: 20–33.

Bermeo, N. 1990. "Review Article: Rethinking Regime Change." *Comparative Politics*, 22: 359–77.

Bratton, M. 1989. "Beyond the State: Civil Society and Associational Life in Africa." *World Politics*, 41: 407–29.

———. 1994. "Civil Society and Political Transitions in Africa." In J.W. Harbeson, D. Rothchild, and N. Chazan (eds.), *Civil Society and the State in Africa*. Boulder: Lynne Rienner Publishers.

Bratton, M. and N. van de Walle. 1994. "Neopatrimonial Regimes and Political Transitions in Africa." *World Politics*, 46: 453–89.

Chabal, P. 1992. *Power in Africa: An Essay in Political Interpretation*. London: Macmillan.

Chazan, N. 1992. "Africa's Democratic Challenge: Strengthening Civil Society and the State." *World Policy Journal*, 9: 279–308.

Coleman, J.S. 1958. *Nigeria: Background to Nationalism*. Berkeley: University of California Press.

Dahl, R. 1989. *Democracy and its Critics*. New Haven: Yale University Press.

Diamond, L. 1988a. *Class, Ethnicity and Democracy in Nigeria: The Failure of the First Republic*. London: Macmillan.

———. 1988b. "Nigeria: Pluralism, Statism and the Struggle for Democracy." In L. Diamond, J.J. Linz, and S.M. Lipset (eds.), *Democracy in Developing Countries: Africa*: 33–91. Boulder: Lynne Rienner Publishers.

———. 1994. "Rethinking Civil Society: Toward Democratic Consolidation." *Journal of Democracy*, 5: 3–17.

———. 1995. "Nigeria: The Uncivic Society and the Descent into Praetorianism." In L. Diamond, J.J. Linz, and S.M. Lipset (eds.), *Politics in Developing Countries: Comparing Experiences with Democracy*: 417–91. Boulder: Lynne Rienner Publishers.

Dresser, D. 1994. "Latin America's Critical Elections: Five Scenarios for Mexico." *Journal of Democracy*, 5: 57–71.
Dudley, B.J. 1968. *Parties and Politics in Northern Nigeria*. London: Frank Cass.
———. 1973. *Instability and Political Order: Politics and Crisis in Nigeria*. Ibadan: Ibadan University Press.
Finer, S.M. 1977. "Space and Politics." *Res Publica*, 19.
Forrest, T, 1985. "The Political Economy of Civil Rule and the Economic Crisis in Nigeria (1979–84)." *Review of African Political Economy*, 35: 4–26.
———. 1995. *Politics and Economic Development in Nigeria*. Boulder: Westview.
Graf, W.D. n.d. Elections 1979: *The Nigerian Citizen's Guide to Parties, Leaders and Issues*. Lagos: Daily Times.
Guyer, J. 1994. "The Spatial Dimensions of Civil Society in Africa: An Anthropologist Looks at Nigeria." In J.W. Harbeson, D. Rothchild, and N. Chazan (eds.), *Civil Society and the State in Africa*: 215–29. Boulder: Lynne Rienner Publishers.
Harbeson, J.W. 1994. "Civil Society and Political Renaissance in Africa." In J.W. Harbeson, D. Rothchild, and N. Chazan (eds.), *Civil Society and the State in Africa*: 1–29. Boulder: Lynne Rienner Publishers.
Harbeson, J.W., D. Rothchild, and N. Chazan, eds. 1994. *Civil Society and the State in Africa*. Boulder: Lynne Rienner Publishers.
Hoffman, J. 1991. "Capitalist Democracies and Democratic States: Oxymorons or Coherent Concepts?" *Political Studies*, 39: 342–49.
Horowitz, D. L. 1985. *Ethnic Groups in Conflict*. Berkeley: University of California Press.
Jordan. G. 1990. "The Pluralism of Pluralism: An Anti-Theory?" *Political Studies*, 38: 286–301.
Joseph, R. 1987. *Democracy and Prebendal Politics in Nigeria: The Rise and Fall of the Second Republic*. Cambridge: Cambridge University Press.
———. 1993a. "Africa in the Latin style." *The Washington Post* (6 July).
———. 1993b. Nigeria: The Way Forward. Testimony before the Subcommittee on Africa, The House Committee on Foreign Affairs, Washington, D.C. (4 August).
Joseph, R., S. Taylor, and A. Agbaje. 1996. "Nigeria." In K. Kesselman, J. Krieger, and W. Joseph (eds.), *Comparative Politics at the Crossroads*: 616–89. Lexington: DC Heath.
Keane, J., ed. 1988. *Civil Society and the State: New European Perspectives*. London: Verso.
Koehn, P. 1989. "Competitive Transition to Civilian Rule: Nigeria's First and Second Experiments." *Journal of Modern African Studies*, 27: 401–30.
Levine, A. 1976. *The Politics of Autonomy*. Amherst: University of Massachusetts Press.

Lewis, P. 1994. "Endgame in Nigeria? The Politics of a Failed Democratic Transition." *African Affairs* 93: 323–40.

———. 1995. "Civil Society, Political Society and Democratic Failure in Nigeria." Paper presented at the annual meeting of the American Political Science Association, Chicago, August 31–September 3.

Lucas, J. 1994. "The State, Civil Society and Regional Elites: A Study of Three Associations in Kano, Nigeria." *African Affairs* 93: 21–38.

Mackenzie, W.J.M. and K.E. Robinson, eds. 1960. *Five Elections in Africa.* Oxford: Clarendon Press.

Mackintosh, J.P. 1966. *Nigerian Government and Politics.* London: George Allen and Unwin.

Mamdani, M. 1990a. *A Glimpse at African Studies, Made in USA.* Codesria Bulletin, 2.

———. 1990b. "State and Civil Society in Contemporary Africa: Reconceptualizing the Birth of State Nationalism and the Defeat of Popular Movements." *Africa Development*, 15.

Manor, J. 1990. "Introduction: Reassessing Third World Politics." *IDS Bulletin*, 21.

Mbembe, A. 1992. "Provisional Notes on the Postcolony." *Africa* (London) 62.

Migdal, J.S. 1988. *Strong Societies and Weak States: State-Society Relations and State Capabilities in the Third World.* Princeton: Princeton University Press.

Okoroji, J.C. 1993. "The Nigerian Presidential Elections." *Review of African Political Economy*, 58: 123–30.

Osaghae, E.E. 1995. "The Study of Political Transitions in Africa." *Review of African Political Economy*, 64: 183–97.

Oyediran, O. ed. 1981. *The Nigerian 1979 Elections.* London: Macmillan.

Oyediran, O. and A. Agbaje. 1991. "Two-Partyism and Democratic Transition in Nigeria." *Journal of Modern African Studies*, 29: 213–35.

Post, K. 1963. *The Nigerian Federal Elections of 1959.* London: Oxford University Press.

———. 1991. "The State, Civil Society, and Democracy in Africa: Some Theoretical Issues." In R. Cohen and H. Goulbourne (eds.), *Democracy and Socialism in Africa*: 34–52. Boulder: Westview Press.

Post, K. and M. Vickers. 1973. *Structure and Conflict in Nigeria, 1960–1966.* London: Heinemann.

Reno, W. 1993. "Old Brigades, Money Bags, New Breeds and the Ironies of Reform in Nigeria." *Canadian Journal of African Studies*, 27: 66–87.

Samudavanija, C.A. 1990. "The Three-Dimensional State." *IDS Bulletin*, 21.

Schatz, S.P. 1977. *Nigerian Capitalism.* Berkeley: University of California Press.

Sklar, R.L. 1963. *Nigerian Political Parties.* Princeton: Princeton University Press.

Suberu, R.T. 1992. "Federalism and the Transition to Democratic Governance in Nigeria." In B. Caron, A. Gboyega, and E. Osaghae (eds.), *Democratic Transition in Africa*: 315–29. Ibadan: CREDU.

———. 1994. "The Democratic Recession in Nigeria." *Current History*, 93: 213–18

Tamuno, T.N. 1966. *Nigeria and Electoral Representation, 1923–1947*. London: Heinemann.

Whitaker, C.S. 1981. "Second Beginnings: The New Political Framework in Nigeria." *Issue*, 11: 1–13.

———. 1984. "The Unfinished State of Nigeria." *Worldview*, 27: 5–8.

Wilson, J.Q. 1992. *American Government*. Lexington: DC Heath.

Young, C. 1988. "The African Colonial State and its Political Legacy." In D. Rothchild, and N. Chazan (eds.), *The Precarious Balance: State and Society in Africa*: 25–66. Boulder: Westview Press.

———. 1994. "In Search of Civil Society." In J.W. Harbeson, D. Rothchild, and N. Chazan (eds.), *Civil Society and the State in Africa*: 33–50. Boulder: Lynne Rienner Publishers.

18

LOCAL INSTITUTIONS, CIVIL SOCIETY AND DEMOCRATIZATION IN NIGERIA, 1986-1993

Alex Gboyega

In June 1993 the tortuous transition program to democratic civil rule that the Babangida administration had implemented for more than seven years came to an abrupt end. The annulment of the presidential election that should have been the culmination of the transition program marked the beginning of a serious political crisis, one of a magnitude unknown since the civil war of 1967 to 1970. Since the annulment, the government has given various reasons for it. While most of those who played key roles in the events leading to the annulment have conveyed the impression that the abortion of the democratic process was purely an elite issue, in 1995 the ex-dictator, General Babangida, has himself provided a significant departure from this perspective. In a rare interview, he blamed the populace for condoning the annulment. In his view, if civil society had resisted him sufficiently, he could not have accomplished his design with its tragic results.

The General's observation is significant for many reasons. First, it shows that the annulment (and by implication the military's decision to intervene in the political arena) was predicated on its being condoned by civil society; if the military thought that the populace would resist it, it would not have been done. Second, the observation should shift our attention from elites and the institutions in which they operate (national political parties, legislative assemblies) to institutions and modalities through which the ordinary people impact the political process. The third import of the statement is Babangida's tacit admission of the failure of his regime to achieve an important goal of his reform program, i.e., to create a new political order based on "grassroots" political participation. Therefore, it is important to examine the government's attempts to empower the grassroots of Nigerian politics and what role grassroots organizations played in the drama of annulment.

The main purpose of this paper is to analyze the local or grassroots dimension of the democratization program from the perspectives of both theory and organization. Additionally, we intend to describe and explain the role of local political institutions in the politics of transition, especially the resistance to the annulment of the presidential election. Lastly, we intend to examine how democracy can be more firmly established in Nigeria if it is built on the foundation of local democratic institutions.

The Philosophy of the Transition

In January 1986 Babangida appointed a Political Bureau to fashion "a system that can guarantee an acceptable and painless succession mechanism" (Babangida 1989a). The Political Bureau proposed a new political order founded on a new political culture that emphasized popular participation in governance and respect for citizens' social, political and economic rights (Federal Republic of Nigeria 1987, 50). Among the many political reforms that the Political Bureau recommended, the most fundamental concerned empowerment of disadvantaged or marginalized groups such as the rural peasantry, urban workers, women and youths.

For example, the Bureau recommended that Government should establish an agency to promote social mobilization to transform passive citizens into active participants in the political process. To achieve this purpose, the Directorate for Social Mobilization (better known by the acronym, MAMSER) was established to:

   a. awaken the consciousness of the mass of Nigerian citizens to their rights and obligations within the Nigerian nation;
   b. inculcate in them the spirit of patriotism and commitment to social justice and self reliance through: (i) mobilizing and harnessing their energies and the natural resources into production; (ii) preparing them to fight internal and external domination of our resources by a few groups or countries; (iii) making them shun waste

and vanity and shedding all pretense to affluence evident in our past life-styles in general; (iv) promoting equality of opportunities in all spheres of our life; (v) creating necessary basic democratic institutions such as farmers' cooperatives, village, clan and ward councils to promote discussion of local affairs and taking decisions on them;
c. make citizens realize that the sovereignty and the resources of the nation collectively belong to them and that it is their right and duty to ensure that they at all times take necessary steps to resist any attempts to deprive them of these valuable rights;
d. make citizens realize that it is equally their right and duty to ensure that those in government primarily serve their collective interests and, if necessary, such people be removed if found wanting;
e. inculcate in the citizens the need to eschew all such vices as corruption, dishonesty, election and census immoral practices, ethnicity and religious bigotry which have bedeviled our body-politic, and uphold the virtues of honesty, hard-work, and commitment to the promotion of national integration; and
f. inculcate in them generally all other virtues of patriotism and active participation in national affairs.

The social mobilization role of the Directorate of Social Mobilization complemented and, in some sense, duplicated the role of the Directorate of Food, Roads and Rural Infrastructures (DFRRI), established in February 1986. The main thrust of DFRRI's functions was the provision and maintenance of rural infrastructures; the strategy proposed was popular mobilization and participation. As General Babangida pointed out in his 1986 budget speech, during which he announced the establishment of the Directorate, it would be "a cardinal role of the Directorate not only effectively to promote a framework for grassroots social mobilization, but also to mount a virile program of developmental monitoring and performance evaluation" (Babangida 1989a).

The desire to ensure more effective participation of rural dwellers in governance through mobilization for political action also found expression in other reforms carried out by the administration. The government established the Better Life for Rural Women Program in September 1987 to (a) raise women's consciousness of their social and political rights, (b) organize them into associations to attract government's support and (c) enable them to better pursue their collective interests (Oyovbaire and Olagunju 1989). The government also established the People's Bank to provide credit for disadvantaged people who could not meet the usual conditions of the normal commercial banks. Community Banks were also promoted to provide banking services in inadequately served communities. The unique aspect of the Community Banks system was that it was conceived to be "a self-sustaining financial institution, owned and managed by a community or group of communities, for the purpose of providing credit, deposit, banking services to its members, largely on the basis of their self-recognition and creditworthiness" (National Board for Community Banks 1992).

The institution of traditional rulers was less a focus of formal reforms than other local institutions were. The government gave the usual assurances of concern that the traditional rulers should play a significant formal role in governance but did nothing practical toward that end. For example, when General Babangida inaugurated the Constitution Review Committee in Abuja on September 7 1987 he enjoined the members to "examine the possibility of giving Traditional Councils a more formal but still advisory function" (Babangida 1989b). To the Constituent Assembly, he commended the role of traditional rulers in helping government to maintain peace, order and political stability and suggested it was up to them to "find ways of giving formal recognition to their role" (Babangida 1989c). In addition, the government nominated some prominent traditional rulers—Alhaji Ibrahim Dasuki, Sultan of Sokoto; Oba Kadiri Momoh, the Olukare of Ikare; Atuwatse II, the Olu of Warri; Alhaji Ibrahim Umar Sanda Ndayako, Etsu Nupe; Dr. Fom Bot, Gbom Gwon of Jos and Alhaji Shuaibu Yakubu Abarshi, the Emir of Yauri—into the Constituent Assembly. The only change in the status of traditional rulers, however, was that the Constituent Assembly wrote into the 1989 Constitution the advisory functions assigned to them under the 1976 local government reform.

At the local government level, however, the Babangida Government made quite fundamental changes. It was at this level of governance that all the measures meant to empower ordinary people discussed above were first expected to have impact under the transition-to-democracy program. The government here combined reform of the system of local government to make local leaders more amenable to the influence of local citizens with efforts to strengthen the localities in their relationship to the states, the intermediate units in the federal structure. In regard to the desire to make the local government system more democratic and accountable, the most fundamental step was the 1987 decision to restore elected local government councils through non-partisan elections. As the transition process continued, local government elections on a partisan basis were held in 1989 and 1991. This was important because the military had inherited a system of local administration manned by appointed Management Committees.

The restoration of democratically elected local governments was reinforced by constitutional guarantee of their boundaries and management structure to prevent the state governments from arbitrarily interfering in their affairs. The 1989 Constitution specified the local governments by name. Therefore, the states could create new local governments only after a constitutional amendment (a process involving all levels of government) and assent by the local community through a referendum. Similarly, the key officials of the local government, their recruitment, and their powers were spelled out in Chapter VIII of the Constitution.

The number of local governments was increased under the transition program from 301 (1984) to 449 (1989) to 589 (1991), ostensibly to enhance participation. The power to conduct local elections was vested in the National Electoral Commission to check the practice by which, previously, state governments could refuse to conduct local government elections so that they could appoint management committees to run local governments. Thus, the federal government became the guarantor of a democratic system of local government. The government's plan, according to General Babangida, was to establish a "Local Government System which should serve as a training ground for democratic politicking and governance and as a springboard for participation at other levels of government" (Babangida 1989d).

The federal government implemented other reforms to strengthen the expression of democratic choice in local governance. These reforms transformed the relationship between the elected leadership of the local governments and the administrative executives. In 1988 the government designated the Local Government Chairman as the Chief Executive and Accounting Officer of his local government. Previously, the administrative secretary of the local government was the chief executive. Consequently, he was really the prime mover of development in his local government. This was not only a source of conflict between the elected and career officials, it often frustrated the expression of democratic choice at the local level. The new policy meant that elected officials could more effectively exercise their electoral mandate.

Within the local government, the position of the chairman was strengthened at the expense of the councilors. In 1987 the chairmen were empowered to appoint the supervisory councilors who, with him, formed the Executive Committee of the local government. In 1991 when the presidential system of government was extended to local administration, the executive was separated from the council and guaranteed a fixed tenure subject to good behavior. Simultaneously, the federal government increased fiscal transfers to local governments. Such transfers were first introduced in 1976 and accorded constitutional guarantee in 1979. Initially pegged at 10 percent of the Federation Account, in 1990 it was raised to 15 percent and in 1992 to 20 percent.

These changes shifted the balance of resources between local government and states significantly in the favor of the former. The sheer volume of the transfers to local government was impressive. In 1989 it was naira 3,347 million, in 1991 naira 8,475 million, in 1992 naira 15,715 million and in 1993 naira 22, 120 million. While the proportion of funds transferred to local governments increased, the transfers to states declined. From 32.5 percent in 1989 these transfers decreased to 30 percent in 1990, 25 percent in January 1992 and 24 percent in June 1992.

Administratively, and politically too, the federal government strengthened local governments against the states. State Ministries for Local Government were abolished in 1988 to "liberate Local Governments from unwholesome bureaucratic constraints; enhance their speed of action; put them in firm control over local affairs and encourage the emergence of local solutions to local problems" (Aikhomu 1988). A new Department of Local Government was established in the State Governor's office to replace the Ministry. However, it was expected to guide and help rather than direct and control the local governments.

Similarly, in 1991 the government abolished the Local Government Service Commission in order to place full control over personnel policies in the hands of each local government. When the government vested the Chairman of each local government with the power to appoint a secretary for his local government, the orientation of local government employees to locally elected officials was expected to change positively. Before then, they were more responsive to state government officials than to elected local officials because their career prospects depended on the Local Government Service Commission established by the state government. However, the Commission was resuscitated within six months because of strong opposition from the staff union of local governments (the National Union of Local Government Employees—NULGE), the civilian governors who assumed office in January 1992, and massive abuses by the local government chairmen who sacked hundreds without due process.

As noted above, in 1991 the federal government decided to extend the presidential system to local government. This step, more than any other policy, freed local governments from the administrative and political controls hitherto exercised by the state governments as it led to the definition of the respective functions of the executive and legislative arms of local government. Thereafter, state governments ceased to have the power to scrutinize and approve local budgets, to vet and approve bylaws, and to authorize the award of contracts. These powers passed to each local government council.

We can summarize the government's objectives in carrying out all of these reforms of the local government system as follows:

a. to establish local government as training ground for "democratic politicking and governance and as a springboard for participation at other levels of government" (Babangida 1989d).
b. to enhance the autonomy of local governments, to reduce agitation for new states and to serve as growth points that would provide the needed push to start and energize productive activities in rural Nigeria and by that reduce the rural-urban drift (Babangida 1991).
c. to enable the local governments to operate according to the spirit and letter of the Constitution by giving them autonomy to perform their statutory functions and play their role in the Federal structure of governance (Babangida 1991).

Government also tried to ensure that ordinary citizens exercised more effective influence on their political leaders by imposing an appropriate party structure and a set of operational rules. The imposition of two political parties (the Social Democratic Party and National Republican Convention) created, funded and directed by the government has appeared to becloud assessment of the thrust of the party system. The party structure had four levels—ward, local government, state and national. Only at the ward level could one join, resign or be expelled from the party. The introduction of primaries to nominate party candidates for elections made popular participation in the selection of candidates compulsory. This was meant to enhance consultations between party leaders and members. For example, a councilor was a member of his party's ward Executive Committee and ward Congress, in which fora he was expected to consult his constituents and account for his stewardship (Nwabuzor 1992).

The electoral reforms, for all their defects, aimed to liberalize and streamline the franchise. The electoral laws stipulated that one could only register and vote in the ward where he was ordinarily a resident. Previously, people had believed and behaved as if they could exercise their right to vote only in their places of origin. In addition, polling stations catered for not more than 500 voters in order to avoid the previously rampant abuses of impersonation and multiple voting at elections. The Government introduced the system of recall to make those elected to legislative bodies behave properly. These aspects of the electoral system and the various manipulations of the voting system—open balloting, "secret-open" balloting and "Option A4"—were intended to make ordinary voters more effective in monitoring elections to check abuses, to make it easier for them to make informed choices based on their knowledge of candidates (their character, credibility and capability) and to reinforce the impact of the political mobilization to be accomplished by the MAMSER and the DFRRI.

It bears repeating that many aspects of the reforms described above undermined or conflicted with accepted democratic values and norms. Although the Political Bureau thought that Nigeria could not have a stable government unless it adopted a two-party system, the government's decision to form and to impose the parties on the electorate negated freedom of association. Nevertheless, there were some positive achievements as well. Although these were far from the "revolutionary change" that the intellectuals who shaped the Babangida administration's political transition program claimed (Oyovbaire and Olagunju 1989) they did aim to transform political relations where it mattered most, the local level. So we must turn to an examination of the impact of these reforms on civil society and the process of democratization.

Civil Society under the Transition Program

If we define civil society as the arena where civil organizations and social movements have the opportunity or freedom to organize and pursue their interests (Stepan 1988) then civil society expanded in scope during the transition period. There was a proliferation of community development associations (CDAs), professional associations, trade unions, civil rights and pro-democracy organizations, cooperative unions, youth associations, and women's groups. The Babangida administration indeed promoted CDAs as a constituency-building measure. The government's shift of attention to rural development and mass mobilization was meant to give it an alternative foothold among the populace to compensate for loss of support of the middle class.

However, the vast majority of the associations operating in the sociopolitical arena were autonomous of the state. These were also welcomed by the Babangida administration because they filled a gap which the state could not cover. By 1985, when Babangida came into office, the Nigerian state that he inherited had ceased to be regarded as *infinitus thesaurus* (Ayoade 1988), as most African leaders had preferred to portray their states. The Nigerian state certainly did not have the means to maintain the social infrastructures which it had been led by surging petro-dollars to erect in more affluent times. With greatly diminished resources, and a loss of confidence in its ability to do anything about the poor state of the economy without outside assistance, the government was compelled to vacate a considerable part of the development space which it previously monopolized (Ekeh 1992). This strengthened the elites who led the associations and made them more independent of the state (Lucas 1994).

The Babangida administration, however, also tried to gain some influence if not control over the NGO community. It was concerned by the profuse number of the NGOs and their autonomy. It therefore sought to bring them into collaboration with its purposes and strategies. In May 1991, the Federal Ministry of Culture and Social Welfare, in collaboration with the United Nations Development Programme, organized a conference at Kaduna on "Strengthening Collaboration Between Government and Non-Governmental organizations in Nigeria." The bargain which the government offered the NGOs was that they should form sectoral apex NGOs that would be registered with the government. The focus and activities of the NGOs would be integrated with national development plans after negotiations with the NGOs. This would mean that the government could intervene in setting priorities for them. In return, the NGOs would have the backing of government in gaining regular access to funds provided by international donors.

The government's attempt to buy its way into collaboration with the NGO community failed for many reasons. First, the Kaduna conference was attended by elite NGOs—those that had computers, mailing lists and regular contacts with government agencies. Second, these NGOs were those that were most concerned to preserve their independence of Government. They welcomed the promise of government assistance to access donor funds, but would not compromise their autonomy. Many had disdain for government policy or for its bureaucratic procedures. At any rate, some of them had been sourcing funds directly from international donors and viewed the promise of government assistance as the thin end of a wedge. They believed that once the government gained the right to intervene between them and donors, the scope of interference would widen to cover what they were allowed to do and when. Third, the vast majority of private, voluntary development associations—especially rural, community-based ones—were not represented. So, even if the bargain had been struck, it would have covered only an insignificant slice of the whole.

Nevertheless, the mobilization carried out by both DFRRI and MAMSER promoted rapid growth in the number and variety of private voluntary associations that sought to participate in the shaping of public policies and the implementation of socioeconomic development programs. Oyo State, for example, had 1,469 Community Development Associations (CDAs) in its twenty-four local governments at the end of 1987 (Olowu, Ayo, and Akande 1991). Most of these were federal organizations that comprised several community-based, private voluntary development associations.

DFRRI concentrated on encouraging communities to establish CDAs for channeling their collective participation in the development effort. The CDAs were also expected to provide political leadership for rural communities to engage in exchanges with the government. To achieve this goal, DFRRI carried out an enumeration of identifiable, distinctive communities (of which there were more than 90,000) and tried to ensure that each had at least one CDA. The CDA was, however, not the only private voluntary development association that DFRRI thought was essential for a community to have. It was to be the "apex" organization for its community bringing within its fold and coordinating the activities of other voluntary development associations sharing the same territorial boundary. Such an apex organization has been described as a "Home Town Association" (Barkan, McNulty, and Ayeni 1991).

The strategy for promoting the establishment of CDAs and ensuring their participation combined central support through advice and incentives with local initiative and direction. DFFRI propagated the advantages of each community organizing an apex CDA and concretized the benefits of so doing by routing the goods and services that it had to distribute through them. Thus, it decentralized its operations through state committees to the local level. Besides the national board that dealt with policies and allocation of resources, state programs were the responsibility of a state Advisory Board headed by the state governor. In addition, there was a State Implementation Committee chaired by the State Director of Rural Development. It comprised local government chairmen and officials of the state and zonal Association of Community Development Councils (Sunmola 1989).

The attempts by DFRRI to organize the communities for effective collective action was not only for the promotion of physical development. It also had an explicitly political objective. As DFRRI admonished

> For those communities who up till now are not convinced about the fundamental need to be properly organised, let a cold fact be stated . . . Government is well organised. When the ban on partisan politics is lifted, parties will also be properly organised. For as long as the people are themselves not organised, so long will Government and political parties exploit them. The current situation where the people are virtually powerless in relation to Government and political parties must be redressed. One of the ways the powerlessness of the people can be redressed is for them to start from the grassroots, organise themselves, not only for their socio-cultural and economic development but also to be able to relate in strength to partisan politics and Government. If this can be achieved, then true sovereignty would have been attained by the people of this country (Koinyan 1987).

The Directorate of Social Mobilization (MAMSER) was even more explicitly concerned with promoting the participation of private voluntary associations in politics and particularly in the process of democratization. It had three main departments: Mass Mobilization, Mass Education, and Political Education. Like DFRRI, MAMSER focused on CDAs, youth organizations, and other popular organizations. Its message was not only similar, but popular participation was in fact the only message. Its Political Education Manual (Directorate of Social Mobilization 1989) highlighted some maxims of its program of mobilization thus:

1. Popular organizations are the engine of democracy;
2. It is important that citizens give their support to popular mass organizations. This is because such organizations strengthen national unity since they promote the interest of the broad masses;
3. Professional associations of well educated citizens are also very important in the building of democracy and rapid national development in Nigeria today . . . It is important that members of these associations realize that their skills are important to national development. However, they can make meaningful contributions to national development only when their work is based on service to the broad masses of our people;
4. Finally, for these unions and associations to play an effective role in national development, their members must ensure internal democracy in the organizations.

The combined effect of the mobilization of DFRRI and MAMSER was to make private voluntary development associations more interested in the politics of the transition period. Furthermore, other aspects of the local reforms of the era drew the community-based associations into closer contact and collaboration with the local governments. For example, when the federal government reorganized the management of primary education in 1988, it made it mandatory for each local government to establish a Local Education Authority (LEA) for the operational control of primary schools in its area of authority. The government assigned more than half the seats on the LEA to representatives of nongovernmental organizations. The LEA was presided over by the local government Chairman. Other official members were the local government Supervisor for Education and the Local Education Officer. Nonofficial members were: a representative of the National Union of Teachers, a representative of women, two citizens who had been intimately connected with primary education, two representatives of religious organizations, and a representative of the Parents-Teachers Association.

While the government was thus consciously promoting the growth and participation of private voluntary development associations, there was also a push toward that same end from another source. In 1986, the government adopted a Structural Adjustment Program (SAP) under which it progressively devalued the naira, privatized or commercialized public enterprises, deregulated prices and interest rates, and liberalized trade. Policymakers assured the country that the liberalization entailed in the SAP would unleash market forces and the entrepreneurial spirit of the people.

However, as Ake (1991) has pointed out, SAP has caused much misery through steep inflation, unemployment, malnutrition and premature death in African countries that have adopted the policy. In Nigeria, these unpalatable consequences of the reforms caused many social groups to oppose the policy specifically and the government generally. The Nigerian Labour Congress (NLC), National Association of Nigerian Students (NANS), Manufacturers Association of Nigeria (MAN), Academic Staff Union of Universities (ASUU), Nigerian Medical Association (NMA), and the Nigerian Bar Association (NBA) became the spearheads of this opposition (Olukoshi 1995). These disaffected groups often acted politically through strikes and demonstrations, while the urban unemployed resorted to riots to protest the adjustment policies (Adejumobi 1995). This raised serious doubts about the extent to which SAP was compatible with democratization (Oyejide 1991). The government responded variously through relaxation of some harsh aspects of the adjustment policies, "selective accommodation of opposition demands, repression and co-optation of opponents, and the erection of its own clientelist network" (Olukoshi 1995). Through such tactics the government succeeded in infiltrating or weakening many professional groups and in restraining opposition to government policies. The NLC's leadership became less radical and bellicose toward government policies after Paschal Bafyau became its President through government intervention. The security forces constantly harassed the leaders of NMA, MBA, and NANS and ASUU. The government's repression diminished the strength of the opposition from the professional associations but did not eliminate it. So Agbaje (1990) was partly correct to observe that SAP had the consequence of weakening the challenges which professional groups could pose to government.

On the other hand, the government's infiltration of professional associations also provoked the establishment of newer associations to challenge its policies and abuses of human rights even more vigorously than professional associations could do. The Civil Liberties Organization (CLO), the Constitutional Rights Project (CRP), the Committee for the Defence of Human Rights (CDHR), the Gani Fawehinmi Solidarity Association (GFSA), and the National Association of Democratic Lawyers (NADL) are some organizations established mainly to fight against the oppressive acts of the Babangida administration (Momoh 1994). These associations which were outside the control of the Government, were well organized and competently led. They became very popular because people perceived that they were the only ones that had the courage and will to seek to protect the oppressed. From civil and human rights protection to more overtly political action was a short step.

An attempt by some of these professional and civil rights organizations to organize a national conference on the "National Question" was aborted by the government because of the fear that it would be a rallying point for its opponents. Perhaps the government was alarmed by the types of organizations invited to the proposed national conference. The organizers invited only non-governmental organizations (NGOs), most of which were radically opposed to government policies. The fact that they were joined by erstwhile pillars of the establishment signalled to the government that the opposition was broadening its front. Secondly, the sponsors had long demanded a sovereign national conference in the model of the one that the Benin Republic convened in 1990. Thirdly, the proposed conference was being convened within a year of the government promulgation of the 1989 Constitution which was to be the foundation of the Third Republic. Thus, the legitimacy of the whole transition program was placed at stake.

The government therefore announced that the conference would be treated as an attempt to undermine the transition program, an offense that carried a penalty of five years jail term! The former permanent secretaries backed out of the conference but their partners—the civil rights organizations and other mass organizations like ASUU and NANS—met clandestinely to discuss plans for resisting the increasingly repressive policies of the government. They formed the Campaign for Democracy (CD) to coordinate the member-organizations' opposition to government.

At this point, the government itself, not just specific policies, became the issue and was viewed as the obstacle to national development. Therefore, the member organizations committed themselves to ensuring that the military handed over power on the scheduled date, in spite of their earlier scepticism regarding the appropriateness of the transition reforms and the genuineness of the government's commitment to its transition plan. The CD committed itself to ensure:

a. restoration of the sovereignty of the Nigerian people to self-determination, to choose how to be governed, who to govern them and the procedure or process through which they will be governed;
b. the right of people to form their own political parties without interference;
c. termination of military rule for all time;
d. the replacement of imposed transitional agencies by independent and impartial electoral bodies;
e. respect of Fundamental Human Rights, the rule of law and the abrogation of all decrees;
f. termination of economic policies which have caused the people hardship, poverty, disease, hunger, unemployment, retrenchment and illiteracy.

From its objectives stated above, it is not surprising that the CD became the strongest source of opposition to the Babangida administration from 1990 to 1993 and especially after the annulment of the presidential election in June 1993.

The government's adoption of SAP also provoked the establishment of several types of community-based, private, voluntary philanthropic organizations. These organizations cater to the needs of destitutes, deprived youths, unemployed people, women, and other disadvantaged peoples. Though they did not engage the government in the same way as the civil rights organizations, the government's policies were the raison d'être of their existence. They were a response to the failure of the government to meet the welfare needs of the people or simply to maintain existing benefits. For example, changes in the funding and administration of primary education led to several cost elements being pushed unto parents. Parents-Teachers Associations and other local, voluntary philanthropic or developmental organizations had to step in to provide school infrastructures and offer scholarships to needy children (Gboyega, Ogunsanya, and Okunade 1995). Such groups were negatively focused on government. All these organizations looked forward to the restoration of democratic rule under which the government could be expected to be more responsive to the needs of the people.

Civil Society and Democratization

The strength of civil society during the period of the transition program was severely tested following the annulment of the June 12 1993 presidential elections. Characteristic of losers in Nigerian electoral contests, the NRC supported the annulment. Thus, Asoluka, an NRC member of the House of Representatives declared that "the SDP's victory will spell doom for our party. . . ." *(African Guardian* 1993) while NRC Governors threatened that there would be chaos, bloodshed and catastrophe of unprecedented proportions should the election results be revalidated. Also, the Peoples Front faction of the SDP thought the annulment could provide an opportunity for its leader, General Yar'Adua, who had won the SDP nomination in late 1992 but had been disqualified, to try again to become president. Therefore, when General Babangida asked the party leaders to choose between immediate fresh elections and an interim national government (*Newswatch*, August 30 1993), it was easy for the national leadership of the SDP to feign helplessness and eventually to abandon the electoral mandate of their presidential candidate.

The irresolute attitude of the political parties toward the annulment was matched by the utter confusion and opportunism of the members of the elected federal National Assembly. They were divided on how to respond to the annulment. Like the party leaders, even some SDP legislators were willing to forego their candidate's electoral victory if they could thereby secure pecuniary benefits or preserve their seats. Apparently they took seriously Babangida's threat that if the parties did not accept immediate fresh elections, then all elected institutions would have to give way to an interim administration. The NRC members, meanwhile, needed little persuasion to support the military authorities. Even then money was liberally distributed (*Newswatch*, August 30 1993) to ensure that the legislators extended Babangida's stay in power.

The battle to seek revalidation of the election results thus fell on other leaders of civil society. The human rights associations uniformly denounced the annulment and were alone responsible for the prolonged street protests and workers' strikes to pressure the government to reverse the decision. The variety of organizations that took part in activities (denunciation, demonstration, and sending delegations to government officials) to make Government reverse the annulment was impressive. For example, Women in Nigeria (WIN) held a meeting at Bauchi on August 7 1993 after which it resolved that "unless General Babangida relinquished power to the winner of the 12th June election unfailingly on August 27, permanent damage will be done to the political and territorial integrity of the nation." Therefore, it resolved to participate actively in all pro-democracy protests to ensure that the wishes of the electorate as expressed during the elections were respected (*The Guardian* June 20 1993, A4).

Similarly, a group of 153 that styled itself as Concerned Professionals placed advertisements in the papers to canvass resistance to the annulment. They expressed alarm at the steep and continuing decline of the quality of life in Nigeria as a result of the political crisis. They asked members of the Transitional Government to stop hiding behind the veil of being technocrats and to declare their stand on the political crisis. In addition, the group pledged to use all legitimate means of expressing their objections to the annulment. Among the most active organizations that denounced the annulment were: the Democratic Forum, Federation of Niger Delta Youths Associations, National Association of Nigerian Students, Academic Staff of Nigerian Universities (ASNU was formed to replace ASUU (then proscribed) as the Universities teachers' union), Committee for the Defence of Human Rights, National Association for Democracy and Development, the Constitutional Rights Project, various branches of the Nigerian Bar Association, Movement for National Reform, and Committee of Concerned Nigerians.

The churches also were firmly and consistently opposed to the annulment. Christian religious leaders considered the annulment immoral and unjust. Even before the results were annulled, the Abuja branch of the Christian Association of Nigeria (CAN) had complained (*The Guardian*, July 30 1993, 32) about the delay in announcing the final election results. It asked Nigerians to be vigilant in prayer. Catholic bishops sent a six-man delegation to Babangida to appeal to him to reverse the annulment on July

29 1993 (*The Guardian* August 4 1993, 32). Following Babangida's rejection of their request, they declared, in a press statement (*The Guardian* August 15 1993, 10), that "a presidential election widely pronounced to be free, fair and peaceful has been held. . . . The wishes of the people, as expressed in that election, should have been, therefore, officially announced and respected." They reminded the military that its role was to serve and defend the nation. In addition, they composed a special prayer to be said daily at the end of every public mass and by every family and individual. They also declared August 15 1993 as a special day on which masses should be offered for Nigeria.

Similarly, Archbishop Abiodun Adetiloye, head of the Anglican Church in Nigeria, led Anglican bishops to condemn the annulment. Bishop Gbonigi of Akure, for instance, in a pastoral letter (a fashionable means by which Church leaders commented on the political crisis) described the Interim National Government as "an illegal, illegitimate and iniquitous national government" that should give way to the popularly elected government of Abiola (*The Guardian* September 17 1993, 5). When General Sani Abacha replaced Shonekan as Head of State, Archbishop Adetiloye began a series of open letters urging him to return to the path of honor by validating the election results. In one such letter (*Tell* October 10 1994, 10), he wrote that "God has decreed your exit from power and nothing can change it. He has directed me to write the final letter to you, so that you may get out in time. I advise you, therefore, to listen to the expressed wishes of the people. . . ." Like the Catholic bishops, he directed Anglican churches to pray regularly that God would restore the sense of justice and fairness of the military cabal intent on subverting the democratic process. The themes of justice and morality were repeated by most churches in their regular and special sessions, thereby keeping their congregations constantly focused on the annulled election results.

The Muslim organizations were, however, divided in their reaction to the annulment. Before the government annulled the elections, the Executive Secretary of the Islamic Forum, Group Captain Jubril Usman, urged the National Electoral Commission to declare the election results and appealed to Nigerians to abide by the verdict (*The Guardian* June 20 1993, A4). The Sultan of Sokoto and President of the Nigerian Supreme Council for Islamic Affairs (NSCIA), Alhaji Ibrahim Dasuki, however, described the annulment as an act of God to which Abiola should be reconciled. This pronouncement provoked many Muslim adherents who thought the Sultan was motivated by partisan political considerations rather than the dictates of justice and morality. Thus, Muslim leaders from the five western states including the secretary-general of NSCIA called on Nigerians to reject the Sultan's position and endorse the truth and justice of June 12 (*The Guardian* September 9 1993, 2). The NSCIA leaders split along a north-south axis and could not take a definite stand on the political crisis. When the NSCIA executive met in July 1993, it decided to meet Babangida and Abiola separately to encourage them to find a peaceful solution to the crisis, and even that could not have been done with any sense of urgency (*The Guardian* July 30 1993, 32).

The press media were generally quite vehement in their support for democracy. The government media were naturally hampered in expressing support for the validation of the election results. The independent press, on the other hand, became staunch proponents of democracy. *The Guardian* in particular wrote trenchant opinions on the political crisis. On August 6 1993 *The Guardian* described the acceptance of an Interim National Government as an evasion of reality that could only lead to the prolongation of military rule. In another opinion, the paper accused the Minister of Information of making "crude, unsubstantiated allegations against editors, publishers, proprietors and even an elected governor" to justify proscription of five newspapers and a magazine by the government (*The Guardian* July 30 1993, 10). Reflecting on the unprincipled role of the members of the National Assembly in accepting the Interim National Government, on October 29 1993, *The Guardian* warned that "if members of the Assembly do not see the unwisdom of supporting arbitrariness and illegality, . . . the inexorable logic of arbitrary power will eventually sweep the unruly crowd away." The *Citizen* (June 21–27 1993, 7) also commented that "In the name of all that is fair and just and in the name of peace and stability, we of this country must let the election be."

Traditional rulers and local government chairmen were generally divided along geographical lines. Most southern traditional rulers and local government chairmen supported the validation of the election results. Their northern counterparts, on the other hand, maintained a silence suggestive of indifference or tacit support of the annulment. Eventually, even the pro-democracy traditional rulers had to modify their position or, at best, keep their opinions to themselves. For example, the Ooni of Ife, Oba Okunade Olubuse II, was one of those strongly in support of Abiola's cause. When the Sultan of Sokoto asked Abiola to regard the cancellation of the election as an act of God, the Ooni had promptly replied that June 12 was fundamental to the peaceful corporate existence of Nigeria and that nobody concerned with justice, fairness and honesty could ask Abiola to forgo his electoral victory (*Tell* September 27 1993, 17). However, he changed his stance after he and other traditional rulers met with Babangida (*Newbreed* November 22 1993, 30). He declared that Babangida's explanation of the cancellation of the results made sense to him, and later he campaigned for Abacha's Constitutional Conference.

Most SDP local government chairmen initially followed the lead of their governors in rejecting the government's decision to annul the elections. However, they were less assertive than the governors and the pro-democracy organizations. One reason for their relatively low-keyed involvement in the resistance to the annulment was the fact that their continued stay in office was literally at the pleasure of the military government. Besides in the face of the government's threat to dissolve all democratic institutions, the local governments were especially vulnerable because their tenure had really expired; it had been verbally extended by the presidency. Therefore, they had reason to fear that they might be summarily dismissed from office.

Government's Reaction

The government's response to the pro-democracy agitations was predictable considering its past record of human rights abuses and arbitrariness. When in early July the Campaign for Democracy called for protests that sparked spontaneous street demonstrations in most parts of the south and pockets of the north, the government rounded up their leaders and detained them for prolonged periods without trial. The street demonstrations were repressed with brutal severity. The security forces were massively deployed in south-western Nigeria, the theater of the fiercest protests. Schools and colleges were closed down to forestall their participation in the pro-democracy agitations.

The government also promulgated The Newspaper Decree No. 43 of 1993 that required all existing newspapers to apply for re-registration from a Board that had not been set up when the decree came into force on June 22 1993. Another law, The Newspapers (Proscription and Prohibitions from Circulation) Decree No. 48 of 1993 was published on July 22 1993 under which *The African Concord, National Concord, Weekend Concord,* and *Sunday Concord* (Abiola's publications) were proscribed. The proscription also affected *Daily Sketch, Sunday Sketch, The Punch, The Sunday Punch, The Nigerian Observer* and *The Sunday Observer. The News, Abuja Newsday* and *The Reporter* were also closed down at different times. The Guardian Newspapers Limited successfully challenged the legality of Decree No. 43 when on November 18 1993 a Lagos High Court declared it unconstitutional and null and void.

It was in large part the valiant performance of civil society that compelled General Babangida to abandon his hopes of prolonging his stay as head of the Interim National Government. On August 27 1993, he bowed out of office and was replaced by Ernest Shonekan. The new administration tried to pacify the pro-democracy forces by releasing activists who had been detained without trial. In addition, the administration made conciliatory gestures to them by appointing a Panel of Inquiry to investigate circumstances leading to the annulment of the elections. Shut media houses were also reopened. However, nothing short of restoration of Abiola's electoral victory would pacify the government's opponents. When the government announced increases in the pump prices of petroleum products, a reluctant Nigerian Labour Congress called workers out on strike. The Lagos High Court's decision in mid-November that the Interim National Government was illegal gave General Abacha the opportunity to shove it aside and seize power.

Conclusion

During the period of Babangida's transition program, a huge number of CDAs, community-based organizations, professional associations, and social movements operated in the political realm outside the purview and control of the state. Even local authorities were less amenable to central dictation. The impact of the autonomy of these associations was more fully tested and felt following the annulment of the presidential election in June 1993. After the political parties and the National Assembly capitulated and abandoned democratization, it was the Campaign for Democracy that mobilized the protests and resistance to the annulment. At the height of the crisis, Babangida had boasted that it was his administration's eleventh crisis and that he would survive it as he did the previous ten. The political class clearly obliged him but not the vast array of popular, voluntary associations that had operated mostly outside the scope of his administration's control or influence under the transition program.

Civil society seemed helpless in the face of the brutal suppression of opposition under Abacha. However, what was most devastating to the strength of civil society under Abacha's administration was the defection of several pro-democracy elites to the government's side. The so-called "progressives" of his first cabinet (Ebenezer Babatope, Lateef Jakande, Olu

Onagoruwa, Wole Oyelese, Abubakar Rimi, Solomon Lar, Jerry Gana, Iyorchia Ayu) had been prominent pro-democracy activists. Not only did they abandon the cause, they became strong advocates of the new military administration and ardent proponents of its "The nation must move forward" message.

The resistance collapsed also because of CD's organizational weakness. To begin with, the member organizations of CD were concentrated in southwestern Nigeria and that was where it had most influence. Because of multiple memberships by those active in these popular organizations, it was possible to draw other organizations into the initial resistance activities. The past protests against human rights abuses under the Babangida administration had also equipped people with exquisite mobilizational skills. In addition, as a result of the political education under the transition program quite a number of organizations had come to associate democratization with a solution to national problems and, therefore, found the abortion of the process intolerable.

Unfortunately, the CD had limited resources against the massive resources of the government. As the crisis became prolonged, weariness set in, particularly as the price to be paid for the battle for democracy got dearer: brutality of the security forces, detention without trial, and assassinations. Undeniably, however, the CD and its allies had fought a valiant battle for democracy and may yet do so again if the opportunity arises. To be more successful, however, the popular private voluntary development associations would need to develop more effective networks and diffuse the organizational skills of the more exposed and experienced ones among them. Contemporary Nigeria remains far from Hirst's (1994) world of "associative democracy," but a robust civil society exists and gives hope for the future.

References

Adejumobi, Said. 1995. "Adjustment Reform and its Impact on the Economy and Society." In Adejumobi and Abubakar Momoh (eds.), *The Political Economy of Nigeria Under Military Rule: 1984–1993*: 163–93. Harare: SAPES Books.

Agbaje, Adigun. 1990. "In Search of Building Blocks: The State, Civil Society, Voluntary Action and Grassroots Development in Africa." *Africa Quarterly*, 30, 3–4: 24–40.

Aikhomu, Vice-Admiral Augustus. 1988. "Address Delivered by the Chief of

General Staff, Vice-Admiral Augustus Aikhomu at the opening of the Seminar on Local Government Autonomy," 19 December, at University of Ibadan, Nigeria.

Ake, Claude. 1991. "Rethinking African Democracy." *Journal of Democracy*, 2, 1 Winter.

Ayoade, John A.A. 1988. "States Without Citizens: An Emerging African Phenomenon." In Donald Rothchild and Naomi Chazan (eds.), *The Precarious Balance: State and Society in Africa*: 100–18. Boulder: Westview Press.

Babangida, General I. B. 1989a. The 1986 Budget: Options for Economic Recovery "Text of the 1986 Budget Speech to the Nation in Lagos on 31 December, 1985." In *Portrait of a New Nigeria: Selected Speeches of IBB*: 131–62. Marlow, Bucks: Precision Press.

———. 1989b. "The Design of a New Constitution." (Speech Delivered at the Inauguration of the Constitution Review Committee in Abuja on 7 September, 1987). In *Portrait of a New Nigeria: Selected Speeches of IBB*: 35–43. Marlow, Bucks: Precision Press.

———. 1989c. "The March to a Viable Political Order" (Address to Members of the Constituent Assembly at Abuja on 11 May, 1988). In *Portrait of a New Nigeria: Selected Speeches of IBB*: 45–55. Marlow, Bucks: Precision Press.

———. 1989d. "Let us Learn From History" (Text of President Babangida's Acceptance Speech on the Draft Nigerian Constitution). In *Portrait of a New Nigeria: Selected Speeches of IBB*: 57–64. Marlow, Bucks: Precision Press.

———. 1991. "The Future of the Past: The Historical Imperative of the Transition" (An Address Delivered on the Occasion of the 12th Graduation Ceremony of the National Institute for Policy and Strategic Studies, Kuru, 20 October, 1990). In *For Their Tomorrow We Gave Our Today: Selected Speeches of IBB Volume II*: 26–36. Ibadan: Safari Books.

Barkan, Joel D, Michael L. McNulty and M. O. Ayeni. 1991. "Hometown Voluntary Associations, Local Development, and the Emergence of Civil Society in Western Nigeria." *The Journal of Modern African Studies*: 29, 3: 457–80.

Directorate For Social Mobilization. 1989. *Political Education Manual*: 21. Abuja.

Ekeh, Peter P. 1992. "The Constitution of Civil Society in African History and Politics." In B. Caron, A. Gboyega and E. Osaghae (eds.), *Democratic Transitions in Africa*: 187–212. Ibadan: CREDU.

Etzioni-Halevy, Eva. 1993. *The Elite Connection: Problems and Potential of Western Democracy*: 78–99. Cambridge: Polity Press.

Federal Republic of Nigeria. 1987. *Report of the Political Bureau*: par. 8.015. Lagos: Federal Government Printer.

Federal Republic of Nigeria. 1988. *Who is Who in the Constituent Assembly 1988–1989*: Appendix A. Lagos: Federal Ministry of Information and Culture.

Gboyega, Alex, Mobolaji Ogunsanya and Bayo Okunade. 1995. "An Evaluation of the Liberalisation of Funding and Administration of Primary Education in Nigeria As a Result of SAP" (Final Research Report Submitted to NISER/Social Science Council of Nigeria).

Hirst, Paul. 1994. *Associative Democracy*. Cambridge: Polity Press.

Koinyan, L.D. 1987. *The Way Forward : How Communities Can Participate in Rural (and National) Development*: Volume 1, 25. Lagos: Federal Government Press.

Lucas, John. 1994. "The State, Civil Society and Regional Elites: A Study of Three Associations in Kano, Nigeria." *African Affairs*, 93: 21–38.

Momoh, Abubakar. 1994. "Some Association Groups and the Transition to Civil Rule in Nigeria." In Omo Omoruyi, Dirk Berg-Schlosser, Adesina Sambo and Ada Okwuosa (eds.), *Democratisation in Africa: Nigerian Perspectives*, Volume Two: 174–201. Benin City: Centre for Democratic Studies.

National Board for Community Banks. 1992. *Community Banks Prospectus*.

Nwabuzor, Elone J. 1992. "The Meaning and Purpose of Grassroots Democracy." In J.A.A. Ayoade, Elone J. Nwabuzor and Adesina Sambo (eds.), *Grassroots Democracy and the New Local Government System in Nigeria*: 7–19. Abuja: Centre for Democratic Studies.

Olowu, Dele. S. Bamidele Ayo and Bola Akande. 1991. *Local Institutions and National Development in Nigeria*. Ile-Ife: Research Group in Local Institutions.

Olukoshi, Adebayo O. 1995. "The Political Economy of the Structural Adjustment Programme." In Said Adejumobi and Abubakar Momoh (eds.), *The Political Economy of Nigeria Under Military Rule: 1984–1993*: 138–62. Harare: SAPES Books.

Oyejide T. A. 1991. "Economic Restructuring, Political Reform and Growth Prospects in Nigeria." In Laolu Akinyele, John Omueti and Tom Ekpeyong (eds.), *Economic and Democratic Reforms in Nigeria's Development*: 9–13. Ibadan: SID.

Oyovbaire, Sam and Tunji Olagunju. 1989. *Foundations of a New Nigeria*: 45. Marlow, Bucks: Precision Press.

Smock, Audrey C. 1971. *Ibo Politics: The Role of Ethnic Unions in Eastern Nigeria*: 111. Cambridge: Harvard University Press.

Stepan, Alfred. 1988. *Rethinking Military Politics: Brazil and the Southern Cone*: 3–4. Princeton: Princeton University Press.

Sunmola, D.O. 1989. "Directorate's Services to the Community: The Case of Ogun State DFRRI." In Aborisade, Oladimeji (ed.), *On Being in Charge at the Grassroots Level in Nigeria*: 276–85. Ile-Ife: Department of Local Government Studies.

19

TRADITIONAL RULERS AND THE DILEMMA OF DEMOCRATIC TRANSITIONS IN NIGERIA

Olufemi Vaughan

Political developments in major African countries reveal the resilience and adaptability of "traditional" political institutions to the structures of the post-colonial nation state. Traditional institutions have not only survived in the contemporary era but have also been integrated into structures of the modern state and society. While undermining overarching national doctrines and institutions, the incorporation of antecedent institutions into the structures of the modern state has consolidated power relations at both the national and sub-national levels. In Botswana, for example, where chieftaincy institutions have been integrated into a relatively viable liberal democratic system, powerful chiefs as representatives of local constituencies have exerted considerable influence in the electoral system and in the implementation of important state policies and programs (Molutsi 1989, 106). This development has often posed local concerns against the interests of the dominant national elites. In Lesotho and Swaziland where chiefly authority in government has been institutionalized by the constitution, chiefs have assumed center stage in the formulation and implementation of key state policies and programs. And in South Africa, extensive powers have been conferred on traditional leaders by the post-Apartheid Constitution. Under specially defined constitutional provisions, South Africa's influential chiefs were granted advisory and executive powers at all levels of government.

At the local level, chiefs continued to exercise traditional functions in the adjudication of indigenous law, and were accorded ex-officio status in local authorities. In provincial legislatures, a second chamber of traditional leaders would have the power to advise both executive and legislative bodies on all matters relating to indigenous customs of diverse local communities. Finally, at the federal level, a national council of traditional leaders secured the constitutional right to advise the national government on local matters and pressing issues of national concern (see Chapter 11 of *The Constitution of the Republic of South Africa* 1993). There is no doubt that this extensive guarantee for chiefly rulers in the late twentieth century is an indication of their critical historical role in South Africa's complex societies. Under white minority rule for example, prominent chiefs were in part the beneficiaries of apartheid's "tribal homeland" policy and its ethnic-focused politics in the black townships. It is widely known that at the basis of Chief Gatsha Buthelezi's politics of ethnicity lies the legitimizing notion of "traditional" authority (Mare and Hamilton 1987; Mzala 1988). Professor Richard Sklar (1993, 97) notes the significance of these indigenous political structures in the politics of the contemporary African state:

> traditional authorities are unmistakably formal and part of the public domain. Furthermore, their existence is often recognized by national constitutions, and they are frequently incorporated into a constitutional order for the performance of specific functions.

The volatile politics of federalism in Nigeria arguably provides the most complex interaction between indigenous political institutions and modern state structures in post-colonial Africa. While possessing its own distinct character, the contemporary political relevance of Nigeria's traditional rulers and chiefs is not essentially different from the forms of traditional leadership found in most post-colonial African states. Yet, while Nigeria's traditional rulers project cherished local values and aspirations, state sponsored political reforms have systematically marginalized them from formal government institutions and agencies. The policies and programs of the holders of state power—especially career politicians, military administrators and senior bureaucrats—have encroached on the authority of traditional rulers and local chiefs since the period of decolonization.

Conversely, within the prevailing ethnoregional political structure of Nigeria, chieftaincy institutions reinforce a complex network of formal and informal political and economic alliances that sustain a fragile structure at the regional and federal levels of government. The dominant regional political elites are yet to devise a mechanism of governance in which the process of political mobilization would require a progressive interplay between antecedent institutions and modern political structures. At the heart of the relationship between traditional rulers, authoritarian regimes, and the struggle of diverse communities for democratization lies a deep and complex engagement between structures of society and state institutions. These critical interactions between grassroots organizations and movements, and the persistent struggle for democratization were aptly described by Pearl Robinson (1993) as "the channels through which a culture of politics is constituted." In Nigeria, the activities of indigenous political institutions are intimately connected to the apparent crises of political authority and legitimacy at the grassroots level. The converging and conflicting interests and values apparent in these institutions have had far reaching implications for the persistence of authoritarian regimes, the recurring constitutional debates on civil-democratic experiments, and the viability of participatory democracy.

Since traditional rulers and chiefs have retained deep relevance in local governance, the present paper will analyze their role in the political programs of Generals Mohammadu Buhari and Ibrahim Babangida. Similar to the programs instituted by their predecessor General Olusegun Obasanjo, these two regimes embarked on elaborate programs to rationalize the crisis of governance throughout the country. Since the demise of the Second Republic, two major military initiatives—the 1984 local government review and the deliberations of the Political Bureau—were expected to serve as the centerpiece of a new democratic order in the succeeding civilian era. The intense debate surrounding these important constitutional and political initiatives not only underscores the central role of indigenous political structures in local communities, but equally reveals the problems of democratic transitions in post-colonial Nigeria. With a view to showing the political relevance of traditional rulers and chiefs in the evolving debates on constitutional democracy in Nigerian politics since the Second Republic, this paper argues that the significance of chieftaincy institutions is not solely sustained by the pressing demands of institutional transformation, but equally by the entrenched interests of dominant regional elites.

The Political Context of "Traditional Rulership" in Post-Colonial Nigeria

Since the period of decolonization, traditional rulers and chiefs have featured prominently in the process of elite formation and in the contrasting style of military and civil rule in all key regions of the country. Their role in contemporary politics lies in a deep engagement with the complex sociopolitical realities in local communities and the prevailing federal structure which has entrenched power in regional-based political elites. As regional political elites consolidate their power base within civic organizations and communal ideologies, chieftaincy structures, in part, provide the legitimating doctrine for these ethnoregional political blocs. Thus, within the context of Nigeria's federal structure, traditional rulers collectively reinforce privileged political classes that draw their legitimacy from diverse communities (Vaughan 1995). Moreover, the underlying colonial origins of the Nigerian state have given impetus to the emergence of a complicated federal structure in the post-colonial period. The saliency of chieftaincy institutions in politics lies in the increasing importance of ethnoregional calculations in the formulation and implementation of national policies.

After nearly four decades of independence, state agencies are still disconnected from the corporate structures of society (Guyer 1992). As the embodiment of cherished local values, absolved from assuming direct responsibility for the affairs of highly corrupt state agencies, traditional rulers and chiefs collectively enjoyed considerable influence in diverse local communities. It is specifically for this reason that various regimes, whether civilian or military, have been at great pains to establish some form of modus vivendi with traditional rulers, attempting in this way to enhance their own popular acceptance (Graf 1986, 1988). The recent resurgence of chieftaincy in both local and national politics is thus not unconnected to the apparent crisis of political legitimacy evident at the local level. This political crisis is further compounded by the seemingly intractable economic problems of the last decade (Bratton 1985). This problem in part explains a recent trend in which while holders of state power confront a deepening crisis of political legitimacy, chiefs and elders continue to enjoy local acceptance. It has been argued quite convincingly that in small towns and remote villages where state institutions are profoundly ineffective, local chiefs and village heads combine their "traditional" and customary functions with the pressing demands of community development (Berry 1985; Osunwale 1984). In many remote areas, the effectiveness of community-based doctrines is strengthened by the utilitarian attributes of local chiefs and leaders.

But questions pertaining to traditional rulership in Nigeria have often transcended the narrow issues of local governance and community development. As implied earlier, influential traditional rulers have contributed significantly to the federal structure that has dominated state affairs since the early 1950s. Central to the extraordinary resilience and adaptability of chieftaincy institutions is an interlocking relationship involving complex economic and political alliances. The structural transformation that has occurred since the terminal years of colonial rule has systematically institutionalized new power relations within the context of fragile postcolonial state structures (Price 1975). Within the context of a highly extractive ethno-clientelist state structure (Falola and Ihonvbere 1985; Joseph 1987), traditional rulers and chiefs have sought to sustain their influence in the modern economy by forging formidable political ties with regional commercial and bureaucratic elites. As far back as the early 1960s, for example, a white paper produced by the northern regional government on the performance of the Northern Nigerian Development Corporation (NNDC) showed that emirs and chiefs had used their position to acquire loans from this public board. Moreover, since the 1970s, prominent traditional rulers have engaged in major commercial enterprises, both through their personal business holdings and their leadership roles in subsidiaries of multi-national corporations (*The Analyst* 1987).

These strong ties with dominant regional elites of conflicting political affiliations have put serious strains on the relationship between individual traditional rulers and their local people. It will suffice to highlight the consequences of prominent cases of these political struggles under civilian and military rule. First, the political alignment that emerged in Yoruba towns during the Action Group (AG) crisis of 1962 to 1966 was expressed in major confrontations between obas, local communities and the Nigerian National Democratic Party (NNDP) government (Sklar 1966). In the case of Owo town, for example, the conspicuous support of the Olowo for this unpopular regional government led to his rejection by townspeople and his ultimate deposition in the early years of military rule. Second, the Agbekoya peasant revolt of 1967 to 1968 in many Yoruba towns and villages highlighted the imminent danger for obas and chiefs seen to represent unpopular government policies (Beer 1976; Williams 1980). Finally, the deposition of the Emir of Muri by the military governor in 1986 exemplifies the ominous fate of a traditional ruler who had lost the confidence of his people.

As these political ties crystallize into regional blocs, traditional rulers remain at great pains to show that they represent the aspirations of local communities. Traditional rulers who ignore local aspirations predictably suffer considerable loss of power and prestige. Yet, while recognizing the significance of local acceptance, these leaders have deployed considerable resources into enlisting the approval of the holders of state power, who are ultimately responsible for the regulation of chieftaincy institutions (Oyemakinde 1977). Individual traditional rulers and chiefs must thus strike a delicate balance between community aspirations and the political objectives of the holders of state power.

Prevailing historical and political factors such as the complex character of specific local communities, the historical rivalry between neighboring communities, the enduring nature of partisan political alliances, the style of military rule, and the modernizing programs of the state, have all combined to influence the status and attitudes of traditional rulers in contemporary politics. In spite of the apparent tendency to coalesce over important grassroots issues such as local government and land reforms,[1] traditional title holders have often embraced conflicting roles and interests. For example, since the period of decolonization traditional rulers and chiefs have featured prominently in acrimonious conflicts at all levels of political engagement. The political alignment which evolved in the parliamentary years and was creatively nurtured throughout the intervening years of military rule, was critical both to the formation of democratic political institutions and the subsequent demise of Nigeria's second experiment with electoral politics (1979–83). These political developments were often complicated by an entrenched federal structure that sustains the domination of regional bureaucratic and commercial elites at the grassroots. Politically motivated organizations with the strong support of prominent traditional rulers often exploit the deep regional, religious and communal divisions in local communities.

Traditional Rulers and the Buhari Regime, 1984–1985

In a country well known for its unfortunate tradition of civil-military governance, the 19-month military regime of General Buhari stands out as one of the most controversial in Nigeria's post-colonial history. The Buhari regime's notoriety is attributable to its flagrant abuse of human rights, excessive authoritarian measures, propensity for embracing unpopular policies, and alienation of powerful regional interest groups throughout the country. But, while alienating the Nigerian Medical Association, labor unions, teachers' unions, university students and the press, the regime embraced influential traditional rulers as an informal mechanism of harnessing grassroots support for government policies and programs. The Federal Military Government's recognition for chieftaincy institutions was declared by Buhari in March 1985, only a year after seizing power, when he stated that the mission of his government coincided with the objectives of traditional rulers in key sections of the country. General Buhari, a Hausa-Fulani, regularly consulted the Sultan of Sokoto on important national and regional issues (*Africa Confidential* April 10 1985). With this endorsement from the Head of State, state military governors and senior government officials embraced traditional rulers and chiefs as an "informal second tier of authority" (Agbese 1986). This spirit of political engagement initiated by the federal government, provided prominent traditional rulers such as the Emir of Kano and the Ooni of Ife with the opportunity to influence the formulation of state policy. Influential emirs and obas demanded the incorporation of chieftaincy institutions into a reconstituted local government system, and a future civilian government (*Africa Now* March 1984). It is highly probable that this rapprochement influenced the military regime's decision, in May 1984, to review the 1976 *Local Government Guidelines*.

On May 29 1984, the Chief of Staff Supreme Headquarters, Major General Tunde Idiagbon, inaugurated a twenty member committee under the chairmanship of the Baraden of Sokoto, Alhaji Ibrahim Dasuki,[2] to make recommendations to the federal government on local government reforms. After a year of deliberation that involved visits to many parts of the country, petitions and testimonies from numerous traditional rulers, local elders and politicians, the Dasuki Committee presented its report to the federal government in April 1985. The Committee reaffirmed its commitment to the 1976 *Local Government Guidelines*, noting that

> the system of local government in the country after the 1976 Local Government Reform had more of an operational, rather than structural problems arising directly from behavior and attitude of the persons who operate the system (*Views and Comments of the Federal Military Government on the Findings and Recommendations of the Committee on the Review of Local Government Administration in Nigeria* 1985, 3).

The Review Committee thus upheld the pre-existing 301 multi-purpose single-tier local authorities established under the 1976 Guidelines. By accepting the boundaries established in 1976, the Committee reversed the decision of several state governments who largely for political motives had dominated local communities by dissolving duly-elected local councils and establishing partisan local authorities. Moreover, the Dasuki Committee maintained that the functions of local authorities defined in the 1976 Guidelines should continue to provide the basis for local administration in the country. On the controversial subject concerning the participation of traditional rulers in local government administration, the Committee granted the traditional councils considerable authority over the executive affairs of local authorities. These included the power to formulate general proposals, and advise the local government councils on all social, customary and economic matters affecting local communities. Local authorities were also duty bound to keep the traditional councils informed of their executive activities by providing them with draft estimates and copies of reports of proposed by-laws for consultation and assessment.

The vocal campaign of influential traditionalists to reverse the steady onslaught on chiefly authority therefore achieved some of its desired objectives under the Buhari regime. By granting the traditional councils considerable control over customary and cultural matters, as well as extensive advisory powers over the executive affairs of local authorities, traditional rulers were accorded new powers through which they could influence the direction of local administration.

The ambitions, and renewed hopes of traditional rulers were demonstrated in their recommendations to the Political Bureau which was constituted by Buhari's successor, General Babangida, in 1986. The strategy of governance adopted by the Babangida regime—especially the political factors that shaped the deliberations of the Political Bureau—illustrates the critical role of powerful traditional rulers in the debate on democratic transitions in post-colonial Nigeria.

Traditional Rulers and the Babangida Regime, 1985–1993

Unlike the Buhari regime, the government of General Babangida, which seized power in a palace coup in August 1985, initially sought to open the political process to the diverse interests hitherto alienated by its predecessors. By projecting itself as a benevolent military regime of consensus, open to debate and dialogue, the Babangida regime, at least initially, interrupted the neo-traditionalist policy of the Buhari administration. Babangida's initial attitude towards traditional rulers was thus to keep them at bay, denying them special privileges in the political affairs of the country. Indeed, the initial disregard in which the regime held traditional rulers had its most blatant expression in a declaration of March 8 1988 which ordered all traditional rulers and chiefs to inform the chairmen of their local authorities before they ventured out of their "domain."

However, this initial disregard for traditional rulers failed to retard the momentum they had acquired from the pro-chieftaincy policies of the preceding era. The influence of traditional rulers was ensured by their active participation in important regional and national issues, and by their consolidation of their ties with powerful regional interests throughout the country. These alliances were institutionalized in the regional and ethnic based sociocultural organizations, which would later influence the direction of politics in the Babangida era. Between 1986 and 1993, powerful traditional rulers, many of them well educated with experience as senior bureaucrats and successful businessmen, featured prominently in political movements which professed to represent regional and ethnic interests. For example, one such organization was the Committee of Elders from the ten northern states which met in Lugard Hall, Kaduna on June 6 1987. The organization, which was dominated by leaders of the proscribed NPC and NPN parties of the First and Second Republics and by influential emirs and traditionalists, claimed to have been formed as a regional response to the wave of religious riots in several northern towns in March 1987. Opponents in other regions, however, contended that the real motive of the organizers was to create a partisan platform in anticipation of the eventual lifting of the ban on party politics. This suspicion is not unwarranted since the leadership of the organization drew its membership from the alliance of emirs, senior bureaucrats and politicians that had dominated regional and national politics since independence. Furthermore, it was suggested that the summit meeting provided the emirs with the opportunity to impress on the military authorities that they retain political influence in the emirate states (*West Africa* July 20 1987).

Early in 1987, ex-politicians and traditional rulers from the eastern states of Anambra, Imo, Rivers and Cross Rivers, who seemed to have taken their lead from the northern elders, formed the Eastern Solidarity Group to advance one "eastern interest" and to encourage a sense of unity among its diverse leadership. In yet another show of solidarity, fifty traditional chiefs, politicians and businessmen from Anambra and Imo states met in July at the Enugu residence of Chief Akanu Ibiam, the former Governor of the old Eastern Region. The meeting, which was "code-named" *ohe n' Eze-Igbo*, (for the people and kings), was an attempt by eminent Igbo leaders to speak with one voice on major federal government policies, especially the government's white paper on the Political Bureau's recommendations on the creation of more states (*West Africa* 20 July 1987).

To complete the dominant tri-partite character of the politics of federalism, prominent Yoruba obas and politicians, after weeks of planning, inaugurated a pan-ethnic association called the *Egbe Ilosiwaju Yoruba* (the

Yoruba Progressive Organization) under the leadership of the Ooni of Ife, Oba Sijuade in Akure in April 1988. This association, which was in response to the other regional solidarity organizations as well as to the death of the Yoruba Leader, Chief Obafemi Awolowo, in May 1987, was established to forge a sense of unity among major political blocs in the southwestern region. For the organizers of this group, an effective strategy that would advance Yoruba interests must now address the serious political problems that were traced back to the Action Group crisis of 1962–1966. At another meeting, in February, the obas decided to promote unity among their people, rally around major Yoruba candidates bidding for national office, and settle personal and group conflicts among Yoruba leaders and communities (*The Nigerian Economist* April 27 1988). This summit meeting of Yoruba obas and elder statesmen formally established a secretariat with the Ooni of Ife as the president and the former military governor of the old Western State, Major-General Adebayo, as coordinator. Similar to the relationship between the *Egbe Omo Oduduwa* and the AG in the early 1950s, leaders of the new Egbe saw the association as the precursor of an ethnic-based party in the next civilian government. In reference to this political objective, one of the obas noted that: "we do not want to be caught napping when the curtain is drawn" on electoral competition. Indeed, the Ooni of Ife was unequivocal about the political motives of the organization; he urged the participants to put their house in order in preparation for 1992 when elections were to start. In a message delivered on behalf of his brother obas the Ooni advised the delegates

> not to see politics as a do or die affair but ensure a constant display of unity of purpose despite political differences . . . I am sure you can do it if you would bury all past misunderstanding and start afresh in brotherhood and sisterly affection to plan together your strategy of putting the Yorubas in their deserved place among our other brothers in Nigeria (*National Concord* April 7 1988).

These three major regional examples are important not only because traditional rulers sought to participate in the debates on the new constitutional arrangement that would shape the conduct of state affairs in a putative Third Republic, but also because they serve as a reminder of the dominant role of regional blocs in Nigerian politics since decolonization. Thus, within the context of the prevailing federal structure, fluid and transient regional organizations conferred on a new generation of influential traditional rulers leadership roles among the dominant regional political elites.

In light of these critical leadership positions within a network of regional power brokers, and the increasing vulnerability of the Babangida regime in key sections of the country,[3] the federal government abandoned its lukewarm attitude for a more conciliatory approach to leading traditional rulers. The most visible demonstration of this can be seen in the June 1988 visit of the President to Sokoto to congratulate Sir Abubakar III on his golden jubilee as Sultan. Moreover, in 1987 and 1988, the Babangida administration took a special interest in chieftaincy politics and at various periods formulated policies to pacify regional traditional and religious leaders. For example, the administration's controversial membership in the Organization of the Islamic Conference (OIC) was perceived by Christian groups in the south and the Middle Belt region as an attempt to placate powerful northern interests, especially emirs and Islamic leaders. Furthermore, by the late 1980s the government "soft pedaled" on the volatile *shari'a* court debates. This controversial issue, which revealed the sharp political divisions between the dominant political class in the emirate north and those of the rest of the country, was advanced by a coalition of emirs, Islamic leaders and prominent northern politicians who forcefully demanded the recognition of *shari'a* law at all levels of adjudication.

The chieftaincy policy of the regime was further tilted in the direction of the emirate north as President Babangida regularly conferred with trusted traditionalists. In addition, the Chief of General Staff, Vice-Admiral Augustus Aikhomu, was forced to withdraw the impertinent directive ordering traditional rulers to report all trips outside of their community to the chairmen of their local authorities. Finally, the government's perception of the significant role of traditional rulers in politics (especially in the emirate states) was demonstrated in its intervention in the selection of a new Sultan, following the death of Sir Abubakar. It is widely known that the military governor of Sokoto state, Mohammed Daku, was under direct instruction to effect succession in accordance with the President's preference. The appointment of the influential and moderate Ibrahim Dasuki over the more conservative choice of the Sokoto kingmakers, Mohammed Maccido, indicates both the importance of this title in contemporary politics, and the increasing insecurity of the regime in the emirate north.[4]

The high visibility of traditional rulers in major political debates, and their pivotal role in defining the cohesion of ethnoregional political interests, prompted intellectual discussions on the role of traditional rulers and chiefs in politics. In 1983 and 1984, two of the country's leading universities, Obafemi Awolowo University, Ile-Ife, and the University of Ibadan, organized major conferences on the relevance of traditional rulers in national politics and local government.[5] Focusing primarily on the northern emirs, another major university, the University of Sokoto, held a national seminar on traditional rulers in regional and national politics in 1986. Some of the views put forth at these conferences later reflected the perspectives of intellectuals who dominated the deliberations of the Political Bureau—the body which, as noted earlier, was constituted by the FMG to recommend a new political system for the next civilian government. The deliberations of the Political Bureau on the role of traditional rulers in a constitutional democracy clearly reveal a major dilemma of democratic transition in Nigeria.

Traditional Rulers and the Political Bureau, 1986–1988

One of the first policy decisions undertaken by the Babangida Administration after seizing power was to appoint a seventeen member Political Bureau under the chairmanship of Professor Samuel Cookey, a distinguished academic and the pro-chancellor of the University of Benin.[6] Established to find a suitable democratic system for the country, this body put forth a number of important recommendations on traditional rulership in local communities and then proceeded to define what their role should be in a new civilian government. At the Political Bureau's inauguration in Abuja on January 13 1986, President Babangida charged the panel with the responsibility of reviewing the country's "political history, [to] identify the basic problems which have led to its failure in the past and suggest ways of resolving these problems" (*Report of the Political Bureau* 1986, 2). Hence, unlike the Constitution Drafting Committee constituted by the Mohammed/Obasanjo administration in 1976, this panel was essentially a fact-finding commission responsible for a thorough reappraisal of existing social and political conditions before recommending a political system that could endure the stress of Nigeria's volatile politics.

Unlike many powerful interest groups which seem apathetic within a culture of democratic transitions under military tutelage, traditional rulers participated actively in the debates that ensued. Whether as individuals or as corporate bodies, they sought to influence the views of members of the panel by making their voices heard on important political issues confronting them and their communities. In at least three cases, they closed ranks forming regional movements and organizations to discuss matters of common interest and to present a united front on the agenda before the Political Bureau. It is instructive here to explore the pressures mounted by traditional rulers and then to examine their substantive contributions to the national debate that unfolded on the country's democratic future.

Again, regional blocs featured prominently. The best organized and cohesive of these regional groups was the assembly of emirs and chiefs from the ten northern states of the federation. In a comprehensive memorandum submitted to the panel, they blamed the failure of preceding governments on what they considered to be the underutilization of traditional rulers in local and national politics. The northern emirs confidently proposed what they considered to be a suitable political structure for the complex problems confronting the country. They recommended a bicameral legislature consisting of a house of representatives and a senate at the federal level of government. Democracy would be served by a popularly elected lower house of representatives, while the essential elements of experience and knowledge of local communities would be found in a senate consisting of nominated leaders of thought, former senior government officials and the chairmen of the state Councils of Chiefs. The emirs' senate would have the power to impeach the president and vice-president, the chief justice and any other senior members of the executive and judiciary found guilty of misconduct and abuse of office. Moreover, the president would be required to consult with, and seek the approval of, the senate on all federal appointments and policies. The emirs also recommended bicameral legislatures consisting of a house of assembly and a house of elders for each of the nineteen states of the federation. These state assemblies would consist of popularly elected members, while the houses of elders would be composed of ex-state governors, chief judges, grand khadis and senior traditional rulers.

The northern emirs also called for the repeal of the customary court reforms instituted by successive governments since the early 1950s. They argued that as an integral component of traditional structure, customary courts still retained considerable popularity among local people. They contended that when the courts were abolished in the old Eastern Region they were revived as soon as the regional government realized that its decision was in grave error. Similarly, in the former Western Region, the customary courts were reconstituted and chiefs who had been excluded by the Action Group government from presiding over them, were reinstated as presidents and members of the courts. In addition, they argued that the people of the northern states had suffered under the arbitrary rule of area court judges since 1967 when the Alkali Courts were withdrawn from the chiefs and taken over by the states. Thus, the emirs argued that a reinstituted customary court system under the firm control of chiefs would not only complement the inadequate modern courts but would also reflect the unique cultural experiences of Nigeria's diverse communities.

The emirs then launched a forceful attack against the 1976 *Local Government Guidelines* and the 1978 Land Use Decree, arguing that in this multi-ethnic country local communities are better served by local government structures suited for specific local conditions. Similarly, they argued that laws governing land tenure should be amended with a view to grant the state council of chiefs control over rural land. With regard to urban land, the emirs suggested the inclusion of traditional rulers in the Land Allocation Committees of each of the nineteen states. Finally the emirs called for constitutional protection against what they considered to be "undue interference by state and federal authorities in chieftaincy affairs." To avoid the partisanship of the past, they recommended that the new constitution should grant the state council of chiefs sole authority over the discipline of traditional title holders found guilty of abusing the privileges of their office.

Traditional rulers from the western and eastern states also contributed to this national debate. Yoruba obas under the leadership of the Ooni of Ife presented a memorandum calling for the complete integration of obas and chiefs into the machinery of government at all levels. At the federal level, they called for the establishment of a national council of traditional rulers to advise the federal government on important national matters. At the state level, they demanded that the constitution grant the council of chiefs the power to advise the state executive on important local matters. On local administration and land matters, the obas called for the appointment of a traditional ruler as president of the council, and for the revocation of the Land Use Decree. On the whole, therefore, traditional rulers from all the key regions of the federation sought a larger national and regional role beyond the advisory functions granted them under the 1976 *Local Government Guidelines,* the 1978 Land Use Decree, and the 1979 Constitution.

But since previous constitutional and political reforms had resolved these issues, most analysts anticipated that members of the Political Bureau would reject these controversial proposals that called for a retreat to the past. As expected, the panel rejected the participation of traditional rulers in the two higher tiers of government on the grounds that their involvement would undermine the fundamental premise of constitutional democracy (*Report of the Political Bureau* 1986, 146). In keeping with the perspective of the liberal intellectuals who dominated the Political Bureau, the panel argued that since traditional office holders draw their claim to authority from specific chiefly lineages, chieftaincy structures inevitably contradict the fundamental notion of egalitarian democracy.[7] Furthermore, the Bureau argued that chieftaincy institutions are anachronistic and dysfunctional in a rapidly changing country such as Nigeria. The Political Bureau thus contended that traditional rulership poses a fundamental threat to "nation building" and the development strategies of the state. In a critical analysis of the contemporary Nigerian state and society, William Graf (1986, 108–09) notes the rationale behind this well known liberal perspective:

> Traditional social systems are thought to impede the growth of national political system and economy, to prevent popular awareness from transcending the horizon of family, kinship group or tribe, and thus to retard the evolution of more literate, more aware, more skilled and more deployable 'citizens'- the human material needed to sustain and nurture this modernizing development strategy.

Yet, political development in Nigeria since the era of decolonization corroborates Arthur Lewis' (1965) assertion over three decades ago, that the conception of a modernizing elite uncompromisingly pitted against a recalcitrant traditional aristocracy is simply a misrepresentation of the facts. Graf himself was quick to note that the politics of institutional transformation and the "nation building" project in Nigeria is definitely more complex than a straightforward portrayal of a progressive modernizing national elite committed to undermining the power base of a reactionary class of chiefly rulers and local elders. However, the liberal pronouncement of the Political Bureau failed to deal with the fundamental discontinuity between indigenous political structures and the concept of constitutional republicanism in Nigeria. The fact remains that by retaining deep relevance in local communities, traditional rulers and chiefs, to borrow Richard Sklar's (1993) phrase, pose an "auxiliary" or "parallel" authority to ineffective and corrupt state institutions. The Political Bureau also failed to acknowledge that the influence of traditional office holders does not only rest on ascriptive values and atavism, but also on a complex clientelist network that has entrenched the power base of regional bureaucratic and commercial elites. Indeed, the immediate outcome of major military reforms in local government and community development, notably the 1976 Guidelines, the 1978 Land Use Decree and, more recently, the implementation of the Directorate of Food, Road and Rural Infrastructure (DFRRI) programs, all reflect the intense communal, regional and class struggles within the context of the prevailing politics of federalism (Vaughan 1995). Piecemeal constitutional and political pronouncements have in reality done little to transform the political importance of chieftaincy institutions at the grassroots level. A carefully managed transition program preoccupied primarily with power sharing and mediating conflict among dominant regional interests actually reinforced the power base of influential traditional rulers within powerful regional blocs. This regional political alliance between traditional rulers and the holders of state power hardly promoted good governance and progressive community development programs. Despite the persistence of these complex issues, the Political Bureau rejected the idea of unfettered executive authority for traditional rulers in politics on familiar constitutional grounds:

> In the context of the new social and political order, traditional rulers should have no place in government beyond the local government level where they have relevance. Furthermore, by virtue of the scope and character of the contemporary Nigerian state, it is a misnomer to designate incumbents of these institutions traditional 'rulers' . . . This official designation must not accord them a rival status with the principal political officers of the Nigerian state (*Report of the Political Bureau* 1986, 48).

In light of this, the Political Bureau recommended that the government should provide a new legal definition for traditional rulers and compile a register of these leaders throughout the country.

Mindful of the complex role of traditional rulers in local governance, the Babangida regime was cautious in its embrace of the liberal pronouncements of the Political Bureau. While rejecting the panel's quibble with the term "traditional ruler," defining it instead simply as a colloquial expression and not a legal designation, the FMG accepted in principle the position of the Political Bureau which limited their role to the non-executive aspect of local administration. Despite this setback, all was not lost for traditional rulers as the Babangida regime also upheld the more pro-chieftaincy Dasuki Report as the benchmark for future local government administration.[8]

The Political Bureau's recommendations gave liberal intellectuals at least a temporary victory in a debate that has lasted over a half century. From the very beginning, this outcome seemed inevitable not because traditional rulers were not organized and powerful enough, but rather because of the composition of the panel itself, dominated as it was by intellectual scholars and professionals (some of them socialists). The panel reflected the perspective of intellectuals who saw chiefly rulers as powerful mischief makers bent on further undermining the stability of an already fragile and conflict-prone country. The position taken by the Political Bureau thus reflects the insightful observation of Richard Sklar (1993, 93) who notes the extent of the discomfort of the African intellectuals[9] with the idea of traditional chiefs assuming executive, legislative and juridical functions in a constitutional democracy. He contends that

> one would be gravely mistaken to minimize the intensity of debates by African intellectuals about the abolition or preservation of traditional rulership. Abolitionists harp on the abuse of authority perpetuated by chiefs, many of whom are the heirs of rulers who were co-opted or installed and nurtured by foreign overlords during the colonial era. They allege that so-called traditional authority is really a form of social parasitism that corrupts the political process.

Beyond the misgivings of liberal intellectuals, a critical assessment of traditional rulers in the governance of Nigerian communities since the late colonial period reveals a trend in which these local leaders have increasingly consolidated their political ties with dominant ethnic and regional political elites. The trend suggests that their complex interactions with the holders of state power have encouraged powerful traditional rulers to pursue private interests, often at the expense of local aspirations. The immediate implication can be seen in the fierce competition by powerful potentates for major titles since the colonial period. For example, it is widely held that the public controversy over the appointment of the Sultan of Sokoto is in keeping with a pattern in which state authorities are often disposed to override the preferences of local communities.

But the favorable response of the 1988 Constituent Assembly (and also the more recent 1994–1995 Constitutional Conference) on the position of traditional title holders indicates the enduring influence of neo-traditionalists in Nigerian politics. The passionate and eloquent plea to the Constituent Assembly by the political scientist Bala Takaya, in which he underscored the contradiction between a constitutional republic and monarchical institutions, did not convince the majority of the delegates. Echoing the sentiments of most delegates, his colleague from Ekiti south in Ondo state, Bamidele Olumilua, reminded him of the crucial role of traditional rulers in community affairs: "In my part of the world, if it does not rain in time, we go to the obas, if there is an outbreak of disease, we first consult our oba." In a debate devoid of substantive questions of local governance and community development strategies, traditionalists won the day in a resounding victory by a vote of 233 in their favor with only 54 against. In contrast to the Political Bureau, the Constituent Assembly, which included prominent traditional title holders, was generally receptive to the idea of granting traditional rulers involvement in Nigeria's third experiment with liberal democracy (*Newswatch* December 19, 1988). Thus the Constituent Assembly granted traditional rulers advisory roles in local, state and federal levels of government. However, while generally sympathetic to traditional authority, the Constituent Assembly did not go beyond the authority granted to traditional rulers under the 1979 Constitution. Constitutional debates and pronouncements aside, previous experience would suggest that the politics of federalism would confer de facto roles on traditional rulers in the next civil-democratic government. Thus, given the prevailing regional structure of power relations, the persistent attempt to curtail the influence of traditional rulers in state institutions is rather simplistic; regional-based politicians, military administrators, senior bureaucrats and influential rulers nurture strong ties within dominant political blocs.

Conclusion

Military transitions to constitutional democracy in Nigeria have often reinforced the politics of federalism in which power is consolidated in the hands of regional commercial and bureaucratic classes. In the context of this regional-based structure "traditional rulership" has remained important in contemporary Nigerian politics. Traditional rulers collectively reinforce the power base of these regional political classes that claim to draw their legitimacy from diverse ethnic, religious and communal groups. The remarkable adaptability and resilience of chieftaincy institutions does not merely reflect the essential elements of the politics of institutional transformation, but also is rooted in an interlocking network of political alliances that have consolidated power at the regional level.

The two major programs instituted by the military regimes of Generals Buhari and Babangida (the Dasuki local government review and the deliberations of the Political Bureau) to address the complex problems of local governance and constitutional democracy examined in this paper were similar to the issues confronted by the preceding military government of General Obasanjo between 1975 and 1979. Within this context of military-imposed transitional programs, traditional rulers engaged in a debate that allowed only the voice of privileged subgroups within the dominant regional blocs. Given their claims to grassroots legitimacy, traditional rulers and their formidable allies forcefully demanded their full integration into the political process. For traditional rulers, the dilemma of democratic transition lies in their sociopolitical importance at the grassroots, and the tendency to reinforce regional political interests on the one hand, while confronting a debate constrained by the rules of constitutional republicanism and participatory democracy on the other. Since these traditional rulers are critical to a process of regional elite formation and consolidation, they will continue to play an important role in Nigeria's complicated debates on constitutional democracy.

Notes

1. For example see the reactions of traditional rulers to major regional and federal government initiatives in local and land reforms, especially the 1976 *Local Government Guidelines*, the *1979 Nigerian Constitution*, and the 1978 *Land Use Decree*.

2. During the time of his appointment as chairman of the Review Committee, Dasuki held a senior chieftaincy title in the Sokoto Sultanate. He was subsequently appointed Sultan of Sokoto following the death of Sir Abubakar in 1988. The appointment of such a distinguished traditional figure as chairman of the Local Government Review Committee was in itself a recognition of the significance of traditional rulers in local communities.

3. The March 1987 religious riots in key northern towns was a clear indication of the vulnerability of the Federal Military Government (FMG) in some parts of the northern emirates. President Babangida who saw the riots as nothing more than "a civilian attempt at a coup" was quick to note that religion was projected by some powerful individuals to undermine the authority of his government. Similarly, realizing that the bitter conflict between the Ooni of Ife and the Alaafin of Oyo in February of the same year could lead to a breakdown of law and order, the FMG secretly intervened in what was essentially a matter for the state authorities.

4. The general consensus in the Nigerian and foreign press suggests that the FMG's preference for Dasuki over his more conservative rival Maccido was crucial in the appointment of the former as Sultan of Sokoto. See the *London Guardian*, 9 November 1988; *Africa Confidential*, 18 November 1988; *New Nigeria*, 15 November 1988; *Newswatch*, 21 November 1988; *Newbreed*, 11 November 1988; *Hotline*, December 1988; and *Africa Events*, December 1988. (Editors' note: After this chapter was prepared, Dasuki was removed and Maccido was installed as Sultan of Sokoto. See *Africa Confidential*, 37, 9 (1996) for discussion.)

5. For detailed discussions of these debates see Oladimeji Aborisade (ed.), *Local Government and Traditional Rulers in Nigeria* (Ile-Ife: University of Ife Press, 1985); see also the papers presented at the National Conference on the Role of Traditional Rulers in the Governance of Nigeria, held at the Institute of African Studies, University of Ibadan, 11–14 September 1984.

6. The panel was dominated by intellectuals that included political scientists Eme Awa, Oyeleye Oyediran, Ali Yahaya, Tunde Adeniran, Sam Oyovbaire, Bala Takaya and Mohammed Zahradeen. Journalists and labor union leaders Haroun Adamu, Ibrahim Halilu, Okon Uya and Paschal Bafyan also served on the panel. Renowned writer Ola Balogun resigned shortly after his appointment for unspecified reasons, while another writer, Edwin Madunagu, was later fired for allegedly disclosing confidential information to the *Nigerian Guardian*, a newspaper in which he had served as member of the editorial board. Two prominent women, Mrs. Hilda Adefarasin, President of the National Council of Women, and Mrs. Hamatu Abdulahi, a community leader, also served on the Bureau.

7. For a good discussion of this perspective see Alex Gboyega, "What Role for Traditional Rulers in Republican Nigeria?", paper presented at the National Conference on the role of traditional rulers in the governance of Nigeria, held at the Institute of African Studies, University of Ibadan, 11–14 September, 1984. See also Ian Shapiro, "Letters from South Africa," *Dissent*, 1994.

8. For a detailed discussion see *Government's Views and Comments on the Findings and Recommendations of the Political Bureau* (Lagos: The Federal Government Printer 1987, 50).

9. This uneasiness with granting traditional rulers power in a modern political system was forcefully expressed in Uganda by a commission of inquiry into local government administration chaired by the eminent socialist scholar, Professor Mahmoud Mamdani of Makerere University in the late 1980s. The commission called on the government of Yoreri Musaveni to abolish chieftaincy institutions and replace them with secretaries who would be more responsive to the resistance councils.

References

Aborisade, Oladimeji, ed. 1985. *Local Government and Traditional Rulers in Nigeria*. Ile-Ife: University of Ife Press.
Agbese, Dan. 1986. "Editorial." *Newswatch*, September 8.
Barkan, Joel, D., McNulty and M.A.O. Ayeni. 1991. "Home-town Voluntary Associations, Local Development and the Emergence of Civil Society in Western Nigeria." *Journal of Modern African Studies*: 29.
Beer, Christopher. 1976. *The Politics of Peasant Groups in Western Nigeria*. Ibadan: Ibadan University Press.

Berry, Sara, S. 1985. *Fathers Work for their Sons: Accumulation, Mobility and Class Formation in an Extended Yoruba Community*. Berkeley: University of California Press.

Bratton, Michael. 1985. "Beyond the State: Civil Society and Associational Life in Africa." *World Politics*: 41.

Ekong, E. 1985. "Traditional Rulership in Contemporary Nigerian Governmental System and the Dilemma of Relevance." In Aborisade, Oladimeji (ed.), *Local Government and Traditional Rulers in Nigeria*. Ile-Ife: University of Ife Press.

Enemuo, F.C. and Oyeleye Oyediran. 1990. "Community Development Associations as Agents of Rural Transformation: A Case of Town Unions in Anambra State." Paper presented at the National Seminar in Integrated Rural Development Policy in Nigeria, Abuja.

Falola, Toyin and Ihonvbere, Julius. 1985. *The Rise and Fall of Nigeria's Second Republic*. London: Zed Press.

Francis, Paul. 1995. "Community Level Institutions and Poverty Alleviation in Nigeria: Consultative Surveys in Thirty-Six Communities." Paper prepared for the *Poverty Alleviation Programme Development Committee*. Washington D.C.: World Bank.

Gboyega, Alex. 1984. "The Role of Traditional Rulers in Republican Nigeria?" Paper presented at the National Conference on the Role of Traditional Rulers in the Governance of Nigeria, held at the Institute of African Studies, University of Ibadan, September 11–14.

Graf, William. 1986. "Nigerian Grassroots Politics: Local Government, Traditional Rule and Class Domination." *Journal of Commonwealth and Comparative Politics*: 24.

———. 1988. *The Nigerian State: Political Economy, State, Class and Political System in the Post-Colonial Era*. London: James Currey.

Guyer, Jane. 1992. "Representation without Taxation: An Essay on Democracy in Rural Nigeria, 1952–1990." Boston University: African Studies Center Working Papers.

Ibrahim, Jibrin. 1983. "The Transition to Civil Rule: Sapping Democracy." In Adebayo, O., Olukoshi, (ed.), *The Politics of Structural Adjustment in Nigeria*. London: James Currey.

Jega, Attahiru. 1993. "Professional Associations and Structural Adjustment." In Adebayo O. Olukoshi (ed.), *The Politics of Structural Adjustment in Nigeria*. London: James Currey.

Joseph, Richard. 1987. *Democracy and Prebendal Politics in Nigeria*. Cambridge: Cambridge University Press.

Lewis, Arthur, W. 1965. *Politics in West Africa*. New York: Oxford University Press.

Mare, Gerhard, P., and Georgina Hamilton. 1987. *An Appetite for Power: Buthelezi's Inkatha and South Africa*. Johannesburg: Ravan Press.

Molutsi, Patrick. 1989. "The Ruling Class and Democracy in Botswana." In John Holm and Patrick Molutsi (eds.), *Democracy in Botswana*. Athens: Ohio University Press.

Molutsi, Patrick, and John Holm. 1990. "Developing Democracy when Civil Society is Weak: The Case of Botswana." *African Affairs*, 89.

Mustapha, Abdul, Raufu. 1993. *Structural Adjustment and Agrarian Change in Nigeria*. London: James Currey.

Mzala. 1988. *Gatsha Buthelezi: Chief with a Double Agenda*. London: Zed Press.

Osunwale, S.A. 1984. "Three Days at the Court of the Timi of Agbale, the Traditional Ruler of Ede." Paper presented at the National Conference on the Role of Traditional Rulers in the Governance of Nigeria, held at the Institute of African Studies, University of Ibadan.

Oyemakinde, Wale. 1977. "The Chiefs Law and the Regulation of Traditional Chieftaincy in Yorubaland." *Journal of the Historical Society of Nigeria*.

Price, Robert. 1975. *Society and Bureaucracy in Contemporary Ghana*. Berkeley: University of California Press.

Robinson, Pearl. 1993. "Approaches to the Study of Democratization: Scripts in Search of Reality." Paper presented at the Annual Conference of the African Studies Association, Boston, (December 5).

Shapiro, Ian. 1994. "Letter from South Africa." *Dissent*.

Sklar, Richard, L. 1966. "Nigerian Politics: The Ordeal of Chief Awolowo, 1960–1965." In Gwendolen M. Carter (ed.), *Politics in Africa, Seven Cases*. New York: Harcourt, Brace and World.

———. 1993. "The African Frontier for Political Science." In Robert H. Bates, V.Y. Mudimbe, and Jean O'Barr, (eds.), *Africa and the Disciplines*. Chicago: Chicago University Press.

Vaughan, Olufemi. 1991. "Chieftaincy Politics and Social Relations in Nigeria." *Journal of Commonwealth and Comparative Politics*, 29.

———. 1994. "Communalism, Legitimation and Party Politics at the Grassroots: The Case of the Yoruba." *International Journal of Politics, Culture and Society*, 7.

———. 1995. "Assessing Grassroots Politics and Community Development in Nigeria." *African Affairs*, 94.

Whitaker, C.S., 1970. *The Politics of Tradition, Continuity and Change in Northern Nigeria, 1946–1966*. Princeton: Princeton University Press.

———. 1967. "Dysrhythmic Process of Change." *World Politics*, 19.

Williams, Gavin. 1980. *State and Society in Nigeria*. Idanre: Afrografika.

INDEX

Compiled by Cathlene Hanaman

Abacha, Maryam 233, 239
Abacha, Sani ascension to power and opening policies, 5, 38–39, 126, 142–43, 171, 233, 257, 303, 316–18, 378, 405; and centralization, 163–64, 349, 322–23, 351, 356; and civil society, 378, 408; and Constitutional Conference, 330, 342, 345; and corruption, 140, 151, 162–63, 303–304, 321–22; and coups, 150–51; and human rights, 137, 237; and military, 146; and permanent transition, 10, 129, 175, 187, 234, 378; proposed transition, 3, 5, 9, 40, 137–38, 146, 152, 175, 184, 186–87, 234, 237, 246, 257–58, 297–98, 318, 331, 345, 356, 380; and regionalism, 41, 243, 246, 249–50, 258; and religion, 297–98; and Saro-Wiwa, 190; and women, 233–35, 237–39
Abiola, Moshood K.O. arrest of, 99, 150, 260; and Babangida, 197–98, 201, 208; election results, 126, 147–48, 171, 186, 195, 206, 254, 315; electoral mandate, 38–39, 150, 202, 205–208; and ethnicity, 99, 248–49, 255–58, 260, 296–97; as leader of SDP, 37; and military, 196–97; and neopatrimony, 148, 204, 210; and regionalism, 152, 248–49, 254–58, 260, 296–97, 406; and religion, 257–58, 296–97, 405–406
Achebe, Chinua 85, 114
Action Group (AG; *See also* UPN) 333, 370, 376, 425; and ethnicity, 332, 370–72, 417, 422; and regionalism, 17–19, 371–72, 417; and religion, 371; and women, 224
Advisory Council for Religious Affairs (ACCRA) 277
African Demos 74, 75, 98
Aikhomu, Augustus 34, 423
Ake, Claude 140, 361, 400
Akintola, Samuel Ladoke 17–20
Alfa, Ibrahim 168
Anenih, Tony 196, 203, 206
Armed Forces Ruling Council (AFRC; 1985–1993), *See also* Supreme Military Council (SMC; before 1985) and *See also* National Defense and Security Council (NDSC; after

January 1993). 30, 31, 36, 228, 292, 295
Assassination attempt on Babangida, 30; of Ironsi (1966), 21, 32; of Muhammed (1976), 23, 32, 284; attempt on Obasanjo (1976), 24; of prime minister (1966), 20
Association for a Better Nigeria (ABN) 37, 148, 183, 194–197, 207, 210n, 212n
Augustus Aikhomu Tripartite Committee 208
Awa, Eme 152n, 169, 432n
Awe, Bolanle 231
Awolowo, Obafemi 19, 332, 333, 422; in Gowon's government, 21, 138; as leader of UPN (1979, 1983 elections), 25–26; 209, 291; and regionalism, 17–18; views of military governance, 138, 141, 146
Azikiwe, Nnamdi 18; and African nationalism democracy, 91; intellectual positions, 332, 334; as leader of NPP, 25–26; and NCNC, 367; in 1979 elections, 26

Baba, Ahmad 87
Babangida, Ibrahim Badamasi and Abacha, 187; ascension to power, 30, 125, 143–44, 162, 303; and centralization, 163, 304, 322–23, 347; and civil society, 139, 378, 389–407; creation of NEC and SDP, 31–32, 34–35; economic policies, 32–33, 303–304, 306–14; 318–19; and ethnicity, 249, 291–97; and June 12 1993 election results, 201–203, 205, 208–209, 315–16; manipulation of transition, 4, 65, 140–42, 144–45, 147–49, 166–71, 178–84, 194–200, 210, 291–97, 315, 342, 356, 389; and permanent transition, 10, 65, 129, 356; and Political Bureau, 125, 293, 390–91, 428–31; and regionalism, 249, 291–97; and religion, 249, 272–73, 285–87, 291–97; resignation as president, 38; and traditional rulers, 415, 420–24; and women, 221, 228–233
Babangida, Maryam 230–32, 239
Bafyau, Paschal 401
Balewa Tafawa, Abubakar 12n, 16, 45, 104n, 329
Bello, Ahmadu (Sardauna of Sokoto) 12n, 19, 52, 249, 333, 340n
Berg Report 71
Better Life for Rural Women Program (BLP; 1987–) 230, 231, 233, 234, 239, 310, 391
Biafra (*See also* Civil War, secession) secession movement, 21, 248, 342; surrender of Biafra (January 12 1970), 21, 138
Bissalla, Major General 23
Borno 35, 37, 41, 244–57, 357
Buhari, Muhammadu ascension to power, 29, 143, 285; and legitimacy, 306; and military, 162, 287, 291; overthrow of,

30, 143, 178, 291, 377; policies, 150, 183, 305, 306, 415, 430; and regionalism, 249; and religion, 285, 291; and traditional rulers, 418, 420; and women, 226, 228

Campaign for Democracy (CD) 37–38, 145, 186, 402, 407, 408, 409
Carter, Jimmy 23, 71, 75, 98
Centralization (degree of centralization or of decentralization at national level) and Abacha, 163–64, 322–23, 349, 351, 356; and Babangida, 163–66, 304, 322–23, 347; at independence, 372; and the military, 116, 164–65, 285, 322, 376; and parties, 19–20; and prebendalism, 320–21
Christian (*See also* religion) and Abacha, 297–98; and Babangida, 292–97, 404; and democratization, 265–68; and ethnicity, 24, 247–49; and Islam 9, 21, 229, 248, 269–74, 277–78, 291–98, 367; and June 12 1993 election results, 148, 256–57, 404; and military, 249, 284–88, and OIC membership, 30, 229, 423; and political parties, 35, 371; and politics, 278; and regionalism, 249 and politics, 267–68; and regionalism, 50–58; and state, 271–73
Christian Association of Nigeria (CAN) 281n, 291, 294; and Buhari, 291; and civil society, 268–69; and class, 279–80; as an interest group, 274–76; and June 12 1993 elections, 257, 404; *Leadership in Nigeria*, 273, 276; and military, 287–288; origins and description, 266, 268; political objectives of, 270; as a political party, 266, 268; and women, 280
Ciroma, Adamu 212n, 213n, 254
Civil Rights 34, 227, 396, 401, 402
Civil Society and Abacha, 378, 408; and Babangida, 141, 182, 378; and democratization, 155, 184–85, 210, 265, 364, 379, 381–83, 389, 396, 403–404, 408; and elites, 50, 58, 98, 182, 209, 210, 368, 377; and ethnicity, 70, 372–74, 377–78; and the military, 139, 143, 160, 162, 180, 185, 284, 286–87, 321, 377–78, 381; and neopatrimony, 377, 378; and parties, 361–70, 373–76, 378–82; and permanent transition, 7, 8, 68, 80, 379; and religion, 265–280, 283, 286, 287, 298, 372; and the state, 49, 59, 78, 101, 106n, 102, 164, 198, 209, 284, 286, 321, 369, 376–77, 379, 389, 408; and women, 238, 373, 377
Civil War Biafran (1967–70), 3, 4, 20–21, 41, 66, 138, 248, 261, 342; between Kano and Sokoto (1890s), 246; and religion, 42; and unity, 60

Civilian Regime alternation of power with military, 80, 142–45; and military, 146

Colonial State Legacy civil society, 365–73, 379, elites, 113–114, 176–77, 266; force, 69; military/civil rule pattern, 115; regionalism, 47–48, 243–45; religion, 283

Community Bank 230, 239, 310, 392

Community Development Associations (CDAs) 396, 398–99, 408

Confederation and ethnicity, 41, 335, 357–59; versus federalism, 41, 358–59; and regionalism, 41–42, 291, 335; and religion, 291; six region confederation proposal, 41, 259–60; Ethno-confedera- tion 352, 357

Consociationalism 3, 117, 128, 329, 331, 335–39

Constituent Assembly in Transition to Second Republic 24–25, 121–22, 226, 272, 339; and religion, 24–25, 290 in Transition under Babangida 31, 181–82, 230, 392; and religion, 294–95; and traditional rulers, 429–30; and women, 230

Constitution Drafting Committee (CDC; October 1975–1979) 1976 report, 25; 1979 Constitution, 121–22; origins of, 289; and women 226–27

Constitution Review Committee (CRC; September 7 1987; Third Republic) 31, 181, 229, 392

Constitutional Conference (1990–95) and Abacha, 39, 188, 234, 345; and Abiola, 407; and ethnicity, 257–58, 330, 342–43, 352; and proposals, 343–45, 349, 352–53; and regionalism, 258, 335, 338, 342–43; and religion, 297; and traditional rulers, 429; and transition, 138, 171, 184, 187, 234, 297, 329, 330; and women, 234

Constitutional Conference Committee on National Values and Lingua Franca 297

Cookey, Samuel J. (*See also* Cookey Political Bureau). 178, 424

Corruption 2, 33; and Abacha, 137, 162–63, 303, 321–22; and centralization, 261; and democracy 120–21; electoral corruption, 36; and ethnicity, 51; in independent state, 47, 114; and legitimacy, 72; and military, 7, 269; and 1992 elections, 36, 296; and oil, 261, 305; and permanent transition, 142–47; and prebendalism, 140; reform, 22, 29, 323; and religion, 266; and Second Republic, 123–24, 305; and state, 49, 59–60; in transition to Third Republic, 126–27, 162–63, 181, 183

Coup (d'état) April 22 1990 (attempted coup), 33, 312; August 27 1985 (Buhari), 30, 285, 291–92, 420; Awolowo's alleged involvement in, 18; coup trials, 151; December 31 1983, 29; ethnicity in 34; February 13 1976 (attempted), 23; January 15 1966, 20, 114–115, 161, 284, 370, 372, 375; July 29 1975 (Gowon), 22; and legitimation, 287; and military, 102; November 1993 (attempted), 171; option of radical military coup, 147; and public opinion, 112; Third Republic coups, 26, 330

Dan Fodio, Shehu Uthman 40, 52, 87–88, 97, 99, 271
Danjuma, Yakubu 23–24, 139, 183
Davies, Abimbola 153n, 183, 194, 210n
Debt 71, 305; and Abiola, 211n; and democratization, 80, and patrimony, 72, 159; reforms, 159, 303, 306–309, 312, 314–18; and Second Republic, 305, 324n
Decentralization (*See* centralization)
Directorate of Social Mobilization (MAMSER) 125, 294, 390, 391, 396, 398–400
Dasuki, Ibrahim (Sultan of Sokoto) 169, 297, 392, 405, 419, 423, 431n
Diya, Ladipo 187
DuBois, W.E.B. 90, 92

Eastern Solidarity Group 421
Economic Community of West African States (ECOWAS) 150

Economic Liberalization 71
Economic Nationalism 352, 359
Egbe Ilosiwaju Yoruba (The Yoruba Progressive Organization) 421
Ekwueme, Alex 256, 261, 335, 344
Elections 3–5; and attitudes toward, 119–20, 130; and colonial state, 368; and democracy, 128, 166, 168; and elites, 49, 128, 367; elsewhere in Africa, 71, 72, 74–76, 78, 318; ethnicity in (*See also* regions in), 19, 41, 49, 56–57, 69, 99, 122, 123, 184, 250–51, 254, 255–58, 260–61, 297, 316, 329n, 343, 370, 422; in 1923–1938, 223; and legitimacy, 124, 128; local elections, 35, 49, 125, 146, 167, 170–72, 226–27, 234–35, 237, 244, 295–96, 380, 393; and the military, 164; and parties, 165; regions in (*See also* ethnicity in), 18–20, 41, 122–23, 245, 250–56, 258, 260–61, 297–98, 343, 370; religion in, 276, 290–298; women in, 223–27, 230–35, 237, 295–98 Elections between 1954 and 1955 16, 69, 224, 245, 373; Elections between 1976 and 1979 25, 41, 145, 146, 226–27, 251–52, 290; Elections in 1983 27–29, 41, 122–24, 142, 225–26, 251, 253, 290, 291 Elections in 1989–June 12 1993 (*See also* June 12 1993) 4–5, 9, 31, 35–39, 56, 59–60, 80, 99, 112,

126–27, 141, 145–48, 152, 157, 166, 169–171, 181–84, 186–87, 193, 197, 199–204, 206–210, 210n, 211n, 212n, 231–34, 246, 248, 254, 256–58, 292–95, 297, 310, 315–16, 339, 342–343, 378, 389, 390, 392, 403–408

Elite and Abacha, 184–86; and Babangida, 180–82, 310; and "class demotion," 130; and colonial state, 113–14, 369–70; and consociationalism, 336–38; and ethnicity, 46, 47, 49–51, 54–56, 58, 267, 373; and legitimacy, 67, 111–131; and military, 161; and parties, 367, 371; and permanent transition, 67, 111–131, 145, 209; and predatory rule, 320–23; and public opinion, 111–131; and regionalism, 177, 250, 267; religion, 267–68; and structural adjustment programs, 310; and traditional rulers, 415–18, 427, 431; values, 118–21, 127–30

Emirate state 244–58; and traditional rulers, 421, 423

Ethnicity 9, 46, 49; and colonial state, 51; and constitutional engineering, 121, 343–46, 376; and democracy, 120–21, 341–42; and elections, 37, 69, 76, 338, 339n; and elites, 46, 55, 56, 77, 373; and language, 48; in military, 23; and neopatrimony, 160; and 1993 elections, 126, 148; in other states, 77–79, 414; and parties, 25, 37, 76, 165, 183, 371–72; as a potential strength, 42; and regionalism, 40–41, 48, 58–59, 251; and religion, 24, 40, 50, 279–80; and Second Republic, 123; strengthening of, 129; and transition, 76–79, 149, 183

Ethnic Nationalism 47, 50, 51

Federalism 7, 8, 10; and consociationalism, 117, 336; and cultural pluralism, 341–59; and ethnicity, 164, 260–61, 421; experiments, 244; history of, 261; horizontal and vertical, 262; and military, 163–65, 172, 262–63, 298, 347–53, 430; and 1995 Constitution, 343–45; options, 261–62, 356–59; and Political Bureau, 31; and regionalism, 20, 164, 260–62, 428; and Second Republic, 25; and state creation, 116, 128, 262; and traditional rulers, 414–15, 430

Federal Capital Territory (FTC; Abuja) 32, 37, 244, 254, 261, 348, 351

Federal Council of Traditional Rulers 297

Federal Electoral Commission (FEDECO) 122, 125, 166, 227

Federation of Muslim Women Association of Nigeria (FOMWAN; formerly known as the Muslim Sisters of Nigeria) 229

First Republic (1960–66) 149; and ethnicity, 3, 41, 116, 121, 284, 373; and parties, 164, 372, 376; reasons for failure of (*See also* ethnicity and regionalism), 164, 177, 329, 336; and regionalism, 41, 116, 121–23, 126, 245–46, 250, 284, 374; and religion, 283, 287, 298; state expenditure in, 70

Fulani (*See also* Hausa and Hausa–Fulani) 21, 26, 41, 48, 52, 58, 87–89, 97, 99, 104n, 105n, 245, 371

Geo-Cultural Zones 243–44, 246, 248, 251, 254, 256–58, 260, 263

Giwa, Dele 150

Gowon, Yakubu 116; and ethnicity, 12n, 21, 22; and federalism, 21; and military, 22, 140, 142, 161, 164, 285, 287, 334; and oil, 158; and parties, 164; and prebendalism, 140; and regionalism, 249, 349; and religion, 249, 284; and transition, 4, 20–24, 66–67, 111, 119, 161; and women, 226

Great Nigeria People's Party (GNPP) 26, 41, 166, 251–53, 376

Gumi, Abubakar 269, 281n, 291

Hausa–Fulani (*See also* Fulani) 48, 52–53; and Abacha, 38; and Babangida, 292, 295; and Buhari coup, 291; and colonial state, 89, 370; and demand for new states, 354; ethnic rivalries in, 9, 258, 261, 297; language, 246–47; and parties, 26, 213n, 332, 370–71; precolonial era, 46, 52, 87; and regionalism, 9, 40–41, 51, 213n, 346, 355; and religion, 58, 284–85, 292, 297; and Tofa, 296

Human rights 50, 58, 95, 98, 402; and Abacha, 137, 172, 186, 237, 317; and Babangida, 144, 321, 377, 401, 404, 409; and Buhari, 418; and Carter, 23, 71; and ethnicity, 99; and First Republic, 283; and military, 285; Muhammed, 23; and women, 236, 239

Ibrahim, Waziri 26, 41

Idiagbon, Tunde 29, 143, 150, 178, 183, 419

Igbo (Ibo) 48, 53–54, 85, 248, 421; and colonial state, 370; coup (January 15 1966), 20, 21; and demand for new states, 354, 421; and elections, 252–53, 255–56; ethnic rivalry, 11–12n, 18, 59, 99, 250, 261; and parties, 25, 26, 37, 251–53, 255–56, 332, 371–72; and precolonial era, 53–54, 86; and regionalism, 18, 25, 41, 51, 59, 148, 244–46, 251–53, 255–58, 335, 355

Ikime, Tom 35

Integral State 117, 121, 123

International Monetary Fund

(IMF) and Abacha, 238; and Babangida, 30, 32, 159, 230, 303, 306–308, 312, 314–16; and Buhari, 305–306; and Shagari, 305

Ironsi, Johnson Aguiyi 12n, 20, 21, 32, 161, 285

Islam (*See also* Muslim, religion) 57, 88, 239, 247, 371; and Christianity, 265–80; and ethnicity, 24, 267, 274; Muslim leaders and the state, 271–73; and OIC, 30; and parties, 35; and regionalism, 46, 50, 58; and transition, 283–99

Izala 285, 287, 298n., 299n., 291, 292, 296

Jama'tu Nasril Islam (JNI) 266, 271–72, 275, 277–78, 287

June 12 1993 (annulled presidential elections) 4, 37, 147, 149, 193–200; and Babangida, 141, 149, 171, 181, 183, 193, 199–200, 210, 211n, 378; and ethnicity, 56, 148, 183–84, 297; and patrimonialism, 157, 197–200, 209–10; and parties' response to, 200–207, 403; and public response to, 112, 126–27, 186, 209, 258, 378, 403–407; results, 37, 126, 171, 255, 315; and regionalism, 56, 148, 258; and religion, 148, 297–98; and women, 232–34

Kaduna (core section of Middle Belt) and assassination of Muhammed (1976), 24; in colonial era, 245; and elections, (1983), 253 and (1993), 255, 295–96; in 30 state federation, 244; People's Redemption Party, 27; and religion, 273, 295–96; and SDP, 36

Kaduna Mafia 285, 291, 292, 298n

Kalu, Kalu I. 316

Kano and Abacha, 38, 41; and elections, (1983), 253 and (1993), 255–58, 296; and Muhammed, 284; and People's Redemption Party, 27, 251; and SDP, 36; in 30 state federation, 244; and Tofa, 37, 56, 126, 254

Kano, Aminu 26, 58, 146, 371

Kanuri 26, 35, 37–38, 41, 46, 58, 89, 245, 247

Kingibe, Baba Gana 35, 37–39, 41, 249, 254, 257, 260

Kinship 49, 85, 93–95, 156, 427

Kusamotu, Hammed 196, 203, 205

Labor 33, 39, 49, 50, 58, 188, 321, 373, 377, 418; in Campaign for Democracy, 186; and Structural Adjustment Program, 307, 310

Lagos Plan of Action 71, 225

Lagos Summit 235, 237

Language 48–49; and elites, 55–56; and ethnicity, 8, 48–49, 50, 56, 95, 160; Hausa, 246–47; and neopatrimony, 160; and precolonial era, 46; and unity, 57, 95

Legitimacy 3–5, 8, 142, 359; and Buhari, 306; definition, 156 and democracy, 112, 129, 131, 342; and economy, 158–60, 322; and elections, 27, 80, 124–28; and local rulers, 415–16; and military, 3–5, 7, 112, 129, 177–78, 286–87; and prebendalism, 139, 156–60; and religion, 278, 287; and rentier state, 156–60; and transition, 3–5, 65–68, 74–80, 111–12, 161–62, 316

Lingua Franca 48, 246, 247

Local Government and Abacha, 38, 146, 163–64, 172, 184, 234, 237; and Babangida, 125, 163, 167, 202, 204, 228, 392–96; and creation of more localities, 353–56; and elections, (1990), 35, 170 and (1992), 36, 142 and (1996) 172, 237; and federalism, 8, 244, 356; and legitimacy, 415; and military, 164; and regionalism, 406–407; and religion, 295–96; and traditional rulers, 415, 418–20, 423–24, 426–30; and women, 224, 226, 228, 235, 237

London Club 306, 314

Lugard, Frederick 88, 89, 97, 104n, 245

Lugard, Lady 89

Macaulay, Herbert Samuel Heelas 223

Maccido, Mohammed 423, 431n

Mahmoud, Bappa 289, 432n

Mandela, Nelson 72, 138, 186

Middle Belt 21, 48, 54, 247; and attempted coup (Babangida 1990), 33–34; and colonial state, 245; and confederation, 41, 357; and elections, 252–56, 296; and ethnicity, 9, 24, 35, 165; and Federal Capital Territory (Abuja), 261; and geo–cultural/political zones, 244–56, 330; and MAMSER, 294; and parties, 251, 371; and regionalism, 24, 33–35, 40, 165, 285, 423; religion, 21, 24, 50, 247, 249, 284–85, 293, 296, 423; United Middle Belt Congress, 165

Military and ethnicity, 23; as an obstacle to democratization, 160–72

Military Elites 152, 304, 342, 357

Military Regime versus civilian rule, 142–44; and democracy, 121, 139; and legitimacy, 4, 129, 177; and regionalism, 248–50; and transition, 4, 80, 129, 145, 175, 177

Mitterand, François 71, 72

Movement for the Survival of Ogoni People (MOSOP) 138, 190

Muhammed, Murtala Ramat 22; assassination of, 23, 32; democratization, 69; and ethnicity, 11n, 32; and human rights, 23; and nonparty elections, 164; and state power, 97; and transition, 4, 23, 67, 69

Muslim (*See also* Islam) 9, 271–75; and Abacha, 297–98; and Babangida, 285, 291–97; and emirate states, 246; and ethnicity, 24, 248; and Christianity, 9, 266, 272–75; 278; and colonial state, 17, 367; and Kingibe, 35; and military, 288–90; and 1993 elections, 148, 254, 256–57, 315, 338, 405; and precolonial era, 87–88; and regionalism, 21, 24; and Second Republic, 290–91; and transition, 288–90, 292

Muslim Brothers Group 287

Muslim Students Society (MSS) 287, 292

National Convention of Nigerian Citizens (NCNC; 1959) 333, 367, 370, 372; and Akintola, 18; and Balewa, 16–17; and ethnicity, 332, 371, 372; and regionalism, 16–19, 371, 372; and women, 224

National Council of Women's Society (NCWS; 1959–) 224, 225, 227–29, 231, 233, 235

National Defense and Security Council (NDSC; before January 1993, *See also* AFRC and SMC) 36, 37, 205, 208

National Democratic Coalition (NADECO) 172, 186, 233

National Electoral Commission (NEC) and Abacha, 38; and candidate discretion, 169, 172; and local government, 393; and party discretion, 31–32, 167, 169, 171, 295; and 1989 Constitution, 125; and 1993 elections, 37, 126, 148, 196, 211n, 197, 202, 207; and religion, 294, 405; and voter registration, 36; and women, 231

National Party of Nigeria (NPN; before 1979, *See also* NPC) and ethnicity, 250, 285; and 1979 elections, 251–53, and prebendalism, 140; and regionalism, 25–27, 209, 250, 343; and religion, 290–91, 371

National Republican Convention (NRC) 32, 34, 35, 213n, 168, 395; and Abacha, 378, 380; and Babangida, 34, 168, 171, 295, 376, 395; 1991 elections, 35; 1993 elections, 195–96, 212n, 200–207, 254–56, 295, 403; and regionalism, 35, 56, 213n, 256–57, 296, 343; and religion, 35, 295–96; and women, 230

National Union of Local Government (NULGE) 394

National Unity Organization (NUO) 250

Neopatrimonialism 181, definition of, 160, 320; democracy and, 197, 204, 209– 210, 378; state and, 160, 320–21, 377–78, 381–82

Nigeria Labour Congress (NLC) 310, 316, 400–401, 408

Nigerian National Alliance (NNA) 18–20, 25

Nigerian Women's Union 223–24
1995 Constitution 188, 234, 334; and consociationalism, 336–39; and federalism, 343–45; strategies, 330–31; tendencies, 331–35
Nkrumah, Kwame 68, 90–92, 102
Nongovernmental Organizations (NGOs) 237, 397, 400, 401
Northern Christian Association 287
Northern People's Congress (NPC; after 1979, *See also* NPN) 370–72; and ethnicity, 332; and regionalism, 16, 18–19, 249–50, 333, 370–72; and religion, 267, 370–72
Nwosu, Humphrey 169, 170, 195, 196
Nyerere, Julius 68, 92, 93, 102
Nzeribe, Arthur 148, 207, 210n, 212n

Obasanjo. Olusegun 34, 97, 142, 214n; ascension to power 23–25; and corruption, 34; and ethnicity, 99, 260; and military, 66, 151; and nationalism, 34, 66; and prison sentence, 39, 99, 151; and regionalism, 12n, 34, 209, 250, 260–61; and transition, 4, 67, 143, 145, 166, 178, 213n, 226–27, 377; and unity, 250, 261; and women, 226–28
Ogoni ethnic mobilization and rivalries, 9, 99, 151–52, 352–54; military, 151–52; Movement for the Survival of the Ogoni People, 138, 190; and 1996 local elections, 172; and oil, 179, 190, 248, 352–54
Oil 67, 68, 115–16, 238, 261, 305, 307, 313, 317; and elites, 124, 146; and federalism, 347–48, 352, 353, 357, 359; and military, 10, 151, 323; and minorities (including Ogoni), 179, 190, 248, 352–53; and nationalization, 31, and patronage, 146; and permanent transition, 7; and regionalism, 41, 151–52, 352; and rents, 158, 311, 377; and Second Republic, 28; and state power, 97, 117; and unity, 60, 151–52;
Oil Mineral Producing Areas Development Commission (OMPADEC) 353
Ojukwu, Chukwuemeka Odumegwu (Emeka) 21, 151
Okogie, Archbishop Olubunmi 270–71, 273, 275, 278
Okpara, Michael I. 19
Onagoruwa, Onu 39, 143, 409
Organization of African Unity (OAU) 22, 71, 77, 226
Organization of Islamic Conference (OIC) 30, 229, 271–73, 289, 293, 297, 423
Organization of Petroleum Exporting Countries (OPEC) 22, 30
Orka, Gideon Oguaza 33, 34, 38, 285

Paris Club 306, 314, 315
Partition (*See also* unity, centralization, and federalism) 260–62

Party 170, 361, 362–65, 378–83, 395; and civil society, 365–78; and constitutions (1979, 1989, and 1994–95); and democracy, 130; and ethnicity, 16–19, 25–27, 35, 165, 183, 332–33, 370–78; and First Republic, 164–65; and regionalism, 16–19, 25–27, 35, 165, 245–46, 249–53, 255–63, 417; and religion, 35, 165, 267, 294–95; restrictions on, 25, 31–32, 125, 140–41, 165–68, 170, 295; and Second Republic, 25–27, 145, 165, 290–91; single–party doctrine, 68–70, 75, 92; in Third Republic Transition, 35–36, 200–207, 209, 254–57, 294–95, 403–404; and women, 223–24, 230, 233–35

Patrimonialism 156, 157, 159–60, 321, 373, 379; and economic crisis, 72, 304

People's Bank (*See also* Community Bank) 230, 239, 310, 391

People's Redemption Party (PRP) 26, 27, 166, 251–53, 376

Permanent Transition 1, 3–11, 67–68, 80; and Abacha, 10, 129; and civil society; definition, 65; and elite, 127–29; and Gowon, 67; and military, 5

Pluralism cultural, 51–52, 54–55, 70, 79, 266, 298, 341, 374; and the electoral system, 329–31, 336–37, 379

Political Bureau (under Babangida) and Babangida, 180–82; and Constitution, 125, 293–94; Cookey Political Bureau (1989), 178, 332, 424; description and purpose, 30–31, 125, 169, 178–80; power–sharing, 345–46; reforms, 144, 179–80, 332, 390–91, 396; and traditional rulers, 424–30; and transition, 415; and women, 228–29

Political Class 52, 56, 59, 177, 213n; and Abacha, 321; and Babangida, 294, 408; and colonial state legacy, 113–14; and democracy, 124, 130, 149, 204, 335; and military, 164, 167, 182, 334; and permanent transition, 5, 80; and state, 197–200, 204, 209–10

Prebendalism 3, 105n; and Babangida, 141; definition, 29, 139–40, 157; and elections, 200; and oil, 7; and military, 163; and permanent transition, 6, 143

Predatory rule 6, 29, 312, 320–22

Provisional Ruling Council (PRC) 39, 40, 188, 244

Qadiriyya 287, 298n

Ransome–Kuti, Beko 145
Ransome–Kuti, Mrs. 223, 224
Reagan, Ronald 71
Regionalism 3, 341; and Abacha, 41, 243, 246, 249–50, 258; and Babangida, 199; in colonial period, 47, 51, 244–45; and elections, 37, 122–23, 126,

246, 251–53, 255, 256–63, 338; and ethnicity, 40–41, 58–59; and Federal Capital Territory, 261; and federalism, 41, 244; in Ironsi's assassination, 21; in June 1993 elections, 148, 152; and 1995 Constitutional Conference, 343–45; and parties, 35, 165 245–46, 251–53, 255, 371, 376; and religion, 40, 58; in Second Republic, 246, 249–50, 376; and traditional rulers, 417–18, 421–26; and transition, 149, 243, 260, 341; and unity, 42, 243, 246, 333

Religion 265–80, 283–98; and constitution, 289–90; and elections, 76, 295–96, 338; and ethnicity, 40, 42, 50, 267, 274, 279–80; and military, 284–88; and neopatrimony, 160; and 1993 elections, 148; and political parties, 76, 262; and regionalism, 40, 42; and Second Republic, 290–91; and transition, 149, 288–90; and women, 239

Rentier state 8, 319; definition, 157; as obstacle to democratization, 156–60, 172

Sarakuna (ruling class; as opposed to *talakawa*) 52

Saro–Wiwa, Ken 8, 99, 106n, 138, 190, 237, 352, 353

Secession Biafran attempt, 21, 248, 261; disintegration, 22; and ethnicity, 59, 258, 260; and religion, 42; and regionalism, 246

Second Liberation 83, 84, 97–101; definition of, 97–98

Second Republic Constitution, 70, 145, 165, 289–90, 343; crisis of, 27–29, 112, 145, 305; and elite, 122; and permanent transition, 122–25, 143; and prebendalism, 139–40; and public opinion, 122–24; and regionalism, 246, 249; and religion, 290–91; transition to, 25–27; and women, 225–28

Secularism and the state, 270–72, 276, 278, 289

Shagari, Shehu 25, 342, 347; and corruption, 142; and crisis, 27–29, 305; and ethnicity, 9, 250, 261; in 1979 elections, 26; in 1983 elections, 27; and religion, 285, 290–91; and women, 225

Shari'a 272; Court of Appeal dispute, 24, 289–90; and state, 265, 272–73, 294; and status of shari'a law, 289, 297, 423

Shekari, Air Vice Marshall 169

Shonekan, Ernest A.O. 233, 315, 316, 405, 408; as interim Head of State, 38, 142, 184, 193, 208–209, 257; in Transitional Council (1992), 36, 208;

Single Party 75–77, 366; doctrine of single party development, 68–70, 76

Social Democratic Party (SDP) 32, 34–37, 168, 171, 260, 295,

376, 395; and Abacha, 378, 380; and ethnicity, 257, 296; and 1993 election results, 195–96, 254–58, 403; and opposition to a new round of elections following 1993 annulment, 196, 200–209, 403, 407; and regionalism, 56, 126, 249, 256–57, 296–97; and religion, 257, 296

Social Justice 31, 35, 121, 339, 390

South Africa 68, 72, 74, 75, 138, 139, 146, 149, 186, 275, 413, 414, 432n

Southern Minorities 244, 246, 248, 250–53, 255, 353, 354

Sovereign 42, 102–103, 163, 399, 401–402

Soviet Union 28, 70, 71

Soyinka, Wole 1, 8, 260, 338

State (creation of new states) 2, 353–56; and Abacha (October 1996, 36 states), 263n; and Babangida (August 1991, 30 states), 35, 51, 128, 163, 310, 395; and centralization, 356; constitutional requirement in elections, 25–26, 37, 207, 209, 343; ethnicity, 333, 355; and Gowan (May 1967, 12 states), 21, 40, 51, 115–16; minority support for, 59; Muhammed (February 1976, 19 states), 23, 115–16; and Political Bureau, 179; and religion, 286, 290

Structural adjustment program (SAP) 71, 159, 166, 168, 230, 286, 303, 306–10, 316, 319, 400–402

Sultan of Sokoto 17, 19, 25, 33, 41, 52, 169, 247, 249, 297, 392, 405–406

Supreme Council of Islamic Affairs (SCIA/NSCIA) 37, 249, 266, 287, 405

Supreme Military Council (1985; *See also* AFRC, 1985–1993; and NDSC, after January 1993) 24, 25, 30

Takaya, Bala 429, 432n

Talakawa (commoner; as opposed to *sarakuna*) 52, 53, 58, 371

Thatcher, Margaret 71

Third Republic 8, 34, 125–27; comparison to Second Republic, 149; constitution of, 3, 31, 293, 331, 343, 401; and corruption, 142; and democratization 71, 131n; and legitimacy, 112; and parties, 167–68, 376; and regionalism, 249, 256; and religion, 288, 294; and traditional rulers, 422; and women, 231

Tijaniyya 287, 298n

Tofa, Bashir 37, 38, 171, 195, 254, 256, 296; as leader of NRC, 37

Traditional Ruler 3, 413–431, 431n., 432n.; and Abacha, 41, 297; and Babangida, 141, 286, 293, 392, 406–407, 420–31; and Buhari, 418–20; and elites, 53, 415; and military, 286; and

Political Bureau, 424–30; and regionalism, 17, 417, 420–22
Transition (*See also* Permanent Transition) 1–11, 144–49, 362; and Abacha, 40, 137, 171–72, 184–89, 234, 237, 246, 298, 318, 331, 339, 356; African transitions, 70–74, 77–79, 145, 152; and Babangida, 140–42, 144–45; and civil society, 362–65, 377–83, 396–409; definition, 15–16; as discourse of legitimation, 65–68, 111, 129, 146, 150, 161–62, 166, 171, 175–76, 187; and economic risks, 79; and elites, 127–29, 146, 182, 185, 209; and ethnicity, 76, 256; and federalism, 262, 346; and First Republic, 176–77; incumbency advantage in, 76, 199–200; and Ironsi, 20; 1992 local elections, 35–36; and military, 175, 184–85, 361; between military and civilian regimes, 142–44; and neopatrimonialism, 187–98, 210; and parties, 362–65, 375–76, 379–83; and religion, 276–77, 283, 288–91, 291–98; to Second Republic (1975), 25, 69–70, 111, 139, 145, 177–78, 226; Third Republic, 29, 32, 34, 71, 80, 125, 140–42, 167–71, 178–83, 210, 291–97, 310, 314–17, 322–23, 356, 389–96; Third Republic termination, 37, 126, 171, 183, 193, 197, 315–16, 389, 403; and traditional rulers, 424–31; Transitional Council 36; and women, 226–27, 236–37, 239

Ugoh, Sylvester 37, 254, 256
Ulama 265, 271; and Babangida, 286–87; The Council of Ulama, 274, 287, 289, 292
United Progressive Grand Alliance (UPGA) 18, 19
Unity (*See also* partition) 10, 40, 58, 60, 118, 260, 333, 356–58 and constitutional formula, 66, 95; and democracy, 76, 120, 127–28, 178; and ethnicity, 40, 42, 46, 54, 95, 118, 250, 346, 422; and federalism, 95, 261–62, 356–58; and military, 164, 191, 260, 342; and regionalism, 40, 243, 246, 258, 260, 263; and religion, 40, 42, 243, 246, 267; and single party system, 76; and women, 232
Unity Party of Nigeria (UPN; *see also* AG) 26, 123, 209, 251–53, 291, 376

Williams, F.R.A. 25
Women 8, 219–40; and Abacha, 233–38; and Babangida, 228–33, 390–91, 396, 400, 402, 404, 432n, background, 220–223; and civil society, 49, 368, 373, 377, 396, 400, 402, 404; and colonial state, 223–24, 238; and democratic regimes, 224–26; and Igbo, 54, 86; and military regimes, 226–28; and

parties, 368; and religion, 42, 280
Women in Nigeria (WIN) 229, 233, 404
World Bank 79–80, 230; and Babangida, 30, 230, 303, 306–308; and Berg Report, 71

Yar'Adua, Shehu Musa 24, 40, 254; imprisonment, 39, 99; and SDP, 202, 212n, 213n, 254, 403
Yoruba 9, 37, 48, 53–54, 87; Abiola, 99, 148, 315; civil society, 377; and geo-cultural zones, 244–58, 260–61; Hausa Fulani, 297, 346; Idiagbon, 29; and Igbo, 99, 148; and new states, 354–55; Obasanjo, 24, 99; and parties, 18–19, 295, 332, 366–67, 370–72; in precolonial era, 53–54; and regionalism, 18–19, 41–42, 51, 59, 244–58, 260–61, 296, 340n, 417; in Second Republic, 25–26; Shonekan, 36; Tofa, 296; and traditional rulers, 417, 426; and women, 240
Yorubaland 20, 50, 232